THE INSTITUTES OF GAIUS AND JUSTINIAN,

THE TWELVE TABLES,

AND

THE CXVIIITH AND CXXVIITH NOVELS,

WITH

INTRODUCTION AND TRANSLATION,

BY

T. LAMBERT MEARS, M.A., LL.D. (LOND.)

OF THE INNER TEMPLE, BARRISTER-AT-LAW;
AUTHOR OF "ANALYSIS OF ORTOLAN'S ROMAN LAW."

THE LAWBOOK EXCHANGE, LTD.
Clark, New Jersey

ISBN 978-1-58477-440-2

Lawbook Exchange edition 2004, 2013

The quality of this reprint is equivalent to the quality of the original work.

THE LAWBOOK EXCHANGE, LTD.
33 Terminal Avenue
Clark, New Jersey 07066-1321

Please see our website for a selection of our other publications and fine facsimile reprints of classic works of legal history:
www.lawbookexchange.com

Library of Congress Cataloging-in-Publication Data

Gaius.
[Institutiones. English & Latin]
The institutes of Gaius and Justinian: the Twelve tables, and the CXVIIIth and CXXVIIth Novels, with introduction and translation / by T. Lambert Mears.
p. cm.
Originally published: London: Stevens and Sons, 1882.
ISBN 1-58477-440-1 (acid-free paper)
1. Roman law—Sources. 2. Gaius. Institutiones. 3. Justinian I, Emperor of the East, 483?-565 I. Mears, T. Lambert (Thomas Lambert), 1839-1918. II. Institutiones. English & Latin. III. Lex duodecim tabularum. English and Latin. IV. Novellae constitutiones. Polyglot. Selections. V. Title.

KJA882.A315713 2004
340.5'4—dc22

2004041800

Printed in the United States of America on acid-free paper

THE INSTITUTES OF GAIUS AND JUSTINIAN,

THE TWELVE TABLES,

AND

THE CXVIIITH AND CXXVIITH NOVELS,

WITH

INTRODUCTION AND TRANSLATION,

BY

T. LAMBERT MEARS, M.A., LL.D. (LOND.)

OF THE INNER TEMPLE, BARRISTER-AT-LAW;
AUTHOR OF "ANALYSIS OF ORTOLAN'S ROMAN LAW."

LONDON:
STEVENS AND SONS, 119, CHANCERY LANE.
1882.

T. RICHARDS, 37, GREAT QUEEN STREET, W.C.

PREFACE.

THE present volume is designed to supplement my Analysis, or rather Digest, of M. Ortolan's Roman law,* by placing before the student the text, and translation, of the *Institutes of Gaius* (not given by M. Ortolan), the text, and translation, of the *Institutes of Justinian*, the fragments of the text, and translation, of the *Twelve Tables*, and the greek text, latin version, and translation of the 118th, and part of the 127th, *Novels.*

In the Introduction, prefixed to these texts, will be found such details as seem necessary to account for the remarkable discovery, in modern times, of the lost Institutes of Gaius, as well as a summary of the contents of that work, and an analytical review of the mode in which it was revised by the editors of the Institutes of Justinian, so as not only to show to what extent the Imperial compilation may be regarded as a second edition of the earlier text-book, but also to indicate the changes which took place in the law of Rome during the centuries intervening between the appearance of the two treatises.

It is intended that the Analysis and this volume should be read together, the fragments of the Twelve Tables being kept before the student whilst perusing, in the first part of the Analysis, the paragraphs (103-140) devoted to an examination of their contents.

In the same way, as the Institutes of Gaius and of Justinian are equally commented upon, under the titles of the latter, in the third part

* This Analysis consists of three parts, viz.: (1) a *history* of Roman legislation, (2) a *generalization* of Roman law, that is a brief comprehensive view of its leading principles, and (3) a *treatise on Roman* law in detail, for though this portion of the Analysis is, (like the original work of M. Ortolan), nominally confined to a commentary on the Institutes of Justinian, and follows the order of that text, it, in fact, embodies in a condensed form, the profound labours of the great French jurist in every department of Roman Law during the forty-six years in which he was engaged in preparing successive editions of his work.

of the Analysis, the student, whilst going through that part, will keep the text of both these Institutes before him. To enable him to do so, and to abridge his labours in mastering the contents of the two Institutes, the portions of the text of Gaius, similar in subject matter to those of Justinian, are arranged, in parallel columns, in the order of the latter, and the passages in Justinian, which are repetitions of Gaius, printed in italics.

The text of the two Novels will be read on concluding the subject of intestate succession in the third part of the Analysis (par. 1143) as, by these novels, the Imperial legislator remodeled that branch of the law, and thereby rendered obsolete the part of his Institutes which deals with this subject.

It is hoped that these two volumes will afford the student, in a compact form, all the information he needs in his preliminary studies in Roman law; and as, on the one hand, he will not have to distract his attention by turning to a separate commentary for the Institutes of Gaius; so, on the other hand, should he desire to proceed further, he will be able indefinitely to extend his inquiries by means of the copious references to other works of the jurists, and to the Digest, Code, and Novels of Justinian.

9, *King's Bench Walk, Temple.*
1st August, 1882.

CONTENTS.

INTRODUCTION.

INSTITUTIONUM.

INSTITUTE

OF

FRAGMENTS OF THE TWELVE TABLES.

NOVELS

INTRODUCTION.

§ 1. OF THE DISCOVERY OF THE INSTITUTES OF GAIUS IN A PALIMPSEST AT VERONA.

THE practice of making palimpsests, that is, again preparing a surface which has been previously written upon (παλιν, again, and ψῆν, to rub or efface), is repeatedly alluded to by the classical authors,* and was greatly facilitated in ancient times by the nature of the materials used for writing. In the case of tablets coated with wax, the letters formed with the point of the metal stilus were easily effaced by the blunted end ;† and in the case of paper or parchment, as the ink was originally a mere mechanical mixture of lampblack, gum, and water, the writing was readily removed by the application of moisture.

When waxen tablets were used for wills, or other documents intended to be preserved, the liability to accidental, or fraudulent, obliteration was prevented by folding them in pairs, with their faces turned inwards, their edges resting on raised rims, and the whole bound together with a sealed string.

To attain the same end where ink was used, the expedient was early

---

* Cicero, writing to the jurisconsult Trebatius, laughingly rebukes his friend's parsimony in having erased some previous communication to make room for his letter. "Sed ut ad epistolas tuas redeam, cætera belle.... Nam quod in *palimpsesto*, laudo equidem parsimoniam: sed miror quid in illa chartula fuerit, quod delere malueris, nisi forte tuas formulas. Non enim puto te meas epistolas delere, ut reponas tuas" (*Ad Familiares*, vii, 18).

Plutarch, in his treatise as to philosophers conversing with princes, and when lamenting on the failure of Plato's visit to Sicily, compares Dionysius of Syracuse to a book, from which what has been written has been erased, (ὥσπερ βιβλίον παλιμψηστον), but the old stains, that nothing can efface, reappear under the new writing.

Ulpian refers to the practice when he says that property can be claimed under a will which is written on fresh paper, or on paper which has been already used (*charta deleticia*), or on the back of paper of which the face is already occupied, "Chartæ appellatio et ad novam chartam refertur, et ad *deleticiam* ; proinde etsi in opistographo quis testatus sit, hinc peti potest bonorum possessio (*Digest*, xxxvii, 11, 4). Observe also the restored passage in Gaius *Institutes*, ii, § 151. In the epigrams of Catullus (*Carm.* 22, *de Suffeno*, v. 3), the reference is rather to paper called palimpsest, because specially made so that the ink could be easily removed by authors correcting and revising their works, see also Martial, xiv, 7.

† "Sæpe stilum vertas", Hor. *Sat.*, 1, 10, 72.

adopted of tempering the mixture with some mordant, such as vinegar, which would penetrate the paper or parchment written upon, and then, at an uncertain date (after other inks, containing animal substances, such as the dark fluid of the cuttle-fish, had been tried,*) a chemical dye, consisting of an infusion of galls, blackened by sulphate of iron (green vitriol), came into use, as the vitriolic acid still more certainly bites or sinks into the medium upon which it is employed; but, as the characters so written are apt in time, from the decay of the vegetable matter, to fade away, a very durable compound ink, consisting of the vegetable dye, with the addition of a good deal of the carbon pigment, was subsequently adopted, and probably became general down into the middle ages.†

With this sort of ink, the characters, at least in the more ancient and best manuscripts which have been preserved to us, were written, or rather painted, on parchment,‡ by means of a broad-pointed reed; and then the separate leaves were allowed to dry slowly before being bound up together.

To remove characters so written, for the purpose of using the surface over again, the carbon in the ink would be washed off, and then the remaining colour, due to the vitriolic portion, would be got rid of mechanically by scraping the parchment with a knife, or rubbing it with pumice-stone, that is, to some extent, repeating the original process of preparing the texture for use.

After subjecting the parchment to treatment of this nature, the surface, especially if subsequently polished, would not show any signs of the original writing. In this way, works which had no sale were obliterated by the ancient booksellers, and the costly material used over again, the practice leading to little inconvenience, as they were sufficiently good judges not to destroy a valuable treatise. Unfortunately, however, in the middle ages, the practice was resuscitated at a time when the scarcity of parchment was combined with a constantly increasing taste for theological discussion, and as, from the fourth to the tenth centuries, the art of writing was mainly practised by ecclesiastics, a systematic destruction took place of those literary treasures

---

* Receipts for the composition of ink are given by Vitruvius, lib. vii, cap. 10; Dioscorides, lib. v. cap. ult.; Pliny, lib. xxxv, cap. 6, § 25; lib. xxvii, cap. 7, § 28.

† The trouble attending the preparation of the carbonaceous portion probably led to its being in later times discarded, and the ink left to depend, as at the present day, for its colour, simply on the black precipitate due to the iron being thrown down, on the union of the galls with the acid portion of the vitriol, but prevented from subsiding by the presence of gum. This tanno-gallate of iron, besides becoming yellow from the decay of the vegetable matter, is further discoloured by the excess of chlorine with which the inferior rags, now used for paper, are bleached. See the whole subject of ancient and modern inks discussed in a paper read before the Society of Arts, by John Underwood, Dec. 16, 1857. See also, as to the nature of inks, the work of Caneparius, *De atramentis cujuscumque generis*, published at Venice, 1619.

‡ Made from the skins of sheep (when made of calves' skin it is called vellum); most of the ancient manuscripts which remain are written on parchment, few on papyrus. As might be expected from the perishable nature of the material, not more than a few fragments of manuscripts older than the Christian era now survive (See Forsyth's *History of Ancient Manuscripts*, Lond., 1872); indeed, it is doubtful whether any known manuscript on parchment is older than the fifth century.

which had tended to accumulate in the libraries of the monasteries during the centuries succeeding the barbarian invasions.*

If, however, the surface of a skin of parchment, which has been so dealt with, be carefully pencilled over with a test for iron, such as an infusion of galls, and then exposed for a time to the action of light, some of the metallic portion of the ink, left by the stroke of the pen, and absorbed in the texture, will be rendered visible, by reason of the formation of a black precipitate, due to the restoration to the ink of the tanning matter and gallic acid, which had either decayed or been artificially removed, and in this way traces of the original characters would become more or less discernible to a practised eye.†

In 1816, Niebuhr (whilst on his way to Rome as envoy for Prussia), so treated the 97th leaf of a manuscript of the 8th century, devoted to the Epistles of St. Jerome, and now numbered xiii in the library of the Chapter of Verona.‡ He deciphered sufficient to satisfy his sagacious mind that the subject matter of the underlying erased writing was a portion of the work of some Roman jurisconsult of the Antonine era, whom he thought to be Ulpian.‖ The results of Niebuhr's observa-

---

* After the seventh century, when, in consequence of the conquests of the Caliph Omar bringing Egypt under the dominion of the Arabs, the manufacture of paper from the papyrus ceased, the rage for theological controversy, and the corresponding oblivion of classical literature, would have deprived us of every line of the ancient authors, had not the art of making paper from cotton or silk (*charta bombycina*) been invented in the ninth century, and supplied material for writing, until the thirteenth century, when it was superseded by the manufacture of paper from linen rags. "Cela (le papier bombycin) vint fort à propos dans un temps où il parait qu'il y avait grande disette de parchemin; ce qui nous a fait perdre plusieurs anciens auteurs.... Après une exacte recherche je puis assurer que des livres écrits sur du parchemin depuis le 12e siècle, j'en ay plus trouvé dont on avait raclé l'ancienne écriture que d'autres". Montfaucon—*Mémoires de Littérature tirés des Régistres de l'Académie Royale des Inscriptions et Belles Lettres*, Paris, 1729.

† This method of rendering erased writing visible is quite a modern idea, not dating earlier than the end of the seventeenth century. It did not for a long time produce any very startling results until inquiry was stimulated by the experiments of Blagden on parchment manuscripts of the ninth to the fifteenth century. See paper on the recovery of the legibility of decayed writings, read before the Royal Society in 1787 (*Phil. Trans.*, vol. 77, part 2, p. 451). See also the whole subject of the recovery of lost writings, ably treated in an article in the *Edinburgh Review*, December 1828, p. 348.

‡ This library is well known for the importance of its manuscripts on Jurisprudence. Scipio Maffei in 1732, in his *Verona Illustrata*, refers to a parchment leaf dealing with the subject of Prescriptions and Interdicts (and to two other leaves treating of the rights of the Crown in respect of property) as follows: "Piu carte lacere, e sciolte d'antico majuscolo, una delle quali par fosse d'un codice delle Pandette, ed altra d'un' opera d'antico Giurisconsulto; quai codici, se si fossero conservati, niente si ha in tal genere, che lor si potesse paragonare." And, in 1742, Maffei published in his *Istoria Teologica* a facsimile of five lines of the writing on this leaf, which had been detached from the manuscript numbered xiii, and is not palimpsest. This same leaf was republished by Haubold in a work entitled *Notitia Fragmenti Veronensis de Interdictis* (Leipsic, 1816); and Niebuhr, on examining the leaf itself at Verona, at once pronounced it, on account of its subject matter, to be part of the *Institutes* of Gaius. Maffei had noticed that the manuscript now numbered xiii was palimpsest, and the existence of a number of such manuscripts in this library is thus alluded to in the catalogue commenced by him and completed by Masotti in 1788: "Multæ ex chartis codicem alium constituerant, dilutis siquidem anterioribus literis ac deletis; quæ nunc cernuntur superinductæ sunt", etc.

‖ Niebuhr communicated his discovery to Savigny in a letter from Venice (dated 4 September 1816) as follows:—"....Nun aber kommt erst die rechte

tions were published by Savigny, coupled with remarks of his own suggesting that the manuscript in question probably contained the lost Institutes of Gaius.*

In the following year, the Berlin Academy of Sciences despatched Goeschen and Bekker to Verona, the place of the latter being subsequently supplied by Hollweg. With the characteristic patient industry of Germans, the greater part of the manuscript was transcribed, and in 1820, Goeschen published a first edition of the work in Berlin. In 1824, an improved edition appeared, which included the results of Blume's attempts at the more difficult passages,† and, after the death of Goeschen, a third edition was completed by Lachmann in 1842. A number of other editions by different editors followed, until, in 1866, Studemund began a fresh examination of the text, and, after being assisted by Mommsen and Krueger, published at Berlin, in 1874, his fac-simile, produced with the aid of type cast in imitation of the written characters.‡

This last work probably contains all that can be gleaned from the Verona text, as it is unlikely that the Italian Government will risk the destruction of the manuscript by allowing it to be further subjected to chemical re-agents.||

The volume in question is a quarto of 126 sheets of parchment of 251 pages of mostly 24 lines each. A fourth part has been twice subjected to erasure, as an intermediate writing (? of the 8th century), resembling the upper in style, and also devoted to the works of St. Jerome, had been obliterated from 61 pages; and as the lines of the original, and of the substituted writing, run in the same direction, and often cover one another, the difficulty of deciphering the underlying text was very greatly increased; added to which the order of the leaves

---

botschaft, welche ich ihnen zu verkündigen habe: nämlich dasz zu Verona von einem alten juristen so viel erhalten ist, als einen mäszigen oktavband anfüllen würde; davon aber habe ich nur ein blatt zur probe und beweis abschreiben können....es ist von der nämlichen hand geschrieben wie das fragment des Gajus" (this refers to the detached leaf mentioned in the previous note)...."Nach meiner vermuthung, die sich auf die manier und citationen grundet, ist es ein werk Ulpians."

* "Der verfasser desselben ist nach dieser probe noch nich zu bestimmen, Niebuhr vermuthet auf Ulpian; ich bin....geneigt, vielmehr die Institutionen des Gajus zu erwarten." *Zeitschrift für geschichtliche Rechtswissenschaft, herausgegeben von Savigny, etc.*, Berlin, 1817, vol. 3, p. 172.

† Blume used his chemicals rather recklessly, and some portions of the manuscript were thereby damaged.

‡ See the elaborate Latin Preface to this work (*Gaii Institutionum Commentarii Quattuor Codicis Veronensis denuo collati apographum confecit et jussu Academiæ Regiæ Scientiarum Berolinensis edidit Guilelmus Studemund*, Leipsic, 1874) for a detailed account of the labours of Studemund and his predecessors, in deciphering the text. This edition of Gaius is interesting rather to the philologist than to the law student, as though Studemund has greatly improved the text by confirming a large number of conjectural readings, he has been able to add little to our knowledge of the fourth commentary, except perhaps a few words as to "secondary" interdicts (§ 170).

|| Studemund used for the outside surfaces of the leaves sulphate of potash, and for the inner surfaces sulphocyanide of potassium or ammonium with a few drops of muriatic acid. See p. 17 of preface to work mentioned in the previous note.

had been altered,* three sheets are missing,† and many passages are hopelessly illegible;‡ still, in the main, the lost work has been reproduced.||

The date of the manuscript cannot be fixed with certainty, but Niebuhr and Kopp decide for the earlier half of the sixth century.¶ From the omission of all greek quotations, the inference is that the amanuensis was not a greek, and that this copy was made in Italy.** The first three books would seem to have been written by one hand, the fourth by another, with occasional corrections and headings by a third not very learned person. A few pages bear traces of previous writing washed off, but this is probably by a hand of the same date. The copyists appear to have been careless in inserting marginal notes in the text, and, from the inaccuracies in the spelling,†† re-

---

* This transposition of the leaves greatly increases the difficulty of recovering the lost works of antiquity, and arises from the fact, that, as the process of erasing the original writing was completed, each loose sheet was thrown on to a heap of others, to be used in the order it happened to come, and the number of sheets employed at any one time would depend on the quantity required for the new work in hand. It was in connecting together the separated leaves in palimpsests, that the ingenuity, patience, learning, and immense perseverance of Cardinal Angelo Mai (whilst librarian of the Ambrosian Library at Milan, and of the Vatican at Rome), were chiefly shown, and which resulted in the discovery and publication, during the years 1813 to 1821, of a number of lost works of classical authors, and particularly of a remarkable manuscript of the second or third century of our era, containing a portion of Cicero's dialogue *de Republica*, underlying a version of St. Augustine's Commentary on the Psalms.

† The missing leaves may possibly yet be found in the library of the monastery founded at Bobbio on the Trebbia near Piacenza by St. Columbanus, a native of Ireland, in the seventh century. The greater number of the palimpsests in the libraries of Rome, Milan, and Verona, were parted with by the monks of this place at the close of the fifteenth century. As to the contents of the three leaves, see notes to the summary of the Institutes of Gaius (ii, § 3; iii, § 1-5; iv, § 17), in the next section of this introduction.

‡ Where these illegible passages cannot be filled up, as is the case to parts of (i) § 21, 22, 32, 35, 45, 135, 137A, 164, 196, 197; (ii) § 26; (iii) § 68, 69; (iv) § 31, 52, 53, 60, 61, 80, 81, 114, 165, 166, 170, dots are inserted in the Latin text, and in the English translation the number of lines illegible is given, and the presumed contents stated. The result of the critical labours of Goeschen, Heffter, Mommsen, Huschke, Krueger, and others has been to partially restore (i) § 133; (ii) § 9, 14, 133, 134, 149, 151; (iii) § 33, part of 34; 43-45, 95, 96; (iv) § 15, 72, 73, 133. See the notes to these passages in the Summary of Gaius in the next section.

|| After taking into account the restorations referred to in the preceding note, about one-thirteenth is still wanting, of which, unfortunately, about half belongs to the fourth Commentary.

¶ Kopp's opinion, which is very guarded, will be found in vol. iv of Savigny's *Zeitschrift*, p. 473. The letters of the manuscript are of the rounded character called "uncial", without any division between the words, or punctuation, and entire words are often represented by initial letters. This is the style of writing of the oldest class of manuscripts, and therefore the date might be placed earlier, but such words as "dimissum" in ii, § 195, seem to be glosses inserted by the copyist from the margin, and as this word appears to be here used in the unclassical sense in which the expression is found in the Epitome of Alaric II, Huschke concludes that the manuscript can only have shortly preceded the reforms of Justinian. Critics, however, are not agreed as to the punctuation and translation of the passage where the word occurs, and therefore there is some doubt as to the precise sense in which the word is intended to be used.

** The Greek quotations omitted in the manuscript (*e.g.* iii, § 93, 141, etc.) can be supplied either from the Institutes of *Justinian*, or from the paraphrase of those Institutes by *Theophilus*.

†† Partly due to the barbarous pronunciation of the period.

petitions, and transpositions, they seem at times to have been half sleepy.*

The text, as given below (on the left hand side of pages 4 to 246), is mainly derived from Gneist's Syntagma,† after a careful comparison of the emendations and additions suggested by later critics, particularly Polenaar,‡ whose edition is based upon the labours of Studemund; but, as my object has been to present the latin original in such a way, that the attention of the student, desirous of mastering the *matter*, may not be distracted by notes and interpolations relating to the *form* in which the text appears, I have avoided fatiguing the eye by the use of different type to indicate parts of words that are not decipherable, but of the existence of which there is no reasonable doubt;|| and for the same reason I have simply enclosed, within brackets, conjectural readings¶ of missing or illegible portions, as, by that means, though they can be at once detected, they do not break the continuity of the latin text.**

---

§ 2. OF THE NATURE AND CONTENTS OF THE INSTITUTES OF GAIUS.

The manuscript which was recovered at Verona, in the manner described in the last section, is the handiwork of an unknown copyist, and bears no author's name. It consists of four commentaries, the

Com. i. first opening abruptly with the division of law into that:—

§ 1. (α) peculiar to each community, and that

(β) common to all nations;

§ 2-7. and, after enumerating and defining the immediate sources of law in the Roman State (viz., laws passed by the whole people, laws passed by the plebeians, decrees of the senate, imperial constitutions, magisterial edicts, and the answers of the learned in the law), the text pro-

* "Minus olei nonnunquam quam vini a semisomnis librariis consumptum esse indicio sunt," p. 29, of Studemund's preface.

† *Institutionum et Regularum Juris Romani Syntagma*, Gneist, Leipsic, 1858.

‡ *Gai Institutiones Juris Civilis Rom.* B. J. Polenaar, Leiden, 1876-9. I have not followed Polenaar where he omits words actually existing in the Verona MS., and also in the text of Justinian, *e.g.*, the word "ætatis", Gai. 1, § 40; Just. 1, 6, § 7. I have also retained some of the headings rejected by Polenaar, as, although these were not inserted by Gaius, and are not always very happy, they help to guide the student to the sub-divisions of the subject matter, and I have tacitly corrected such inconsistencies of style as are due to the copyist, and not to the original author of the work, for example, spelling "apud" at times "aput," and "sed" as "set," so substituting v for b, and vice versa.

|| However valuable such indications may be to the critical scholar, they are of no practical utility to the law student.

¶ The authorities for conjectural readings will be found in the summary of the Institutes contained in the next section of this introduction. References from one part of the Institutes to another will be found in the English translation.

** I have retained the separation of the text into sections, introduced, for the convenience of reference, by Goeschen, as, though the division of the paragraphs might now, in some places, be improved, the arrangement has become consecrated by usage.

ceeds to deal with the whole subject of private law, under the three heads of persons, things, and actions. § 8.

Persons are divided into:—

(α) *free* and *slaves.* The former are subdivided into *free-born* and *freed*, and a lengthy description follows of the different classes of freed persons, viz., those ranking as Roman citizens, those assimilated to the condition of Latins by the Junian law, and those reduced to the class of surrendered persons by the Ælian-Sentian law. The various modes of attaining a higher status are then discussed, together with the restrictions imposed by the Ælian-Sentian and Fusian-Caninian laws on the power of enfranchisement. § 9-11 § 12-35. § 36 47.

(β) Those *free from power*, and those *subject to the power of others.* The latter are subdivided into:— § 48. § 49, 50.

(1) Those in the *power of their masters*, whether by a legal or equitable title. § 51-54.

(2) Those in the *power of their ascendants*, involving a statement of the essentials of a legal marriage and of the impediments thereto, together with a long digression concerning the provisions of the Ælian-Sentian and Junian laws, and certain decrees of the senate, by which those who are married to aliens,* whether by mistake or otherwise, may get their children legitimated, and into their power, with some remarks on the position of children born through the union of slaves and free persons, and on the effect, as to the children, of the grant by the emperor of roman citizenship to an alien. § 55. § 56-64. § 65-81. § 82-91 § 92-96.

The law of *adoption* is then explained as being a fictitious extension of the power of ascendants; and as the power of a husband over his wife reduced her to the rank of a daughter, a description is given of the modes of creating *marital power*, and of the fictitious use of such power in the case of the guardian of a female ward.† § 97-107. § 108-115*b*

(3.) Those *free persons in a position analogous to slavery.* This subdivision involves a detailed account of the origin, and mode of conducting, by way of copper and scale, formal conveyances of property, whether consisting of things or persons fictitiously sold for the purpose of emancipating them. § 116. § 117-123.

The means are then discussed by which persons, whether slaves, § 124-141.

---

* I have translated "peregrinus" by "alien", meaning an alien friend, as being the nearest approach to the true idea, that is a person who belonged to a conquered community and was then living within the limits of the Roman Empire, though not admitted to all the rights of a Roman citizen. The term "provincial" would be more accurate, if not misleading on other grounds, as the term alien does not imply, as it should, that the "peregrinus" was a subject of Rome. See Austin's *Jurisprudence*, 4th edit. p. 571.

† It may be objected to my translation of the word "manus" by "marital power" that a woman could through *co-emptio* be *in manu* towards a person who was not her husband, but in fact, she was temporarily in the position, as if under the power of a husband. in order to accomplish a given end (*e.g.* change of guardians) by the fictitious use of a method properly applicable to another purpose, as is done in the infancy of all legal institutions.

Com. i.

descendants, adopted children, wives, or free persons in a state of
bondage, are *released* from power.*
§ 142,143. (γ) Those under *guardianship*. Here the difference is pointed out
§ 144. between male and female wards, and the modes are described of ap-
§ 145-154. pointing the class of guardians called *tutors*, together with the rights of rela-
§ 155. tions to fill the office, involving the definition of *agnation* and *cognation*,
§ 156,157. and (by reason of its effect on agnation) also a discussion on the changes
§ 158-164. of legal position† resulting from crime, adoption, or fictitious sales.‡
§ 165. The right of *patrons* to act as guardians is next dealt with, as well as
§ 166. the rights of fictitious purchasers, and of those who have the legal or
§ 167. equitable ownership of the person in respect of whom the question of
guardianship arises, followed by a lengthy description of the methods
§ 168-183. available to women for shifting their guardians, the divergence of
opinion being noted as to the proper course to adopt for the appoint-
§ 184. ment of a new tutor, when a civil law action is commenced between a
tutor and a woman or pupil.
§ 185-187. The laws relating to the appointment of guardians by magistrates
§ 188. are then mentioned, the reader being referred for fuller details to other
works|| of the author dealing with the whole subject of guardianship.

---

* The passage included in § 133 is illegible in the manuscript, but is filled up by means of the extract from the Institutes of Gaius in *Dig.*, i, 7, 28. Unfortunately, the blanks occurring in § 137, as to the modes of dissolving marital power (? emancipation or deed of divorce), cannot be supplied.

† The translation of the expression "capitis deminutio" is beset with difficulties, owing to the confusion which has arisen from the elasticity of the two words "caput" and "status", and the loss of the true meaning of the former word as republican institutions disappeared. The word "caput" probably had a more restricted meaning than "status", the former implying the possession of civil rights, whilst the latter referred only to the possession of a recognised, though not necessarily beneficial, condition, hence a slave was looked upon as having no *caput*, but had a *status*. The origin of the expression "capitis deminutio" has been traced to the caput, chapter, or page, in the register of voters from which, at the quinquennial survey, established by Servius Tullius, the censors could remove the name of a citizen who had been guilty of certain grave offences, and so actually degrade him, or, in the case of the arrogation of the head of a family, technically degrade him by transferring his name to a subordinate position under the caput of the head of the house who now represented him (see my *Ort. Anal.*, part i, par. 55, 56, pp. 5, 6; and part iii, par. 208 (3) p. 123). The definition of "capitis deminutio" given by Gaius in these Institutes (§ 159), is "prioris *capitis* permutatio", whilst Justinian (i, tit. 16, pr.) words it "prioris *status* mutatio" (or "commutatio" according to some readings), and adhering to this distinction, I have translated the words where they occur in the Institutes of *Gaius* as "a change of one's former legal position", so as to recognise the fact that in his time there was a distinct change caused, even in the minima c. d. by, *e.g.*, the state of temporary technical degradation to which a person was reduced whilst going through the legal forms necessary to effect his emancipation from the power of his father, or in the case of a woman, to bring her under the marital power of her husband; though it would be a perversion of terms to say that any loss of general *status* resulted from a son improving his social condition by becoming a free agent, or from a woman acquiring the right of succession to her husband and escaping from the thraldom of her relations. On the other hand, I have used the word "status", in the translation of *Justinian's* Institutes, as in his time the fictitious ancient forms had disappeared. For the perplexities connected with the distinction between "caput" and "status", see Austin's *Jurisprudence*, 4th edit., pp. 362, 747.

‡ The next 17 lines are illegible, but probably stated that, on failure of agnates, the right of guardianship passed to the gentiles.

|| Viz., the Commentaries on the works of Quintus Mucius Scævola, and on the Urban Prætor's Edict.

Com. i.

The grounds for placing young persons under guardianship are next § 189.
stated, and the reasons commonly assigned for keeping women of full § 190.
age under perpetual guardianship scouted as absurd.

The rights and duties of guardians are then briefly reviewed, and the § 191-193.
modes by which the guardianship of tutors comes to an end, whether
in the case of women, by having the necessary number of children, or § 194-196.
in the case of males, by reaching the age of puberty, with a reference
to the different views of the schools as to the period for fixing puberty
in the case of males.

The guardianship of *curators* is then discussed,* and the subject § 197, 198.
completed by remarks as to the *security* required to be given by both § 199, 200.
classes of guardians, with the exceptions thereto.

Com. ii.

Things are divided into:—

1. Those (α) subject to *divine* law as being consecrated to the gods § 1-9.
or abandoned to departed spirits, or sanctioned for their preservation, and those (β) subject to *human* law. These latter being § 10, 11.
subdivided into those (*a*) belonging to the whole community, and
those (*b*) belonging to private individuals.
2. *Corporeal* and *incorporeal*, with illustrations,† and an explanation § 12-14.
given of such incorporeal things as *servitudes*. § 14*a*.
3. Those (α) requiring a formal *civil law conveyance* for their § 15-23.
transfer, and those (β) capable of alienation by *simple delivery*
with illustrations; followed by a description of a *surrender in*
court as an alternative mode of transfer for the former class of § 24-27.
things, with illustrations of the cases to which the last-mentioned § 28-37.
form of transfer is particularly applicable, and the point noted that § 38, 39.
this method is not available for obligations.

The effect of not complying with the rules laid down for the conveyance of property is then used to illustrate the division, which had § 40, 41.
grown up, of ownership into *legal* and *equitable*;‡ and the doctrine of
acquiring property by possession during a fixed statutory period is § 42-44.

---

* One page of the manuscript is here illegible.

† Part of § 9 and § 14 are illegible but have been filled up from *Digest*, i, 8, 1.

‡ Although the words "legal" and "equitable" here used in summarising the text, convey a very good idea of the distinction between a title resting on the civil law, and one based on the jurisdiction of the prætor, still it must be borne in mind, that the equitable (or prætorian) title in Roman law—

(α) was originally introduced in furtherance of the civil law, and to support the heir-at-law in his possession (see *Ort. Anal.*, part iii, par. 1099, p. 249).

(β) ripened, in a very short time, by possession, into full legal ownership (see Gai *Inst.*, ii, § 41, and Maine's *Ancient Law*, p. 288).

(γ) when it had done its work, and the civil law was capable, unaided, of meeting all the complicated cases of proprietary rights; the equitable title, as being a purely accidental and historical peculiarity in Roman law (see Austin's *Jurisprudence*, 4th edit., p. 634). died out, and was suppressed by Justinian (see *Ort. Anal.*, part iii, par. 342, p. 144);

whereas in English law, equitable titles were (and still, in fact, are), only protected by a distinct set of Courts, viz., the so called Courts of Equity (Chancery Division of the High Court), and unfortunately depending upon the doctrine of trusts, the eradication of this totally unnecessary disfigurement of any refined system of jurisprudence seems somewhat hopeless.

Com. ii.

brought in here by way of showing how a thing which has not been properly transferred, and is, therefore, only equitably held, may fall
§ 45-58. by time into the legal ownership of the transferee, with the exceptions in the case of things stolen, taken by force, etc., followed by an ex-
§ 59-61. planation of the doctrine of re-acquiring by use that which we once possessed, and illustrated by the case of a mortgagor in possession, with and without the debt being paid off.

§ 62-64. The principle that owning a thing does not necessarily imply the power of alienating it, and vice versâ, is next dwelt upon, and the distinction between things requiring a formal conveyance and those
§ 65. passing by simple delivery, ascribed to the *civil* and to *natural*
§ 66. law respectively; the rules governing the acquisition of property by
§ 67, 68. *occupation* being traced to the latter, with illustrations of the ap-
§ 69, 70. plication of the doctrine to the case of wild animals, property of
§ 71, 72. an enemy, alluvion, islands formed in rivers; buildings, or plants,
§ 73-76. or corn, on another's land; writing, or painting, on another's parch-
§ 77-79. ment or canvas; and the making new things out of another's materials.

§ 80. The restrictions in the way of a ward alienating a thing without the authority of the guardian, are then adverted to, with the distinc-
§ 81-85. tions drawn in the case of persons under age, and women.

§ 86-88. The acquisition of things through those in our power is next con-
§ 89-95. sidered, followed by a discussion as to the effect of such persons being
§ 96. in *possession* on our behalf, and notice taken of the incapacity of such persons to acquire by way of surrender in court.

§ 97-99. From the acquisition of particular things, the text passes to their acquisition in the aggregate, that is, by—

Universal succession, first dealing with the case of the devolution
§ 100. of an inheritance by virtue of a *testament*, involving a reference to the two forms of wills which had fallen into disuse, viz.:—

§ 101. (1), that made in the public assembly, and

(2), that made in the presence of the army;

§ 102-104. This is followed by a graphic description of the existing mode of making a testament by way of—

(3), the copper and scale, with observations on the restrictions
§ 105-108. as to the witnesses to such a will.

§ 109-111. The privileges accorded to *soldiers* in respect of their wills is then dwelt upon,* and allusion made to the advantageous position of *women*
§ 112, 113. in respect of the power of making a will.

§ 114, 115. The essentials to the validity of a will are next discussed, particularly
§ 116, 117. as to the due *appointment of the heir*, and the necessity, in the case
§ 118. of a woman, for the guardian's authority, as also the rights at law of the successor ab intestato, either against claimants under a will
§ 119-122. deficient in some formality, or against a prætorian will passing only the equitable estate. The necessity of expressly appointing or excluding

---

* The next sheet of parchment is missing, but the subject matter of the leaf, viz., the testamentary incapacity of persons in the power of others, and of lunatics and pupils, may be gathered from the Epitome of Gaius (bk. ii, tit. 2) in the *Breviarium Alaricianum*.

Com. ii.

a son in power is also dwelt upon, together with the effect of omitting § 123.
to mention other descendants, and reference made to the interference § 124-129.
of the prætor on behalf of these latter. The claims of posthumous*
children are then considered, and the mode of excluding them,† as § 130-134.
also the necessity (on account of the prætor's interference in their
behalf) of mentioning in the will children released from power; and, § 135.
incidentally, the position of children in the power of their father, as § 135*a*.
the result of a petition to the Emperor, is referred to, as also the § 136,137.
effect of emancipating adopted children.

Testaments are shown to be rendered *invalid* by the arrogation, or § 138.
adoption, of an heir, or by a wife coming under marital power, and the § 139,140.
effect, on the testament, of the three sales of a son not having been
completed, is alluded to, together with the existing law (as opposed § 141.
to the old law) on the subject of the result of proving a case of error,
so as to bring a son under power after the making of the testament. § 142,143.
The revocation of a first will, either by the execution of a second or § 144.
a change in the legal position of the testator, together with the § 145,146.
circumstances under which such a will may nevertheless be upheld § 147.
by the prætor, are then dealt with, as also the conflict of rights of the
equitable possessor, and the civil law heir, in the case of a will so § 148-150.
upheld by the prætor, concluding with an inquiry into the effect, on
a validly executed testament, of a mere contrary intention, or an actual § 151.
obliteration of the writing.‡

The different classes of *heirs* are now entered upon. The reasons § 152.
for appointing a *necessary* heir, and the position of heirs succeeding § 153-155.
as *co-owners of the patrimony*,|| explained, together with the right § 156,157.
granted by the prætor to these heirs, and others of a similar class, § 158-160.
of abstaining from the inheritance. *Stranger* heirs are then defined, § 161.
and the power they possess of deliberating whether they will accept § 162.
the inheritance mentioned, together with the special privileges as to
renouncing inheritances accorded to minors, and the formal mode of § 163.
giving stranger heirs the power to deliberate is detailed, with the § 164-169.
method adopted by the prætor, at the instance of creditors, to compel
all classes of heirs to decide; and the distinction is pointed out be- § 170-173.
tween the common, and the continuous, period of deliberation.

---

* The word "posthumous" relates here to the period of the making of the testament. For the different classes of *postumi*, see my *Ort. Anal.*, part iii, par. 697 (3) p. 184.

† The passage included in § 131-134 is illegible in the manuscript, but is filled up from Justinian's *Institutes*, ii, xiii, § 1, 2, and *Digest*, xxviii, 3, 13.

‡ The passage included in § 149-151 is illegible in the manuscript, but may be partially restored from the context.

|| This mode of translating the words "sui heredes" seems to hit the true idea intended to be conveyed by Gaius. The difficulty of finding any English equivalent expression for "suus heres" arises from the fact that early Roman law is saturated with a principle existing in the infancy of all communities possessing, like the Roman, a really long legal history, viz., *potestas* (of which *manus*, etc., are only derivative forms), that is, the supremacy of the eldest male ascendant, or political chief, combined with the co-proprietorship of his children and wife (as a daughter), in the common property of which he was morally only steward, but, owing to the want of an effective system of law and procedure, legally owner. See *Ort. Anal.*, part iii, par. 804 (2), p. 194; and Maine's *Ancient Law*, p. 228.

Com. ii.

§ 174-176. The modes of *substituting* one or more heirs in the place of the first named, are next dealt with, and the effect of not expressly disinheriting
§ 177,178. the first named discussed, together with the manner in which a descendant's will may be made, by substituting an heir to him in case he
§ 179-184. should die under the age of puberty after having succeeded to the inheritance.

§ 185,186. The mode of appointing a *slave heir* is then pointed out, the necessity
§ 187. being shown in the case of a person's own slave, of, at the same time, giving him his freedom, followed by remarks as to the result of
§ 188-190. the manumission or alienation of the slave, subsequent to the making of the will.

§ 191. *Legacies* are here discussed as being involved in the subject of testa-
§ 192-223. mentary succession. The four kinds are defined, their distinct characters detailed, and the formal words necessary for the creation of each specified, together with the modes of enforcing them, the kinds of property to which they can severally be applied, the effect of alienating the property bequeathed, or leaving it conjointly, or disjunctively, or subjecting it to a condition, the period at which each kind of legacy vests in the legatee, followed by a lengthy dissertation on the complicated state of the law relating to the fourth kind of legacy.

§ 224-228. The effect of the generality of the *Twelve Tables* in the matter of testamentary power is then referred to, and the defects in the *Furian*, and the *Voconian* law, pointed out in order to show the necessity for the passing of the *Falcidian* law, to check the liberality of testators at the expense of the heir.

§ 229-231. The *invalidity* of legacies is shown to arise from various causes, such as the bequest preceding the appointment of the heir, or because
§ 232-234. the legacy is to take effect after the death of the heir, or is by way
235-237. of a penalty on the heir, or is given to an uncertain person, or to a
§ 238-243. posthumous stranger; and the question of the invalidity of a legacy
§ 244. to a person in the power of the heir is discussed, as well as the cases
§ 245. in which a legacy to a person through another in his power will be valid.

§ 246,247. *Bequests in trust** are now dealt with as being indirectly connected with the last subject. Those relating to *inheritances* are taken
§ 248. first, and the necessity stated for an heir to be legally appointed, after
§ 249,250. which the appropriate words are to be added creating the bequest in trust. The fact that the position of the person beneficially entitled

---

* The translation of "fidei-commissum" by "bequest in trust" is not quite accurate, owing to the dual system of words in English law applicable to personalty and realty respectively, so that the word "bequest" refers to a gift of the former class of property, and the word "devise" to the latter, whereas a fidei-commissum might relate to either. This is a difficulty which must continue to embarrass the English student so long as the slow but steady process of absorption of the law of realty in that of personalty is incomplete, as until then the rules of descent of realty in this country will continue to be hampered by distinctions based not on logical, scientific, and natural principles, but on the feudal tenure of land arising out of the exigencies of military service in a past and semi-barbarous age. See Austin's *Jurisprudence*, 4th edit., pp. 59, 60; Maine's *Ancient Law*, ch. viii, p. 283; Williams on *Personal Property*, 10th edit., p. 408.

Com. ii.

is sometimes that of heir, and sometimes that of legatee, is noted, § 251.
though, formerly, he assumed the character of a purchaser of the estate from the heir, and the stipulations usual in the case of sales were there- § 252.
fore entered into, until they were rendered unnecessary by the interference of the prætor consequent upon the *Trebellian* decree of the § 253.
senate settling the respective liabilities of the heir and the person beneficially entitled. Owing, however, to bequests in trust often failing through the heir-at-law refusing to accept an inheritance from which he was to derive no benefit, the latter was authorised by the *Pegasian* § 254.
decree of the senate to retain a fourth, and consequently stipulations analogous to those customary between an heir and a legatee of a share of the inheritance became necessary, and, in the result, these two decrees of the senate were respectively invoked according as the heir § 255-258.
was entitled to retain, or claimed the right to retain, a fourth of the estate, the last-mentioned decree being held equally applicable to an § 259.
heir of part of the inheritance only.

Bequests in trust of *specific things* may be made through the medium § 260.
of the heir, or of a legatee, and the things bequeathed need not be § 261.
the property of the testator, though a doubt existed as to the effect § 262.
of the bequest where the actual owner refused to sell. In the case § 263-265.
of the freedom of a slave, it was held that the bequest failed if the owner refused to sell the slave, but in any case the slave so freed was § 266, 267.
the freed-man of the manumittor, and not of the testator. This subject is concluded by a lengthy description of the differences between § 268-289.
legacies, and bequests in trust, whether as to the things which may be bequeathed, the mode of doing so, the courts for enforcing them, or the language in which they may be expressed, and a brief reference made to distinctions which had been removed by legislative interference.

Intestate succession is now entered upon as the second division of Com. iii.
the acquisition of things in the aggregate, and the descent of inheritances, according to the law of the Twelve Tables,* is shown to be in the following order, viz., to the:—

(1.) *Co-owners of the patrimony*, the succession being by repre- § 1-8.
sentation in the event of the decease of those primarily entitled.

(2.) *Agnates*, there being no devolution in their case, and the § 9-13.
state of the law very anomalous in respect of the claims § 14
of *women* as agnates, whilst in the case of default of agnates primarily entitled the succession is held to be by § 15, 16.
individuals.

(3.) *Gentiles*, but this class of heirs is only cursorily alluded § 17.
to, as the law affecting them had fallen into disuse.†

The defects in these rules of succession are then commented upon, § 18-24.
by way of introduction to the equitable interference of the prætor, and

* The sheet of parchment is missing, but the contents are known through the extract in the *Mosaicarum et Romanorum legum collatio*, tit. xvi. cap. ii, § 1-5.

† See *Ort. Anal.*, part iii, par. 1032, p. 325.

Com. iii.
§ 25, 26. the consequent recognition of the claims of emancipated children, of
§ 27-29. excluded agnates (to rank as cognates), women, and adopted children
§ 30. (in respect of their actual family); but the inability of the prætor to
§ 31. give a legal title to those he introduces into the succession is pointed
§ 32. out,* the reader being referred for further information to the author's
§ 33. special work on this subject,† and after showing that the prætor
§ 34. sometimes aids the heir-at-law, examples are given of the title at law,
§ 35-38. and the beneficial interest existing in different hands, in consequence
of the conflict between the legal and equitable rules.

§ 39, 40. In tracing the rules laid down by the Twelve Tables as to suc-
§ 41. cession to the property of *freed-men*, reasons are given for the inter-
ference of the prætor in favour of the patron, where the latter had been
§ 42. excluded by testament, and mention is made of the further extension
of the patron's rights by the Papian law. The rights of patrons and
patronesses in respect of freed-*women* are then discussed at considerable
length, and notice taken of the way in which these rights had been
interfered with by the conflicting privileges accorded to fecundity by
§ 43-53. the Papian law,‡ the reader being referred for further information
§ 54. to a special work of the author on the subject.||

§ 55. The succession to the property of *Latin* freed-men entails a long
§ 56-62. digression to notice the effect of the *Junian* law in establishing the
§ 63-71. rights of their patrons, as well as the conflicting views existing as to the
result of subsequent legislation. Remarks follow on the anomalous
§ 72, 73. condition of Latins, who have been freed by the Emperor, but with
a reservation of the rights of their patrons, and on the succession to the
§ 74-76. property of persons belonging to the lowest class of freed persons.

§ 77-81. The rules introduced by the prætor, in the interests of creditors, for
regulating the kind of succession resulting from the sale to the highest
bidder of the whole property of *insolvent debtors*, in their lifetime, or
§ 82, 83. on their decease, are then incidentally noticed, as also the succession
arising from adoption and marital power; with remarks on the inter-
§ 84. ference of the prætor in favour of creditors, rendered necessary in such
cases by the operation of the strict rules of law, concluding with a
§ 85-87. reference to the dispute as to the effect of an heir going through the
process of surrendering the property in court before, or after, his
acceptance of the inheritance.¶

---

* Part of § 33, 34, is illegible in the manuscript, but can be, to some extent, filled up from the *Institutes of Justinian*, iii, ix, § 1, 2.

† Namely to the ten books on the Urban Edict. The next sheet of the MS. is illegible, but possibly contained an account of the senatus-consultum Tertullianum, see *post*, p. xxviii, note ||. For the order of succession introduced by the prætor, see my *Ort. Anal.*, part iii, par. 1008, 1022, pp. 242, 244. For a tabular view of the different degrees of cognates called to the prætorian succession, see Domenget's Gaius, Paris, 1866, p. 307.

‡ Part of the passage included in § 43-45, is illegible in the manuscript, but may be filled up from the context and from Ulpian's Rules, xxix, § 3-5.

|| Namely the fifteen books on the Julian and Papian laws.

¶ The matter contained in § 85-87 seems a mere repetition of Com. ii, § 35-37, and on this account Polenaar (p. 341, *Syntagma*) rejects them as spurious, but his arguments do not seem conclusive.

Com. iii.

The author next proceeds to the subject of :—

Obligations, as being incorporeal things,* and divides them into those :— § 88.

(α) Arising from *contract*, and those

(β) Arising from *wrongs*.

The former are subdivided into four kinds, viz., those resulting from:— § 89.

(1) The delivery of the *thing*, illustrated by a loan in kind, and payment by mistake. § 90, 91.

(2) *Words*, with examples of verbal obligations, and the distinc- § 92.
tion is shown between those exclusively used by Roman § 93, 94.
citizens and those available to aliens, with the cases where
there is no previous interrogation, or the promise and answer § 95, 96.
are in different languages.† Various illustrations are given
of useless stipulations,‡ whether arising from the nature § 97.
of the thing stipulated for, or its non-existence, or because § 97*a*.
subject to an impossible condition, or because the thing § 98.
is already the property of the stipulator, or because it can § 99.
only take effect after the death or change of legal position of § 100, 101.
the stipulator, or on account of the question and answer not § 102.
agreeing, or because the person was not in the power of him § 103.
on whose behalf he stipulated, or because we have stipulated § 104.
with a person in our power or vice versâ, or being in power § 105.
have attempted to render ourselves liable by a promise, or
the invalidity may arise from the stipulator or promisor being § 106.
totally deaf or dumb, or insane, with the distinction to be § 107-109.
drawn in the case of a ward who is above tender years, and
women.

The position of an additional *creditor* (*adstipulator*) is then dis- § 110-114.
tinguished from the opposite case of an additional *debtor* (or *surety*), § 115-117.
whether in the shape of a *sponsor*, *fidepromissor*, or *fidejussor*. The
similarity of the character of the sponsor and fidepromissor, as opposed § 118
to the fidejussor is noted, and illustrated by the restricted sphere of the
two former, whether in respect of their own liability, or that of their § 119, 120.
heir. Their position is further contrasted with that of the fidejussor
by reference to the *Furian* law, the *rescript of Hadrian*, the *Apuleian*, § 121-123.
and the *Cicereian* laws, and the limitations of liability under the
Cornelian law in favour of all classes of sureties are dwelt upon, with § 124.
the exceptions in the cases of dowry, of debts due under testaments, § 125.
security ordered by a judge, or under the *Julian* law as to the tax

---

* Whether obligations were intended to fall under things, or to occupy an intermediate position between things and actions, or to be introductory to the latter (as Theophilus in his Paraphrase, iii, 13, pr.; iv, 6, pr. has made them), has been much discussed, but with little practical result; the weight of opinion seems to incline to the view I have adopted. See note ii (by Rudorff) p. 464, Puchta, Cursus (4th edit.).

† The passage included in § 95, 96, is illegible in the manuscript, but the contents may be conjectured from the Epitome of Gaius, ii, ix, §§ 3, 4. See *post*, p. 455.

‡ The remarks here made, though confined to the stipulation, rather belong to an examination into the conditions necessary to the validity of *all* contracts. See my *Ort. Anal.*, part iii, par. 1324, p. 267.

Com. iii.

§ 126, 127. on inheritances. Reference is then made to the fact that all sureties are alike in not being liable for more, though they may be liable for less than the principal obligation, as also in their right to recover from the principal debtor any sum they may have been compelled to pay, and the exceptional favour shown to sponsors by the *Publilian* law is pointed out.

The nature of obligations belonging to the third subdivision is next considered, viz., those resulting from :—

§ 128-130. (3.) *Writing*, the contract by written entries being effected either by (α) an entry of a previous transaction, such as a sale, or (β) by an entry substituting a new debtor for an old one.
§ 131. These are distinguished from those mere entries which only afford evidence of obligations already existing, and which, as
§ 132, 133. belonging to the law of nations, are available to aliens, to
§ 134. whom also the form of contract consisting in a written acknowledgment, whether single or in duplicate, is peculiar.

Obligations falling under the fourth subdivision, viz., those created by :—

§ 135. (4.) *Consent*, are shown to be distinguished by their mutuality
§ 136-138. from the obligations previously considered. These contracts are dealt with in order, viz. :—

§ 139. (α.) *Sale*, which is complete when the price is agreed upon, if
§ 140. certain, and consisting in money, though doubts existed on
§ 141. this point.

§ 142-144. (β.) *Letting and hiring*, which is subject to similar rules, and often approaches very nearly the last-mentioned contract,
§ 145. especially in the case of the letting out of estates in perpetuity, on condition of due payment of rent, and the event may determine which class of contract has been entered into, as in the
§ 146. case of gladiators in respect of whom a sum for the hire, or a price per head, may be due according as each one comes out unhurt, or is killed or maimed, whilst, according to the better opinion, it was entirely a contract of sale, where a goldsmith
§ 147. agrees to make rings, of a certain weight and form, out of his own gold, for a certain sum.

§ 148. (γ.) *Partnership* may involve our whole property, or only relate to some particular business. The shares of profit and loss
§ 149, 150. may be unequal, and a dissolution of the partnership may
§ 151. result from one partner renouncing, or dying, or undergoing
§ 152-154. a change of legal position, or becoming insolvent.

§ 155-158. (δ.) *Gratuitous agency* arises when a person is commissioned to do something for another, or for a third person, but not for himself, as in the case of advising him to purchase something, or to lend money at interest, provided in the latter case the borrower is not specified. The commission must not be contrary to good morals, or in respect of something to be done after
§ 159-162. the mandator's death. The dissolution of such contracts may result from revocation before anything has been done, or through the death of either party, unless the contract has been performed in ignorance of the fact. The effect of the agent not

Com. iii.

complying strictly with his instructions is then discussed, and the point noted that an action of mandate will lie, whenever, if a sum had been fixed, a contract of letting and hiring would have arisen.

The benefit of contracts is stated to be acquired for us by those in our power, whether descendants, slaves, wife, or freemen in bondage, as well as by the slaves, and freemen in bondage, of others, whom we bona fide possess, but only in respect of their labour, or by means of our own property, a rule applying also to the case of the usufruct of a slave, the bare legal owner having no claim in respect of his contracts, and masters owning a slave in common acquire in proportion to their several interests, unless one only is expressly named. § 163. § 164. § 165. § 166. § 167, 167a

The *dissolution* of obligations is shown to result from— § 168.

(1.) *Performance.*

(2.) *Release*, that is, by formally crediting the obligation as fulfilled, in which way all obligations may be dissolved, if first thrown into the form of a verbal contract, though women cannot do this without the authority of their guardians, and whether this method will apply to part only is doubtful. The special form of release by the process of the copper and the scale is applicable to obligations so formed, or to those arising out of debts due by way of legacy, or to those resulting from the judgment of a court of justice. § 169. § 170. § 171. § 172. § 173-175.

(3.) *Novation.* This mode of dissolution is effectual even in some cases where no new obligation is formed; but if the parties are the same, there must be something new inserted, in order that novation may arise, as in the case of adding, or withdrawing a condition, a term, or a surety, though the effect of the last mentioned was disputed, and it was essential that where a condition was added it must be fulfilled. *Joinder of issue* in a civil law action also dissolved the original obligation, though the new one created was again dissolved by that resulting from the judgment; but these involuntary novations did not occur in actions based on the authority of the magistrate. § 176. § 177. § 178. § 179. § 180, 181.

Obligations arising from *wrongs** are next dealt with, and illustrated by :— § 182.

(1.) *Theft*, of which, according to the better opinion, there are two kinds: manifest, and non-manifest; the other two kinds, that arising from discovery after solemn search, and that arising from the stolen thing having been deposited elsewhere, being considered rather as forms of actions relating to theft. The conflicting views on the subject of what is manifest theft are given, and that which is not manifest theft is deemed non-manifest. The meaning of "conceptum" and "oblatum", as § 183. § 184. § 185. § 186, 187.

---

* Much that is here dealt with in connection with civil injuries would, in modern times, appear under the head of *criminal* law. For the reason of this see Maine's *Ancient Law*, ch. x.

Com. iii.
§ 188. applied to theft, is explained, and the action for opposing a search for stolen goods adverted to.

§ 189-191. The law of the Twelve Tables, as to the punishment for manifest and non-manifest theft, and for theft discovered after formal search, is then stated, with the modification introduced by the prætor in respect of the first, and reference made to the dispute as to the status of a freeman found guilty of theft. The penalty for preventing a search for stolen property is shown to have been introduced by the prætor, and the author
§ 192, 193. turns into ridicule the whole of the solemnities enjoined by the Twelve Tables in the case of a solemn search, and he re-
§ 194. gards as groundless the distinction as to theft being manifest
§ 195. by law, or by nature. Theft is extended to include dealing with another's property against that other's will, so that using
§ 196. a thing deposited, or using a thing differently to that intended,
§ 197. amounts to theft, if without the owner's consent, and therefore
§ 198. neither an action of theft, nor one for corrupting a slave, will lie, where, in order to detect a would-be thief, a person allows
§ 199. his slave to take things to him. Examples of theft of free
§ 200. persons, and of a person's own property, are then given, as
§ 201. well as of cases where a person becomes possessed of another's property, and yet does not commit theft. Intentional co-
§ 202. operation in a theft may make the person liable as a principal.
§ 203-207. The right to bring an action for theft rests not on ownership, but on the question whose interest it is that the property
§ 208. should be safe, and as intention is involved in theft, only those who are above tender years can be held liable.

§ 209. (2.) *Robbery with violence.* This is shown to expose the offending party to a special action introduced by the prætor, and the three heads of the *Aquilian law* are then detailed relating to—

§ 210-214. (3.) *Damage wrongfully inflicted,* whether (α) by killing slaves
§ 215, 216. or quadrupeds, or (β) by an adstipulator fraudulently releasing
§ 217, 218. a debtor, or (γ) by inflicting any other kind of damage, pro-
§ 219. vided it was done by the person's own bodily act; for, if otherwise, only equitable actions lie.

§ 220. (4.) *Outrages.* In this class of wrongs an action lies in favour
§ 221. of all persons who suffer injury through the person actually
§ 222. outraged, the case of a slave being separately commented
§ 223. upon. The scale of penalties* according to the Twelve
§ 224. Tables is stated to be subject to modifications introduced by
§ 225. the prætor, and, finally, reference is made to outrages deemed *grave.*

Com. iv
§ 1-3. **Actions** are divisible, according to the better opinion, into two kinds only, viz.:—

(α) *real* and (β) *personal.*

Examples of both kinds are given, and the grounds explained for

* See note ¶, at p. xlvi, *post*, § 4 of Introduction.

Com. iv.

the existence of the anomalous personal action against thieves for the § 4. 5.
recovery of property. Illustrations follow of actions for the recovery § 6, 7.
of the thing only, for the recovery of the penalty only, and for the § 8, 9.
recovery of both.

The old *actions of the law* are then elaborately reviewed, their § 10, 11.
perilous nature referred to, and their five forms dealt with in order, § 12.
viz.:—

(1.) The *sacramental* action, a general form applicable in all § 13.
cases where the others were not provided. By the Twelve
Tables, the amount of the wager staked varied according to § 14.
the value of the property in dispute, or because liberty was
involved; but, with regard to the old rules as to the time for § 15.
the appointment of the judge,* an alteration was introduced
by the *Pinarian* law. A lively picture of the formal proceed- § 16.
ings taken before the prætor in the case of a real action, is
followed by an explanation of the expedients adopted where § 17.
the subject-matter of the suit was an immovable.†

The mis-use of the term "condictio", to indicate generally § 18.
a personal action, is commented upon, and the laws originating § 19.
this action pointed out, with a hint of the necessity for its § 20.
introduction not being apparent.

(4.) The action by way of *execution for a judgment debt* is shown § 21.
to have had its use extended to other cases by the *Publilian*, § 22.
the *Furian*, and other laws; as, for example, the *Marcian*, § 23.
which had made use of it, without assuming a judgment debt
to have been incurred, and hence an alteration in the mode of § 24.
conducting the defence followed, which led to its use being
further extended by the (?) *Vallian* law. § 25.

(5.) The action by way of *distraining on the debtor* is referred § 26.
for its origin partly to custom and partly to statute, and exam- § 27. 28.
ples of each class given, followed by remarks on the doubts § 29.
raised as to this being properly an action of the law.

The discredit brought upon these actions by their unbending cha- § 30.
racter is then stated to have led to their abolition by the *Æbutian* and
the two *Julian* laws, and the substitution of the—

Formulary system, though the old forms were retained when the case § 31.
went before the Centumviral tribunal.‡

The *fictions* used in certain formulæ to accommodate them to the § 32, 33.
old forms of action, are next adverted to, followed by examples of § 34.
fictions so introduced in order to get over the difficulty occasioned by
actions given by the prætor not being available in assertion of a legal
title, as in the case of the *Rutilian*, *Servian*, and *Publician* actions, § 35.

---

* Part of the passage included in § 15 is illegible in the manuscript, but the contents may be inferred from the context. See *post*, p. 518.

† A leaf of the manuscript is missing, and it can only be conjectured that a description followed of—

(2) the action demanding a judge, and of—

(3) the action in which the defendant is formally warned to appear in thirty days for the appointment of a judge.

‡ The next page of the manuscript is illegible.

Com. iv.
§ 36. and further examples of these fictions are given as applied to the case
§ 37. of a suit by or against an alien, or against a person who has under-
§ 38. gone a change of legal position.
§ 39-43. The principal *parts of a formula* are then taken in their order, with
§ 44. examples of their use, and an illustration given of actions where only
the one part stating the precise legal point involved is required.
§ 45. The distinction is explained between formulæ involving a *civil law*
§ 46. *issue*, and those *based upon the facts* of the case,* with examples of
§ 47. each class drawn from that part of the edict which deals with the
summons into court, and further examples are given of formulæ
adapted to both classes.
§ 48. The *pecuniary* nature of all judgments under the formulary system is
§ 49, 50. pointed out, with the distinction as to *certain* and *uncertain* sums being
named in the condemnation, and attention drawn to the necessity for
§ 51, 52. care on the part of the judge to name a precise sum, but not to ex-
ceed any limit fixed in the instructions addressed to him by the prætor.
§ 53, 53*a*. The rules relating to the penalties for *claiming too much*, are
elaborately reviewed, such claims being distributed under four heads,
§ 54. and formulæ of the uncertain class shown to be outside these rules,
§ 55. as also a real action claiming only an uncertain part of the whole, or a
claim of one thing instead of another; but, if less is claimed than is
§ 56. due, the residue cannot be demanded during the same prætorship. If
the condemnation is too great, the matter may be put right by the
§ 57. defendant applying to set the judgment aside, though, when the con-
demnation is for too small a sum, the plaintiff (unless a minor) loses
§ 58. the balance. An inaccurate preliminary statement does not vitiate the
§ 59, 60. proceedings, but conflicting views were entertained on this point, and
the matter is discussed at length, using, as an illustration, the case of
an action of deposit.†
§ 61. The subject of *set off* is introduced by showing that the powers of
the judge, in actions of good faith, include the right of taking into
account any claim the defendant may have in respect of the same
§ 62. matter, condemning him only in the balance; but, after giving a list
§ 63. of such actions, it is noted that these powers of the judge are due to
the nature of the action, and are distinguishable from such true cases
§ 64. of set off as are exemplified in an action by a banker; and these, again,
§ 65-68. are shown to differ from deductions of cross accounts made in an
action brought by the purchaser of an insolvent's estate against the
latter's debtors.
§ 69-70. Actions given against a father or master, on account of transactions
entered into by a son or slave, are next considered, together with the
§ 71. special actions available where the person in power has acted as
§ 72-74. master of a vessel, or manager of a shop, or has traded with his private
savings, and turned them to the profit of the father or master.‡

* For the meaning of this distinction, see *Ort. Anal.*, part iii, par. 1971, p. 347.
† The result of the argument is illegible.
‡ The greater part of the passage included in § 72, 73, is illegible in the manuscript, but may be filled up from *Justinian's* Institutes, iv, vii, § 4.

Com. iv.

Noxal actions are shown to involve the power of surrendering the § 75.
delinquent. Their origin is traced to the Twelve Tables, the Aquilian § 76.
law, and the prætor's edict. They are peculiar in following the § 77.
offending party, but do not lie between masters, or fathers, and their slaves or children, though conflicting views were entertained as to the § 78.
result in the case of the wrong doer falling into the power of the injured party, as also whether three formal sales were required when a § 79.
son in power was surrendered.

The mode of making the property of women under marital power, § 80.
or of freemen in a state of bondage, answerable, in the event of the person, into whose power they have fallen, not defending the suit, is next pointed out, and the question of the death of the offending party con- § 81.
sidered.*

The right of bringing or defending a suit through the instrumentality § 82-85.
of another, is stated to have not formerly been permitted, except in certain cases; but that the appointment of a cognitor, or a procurator, was now allowed, and the method of turning the condemnation against, § 86, 87.
or in favour of, the person suing in the name of another, is illustrated.

The rules as to the *security* required of the plaintiff, or of the de- § 88.
fendant, or of both, are next reviewed, involving the consideration of the stipulations by which this end was attained in the case of *real* § 89-94.
actions framed to claim the thing itself, as well as in those adopting the wager method, with the distinction to be drawn where the action comes § 95.
before the centumvirs. Plaintiffs suing by real actions, in their own § 96, 97.
name, or by cognitors, do not need to give security, though procu- § 98.
rators must do so as a guarantee that their acts will be ratified, and tutors and curators are also sometimes required to give it. In the case of plaintiffs in *personal* actions similar rules are shown to apply. Security is always required of persons acting on behalf of *defendants;* § 99, 100.
but, if the defendant himself appears, then only when the peculiar § 101.
nature of the action requires it, or when his credit is not good. § 102.

The distinction between actions resulting from the *civil law*, and § 103.
those based on the *authority of the magistrate*, is then explained, with the limitation of eighteen months as the period (by the Julian law) for § 104, 105.
barring the first, when not further proceeded with after delivery of the formula, and the term of office of the magistrate, as the period for barring the right of action in the second. The necessity is then § 106, 107.
pointed out for pleas of judgment awarded, or pending suit, in the second case, or where the actions of the first class are real, or based § 108.
on the facts, though this was not so with the old actions of the law; and examples are given of actions which, though resulting from some § 109.
law, yet were not of the civil law, or which were of the civil law, though not resulting from a law.

Actions springing from the prætor's jurisdiction are shown to be § 110, 111.
limited to one year, except where a civil law right has been taken as a precedent, and the non-liability of heirs to penal actions arising out § 112, 113.
of torts, or even, sometimes, to actions arising out of contract (as in the case of sponsors and fidepromissors), is dwelt upon, though such

* But the paragraph is illegible.

Com. iv.

actions are open to heirs, except, in torts, the action for outrage and others of that nature; and, in contract, the heir of an adstipulator has no action open to him.

§ 114. According to the Sabinians, it was the duty of the judge to absolve a defendant on his making satisfaction before judgment; but the Proculeians were opposed to this in the case of actions of strict law.

§ 115. *Exceptions* are stated to have been introduced as a mode of defence
§ 116, 117. to actions, and their use is explained by examples. They arose from
§ 118. laws, or from the prætor's jurisdiction. They are always negative
§ 119, 120. in form and are either peremptory or dilatory, the first barring the
§ 121, 122. action at any time, but the second, whether applying to persons or to
§ 123, 124. time, only acting temporarily, though whether a mistake in the use of
§ 125. a dilatory exception, could not be rectified by a restitution of rights was doubtful.

§ 126-129. *Replications* are used by the plaintiff to meet the defendant's exceptions; and these, in their turn, may be met by the defendant's rejoinder, and these by the plaintiff's surrejoinder, and so on, until the parties are at issue.

§ 130-132. *Prescriptions* are required by the *plaintiff* in order to limit his action
§ 133. to that part of the entire claim which is now due. The use formerly made of them by *defendants* is illustrated,* as also their application
§ 134, 135. to such cases as a master or father suing on his slave's or son's stipu-
§ 136-137. lation,† or where the action is brought in respect of an uncertain thing, against the promisor himself or against a sponsor or fidejussor.

§ 138. *Interdicts* arise out of the interposition of the authority of the prætor
§ 139. for the settlement of disputes, chiefly in cases of possession, and they are divided into:—

§ 140. (1.) *Restitutory*, *exhibitory*, or *prohibitory*.

§ 141-142. The action arising out of the issue of an interdict involves a penalty when it is by way of wager, as is usual with prohibitory interdicts, but not when an arbitrator is claimed, as is sometimes the case after the issue of the other two kinds.

§ 143. (2.) Those for *acquiring*, or *retaining*, or *recovering* possession.
§ 144, 145. The interdict, commencing "quorum bonorum", as well as
§ 146. the interdicts called "possessorum", "sectorium", and Sal-
§ 147. vianum", being examples of the first class. The interdicts,
§ 148. "uti possidetis" and "utrubi", belong to the second class.
§ 149. They are available for immovables and movables respectively,
§ 150. and involve the question of bona fide possession as against
§ 151. the adversary, whether this possession is that of others joined
§ 152. to our own or the possession of others on our behalf, some
§ 153. holding that possession may be retained even by the intention
§ 154, 155. only. The third class are usually applied for in cases of deprivation of possession by force, provided the applicant (un-

---

* The passage included in the page of the manuscript following § 133, is wholly illegible, but the contents may be conjecturally filled up as indicated above, and at p. 558.

† The portion of the text included between § 134-144 is contained on the sheet of parchment which had been detached from the rest, and is not palimpsest. See *ante*, p. iii, note ‡.

Com. iv.

less ejected by force of arms) had not been in possession by force, or secretly, or at will.

(3.) *Simple* and *double*, that is, those in which one party is plaintiff and the other defendant (as in the case of all restitutory and exhibitory interdicts), or those in which both parties occupy the same position, as is the case with some prohibitory interdicts. § 156-160.

The procedure, in respect of interdicts, is detailed at considerable § 161.
length, and it is shown that, in the case of simple interdicts, a penalty § 162, 163.
need not be involved, if an arbitrator be demanded; and, on his award, the thing sued for be restored, or produced, unless the defendant has opposed an action for vexatious litigation (involving the tenth part of the value), or the defendant has omitted to claim the arbitrator at once, § 164.
in which cases wagers and counterwagers are staked by plaintiff and defendant respectively. On these wagers, the formula is framed, to- § 165.
gether with a claim joined by the plaintiff for the restitution or production of the thing. Interim possession is then granted to that one of the litigants who makes the highest bidding for, and gives security for the restoration if necessary of, the produce. The judge next proceeds to ascertain, in the case of an interdict about possession, who was entitled to possess at the time the controversy arose, and then the amount of the wagers has to be paid by him against whom judgment § 166-168.
goes; and, if he is interim possessor, he has also to deliver up the property together with the produce, the Cascellian, secutorian, and § 169.
fructuarian actions being available by way of subsidiary aids in enforcing § 170.
these liabilities, as well as so-called *secondary* interdicts granted by the prætor in aid of the objects contemplated by the interdict first issued.*

Vexatious litigation is checked in the case of— § 171-173.

(1) the *defendant*, by actions for double the amount, by wagers, by the exaction of an oath that the defence is not vexatious, or by the fact that the nature of the original action involves the quadruple, treble, or double value.

(2) the *plaintiff*, by an action based on the fact, or by a cross- § 174-181.
action, or by an oath, or by the penalty involved in a restipulation. The first and third can always be used, the second only in special cases (examples of which are given), and is the most effective, as it always lies where the plaintiff fails in certain kinds of actions, but only one of the four remedies is available.

Certain actions also involve the loser in infamy, even if § 182, 183.
compromised, and a penalty is incurred by plaintiffs, who, without the permission of the prætor, commence an action against those who stand in peculiar positions towards them, as ascendants, or patrons, or the ascendants or children of the latter.

Finally, it is noted that, if the matter cannot be concluded on the § 184, 185.
day the defendant is summoned into court, he will have to find security for his reappearance. This is effected, at times with, at times without,

* The further explanation of the use of these secondary interdicts is illegible.

sureties; and an oath may be exacted, or recuperators appointed to at once condemn the defendant on non-appearance, in the amount of the security. This amount, in some cases, equals that involved in the
§ 186. action, otherwise it is ascertained by the oath of the plaintiff, but it cannot then be fixed at more than half the sum involved, nor over
§ 187. 100,000 sesterces, and a special application is necessary if security is required against the will of those whom we cannot summon into court without the prætor's permission.

From the foregoing summary of the contents of the manuscript the following conclusions may be drawn :—

(1) As to the *nature* of the work, that it is a treatise on law arranged so as to approach a scientific division of the subject, the reader being presented with a synoptical review of the private law of Rome under the three heads of persons, things, and actions, or, more accurately, the matter is grouped under—

(α) The law affecting special classes of persons, and relations of life, as parent and child, husband and wife, master and slave, patron and freedman, guardian and ward.

(β) The general law governing the mutual rights and duties of individuals, dealing with them under the heads of property or ownership, obligations, and inheritance.

(γ) The rules of civil procedure.*

As much of the matter detailed in these commentaries was previously unknown, the discovery of the work has thrown a flood of light on many interesting portions of Roman law, clearing up difficulties which embarrassed the student, and affording a fresh starting point on many important subjects,† but the work cannot strictly be said to

---

* For a criticism of the method observed by Gaius, see Austin's *Jurisprudence*, 4th edit., p. 764.

† These subjects are mainly :—

In the *first* commentary, the details as to the *lex regia* (§ 5), proving that this was not, as some have suggested, a falsification introduced by Tribonian to support the pretensions of absolute power asserted by his master, but an institution dating from the infancy of the state. (See *Ort. Anal.*, part i, par. 350, p. 40.) The rescript of Hadrian making the unanimous opinion of the privileged juris-consults binding on the judge (§ 7). The class of Latin Junians (§ 17). The application to aliens of the rules as to freedoms in fraud of creditors (§ 47). True notions as to marital power and the older forms of marriage (§ 108-115), and the power over a free man acquired by mancipatio (§ 116-123). The perpetual tutelage of women (§ 190-195A), as to which, see Maine's remarks at page 153, *Ancient Law*.

In the *second* commentary, the rules as to the possession of property with, and without, the beneficial interest (§ 148, 149). The rules as to the time allowed for deliberating as to the acceptance of an inheritance (§ 164-173). The four kinds of legacies (§ 192-223). The original state of the caduca laws before the alteration made by Caracalla in favour of the treasury (§ 206, 286).

In the *third* commentary, some details as to the kinds of theft, and the various actions relating thereto (§ 183-194). The second head of the Aquilian law (§ 215, 216).

In the *fourth* commentary, the forms of the actions of the law (§ 11-29), formulæ (§ 31-52), and the procedure in respect of interdicts (§ 161-170).

It is also from these commentaries that our knowledge of the points of difference between the Sabinian and Proculeian Schools of Law (*Ort. Anal.*, part i, par. 362,

come under the denomination of "Institutes", as that term specially applies, in Roman jurisprudence, to treatises devoted to the exposition in a simple and methodical manner of the general principles and elements of private law;* and from this point of view the four commentaries seem defective, as they are for the most part wanting in defini-

p. 41) is mainly derived. These differences seem chiefly to have arisen from the tendency of the Proculeians to push a legal principle to all its logical consequences, apart from the question of utility or convenience, and there are twenty-two references, in the commentaries, to the resulting differences of opinion on isolated points of detail, viz.: As to fixing an arbitrary age for puberty, i, § 196 (decided by Justinian in favour of the Proculeians): As to when domestic animals were res mancipi, ii, § 15, (the distinction between res mancipi and nec mancipi died out in time, and was abolished by Justinian): As to the effect of a surrender in court by a necessary heir, § 37 (and iii § 87), (the process of in jure cessio was falling into disuse in the time of Gaius, see ii, § 25, and was superseded before the time of Justinian): As to the property in a thing made out of another's materials, § 79 (an intermediate opinion adopted by Justinian, *Inst.* ii, 1, 25): As to the invalidity of an appointment of an heir in a testament in which a son was omitted § 123 (decided in favour of the Sabinians by Justinian): As to a legacy, bequeathed by way of giving the legatee the right to claim it, not vesting in the legatee until he assented to it, § 195 (decided by Antoninus Pius in favour of the Proculeians, but the opinion did not prevail, *Dig.* xxx, 86, § 1.): As to the person in whom it vested pending a condition, § 200 (also decided in favour of Proculeians): As to a legacy, by way of giving the legatee the right to take it before the division of the inheritance, being left to a person not the heir § 221 (decided by Hadrian in favour of the Proculeians): As to the appointment of a tutor before the heir, § 231 (the opinion of the Proculeians prevailed, Code vi, 23, l. 24): As to the validity of a legacy to a person in the power of the appointed heir, § 244 (settled in favour of Sabinians when conditional): As to the validity of a legacy in spite of its being left subject to an impossible condition, iii, § 98 (opinion of Sabinians prevailed): As to the effect of a stipulation made by a person in favour of himself, and another to whom he is not subject, § 103 (opinion of Proculeians confirmed by Justinian, Inst. iii, 19, 4): As to the effect of aliens contracting by means of written entries, § 133, (this form of contract disappeared before the point was settled): As to the validity of a sale at a price to be fixed by a third person, and as to an exchange not being a contract of sale, § 140, 141 (both points decided in favour of Proculeians): As to being able to bring an action of mandate up to the amount a person had been instructed to go, although he had exceeded the limit, § 161 (decided by Justinian in favour of Proculeians): As to the effect of the stipulation of a slave owned in common, but made by the order of one master, § 167A (opinion of Sabinians confirmed by Justinian): As to the effect of the payment of one thing for another with the consent of the creditor, § 168 (opinion of Sabinians confirmed by Justinian): As to novation in the case of the addition or withdrawal of a surety, § 178 (opinion of Sabinians in the special case of sponsors prevailed generally): As to the extinction of a noxal action by the wrongdoer falling into the power of the injured party, iv, § 78 (opinion of Sabinians confirmed by Justinian): As to the mode of surrendering a son in power, § 79 (the noxal abandonment of children fell into disuse, see *Just.* Inst., iv, viii, § 7): As to the effect of satisfaction before judgment absolving a defendant in all cases, § 114 (opinion of Sabinians confirmed by Justinian): As to the effect of demanding an arbitrator in the action for vexatious litigation, § 163 (opinion of Sabinians prevailed).

* During the period between Antoninus Pius and Alexander Severus (A.D. 138-222), we know of the publication of six *Institutes*, viz., those of Gaius in four books, those of Florentinus in twelve books, those of Callistratus in three books, those of Paul and those of Ulpian each in two books, and those of Ælius Marcianus in sixteen books; but only the first has come down to us, the contents of the rest being gathered from scattered fragments in the *Digest.* Celsus the younger, is said, on very doubtful authority, to have written seven books of Institutes during the reign of Hadrian, and if so, these would have been somewhat earlier than those of Gaius.

tions,* the boundaries of the threefold division are not maintained, and subjects are omitted which seem to stand on the threshold of an elementary work,† whilst, throughout, details wholly unsuited to a student's first book are treated at inordinate length.‡

From this, it may, perhaps, be concluded that the work consists of notes, which were subsequently drawn up methodically, and published in a collected form, but which were originally used as the basis of a series of oral lectures,|| devoted to the exposition in outline of the leading principles of Roman law, the lecturer having particularly in view the explanation of such points of practical difficulty as arose out of the peculiar condition of freed persons and aliens at the time,¶ together with the attempts of the prætor to meet the wants of such persons by means of a highly artificial system of pleading.**

(2) As to the *date* of the work, it will be noted that the law with which the author is dealing is in a transitional state, so that whilst some of the more ancient and salient features of Roman law (such as the perpetual tutelage of women, and the mancipium of free persons), are still in force, though softened in character, and eluded by the ingenuity of lawyers,†† others are treated as obsolete, such as the

---

* This possibly arose from the evident dislike of the author to commit himself to them, whilst the compilers of the Institutes of *Justinian* are conspicuous for their rashness in incorporating very doubtful definitions and derivations from other sources.

† Such as introductory matter by way of explanation of the nature of law and jurisprudence. Under the head of persons, the rules relating to marriage, the administration of the property of minors and wards, and the nature of the private property a son could hold. This last omission seems remarkable, as the rules relating to the peculium castrense were certainly in existence in the time of Gaius, if not those of the peculium quasi-castrense (see *Ort. Anal.*, part iii, par. 611, p. 176). Under the law of things, only the commencement and termination of the rights and duties relating to them are discussed, omitting such subjects as gifts, and the wife's dowry, inofficious testaments, the quarta legitima, and in the law of succession the degrees of relationship. In contracts a description of specific loan, deposit, pledge, and the innominate contracts is wanting. So, under actions, the mode of redress in the case of damage caused by animals is omitted.

‡ As for example, the position of Latins, aliens, and others with imperfect rights of citizenship, the mode of bringing children under power in the case of marriage by mistake with aliens, the old forms for creating marital power, and the intricacies of the law relating to legacies. In the fourth commentary, under the law of actions, there are long historical disquisitions on obsolete forms of procedure, and highly technical details of pleading are introduced which are outside the elements of the subject; but the keen interest of the author in the antiquities of his subject has rendered these very digressions invaluable to those students of the science of comparative jurisprudence who follow the historical method and find here careful notes on "survivals" by a painstaking and accurate observer. See Maine's *Early Institutions*, ch. ix.

|| See this matter discussed in Abdy and Walker's *Gaius*, preface, pp. ix, x.

¶ The condition of alien friends was a matter of infinite detail, and continued to be of primary importance for some half century longer. The differences between such aliens and citizens, and the distinctions between the classes of freed-persons were not finally suppressed until the reforms of Justinian. See my *Ort. Anal.*, part i, par. 181-197, pp. 20, 21; and par. 396 (2) pp. 45, 46; and part ii, par. 31, 32, p. 75; part iii, par. 65, p. 106.

** See my *Ort. Anal.*, part i, par. 222, p. 25; par. 252, p. 29; part iii, par. 1911, etc., p. 341.

†† *Gai.* i, § 190 (*Ort. Anal.*, part iii, par. 254, pp. 128, 129); *Gai.* i, § 141 (*Ort. Anal.*, part ii, par. 46 (3) p. 77). So the weight of the paternal power, the distinc-

actions of the law,* which are shown to be supplanted by the formulary system.

It also appears that another striking and characteristic feature of Roman law has long been in existence, and gives rise to perpetual intricate distinctions throughout the work, viz., that difference between civil and prætorian rights which had grown up, in consequence of the efforts of the prætor to undermine the principles of exclusion upon which the old civil law of Rome was grounded,† and with the aid of fictions, and by the manipulation of the formula, so work in equitable doctrines,‡ based upon the law of nations, as to mould the rude unbending legal institutions of a primitive race, and make them capable of dealing with the complicated interests arising from a constantly increasing territory and an advancing civilisation.

On the other hand, a close examination of the text shows that the legislative innovations of the prætors had just come to an end, for Julianus, the author of the Perpetual Edict, is mentioned; and though Hadrian, in whose reign this change was carried out, is always spoken of as deceased, his successor, Antoninus Pius, is, in the first portion of the work, alluded to as if living, and only in the later portion referred to as of pious memory, whilst the epithets applied to Marcus Aurelius, indicate that he is the occupant of the throne.|| It may be further remarked, by way of negative evidence, that there are no re-

---

tion of things into those requiring a formal civil law conveyance, and those passing by delivery, and the classes of Latin junians, dediticii, etc., show the vigour of the old law still existing.

* *Gai.* iv, § 30. So of patrician agnation (gens) iii, § 17.

† The history of Rome "is little more than a narrative of conflicts between a stubborn nationality and an alien population". Maine's *Ancient Law*, p. 47.

‡ These Commentaries clearly show (*e.g.*, iv. § 34-38) that it was mainly by the manipulation of the formula, and not as in England (until recently in theory, and still in fact), by the existence of an independent set of courts administering a system (styled equity) different from that of the ordinary courts, that the prætor obtained his results.

|| The word "divus" (which, for the sake of brevity, I have translated by "late", though "of pious" or "blessed memory", would be perhaps more accurate) always precedes the name of Hadrian (except in i, § 47, and ii, § 57, where reference is only made to senatus-consulta "ex auctoritate Hadriani"); and at ii, § 195, the word is prefixed to the name of Antoninus Pius, although at i, § 53, 74, 102; ii, § 120, 126, he is alluded to as if then living; hence, it is supposed that that emperor had died in the interval, though too much reliance must not be placed on such details in the only and defective manuscript that has reached us. Again, Ulpian mentions (*Rules*, xxii, 34) that Marcus Aurelius had altered the harsh doctrine referred to in *Gai.* ii, § 177 (as to the appointed heir, by omitting the formality of making the sacramental declaration of acceptance of the inheritance, letting in the substituted heir for a share), and therefore it is supposed that the work was completed before that time, and, as in iii, § 23, 24, there is a statement of the hardships sustained by women in the matter of succession, it is further supposed that this portion of the treatise was not consecutive, and was written before the passing of the senatus-consultum Tertullianum in A.D. 158, under Antoninus Pius, but it is not improbable that an account of this decree filled up the illegible portion of the manuscript following, iii, § 33. As to the reciprocal senatus-consultum (Orphitianum) passed in favour of children twenty years later, see note ||, *post*, p. xxviii. Again, at iii, § 78, when speaking of the sale of the property of insolvent debtors, no mention is made of the rescript of Marcus Aurelius authorising the grant of the property to one of the freed slaves in order to secure the liberty of the other slaves freed by testament (*Ort. Anal.*, part iii, par. 1154, p. 255), and it seems clear that the work was

ferences to any constitutions subsequent to these emperors, and no quotations or opinions of any jurisconsult* belonging to a later period.

From this internal evidence, it may with confidence be assumed that the four commentaries must have been composed under the Antonine Cæsars, in the second century of our era, during the most brilliant and classical period of Roman jurisprudence.

(3) As to the *authorship* of the work, it will be found that the manuscript contains all the passages quoted from the Institutes of Gaius in the Digest, as well as the passages referred to by Priscian in his work on grammar, and by Boethius in his commentaries on the Topica of Cicero. It also includes the passages used by the author of the Mosaicarum et Romanorum legum collatio, and is the apparent source of the mutilated abridgment of the first three books contained in the Breviarium Alaricianum. These facts, combined with the parallelism of the four commentaries with the Institutes of Justinian, which are admitted, in the preface to the latter, to be founded upon the former, lead irresistibly to the conclusion that the manuscript in question contains the genuine text of that elementary work of Gaius, which, for centuries preceding the reforms of Justinian, was in the hands of every law student during his first year's course at the schools.†

§ 3. OF GAIUS.

Of the personal history, or even the family name, of the author of the work described in the last section, nothing is positively known, and the mode of spelling and pronouncing the prænomen has been the subject of dispute.‡

The evidence already detailed as to his Institutes, combined with the references made to dates and facts, in the extracts we possess of his other works,|| all tend to show that he was born under Hadrian, that

---

written previous to Caracalla, because lapsed legacies are stated (ii, § 206, 286) to fall, by the provisions of the Julian and Papian laws, to those heirs or legatees named in a will who had legitimate offspring, whereas that emperor made such legacies go at once into the Treasury. See Ulpian, *Reg.*, xvii, § 2, and my *Ort. Anal.*, part i, par. 369, p. 43.

* The jurists mentioned in the manuscript are:—Cassius, Fufidius, Javolenus, Julianus, Labeo, Nerva, Ofilius, Proculus, Sabinus, Scævola (Quintus Mucius), Servius Sulpicius, Sextus. For the dates of these jurisconsults, see my *Ort. Anal.*, and, for the places where they are mentioned in the MS., consult index to present volume.

† See note **, *post*, p. liv.

‡ In classical times the word was trisyllabic, and spelt with a C. See the whole matter exhaustively discussed in the article on Gaius, by J. T. Graves, in Dr. Smith's *Dict. of Gr. and R. Biog.*

|| In addition to the evidence afforded by his Institutes as given, *ante*, p. xxvi, it may be added that in his work on bequests in trust, quoted in the *Digest*, xxxiv, 5, 7, Gaius speaks of a remarkable case of childbirth having occurred during the reign of Hadrian, and apparently in his own lifetime; but the expression "nostra ætate" is somewhat indefinite. If the heading in the extract in the *Digest*, xxxviii, 17, 9, is to be trusted, Gaius wrote a treatise on the Orphitian decree of the senate passed under Marcus Aurelius, A.D. 178. This, if correct, would bring his writings down to two years before the death of that Emperor.

he wrote at a time when the empire was ruled in succession by two of the noblest beings that ever lived, Antoninus Pius and Marcus Aurelius, and that he probably died under Commodus.*

The writings of Gaius include commentaries on the elements of law (the Institutes), on the Twelve Tables, on the Urban, Ædilitian and Provincial Edicts, Rules for Practice, and an Every-day book, which subsequently acquired the name of the Golden Treasury.

These works, which, with the exception of the Institutes, are only known through the passages extracted from them in other works, entitle Gaius to a place amongst the greatest of the Roman writers on law; and the use made of them in the compilation of Justinian's Digest,† shows the high estimation in which they were held. It is, therefore, surprising that we possess so little knowledge of their author. Some would explain this by assuming, on very insufficient grounds, that he was a provincial,‡ whilst others would identify him with some other jurisconsult referred to under his family name;|| but there seem to be two satisfactory reasons why Gaius is not quoted by other writers. These are, first, that it was not until two centuries after the period usually assigned for his death, that, by the citation law, imperial authority gave formal recognition to his works;¶ and, there-

---

* "If a man were called to fix the period in the history of the world, during which the condition of the human race was most happy and prosperous, he would without hesitation name that which elapsed from the death of Domitian to the accession of Commodus (A.D. 96-180). The vast extent of the Roman empire was governed by absolute power, under the guidance of virtue and wisdom. The armies were restrained by the firm, but gentle, hand of four successive Emperors, whose characters and authority commanded involuntary respect. The forms of the civil administration were carefully preserved by Nerva, Trajan, Hadrian, and the Antonines, who delighted in the image of liberty, and were pleased with considering themselves as the accountable ministers of the laws." Gibbon's *Decline and Fall of the Roman Empire;* Dr. Smith's edit. 1854. vol. i, p. 216.

† Out of upwards of fifteen works attributed to Gaius, the compilers of the *Digest* extracted 535 fragments from the following:—1, fifteen books *Ad leges Juliam et Papiam* (28 extracts); 2, seven books *Rerum cottidianarum sive aureorum* (26 extracts); 3, one book *De Casibus* (7 extracts); 4, two books *Ad Edictum Ædilium Curulium* (11 extracts); 5, ten books *Ad Edictum Prætoris Urbani* (47 extracts); 6, thirty books *Ad Edictum Provinciale* (340 extracts); 7, two books *Fidei Commissorum* (12 extracts); 8, one book *Ad Formulam Hypothecariam* (6 extracts); 9, four books *Institutionum* (14 extracts); 10, three books *De Verborum Obligationibus* (12 extracts); 11, three books *De Manumissionibus* (5 extracts); 12, one book *Regularum* (1 extract); 13, one book *Ad Legem Gliciam* (?) (1 extract); 14, six books *Ad Legem Duodecim Tabularum* (20 extracts); and the remaining 5 extracts from single books, probably entitled, *De Tutelis, De Testamentis et De Legatis, De Re Uxoria, De Tacitis Fideicommissis,* and *Ad S. C. Tertullianum* and *Orphitianum,* but the authenticity of some of these latter works is doubtful.

‡ Relying upon the passage in his Institutes, ii. § 7.

|| See this argument refuted in the article on Gaius in Dr. Smith's *Dict. of Gr. and R. Biog.*

¶ The practice of making the opinions of eminent jurisconsults rest, not on the professional reputation of their authors, but on their selection by the emperor, was introduced by Augustus (*Dig.* i, 2, 2, § 47), probably in furtherance of his general scheme for the centralization of power by covertly converting troublesome republican institutions into engines of his own will. By the time of Hadrian, the Roman world had become sufficiently accustomed to imperial despotism for the head of the state to legislate avowedly as a monarch, and, as a consequence, the legal reforms

fore, previous to that time, these works, however intrinsically valuable, could not be cited as of binding authority in support of a proposition of law; and, secondly, that, as his writings do not include Quæstiones or Responsa, as in the case of other jurisconsults who published notes of the cases arising in their own practice,* it may be inferred that he

introduced by the prætor's edict were put a stop to, and at the same time the unanimous opinion of a few selected jurisconsults was made binding on the judge (*Gai* i, § 7; *Just.* Inst. i, ii, § 8), so that the indirect influence of the unprivileged, and possibly little subservient, portion of the legal profession in the growth of law was practically destroyed.

The system, however, combined with the growth of despotism generally, was inconsistent with the independence required for the voluntary elaboration of the principles of law. By the end of the reign of Alexander Severus (A.D. 235) or at least, by the time of Diocletian, the whole of the brilliant professors of law, who had held the highest dignities in the State, died out; and the steady decline of law, science, and letters commenced. During the troublous times that ensued, the best intellects gradually forsook the bar, and engaged in the more exciting field of religious controversy, whilst the jurists degenerated into a class who, in their pleadings before the judges or in their lectures in the public schools, simply quoted the writings of the prudentes and the imperial constitutions. These men were, not only unequal, but unwilling to wade through the mass of treatises on law which had descended from classical times, and it may, perhaps, be assumed, that, without much judgment in the selection, the method grew gradually into favour of taking the opinions given in the works of a few of the leading jurisconsults as decisive of controverted points, for we know that Constantine (A.D. 321) had to interfere, to prevent the notes of Paul, Ulpian, and Marcian, on the writings of Papinian, overriding the text, and a few years later (A.D. 327), he had again to interfere to give authority to the opinions of Paul himself. In this state of things, and in the struggle amongst the works of deceased writers for pre-eminence, and the survival of the fittest, it is probable that five great luminaries of the law, Gaius, Papinian, Ulpian, Paul, and Modestinus, became tacitly accepted as authoritative guides, for we find these five selected by the author of the *Mosaicarum et Romanorum legum collatio*, or *Lex Dei*, a work which probably appeared about A.D. 410. (See *Ort. Anal.* part i, par. 511 (2), p. 55). The want, however, of legislative sanction to this mode of compromising the embarrassing position arising out of the multitude of legal works which could be appealed to, appears to have pressed itself at this time upon the attention of the leaders of the legal profession, and in connection with the establishment of a school of law at Constantinople in A.D. 425, the idea was conceived of presenting an embodiment of the actual living law by uniting in one mass, and publishing, under imperial authority, all the valuable portions of the writings of the classical jurisconsults, together with such parts of the rescripts of the emperors, as were then in force, but this grand scheme for consolidating the law of Rome, the necessity for which had, centuries before this, haunted the minds of Cicero, Julius Cæsar (*Ort. Anal.*, part 1, par. 237, p. 27), and others, was never carried out, and all that the commissioners appointed by Theodosius II actually accomplished was :—

(1) the issue in A.D. 426 of the *Lex de responsis prudentum*, or constitution known as the "Citation" Law (*Cod. Theod.* i, 43), by which the authority of the five deceased jurists mentioned above (including the passages from other authors referred to by them) was formally recognised, that is, Papinian, Paul, Gaius, Ulpian, and Modestinus, were created members of a sort of Council giving binding opinions by the majority, with a casting vote in the hands of Papinian in the event of a difference of opinion.

(2) the publication in A.D. 438 of the Theodosian Code, which embodied all the Imperial Constitutions which had appeared up to that date, and formed a continuation of the collection made by the private labours of Hermogenianus and Gregorianus (see *Ort. Anal.*, part i, par. 499 and 502, p. 54, and Puchta, *Cursus*, § 134, *et seq.*).

* The work of Gaius entitled *de Casibus*, did not relate to cases within his own practice, see for example the extract in Digest xii, 6, 63.

did not give opinions as a practising lawyer, but occupied the position of a private teacher.

The style of Gaius, as shown in the Institutes, and in the extracts from his other works, is, like that of the majority of the classical jurists of his time, pure and concise,* with an entire absence of any ostentatious display of a knowledge of greek theories, though he understood greek.† His works exhibit some acquaintance with foreign law.‡ They also prove that he was well read in the history, theory, and practice of his profession, and, though his perception of the defects of the legal institutions he explained, occasionally leads him to indulge in a little dry humour at their expense,|| it is evident that he was keenly sensible of the caution necessary in introducing innovation, as well as of the risk attending hasty definitions or sweeping generalisations. With the true instincts of an educated lawyer, he

---

* This conciseness and terseness render the Commentaries difficult to translate, and the fondness of the author for dilating on archaic forms increases the difficulty. If English law had not been saturated with feudal rules, the task would have been easier; but any attempt to introduce English technical law terms as equivalent expressions in the domain of proprietary rights, whether real or personal, would be fatally misleading to a student of a legal system like the Roman, which is free from the feudal taint (see *ante*, p. xii, note *). On the other hand, I have not hesitated to use such latin technical terms as are employed in their correct sense in the daily practice of the English courts (*e. g.*, gifts *inter vivos*, or *mortis causa*, inofficious testaments, etc.). The French translations of Boulet and Domenget have been of use to me, but they do not contain the new passages which have been recently deciphered. The numerous English translations, which have already appeared, do not afford so much assistance as might be expected, for they all, more or less, err (if I may venture to say so), in assuming that when a difficult latin word occurs, all that is required is to tack on an english termination to it, and so give it the ring of the latin original; but when the genius of the language and the institutions of the people are different, the terms are not convertible, and all the student really acquires by this method is a knowledge of a number of meaningless barbarisms that do not belong to any known language; for example, in Poste's Gaius, *jus gentium* (*i.e.*, the law common to all nations), is translated "gentile law", which conveys a totally misleading idea; so *jus postliminii* (*i.e.*, the law as to the resumption of rights on return from captivity), is translated "the right of retrospective rehabilitation". So, for example, in both Abdy and Walker's, and Muirhead's, Gaius, the *legatum per damnationem* (*i.e.*, the legacy bequeathed by way of ordering the heir to give it) is translated as the legacy "by damnation", an expression which can only provoke a smile. The result of translating in this way is that the subject wears a strange uncouth dress, which repels the beginner; whereas, if intelligible terms and paraphrases are used, the path is smoothed to the understanding of those peculiarities which otherwise form such stumbling-blocks in the student's path, such as the *mancipium*, the *co-emptio*, the *manus*, etc., expressions which, though afterwards twisted, by the ingenuity of counsel, to cope with the more complex requirements of an advancing civilisation, really only indicate the crude attempts of a peasant population to meet the legal necessities of an infant society, and which, when stripped of technical phraseology, and expressed in words of everyday use, will be found not to be necessarily bound up with a past age; but, even the most primitive, to be rudimentary forms of analogous legal institutions existing at the present moment. Compare, for example, as Maine has done (*Ancient Law*, p. 159), the patria potestas of Roman law, and the position of wives at common law apart from statutory or equitable interference.

† See *Com.*, iii § 141, etc. These quotations from Homer were probably those usually cited in support of the propositions they illustrated.

‡ For example, *Com.* i, § 55, 189, 193, 197; *Com.* ii, § 40; *Com.* iii, § 96, 120.

|| For example, *Com.* iii, § 193.

shrinks from unnecessarily advancing his own opinion;* and, though he admits himself a Sabinian,† he was not a bigoted adherent of the school;‡ indeed, he never quotes its founder Capito. It will be found, in the Institutes, that he usually contents himself with placing, side by side, the different views of the two schools,|| adding such remarks, bearing on the history of the subject, as tend to throw light on the growth of the doctrine, and summing up the matter, where practicable, by stating that view which had been held to be the better, either by some imperial rescript involving the point,¶ or by the weight of professional opinion.**

---

§ 4. OF THE INSTITUTES OF JUSTINIAN.††

On the accession of Justinian, in A.D. 527, the law in force in the Eastern Empire may be said practically to have consisted‡‡ of:—

(1) the *jura*, or writings, of those classical prudentes whose opinions had been rendered authoritative by the citation law|||| of Valentinian III, and Theodosius II, for these commentaries had, in fact, superseded the law which they professed to explain, viz., the plebiscita, the senatus-consulta, the pretorian edicts, and the rest of the chaotic mass of the legislative enactments of Ancient Rome.

(2) the *leges*, or imperial constitutions, as contained in the Gregorian, Hermogenian, and Theodosian codes, and in the novellæ, which had been published subsequently.

The revision of these two bodies of law was undertaken by Justinian with a view, as to the *jura*, to condense them into a digest, so as to get rid of the necessity for the method of numerical computation, which had been in use for a century; and, as to the *leges*, to bring the collection of constitutions down to the latest date.

The second and easier of the two tasks was first dealt with; the commission appointed by Justinian, publishing under his authority in A.D. 529, the collection of imperial constitutions now known as the first Code,¶¶ and which was subsequently suppressed on the appearance, five years later, of an amended edition.

---

* But see *Com.* i, § 172, 190; *Com.* ii, § 78, 232; *Com.* iii, § 64, 76, 94, 98, 120, 184, 193; *Com.* iv, § 1, 24, 60, 152, 163.

† *Com.* ii, § 15, 195.

‡ See, for example, *Com.* ii, § 154; *Com.* iii, § 98.

|| See, for example, *Com.* ii, § 15, 231; *Com.* iii, § 87, 141, 168.

¶ See, for example, *Com.* ii, § 195, 221.

** See, for example, *Com.* ii, § 198 (cf. *Just.* Inst., ii, xx, § 12).

†† The third part of my analysis of M. Ortolan's work is devoted to an historical exposition of the contents of the Institutes of *Justinian*, and therefore this section is confined to such matters as tend to indicate the differences between these Institutes and the Commentaries of *Gaius*.

‡‡ See Puchta, *Cursus, etc.*, vol. i, § 139; and Savigny, *Geschichte des Römischen Rechts im Mittelalter*, 2nd edit., 1834, vol. i, p. 31, etc.

|||| *Ante*, note ¶, p. xxix.

¶¶ See *Ort. Anal.*, part i, par. 539, 540, 550, pp. 58, 59, 60.

In A.D. 530 the first, and more formidable, undertaking was entered upon, but whilst this great work was in progress, it became apparent that neither the Digest, nor the Code, was suited to the first stages of a law student's studies, and Justinian therefore confided to Tribonian, his principal law officer, and the editor of all his works,* together with Theophilus and Dorotheus, professors of law at Constantinople and Berytus respectively, the task of preparing a work which would serve as an introductory manual.

The text-book at that time in the hands of students in the law schools was the Institutes of Gaius, but three and a half centuries had elapsed since this work was composed, and in the interval the law of Rome had undergone very great modification by reason of a number of important influences which had been brought to bear upon it, and which may be roughly grouped under four heads, viz. :—

(1.) Constitutional changes due to the growth of despotism, under which all traces of the republican institutions still lingering in the time of Gaius were eradicated, and, by the absorption of the ordinary in the extraordinary procedure, an entire change was effected in the organisation of the courts of law.†

(2.) The transfer of the seat of government from Rome to Byzantium, involving the change of language, the extinction of italian privileges, and the gradual disappearance of those technical distinctions and subtleties which depended on the legal atmosphere of ancient Rome.‡

(3.) The cessation of foreign conquest, and that slow fusion of races and classes within the Empire, which tended to bring about an equality in the condition of citizens and aliens, free-born and freed.

(4.) The influence of christianity. This religion had at first, by separating itself from the existing institutions, excited the

---

* Tribonian, though not a man of any originality, was well acquainted with law, and possessed one of the best libraries then in existence. See *Ort. Anal.*, part i, par. 565, p. 61; and p. 281, chap. 44, Gibbon's *Decline and Fall, etc.*, Dr. Smith's edit. 1854.

† That is, the formulary system, with its trial by a judge and one or more jurymen, was abolished, and trial by a judge alone substituted. (See *Ort. Anal.*, part i, par. 427, 442, 493, 579, pp. 47, 49, 62). In consequence of this change, much of the learning as to the use of exceptions and prescriptions in pleading by formula; and as to the practice relating to interdicts, which occupies so many pages of the fourth Commentary of *Gaius*, became obsolete. See *post*, note **, p. lii.

‡ Examples of such results are shown in the disappearance of the modes of acquiring marital power in the form of *manus*, and power over a freeman in a state of bondage called *mancipium* (see *Ort. Anal.*, part iii, par. 150 and 153, p. 117), together with the process of *mancipatio* itself, and practically (so far as the Eastern Empire was concerned) of the testament *per æs et libram* (see Maine's *Ancient Law*, ch. vi, p. 214; and Just. *Inst.*, ii, x, § 1). So of the distinction between *bonorum possessio cum re* and *sine re* (*Ort. Anal.*, part iii, par. 1123, p. 252). So as to the technical modes of appointing an heir in the testament (law of Constantine ii, in A.D. 339; *Ort. Anal.*, part iii, par. 715, p. 185). So as to the rules relating to "cretio" (suppressed in A.D. 407, *Ort. Anal.*, part iii, par. 821, p. 196). So as to the universal succession to an insolvent debtor's property (*Ort. Anal.*, part iii, par. 1161, p. 257). So as to sponsors and fidepromissors as special classes of sureties (*Ort. Anal.*, part iii, par. 1384, 1392, pp. 271, 272). So as to the contract *litteris* (*Ort. Anal.*, part iii, par. 1414, p. 276), and the necessity for a cognitor as a representative of plaintiff or defendant in a law suit (*Ort. Anal.*, part iii, par. 2228, 2233, pp. 379, 380).

hostility of the governing powers, but on its subsequent adoption by the state, it caused a still greater reactionary antipathy against adherents of the old, or any other faith, and directly affected the administration of justice by leading to the creation of an episcopal jurisdiction. It also, through the rise of monastic institutions and charitable foundations, brought about alterations in the law affecting the power of corporate bodies to acquire and hold property.* In other departments of law its influence resulted from its principles, and was therefore less direct, but its tendency to further equitable views made it everywhere felt. By fostering the doctrine of equality, it tended, in the domestic forum, to ameliorate the condition of slaves, as well as to soften the rigours of the ancient law in respect of the power of the father over the person or property of his children,† and, on the death of the head of the family intestate, it favoured the claims of blood relations as against the civil law heirs. By reproving second marriages, and encouraging celibacy, it led to the suppression of the incapacities of childless legatees,‡ and it directly tended to the removal of such brutalising influences as gladiatorial exhibitions.||

These powerful influences had not, however, prior to Justinian, borne their full fruit: for legislation had been checked, and rendered spasmodic and temporary, by various causes, such as the anxiety arising from the incessant inroads of the barbarians, the constant uncertainty as to the next successor to the throne, together with the division of the Empire, and the fall of the Western portion. In the result, therefore, a number of distinctions, long worn threadbare by time, were not authoritatively abolished until the reforms of Justinian; but, in the course of the six years intervening between his accession and the publication of the Institutes, he suppressed the old civil law distinctions between the classes of freedmen,¶ between italian and provincial soil, between quiritarian and bonitarian ownership, and between things requiring a formal conveyance, and things passing by delivery. He assimilated the rules relating to gifts *mortis causa*, bequests in trust, and legacies, and gifts before and after marriage. He rendered valid obligations entered into for the benefit of heirs;** and he made radical changes in the laws affecting manumission, prescription, adoption, insolvency, and testamentary and intestate succession, besides withdrawing the ownership of the son's property from the father, and destroying the power of the father over the son on the attainment by the latter of certain dignities.

In consequence of these great changes, the editors of the Institutes

* See *Ort. Anal.*, part i, par. 467, 471 (1), 495, 581, part ii, par. 99, pp. 51, 54, 62, 81.

† See *Ort. Anal.*, part i, par. 479, p. 52.

‡ See *Ort. Anal*, part i, par. 369, p. 43.

|| Mentioned by Gaius at iii, § 146, and finally put down by Honorius.

¶ *Ort. Anal.*, part iii, par. 67, p. 106.

** So that the necessity for an additional creditor (adstipulator) became unnecessary (*Ort. Anal.*, part iii, par. 1377, 1746, pp. 271, 325), and the rule was extended to cover such cases as mandates to do something after the mandatee's death (cf. *Gai. Com.* iii, § 158, with *Ort. Anal.*, part iii, par. 1361, p. 269).

of Justinian, whilst following closely the method, the arrangement, and, wherever possible, the very words of the Commentaries of Gaius,* found it necessary, on the one hand, to cut out large portions of the latter work as obsolete; and, on the other hand, to interpolate a quantity of new matter so as to adapt the commentaries to the existing state of the law. They also borrowed, from the works of other jurists,† passages on such additional subjects as, in their opinion, it seemed advisable, in an elementary treatise, to notice in outline, and, in the course of the preparation of the Institutes, they settled (or referred to the Imperial Constitutions, particularly those of Justinian, which had settled) a large number of controverted points suggested by Gaius himself, or by the other jurists from whose works passages were incorporated.

In the result, the following passages were respectively—‡

Struck out.	*Added.*
	A *preface*, in the form of a constitution, drawn in the laudatory style usual in the case of a chancellor writing in the name of the Emperor, ‖ and stating

* On turning over the following pages (4 to 246) it will be seen at a glance to what extent the Commentaries of *Gaius* were reproduced by the compilers of the Institutes of *Justinian*, as identical passages are shown in the latter in *italics*. The labour of the student, in attempting to master the two works, is thereby greatly abridged; but I have not gone the length of showing the identity in *parts* of words, as when, for example, Gaius uses the *present*, and Justinian the *past* tense, I have thought that the eye of the student would be more readily attracted to the alteration in the law by letting the whole word appear in Justinian as an alteration, *e.g.*, *legatur* and *legabatur* (*Gai.*, ii, § 229, 232; *Just.*, ii, 20, § 34, 35); but on immaterial points, as the manuscript before Tribonian and his colleagues may have differed from the Verona palimpsest, I have been guided by Polenaar in treating the text as identical, in spite of the use of equivalents, such as "vel" for "aut", "veluti" for "velut", the subjunctive for the indicative; or, again, the use of the second person for the first or third, or the singular for the plural, or conventional names, such as Mævius, etc. (cf. *Gai.*, iii, § 221, 222; iv, § 4, 78, 126; and *Just.*, iv, 4, § 2, 3; 6, § 14; 8, § 6).

† Viz., from the works of Celsus, Julianus, Pomponius, Papinian, Tryphoninus, Ulpian, Paul, Callistratus, Marcianus, Florentinus, and particularly from the *Every Day Book* of Gaius, which seems to have been somewhat later in date than his Institutes, and from which probably more was taken than can be traced, as the original is not extant, and, like the works of the other jurists, chiefly known by the extracts in the Digest. As the jurists mentioned above all lived prior to, during the life of, or shortly after the death of, Gaius, the passages from their works must have been introduced rather as amplifications of such subjects as were deemed by the editors necessary for a work of this class, than as embodying alterations of the law. For the dates and works of the above-mentioned jurists, see Index to *Ort. Anal.*, and for the places where the various extracts are inserted, see the foot-notes to the rest of this section of the Introduction. The majority of the extracts are given in full in Pellat's *Manuale Juris Synopticum*, and copious references to them will be found in the side and foot notes to Gneist's *Syntagma*, a work to which all English editors of Gaius and Justinian are greatly indebted.

‡ The number of passages shown in the following pages as struck out include 478 of the sections into which Goeschen's arrangement divides the work. To these must be added 8 sections (viz., Com. i, § 2, 5, 6; Com. ii, § 2, 3, 5, 10, 11) which were omitted by the editors, owing to the same matter being taken by preference from the works of Ulpian, Marcianus, and the Every Day Book of Gaius. On the whole the editors appear to have used about 415 out of a total of 901 sections.

‖ The fulsome and debased style which characterises the portions of the Institutes of *Justinian* actually due to the pen of the editors contrasts very unfavourably with the terse periods of the underlying Commentaries of *Gaius*.

Com. i. *Struck out.* *Added.* Bk. i.

the nature of the work, the sources from which it
was derived, and giving to the contents of the book
the force of law.*

Preliminary chapter† containing definitions of Tit. i.
justice and *jurisprudence*, the *maxims* of the law,
and dividing law into *public* and *private*, deriving
the latter from *natural* law, the law of *nations*, and
the *civil* law. An attempt is made to discriminate Tit. ii.
between the two first‡ of these three, grounded on pr.
a supposed conflict between them on the subject (Tit. v, pr.)
of slavery, and illustrations follow of the distinction § 2.
between the two last. Law is then divided into § 3.
written and *unwritten*, and constitutions affecting
particular persons are distinguished from those of § 6.
general application. || Unwritten law is derived from § 9.
custom, and its origin fancifully traced to the laws of § 10.
Lacedemon, with remarks on the immutability of § 11.
natural law as compared with the civil law.

In the law of *persons* definitions are given of Tit. iii.
freedom and slavery, with the origin of the latter, ¶ § 1-4.
and the definition of the free born is amplified in
accordance with the tendency of legislation subse- Tit. iv.
quent to Gaius, the views of his contemporary Mar- pr.
cellus in favour of liberty being incidentally con-
firmed.**

The various authorised modes of conferring liberty Tit. v.
on slaves are enumerated, including that in church.†† § 1.

	Struck out.	Added.
§ 12-19. § 21-35.	All the details as to the two descriptions of freedmen classed as latins and surrendered persons.	The two obsolete classes of freedmen stated to be formally abolished.‡‡

The appointment of a slave as heir is in all cases Tit. vi.
to imply the gift of freedom.|||| Gifts of freedom by § 1-3.
insolvent masters only to be void if done with

---

* And so taking the book out of the class-room and rendering it binding on the law courts in respect of any disputed points it incidentally decided.

† Borrowed from the Rules and Institutes of *Ulpian*. See Dig. i, 1, 1 pr. § 1-3; Dig. i, 1, 10 pr. § 1, 2; Dig. i, 1, 4.

‡ See *Ort. Anal.*, part iii, par. 19, 20, p. 101, and Austin's *Jurisprudence*, 4th edit., pp. 215, 216, 569, 584. This useless distinction between natural law, and the law of nations, of which no further use is made, is one of the many examples of the defective nature of the Institutes of *Justinian*, as compared with the original Commentaries of *Gaius*. The want of originality here becomes evident, the labours of the Commission in drawing additional matter from various sources having been at times very unskilfully performed. For further examples of unnecessary distinctions and inaccuracies, see *post*, notes to bk. iii, tit. 13, § 1; 25, § 2, and bk. iv, tit. 6; and *Ort. Anal.*, part iii, par. 2246, p. 383.

|| Institutes of *Ulpian*, *Dig.* i, 1, 6, § 1; *Dig.* 1, 4, 1 pr. § 1, 2.

¶ Institutes of *Florentinus*, *Dig.* i, 5, 4 pr. § 1-3.

** Principally from Institutes of *Marcianus*, *Dig.* i, 5, 5 pr. § 1-3.

†† Introduced by Constantine (C. i, 13).

‡‡ By Justinian (C. vii, 5 and 6, 1).

|||| Justinian (C. vi, 27, 5).

Com. i. *Struck out.* | *Added.* Bk. i.

fraudulent intent. Masters over seventeen to be § 7.
able to free their slaves by testament.

§ 42-47. The restrictions imposed by the Fusian-Caninian law on manumission. | The Fusian-Caninian law imposing restrictions on manumission, repealed.* Tit. vii.

The terms of the rescript, referred to by Gaius, of Tit. viii.
the Emperor Antoninus, as to the protection to be afforded to slaves fleeing to the statues of the Emperor, set out.

§ 54. The distinction between the legal and equitable ownership of a slave.

The subject of *marriage* is amplified by a defini- Tit. ix.
tion, and the point settled as to the liberty to marry Tit. x.
allowed to the son of a lunatic,† whilst marriage with pr.
a brother's daughter is stated to be unlawful,‡ and § 3.
a lengthy statement added of the obstacles resulting § 7-11.
from affinity, followed by the rights of children as § 13.
affecting the rules of marriage by falling under the power of their ascendants in consequence of their being enrolled in the local senate,|| or by the subsequent marriage of their parents.¶

§ 57. The paragraphs relating to the right of intermarriage accorded to veteran soldiers with latins or
§ 67-96. aliens, and as to the position of children resulting from a marriage by mistake with latins or aliens.

§ 100, 101. The restrictions in the mode of adoption by the authority of the people and its non-application to women. | In the law of *adoption*, the authority of the Emperor is substi- Tit. xi. § 1.
tuted for that of the people. The
change** in the law as to the effect § 2.
of adoption noted, and the statement as to the con- § 3.
ditions required in arrogation amplified. The doubt
as to the power of a younger person to adopt an § 4.
older one decided in the negative. The right of § 10.
women to adopt by special permission of the Emperor stated, and Cato's opinion confirmed†† that the adoption of slaves by their masters gives them their freedom.

§ 108-123. The paragraphs relating to the position of women under marital power, and of freemen in a state of bondage.

---

* By Justinian (C. vii, 3, 5). † Justinian (C. v, 4, 25).

‡ The law passed to enable Claudius to marry his niece Agrippina having been repealed by Constantine. || A provision of Theodosius II.

¶ Introduced by Constantine, see *post*, book iii, tit. i, § 1.

** Made by Justinian (C. viii, 48, 10). †† Justinian (C. vii, 6, 10).

Com. i.	*Struck out.*	*Added.*	Bk. i.
		The rights appertaining to *paternal power* are shown to be affected by banishment, or penal servitude,* or in the case of the son, the attainment of the dignity of the patriciate.	Tit. xii. § 2-4.
§ 130, 131.	Release of children from power when consecrated as priests of Jupiter, or selected to be vestal virgins.	The point settled that children become free from power from the time their father was taken prisoner, if he die in captivity,† and postliminium defined, followed by a statement of the simplification introduced in the methods of emancipation.‡	§ 5. § 6-8.
§ 134-141.	The paragraphs relating to the mode of emancipating women under marital power and freemen in a state of bondage.		
§ 145. § 148-154.	The paragraphs relating to the guardianship of free women of full age.	Under the head of *guardianship*, Servius' definition is added,‖ and a title inserted as to guardians by testament; and, as affecting this subject, the examples of causes of changes of status are altered, and the tie of cognation shown to be affected by the greatest change. A few words are added as to the guardianship by law of ascendants, and the effect pointed out of recent legislation¶ on the methods for the appointment of guardians by magistrates, as also the necessity for, and the mode of giving, the authority of guardians, and it is noted that a *curator* must be appointed, when an action arises between guardian and ward.	Tit. xiii. Tit. xiv. Tit. xv. Tit. xvi. § 6. Tit. xviii. Tit. xx. § 3-5. Tit. xxi.
§ 157.	The reference to the lex Claudia abolishing the agnate tutorship of women.		
§ 163.	The effect of change of legal position on agnation.		
§ 167-183.	The paragraphs relating to the guardianship of freed women of full age, and the mode of shifting guardians.		
§ 188.	Remarks on the difference of opinion as to the kinds of guardianship.		
§ 190-193.	The reasons assigned for the guardianship of women of full age.		
§ 194-195*a*	The grounds on which women of full age may be released from guardianship.	The puberty of males is fixed at fourteen.**	Tit. xxii.
		The subject of guardianship by *curators*, and of the security to be given by both tutors, and curators, amplified, concluding with the grounds of exemption available to guardians,†† and the method of removing them on suspicion.‡‡	Tit. xxiii. Tit. xxiv. Tit. xxv. Tit. xxvi.

---

* Rules and Institutes of *Marcianus; Dig.* xlviii, 22, 4 and 5; *Dig.* xlviii, 19, 17 pr. § 1.

† In accordance with views of Tryphoninus and Ulpian, *Dig.* xlix 15, 12, § 1 and 18.

‡ By Anastasius and Justinian, C. viii, 49, 6.

‖ Paul on the Edict, *Dig.* xxvi, 1, 1, pr.

¶ Justinian, C. i, 4, 30.

** Justinian, C. v, 60, 3.

†† Partly from Ulpian and Marcianus, see *Dig.* xxvii, 1.

‡‡ Principally from Ulpian on the Edict, *Dig.* xxvi, 10; and one passage (part of § 12) from Callistratus, *Dig.* xxvi, 10, 6.

Com. ii. *Struck out.* *Added.* Bk. ii.

Things further subdivided so as to separate such as are *common* to all by natural law, and the use of them illustrated. Tit. i, pr. § 1-7.

The shore of the sea defined, and things subject to divine law stated to belong to no one.*

§ 7. The distinction as to provincial soil in respect of religious things.

The definition of sacred things altered, their alienation (unless in certain exceptional cases) prohibited† and *natural* law stated to be older than the *civil* law. § 8. § 11.

The point settled in the negative as to the property in an animal wounded but not yet caught, and the doctrine of *occupation* further illustrated as applied to wild animals, prisoners of war, precious stones, the offspring of animals, portions of land swept away by a stream, and islands formed in the sea or rivers.‡ § 13. § 14-24.

The dispute as to the ownership of a thing made out of another's materials settled by the adoption of an intermediate rule favouring the owner of the materials when the thing can be reduced to its former state. § 25.

The doctrine of *accession* amplified and illustrated, and the question whether the tablet is an accessory to the picture painted on it decided in the affirmative. § 26-33. § 34.

The law as to *produce*, gathered or consumed by a person not the owner of the land, incidentally laid down, and the distinction, in respect of produce, between the young of animals and the offspring of slaves stated. § 35, 36. § 37, 38.

The rules relating to *treasure-trove* inserted, and *delivery* shown to be another mode of acquiring things by natural law, with illustrations drawn from the transfer of land of any description (as the distinction between provincial and italian land had been abolished||), followed by an explanation of those sales which are perfected by the intention without delivery, and cases of abandonment discussed, and distinguished from jettison.¶ § 39. § 40-48.

In treating of rights over the property of others, Tit. iii, pr.

---

* Institutes of *Marcianus*, *Dig.* i, 8, 2, pr. § 1, and 4 pr. § 1. Digest of *Celsus*, *Dig.* l, 16, 96; Every-Day Book of *Gaius*, *Dig.* i, 8, 5, pr. § 1.

† By Justinian, C. 1, 2. 21.

‡ Every-Day Book of *Gaius*, *Dig.* xli, 1, 1, pr. § 1; and 3, pr. § 1, 2 and 5, § 1-7; and 7, pr. § 1-7. Institutes of *Florentinus*, *Dig.* i, 8, 3, xli, i, 6.

|| By Justinian, C. vii, 31.

¶ The greater part of § 26-48 is taken from the Every Day-Book of *Gaius*, *Dig.* xli, i, 7, § 8-13; and 9 pr. § 1-8; xxii, i, 28, pr. § 1.

Com. ii. *Struck out.* *Added.* Bk. ii.

rural servitudes are defined,* the mode of creating them explained,† and the law noticed affecting the § 4. so-called personal servitudes, *usufruct*, *use*, and Tit. iv, v. *habitation*.‡

§ 15-23. The paragraphs relating to the distinction between things requiring a formal transfer and those passing by delivery.

§ 24-39. The description of the process of surrender in court and of its uses.

§ 40, 41. The distinction between legal and equitable titles.

§ 46, 47. Paragraphs stating that provincial land, and such property of a woman under agnate guardianship as required a formal conveyance, could not be acquired by use.

§ 52-58. Paragraphs relating to the acquisition by use, in one year, of property belonging to an inherit-

§ 59-61. ance, and paragraphs as to re-acquisition by use of our own property.

In the matter of *prescription*, Tit. vi, pr. the alterations in the statutory periods of acquisition by use‖ are inserted, and the rules as to ac- § 8-11. quiring by use things infected with any vice, such as theft, are amplified, in part, according to the decisions of the Emperors Severus and Antoninus, whilst the doc- § 12-14. trine of tacking the possession of our predecessor in title, and the rules applying to property purchased from the imperial treasury are inserted in accordance with imperial rescripts.¶

As to *gifts*, the law in respect of those *inter vivos* Tit. vii. (including gifts on account of marriage), and *mortis causa*,** stated in accordance with Justin and Jus- § 4. tinian's legislation,†† and an indemnity substituted by Justinian for the right of accrual formerly existing in the case of the gift of liberty by one master to a slave owned in common.‡‡

In respect of the impediments to the alienation of Tit. viii. property, mention is made of the amendments introduced by Justinian in the Julian law, so that the alienation or mortgage, by the husband, of the wife's immovable property, is altogether forbidden,‖‖ and reference made to the new procedure by which, in the alienation of a debtor's property, Justinian protected the interests of both creditors § 1. and debtors, as also in the case of a debtor to a ward paying the § 2. amount to a guardian.¶¶

§ 85. Paragraph as to the effect of a payment to a woman without the authority of her guardian.

---

* Institutes of *Ulpian*, *Dig.* viii, 3, 1, pr., § 1, and 4, 1, pr. § 1.
† Every Day Book of *Gaius*, *Dig.* viii, 4, 16.
‡ Paul on *Vitellius*, *Dig.* vii, 1, 1; Digest of *Celsus*, *Dig.* vii, 1, 2; Every Day Book of *Gaius*, *Dig.* vii, 1, 3, pr. § 1, 2. ‖ Justinian, C. vii, 31.
¶ Severus and Antoninus, Zeno, and Justinian, C. vii, 31 and 37. 2, 3.
** The illustration as to gifts *mortis causa* is from the Institutes of *Marcianus*, *Dig.* xxxix, 6, 1. †† C. viii, 57. 4, v, 3, 19 and 20; viii, 54, 35, § 5 and 36.
‡‡ C. vii, 7, 1. ‖‖ C. v, 13, 15. ¶¶ C. viii, 24, 3; v, 37, 25 and 27.

Com. ii. *Struck out.* *Added.* Bk. ii.

§ 88-90. As to acquisitions by the equitable, not by the legal, owner of a
§ 96. slave; and as to the doubt about acquiring the possession of things through those in our marital power, or through free persons in bondage, and as to the effect of a surrender in court to such persons.

Under the head of *acquiring* Tit. ix.
property through others, the changes made by Justinian in the law as
to the power of the father over § 1.
his son's property,* are stated, as well as the effect of the constitu-
tion of Severus on the acquisition § 5.
of ownership by means of the possession of an agent.†

In opening the subject of *testamentary succession*, a Tit. x.
testament is defined,‡ and the testament made by the § 1.
process of the copper and the scale

§ 103,104. The description of the mode of
§ 107. making a testament *per æs et libram*.

is stated to be little used, whilst the § 2-12.
formalities are described necessary to the existing testament, together with the alterations in the law made by Theodosius and Valentinian, and Justinian, as to who
may be witnesses; and the right of § 14.
making an oral will, is confirmed.||

§ 110,111. The power possessed by soldiers, of appointing as heirs, and bequeathing property to, latins or aliens, or persons subject to incapacities under the Julian and Papian laws.

The relaxation of the rules in fa- Tit. xi.
vour of the testaments of *soldiers*¶ is further exemplified, and restricted to the period of actual service,** and reference made to the right accorded to all persons, by Justinian, holding private property, by analogy to that acquired in war, to dispose of it by testament, but with the customary formalities.†† This is followed by the rules, as settled by Justin and Justinian,‡‡
governing the making of testaments by lunatics in Tit. xii.
lucid intervals, by the deaf, the dumb, blind persons, and prisoners of war.

§ 114. The inquiry as to the *testamenti factio* of the testator, and the legality of the testament according to the civil law.

§ 116-117. The technical modes of appointing an heir.

§ 118-122. The rules invalidating the testaments of women unauthorised by their guardians.

Several questions affecting the Tit. xiii,
invalidity of a will are then set- pr.
tled, as that a son cannot be passed over in silence, though he has predeceased the testator, that
males and females are to be dealt § 5.
with on the same footing with re-

---

* C. vi, 61, 6. † C. vii, 32, 1. ‡ Partly from Rules of *Ulpian*, xx, 1.
|| C. vi, 23, 21 and 29, and 11, 2.
¶ Institutes of *Florentinus*, *Dig.* xxix, 1, 24; Institutes of *Marcianus*, *Dig.* xxix, 1, 22.
** Justinian, C. iv, 21, 17.
†† C. vi, 22, 12.
‡‡ C. vi, 22, 10.

Com. ii.	*Struck out.*	*Added.*	Bk. ii.
§ 125-128.	The interposition of the prætor in favour of persons improperly excluded.	gard to being appointed or excluded by name;* and that it is not necessary to give a slave his freedom when appointing him heir;† but the invalidity is insisted upon of the appointment, as her heir, of a slave accused of adultery with his mistress, in accordance with a decision of Severus and Antoninus.‡	Tit. xiv, pr.
§ 135*a*.	As to children not specially brought under the power of their father when the latter was made a citizen by the Emperor.		
§ 190.	The rules as to the time running where a term for deliberation has been given, in the case of the slave of another being appointed heir.		

The rules are noticed as to the appointment of the slave of another, or of several masters, the mode indicated of dividing an inheritance into ounces,‖ and the question of conditional appointments considered. § 2. § 4-8. § 9-11.

§ 174-178.	The formal modes of appointing and substituting heirs.	The case of *substituted* heirs, whose shares had not been mentioned, is settled in accordance	Tit. xv.

with decisions of Severus and Antoninus, as well as of substitutes to a slave appointed heir, whom the testator thought was free,¶ and the rules as to pupillary substitutions extended by Justinian** to the case of insane descendants, but the effect of the pupillary testament being an accessory of the paternal testament and sharing its fate, is pointed out, together with the mode by which a father can make substitutions to all his children.†† § 2, 3. § 4. Tit. xvi. § 1. § 5, 6. § 8.

§ 139-143. The invalidity of a will arising from a woman falling into the marital power of the testator, or from a son falling into power again after a first or second sale, or from children falling into the power of their father after a mistake has been proved as to a marriage with an alien or with a latin.

§ 148-151.	The rules as to passing the equitable title, with or without the beneficial interest according to the nature of the invalidity of the testament.	The law stated as to the revocation of a first will by a second one, though the latter only covers a portion of the property,‡‡ together with the rules partly based on decisions of Severus and Antoninus	Tit. xvii § 3. § 7, 8.

* Justinian, C. vi, 28, 4. † C. vi, 27, 5.
‡ Institutes of *Marcianus*, *Dig.* xxviii, 5, 48, § 2.
‖ Rules of *Ulpian*, *Dig.* xxviii, 5, 50, § 2.
¶ Institutes of *Marcianus*, *Dig.* xxviii, 6, 36; xxxviii, 16, 9.
** C. vi, 26, 9. †† Institutes of *Florentinus*, *Dig.* xxviii, 6, 37.
‡‡ Institutes of *Marcianus*, *Dig.* xxxvi, 1, 29.

Com. ii. *Struck out.* *Added.* Bk. ii.

and of Pertinax, as to a will not being invalid from the mere wish of the testator, and as to defective wills not being necessarily valid because the Emperor is made heir, followed by a statement of the law regard- Tit. xviii.
ing *inofficious* testaments* as settled by Justinian.†

§ 159-160. The power of abstaining from the inheritance given to a wife under marital power, and to a freeman in a state of bondage.

§ 164-166.
§ 168.
§ 170-173. The two formal modes of giving the appointed heir a limited period for deliberation, and the mode of declaring acceptance.

In respect of the different classes Tit. xix.
of *heirs*, the three periods are noted at which the capacity of stranger-heirs to take the inherit- § 4.
ance is determined.‡ Reference is § 6.
also made to the provision extended by Justinian to all classes of heirs as to being liable only to the extent of the value of the inheritance,|| and the power of the § 7.
deaf and dumb to become heirs pointed out.

A *legacy* is defined, the four kinds suppressed, the Tit. xx.
nature of all declared to be the same, and put § 1.
on the same footing as bequests in § 2, 3.
trust.¶

§ 192-223. The four kinds of legacies.

A series of rules are then given applying to such § 4.
legacies as that of the property of others (with the burden of proof in such cases**); property pledged; § 5.
the property of another which has come to the § 6.
legatee; a thing not in existence; the same thing to § 7, 8.
two persons; an estate which the legatee had already § 9.
purchased minus the usufruct;†† the legatee's own § 10.
property; testator's property bequeathed as if that § 11.
of another; testator's property bequeathed, and sub- § 12.
sequently alienated, or mortgaged;‡‡ a release to a § 13.
debtor; a debt to a creditor;|||| her dowry to a wife; § 14, 15.
and this is followed by a discussion as to the result § 16.
of the loss of the thing, or slave, bequeathed;¶¶ and the effect of bequeathing the offspring with a female § 17.
slave, head slaves with assistants, slave with private savings, an estate with its appurtenances, a flock, a § 18.
building, the private savings of a slave (rescript of § 19, 20.
Severus and Antoninus), incorporeal rights, a § 21. § 22.
thing generally, and a right of election (law settled § 23.

* Institutes of *Marcianus*, *Dig* v, 2, 2. † C. iii, 28, 30 and 35.
‡ Institutes of *Florentinus*, *Dig*. xxviii, 5, 49, § 1. || C. vi, 30, 22.
¶ Justinian, C. vi, 37, 21 and 43, 1 and 2.
** Institutes of *Marcianus*, *Dig*. xxii, 3, 21.
†† Digest of *Julianus*, *Dig*. xxx, 1, 82, § 2, 3.
‡‡ The opinion of the majority (according to *Gaius*, ii, § 198), being overruled, and the question held, in accordance with rescripts of Severus and Antoninus, to depend on intention (C. vi, 37, 3).
|||| Answers of *Papinian*, *Dig*. xxxv, 2, 5.
¶¶ (Opinion of *Julianus*) Institutes of *Marcianus*, *Dig*. xxx, 1, 112, § 1.

Com. ii. *Struck out.* | *Added.* Bk. ii.

by Justinian).* The alteration of the law is then referred to, allowing legacies and bequests in trust to be given to uncertain persons,† and certain rules in construing legacies referred to, as that a false description, or false reasons, do not invalidate legacies,‡ and some further points settled, as that a conditional legacy may be left to the slave of the heir; that a legacy, or liberty, may be given before the appointment of the heir, that legacies may take effect after the death of the heir, or legatee; and that those by way of penalty are to be held valid.‖ § 25-27. § 30, 31. § 32. § 34. § 35. § 36.

§ 233, 234. Remarks as to gifts of freedom, or appointment of a guardian to take effect after the death of the heir.

Reference is then made to the power of revoking or transferring legacies, and the mode discussed of applying the *Falcidian law* to the case of two heirs unequally burdened with legacies, together with the time when the value of the estate is to be estimated, and the deductions to be first made.¶ Tit. xxi. Tit. xxii.

§ 252. The description of the character of purchaser occupied, before the time of Gaius, by the person beneficially entitled to a bequest in trust.

In *bequests in trust*, the origin of the jurisdiction of the special prætor is shortly noticed, as well as the merger by Justinian of part of the *Pegasian* in the *Trebellian* decree of the senate, with supplemental provisions, including the power of exacting an oath of the trustee, as to the existence of the bequest in trust, if the evidence required by law is wanting,** and reference made to the confirmation of the rescript of Alexander, by which freedom is only deferred, not lost, where the owner of the slave, freed by way of bequest in trust, refuses to sell.†† Tit. xxiii § 1. § 7-9. § 12. Tit. xxiv § 2.

§ 268-289. The differences between legacies and bequests in trust.

Finally, a short historical account is given of *codicils*, and the law stated in accordance with the decisions of Severus and Antoninus overruling the opinion of Papinian.‡‡ Tit. xxv.

---

* C. vi, 43, 3.

† In accordance with the legislation of Justinian, as contained in his first Code, of which only a short abstract is to be found in the second, see *Ort. Anal.*, part iii, par. 908, p. 208.

‡ Institutes of *Marcianus*, *Dig.* xxxv, 1, 33, pr. § 1.

‖ C. vi, 23, 24; viii, 38, 11; vi, 41.

¶ *Gaius* on the Provincial Edict, *Dig.* xxxv, 2, 73, § 1-5 and 77.

** C. vi, 42, 32.

†† C. vii, 4, 6.

‡‡ Answers of *Papinian*, *Dig.* xxix, 7, 5; Institutes of *Marcianus*, *Dig.* xxix, 7, 6, § 1-4.

Com. iii. *Struck out.* *Added.* Bk. iii.

Under the head of ***intestate succession*** the sweeping changes in the law are introduced by a definition of intestacy, and by including in the class of heirs succeeding as co-owners of the patrimony, children given to the local senate,* as well as those legitimated by the subsequent marriage of their parents.† And, as the acquisition of the inheritance results from the operation of law, it is shown that the lunacy of the heir is no obstacle, though captivity, or the father's condemnation for treason after death, may affect the devolution of the property, as the succession opens at the time that the fact of intestacy has become apparent. In the review which follows of the prætor's interference in favour of emancipated and adopted children, and descendants of daughters, the alterations are noted which had been introduced by Valentinian, Theodosius, and Arcadius,‡ as well as by Justinian;|| and reference is made to the latter's amendments of the law as to the succession of women¶ and the children of uterine sisters, by restoring the first to an equality with male agnates and placing the second on an equality with consanguineous sisters towards their maternal uncle. Tit. i. § 2. § 3. § 4. § 5. § 7, 8. § 9-15. Tit. ii. § 3. § 4

§ 3, 5, 6. Paragraphs relating to wives under marital power, and children coming under paternal power, after cause has been shown, or they have not been effectually sold, succeeding as co-owners of the patrimony on an intestacy.

§ 15, 16. The difference between the succession of the descendants of agnates, and of co-owners of the patrimony.

An explanation of the law of the Twelve Tables as to the "nearest" agnate, is then given, in order to show the alteration** of the law, so as to admit devolution in their case, whilst emancipations are stated to be deemed always made with a redemption clause, so that the ascendant may invariably be called to the succession. § 5. § 6. § 7. § 8.

§ 17. The reference to the succession of the gentiles.

The reciprocal rights of succession of a mother and her children under the *Tertullian* and *Orphitian* decrees of the senate are next detailed, with the alterations in the first by Theodosius, and Valentinian,†† and Justinian;‡‡ and, in the second, by Tit. iii. Tit. iv.

---

* C. v, 27, 3 and 4, and 9.

† C. v, 27, 11, *ante*, bk. i, tit. 10, § 13.

‡ C. vi, 55, 9 and 12.

|| C. viii, 48, 10.

¶ C. vi, 58, 14.

** By Justinian, C. vi, 4, 4; viii, 49, 6.

†† C. vi, 56, 5.

‡‡ C. viii, 59, 2, vi, 57, 7. The Institutes say that the Tertullian decree of the senate was passed in the reign of Hadrian, but probably Antoninus Pius is thereby referred to under his adoptive name.

Com. iii.	*Struck out.*	*Added.*	Bk. iii.
		Valentinian, Theodosius, and Arcadius* and Justinian,† and a reference made to the right of accrual as between statutory heirs.‡	§ 4.
§ 18-24.	The comments on the strictness of the law of succession under the Twelve Tables.	In the succession of *cognates,* remarks are inserted as to the position of children born of an uncertain father, and as to the claims of cognation extending only to the sixth degree.	Tit. v. § 4.
§ 35-38.	Examples of cases where the grant of the possession of the property may not be accompanied by the beneficial interest.	The *degrees of relationship* are then described at length and illustrated by a *table of consanguinity.*‖	Tit. vi.
§ 43-76	Paragraphs relating to the right of patrons in respect of freedwomen and latins, and those classed as surrendered persons; and the rights of patronesses in respect of freedmen and latins.	In dealing with the succession of *freedmen,* the Junian law, the Largian decree of the senate, the edict of Trajan, and the class of latins are stated to be abolished. The law as to the rights of patrons and patronesses to the succession of freedmen and freedwomen is shown to be amended,¶ so as to be similar to that of the free-	Tit. vii. § 3, 4. (Tit. ix, § 5.)

* C. vi, 55, 4, § 2 and 9. † C. vi, 57, 5.

‡ Institutes of *Marcianus, Dig.* xxxviii, 16, 9.

‖ Gaius on the Provincial Edict, *Dig.* xxxviii, 10, 1, pr. 1, 3-7, and 3, pr. § 1. Sentences of Paul, *Dig.* xxxviii, 10, 10, § 9. The *table of consanguinity* is taken from the paraphrase of Theophilus, and the blank left in the MS. of Justinian's Institutes for its insertion led to the mistake of assuming that a new title on the relationship of slaves commenced here.

The table is fuller than the text, as it includes two cases of the sixth degree, not mentioned by Justinian, viz., the paternal and maternal uncle and aunt's great-grandchildren, and the paternal and maternal great-great uncle and aunt's son and daughter, that is, in both cases, first cousins twice removed. In translating the table I have followed the distinction laid down by the Master of the Rolls In re Parker, Bentham *v.* Wilson (L. R., 15 Ch. D., 528), as to first cousins (or cousins german), first cousins once and twice removed, and second cousins, *i.e.*, persons descended from the same great grandfather. The term "german", as applied to first cousins, is sanctioned by use; but "germani" are properly those who are of the same blood by both parents as opposed to "consanguinei" who have a common father only, and "uterini" who have a common mother only.

The mode of reckoning the degrees in Roman law (as opposed to the canon law) is followed in England in ascertaining the persons who are entitled as next of kin to the personal estate of an intestate, and also as to the incapacity to marry, by reason of being within the prohibited degrees of consanguinity or affinity. The degree of relationship is traced by counting from either of the two persons to the other through the common ancestor. (See Williams' *Personal Property,* 10th edit., p. 405; Stephens' *Blackstone,* 6th edit., vol. ii, pp. 212, 263.)

¶ Justinian, C. vi, 4, 4, § 9-19, vii, 6. In dealing with the subject of the claims of patrons to the succession of their freedmen, the editors of Justinian's Institutes found themselves hampered by the depreciation in the value of money which had taken place since the Papian law was passed in the reign of Augustus, and they therefore at iii, vii, § 3, by way of parenthesis, note that they have reckoned the *aureus* as equivalent to about the 1000 sesterces mentioned in that law, and assuming the aureus to be worth nearly £8, this would make the centenarii to possess about £800 of English money. It will be noticed that Gaius at iii, § 223, and Justinian in the corresponding passage (iv, iv, § 7) allude to the poverty of the times when the

Com. iii. *Struck out.* *Added.* Bk. iii.

born, except that the succession is limited to the fifth degree; and notice is taken of the power given by a decree of the senate, under Claudius,* to testators of assigning freedmen to one only of their descendants. Tit. viii.

§ 77-81. Paragraphs as to the mode of universal succession arising out of the purchase of the estates of insolvent persons.

Tit. ix. pr. § 3-10. In respect of the prætors' grant of the possession of the property, a description is given of such grants arising out of testamentary dispositions, with the changes introduced by Justinian,† and, under the head of *arrogation*, the restrictions imposed by Justinian‡ on the rights and liabilities of the arrogator, in respect of the property of the persons arrogated, are noticed. Tit. x. § 2, 3.

§ 85-87. The effect of a surrender in court by an heir before acceptance of the inheritance.

Another mode of succession is shown to result from the assignment of property in order to preserve gifts of freedom, as based on a rescript of Marcus Aurelius,|| amended by Justinian;¶ and the subject of succession is closed by a reference to the disused sales of debtors' property in the aggregate,** and to the abolition, by Justinian, of the loss of her entire property by a woman uniting herself with a slave.†† Tit. xi. Tit. xii.

The text then passes to *obligations*, which are defined, and divided into civil and prætorian, with a further subdivision into *quasi* contracts and *quasi* delicts.‡‡ Tit. xiii. pr. § 1. § 2.

The contracts *re* are illustrated by the cases of specific loans, deposits, and pledges.|||| Tit. xiv. § 2-4.

---

penalties for outrages were fixed by the Twelve Tables, and only copper was in use (*Gai.* Com. i, § 122); but it would be more accurate to say that the value of money had diminished as compared with the equivalents it would purchase, and as the substitution of coins of nominal, instead of real value, continued up to and after the time of Gaius, I have thought it better in the translation to avoid using any expressions indicative of the value of the coins referred to by either Gaius or Justinian, especially as the actual value of the coinage mentioned is of little practical importance to the law student. For information on this subject, consult the appendix to any large Latin dictionary, or for an exhaustive account, see Dr. Smith's *Dict. of Gr. and R. Antiq.*

* *Dig.* xxxviii, 4, 1.

† C. viii, 49, 6, vi. 4, 4 and 9, 8 and 9.

‡ C. iii, 33, 16, vi, 59, 11.

|| Ulpian on the Edict, *Dig.* xl, 5, 2.

¶ C. vii, 2, 15, § 1-6.

** Details given in *Dig.* xlii, 4 and 5.

†† C. vii, 24.

‡‡ The introduction by the compilers of the Institutes of *Justinian*, of the division of obligations into *civil* and *prætorian* seems unnecessary in the existing state of the law in the sixth century at Constantinople, and as to *quasi*-delicts, see Austin's *Jurisprudence*, 4th edit., pp. 945, 948, 1017, 1018.

|||| Every Day Book of *Gaius*, *Dig.* xliv, 7, 1, § 3-6.

Com. iii. *Struck out.* *Added.* Bk. iii.

§ 94-96. Special terms of stipulations restricted to citizens, and stipulations as to wife's dowry.

A derivation is given of the word stipulation, and the abolition of the necessity of solemn words by the Emperor Leo* stated, with the distinction between absolute and conditional stipulations, and the advantage of adding a penal clause, where some act on the part of the promisee is involved. Tit. xv. § 1. § 2-6. § 7.

Three separate titles are then devoted to the subjects of joint promisors and joint promisees,† stipulations entered into by slaves,‡ and the classification of stipulations.|| Tit. xvi. Tit. xvii Tit. xvii

Further illustrations are given of useless stipulations, whether through the thing subsequently becoming unmarketable, or because the promise involves performance by another, and the point settled as to the effect of stipulations for payment to self and to another to whom not subjected.¶ Tit. xix. pr. § 1, 2. § 3. § 4.

§ 108. Necessity for the guardian of a woman being a party to any business transaction entered into by her.

The restrictions are mentioned, imposed by Justinian, on the power of proving an alibi where a document in proof of the stipulation is produced; and the amendment is referred to rendering valid, stipulations the benefit of which would only arise in favour of heirs;** so, also, the new rules rendering preposterous stipulations†† valid in all cases; and further points relating to the validity of conditional and other forms of stipulations considered.‡‡ § 12. § 13. § 14. § 15-27.

§ 110-114. Paragraphs as to the mode of creating an additional creditor (adstipulator).

§ 115-119. § 123-125. As to the distinctions between sponsors, fidepromissors, and fidejussors, and the consequent effect of the Furian, Apuleian, Cicereian, Cornelian, and Publilian laws.

§ 128-134. § 138. Rules as to obligations created by entries in writing.

As to *sureties*, a promise in the Greek language is held to be binding; and reference is made to the presumption of law in favour of the validity of a written statement|||| made by a surety, but the kind of contract formed by *written entries* stated to be no longer in Tit. xx. § 7-8. Tit. xxi.

---

* C., viii, 38, 10. † Partly from Institutes of *Florentinus*, *Dig*. xlv, 2, 7.
‡ Partly from Institutes of *Florentinus*, *Dig*. xlv, 3, 15.
|| Pomponius on Sabinus, *Dig*. xlv, 1, 5.
¶ Partly from Every Day Book of Gaius, *Dig*. xliv, 7, 15, § 9-15.
** Justinian, C. viii, 38, 14 and 11. †† Justinian, C. vi, 23, 25.
‡‡ Sentences of Paul, v, 7, 2; Ulpian on Sabinus, *Dig*. xlv, 1, 38, § 17, 20; Paul on the Edict, *Dig*. xlv, 1, 87; Pomponius on Sabinus, *Dig*. xlv, 1, 42.
|||| Ulpian on Sabinus, *Dig*. xlvi, 1, 8; xlv, 1, 30.

Com. iii. *Struck out.* *Added.* Bk. iii.

use, and the period of five years, allowed by the imperial constitutions, for a plea of not having received the money, in spite of a written admission of the debt, restricted to two years.*

In the contract of *sale*, the alterations in the law as to contracts put into writing† and as to the use and effect of earnest money, are noticed, and the points settled as to the validity of a sale where the sum is to be (and is) fixed by a third person;‡ and that *exchange* is a separate contract,|| together with remarks as to the party on whom, after the contract of sale is complete, the risk of loss attaches and gain accrues,¶ and as to absolute, conditional, and impossible sales.** Tit. xxiii. § 1. § 2. § 3. § 4.

The contract of *letting and hiring* is also stated to be formed though the sum to be paid is left to the decision of a third party;‡ but this contract does not include the case of an *exchange* of things;†† and the law of Zeno is referred to by which the special contract of *emphyteusis* was created.‡‡ Tit. xxiv. § 1. § 2. § 3.

146. Examples of gladiators partly let out and partly sold.

The point is also discussed whether, and it is settled that, it is a contract of sale, where a goldsmith is ordered to make rings of a given weight and form out of his gold at a fixed price. § 4.

It is further shown that it is the duty of the hirer to use due care|||| to do what is fair and equitable; and it is stated that the benefit of the contract survives to his heir. § 5. § 6.

In *partnership*, the point is settled that one partner may share the profit and not be liable for the loss; and the degree of negligence is considered for which one partner is liable to the other.¶¶ Tit. xxv. § 2. § 9.

The contract of *gratuitous agency**** is shown to be capable of being formed in five modes, and the Tit. xxvi. pr.

---

* Justinian, C. iv, 30, 14. † Justinian, C. iv, 21, 17.

‡ Justinian, C. iv, 38, 15.

|| In accordance with constitutions of Diocletian and Maximian, C. iv, 64, 3 and 7; and partly from opinions of Nerva, Proculus, Celsus and Paul, *Dig.* xviii, 1, 1, § 1; xii, 4, 16; xix, 4, 1, and 5, 5, § 1.

¶ Partly from Gaius on the Provincial Edict, *Dig.* xviii, 1, 35, § 4.

** In accordance with views of Ulpian and Paul, *Dig.* xviii, 1, 3 and 34, § 1; xli, 4, 2, § 5.

†† Ulpian on the Edict, *Dig.* xix, 5, 17, § 3.

‡‡ C. iv, 66, 1.

|||| Partly from Gaius on the Provincial Edict, *Dig.* xix, 2, 25, § 3, 6, 7.

¶¶ Every-Day Book of Gaius, *Dig.* xvii, 2, 72. The example inserted by the editors, in § 2, of the surety authorising the creditor to sue the principal debtor at his risk, is inaccurate, as the law had been altered two years previously. See *Ort. Anal.*, part iii, par. 1557 (2); p. 288.

*** Every-Day Book of Gaius, *Dig.* xvii, 1, 2, § 1-6.

Com. iii. *Struck out.* *Added.* Bk. iii.

point is settled that a party would be liable who § 1-6.
commissioned another to lend money to a particular
person, as also that an action of mandate lies if the § 8.
claim is limited to the amount for which the mandatee had authority to purchase an estate.*

§ 158. Uselessness of mandate for something to be done after the mandatee's death.

The renunciation of a mandate § 11.
without notice is not allowed;†
but a mandate may be condi- § 12.
tional.‡ If remuneration is agreed upon, the contract
is one of letting and hiring, but, if otherwise, then an § 13.
action of mandate lies.

In *quasi*-contracts, || the rule as to the non-recovery Tit. xxv
of certain legacies, paid by mistake, is extended to all legacies and bequests in trust so paid in furtherance of religious objects.¶

In respect of acquisitions resulting from obliga- Tit. xxv
tions contracted by children in our power, the rule is pr.
laid down that they divide as to the ownership and the use and enjoyment;** and the

§ 166. Point as to non-acquisition by slave, of whom we have only the bare legal right.

point settled that a slave, stipulat- § 3.
ing by order of one master, acquires for that one only.††

In dealing with the *dissolution* of obligations, the
point is settled that this would result from the pay- Tit. xxi
ment of an equivalent, with the consent of the cre- pr.
ditor, and that a release of part only may be
effected by crediting it as paid. The terms of the § 1.
Aquilian form of release‡‡ are then

§ 173-175. The process of release by way of the copper and the scale.

set out, and in respect of a disso- § 2.
lution by novation, the rule is settled to be that the addition or
withdrawal of a surety imports something new into § 3.
a stipulation, and, therefore, may have this effect; but novation is to be deemed only to occur when the parties expressly so intend:|||| and it is finally noted that all obligations resulting from consent may be
dissolved by a contrary intention. § 4.

§ 180-181. Paragraphs as to novation resulting from joinder of issue in a civil law case.

---

* Every-Day Book of Gaius, *Dig.* xvii, 1, 4.
† Paul on the Edict, *Dig.* xvii, i, 22, § 11.
‡ Paul on the Edict, *Dig.* xvii, i, § 3.
|| The matter generally is derived from the Every-Day Book of Gaius, *Dig.* xliv, 7, 5, pr. § 1-3.
¶ Justinian, C. vi, 43, 2.
** Justinian, C. vi, 61, 6 and 8, § 3.
†† C. iv, 27, 3.
‡‡ Institutes of *Florentinus*, *Dig.* xlvi, 4, 18.
|||| C. viii, 42, 8.

Com. iii. *Struck out.* *Added.* Bk.iv.*

In dealing with obligations arising from *wrongs*, Tit. i.
a derivation of the word *theft* is given,† the offence § 1, 2.
defined, and manifest theft explained;‡ and it is held that a § 3.
person, knowingly receiving and § 4.
concealing stolen property, is liable to an action for non-manifest theft, whilst the four actions relating to the kinds of theft termed conceptum, oblatum, prohibitum, and non-exhibitum, are stated to have fallen into disuse, and the point settled in the affir- § 8.
mative as to the liability of a person both to the action for theft and for corrupting a slave, when the slave had been incited by him to steal from his master, and the latter had allowed the slave to take the thing, with a view to detection.|| This is followed by examples of intentional co-operation in § 11.
theft, and of the effect of theft by persons in power from those to whom they are subject; and a right of § 16.
election is given to the owner to bring an action of loan against him who borrowed a thing, or an action of theft against him who stole it.¶ It is further noted that the owner has concurrent rights to sue § 19.
for the stolen thing itself, besides bringing an action for the penalty.

§ 189-194. *Struck out:* Historical account of the law of the Twelve Tables as to manifest
§ 201. theft, and paragraphs as to there being no theft of property not yet acquired by the heir, or of property re-acquired by use.

The action for *robbery with violence* is shown only Tit. ii.
to lie where the act was done with fraudulent intent, § 1.
forcible acts being punished in other ways,** and it is not essential that the thing should be owned by the prosecutor.††

In respect of the action for *damage wrongfully inflicted*, the first head of the *Aquilian* law is inter- Tit. iii.
preted to include only animals feeding in flocks,‡‡ § 1.
and examples of homicide by misadventure are given, § 4-8.
and distinguished from injuries resulting from culpable negligence;|||| but, as the action is penal, it § 9.
does not lie against the heir.

§ 215, 216. *Struck out:* The second head of the Aquilian law against an adstipulator.

Added: The second head of the Aquilian law, relating to the obsolete ad- § 12.

---

* As Justinian commences the fourth book here, he seems to have abandoned the arrangement of Gaius, and made the division turn rather on bulk than on matter. See *Ort. Anal.*, part iii, par. 1, p. 99.

† Paul on the Edict, *Dig.* xlvii, 2, 1, § 1-3.

‡ Partly from Ulpian on Sabinus, *Dig.* xlvii, 2, 3.

|| C. vi, 2, 20.

¶ Justinian, C. vi, 2, 22.

** Constitutions of Valentinian, Theodosius, and Arcadius (C. viii, 4, 7).

†† Ulpian on the Edict, *Dig.* xlvii, 8, 2, § 22, 23.

‡‡ Institutes of *Marcianus*, *Dig.* xxxii, 65, § 4.

|||| Partly from Ulpian on the Edict, and Gaius on the Provincial Edict, *Dig.*, ix, 2, 7, § 8; and 8, § 1.

Com. iv. *Struck out.* *Added.* Bk. iv.

stipulation, is stated not to be in use, and in respect
of the third head of the same law, the view of Sabinus § 15.
is affirmed, and the word "highest" value deemed
included, whilst the distinction between damage § 16.
being done by bodily act or not is amplified.

In dealing with *outrages*, the different meanings of Tit. iv.
the word "injuria" are given,* and it is laid down
that a wife cannot bring an action for an outrage to § 2.
her husband.† The case of outrage committed on a § 4, 5.
slave held in common, or in different rights, is con-
sidered, and the scale of compensation is shown to § 7.
vary with the rank of the individual injured, whether
master or slave, and the provisions of the Cornelian § 8.
law noticed.‡ It is further pointed out that proceed-
ings may be taken either civilly or criminally, and § 10.
that persons of rank may sue or defend by a pro-
curator,‖ as also that the instigator of the outrage is
liable to an action. The subject of obligations is
closed by examples of those arising from *quasi*- Tit. v.
delicts.¶

*Actions*** are then entered upon, and a definition†† Tit. vi.
given, followed by examples of real actions, with § 2-13.
the alterations made by Justinian‡‡ in others, whether
real or personal, originally introduced by the prætor.
After classifying mixed actions, examples are given § 16-20.
of other actions apparently so, and also examples of
those actions (some introduced by Justinian‖‖) which § 21-27.
are available for recovering the single, double, triple,
or quadruple value.

Com. iv. § 10-52. Account of the actions of the law, and of the introduction of *formulæ*, and of their parts and uses.

§ 64-68. Difference between the set off allowed by a banker when bringing an action, and the deduction

The list of actions of good faith § 28-29.
is enlarged¶¶ and set off shown to § 30.
be allowed*** in all actions except

* Paul on Outrages, *Mos. et Rom. leg. collat.*, ii, 5.
† Paul on the Edict, *Dig.* xlvii, 10, 2.
‡ Ulpian on the Edict, *Dig.* xlvii, 10, 5. ‖ Zeno, C. ix, 35, 11.
¶ Nearly the whole title taken from Every-Day Book of Gaius, *Dig.* l, 13, 6; xliv, 7, 5, § 4-6. Gaius on the Provincial Edict, *Dig.* ix, 3, 7.
** As the formulary system had disappeared two centuries before the editors of the Institutes of *Justinian* entered upon their task, much of the language relating to actions generally, to interdicts, and to the use of exceptions in pleading, etc., which has been hastily borrowed from Gaius, and other classical jurists, who wrote under the system of formulæ, conveys a wrong impression of the civil procedure in force in the sixth century at Constantinople. See *Ort. Anal.*, part i, par. 427, p. 47; and *post*, note *, p. liv.
†† Digest of Celsus, *Dig.* xliv, 7, 51. ‡‡ *E.g.*, C. iv, 18, 2.
‖‖ *E.g.*, C. iii, 10, 2, § 2, and 2, 4.
¶¶ Justinian, C. iii, 31, 12, § 3; v, 13, and 12, 30; viii, 18, 12, § 1.
*** Justinian, C. iv, 31, 14, pr. § 1, and 34, 11.

Com. iv. *Struck out.*

of cross claims by a purchaser of an insolvent's goods.

54. That too much cannot be claimed in formulæ of the uncertain class.

56-60. Pleas available to defeat claim of residue during the same prætorship, and the result of claiming too much in formulæ framed in a case of deposit, etc.

Added. Bk. iv.

that of deposit. Examples follow § 31-32.
of "arbitrary" actions, and notice
taken of both the alteration of the § 33.
law as to the penalty for claiming
more than due, and as to the
balance being recoverable in the § 34.
same action where too little has
been claimed.* The class of ac- § 36-40.
tions are next referred to in which
less is recovered than was claimed,
whether on account of the nature
of the action, or from the right of set-off; and
cases where all redress is denied are illustrated by Tit. vii.
the provisions of the *Macedonian decree* of the § 6.
senate.

In discussing *noxal* actions, it is shown that if a Tit. viii.
slave is surrendered to the person injured, the slave § 3.
can obtain his freedom on raising the money re-
quired for compensation;† and the point is settled § 6.
that the action is lost where you have been injured
by the slave of another, and then that slave has
passed into your power.

79-81. Paragraphs as to the surrender of sons by way of formal sale, and as to the mode of dealing with the property of women under marital power, or of freemen in a state of bondage, in such cases.

Finally, it is noted that noxal § 7.
actions only now apply to slaves.

A special title is devoted to the subject of the Tit. ix.
noxal, and Ædilitian,‡ actions available in respect of damage caused by animals.

83. Mode of appointing cognitors,
86, 87. and mode of drawing up the formula in the name of another.

91-95. Two forms of formulæ for real
97. actions, involving the giving of
102. security, and as to security when defending personal actions.

103-109. Distinction between actions resulting from the civil law, and those based on the authority of the magistrate.

The origin of the law relating Tit. x.
to suits conducted by procurators
is shortly stated, and the modern
system of finding *security* is shown Tit. xi.
to have arisen from custom, and
details of the methods in use are § 2-7.
given.

In respect of *defences* to actions, Tit. xii.
the disputed point whether a judge § 2.
should absolve the defendant in all
cases, if he make satisfaction, is de-

* Zeno and Justinian, C. iii, 10, 1 and 2.
† Papinian. See *Mos. et Rom. leg. collat.*, ii, 3.
‡ Ulpian on the Edict, *Dig.* ix, 1, 1, pr. § 1-3; l, 17, 130.

Com. iv. *Struck out.*

§ 118,119. Details as to the mode in which
§ 125. exceptions were drawn up, and the doubt referred to as to a defendant being able to get a restitution of rights who had neglected to avail himself of a dilatory plea.

§ 126. Example of replication used by a banker.

§ 130-137. Paragraphs as to prescriptions used by plaintiff.

§ 140,141.
§ 145,146. Procedure in respect of *inter-*
§ 161-170. *dicts.*

§ 174-181. Paragraphs relating to the mode of restraining vexatious litigation, and as to the restipulations by way of check on litigation.

§ 184-187. As to the defendant giving security for his reappearance.

Added. Bk. iv.

cided in the affirmative, the provisions of the constitution of Zeno* Tit. xii
are made applicable to an action § 10.
commenced before the time, whilst
exceptions† on account of infamy § 11.
are abolished, and the *defences open* Tit. xiv
to sureties explained.‡ § 4.

The details as to *injunctions* are amplified by ex- Tit. xv.
amples of prohibitory, restitutory, and exhibitory § 1.
interdicts, and it is shown that the procedure in re-
spect of interdicts has been super- § 8.
seded by actions under the extra-
ordinary system. To check the Tit. xvi
abuse of the process of the courts,‖
the action for *vexatious litigation*
is replaced by a *judicial oath* re- § 1, 2.
quired of defendants and of plaintiffs, that they are not defending or proceeding litigiously, and also of the advocates, that there is a good cause of action.

Observations upon the *duty of a judge*¶ in pro- Tit. x
nouncing judgment occupy a separate title, and a few
examples of criminal statutes to illustrate the subject Tit. xv
of *public prosecutions*,** conclude the fourth book.

On the completion of the Institutes, in A.D. 533, Justinian published a constitution by which he directed that the course of study in the law

---

* C. iii, 10, 1.

† Under Justinian there was not, properly speaking, any such thing as an *exception* in the technical sense, *i.e.*, a negative clause inserted in the formula by the prætor on behalf of the defendant. (See *Ort. Anal.*, part iii, par. 1945, p. 345.) The word now applied to any defence other than a denial of the right of action.

‡ Partly from Institutes of *Marcianus*, *Dig.* xliv, 1, 19.

‖ Justinian, C. ii, 59, 2; iii, 1, 14, § 1.

¶ The word *judex* in the time of Justinian meant an (inferior) magistrate; but, in the time of Gaius, when the formulary system was in force, it meant rather a juryman appointed for the particular case, and who, after receiving precise written instructions from the magistrate, heard the evidence and gave judgment for plaintiff or defendant. See *Ort. Anal.*, part i, par. 162; 427, pp. 18, 47. Austin's *Jurisprudence*, 4th edit., pp. 606, 607.

** Principally from Paul on the Edict, *Dig.* xlviii, 1, 2; Gaius on the Twelve Tables, *Dig.* l, 16, 233, § 2; Institutes of *Marcianus*, *Dig.* xlviii, 8, 1; and 3 tit. 9, 1; and 3, tit. 10, 1; tit. 6, 1; and 3 and 5, tit. 7, 1; tit. 13, 4; *Code*, ix, 13, 1, pr. § 1-3. The subject of public prosecutions is very briefly treated, as criminal law was held by Roman Institutional writers to be outside the province of private law. See Austin's *Jurisprudence*, 4th edit., pp. 764, 765.

schools* should be opened by this elementary treatise, and thereupon the Imperial text-book usurped the place hitherto occupied by the Commentaries of Gaius. These latter then disappeared, and were only known to jurists by the epitome in the Breviarium Alaricianum,† and by the references in other works, until, after the lapse of twelve centuries, they were disinterred at Verona.‡

---

§ 5. OF THE TWELVE TABLES.||

In theory the Twelve Tables were not superseded until the reforms of Justinian. They had been in part repealed by direct legislation,¶ in

---

* For the course of study pursued in the law schools, both before and after Justinian's time, see *Ort. Anal.*, part i, par. 570, p. 61.

† *Ante*, p. xxviii, and *Ort. Anal.*, part 1, par. 529 (1), p. 56.

‡ In arranging the text of the Institutes of *Gaius* in parallel columns with the Institutes of *Justinian*, I decided, after considerable hesitation, to make the sequence of the former yield to that of the latter. In doing so, I am supported by Klenze and Böcking in Germany, Polenaar in Holland, and Pellat in France, as opposed to those who follow the well-known arrangement of Gneist; and I would venture to urge in further support of my plan, that the only manuscript we possess of the Institutes of *Gaius* is defective, the order of the sheets of parchment in part conjectural, and the absence of any division into titles inconvenient for reference; whereas the text of the Institutes of *Justinian* is complete, and, however inferior in style, is, in respect of matter, a second edition of the former, and, being several centuries later in date, embodies the leading doctrines of that developed Roman law, which it is more particularly the object of the student to master.

The transpositions of the text of Gaius in order to suit that of Justinian are as follows:—

In *Com.* i, §§ 106, 105, are interpolated between §§ 102, 103; and § 184 follows § 193.

In *Com.* ii, §§ 65 to 72, 79, 73 to 78, follow § 11; §§ 185 to 190, 174 to 184, follow § 137; §§ 191 to 223, 238, 239, 241, 240, 242 to 245, 229 to 237, 224 to 228, 246 to 248, 250 to 207, 249, 268 to 289, follow § 173.

In *Com.* iii, §§ 35 to 76, follow § 31; §§ 32, 33, follow § 34; § 77 follows § 33; §§ 103, 102, 104, 105 to 109, follow § 97A; § 110 follows § 101; § 161 follows § 157; § 214 follows § 211.

In *Com.* iv, §§ 61 to 68, follow § 52.

The text of the Institutes of *Justinian*, given on the right hand side of pp. 1 to 250, is mainly that of Schrader, as used by Gneist, with occasional emendations suggested by other and later critics. For convenience of reference I have followed the customary division of the subject-matter of each title into numbered paragraphs, though these divisions do not exist in the original manuscripts.

In translating the Institutes of *Justinian*, I have carefully perused the rendering by Harris and Cooper, and in ascertaining the meaning of obscurely worded passages, I have sought assistance in the French of Ortolan, and in the able German translation of Dr. Sintenis.

|| For a review of the nature, and a complete analysis of the contents of the Twelve Tables, see my *Ort. Anal.*, part i, par. 112, pp. 10 to 16. In this section only such information is given as tends to throw light on the form in which the Twelve Tables appeared, and in which they have reached us.

¶ For example, Table v, § 3, as to the unlimited power of testamentary disposition, by the *lex Falcidia* (see *Ort. Anal.*, part iii, par. 940, p. 211). Table xi, as to marriage, by the *lex Canuleia* (*Ort. Anal.*, part i, par. 150, p. 17). Table viii, so far as relating to wrongful damage, by the *lex Aquilia* (*Ort. Anal.*, part iii, par. 1746, p. 324); and the actions of the law, by the *lex Æbutia* (*Ort. Anal.*, part i, par. 244, p. 27).

part overruled by the equitable intervention of the prætor*, and practically buried under those works of the jurists which were ostensibly devoted to the interpretation of their meaning†; still, for one thousand years, the language of the Roman lawyer always assumes that these tables were not only the source,‡ but the actual embodiment of the civil law of Rome, || and, for upwards of four centuries after their promulgation, they were regarded with pride by every Roman citizen, and learnt by heart by every Roman schoolboy.¶

From an historical point of view, their importance can hardly be overrated. The fixing of the brazen tablets, in a conspicuous position in the heart of the city, marks, at a critical period in the infancy of the commonwealth, the successful issue of one of the many struggles of the plebeian element for that equality of rights which was denied them by the patricians, and which it was vain to look for until a preliminary step had been attained, viz., the withdrawal, from the hands of a dominant caste, of the exclusive knowledge of, and power of perverting to their own ends, those hitherto unwritten usages which had served the purposes of law.

It was in this publicity, as Sir H. Maine has so eloquently pointed out,** that the real value of the code consisted, for, with the exception of the legalisation of the testament made by way of the copper and the scale,†† and the settlement of the question of usurious interest,‡‡ the provisions of these Tables extended no peculiar favour to the plebeians, effected no improvement in their condition; and the prohibition against marriage between patricians and plebeians was highly prejudicial to the interests of the latter.

From an antiquarian point of view, also, the Twelve Tables are of very great interest, as revealing the actual habits and degree of civilisation of the Romans in the fifth century before the Christian era.

In the study of comparative jurisprudence, the Twelve Tables are valuable as containing the germ of a number of institutions developed in the law of a later period; and, to the student of Roman law, a

---

* Particularly shown in giving blood relations an equitable title to the property, and so gradually extinguishing the artificial family system of succession on intestacy, see *Ort. Anal.*, part iii, par. 1008, p. 242.

† The more important works interpreting the Twelve Tables were those of *Sextus Ælius* (see *Ort. Anal.*, part i, par 239, p. 27); of *Labeo* (mentioned by Aulus Gellius, *Noc. Att.*, i, c. 12; vii, c. 15; xx, c. 1); and of *Gaius* (see *ante*, note †, p. xxix).

‡ "Fons omnis publici privatique juris" Liv. *Hist.*, iii, 34. "Finis æqui juris". Tac. *Ann.*, iii, 27.

"The expositors of Roman law consistently employed language which implied that the body of their system rested on the twelve Decemviral tables." Maine's *Ancient Law*, c. 1, p. 1.

|| Hence the word *lex* is sometimes used by them as meaning the Twelve Tables.

¶ Cicero regrets that, in his lifetime, this practice had died out, and, with the exception of the two last, he praises the Twelve Tables very highly, Cic., *De Leg.*, ii, c. 23; *De Orat.*, i, c. 43; *De Rep.*, ii, c. 36, 37, iv, c. 4; and see *Ort. Anal.*, part i, par. 236, p. 27.

** Maine's *Ancient Law*, c. i, p. 15.

†† Table v, § 3, Maine's *Ancient Law*, c. vi, p. 202.

‡‡ Table viii, § 18, see *Ort. Anal.*, part iii, par. 1658, p. 299.

knowledge of them is, of course, essential, as they are the subject of continual reference in the works of the jurists, and formed the model upon which subsequent legislation was founded;* but regarded as a body of law in themselves, and more particularly as a code, in the modern sense, these tables are miserably crude and defective. They practically omit all mention of the political constitution of the state, and of the fundamental principles essential to its existence. They assume that the details necessary for carrying on the machinery of government, law, and police, are well known and in full working order; and, in fact, the Twelve Tables bear internal evidence of being, with a few exceptions, and with some slight assistance from Attic legislation,† a mere enunciation of existing local customs, some of them not only in a transitional state, but in process of disintegration,‡ many of them rude, harsh, and barbarous in the extreme,|| and all of them expressed in abrupt, imperative terms, affecting a brevity wholly inconsistent with the subject-matter.

The Ten Tables were completed in B.C. 451, two supplementary Tables being added in the following year. The actual brazen tablets, publicly exhibited by the decemvirs in the Comitium, survived the destruction of the city by the Gauls, in B.C. 390; but, after an existence of upwards of five more centuries, they disappeared, and all trace of their contents, as a whole, was lost.¶ Vigorous efforts have, however, been

---

* For example, the Edict of the prætors, the Code of Theodosius, the Code and Digest of Justinian.

† For example, according to an extract in the *Digest* (x, 1, 13), from the work of Gaius on the Twelve Tables, the details in Table vii, 2 and 3, as to the distances and depths to be observed in respect of neighbouring plantations, constructions, and excavations, were taken from Solon's Athenian Code; and with reference to Table viii, § 27, as to the power of corporations to make their own bye-laws, if not inconsistent with the general law, the same jurist quotes a law of Solon as a source of this clause (see *Dig.* xlvii, 22, 4); and, according to Cicero (*De Leg.*, b. ii, c. 25) the same code was the source of the regulations in Table x, as to funerals. The account of the three deputies sent to Athens and other Greek cities to obtain materials for the code, rests principally on the statements of Pomponius (*Dig.* i, 2, 2, § 4); Livy (b. iii, c. 31, 32, 33); and Dionysius of Halicarnassus (*Antiq. Rom.*, b. 10, c. 56); and it seems in itself not an improbable story, but the fact of such an embassy having visited Greece for the purpose, is doubted by some modern writers, including Gibbon (*Hist.*, c. 44); and Sir G. C. Lewis (*Credibility of Early Roman Hist.*, c. xii, § 54); whilst Niebuhr (*Hist. of Rome;* and lect. xxiv, on *Hist. of Rome*) thinks the commission was sent, but derived no assistance as to personal rights, or judicial proceedings from the Attic code. The Decemvirs are also said (Pomponius, *Dig.*, i, 2, 2, § 4) to have had assistance in the interpretation of the Greek laws from the exile Hermodorus of Ephesus; and Pliny (*Hist. Nat.*, xxxiv, 11) refers to a statue erected to him, at the public expense, in the Comitium; but Sir G C. Lewis, after examining the authorities (*Credibility, etc.*, c. xii, § 54), throws doubt on the story, and is followed by Ihne (*Hist. Rome*, bk. ii, c. 9 and 16).

‡ For example, Table iv, § 3, by which a son could become released from the power of the head of the family; and Table vi, § 4, by which a wife could defeat the acquisition of marital power by the husband, when the circumstances of her family and fortune made such a course desirable.

|| For example, Table iii, § 6, towards debtors; and Table viii, in respect of retaliation in the case of bodily injuries. As to the power of noxal abandonment, see *Ort. Anal.*, part iii, par. 2226, p. 378.

¶ See the evidence on this subject collected in Puchta, *Cursus, etc.*, vol. i, § 55, 4th edit., 1853.

made to reconstruct them from the materials furnished by the references to, and extracts from, them in the works of the jurists, and in the result, probably about two-thirds have been recovered, particularly through the industry of Jacobus Gothofredus (Jacques Godefroy),* in the seventeenth century. His work was, however, published before the discovery of the Republic of Cicero,† or the Institutes of Gaius,‡ from both of which much additional information has been since derived and embodied by Dirksen in his exhaustive treatise.|| A few further indications of the contents of the Twelve Tables have been subsequently drawn from the Fragmenta Vaticana.¶

Some editors, in their anxiety to preserve the integrity of the text, object to insert any word of the Twelve Tables for which there is not very satisfactory authority; but, to enable the student to grasp their general scope, it seems advisable to include within brackets conjectural readings, headings, and summaries of the supposed contents of lost portions of the tables.

In the translation, I have endeavoured faithfully to convey the meaning, whilst avoiding the use of latin words simply anglicised.

§ 6. OF THE NOVELS OF JUSTINIAN RELATING TO INTESTATE SUCCESSION.

The modifications introduced into the law of intestate succession in the early years of the reign of Justinian, and embodied in the third book of his Institutes, were intended to supplement and extend the efforts of the prætors of ancient Rome to recognise the claims of the natural family; but the underlying rules of agnation, upon which the constitution of the ancient civil family rested, together with those rules of later date, which depended upon the difference of sex, were inconsistent with the principle of kinship in blood upon which the new rules were founded, and, as a necessary consequence, the body of law governing the devolution of property on intestacy was a complicated and defective patchwork.

To remedy this state of things Justinian, in A.D. 544, published the CXVIIIth Novel, by which the civil constitution of the family was abolished, together with the distinction between the hereditas, and the bonorum possessio, and between agnatio and cognatio. At the same time the sexes were put on an equality,** and a succession

---

* *Quattuor Fontes Juris Civilis* (amended edit.), Geneva, 1653.

† But as this is an ideal republic the statements must be accepted with caution.

‡ For the references to the Twelve Tables in the Institutes of *Gaius*, see Index.

|| Entitled *Uebersicht der bisherigen versuche zum kritik und herstellung des Textes der Zwölf Tafel-Fragmente*, Leipsic, 1824.

¶ Published in 1828 (*Ort. Anal.* part i, par 511 (1), p. 55.) For a list of all the authorities for reconstructing the Twelve Tables, see the notes to each Table in M. Ortolan's *Legislation Romaine*, 10th edit., vol. i, pp. 102-122; see also Gneist's *Syntagma*, pp. xii to xxvii.

** Hence the law of intestate succession, as laid down in bk. iii, titles 1, 2, 3, 5, and 9, of the Institutes (*Ort. Anal.*, part iii, par. 994-1138, pp. 242-253, summarised at pp. 306-310) became obsolete eleven years after the publication of the work,

established, based simply upon blood relationship, in the order of descendants, ascendants, and collaterals.*

This reform was completed, in A.D. 548, by the CXXVIIth Novel, by which an omission in the previous Novel was rectified, and the right of representation accorded to the children of deceased brothers or sisters when competing with ascendants.†

It will be seen, however, from the text of the sixth chapter of the CXVIIIth Novel, that religious intolerance prevented these important changes in the law of intestate succession being of universal application, and that their benefits were confined to those holding the catholic faith. By this restriction, a great part of the inhabitants of the empire were shut out,‡ but as the principle upon which these Novels were based, was sound, and in accordance with the natural instincts of mankind, it has struggled through the trammels placed upon its use, so that these Novels have become the basis of most of the rules of modern times on the subject; and the statute law of England governing the distribution of personal estate on intestacy is in great measure borrowed from them.‖

These two Novels, representing the final stage of intestate succession, as settled by Justinian, were published separately, on their respective dates, at Constantinople in the greek language; but towards the close of Justinian's reign, an abridged latin version¶ of the substance of them, together with one hundred and twenty-three others, was made by Julianus,** probably for use in Italy, which had at that time refallen under the dominion of the Eastern Empire; and, shortly afterwards, a very inac-

---

but in the matter of guardianship a distinction continued to exist between the sexes, as, by ch. v of this novel, females were excluded, except the mother or grandmother of the ward, who could be entrusted with the guardianship in her order of successsion, and in default of a guardian appointed by testament, if she renounced second marriage, and the benefit of the senatus-consultum Velleianum.

* This order being based upon the fact recognised from the earliest times by philosophers that the parent has more affection for the child than the child for the parent, because a person regards his issue as peculiar to himself. (Aristotle, *Ethic., ad Nicom.*, lib. 8, cap. 12.)

† For an analysis of the contents of the CXVIIIth and CXXVIIth Novels, see my *Ort. Anal.*, part iii, par. 1143, p. 253; and see Demangeat, *Cours élémentaire de Droit Romain*, 3rd edit., 1876, vol. ii, pp. 129-136.

‡ The term catholic excluded all who were not sufficiently orthodox to subscribe to the whole of the dogmas of the four œcumenical councils mentioned in Novel CXXXI, c. 1. In respect of such heretics, the CXVth Novel, c. 3, § 14, provided that their catholic ascendants should have the right of disinheriting them, and in the case of a deceased person leaving several children, the whole property would pass to those who were catholics, to the exclusion of such as were heretics.

‖ Blackstone (*Com.*, vol. ii, p. 516) does not give full credit to the civil law as the ground work of the statute of Distributions (22 and 23 Car. II, c. 10, amended by 1 Jac. II, c. 17, § 7), but it is well known that it was framed principally upon the model of the CXVIIIth Novel of Justinian, by a professional civilian, Sir Leoline Jenkins, Judge of the High Court of Admiralty, who died shortly after the accession of James II. See Phillimore's *International Law*, 2nd edit., 1871, vol. i, p. lxxii. See also Pett's case, 1 P. Wms. 27, and Reports of all the cases determined by Sir John Holt, p. 259, and Prec. Chan. 593. For comments on the working of this statute, and its defect in placing the half blood on an equality, see William's *Personal Property*, 10th edit., p. 407.

¶ The so-called Epitome Juliani.

** A professor in Constantinople.

curate latin translation* of one hundred and thirty-four of the Novels was made by an unknown author. These two latin versions seem to have been the only texts of the Novels used by the glossators, though a greek collection of one hundred and sixty-eight Novels of Justinian and of his successors was in existence as early as A.D. 578.

The latin versio vulgata is that commonly introduced into treatises on Roman law; but I have preferred printing the CXVIIIth, and the first chapter of the CXXVIIth Novel,† in the original greek, placing by its side the very elegant literal latin rendering of Hombergk,‡ by which I have been greatly assisted in the english translation added at the foot.||

---

* The so-called *versio vulgata.*

† The remaining chapters (2, 3, and 4) relate to other matters not affecting the law of succession, viz., marriage portions, and the penalties for divorce without lawful grounds.

‡ Made in 1717, but I have used the text as given, with corrections, by the Kriegel Brothers, in their edition (1868) of the Corpus Juris Civilis.

|| I have also derived much help from the very accurate German translation of the Greek text by Dr. Schneider, contained in the seventh volume of the "Corpus Juris Civilis ins Deutsche übersetzt von einem vereine rechtsgelehrter", Leipsic, 1833.

INSTITUTIONUM JUSTINIANI

PROOEMIUM.

IN NOMINE DOMINI NOSTRI JESU CHRISTI.

IMPERATOR CAESAR FLAVIUS JUSTINIANUS,
ALAMANNICUS, GOTHICUS, FRANCICUS,
GERMANICUS, ANTICUS, ALANICUS,
VANDALICUS, AFRICANUS, PIUS,
FELIX, INCLYTUS VICTOR AC
TRIUMPHATOR, SEMPER
AUGUSTUS

CUPIDAE LEGUM JUVENTUTI.

IMPERATORIAM majestatem non solum armis decoratam, sed etiam legibus oportet esse armatam, ut utrumque tempus et bellorum et pacis recte possit gubernari, et princeps romanus victor existat non solum in hostilibus proeliis, sed etiam per legitimos tramites calumniantium iniquitates expellens, et fiat tam juris religiosissimus, quam victis hostibus triumphator.

§ 1. Quorum utramque viam cum summis vigiliis summaque providentia, annuente Deo, perfecimus. Et bellicos quidem sudores nostros barbaricae gentes sub juga nostra deductae cognoscunt; et tam Africa quam aliae innumerosae provinciae post tanta temporum spatia nostris victoriis a caelesti numine praestitis iterum dicioni Romanae nostroque additae imperio protestantur. Omnes vero populi legibus tam a nobis promulgatis quam compositis reguntur. § 2. Et cum sacratissimas constitutiones antea confusas in luculentam ereximus consonantiam, tunc nostram extendimus curam ad immensa veteris prudentiae volumina, et opus desperatum quasi per medium profundum euntes, caelesti favore jam adimplevimus. § 3. Cumque hoc Deo propitio peractum est, Triboniano, viro magnifico, magistro et exquaestore sacri palatii nostri, nec non Theophilo et Dorotheo, viris illustribus, antecessoribus, quorum omnium sollertiam et legum scientiam et circa nostras jussiones fidem jam ex multis rerum argumentis accepimus, convocatis, specialiter mandavimus, ut nostra auctoritate nostrisque suasionibus Institutiones componerent, ut liceat vobis prima legum cunabula non ab antiquis fabulis discere, sed ab imperiali splendore appetere, et tam aures quam animae vestrae nihil inutile nihilque perperam positum, sed quod in ipsis rerum obtinet argumentis, accipiant, et quod in priore tempore vix post quadriennium prioribus contingebat, ut tunc constitutiones imperatorias legerent, hoc vos a primordio ingrediamini, digni tanto honore tantague reperti felicitate, ut et initium vobis et finis legum eruditionis a voce principali procedat. § 4. Igitur post libros quinquaginta digestorum seu pandectarum in quibus omne jus antiquum collatum est, quos per eundem virum excelsum Tribonianum nec non ceteros viros illustres et facundissimos confecimus, in hos quatuor libros easdem Institutiones partiri jussimus, ut sint totius legitimae scientiae prima elementa. § 5. In quibus breviter expositum est et quod antea obtinebat et quod postea desuetudine inumbratum ab imperiali remedio illuminatum est. § 6. Quas ex omnibus antiquorum institutionibus, et praecipue ex commentariis Gaii nostri tam institutionum quam rerum quotidianarum, aliisque multis commentariis compositas, cum tres praedicti viri prudentes nobis obtulerunt, et legimus et cognovimus, et plenissimum nostrarum constitutionum robur eis accommodavimus.

§ 7. Summa itaque ope et alacri studio has leges nostras accipite, et vosmetipsos sic eruditos ostendite, ut spes vos pulcherrima foveat, toto legitimo opere perfecto, posse etiam nostram rempublicam in partibus ejus vobis credendis gubernare.

Data undecimo calendas decembres, Constantinopoli, Domino nostro Justiniano perpetuo Augusto tertium Consule.

INSTITUTIONUM

GAII COMMENTARIUS I. JUSTINIANI LIBER I.

Tit. i. De justitia et jure.

Justitia est constans et perpetua voluntas jus suum cuique tribuendi.

§ 1. Jurisprudentia est divinarum atque humanarum rerum notitia, justi atque injusti scientia.

§ 2. His igitur generaliter cognitis, et incipientibus nobis exponere jura populi Romani ita maxime videntur posse tradi commodissime, si primo levi ac simplici, post deinde diligentissima atque exactissima interpretatione singula tradantur. Alioquin, si statim ab initio rudem adhuc et infirmum animum studiosi multitudine ac varietate rerum oneraverimus, duorum alterum, aut desertorem studiorum efficiemus, aut cum magno labore ejus saepe etiam cum diffidentia quae plerumque juvenes avertit, serius ad id perducemus, ad quod, leviore via ductus, sine magno labore et sine ulla diffidentia maturius perduci potuisset.

§ 3. Juris praecepta sunt haec: honeste vivere, alterum non laedere, suum cuique tribuere.

§ 4. Hujus studii duae sunt positiones, publicum et privatum. Publicum jus est, quod ad statum rei Romanae spectat; privatum, quod ad singulorum utilitatem pertinet. Dicendum est igitur de jure privato, quod tripertitum est collectum: est enim ex naturalibus praeceptis, aut gentium, aut civilibus.

Tit. ii. De jure naturali, gentium, et civili.

Jus naturale est, quod natura omnia animalia docuit. Nam jus istud non humani generis proprium est, sed omnium animalium quae in caelo, quae in terra, quae in mari nascuntur. Hinc descendit maris atque feminae conjunctio quam nos matrimonium appellamus; hinc liberorum procreatio et educatio. Videmus etenim cetera quoque animalia istius juris peritia censeri.

De jure gentium et civili. § 1. [Omnes populi qui legibus et moribus reguntur, partim suo proprio, partim communi omnium hominum jure utuntur: nam quod quis]que populus ipse sibi jus constituit, id ipsius proprium est, vocaturque jus civile, quasi jus proprium civitatis; quod vero naturalis ratio inter omnes homines constituit, id apud omnes populos peraeque custoditur vocaturque jus gentium, quasi quo jure omnes gentes utuntur. Populus itaque Romanus partim suo proprio, partim communi omnium hominum jure utitur: quae singula qualia sint, suis locis proponemus.

§ 1. Jus autem civile, vel gentium, ita dividitur. *Omnes populi qui legibus et moribus reguntur, partim suo proprio, partim communi omnium hominum jure utuntur: nam quod quisque populus ipse sibi jus constituit, id ipsius civitatis proprium est, vocaturque jus civile, quasi jus proprium ipsius civitatis; quod vero naturalis ratio inter omnes homines constituit, id apud omnes populos peraeque custoditur vocaturque jus gentium, quasi quo jure omnes gentes utuntur. Et populus itaque Romanus partim suo proprio, partim communi omnium hominum jure utitur: quae singula qualia sint, suis locis proponemus.*

§ 2. Sed jus quidem civile ex unaquaque civitate appellatur, veluti Atheniensium: nam si quis velit Solonis vel Draconis leges appellare jus civile Atheniensium, non erraverit. Sic enim et jus quo populus Romanus utitur jus civile Romanorum appellamus; vel jus Quiritium, quo Quirites utuntur; Romani enim a Quirino Quirites appellantur. Sed quotiens non addimus nomen, cujus sit civitatis, nostrum jus significamus: sicuti cum poetam dicimus, nec addimus nomen, subauditur apud Graecos egregius Homerus, apud nos Virgilius. Jus autem gentium omni humano generi commune est. Nam, usu exigente et humanis necessitatibus, gentes humanae quaedam sibi constituerunt: bella etenim orta sunt et captivitates secutae, et servitutes, quae sunt juri naturali contrariae; jure enim naturali ab initio omnes homines liberi nascebantur. Et ex hoc jure gentium omnes pene contractus introducti sunt, ut emptio venditio, locatio conductio, societas, depositum, mutuum, et alii innumerabiles.

§ 2. Constant autem jura populi Romani ex legibus, plebiscitis, senatus-consultis, constitutionibus principum, edictis eorum qui jus edicendi habent, responsis prudentium.

§ 3. Constat autem jus nostrum aut ex scripto, aut ex non scripto: ut apud Graecos, τῶν νόμων οἱ μὲν ἔγγραφοι, οἱ δὲ ἄγραφοι. Scriptum jus est lex, plebiscita, senatus-consulta, principum placita, magistratuum edicta, responsa prudentium.

§ 3. Lex est quod populus jubet atque constituit. Plebiscitum est quod plebs jubet atque constituit.

§ 4. *Lex est quod populus* Romanus, senatorio magistratu interrogante, veluti consule, constitu-

Plebs autem a populo eo distat, quod populi appellatione universi cives significantur, connumeratis etiam patriciis; plebis autem appellatione sine patriciis ceteri cives significantur. Unde olim patricii dicebant plebiscitis se non teneri, quae sine auctoritate eorum facta essent: sed postea lex Hortensia lata est, qua cautum est ut plebiscita universum populum tenerent; itaque eo modo legibus exaequata sunt.

ebat. *Plebiscitum est quod plebs*, plebeio magistratu interrogante, veluti tribuno, constituebat. *Plebs autem a populo eo* differt, quo species a genere: nam *appellatione populi universi cives significantur, connumeratis etiam patriciis* et senatoribus; *plebis autem appellatione, sine patriciis* et senatoribus *ceteri cives significantur.* Sed et plebiscita lege *Hortensia lata* non minus valere quam leges coeperunt.

§ 4. Senatus-consultum est quod senatus jubet atque constituit, idque legis vicem obtinet, quamvis fuerit quaesitum.

§ 5. *Senatus-consultum est quod senatus jubet atque constituit.* Nam cum auctus est populus Romanus in eum modum, ut difficile sit in unum eum convocari legis sanciendae causa, aequum visum est senatum vice populi consuli.

§ 5. Constitutio principis est quod imperator decreto, vel edicto, vel epistola constituit: nec umquam dubitatum est, quin id legis vicem obtineat, cum ipse imperator per legem imperium accipiat.

§ 6. Sed et quod principi placuit legis habet vigorem, cum lege regia quae de imperio ejus lata est, populus ei et in eum omne suum imperium et potestatem concessit. Quodcumque igitur Imperator per epistolam constituit, vel cognoscens decrevit, vel edicto praecepit, legem esse constat: hae sunt, quae constitutiones appellantur. Plane ex his quaedam sunt personales, quae nec ad exemplum trahuntur, quoniam non hoc princeps vult, nam quod alicui ob merita indulsit, vel si cui poenam irrogavit, vel si cui sine exemplo subvenit, personam non transgreditur. Aliae autem, cum generales sint, omnes procul dubio tenent.

§ 6. Jus autem edicendi habent magistratus populi Romani; sed amplissimum jus est in edictis duorum praetorum, urbani et peregrini: quorum jurisdictionem in provinciis praesides earum habent; item in edictis aedilium curulium, quorum jurisdictionem in provinciis populi Romani quaestores habent; nam in provincias Caesaris omnino quaestores non mittuntur, et ob id hoc edictum in his provinciis non proponitur.

§ 7. Praetorum quoque edicta non modicam juris obtinent auctoritatem. Haec etiam jus honorarium solemus appellare, quod qui honorem gerunt, id est magistratus, auctoritatem huic juri dederunt. Proponebant et Aediles curules edictum de quibusdam causis, quod edictum juris honorarii portio est.

§ 7. Responsa prudentium sunt sententiae et opiniones eorum quibus permissum est jura condere: quorum omnium si in unum

§ 8. *Responsa prudentium sunt sententiae et opiniones eorum quibus permissum* erat *jura condere.* Nam antiquitus institutum erat, ut essent qui jura publice interpretarentur, quibus a Caesare jus

sententiae concurrant, id quod ita sentiunt legis vicem obtinet; si vero dissentiunt, judici licet quam velit sententiam sequi, idque rescripto divi Hadriani significatur.

respondendi datum est, qui jurisconsulti appellabantur: *quorum omnium sententiae* et opiniones eam auctoritatem tenebant, ut judici recedere a responso eorum non liceret, ut est constitutum.

§ 9. Ex non scripto jus venit quod usus comprobavit. Nam diuturni mores consensu utentium comprobati legem imitantur.

§ 10. Et non ineleganter in duas species jus civile distributum videtur; nam origo ejus ab institutis duarum civitatium, Athenarum scilicet et Lacedaemonis, fluxisse videtur. In his enim civitatibus ita agi solitum erat, ut Lacedaemonii quidem magis ea quae pro legibus observarent, memoriae mandarent; Athenienses vero ea quae in legibus scripta comprehendissent, custodirent.

§ 11. Sed naturalia quidem jura quae apud omnes gentes peraeque servantur, divina quadam providentia constituta, semper firma atque immutabilia permanent; ea vero quae ipsa sibi quaeque civitas constituit, saepe mutari solent, vel tacito consensu populi, vel alia postea lege lata.

De juris divisione.

§ 8. Omne autem jus quo utimur, vel ad personas pertinet, vel ad res, vel ad actiones: sed prius videamus de personis.

§ 12. *Omne autem jus quo utimur vel ad personas pertinet, vel ad res, vel ad actiones. Et prius de personis videamus;* nam parum est jus nosse, si personae quarum causa statutum est, ignorentur.

De conditione hominum.

§ 9. Et quidem summa divisio de jure personarum haec est, quod omnes homines aut liberi sunt aut servi.

Tit. iii. De jure personarum.

Summa itaque *divisio de jure personarum haec est, quod omnes homines aut liberi sunt, aut servi.*

§ 1. Et libertas quidem (ex qua etiam liberi vocantur) est naturalis facultas ejus quod cuique facere libet, nisi si quid aut vi aut jure prohibetur.

§ 2. Servitus autem est constitutio juris gentium, qua quis dominio alieno contra naturam subjicitur.

§ 3. Servi autem ex eo appellati sunt, quod imperatores captivos vendere jubent, ac per hoc servare, nec occidere solent: qui etiam mancipia dicti sunt, quod ab hostibus manu capiuntur.

§ 4. Servi autem aut nascuntur, aut fiunt. Nascuntur ex ancillis nostris: fiunt aut jure gentium, id est ex captivitate; aut jure civili, cum homo liber major viginti annis ad pretium participandum sese venundari passus est.

§ 10. Rursus liberorum hominum alii ingenui sunt, alii libertini.

§ 5. In servorum conditione nulla est differentia. In liberis multae differentiae sunt: aut enim ingenui sunt, aut libertini.

Tit. iv. De ingenuis.

§ 11. Ingenui sunt, qui liberi nati sunt.

Ingenuus est, qui statim ut nascitur liber est; sive ex duobus ingenuis matrimonio editus, sive ex libertinis duobus, sive ex altero libertino, altero ingenuo. Sed etsi quis ex matre libera nascatur, patre servo, ingenuus nihilominus nascitur; quemadmodum qui ex matre libera et incerto patre natus est, quoniam vulgo conceptus est. Sufficit autem liberam fuisse matrem eo tempore quo nascitur, licet ancilla conceperit. Et ex contrario si libera conceperit, deinde ancilla facta pariat, placuit eum qui nascitur liberum nasci, quia non debet calamitas matris ei nocere qui in utero est. Ex his illud quaesitum est, si ancilla praegnans manumissa sit, deinde ancilla postea facta pepererit, liberum an servum pariat? et Marcellus probat liberum nasci; sufficit enim ei qui in ventre est liberam matrem vel medio tempore habuisse: quod et verum est.

§ 1. Cum autem ingenuus aliquis natus sit, non officit illi in servitute fuisse et postea manumissum esse; saepissime enim constitutum est, natalibus non officere manumissionem.

Tit. v. De libertinis.

Libertini, qui ex justa servitute manumissi sunt.

Libertini sunt, *qui ex justa servitute manumissi sunt.*

Manumissio autem est datio libertatis; nam quamdiu quis in servitute est, manui et potestati suppositus est, et manumissus liberatur potestate. Quae res a jure gentium originem sumpsit: utpote cum jure naturali omnes liberi nascerentur, nec esse nota manumissio, cum servitus esset incognita. Sed posteaquam jure gentium servitus invasit, secutum est beneficium manumissionis; et cum uno naturali nomine homines appellaremur, jure gentium tria genera hominum esse coeperunt: liberi, et his contrarium servi, et tertium genus libertini, qui desierant esse servi. § 1. Multis autem modis manumissio procedit: aut enim ex sacris constitutionibus in sacrosanctis ecclesiis, aut vindicta, aut inter amicos, aut per epistolam, aut per testamentum aut per aliam quamlibet ultimam voluntatem. Sed et aliis multis modis libertas servo competere potest, qui tam ex veteribus quam nostris constitutionibus introducti sunt.

§ 12. Rursus libertinorum [tria sunt genera: nam aut cives Romani, aut Latini, aut dedititiorum] numero sunt; de quibus singulis dispiciamus; ac prius de dedititiis.

De dedititiis vel lege Aelia Sentia.

§ 13. Lege itaque Aelia Sentia cavetur, ut qui servi a dominis poenae nomine vincti sint, quibusve stigmata inscripta sint, deve quibus ob noxam quaestio tormentis habita sit et in ea noxa fuisse convicti sint, quive ut ferro aut cum bestiis depugnarent traditi sint, inve ludum custodiamve conjecti fuerint, et postea vel ab eo domino vel ab alio manumissi, ejusdem conditionis liberi fiant, cujus conditionis sunt peregrini dedititii.

De peregrinis dedititiis.

§ 14. Vocantur autem peregrini dedititii hi, qui, quondam adversus populum Romanum armis susceptis, victi se dediderunt.

§ 15. Hujus ergo turpitudinis servos quocumque modo et cujuscumque aetatis manumissos, etsi pleno jure dominorum fuerint, nunquam aut cives Romanos aut Latinos fieri dicemus, sed omni modo dedititiorum numero constitui intelligemus. § 16. Si vero in nulla tali turpitudine sit servus, manumissum modo civem Romanum modo Latinum fieri dicemus. § 17. Nam in cujus persona tria haec concurrent, ut major sit annorum triginta, et ex jure quiritium domini, et justa ac legitima manumissione liberetur, id est, vindicta aut censu aut testamento, is civis Romanus fiet: sin vero aliquid eorum deerit, Latinus erit.

De manumissione vel causae probatione.

§ 18. Quod autem de aetate servi requiritur, lege Aelia Sentia introductum est; nam ea lex minores XXX annorum servos non aliter voluit manumissos cives Romanos fieri, quam si vindicta, apud consilium justa causa manumissionis adprobata, liberati fuerint. § 19. Justa autem causa manumissionis est, veluti si quis filium filiamve, aut fratrem sororemve naturalem, aut alumnum, aut paedagogum, aut servum procuratoris habendi gratia, aut ancillam matrimonii causa, apud consilium manumittat.

De recuperatoribus.

§ 20. Consilium autem adhibetur in urbe Roma quidem quinque senatorum et quinque equitum Romanorum puberum; in provinciis autem, viginti recuperatorum civium Romanorum, idque fit ultimo die conventus: sed Romae certis diebus apud consilium manumittuntur. Majores vero triginta annorum servi semper manumitti solent, adeo ut vel in transitu manumittantur, veluti cum praetor aut proconsule in balneum vel in theatrum eat. § 21. Praeterea minor triginta annorum servus manumissione potest civis Romanus fieri, si ab eo domino qui solvendo non erat, testamento eum liberum ei heredem relictus sit. . . . . . § 22. . . . . . homines Latini Juniani appellantur: Latini ideo, quia adsimulati sunt Latinis coloniariis; Juniani ideo, quia per legem Juniam libertatem acceperunt cum olim servi viderentur esse. § 23. Non tamen illis permittit lex Junia vel ipsis testamentum facere, vel ex testamento alieno capere, vel tutores testamento dari. § 24. Quod autem diximus, ex testamento eos capere non posse, ita intelligemus, ne quid inde directo hereditatis legatorumve nomine eos posse capere dicamus: alioquin per fideicommissum capere possunt. § 25. Hi vero qui dedititiorum numero sunt, nullo modo ex testamento capere possunt, non magis quam quilibet peregrinus; quin nec ipsi testamenta facere possunt, secundum id, quod magis placuit. § 26. Pessima itaque libertas eorum est, qui dedititiorum numero sunt: nec ulla lege, aut senatus-consulto, aut constitutione principali aditus illis ad civitatem Romanam datur. § 27. Quin etiam in urbe Roma vel intra centesimum urbis Romae milliarium morari prohibentur; et si contra ea fecerint, ipsi bonaque eorum publice venire jubentur, ea conditione, ut ne in urbe Roma vel intra centesimum urbis Romae milliarium serviant, neve unquam manumittantur; et, si manumissi fuerint, servi populi Romani esse jubentur: et haec ita lege Aelia Sentia comprehensa sunt.

§ 2. *Servi vero a dominis semper manumitti solent: adeo; ut vel in transitu manumittantur, veluti cum praetor aut proconsul* aut praeses *in balneum vel in theatrum eat.*

Quibus modis latini ad civitatem romanam perveniant.

§ 28. Latini vero multis modis ad civitatem Romanam perveniunt. § 29. Statim enim ex lege Aelia Sentia cautum est, ut minores triginta annorum manumissi et Latini facti, si uxores duxerint vel cives Romanas, vel Latinas coloniarias, vel ejusdem conditionis cujus ei ipsi essent, idque testati fuerint, adhibitis non minus quam septem testibus civibus Romanis puberibus, et filium procreaverint, cum is filius anniculus esse coeperit, datur eis potestas, per eam legem adire praetorem, vel in provinciis praesidem provinciae, et adprobare se ex lege Aelia Sentia uxorem duxisse et ex ea filium anniculum habere; et si is apud quem causa probata est, id ita esse pronuntiaverit, tunc et ipse Latinus et uxor ejus, si et ipsa ejusdem conditionis est, [et ipsorum filius, si et ipse ejusdem conditionis sit,] cives Romani esse jubentur. § 30. Ideo autem in persona filii adjecimus "si et ipse ejusdem conditionis sit", quia, si uxor Latini civis Romana est, qui ex ea nascitur, ex novo senatus-consulto quod auctore divo Hadriano factum est, civis Romanus nascitur. § 31. Hoc tamen jus adipiscendae civitatis Romanae, etiam si servi modo minores triginta annorum manumissi et Latini facti ex lege Aelia Sentia habuerunt, tamen postea senatus-consulto quod Pegaso et Pusione consulibus factum est, etiam majoribus triginta annorum manumissis et Latinis factis concessum est. § 32. Ceterum etiamsi ante decesserit Latinus, quam anniculi filii causam probaret, potest mater ejus causam probare, et sic et ipsa fiet civis Romana et Latin . . . . debet causam probare ut . . . . . supra diximus de fili anniculo dicta intelligemus id est, fiunt cives Romani si Romae inter vigiles sex annis militaverint; postea dicitur factum esse senatus-consultum, quo data est illis civitas Romana, si triennium militiae expleverint. Item edicto Claudii Latini jus quiritium consequuntur, si navem marinam aedificaverint, quae non minus quam decem millia modiorum frumenti capiat, eaque navis, vel quae in ejus locum substituta sit, sex annis frumentum Roman portaverit. § 33. Praeterea Ne[rone auctore senatus permisit] ut si Latinus, qui patrimonium SS CC millium plurisve habebit, in urbe Roma domum aedificaverit, in qua non minus quam partem dimidiam patrimonii sui impenderit, jus quiritium consequatur. § 34. Denique Trajanus constituit; ut si Latinus in urbe triennio pistrinum exercuerit in quo in dies singulos non minus quam centenos modios frumenti pinserit, ad jus quiritium perveniret. § 35. . . . . . datur quocunque modo jus quiritium fuerit consecutus . . . . . in bonis et ex jure quiritium sit manumissus ab eodem scilicet et Latinus fieri potest, et jus quiritium consequi.

§ 3. Libertinorum autem status tripertitus antea fuerat. Nam qui manumittebantur, modo majorem et justam libertatem consequebantur, et fiebant cives Romani; modo minorem, et Latini ex lege Junia

Norbana fiebant; modo inferiorem, et fiebant ex lege Aelia Sentia dedititiorum numero. Sed dedititiorum quidem pessima conditio jam ex multis temporibus in desuetudinem abiit; Latinorum vero nomen non frequentabatur; ideoque nostra pietas omnia augere et in meliorem statum reducere desiderans, in duabus constitutionibus hoc emendavit, et in pristinum statum reduxit; quia et a primis urbis Romae cunabulis una atque simplex libertas competebat, id est eadem quam habebat manumissor, nisi quod scilicet libertinus sit qui manumittitur, licet manumissor ingenuus sit, et dedititios quidem per constitutionem nostram expulimus quam promulgavimus inter nostras decisiones, per quas, suggerente nobis Triboniano, viro excelso, quaestore, antiqui juris altercationes placavimus; Latinos autem Junianos, et omnem quae circa eos fuerat observantiam, alia constitutione, per ejusdem quaestoris suggestionem, correximus, quae inter imperiales radiat sanctiones. Et omnes libertos, nullo, nec aetatis manumissi, nec dominii manumissoris, nec in manumissionis modo discrimine habito, sicuti antea observabatur, civitate romana donavimus; multis additis modis, per quos possit libertas servis cum civitate romana, quae sola in praesenti est, praestari.

Tit. vi. Qui, et quibus ex causis, manumittere non possunt.

GAI.	JUST.
§ 36. [Non tamen cuicumque volenti manumittere licet. § 37. Nam is qui] in fraudem creditorum vel in fraudem patroni manumittit, nihil agit, quia lex Aelia Sentia impedit libertatem.	*Non tamen cuicumque volenti manumittere licet: nam is qui in fraudem creditorum manumittit, nihil agit; quia lex Aelia Sentia impedit libertatem.* § 1. Licet autem do-

mino, qui solvendo non est, in testamento servum suum cum libertate heredem instituere, ut liber fiat heresque ei solus et necessarius, si modo ei nemo alius ex eo testamento heres extiterit, aut quia nemo heres scriptus sit, aut quia is qui scriptus est, qualibet ex causa, heres non extiterit. Idque eadem lege Aelia Sentia provisum est, et recte; valde enim prospiciendum erat, ut egentes homines, quibus alius heres extiturus non esset, vel servum suum necessarium heredem haberent, qui satisfacturus esset creditoribus; aut hoc eo non faciente, creditores res hereditarias servi nomine vendant, ne injuria defunctus afficiatur. § 2. Idemque juris est, etsi sine libertate servus heres institutus est. Quod nostra constitutio non solum in domino qui solvendo non est, sed generaliter constituit, nova humanitatis ratione, ut ex ipsa scriptura institutionis etiam libertas ei competere videatur; cum non est verisimile, eum quem heredem sibi elegit, si praetermiserit libertatis dationem, servum remanere voluisse, et neminem sibi heredem fore. § 3. In fraudem autem creditorum manumittere videtur, qui, vel jam eo tempore quo manumittit, solvendo non est, vel qui, datis libertatibus, desiturus est solvendo esse. Praevaluisse tamen videtur, nisi animum quoque fraudandi manumissor habuit, non impediri libertatem, quamvis bona ejus creditoribus non sufficiant: saepe enim de facultatibus suis amplius quam in his est sperant homines. Itaque tunc intelligimus impediri libertatem, cum utroque modo fraudantur creditores, id est et consilio manumittentis et ipsa re, eo quod ejus bona non suffectura sunt creditoribus.

§ 38. Item eadem lege minori xx annorum domino non aliter manumittere permittitur, quam si vindicta apud consilium justa causa manumissionis adprobata fuerit. § 39. Justae autem causae manumissionis sunt: veluti si quis patrem, aut matrem, aut paedagogum, aut collactaneum manumittat. Sed et illae causae, quas superius in servo minore xxx annorum exposuimus, ad hunc quoque casum de quo loquimur adferri possunt; item ex diverso hae causae, quas in minore xx annorum domino rettulimus, porrigi possunt et ad servum minorem xxx annorum.

§ 4. *Eadem lege* Aelia Sentia *domino minori viginti* annis *non aliter manumittere permittitur, quam si vindicta apud consilium justa causa manumissionis adprobata fuerit.* § 5. *Justae autem manumissionis causae sunt: veluti, si quis patrem aut matrem, aut filium filiamve, aut fratrem sororemve naturales, aut paedagogum,* aut nutricem, educatoremve, aut alumnum, alumnamve, *aut collactaneum manumittat, aut servum, procuratoris habendi gratia, aut ancillam, matrimonii causa,* dum tamen intra sex menses uxor ducatur, nisi justa causa impediat; et qui manumittitur procuratoris habendi gratia non minor decem et septem annis manumittatur. § 6. Semel autem causa adprobata, sive vera sive falsa sit, non retractatur.

§ 40. Cum ergo certus modus manumittendi minoribus xx annorum dominis per legem Aeliam Sentiam constitutus sit, evenit ut qui xiv annos aetatis expleverit, licet testamentum facere possit, et in eo heredem sibi instituere legataque relinquere possit, tamen, si adhuc minor sit annorum xx, li-

§ 7. *Cum ergo certus modus manumittendi minoribus viginti* annis *dominis per legem Aeliam Sentiam constitutus sit,* eveniebat, *ut qui quatuordecim annos aetatis expleverit, licet testamentum facere possit, et in eo heredem sibi instituere, legataque relinquere posset, tamen, si adhuc minor sit*

bertatem servo dare non possit. § 41. Et quamvis Latinum facere velit minor xx annorum dominus, nihilominus tamen debet apud consilium causam probare, et ita postea inter amicos manumittere.

viginti annis, libertatem servo dare non posset. Quod non erat ferendum, si is cui totorum bonorum in testamento dispositio data erat, uni servo libertatem dare non permittebatur. Quare nos similiter ei, quemadmodum alias res, ita et servos suos in ultima voluntate disponere, quemadmodum voluerit, permittimus, ut et libertatem eis possit praestare. Sed cum libertas inaestimabilis est, et propter hoc ante vicesimum aetatis annum antiquitas libertatem servo dare prohibebat: ideo nos, mediam quodammodo viam eligentes, non aliter minori viginti annis libertatem in testamento dare servo suo concedimus, nisi septimum et decimum annum impleverit et octavum decimum tetigerit. Cum enim antiquitas hujusmodi aetati et pro aliis postulare concessit, cur non etiam sui judicii stabilitas ita eos adjuvare credatur, ut et ad libertates dandas servis suis possint pervenire?

42. Praeterea lege Fusia Caninia certus modus constitutus est in servis testamento manumittendis. § 43. Nam ei, qui plures quam duos, neque plures quam decem servos habebit, usque ad partem dimidiam ejus numeri manumittere permittitur; ei vero qui plures quam x neque plures quam xxx servos habebit, usque ad tertiam partem ejus numeri manumittere permittitur; at ei, qui plures quam xxx, neque plures quam centum habebit, usque ad partem quartam potestas manumittendi datur; novissime si qui plures quam C habebit, nec plures quam D, non plures ei manumittere permittitur, quam quintam partem, neque plures numerantur. Sed praescribit lex, ne cui plures manumittere liceat quam C; contra si quis unum servum omnino aut duos habet, ad hunc haec lex non pertinet; et ideo liberam habet potestatem manumittendi. § 44. Ac ne ad eos quidem omnino haec lex pertinet, qui sine testamento manumittunt: itaque licet iis, qui vindicta, aut censu, aut inter amicos manumittunt, totam familiam suam liberare, scilicet si alia causa non impediat libertatem. § 45. Sed quod de numero servorum testamento manu-

Tit. vii. De lege Fusia Caninia sublata.

Lege Fusia Caninia certus modus constitutus erat *in servis testamento manumittendis.* Quam, quasi libertatibus impedientem et quodammodo invidam, tollendam esse censuimus, cum satis fuerat inhumanum, vivos quidem licentiam habere totam suam familiam libertate donare, nisi alia causa impediat libertati, morientibus autem hujusmodi licentiam adimere.

mittendorum diximus, ita intelligemus, ne unquam ex eo numero ex quo dimidia, aut tertia, aut quarta, aut quinta pars liberari potest [pauciores manumitti] liceat, quam ex antecedenti numero licuit, et hoc ipsa ratione provisum est: erat enim sane absurdum, ut x servorum domino quinque liberare liceret, quia usque ad dimidiam partem ejus numeri manumittere ei conceditur, at xii servos habenti non plures liceret manumittere quam iv, at eis qui plures quam x, neque . . . . . . § 46. Nam etiam si testamento scriptis in orbem servis libertas data sit, quia nullus ordo manumissionis invenitur, nulli liberi erunt; quia lex Fusia Caninia, quae in fraudem ejus facta sint, rescindit. Sunt etiam specialia senatus-consulta, quibus rescissa sunt ea, quae in fraudem ejus legis excogitata sunt.

§ 47. In summa sciendum est, cum lege Aelia Sentia cautum sit ut, creditorum fraudandorum causa manumissi, liberi non fiant, etiam hoc ad peregrinos pertinere: senatus ita censuit ex auctoritate Hadriani; cetera vero jura ejus legis ad peregrinos non pertinere.

§ 48. Sequitur de jure personarum alia divisio: nam quaedam personae sui juris sunt, quaedam alieno juri sunt subjectae. § 49. Sed rursus earum personarum, quae alieno juri subjectae sunt, aliae in potestate, aliae in manu, aliae in mancipio sunt. § 50. Videamus nunc de his quae alieno juri subjectae sint: nam si cognoverimus quae istae personae sint, simul intelligemus quae sui juris sint.

§ 51. Ac prius dispiciamus de his qui in aliena potestate sunt.

§ 52. In potestate itaque sunt servi dominorum; quae quidem potestas juris gentium est; nam apud omnes peraeque gentes animadvertere possumus, dominis in servos vitae necisque potestatem esse, et quodcumque per servum adquiritur, id domino adquiri. § 53. Sed hoc tempore neque civibus Romanis, nec ullis aliis hominibus qui sub im-

Tit. viii. De his qui sui, vel alieni juris sunt.

Sequitur de jure personarum alia divisio: nam, quaedam personae sui juris sunt, quaedam alieno juri subjectae sunt. Rursus earum, quae alieno juri subjectae sunt, aliae in potestate parentum, *aliae* in potestate dominorum sunt. *Videamus* itaque *de his quae alieno juri subjectae sunt: nam si cognoverimus quae istae personae sunt, simul intelligemus quae sui juris sunt.*

Ac prius dispiciamus de his qui in potestate dominorum sunt.

§ 1. *In potestate itaque dominorum sunt servi; quae quidem potestas juris gentium est; nam apud omnes peraeque gentes animadvertere possumus, dominis in servos vitae necisque potestatem esse, et quodcumque per servum adquiritur, id domino adquiri.* § 2. *Sed hoc tempore nullis hominibus qui sub imperio* nostro *sunt, licet, sine*

perio populi Romani sunt, licet supra modum et sine causa in servos suos saevire: nam ex constitutione sacratissimi imperatoris Antonini, qui sine causa servum suum occiderit, non minus teneri jubetur, quam qui alienum servum occiderit. Sed et major quoque asperitas dominorum per ejusdem principis constitutionem coercetur: nam consultus a quibusdam praesidibus provinciarum de his servis, qui ad fana deorum vel ad statuas principum confugiunt, praecepit, ut, si intolerabilis videatur dominorum saevitia, cogantur servos suos vendere; et utrumque recte: male enim nostro jure uti non debemus; qua ratione et prodigis interdicitur bonorum suorum administratio.

causa legibus cognita, *in servos suos supra modum saevire: nam ex constitutione* divi Pii *Antonini, qui sine causa servum suum occiderit, non minus* puniri *jubetur, quam qui servum alienum occiderit. Sed et major asperitas dominorum ejusdem principis constitutione coercetur; nam consultus a quibusdam praesidibus provinciarum de his servis qui* ad aedem sacram *vel ad statuas principum confugiunt, praecepit ut, si intolerabilis videatur dominorum saevitia, cogantur servos suos* bonis conditionibus *vendere,* ut pretium dominis daretur; *et recte:* expedit enim reipublicae, ne quis re sua male utatur. Cujus rescripti, ad Aelium Marcianum emissi, verba haec sunt:

"Dominorum quidem potestatem in servos suos illibatam esse oportet, nec cuiquam hominum jus suum detrahi; sed dominorum interest, ne auxilium contra saevitiam, vel famem, vel intolerabilem injuriam, denegetur his qui juste deprecantur. Ideoque cognosce de querelis eorum qui ex familia Julii Sabini ad statuam confugerunt; et si vel durius habitos quam aequum est, vel infami injuria affectos cognoveris, veniri jube, ita ut in potestatem domini non revertantur. Qui Sabinus, si meae constitutioni fraudem fecerit, sciet me admissum severius executurum."

§ 54. Ceterum, cum apud cives Romanos duplex sit dominium, nam vel in bonis, vel ex jure quiritium, vel ex utroque jure cujusque servus esse intelligitur, ita demum servum in potestate domini esse dicemus, si in bonis ejus sit, etiam si simul ex jure quiritium ejusdem non sit; nam qui nudum jus quiritium in servo habet, is potestatem habere non intelligitur.

Tit. ix. De patria potestate.

§ 55. Item in potestate nostra sunt liberi nostri, quos justis nuptiis procreavimus. Quod jus proprium civium Romanorum est; fere enim nulli alii sunt homines, qui talem in filios suos habent

In potestate nostra sunt liberi nostri quos ex justis nuptiis procreaverimus. § 1. Nuptiae autem, sive matrimonium, est viri et mulieris conjunctio, individuam consuetudinem vitae continens. § 2. *Jus* autem potestatis, quod in liberos habemus, *proprium est civium Romanorum;*

potestatem, qualem nos habemus: idque divi Hadriani edicto, quod proposuit de his, qui sibi liberisque suis ab eo civitatem Romanam petebant, significa[tur sic]: "Nec me praeterit Galatarum gentem credere, in potestatem parentum liberos esse."

§ 56. [Justas autem nuptias contrahunt cives Romani,] si cives Romanas uxores duxerint, vel etiam Latinas peregrinasve cum quibus connubium habeant. Cum enim connubium id efficiat, ut liberi patris conditionem sequantur, evenit ut non modo cives Romani fiant, sed etiam in potestate patris sint. § 57. Unde causa cognita veteranis quibusdam concedi solet principalibus constitutionibus connubium cum his Latinis peregrinisve quas primas post missionem uxores duxerint; et qui ex eo matrimonio nascuntur, et cives Romani et in potestate parentum fiunt.

§ 58. [Sciendum autem est non omnes nobis uxores ducere licere]; nam a quarundam nuptiis abstinere debemus.

§ 59. Inter eas enim personas quae parentum liberorumve locum inter se obtinent, nuptiae contrahi non possunt, neque inter eas connubium est, veluti inter patrem et filiam, vel matrem et filium, vel avum et neptem; et si tales personae inter se coierint, nefarias et incestas nuptias contraxisse dicuntur. Et haec adeo ita sunt, ut, quamvis per adoptionem parentum liberorumve loco sibi esse coeperint, non possint inter se matrimonio conjungi, in tantum, ut etiam

nulli enim alii sunt homines, qui talem in liberos habeant potestatem qualem nos habemus.

§ 2. Qui igitur ex te et uxore tua nascitur in tua potestate est. Item qui ex filio tuo et uxore ejus nascitur, id est nepos tuus et neptis, aeque in tua sunt potestate, et pronepos et proneptis, et deinceps ceteri. Qui tamen ex filia tua nascitur in tua potestate non est, sed in patris ejus.

Tit. x. De nuptiis.

Justas autem nuptias inter se *cives Romani contrahunt*, qui secundum praecepta legum coëunt, masculi quidem puberes, feminae autem viripotentes, sive patresfamilias sint sive filiifamilias; dum tamen si filiifamilias sint, consensum habeant parentum, quorum in potestate sunt. Nam hoc fieri debere, et civilis et naturalis ratio suadet in tantum ut jussum parentis praecedere debeat. Unde quaesitum est, an furiosi filia nubere, aut furiosi filius uxorem ducere possit? cumque super filio variabatur, nostra processit decisio, qua permissum est, ad exemplum filiae furiosi filium quoque posse et sine patris interventu matrimonium sibi copulare secundum datum ex constitutione modum.

§ I. Ergo *non omnes nobis uxores ducere* licet; *nam a quarundam nuptiis abstinendum est.*

Inter eas enim personas quae parentum liberorumve locum inter se obtinent, nuptiae contrahi non possunt, veluti inter patrem et filiam, vel avum et neptem, vel matrem et filium, vel aviam et nepotem, et usque ad infinitum; *et si tales personae inter se coierint, nefarias atque incestas nuptias contraxisse dicuntur. Et haec adeo ita sunt, ut quamvis per adoptionem parentum liberorumve loco sibi esse coeperint, non possint inter se matrimonio jungi, in tan-*

dissoluta adoptione idem juris maneat: itaque eam, quae mihi per adoptionem filiae seu neptis loco esse coeperit, non potero eam uxorem ducere, quamvis eam emancipaverim.

§ 60. Inter eas quoque personas quae ex transverso gradu cognatione junguntur, est quaedem similis observatio, sed non tanta. § 61. Sane inter fratrem et sororem prohibitae sunt nuptiae, sive eodem patre eademque matre nati fuerint, sive alterutro eorum; sed si qua per adoptionem soror mihi esse coeperit, quamdiu quidem constat adoptio, sane inter me et eam nuptiae non possunt consistere; cum vero per emancipationem adoptio dissoluta sit, potero eam uxorem ducere; sed etiam, si ego emancipatus fuero, nihil impedimento erit nuptiis.

§ 62. Fratris filiam uxorem ducere licet: idque primum in usum venit, cum divus Claudius Agrippinam, fratris sui filiam, uxorem duxisset; sororis vero filiam uxorem ducere non licet; et haec ita principalibus constitutionibus significantur. Item amitam aut materteram uxorem ducere non licet.

§ 63. Item eam, quae mihi quondam socrus, aut nurus, aut privigna, aut noverca fuit. Ideo autem diximus

tum, ut, etiam dissoluta adoptione, idem juris maneat: itaque eam, quae tibi *per adoptionem filia aut neptis esse coeperit, non poteris uxorem ducere, quamvis eam emancipaveris.*

§ 2. *Inter eas quoque personas quae ex transverso gradu cognationis junguntur, est quaedam similis observatio, sed non tanta. Sane enim inter fratrem et sororem nuptiae prohibitae sunt, sive ab eodem patre eademque matre nati fuerint, sive ex alterutro eorum; sed si qua per adoptionem soror tibi esse coeperit, quamdiu quidem constat adoptio sane inter te et eam nuptiae consistere non possunt; cum vero per emancipationem adoptio dissoluta sit, poteris eam uxorem ducere; sed et si tu emancipatus fueris, nihil est impedimento nuptiis.* Et ideo constat: si quis generum adoptare velit, debere eum ante filiam suam emancipare; et si quis velit nurum adoptare, debere eum ante filium emancipare. § 3. *Fratris* vero, vel sororis *filiam, uxorem ducere* non *licet.* Sed nec neptrem fratris vel sororis ducere quis potest, quamvis quarto gradu sint: cujus enim filiam uxorem ducere non licet, ejus neque neptem permittitur. Ejus vero mulieris quam pater tuus adoptavit filiam non videris impediri uxorem ducere, quia neque naturali neque civili jure tibi conjungitur. § 4. Duorum autem fratrum vel sororum liberi, vel fratris et sororis, jungi possunt. § 5. *Item amitam,* licet adoptivam, *uxorem ducere non licet* item nec *materteram,* quia parentum loco habentur. Qua ratione verum est, magnam quoque amitam et materteram magnam prohiberi uxorem ducere.

§ 6. Affinitatis quoque veneratione quarundam nuptiis abstinere necesse est, ut ecce: privignam aut nurum uxorem ducère non licet, quia utraeque filiae

"quondam", quia si adhuc constant eae nuptiae per quas talis affinitas quaesita est, alia ratione mihi nupta esse non potest, quia neque eadem duobus nupta esse potest, neque idem duas uxores habere.

loco sunt. Quod scilicet ita accipi debeat si *fuit nurus aut privigna.* Nam *si adhuc* nurus tua est, id est, si adhuc nupta est filio tuo, *alia ratione* uxorem eam ducere *non possis, quia eadem duobus nupta esse non potest.* Item si adhuc privigna tua est, id est si mater ejus tibi nupta est, ideo eam uxorem ducere non poteris, quia duas uxores eodem tempore habere non licet. § 7. Socrum quoque et novercam prohibitum est uxorem ducere, quia matris loco sunt. Quod et ipsum, dissoluta demum affinitate, procedit. Alioquin, si adhuc noverca est, id est, si adhuc patri tuo nupta est, communi jure impeditur tibi nubere, quia eadem duobus nupta esse non potest. Item si adhuc socrus est, id est, si adhuc filia ejus tibi nupta est, ideo impediuntur nuptiae, quia duas uxores habere non possis. § 8. Mariti tamen filius ex alia uxore et uxoris filia ex alio marito, vel contra, matrimonium recte contrahunt, licet habeant fratrem sororemve ex matrimonio postea contracto natos. § 9. Si uxor tua post divortium ex alio filiam procreaverit, haec non est quidem privigna tua; sed Julianus hujusmodi nuptiis abstinere debere ait; nam nec sponsam filii nurum esse, nec patris sponsam novercam esse, rectius tamen et jure facturos eos qui hujusmodi nuptiis se abstinuerint. § 10. Illud certum est, serviles quoque cognationes impedimento nuptiis esse, si forte pater et filia, aut frater et soror manumissi fuerint. § 11. Sunt et aliae personae, quae propter diversas rationes nuptias contrahere prohibentur, quas in libris Digestorum seu Pandectarum ex veteri jure collectorum enumerari permisimus.

§ 64. Ergo si quis nefarias atque incestas nuptias contraxerit, neque uxorem habere videtur, neque liberos. Itaque hi, qui ex eo coitu nascuntur, matrem quidem habere videntur, non vero patrem, nec ob id in potestate ejus sunt, quales utique sunt hi, quos mater vulgo conceperit; nam et ei patrem habere non intelliguntur, cum is etiam incertus sit; unde solent spurii filii appellari, vel a graeca voce quasi σποράδην concepti, vel quasi sine patre filii.

§ 12. Si adversus ea quae diximus aliqui coierint, nec vir, nec uxor, nec nuptiae, nec matrimonium, nec dos intelligitur. *Itaque hi qui ex eo coitu nascuntur in potestate* patris *non sunt:* sed tales sunt, quantum ad patriam potestatem pertinet, *quales sunt hi quos mater vulgo concepit. Nam nec hi patrem habere intelliguntur, cum his etiam pater incertus* est : *unde solent filii spurii appellari, vel a graeca voce quasi σποράδην concepti, vel quasi sine patre filii.* Sequitur ergo, ut et dissoluto tali coitu nec dotis exactioni locus sit. Qui autem prohibitas nuptias contrahunt et alias poenas patiuntur, quae sacris constitutionibus continentur.

§ 65. [Aliquando autem evenit ut liberi, qui, statim ut na]ti sunt, parentum in potestate non fiant, ii postea tamen redigantur in potestatem. § 66. Velut si Latinus ex lege Aelia Sentia uxore ducta, filium procreaverit, aut Latinum ex Latina, aut civem Romanum ex cive Romana, non habebit eum in potestate; [sed causa postea probata civitatem Romanam consequitur]: simul ergo eum in potestate sua habere incipit.

§ 13. *Aliquando autem evenit, ut liberi qui, statim ut nati sunt, in potestate parentum non fiant, postea autem redigantur in potestatem.* Qualis est is qui, dum naturalis fuerat, postea curiae datus, potestati patris subjicitur. Nec non is qui, a muliere libera procreatus cujus matrimonium minime legibus interdictum fuerat, sed ad quam pater consuetudinem habuerat, postea ex nostra constitutione dotalibus instrumentis compositis in potestate patris efficitur: quod et aliis liberis qui ex eodem matrimonio postea fuerint procreati, similiter nostra constitutio praebuit.

§ 67. Item si civis Romanus Latinam aut peregrinam uxorem duxerit per ignorantiam, cum eam civem Romanam esse crederet, et filium procreaverit, hic non est in potestate ejus, quia ne civis Romanus quidem est, sed aut Latinus aut peregrinus, id est, ejus conditionis cujus et mater fuerit, quia non aliter quisquam ad patris conditionem accedit, quam si inter patrem et matrem ejus connubium sit: sed ex senatus-consulto permittitur ei causam erroris probare, et ita uxor quoque et filius ad civitatem Romanam perveniunt, et ex eo tempore incipit filius in potestate patris esse. Idem juris est, si eam per ignorantiam uxorem duxerit, quae dedititiorum numero est, nisi quod uxor non fit civis Romana. § 68. Item si civis Romana per errorem nupta sit peregrino, tamquam civi Romano, permittitur ei causam erroris probare, et ita filius quoque ejus et maritus ad civitatem Romanam perveniunt, et aeque simul incipit filius in potestate patris esse. Idem juris est, si peregrino, tamquam Latino, ex lege Aelia Sentia nupta sit: nam et de hoc specialiter senatus-consulto cavetur. Idem juris est aliquatenus, si ei, qui dedititiorum numero est, tamquam civi Romano aut Latino ut secundum legem Aeliam Sentiam nupta sit: nisi quod scilicet qui dedititiorum numero est, in sua conditione permanet, et ideo filius, quamvis fiat civis Romanus, in potestatem patris non redigitur. § 69. Item si Latina peregrino, cum eum Latinum esse crederet, nupserit, potest ex senatus-consulto, filio nato, causam erroris probare, quo modo omnes fiunt cives Romani, et filius in potestate patris esse incipit. § 70. Idem constitutum est utique, si Latinus per errorem peregrinam, quasi Latinam, aut civem Romanam, e lege Aelia Sentia uxorem duxerit. § 71. Praeterea si civis Romanus, qui se credidisset Latinum esse, duxerit Latinam, permittitur ei, filio nato, erroris causam probare, tamquam e lege Aelia Sentia uxorem duxisset. Item si qui, cum civis Romanus esset, peregrinum se esse credidisset et peregrinam uxorem duxisset, permittitur ei ex senatus-consulto, filio nato, causam erroris probare : quo facto, fiet peregrina uxor civis Romana et filius quoque statim non solum ad civitatem Romanam perveniet, sed etiam in potestatem patris redigetur. § 72. Quaecumque de filio diximus, eadem et de filia dicta intelligemus. § 73. Et quantum ad erroris causam probandam attinet, nihil interest, cujus aetatis filius sive filia sit. . . . . Latinus . . . . . qui . . . . . nisi minor anniculo sit filius filiave, causa probari non potest : nec me praeterit in aliquo rescripto divi Hadriani ita esse constitutum, tamquam quod ad erroris quoque causam probandam . . . . . imperator . . . . . tuendam dedit. § 74. Si peregrinus civem Romanam uxorem duxerit . . . . . hoc ei specialiter concessum est; sed cum peregrinus civem Romanam uxorem duxisset, et, filio nato, alias civitatem Romanam consecutus esset, deinde cum quaereretur an causam probare posset, rescripsit imperator Antoninus, perinde posse eum causam probare atque si peregrinus mansisset; ex quo colligimus etiam peregrinum causam probare posse. § 75. Ex iis, quae diximus, apparet, sive civis Romanus peregrinam, sive peregrinus civem Romanam uxorem duxerit, eum, qui nascitur peregrinum esse; sed si quidem per errorem tale matrimonium contractum fuerit, emendari vitium ejus existimatur, secundum scilicet ea, quae superius diximus; si vero nullus error intervenerit, sed scientes suam conditionem, ita coierint, nullo casu emendatur. § 76. Loquimur autem, de his scilicet, inter quos connubium non sit; nam alioquin si civis Romanus peregrinam, cum qua ei connubium est, uxorem duxerit, sicut supra quoque diximus, justum matrimonium contrahitur; et tunc ex his qui nascetur, civis Romanus et in potestate patris erit. § 77. Itaque si civis Romana peregrino, cum quo ei connubium est, nupserit, peregrinus sane procreatur at is justus patris filius est, tamquam si ex peregrina eum procreasset. Hoc tamen tempore e senatus-consulto quod auctore divo Hadriano sanctissimo factum est, etiam si non fuerit connubium inter civem Romanam et peregrinum, qui nascitur justus patris filius est. § 78. Quod autem diximus, inter civem Romanam peregrinum[que matrimonio contracto eum qui] nascitur, peregrinum esse . . . . . est, ut si is quidem . . . . . parentis conditionem sequi; eadem lege . . . . . si peregrinam, cum qua ei connubium non sit, uxorem duxerit civis Romanus, peregrinus ex eo coitu nascatur; sed hoc maxime casu necessaria lex Minicia est; nam remota ea lege . . . . . conditionem sequi . . . . est connubium, qui nascitur jure gentium matris conditioni accedit; qua parte autem jubet lex ex civi Romano et peregrina peregrinum nasci, supervacua videtur; nam etiam remota ea lege hoc utique jure gentium futurum erat. § 79. Adeo autem hoc ita est, ut . . . . . solum exterae nationes et gentes sed etiam qui Latini nominantur; sed ad alios Latinos pertinet, qui proprios populos propriasque civitates habebant, et erant peregrinorum numero. § 80. Eadem ratione ex contrario, ex Latino et cive Romana, sive ex lege Aelia Sentia sive aliter contractum fuerit matrimonium, civis Romanus nascitur. Fuerunt tamen qui putaverunt, ex lege Aelia Sentia contracto matrimonio, Latinum nasci, quia videtur eo casu per legem Aeliam Sentiam et Juniam connubium inter eos dari, et semper connubium efficit ut qui nascitur patris conditioni accedat; aliter vero contracto matrimonio eum qui nascitur, jure gentium matris conditionem sequi et ob id esse civem Romanum. Sed hoc jure utimur ex senatus-consulto, quo, auctore divo Hadriano [sanctissimo factum est, quo] significatur, ut quoquo modo ex Latino et cive Romana natus, civis Romanus nascatur. § 81. His convenienter et illud senatus-consultum, divo Hadriano sanctissimo auctore significavit, ut ex Latino et peregrina, item contra ex peregrino et Latina qui nascitur, is matris conditionem sequatur. § 82. Illud quoque his consequens est, quod ex ancilla et libero jure gentium servus nascitur, et contra ex libera et servo liber nascitur. § 83. Animadvertere tamen debemus, nec ubi juris gentium regulam vel lex aliqua, vel quod legis vicem obtinet commutaverit. § 84. Ecce enim ex senatus-consulto Claudiano poterat civis Romana, quae cum alieno servo, volente domino ejus, coiit, ipsa ex pactione libera permanere, sed servum procreare: nam quod inter eam et dominum istius servi convenerit, ex senatus-consulto ratum esse jubetur. Sed postea divus Hadrianus, iniquitate rei et inelegantia juris motus, restituit juris gentium regulam, ut, cum ipsa mulier libera permaneat, liberum pariat. § 85. Ex contrario per legem . . . . ex ancilla et libero poterant liberi nasci : nam ea lege cavetur, ut si quis cum aliena ancilla, quam credebat liberam esse, coierit; si quidem masculi nascantur, liberi sint, sin vero feminae, ad eum pertineant, cujus mater ancilla fuerit. Sed etiam in hac specie divus Vespasianus, inelegantia juris motus, restituit juris gentium regulam, ut omnimodo, etiam si masculi nascantur, servi sint ejus, cujus et mater fuerit. § 86. Sed illa pars ejusdem legis salva est, ut ex libera et servo alieno, quem sciebat servum esse, servi nascantur. Itaque apud quos talis lex non est, qui nascuntur jure gentium matris conditionem sequuntur.

§ 87. Quibus autem casibus matris et non patris conditionem sequitur qui nascitur, eisdem casibus in potestate eum patris, etiam si is civis Romanus sit, non esse plus quam manifestum est. Et ideo superius rettulimus, quibusdam casibus per errorem non justo contracto matrimonio, senatum intervenire et emendare vitium matrimonii, eoque modo plerumque efficere, ut in potestatem patris filius redigatur. § 88. Sed si ancilla ex cive Romano conceperit, deinde manumissa civis Romana facta sit, et tunc pariat, licet civis Romanus sit qui nascitur, sicut pater ejus, non tamen in potestate patris est, quia neque ex justo coitu conceptus est, neque ex ullo senatus-consulto talis coitus quasi justus constituitur.

§ 89. Quod autem placuit, si ancilla ex cive Romano conceperit, deinde manumissa pepererit, qui nascitur liberum nasci, naturali ratione fit; nam hi qui illegitime concipiunter, statum sumunt ex eo tempore quo nascuntur : itaque si ex libera nascuntur, liberi fiunt, nec interest ex quo mater eos conceperit, cum ancilla fuerit. At hi qui legitime concipiuntur, ex conceptionis tempore statum sumunt. § 90. Itaque si cui mulieri civi Romanae praegnanti aqua et igni interdictum fuerit, eoque modo peregrina facta tunc pariat, complures distinguunt et putant, si quidem ex justis nuptiis conceperit, civem Romanum ex ea nasci, si vero vulgo conceperit, peregrinum ex ea nasci. § 91. Item, si qua mulier civis Romana praegnans ex senatus-consulto Claudiano ancilla facta sit, ob id quod cum alieno servo, invito et denuntiante domino ejus, coiit, complures distinguunt et existimant, si quidem ex justis nuptiis conceptus sit, civem Romanum ex ea nasci, si vero vulgo conceptus sit, servum nasci ejus cujus mater facta esset ancilla.

92. Peregrina quoque si vulgo conceperit, deinde cum civis Romana sit tunc pariat, civem Romanum parit; si vero ex peregrino, secundum legem moresque peregrinorum conceperit, ita videtur ex senatusconsulto, quod auctore divo Hadriano factum est, civem Romanum parere, si et patri ejus civitas Romana donetur. § 93. Si peregrinus sibi liberisque suis civitatem Romanam petierit, non aliter filii in potestate ejus fient, quam si imperator eos in potestatem redegerit; quod ita demum is facit, si causa cognita aestimaverit, hoc filiis expedire: diligentius autem exactiusque causam cognoscit de impuberibus absentibusque; et haec ita edicto divi Hadriani significantur. § 94. Item si quis cum uxore praegnante civitate Romana donatus sit, quamvis is qui nascitur, ut supra dixi, civis Romanus sit, tamen in potestate patris non fit; idque subscriptione divi sanctissimi Hadriani significatur. Qua de causa, qui intelligit uxorem suam esse praegnantem, dum civitatem sibi et uxori ab imperatore petit, simul ab eodem petere debet, ut eum qui natus fuerit in potestate sua habeat. § 95. Alia causa est eorum qui latii jure cum liberis suis ad civitatem Romanam perveniunt: nam horum in potestate fiunt liberi. § 96. Quod jus quibusdam peregrinis civitatibus datum est vel a populo Romano vel a senatu vel a Caesare, ... aut majus est latium, aut minus, majus est latium, cum et hi, qui decuriones leguntur, et ei qui honorem aliquam aut magistratum gerunt, civitatem Romanam . . . . . . consequuntur; minus latium est, cum hi tantum . . . . . vel qui magistratum, vel honorem gerunt, ad civitatem Romanam perveniunt: idque compluribus epistolis principum significatur . . . . .

Tit. xi. De Adoptionibus.

§ 97. [Non solum autem naturales liberi, secundum ea quae] diximus, in potestate nostra sunt, verum etiam hi quos adoptamus.	*Non solum autem naturales liberi, secundum ea quae diximus, in potestate nostra sunt, verum etiam hi quos adoptamus.*
§ 98. Adoptio autem duobus modis fit, aut populi auctoritate, aut imperio magistratus, velut praetoris. § 99. Populi auctoritate adoptamus eos qui sui juris sunt: quae species adoptionis dicitur adrogatio, quia et is qui adoptat, rogatur, id est, interrogatur an velit eum quem adoptaturus sit justum sibi filium esse; et is qui adoptatur, rogatur an id fieri patiatur; et populus rogatur an id fieri jubeat. Imperio	§ 1. *Adoptio autem duobus modis fit: aut* principali rescripto, *aut imperio magistratus. Imperatoris auctoritate adoptamus eos* easve *qui* quaeve *sui juris sunt. Quae species adoptionis dicitur adrogatio. Imperio magis-*

magistratus adoptamus eos qui in potestate parentum sunt, sive primum gradum liberorum obtineant, qualis est filius et filia, sive inferiorem, qualis est nepos, neptis, pronepos, proneptis.

tratus adoptamus eos easve *qui* quaeve *in potestate parentum sunt, sive primum gradum liberorum obtineant, qualis est filius, filia, sive inferiorem, qualis est nepos, neptis, pronepos, proneptis.*

§ 100. Et quidem illa adoptio quae per populum fit, nusquam nisi Romae fit; at haec etiam in provinciis apud praesides earum fieri solet. § 101. Item per populum feminae non adoptantur; nam id magis placuit. Apud praetorem vero, vel in provinciis apud proconsulem legatumve, etiam feminae solent adoptari.

§ 2. Sed hodie, ex nostra constitutione, cum filiusfamilias a patre naturali extraneae personae in adoptionem datur, jura potestatis naturalis patris minime dissolvuntur, nec quicquam ad patrem adoptivum transit, nec in potestate ejus est, licet ab intestato jura successionis ei a nobis tributa sint. Si vero pater naturalis non extraneo, sed avo filii sui materno, vel si ipse pater naturalis fuerit emancipatus, etiam avo paterno vel proavo simili modo paterno vel materno filium suum dederit in adoptionem, in hoc casu, quia in unam personam concurrunt et naturalia et adoptionis jura, manet stabile jus patris adoptivi, et naturali vinculo copulatum, et legitimo adoptionis modo constrictum, ut et in familia et potestate hujusmodi patris adoptivi sit.

§ 102. Item impuberem apud populum adoptari aliquando prohibitum est, aliquando permissum; sed nunc ex epistola optimi imperatoris Antonini, quam scripsit pontificibus, si justa causa adoptionis esse videbitur, cum quibusdam condicionibus permissum est. Apud praetorem vero, et in provinciis apud proconsulem legatumve, cujuscumque aetatis adoptare possumus.

§ 3. Cum autem impubes per principale rescriptum adrogatur, causa cognita adrogatio permittitur, et exquiritur causa adrogationis, an honesta sit expediatque pupillo, et cum quisbusdam condicionibus adrogatio fit, id est, ut caveat adrogator personae publicae, hoc est tabulario, "si intra pubertatem pupillus decesserit, restituturum se bona illis, qui, si adoptio facta non esset, ad successionem ejus venturi essent". Item non alias emancipare eos potest adrogator, nisi causa cognita digni emancipatione fuerint, et tunc sua bona eis reddat. Sed etsi decedens pater eum exheredaverit, vel vivus sine justa causa eum emancipaverit, jubetur quartam partem ei suorum bonorum relinquere, videlicet, praeter bona quae ad patrem adoptivum transtulit, et quorum commodum ei postea acquisivit.

§ 106. Sed et illud de quo questio est, an minor natu majorem natu adoptare possit: utri-

§ 4. Minorem natu majorem non posse adoptare placet: adoptio enim naturam imitatur, et pro monstro est, ut major sit filius quam pater. Debet itaque is qui sibi per adrogationem vel adoptionem filium facit plena pubertate, id est decem et octo annis praecedere. § 5. Licet autem et in locum nepotis vel

usque adoptionis commune est.

pronepotis, vel in locum neptis vel proneptis, vel deinceps adoptare, quamvis filium quis non habeat. § 6. Et tam filium alienum quis in locum nepotis potest adoptare quam nepotem in locum filii. § 7. Sed si quis nepotis loco adoptet, vel quasi ex eo filio quem habet jam adoptatum, vel quasi ex illo quem naturalem in sua potestate habet: in eo casu et filius consentire debet, ne ei invito suus heres agnascatur; sed ex contrario, si avus ex filio nepotem det in adoptionem, non est necesse filium consentire.

§ 105. Item sive quis per populum, sive apud praetorem, vel apud praesidem provinciae adoptaverit, potest eundem alii in adoptionem dare. § 103. Illud vero utriusque adoptionis commune est, quod et hi qui generare non possunt, quales sunt spadones, adoptare possunt. § 104. Feminae vero nullo modo adoptare possunt, quia ne quidem naturales liberos in potestate habent.

§ 8. In plurimis autem causis assimilatur is qui adoptatus vel adrogatus est, ei qui ex legitimo matrimonio natus est. Et ideo si quis per imperatorem, *sive apud praetorem, vel apud praesidem provinciae* non extraneum *adoptaverit, potest eundem alii in adoptionem dare.* § 9. Sed et *illud utriusque adoptionis commune est, quod et hi qui generare non possunt, quales sunt spadones, adoptare possunt;* castrati autem non possunt. § 10. *Feminae quoque adoptare non possunt, quia nec naturales liberos in potestate sua habent;* sed ex indulgentia principis ad solatium liberorum amissorum adoptare possunt.

§ 107. Illud proprium est ejus adoptionis quae per populum fit, quod is qui liberos in potestate habet, si se adrogandum dederit, non solum ipse potestati adrogatoris subjicitur, set etiam liberi ejus in ejusdem fiunt potestate, tamquam nepotes.

§ 11. *Illud proprium est illius adoptionis quae per* sacrum oraculum *fit, quod is qui liberos in potestate habet, si se adrogandum dederit, non solum ipse potestati adrogatoris subjicitur, sed etiam liberi ejus in ejusdem fiunt potestate tamquam nepotes.* Sic enim et divus Augustus non ante Tiberium adoptavit, quam is Germanicum adoptavit, ut protinus, adoptione facta, incipiat Germanicus Augusti nepos esse.

§ 12. Apud Catonem bene scriptum refert antiquitas, servos si a domino adoptati sint, ex hoc ipso posse liberari. Unde et nos eruditi in nostra constitutione etiam eum servum quem dominus actis intervenientibus filium suum nominaverit liberum esse constituimus, licet hoc ad jus filii accipiendum non sufficiat.

§ 108. [Nunc de his personis videamus quae in manu nostra sunt: quod] et ipsum jus proprium civium Romanorum est. § 109. Sed in potestate quidem et masculi et feminae esse solent, in manum autem feminae tantum conveniunt. § 110. Olim itaque tribus modis in manum conveniebant: usu, farreo, coemptione. § 111. Usu in manum conveniebat quae anno continuo nupta perseveranter [in domo mariti commorabatur] nam velut annua possessione usucapiebatur, in familiam viri transibat, filiaeque locum obtinebat. Itaque lege Duodecim Tabularum cautum est, si qua nollet eo modo in manum mariti convenire, ea quotannis trinoctio abesset, atque eo modo cujusque anni [usum] interrumperet. Sed hoc totum jus partim legibus sublatum est, partim ipsa desuetudine obliteratum est. § 112. Farreo in manus conveniunt per quoddam genus sacrificii quod Jovi Farreo fit, in quo farreus panis adhibetur: unde etiam confarreatio dicitur; Complura praetera hujus juris ordinandi gratia cum certis et sollemnibus verbis, praesentibus decem testibus, aguntur et fiunt. Quod jus etiam nostris temporibus in usu est: nam flamines majores (id est, Diales, Martiales, Quirinales), item reges sacrorum, nisi ex farreatis nati non leguntur, ac ne ipsi quidem sine confarreatione sacerdotium habere possunt. § 113. Coemptione vero in manum conveniunt per mancipationem, sive per quamdam imaginariam venditionem. Nam adhibitis non minus quam v testibus, civibus Romanis puberibus item libripende, emit eam mulierem cujus in manum convenit. § 114. Potest autem coemptionem facere mulier non solum cum marito suo, sed etiam cum extraneo: scilicet, aut matrimonii causa facta coemptio dicitur, aut fiduciae. Quae enim cum marito suo facit coemptionem, ut apud eum filiae loco sit, dicitur matrimonii causa fecisse coemptionem: quae vero alterius rei causa facit coemptionem, aut cum viro suo, aut cum extraneo, dicitur fiduciae causa fecisse coemptionem, veluti tutelae evitandae causa. § 115. Quod est tale: si qua velit quos habet tutores reponere et alium nancisci, illis tutoribus coemptionem facit; deinde a coemptionatore remancipata ei cui ipsa velit, et ab eo vindicta manumissa, incipit eum habere tutorem, a quo manumissa est: qui tutor fiduciarius dicitur, sicut in inferioribus apparebit. § 115A. Olim etiam testamenti faciendi gratia fiduciaria fiebat coemptio: tunc enim non aliter feminae testamenti faciendi jus habebant, exceptis quibusdam personis, quam si coemptionem fecissent remancipataeque et manumissae fuissent. Sed hanc necessitatem coemptionis faciendae ex auctoritate divi Hadriani senatus remisit. . . . . . femina . . . . § 115B. [Licet autem mulier fiduciae causa cum viro suo fecerit coemptionem] nihilominus filiae loco incipit esse; nam si omnino qualibet ex causa uxor in manu viri sit, placuit eam jura filiae nancisci.

§ 116. Superest ut exponamus quae personae in mancipio sint. § 117. Omnes igitur liberorum personae, sive masculini, sive feminini sexus, quae in potestate parentis sunt, mancipari ab hoc eodem modo possunt, quo etiam servi mancipari possunt. § 118. Idem juris est in earum personis quae in manu sunt; nam feminae a coemptionatoribus eodem modo possunt [mancipari quo liberi a parente mancipantur: adeo quidem ut, quamvis ea sola] apud coemptionatorem [filiae loco sit, quae ei nupta sit, tamen] nihilominus etiam quae ei nupta non sit, nec ob id filiae loco sit, ab eo mancipari possit. § 118A. Sed plerumque solum et a parentibus et a coemptionatoribus mancipantur, cum velint parentes coemptionatoresque e suo jure eas personas dimittere, sicut inferius evidentius apparebit. § 119. Est autem mancipatio, ut supra quoque diximus, imaginaria quaedam venditio; quod et ipsum jus proprium civium Romanorum est. Eaque res ita agitur: adhibitis non minus quam quinque testibus civibus Romanis puberibus, et praeterea alio ejusdem conditionis, qui libram aeneam teneat, qui appellatur libripens, is qui mancipio accipit rem tenens ita dicit: "Hunc ego hominem ex jure quiritium meum esse aio, isque mihi emptus est hoc aere aeneaque libra;" deinde aere percutit libram, idque aes dat ei a quo mancipio accipit, quasi pretii loco. § 120. Eo modo et serviles et liberae personae mancipantur; animalia quoque quae mancipi sunt, quo in numero habentur boves, equi, muli, asini; item praedia tam urbana quam rustica, quae et ipsa mancipi sunt, qualia sunt italica, eodem modo solent mancipari. § 121. In eo solo praediorum mancipatio a ceterorum mancipatione differt, quod personae serviles et liberae, item animalia quae mancipi sunt, nisi in praesentia sint, mancipari non possunt: adeo quidem ut eum qui mancipio accipit adprehendere id ipsum quod ei mancipio datur necesse sit; unde etiam mancipatio dicitur, quia manu res capitur: praedia vero absentia solent mancipari. § 122. Ideo autem aes et libra adhibetur, quia olim aereis tantum nummis utebantur, et erant asses, dupondii, semisses et quadrantes, nec ullus aureus vel argenteus nummus in usu erat, sicut ex lege xii Tabularum intelligere possumus; eorumque nummorum vis et potestas non in numero erat, sed in pondere [nummorum: veluti] asses librales erant, et dupondii [tum erant bilibres]; unde etiam dupondius dicitur . . . . . si duo pondo: quod nomen adhuc in usu retinetur; semisses quoque et quadrantes pro rata scilicet portione ad pondus examinati erant . . . . . . pecuniam non numerabat eam, sed appendebat: unde servi quibus permittitur administratio pecuniae dispensatores appellati sunt, et adhuc [appellantur. § 123. Si tamen quaerat aliquis quid inter coemptionem feminae et mancipationem intersit], ea quidem, quae coemptionem facit, [non deducitur in] servilem conditionem; [a parentibus vero et a coemptionatoribus] mancipati mancipataeve servorum loco constituuntur: adeo quidem, ut ab eo cujus in mancipio sunt, neque hereditatem neque legata aliter capere possunt, quam si simul eodem testamento liberi esse jubeantur, sicuti juris est in persona servorum. Sed differentiae ratio manifesta est, cum a parentibus et a coemptionatoribus iisdem verbis mancipio accipiantur quibus servi; quod non similiter fit in coemptione.

§ 124. Videamus nunc, quo modo hi qui alieno juri subjecti sunt, eo jure liberentur. § 125. Ac prius de his dispiciamus, qui in potestate sunt. § 126. Et quidem servi quemadmodum potestate liberentur, ex iis intelligere possumus, quae de servis manumittendis superius exposuimus.

§ 127. Hi vero qui in potestate parentis sunt, [mortuo eo, sui juris fiunt. Sed hoc di]stinctionem recipit: nam [mortuo patre, sane] omnimodo filii filiaeve sui juris efficiuntur; mortuo vero avo [non omnimodo nepotes neptesve sui juris fiunt, sed ita, si post mortem avi] in patris sui potestatem recasuri non [sunt. Itaque si moriente avo pater eorum et vivit et in potestate] patris sui fuerit, tunc post [obitum avi in patris] potestate sui fiunt: si vero is, quo tempore avus moritur, [aut jam mortuus erat, aut exiit de potestate patris, tunc hi, quia in potestatem] ejus cadere non possunt, sui juris fiunt. § 128. Cum autem is cui ob aliquod maleficium ex lege Cornelia aqua et igni interdicitur, civi-

Tit. xii. Quibus modis jus potestatis solvitur.

Videamus nunc, quibus modis hi qui alieno juri subjecti sunt, eo jure liberantur.

Et quidem servi quemadmodum potestate liberantur, ex iis intelligere possumus quae de servis manumittendis superius exposuimus.

Hi vero qui in potestate parentis sunt, mortuo eo, sui juris fiunt. Sed hoc distinctionem recipit; nam mortuo patre sane omnimodo filii filiaeve sui juris efficiuntur. Mortuo vero avo non omnimodo nepotes neptesque sui juris fiunt, sed ita, si post mortem avi in potestatem patris sui recasuri non sunt. Itaque, si moriente avo pater eorum et vivit et in potestate patris sui est, tunc post obitum avi in potestate patris sui fiunt. Si vero is, quo tempore avus moritur, aut jam mortuus est, aut exiit de potestate patris, tunc hi quia in potestate ejus cadere non possunt, sui juris fiunt. § 1. *Cum autem is qui ob aliquod maleficium* in insulam deportatur *civitatem amittit, sequitur, ut qui eo modo ex*

tatem Romanam amittat, sequitur ut, qui eo modo ex numero civium Romanorum tollitur, perinde ac mortuo eo desinant liberi in potestate ejus esse : nec enim ratio patitur, ut peregrinae conditionis homo civem Romanum in potestate habeat. Pari ratione etiam, si ei qui in potestate parentis sit, aqua et igni interdictum fuerit, desinit in potestate parentis esse, quia aeque ratio non patitur ut peregrinae conditionis homo in potestate sit civis Romani parentis.

numero civium Romanorum tollitur perinde ac si eo mortuo, desinant liberi in potestate ejus esse. Pari ratione et si is qui in potestate parentis sit in insulam deportatus fuerit, *desinit in potestate parentis esse.* Sed si, ex indulgentia principis, restituti fuerint per omnia, pristinum statum recipiunt. § 2. Relegati autem patres in insulam in potestate sua liberos retinent, et ex contrario, liberi relegati in potestate parentum remanent. § 3. Poenae servus effectus filios in potestate habere desinit. Servi autem poenae efficiuntur qui in metallum damnantur, et qui bestiis subjiciuntur. § 4. Filiusfamilias si militaverit, vel si senator vel consul fuerit factus, manet in patris potestate, militia enim, vel consularia dignitas de patris potestate filium non liberat. Sed ex constitutione nostra summa patriciatus dignitas illico, ab imperialibus codicillis praestitis, filium a patria potestate liberat. Quis enim patiatur patrem quidem posse per emancipationis modum suae potestatis nexibus filium relaxare, imperatoriam autem celsitudinem non valere eum quem sibi patrem elegit ab aliena eximere potestate?

§ 129. Quod si ab hostibus captus fuerit parens, quamvis servus eo modo hostium fiat, pendet jus liberorum propter jus postliminii, quia hi qui ab hostibus capti sunt, si reversi fuerint, omnia pristina jura recipiunt, itaque reversus is habebit liberos in potestate. Si vero illic mortuus sit, erunt quidem liberi sui juris ; sed utrum ex hoc tempore quo mortuus est apud hostes parens, an ex illo quo ab hostibus captus est, dubitari potest. Ipse quoque filius neposve si ab hostibus captus fuerit, similiter dicimus, propter jus postliminii, potestatam quoque parentis in suspenso esse.

§ 5. *Si ab hostibus captus fuerit parens, quamvis servus hostium fiat, tamen pendet jus liberorum propter jus postliminii, quia hi qui ab hostibus capti sunt, si reversi fuerint, omnia pristina jura recipiunt ; idcirco reversus et liberos habebit in potestate,* quia postliminium fingit eum qui captus est semper in civitate fuisse. Si vero ibi decesserit, exinde ex quo captus est pater, filius sui juris fuisse videtur. *Ipse quoque filius, neposve, si ab hostibus captus fuerit, similiter dicimus propter jus postliminii jus quoque potestatis parentis in suspenso esse.* Dictum est autem postliminium a "limine" et "post", ut eum, qui ab hostibus captus in fines nostros postea pervenit, postliminio reversum recte dicimus.

§ 130. Praeterea exeunt liberi virilis sexus de patris potestate, si flamines Diales inaugurentur et feminini sexus si virgines Vestales capiantur. § 131. Olim quoque, quo tempore populus Romanus in Latinas regiones colonias deducebat, qui jussu parentis in Latinam coloniam nomen dedissent, desinebant in potestate parentis esse, quia efficerentur alterius civitatis cives.

Nam limina sicut in domibus finem quendam faciunt, sic et imperii finem limen esse veteres voluerunt. Hinc et limes dictus est, quasi finis quidam et terminus: ab eo postliminium dictum, quia eodem limine revertebatur quo amissus erat. Sed et qui captus victis hostibus recuperatur postliminio redisse existimatur.

§ 132. Praeterea emancipatione quoque desinunt liberi in potestatem parentium esse, et filius quidem tribus mancipationibus, ceteri vero liberi, sive masculini sexus, sive feminini, una mancipatione exeunt de parentum potestate: lex enim xii tabularum tantum in persona filii de tribus mancipationibus loquitur his verbis: "si pater filium ter venumdabit, filius a patre liber esto". Eaque res ita agitur: mancipat pater filium alicui; is eum vindicta manumittit: eo facto revertitur in potestatem patris. Is eum iterum mancipat vel eidem, vel aliis; sed in usu est eidem mancipare; isque eum postea similiter vindicta manumittit: postea cum rursus in potestatem patris fuerit reversus tertio pater eum mancipat vel eidem, vel alii; sed etiam hoc in usu est ut eidem mancipetur; [eaque mancipatione desinit in potestate patris esse, etiam] si nondum manumissus sit, et adhuc in causa mancipii.

§ 6. *Praeterea emancipatione quoque desinunt liberi in potestate parentium esse.* Sed ea emancipatione antea quidem vel per antiquam legis observationem procedebat, quae per imaginarias venditiones et intercedentes manumissiones celebrabatur, vel ex imperiali rescripto. Nostra autem providentia et hoc in melius per constitutionem reformavit, ut fictione pristina explosa, recta via ad competentes judices vel magistratus parentes intrent, et filios suos, vel filias, vel nepotes, vel neptes, ac deinceps, sua manu dimittant. Et tunc ex edicto praetoris in hujus filii, vel filiae, nepotis vel neptis bonis, qui vel quae a parente manumissus vel manumissa fuerit, eadem jura praestantur parenti quae tribuuntur patrono in bonis liberti; et praeterea si impubes sit filius vel filia vel ceteri, ipse parens ex manumissione tutelam ejus nanciscitur.

§ 133. [Admonendi autem sumus, liberum esse arbitrium ei qui filium et ex eo nepotem in potestate habebit, filium quidem e potestate dimittere, nepotem vero vel neptem in potestate retinere; vel ex diverso, filium quidem in potestate retinere, nepotem vero vel neptem manumittere; vel omnes sui juris efficere. Eadem et de pronepote vel pronepte dicta esse intelligemus.

§ 7. *Admonendi autem sumus liberum esse arbitrium ei qui filium et ex eo nepotem vel neptem in potestate habebit filium quidem de potestate dimittere, nepotem vero vel neptem retinere; et ex diverso filium quidem in potestate retinere, nepotem vero vel neptem manumittere vel omnes sui juris efficere. Eadem et de pronepote vel pronepte dicta esse intellegantur.*

§ 134. Praeterea parentes, etiam liberos in adoptionem datos, in potestate habere desinunt; et in filio quidem tres mancipationes] et duae intercedentes manumissiones perinde fiunt, ac fieri solent, cum ita eum pater de potestate dimittit, ut sui juris efficiatur. Deinde aut patri remancipatur, et ab eo is qui adoptat, vindicat apud praetorem filium suum esse, et, illo contra non vindicante, praetore vindicanti filius addicitur aut non remancipatur patri, sed ab eo vindicat, is qui adoptat, apud quem in tertia mancipatione est: sed sane commodius est patri remancipari. In ceteris vero liberorum personis seu masculini, seu feminini sexus, una scilicet mancipatio sufficit, et aut remancipantur parenti, aut non remancipantur. Eadem et in provinciis apud praesides provinciae solent fieri. § 135. Qui ex filio semel iterumve mancipato . . . . . conceptus est, licet post tertiam mancipationem patris sui nascatur, tamen in avi potestate est, et ideo ab eo et emancipari et in adoptionem dari potest. At is qui ex eo filio conceptus est, qui in tertia mancipatione est, non nascitur in avi potestate; sed eum Labeo quidem existimat in ejusdem mancipio esse cujus et pater sit utimur autem hoc jure, ut: quamdiu pater ejus in mancipio sit, pendeat jus ejus: et si quidem pater ejus ex mancipatione manumissus fuerit cadat in ejus potestatem; si vero is, dum in mancipio sit, decesserit, sui juris fiat. Eadem scilicet . . . . . . ut supra diximus, quod in filio faciunt tres mancipationes, hoc facit una mancipatio in nepote.

§ 8. Sed et si pater filium, quem in potestate habet, avo vel proavo naturali, secundum nostras constitutiones super his habitas, in adoptionem dederit: id est, si hoc ipsum actis intervenientibus apud competentem judicem manifestaverit, praesente eo qui adoptatur, et non contradicente, nec non eo praesente qui adoptat, solvitur quidem jus potestatis patris naturalis; transit autem in hujusmodi parentem adoptivum, in cujus persona et adoptionem plenissimam esse antea diximus. § 9. Illud autem scire oportet, quod si nurus tua ex filio tuo conceperit, et filium postea emancipaveris vel in adoptionem dederis, praegnante nuru tua, nihilominus quod ex ea nascitur in potestate tua nascitur; quod si post emancipationem vel adoptionem fuerit conceptus, patris sui emancipati vel avi adoptivi potestati subjicitur; § 10. et quod neque naturales liberi, neque adoptivi, ullo paene modo possunt cogere parentes de potestate sua eos dimittere.

§ 136. [Mulieres, quamvis in manu sint, nisi coemptionem fecerint, potestate parentis non liberantur. Hoc in Flaminica Diali senatus-consulto confirmatur, quo ex auctoritate consulum] Maximi et Tuberonis cavetur, ut haec quod ad sacra tantum videatur in manu esse, quod vero ad ceteras causas perinde habeatur, atque si in manum non convenisset. [Sed mulieres quae coemptionem fecerunt per mancipationem] potestate parentis liberantur: nec interest, an in viri sui manu sint, an extranei; quamvis hae solae loco filiarum habeantur, quae in viri manu sint.

§ 137. . . . . . tunc desinunt in manu esse, et si ex ea mancipatione manumissae fuerint, sui juris efficiuntur . . . . . enim magis potest cogere, quam et filia patrem. Sed filia quidem nullo modo patrem potest cogere, etiamsi adoptiva sit: haec autem repudio misso perinde compellere potest, atque si ei numquam nupta fuisset.

§ 138. Ii, qui in causa mancipii sunt, quia servorum loco habentur, vindicta, censu, testamento manumissi, sui juris fiunt. § 139. Nec tamen in hoc casu lex Aelia Sentia locum habet: itaque nihil requirimus, cujus aetatis sit is qui manumittit, et qui manumittitur, ac ne illud quidem, an patronum creditoremve manumissor habeat; ac ne numerus quidem legis Fusiae Caniniae finitus in his personis locum habet. § 140. Quin etiam invito quoque eo cujus in mancipio sunt, censu libertatem consequi possunt, excepto eo quem pater ea lege mancipio dedit, ut sibi remancipetur; nam quodammodo tunc pater potestatem propriam reservare sibi videtur eo ipso, quod mancipio recipit. Ac ne is quidem dicitur, invito eo cujus in mancipio est, censu libertatem consequi, quem pater ex noxali causa mancipio dedit, veluti si, quod furti ejus nomine damnatus esset, eum mancipio actori dederit: nam hunc actor pro pecunia habet. § 141. In summa admonendi sumus, adversus eos quos in mancipio habemus, nihil nobis contumeliose facere licere: alioquin injuriarum actione tenebimur; ac ne diu quidem in eo jure detinentur homines, sed plerumque hoc fit dicis gratia uno momento; nisi scilicet ex noxali causa mancipati sint a parente.

§ 142. Transeamus nunc ad aliam divisionem: nam ex his personis, quae neque in potestate, neque in manu, neque in mancipio sunt, quaedam vel in tutela sunt, vel in curatione, quaedam neutro jure tenentur. Videamus igitur, quae in tutela, quae in curatione sint: ita enim intelligemus deinde ceteras personas quae neutro jure tenentur.

§ 143. Ac prius dispiciamus de his quae in tutela sunt.

Tit. xiii. De tutelis.

Transeamus nunc ad aliam divisionem: nam ex his personis quae iu potestate non sunt, quaedam vel in tutela sunt vel in curatione, quaedam neutro jure tenentur. Videamus igitur de his quae in tutela vel in curatione sunt: ita enim intelligemus ceteras personas quae neutro jure tenentur.

Ac prius dispiciamus de his quae in tutela sunt.

§ 1. Est autem tutela, ut Servius definit, vis ac potestas in capite libero, ad tuendum eum qui propter aetatem se defendere nequit, jure civili data ac permissa. § 2. Tutores autem sunt qui eam vim ac potestatem habent, ex qua re ipsa nomen ceperunt: itaque appellantur tutores, quasi tuitores atque defensores; sicut aeditui dicuntur qui aedes tuentur.

§ 144. Permissum est itaque parentibus, liberis, quos in potestate habent, testamento tutores dare: masculini quidem sexus impuberibus [dumtaxat, feminini autem etiam puberibus]; veteres enim voluerunt feminas, etiam si perfectae aetatis sint, propter animi levitatem in tutela esse. § 145. Itaque si quis filio filiaeque testamento tutorem dederit, et ambo ad pubertatem pervenerint, filius quidem desinit habere tutorem, filia vero nihilominus in tutela permanet; tantum enim, ex lege Julia et Papia Poppaea, jure liberorum a tutela liberantur feminae. Loquimur autem exceptis virginibus vestalibus, quas etiam veteres in honorem sacerdotii liberas esse voluerunt: itaque etiam lege xii tabularum cautum est. § 146. Nepotibus autem neptibusque ita demum possumus testamento tutores dare, si post mortem nostram in patris sui potestatem jure recasuri non sint. Itaque si filius meus mortis meae tempore in potestate mea sit, nepotes, quos ex eo habeo, non poterunt ex testamento meo habere tutorem, quamvis in potestate mea fuerint, scilicet, quia, mortuo me, in patris sui potestate futuri sunt. § 147. Cum tamen in compluribus aliis causis postumi pro jam natis habeantur, et in hac causa placuit, non minus postumis quam jam natis testamento tutores dari posse: si modo in ea causa sint, ut, si vivis nobis nascantur, in potestate nostra fiant. Hos etiam heredes instituere possumus, cum extraneos possumus heredes instituere permissum non sit. § 148. Uxori quae in manu est, perinde ac filiae, item nurui quae in filii manu est, perinde ac nepti, tutor dari potest. § 149. Rectissime autem tutor sic dari potest: "Lucium Titium liberis meis tutorem do." Sed etiam si ita scriptum sit "Liberis meis" vel "Uxori meae Titius tutor

§ 3. *Permissum est itaque parentibus liberis impuberibus quos in potestate habent testamento tutores dare.* Et hoc in filios filiasque omnimodo procedit; *nepotibus tamen neptibusque ita demum parentes possunt testamento tutores dare, si post mortem eorum in patris sui potestatem non sint recasuri. Itaque si filius tuus mortis tuae tempore in potestate tua sit, nepotes ex eo non poterunt testamento tuo tutorem habere, quamvis in potestate tua fuerint; scilicet quia, mortuo te, in patris sui potestatem recasuri sunt.* § 4. *Cum autem in compluribus aliis causis postumi pro jam natis habentur, et in hac causa placuit non minus postumis quam jam natis testamento tutores dari posse, si modo in ea causa sint, ut, si vivis* parentibus *nascerentur,* sui heredes et *in potestate* eorum *fierent.* § 5. Sed si emancipato filio tutor a patre testamento datus fuerit, confirmandus est ex sententia Praesidis omnimodo, id est sine inquisitione.

esto", recte datus intelligitur. § 150. In persona tamen uxoris, quae in manu est, recepta est etiam tutoris optio, id est, ut liceat ei permittere quem velit ipsa tutorem sibi optare, hoc modo: "Titiae uxori meae tutoris optionem do": quo casu licet uxori [eligere tutorem], vel in omnes res, vel in unam forte aut duas. § 151. Ceterum aut plena optio datur aut angusta. § 152. Plena ita dari solet, ut proxime supra diximus; angusta ita dari solet: "Titiae uxori meae duntaxat tutoris optionem semel do", aut "duntaxat bis do". § 153. Quae optiones plurimum inter se differunt; nam quae plenam optionem habet, potest semel et bis et ter et saepius tutorem optare: quae vero angustam habet optionem, si duntaxat semel data est optio, amplius quam semel optare non potest: si tantum bis, amplius quam bis optandi facultatem non habebit. § 154. Vocantur autem hi, qui nominatim testamento tutores dantur, dativi; qui ex optione sumuntur, optivi.

Tit. xiv. Qui dari tutores testamento possunt.

Dari autem potest tutor non solum paterfamilias, sed etiam filiusfamilias. § 1. Sed et servus proprius testamento cum libertate recte tutor dari potest. Sed sciendum est, eum et sine libertate tutorem datum, tacite libertatem directam accepisse videri, et per hoc recte tutorem esse. Plane si per errorem quasi liber tutor datus sit, aliud dicendum est. Servus autem alienus pure inutiliter testamento datur tutor; sed ita, "cum liber erit", utiliter datur: proprius autem servus inutiliter eo modo tutor datur. § 2. Furiosus, vel minor vigintiquinque annis tutor testamento datus, tunc tutor erit, cum compos mentis, aut major vigintiquinque annis factus fuerit.

§ 3. Ad certum tempus, vel ex certo tempore, vel sub conditione, vel ante heredis institutionem, posse dari tutorem non dubitatur. § 4. Certae autem rei vel causae tutor dari non potest, quia personae, non causae vel rei datur.

§ 5. Si quis filiabus suis vel filiis tutores dederit, etiam postumae vel postumo dedisse videtur quia "filii" vel "filiae" appellatione et postumus vel postuma continetur. Quod si nepotes sint, an appellatione filiorum et ipsis tutores dati sint? Dicendum est, ut ipsis quoque dati videantur, si modo liberos dixit. Ceterum, si filios, non continebuntur; aliter enim filii, aliter nepotes appellantur. Plane si postumis dederit, tam filii postumi, quam ceteri liberi continebuntur.

Tit. xv. De legitima agnatorum tutela.

§ 155. Quibus testamento quidem tutor datus non sit, iis ex lege xii tabularum agnati sunt tutores, qui vocantur legitimi. § 156. Sunt autem agnati per virilis sexus personas cognatione juncti, quasi a patre cognati: veluti frater eodem patre natus, fratris filius neposve ex eo, item patruus et patrui filius et nepos ex eo. At hi qui per feminini sexus personas cognatione junguntur, non sunt agnati, sed alias, naturali jure, cognati: itaque inter avunculum et sororis filium non agnatio est, sed cognatio; item amitae, materterae filius non est mihi agnatus, sed cognatus, et invicem scilicet ego illi eodem jure conjungor, quia qui nascuntur patris, non matris, familiam sequuntur.

Quibus autem testamento tutor datus non sit, his ex lege Duodecim Tabularum agnati sunt tutores qui vocantur legitimi. § 1. *Sunt autem agnati, per virilis sexus personas cognationem conjuncti, quasi a patre cognati: veluti frater eodem patre natus, fratris filius neposve ex eo, item patruus et patrui filius neposve ex eo. At hi qui per feminini sexus personas cognatione junguntur, non sunt agnati, sed alias, naturali jure, cognati: itaque amitae tuae filius non est* tibi *agnatus, sed cognatus, et invicem scilicet* tu *illi eodem jure conjungeris; quia qui nascuntur patris, non matris familiam sequuntur.*

§ 157. Sed olim quidem, quantum ad legem xii tabularum attinet, etiam feminae agnatos habebant tutores; sed postea lex Claudia lata est, quae, quod ad feminas attinet, tutelas istas sustulit. Itaque masculus quidem impubes fratrem puberem, aut patruum habet tutorem; femina vero talem habere tutorem non poterit.

§ 2. Quod autem lex ab intestato vocat ad tutelam agnatos, non hanc habet significationem, si omnino non fecerit testamentum is qui poterat tutores dare, sed si, quantum ad tutelam pertinet, intestatus decesserit: quod tunc quoque accidere intelligitur, cum is qui datus est tutor vivo testatore decesserit.

§ 158. Sed agnationis quidem jus capitis deminutione perimitur, cognationis vero jus eo modo non commutatur: quia civilis ratio civilia quidem jura corrumpere potest, naturalia vero non potest.

§ 3. *Sed agnationis quidem jus* omnibus modis *capitis deminutione* plerumque *perimitur:* nam agnatio juris nomen est; *cognationis vero jus non* omnibus modis *commutatur, quia civilis ratio civilia quidem jura corrumpere potest, naturalia vero non utique.*

Tit. xvi. De capitis deminutione.

§ 159. Est autem capitis deminutio prioris capitis permutatio, eaque tribus modis accidit; nam aut maxima est capitis deminutio, aut minor, quam quidam mediam vocant, aut minima.

Est autem capitis deminutio prioris status *mutatio. Eaque tribus modis accidit: nam aut maxima est capitis deminutio, aut minor quam quidam mediam vocant, aut minima.*

§ 160. Maxima est capitis deminutio, cum aliquis simul et civi-

§ 1. *Maxima est capitis deminutio, cum aliquis simul et civita-*

tatem et libertatem amittit; quae accidit incensis, qui ex forma censuali venire jubentur, quod jus . . . . . qui contra eam legem in urbe Roma domicilium habuerint. Item feminae, quae ex senatusconsulto Claudiano ancillae fiunt eorum dominorum, quibus invitis et denuntiantibus dominis cum servis eorum coierint.

tem et libertatem amittit; quod accidit in his qui servi poenae efficiuntur atrocitate sententiae, vel libertis ut ingratis circa patronos condemnatis; vel his qui ad pretium participandum se venumdari passi sunt.

§ 161. Minor, sive media est capitis deminutio cum civitas quidem amittitur, libertas vero retinetur; quod accidit ei cui aqua et igni interdictum fuerit.

§ 2. *Minor, sive media est capitis deminutio, cum civitas quidem amittitur, libertas vero retinetur; quod accidit ei cui aqua et igni interdictum fuerit,* vel ei qui in insulam deportatus est.

§ 162. Minima est capitis deminutio cum et civitas et libertas retinetur, sed status hominis commutatur; quod accidit in his qui adoptantur, item in his quae coemptionem faciunt, et in his qui mancipio dantur, quique ex mancipatione manumittuntur; adeo quidem ut, quotiens quisque mancipetur, ut manumittatur, totiens capite diminuatur. § 163. Nec solum majoribus deminutionibus jus agnationis corrumpitur, sed etiam minima; et ideo si ex duobus liberis alterum pater emancipaverit, post obitum ejus neuter alteri agnationis jure tutor esse poterit.

§ 3. *Minima capitis deminutio est, cum et civitas et libertas retinetur, sed status hominis commutatur; quod accidit in his qui,* cum sui juris fuerunt, coeperunt alieno juri subjecti esse, vel contra si filius emancipatus fuerit a patre, est capite deminutus. § 4. Servus autem manumissus capite non minuitur, quia nullum caput habuit. § 5. Quibus autem dignitas magis quam status permutatur, capite non minuuntur: et ideo a senatu motum capite non minui constat.

§ 6. Quod autem dictum est, manere cognationis jus et post capitis deminutionem, hoc ita est, si minima capitis deminutio interveniat; manet enim cognatio. Nam si maxima capitis deminutio incurrat, jus quoque cognationis perit, ut puta servitute alicujus cognati; et ne quidem si manumissus fuerit, recipit cognationem. Sed et si in insulam deportatus quis sit, cognatio solvitur.

§ 164. Cum autem ad agnatos tutela pertineat, non simul ad omnes pertinet, sed ad eos tantum qui proximo gradu sunt.

§ 7. *Cum autem ad agnatos tutela pertineat, non simul ad omnes pertinet, sed ad eos tantum qui proximiores gradu sunt,* vel si plures ejusdem gradus sunt, ad omnes pertinet.

Tit. xvii. De legitima patronorum tutela.

§ 165. Ex eadem lege Duodecim Tabularum libertarum et impu-

Ex eadem lege Duodecim Tabularum, libertorum et libertarum

berum libertorum tutela ad patronos liberosque eorum pertinet, quae et ipsa legitima tutela vocatur, non [quia nominatim] in ea lege de hac tutela caveatur, sed quia perinde accepta est per interpretationem, atque si verbis legis introducta esset. Eo enim ipso, quod hereditates libertorum libertarumque, si intestati decessissent, jusserat lex ad patronos liberosve eorum pertinere, crediderunt veteres voluisse legem etiam tutelas ad eos pertinere, quia et agnatos, quos ad hereditatem vocavit, eosdem etiam tutores esse jusserat.

tutela ad patronos liberosque eorum pertinet, quae et ipsa legitima tutela vocatur, non quia nominatim in ea lege de hac tutela caveatur, sed quia perinde accepta est per interpretationem, atque si verbis legis introducta esset. Eo enim ipso, quod hereditates libertorum libertarumque, si intestati decessissent, jusserat lex ad patronos liberosve eorum pertinere, crediderunt veteres voluisse legem etiam tutelas ad eos pertinere, cum et agnatos quos ad hereditatem lex vocat, eosdem et tutores esse jusserit; quia plerumque ubi successionis est emolumentum, ibi et tutelae onus esse debet. Ideo autem diximus "plerumque", quia, si a femina impubes manumittatur, ipsa ad hereditatem vocatur, cum alius erit tutor.

Tit. xviii. De legitima parentum tutela.

Exemplo patronorum recepta est et alia tutela, quae et ipsa legitima vocatur: nam si qui filium aut filiam, nepotem aut neptem ex filio, et deinceps, impuberem emancipaverit, legitimus eorum tutor erit.

§ 166. Exemplo patronorum receptae sunt et aliae tutelae, quae fiduciariae vocantur, id est, quae ideo nobis competunt, quia liberum caput mancipatum nobis vel a parente vel a coemptionatore manumiserimus. § 167. Sed Latinarum et Latinorum impuberum tutela non omnimodo ad manumissores pertinet, sed ad eos quorum ante manumissionem ex jure quiritium fuerunt: unde si ancilla ex jure quiritium tua sit, in bonis mea, a me quidem solo, non etiam a te manumissa, Latina fieri potest, et bona ejus ad me pertinent, sed ejus tutela tibi competit: nam ita lege Junia cavetur. Itaque si ab eo cujus et in bonis et ex jure quiritium ancilla fuerit, facta sit Latina, ad eumdem et bona et tutela pertinent.

§ 168. Agnatis, et patronis et liberorum capitum manumissoribus permissum est feminarum tutelam alii in jure cedere: pupillorum

Tit. xix. De fiduciaria tutela.

Est et alia tutela, quae *fiduciaria* appellatur; nam si parens filium vel filiam, nepotem vel neptem, vel deinceps impuberes manumiserit, legitimam nanciscitur eorum tutelam. Quo defuncto, si liberi virilis sexus ei extant, fiduciarii tutores filiorum suorum, vel fratris, vel sororis, et ceterorum efficiuntur. Atqui patrono legitimo tutore mortuo, liberi quoque ejus legitimi sunt tutores: quoniam filius quidem defuncti, si non

autem tutelam non est permissum cedere, quia non videtur onerosa, cum tempore pubertatis finiatur. § 169. Is autem cui ceditur tutela, cessicius tutor vocatur. § 170. Quo mortuo aut capite deminuto, revertitur ad eum tutorem tutela, qui cesserat. Ipse quoque qui cessit, si mortuus aut capite deminutus sit, a cessicio tutela discedit, et revertitur ad eum, qui post eum qui cesserat, secundum gradum in tutela habuerit. § 171. Sed quantum ad agnatos pertinet, nihil hoc tempore de cessicia tutela quaeritur, cum agnatorum tutelae in feminis lege Claudia sublatae sint. § 172. Sed fiduciarios quoque quidam putaverunt cedendae tutelae jus non habere, cum ipsi se oneri subjecerint: quod etsi placeat, in parente tamen, qui filiam neptemve aut proneptem alteri ea lege mancipio dedit, ut sibi remanciparetur, remancipatamque manumisit, idem dici non debet, cum is etiam legitimus tutor habeatur; et non minus huic quam patronis honor praestandus est.

esset a vivo patre emancipatus, post obitum ejus sui juris efficeretur, nec in fratrum potestatem recideret, ideoque nec in tutelam. Libertus autem, si servus mansisset, utique eodem jure apud liberos domini post mortem ejus futurus esset. Ita tamen hi ad tutelam vocantur, si perfectae sint aetatis. Quod nostra constitutio generaliter in omnibus tutelis et curationibus observari praecepit.

§ 173. Praeterea senatus-consulto mulieribus permissum est, in absentis tutoris locum alium petere: quo petito prior desinit, nec interest quam longe abierit is tutor. § 174. Sed excipitur, ne in absentis patroni locum liceat libertae tutorem petere. § 175. Patroni autem loco habemus etiam parentem, qui ex eo, quod ipse sibi remancipatam filiam, neptemve aut proneptem, manumisit, legitimam tutelam nactus est. Sed hujus quidem liberi fiduciarii tutoris loco numerantur: patroni autem liberi eandem tutelam adipiscuntur, quam et pater eorum habuit. § 176. Sed aliquando etiam in patroni absentis locum permittitur tutorem petere, veluti ad hereditatem adeundam. § 177. Idem senatus censuit etiam in persona pupilli patroni filii. § 178. Item lege Julia de maritandis ordinibus, ei quae in legitima tutela pupilli sit, permittitur dotis constituendae gratia a praetore urbano tutorem petere. § 179. Sane enim patroni filius, etiam si impubes sit, libertae efficietur tutor, quamquam in nulla re auctor fieri potest, cum ipsi nihil permissum sit, sine tutoris auctoritate agere. § 180. Item si qua in tutela legitima furiosi aut muti sit, permittitur ei senatus-consulto, dotis constituendae gratia, tutorem petere. § 181. Quibus casibus salvam manere tutelam patrono patronique filio manifestum est. § 182. Praeterea senatus censuit, ut, si tutor pupilli pupillaeve suspectus a tutela remotus sit, sive ex justa causa fuerit excusatus, in locum ejus alius tutor detur, quo facto prior tutor amittet tutelam. § 183. Haec omnia similiter Romae et in provinciis observantur, nisi scilicet [quod Romae a praetore urbano vel peregrino praetore], et in provinciis a praeside provinciae tutor peti debet.

Tit. XX. De Atiliano tutore, et eo qui ex lege Julia et Titia dabatur.

§ 185. Si cui nullus omnino tutor sit, ei datur in urbe Roma ex lege Atilia a praetore urbano et majore parte tribunorum plebis, qui Atilianus tutor vocatur; in provinciis vero a praesidibus provinciarum ex lege Julia et Titia. § 186. Et ideo si cui testamento tutor sub conditione aut ex die certo datus sit, quamdiu conditio aut dies pendet, tutor dari potest; item si pure datus fuerit, quamdiu nemo heres existat, tamdiu ex iis legibus tutor petendus est: qui desinit tutor esse posteaquam aliquis ex testamento tutor esse coeperit. § 187. Ab hostibus quoque tutore capto, ex iis legibus tutor peti debet, qui desinit tutor esse, si is, qui captus est, in civitatem reversus fuerit: nam reversus recipit tutelam jure postliminii.

Si cui nullus omnino tutor fuerat, ei dabatur, in urbe quidem Roma a praetore urbano et majore parte tribunorum plebis tutor ex lege Atilia; in provinciis vero a praesidibus provinciarum ex lege Julia et Titia. § 1. Sed *et si testamento tutor sub conditione, aut die certo, datus fuerat, quamdiu conditio aut dies pendebat, ex* iisdem legibus *tutor dari poterat. Item si pure datus fuerat, quamdiu nemo* ex testamento *heres existat, tamdiu ex iisdem legibus tutor petendus erat: qui desinebat esse tutor,* si conditio existeret aut dies veniret aut heres existeret. § 2. *Ab hostibus quoque tutore capto, ex iis legibus tutor petebatur, qui desinebat esse tutor, si is, qui captus erat, in civitatem reversus fuerat, nam, reversus, recipiebat tutelam jure postliminii.*

§ 3. Sed ex iis legibus tutores pupillis desierunt dari, posteaquam primo consules pupillis utriusque sexus tutores ex inquisitione dare coeperunt; deinde praetores ex constitutionibus. Nam supradictis legibus neque de cautione a tutoribus exigenda, rem salvam pupillis fore, neque de compellendis tutoribus ad tutelae administrationem quidquam cavebatur. § 4. Sed hoc jure utimur, ut Romae quidem praefectus urbi vel praetor secundum suam jurisdictionem; in provinciis autem praesides, ex inquisitione tutores crearent, vel magistratus, jussu praesidum, si non sint magnae pupilli facultates. § 5. Nos autem, per constitutionem nostram et hujusmodi difficultates hominum resecantes, nec expectata jussione praesidum, disposuimus, si facultates pupilli vel adulti usque ad quingentos solidos valeant, defensores civitatum una cum ejusdem civitatis religiosissimo antistite, vel alias publicas personas, id est magistratus, vel juridicum Alexandrinae civitatis, tutores vel curatores creare, legitima cautela secundum ejusdem constitutionis normam praestanda, videlicet eorum periculo qui eam accipiunt.

§ 188. Ex his apparet quot sint species tutelarum. Si vero quaeramus in quot genera hae species deducantur, longa erit disputatio : nam de ea re valde veteres dubitaverunt. Nos, qui diligentius hunc tractatum exsecuti sumus et in edicti interpretatione, et in his libris, quos ex Quinto Mucio fecimus, hoc tantum tantisper sufficit admonuisse, quod quidam quinque genera esse dixerunt, ut Quintus Mucius; alii tria, ut Servius Sulpicius; alii duo, ut Labeo : alii tot genera esse crediderunt, quot etiam species essent.

§ 189. Sed impuberes quidem in tutela esse omnium civitatium jure contingit; quia id naturali rationi conveniens est, ut is, qui perfectae aetatis non sit, alterius tutela regatur; nec fere ulla civitas est in qua non licet parentibus liberis suis impuberibus testamento tutorem dare: quamvis, ut supra diximus, soli cives Romani videantur tantum liberos suos in potestate habere. § 190. Feminas vero perfectae aetatis in tutela esse fere nulla pretiosa ratio suasisse videtur; nam quae vulgo creditur, quia levitate animi plerumque decipiuntur, et aequum erat eas tutoris auctoritate regi, magis speciosa videtur quam vera. Mulieres enim, quae perfectae aetatis sunt, ipsae sibi negotia tractant, et in quibusdam causis dicis gratia tutor interponit auctoritatem suam : saepe etiam invitus auctor fieri a praetore cogitur. § 191. Unde cum tutore nullum ex tutelae gestione judicium mulieri datur; at ubi pupillorum pupillarumve negotia tutores tractant, eis post pubertatem tutelae judicio rationem reddunt. § 192. Sane patronorum et parentum legitimae tutelae vim aliquam habere intelliguntur eo, quod hi neque ad testamentum faciendum, neque ad res mancipi alienandas, neque ad obligationes suscipiendas auctores fieri coguntur, praeterquam si magna causa alienandarum rerum mancipi, obligationisve suscipiendae interveniat; eaque omnia ipsorum causa constituta sunt, ut, quia ad eos intestatarum mortuarum hereditates pertinent, neque per testamentum excludantur ab hereditate, neque alienatis pretiosioribus rebus, susceptoque aere alieno minus locuples ad eos hereditas perveniat. § 193. Apud peregrinos non similiter, ut apud nos, in tutela sunt feminae; sed tamen plerumque quasi in tutela sunt : ut ecce lex Bithy-

§ 6. *Impuberes autem in tutela esse naturali* juri *conveniens est, ut is, qui perfectae aetatis non sit, alterius tutela regatur.*

§ 7. Cum igitur *pupillorum pupillarumque tutores negotia* gerunt, *post pubertatem tutelae iudicio rationem reddunt.*

norum, si quid mulier contrahat, maritum auctorem esse jubet, aut filium ejus puberem.

Tit. xxi. De auctoritate tutorum.

Auctoritas autem tutoris in quibusdam causis necessaria pupillis est, in quibusdam non est necessaria ; ut ecce : si quid dari sibi stipulentur, non est necessaria tutoris auctoritas ; quod si aliis pupilli promittant, necessaria est. Namque placuit meliorem quidem suam conditionem licere eis facere etiam sine tutoris auctoritate ; deteriorem vero, non aliter quam tutoris auctoritate. Unde in his causis ex quibus obligationes mutuae nascuntur, ut in emptionibus venditionibus, locationibus conductionibus, mandatis, depositis, si tutoris auctoritas non interveniat, ipsi quidem qui cum his contrahunt obligantur ; at invicem pupilli non obligantur. § 1. Neque tamen hereditatem adire, neque bonorum possessionem petere, neque hereditatem ex fideicommisso suscipere aliter possunt, nisi tutoris auctoritate, quamvis illis lucrosa sit, neque ullum damnum habeat. § 2. Tutor autem statim, in ipso negotio praesens, debet auctor fieri, si hoc pupillo prodesse existimaverit. Post tempus vero aut per epistolam interposita auctoritas nihil agit.

§ 184. Olim cum legis actiones in usu erant, etiam ex illa causa tutor dabatur, si inter tutorem, et mulierem pupillumve lege agendum erat : nam quia ipse tutor in re sua auctor esse non poterat, alius dabatur, quo auctore legis actio perageretur ; qui dicebatur praetorius tutor, quia a praetore urbano dabatur ; sed post sublatas legis actiones quidam putant hanc speciem dandi tutorem in usu esse desisse, aliis autem placet, adhuc in usu esse, si legitimo judicio agatur.

§ 3. *Si inter tutorem pupillumve* judicium *agendum* sit, *quia ipse tutor in rem suam auctor esse non potest*, non *praetorius tutor*, ut olim, constituitur, sed curator in locum ejus datur, quo interveniente judicium peragitur, et, eo peracto, curator esse desinit.

§ 194. Tutela autem liberantur ingenuae quidem trium [liberorum jure, libertinae vero quatuor, si in patroni] liberorumve ejus legitima tutela sint ; nam et ceterae, quae alterius generis tutores habeant, velut Atilianos aut fiduciarios, trium liberorum jure liberantur. § 195. Potest autem pluribus modis libertina alterius generis [tutores] habere, velut, si a femina manumissa sit ; tunc enim e lege Atilia petere debet tutorem vel in provincia e lege Julia et Titia : nam in patronae tutela esse non potest. § 195A. Item si a masculo manumissa [sit,] et auctore eo coemptionem fecerit, [et] deinde remancipata et manumissa sit, patronum quidem habere

Tit. xxii. Quibus modis tutela finitur.

tutorem desinit, incipit autem habere eum tutorem a quo manumissa est, qui fiduciarius dicitur. Item si patronus ejusque filius in adoptionem se dederit, debet liberta e lege Atilia vel Julia et Titia tutorem petere. Similiter ex iisdem legibus petere debet tutorem liberta, si patronus decesserit, nec ullum virilis sexus liberorum in familia retinuerit.

§ 196. Masculi autem, cum puberes esse coeperint, tutela liberantur. Puberem autem Sabinus quidem et Cassius ceterique nostri praeceptores eum esse putant tantum, qui habitu corporis pubertatem ostendit, id est eum, qui generare potest; sed in his qui pubescere non possunt, quales sunt spadones, eam aetatem esse spectandam, cujus aetatis puberes fiunt. Sed diversae scholae auctores annis putant pubertatem aestimandam, id est, eum puberem esse existimant [qui xiv annos expleverit . . . . .]

Pupilli pupillaeque, cum *puberes esse coeperint, tutela liberantur. Pubertatem autem* veteres *quidem* non solum ex annis, sed etiam *ex habitu corporis* in masculis aestimari volebant. Nostra autem majestas dignum esse castitate temporum nostrorum bene putavit, quod in feminis et antiquis impudicum esse visum est, id est inspectionem habitudinis corporis, hoc etiam in masculos extendere. Et ideo, sancta constitutione promulgata, pubertatem in masculis post decimum quartum annum completum illico initium accipere disposuimus; antiquitatis normam in feminis personis bene positam, suo ordine relinquentes, ut post duodecimum annum completum viripotentes esse credantur. § 1. Item finitur tutela, si adrogati sint adhuc impuberes, vel deportati; item si in servitutem pupillus redigatur vel si ab hostibus captus fuerit. § 2. Sed et si usque ad certam conditionem datus sit in testamento, aeque evenit, ut desinat esse tutor existente conditione. § 3. Simili modo, finitur tutela morte vel pupillorum vel tutorum. § 4. Sed et capitis deminutione tutoris, per quam libertas vel civitas ejus amittitur, omnis tutela perit. Minima autem capitis deminutione tutoris, veluti si se in adoptionem dederit, legitima tantum tutela perit; ceterae non pereunt. Sed pupilli et pupillae capitis deminutio, licet minima sit, omnes tutelas tollit. § 5. Praeterea qui ad certum tempus testamento dantur tutores, finito eo deponunt tutelam. § 6. Desinunt autem esse tutores qui vel removentur a tutela ob id quod suspecti visi sunt; vel ex justa causa sese excusant, et onus administrandae tutelae deponunt, secundum ea quae inferius proponemus.

Tit. xxiii. De curatoribus.

§ 197. . . . . aetatem pervenerit, in qua res suas tueri possit, sicuti apud pere-

Masculi puberes et feminae viripotentes usque ad vicesimum quintum annum completum curatores accipiunt; quia licet puberes sint, adhuc tamen ejus aetatis sunt ut negotia sua tueri non possint. § 1. Dantur autem curatores ab iisdem magistratibus a

grinas gentes custodiri superius indicavimus. § 198. Ex iisdem causis et in provinciis a praesidibus earum curatores dari volunt.

quibus et tutores. Sed curator testamento non datur: sed datus, confirmatur decreto praetoris vel praesidis. § 2. Item inviti adolescentes curatores non accipiunt, praeterquam in litem; curator enim et ad certam causam dari potest. § 3. Furiosi quoque et prodigi, licet majores vigintiquinque annis sint, tamen in curatione sunt agnatorum ex lege Duodecim Tabularum. Sed solent Romae praefectus urbi, vel praetor, et in provinciis praesides ex inquisitione eis dare curatores. § 4. Sed et mente captis et surdis et mutis et qui morbo perpetuo laborant, quia rebus suis superesse non possunt, curatores dandi sunt. § 5. Interdum autem et pupilli curatores accipiunt, utputa si legitimus tutor non sit idoneus, quoniam habenti tutorem tutor dari non potest. Item si testamento datus tutor, vel a praetore vel a praeside, idoneus non sit ad administrationem, nec tamen fraudulenter negotia administret, solet ei curator adjungi. Item in locum tutorum qui non in perpetuum, sed ad tempus, a tutela excusantur, solent curatores dari.

§ 6. Quodsi tutor, adversa valetudine, vel alia necessitate, impediatur quominus negotia pupilli administrare possit, et pupillus vel absit, vel infans sit, quem velit actorem, periculo ipsius tutoris praetor, vel qui provinciae praeerit, decreto constituet.

Tit. xxiv. De satisdatione tutorum vel curatorum.

§ 199. Ne tamen et pupillorum, et eorum qui in curatione sunt, negotia a tutoribus curatoribusque consumantur, aut deminuantur, curat praetor, ut et tutores et curatores eo nomine satisdent. § 200. Sed hoc non est perpetuum; nam et tutores testamento dati satisdare non coguntur, quia fides eorum et diligentia ab ipso testatore probata est; et curatores ad quos non e lege curatio pertinet, sed vel a consule, vel a praetore, vel a praeside provinciae dantur, plerumque non coguntur satisdare, scilicet quia satis honesti electi sunt.

Ne tamen pupillorum pupillarumve, *et eorum qui* quaeve *in curatione sunt, negotia a tutoribus curatoribusve consumantur, aut deminuantur, curat praetor, ut et tutores et curatores eo nomine satisdent. Sed hoc non est perpetuum; nam tutores testamento dati satisdare non coguntur, quia fides eorum et diligentia ab ipso testatore approbata est.* Item, ex inquisitione tutores vel *curatores* dati, satisdatione non onerantur, *quia* idonei *electi sunt.*

§ I. Sed si ex testamento vel inquisitione duo pluresve dati fuerint, potest unus offerre satis de indemnitate pupilli vel adolescentis, et contutori suo vel concuratori praeferri, ut solus administret; vel ut contutor satis offerens praeponatur ei, et ipse solus administret. Itaque per se non potest petere satis a contutore vel concuratore suo; sed offerre debet, ut electionem det contutori vel concuratori suo, utrum velit satis accipere, an satisdare. Quod si nemo eorum satis offerat, si quidem adscriptum fuerit a testatore quis gerat, ille gerere debet: quodsi non fuerit adscriptum, quem major pars elegerit ipse gerere debet; ut edicto praetoris cavetur. Sin autem ipsi tutores dissenserint circa eligendum eum vel eos qui gerere debent praetor partes suas interponere debet. Idem et in pluribus ex inquisitione datis comprobandum est, id est, ut major pars eligere possit per quem administratio fieret.

§ 2. Sciendum autem est, non solum tutores vel curatores pupillis, vel adultis, ceterisque personis, ex administratione rerum teneri; sed etiam in eos qui satisdationem accipiunt subsidiariam actionem esse, quae ultimum eis praesidium possit afferre. Subsidiaria autem actio datur in eos qui aut omnino a tutoribus vel curatoribus satisdari non curaverint, aut non idonee passi essent caveri: quae quidem, tam ex prudentum responsis, quam ex constitutionibus imperialibus etiam in heredes eorum extenditur. § 3. Quibus constitutionibus et illud exprimitur, ut, nisi caveant tutores vel curatores, pignoribus captis coerceantur. § 4. Neque autem praefectus urbi, neque praetor, neque praeses provinciae, neque quis alius, cui tutores dandi jus est, hac actione tenebitur; sed hi tantummodo qui satisdationem exigere solent.

Tit. xxv. De excusationibus tutorum vel curatorum.

Excusantur autem tutores vel curatores variis ex causis; plerumque propter liberos, sive in potestate sint, sive emancipati. Si enim tres liberos superstites Romae quis habeat, vel in Italia quatuor, vel in provinciis quinque, a tutela vel cura potest excusari, exemplo ceterorum munerum: nam et tutelam vel curam placuit publicum munus esse. Sed adoptivi liberi non prosunt: in adoptionem autem dati, naturali patri prosunt. Item nepotes ex filio prosunt, ut in locum patris succedant; ex filia non prosunt. Filii autem superstites tantum ad tutelae vel curae muneris excusationem prosunt; defuncti non prosunt. Sed si in bello amissi sunt, quaesitum est an prosint? Et constat eos solos prodesse qui in acie amittuntur; hi enim, qui pro republica ceciderunt, in perpetuum per gloriam vivere intelliguntur. § 1. Item divus Marcus in Semestribus rescripsit, eum qui res fisci administrat a tutela vel cura, quamdiu administrat, excusari posse. § 2. Item qui reipublicae causa absunt a tutela et cura excusantur. Sed et si fuerint tutores vel curatores, deinde reipublicae causa abesse coeperint, a tutela vel cura excusantur, quatenus reipublicae causa absunt, et interea curator loco eorum datur. Qui, si reversi fuerint, recipiunt onus tutelae, nam nec anni habent vacationem, ut Papinianus libro quinto responsorum scripsit; nam hoc spatium habent ad novas tutelas vocati. § 3. Et qui potestatem aliquam habent se excusare possunt, ut divus Marcus rescripsit, sed coeptam tutelam deserere non possunt. § 4. Item, propter litem quam cum pupillo vel adulto tutor vel curator habet, excusare se nemo potest; nisi forte de omnibus bonis vel hereditate controversia sit. § 5. Item, tria onera tutelae non affectatae, vel curae, praestant vacationem quamdiu administrantur; ut tamen plurium pupillorum tutela vel cura eorundem bonorum, veluti fratrum, pro una computetur. § 6. Sed et propter paupertatem excusationem tribui, tam divi fratres quam per se divus Marcus rescripsit, si quis imparem se oneri injuncto possit docere. § 7. Item propter adversam valetudinem propter quam nec suis quidem negotiis interesse potest, excusatio locum habet. § 8. Similiter, eum qui literas nesciret, excusandum esse divus Pius rescripsit; quamvis et imperiti literarum possint ad administrationem negotiorum sufficere. § 9. Item, si propter inimicitias aliquem testamento tutorem pater dederit, hoc ipsum praestat ei excusationem; sicut per contrarium; non excusantur qui se tutelam patri pupillorum administraturos promiserant. § 10. Non esse autem admittendam excusationem ejus qui hoc solo utitur, quod ignotus patri pupillorum sit, divi fratres rescripserunt. § 11. Inimicitiae, quas quis cum patre pupillorum vel adultorum exercuit, si capitales fuerunt, nec reconciliatio intervenit, a tutela vel cura solent excusari. § 12. Item si quis status controversiam a pupillorum patre passus est, excusatur a tutela. § 13. Item major septuaginta annis a tutela vel cura excusare se potest. Minores autem viginti quinque annis olim quidem excusabantur: nostra autem constitutione prohibentur ad tutelam vel curam aspirare, adeo ut nec excusatione opus sit. Qua constitutione cavetur, ut nec pupillus ad legitimam tutelam vocetur, nec adultus; cum erat incivile, eos qui alieno auxilio in rebus suis administrandis egere noscuntur, et ab aliis reguntur, aliorum tutelam vel curam subire. § 14. Idem et in milite observandum est ut, nec volens, ad tutelae onus admittatur. § 15. Item, Romae grammatici rhetores et medici, et qui in patria sua id exercent, et intra numerum sunt, a tutela vel cura habent vacationem.

§ 16. Qui autem se vult excusare, si plures habeat excusationes, et de quisbusdam non probaverit, aliis uti intra tempora constituta non prohibetur. Qui autem excusare se volunt, non appellant; sed, intra dies quinquaginta continuos, ex quo cognoverint se tutores datos, excusare se debent, cujuscumque generis sint id est, qualitercumque dati fuerint tutores, si intra centesimum lapidem sunt ab eo loco ubi tutores dati sunt. Si vero ultra centesimum habitant, dinumeratione facta viginti millium diurnorum, et amplius triginta dierum: quod tamen, ut Scaevola dicebat, sic debet computari, ut ne minus sint quam quinquaginta dies. § 17. Datus autem tutor, ad universum patrimonium datus esse creditur. § 18. Qui tutelam alicujus gessit, invitus curator ejusdem fieri non compellitur: in tantum ut, licet paterfamilias qui testamento tutorem dedit adjecerit se eundem curatorem dare, tamen invitum eum curam suscipere non cogendum, divi Severus et Antoninus rescripserunt. § 19. Iidem rescripserunt maritum uxori suae curatorem datum, excusare se posse, licet se immisceat. § 20. Si quis autem falsis allegationibus excusationem tutelae meruerit, non est liberatus onere tutelae.

Tit. XXVI. De suspectis tutoribus vel curatoribus.

Sciendum est, suspecti crimen ex lege Duodecim Tabularum descendere. § 1. Datum est autem jus removendi suspectos tutores Romae praetori et in provinciis praesidibus earum et legato proconsulis. § 2. Ostendimus qui possunt de suspecto cognoscere, nunc videamus qui suspecti fieri possunt. Et quidem omnes tutores possunt, sive testamentarii sint, sive non, sed alterius generis tutores. Quare et si legitimus fuerit tutor, accusari poterit. Quid si patronus? Adhuc idem erit dicendum; dummodo meminerimus famae patroni parcendum, licet ut suspectus remotus fuerit. § 3. Consequens est ut videamus qui possunt suspectos postulare. Et sciendum est, quasi publicam esse hanc accusationem, hoc est, omnibus patere. Quinimo et mulieres admittuntur, ex rescripto divorum Severi et Antonini, sed hae solae quae, pietatis necessitudine ductae, ad hoc procedunt, utputa mater; nutrix quoque, et avia possunt; potest et soror. Sed et si qua alia mulier fuerit, cujus praetor perpensam pietatem intellexerit, non sexus verecundiam egredientem, sed pietate productam, non continere injuriam pupillorum, admittet eam ad accusationem. § 4. Impuberes non possunt tutores suos suspectos postulare, puberes autem curatores suos ex consilio necessariorum suspectos possunt arguere: et ita divi Severus et Antoninus rescripserunt. § 5. Suspectus est autem qui non ex fide tutelam gerit, licet solvendo sit, ut Julianus quoque scripsit. Sed et antequam incipiat tutelam gerere tutor, posse eum quasi suspectum removeri, idem Julianus scripsit, et secundum eum constitutum est. § 6. Suspectus autem remotus, si quidem ob dolum, famosus est; si ob culpam, non aeque. § 7. Si quis autem suspectus postulatur, quoad cognitio finiatur, interdicitur ei administratio, ut Papiniano visum est. § 8. Sed si suspecti cognitio suscepta fuerit, posteaquam tutor vel curator decesserit, extinguitur cognitio suspecti. § 9. Si quis tutor copiam sui non faciat ut alimenta pupillo decernantur, cavetur epistola divorum Severi et Antonini, ut in possessionem bonorum ejus pupillus mittatur; et quae mora deteriora futura sunt, dato curatore distrahi jubentur. Ergo ut suspectus removeri poterit, qui non praestat alimenta. § 10. Sed si quis praesens negat propter inopiam alimenta non posse decerni, si hoc per mendacium dicat, remittendum eum esse ad praefectum urbi puniendum placuit, sicut ille remittitur qui, data pecunia, ministerium tutelae redemerit. § 11. Libertus quoque, si fraudulenter tutelam filiorum vel nepotum patroni gessisse probetur, ad praefectum urbi remittetur puniendus. § 12. Novissime sciendum est eos qui fraudulenter tutelam vel curam administrant, etiam si satis offerant, removendos esse a tutela, quia satisdatio propositum tutoris malevolum non mutat, sed diutius grassandi in re familiari facultatem praestat. § 13. Suspectum enim eum putamus qui moribus talis est, ut suspectus sit. Enimvero tutor vel curator, quamvis pauper est, fidelis tamen et diligens, removendus non est quasi suspectus.

INSTITUTIONUM

GAII COMMENTARIUS II.

§ 1. [Superiore commentario de jure personarum] exposuimus : modo videamus de rebus, quae vel in nostro patrimonio sunt, vel extra nostrum patrimonium habentur.

§ 2. Summa itaque rerum divisio in duos articulos deducitur : nam aliae sunt divini juris, aliae humani.

JUSTINIANI LIBER II.

Tit. i. De rerum divisione.

Superiore libro *de jure personarum exposuimus: modo videamus de rebus, quae vel in nostro patrimonio, vel extra nostrum patrimonium habentur.* Quaedam enim naturali jure communia sunt omnium, quaedam publica, quaedam universitatis, quaedam nullius, pleraque singulorum, quae ex variis causis cuique acquiruntur sicut ex subjectis apparebit.

§ 1. Et quidem naturali jure communia sunt omnium haec : aer, aqua profluens, et mare, et per hoc litora maris. Nemo igitur ad litus maris accedere prohibetur, dum tamen villis et monumentis et aedificiis abstineat, quia non sunt juris gentium, sicut et mare. § 2. Flumina autem omnia, et portus publica sunt, ideoque jus piscandi omnibus commune est in portu fluminibusque. § 3. Est autem litus maris, quatenus hibernus fluctus maximus excurrit. § 4. Riparum quoque usus publicus est juris gentium, sicut ipsius fluminis. Itaque navem ad eas applicare, funes arboribus ibi natis religare, onus aliquod in his reponere, cuilibet liberum est, sicuti per ipsum flumen navigare. Sed proprietas earum illorum est quorum praediis adhaerent : qua de causa arbores quoque in iisdem natae eorundem sunt. § 5. Litorum quoque usus publicus juris gentium est, sicut ipsius maris ; et ob id quibuslibet liberum est casam ibi ponere in qua se recipiant, sicut retia siccare, et ex mari deducere. Proprietas autem eorum potest intelligi nullius esse, sed ejusdem juris esse cujus et mare, et, quae subjacent mari, terra vel arena. § 6. Universitatis sunt, non singulorum, veluti quae in civitatibus sunt, theatra, stadia et similia, et si qua alia sunt communia civitatum.

Gaius:

§ 3. Divini juris sunt, veluti res sacrae et religiosae. § 4. Sacrae sunt, quae Diis superis consecratae sunt ; religiosae, quae Diis manibus relictae sunt. § 5. Sed sacrum quidem hoc solum existi-

Justinian:

§ 7. Nullius autem sunt *res sacrae, et religiosae*, et sanctae, *quod enim divini juris est, id nullius in bonis est.* § 8. *Sacrae res sunt quae* rite et per Pontifices *Deo consecratae sunt*, veluti aedes sacrae, et dona quae rite ad ministerium Dei dedicata sunt, quae etiam per nostram constitutionem alienari et obligari prohibuimus, excepta

matur quod ex auctoritate populi Romani consecratum est, veluti lege de ea re lata, aut senatusconsulto facto.

causa redemptionis captivorum. Si quis vero auctoritate sua quasi sacrum sibi constituerit, sacrum non est, sed profanum. Locus autem in quo aedes sacrae aedificatae sunt, etiam diruto aedificio, adhuc sacer manet, ut et Papinianus scripsit.

§ 6. Religiosum vero nostra voluntate facimus, mortuum inferentes in locum nostrum, si modo ejus mortui funus ad nos pertineat. § 7. Sed in provinciali solo placet plerisque, solum religiosum non fieri, quia in eo solo dominium populi Romani est, vel Caesaris, nos autem possessionem tantum et usumfructum habere videmur: utique tamen etiam si non sit religiosus, pro religioso habetur. Item quod in provinciis non ex auctoritate populi Romani consecratum est, proprie sacrum non est, sed tamen pro sacro habetur.

§ 9. *Religiosum locum* unusquisque sua *voluntate facit, dum mortuum infert in locum* suum. In communem autem locum purum invito socio inferre non licet. In commune vero sepulcrum etiam invitis ceteris licet inferre. Item, si alienus ususfructus est, proprietarium placet, nisi consentiente usufructuario, locum religiosum non facere. In alienum locum, concedente domino, licet inferre; et licet postea ratum habuerit quam illatus est mortuus, tamen religiosus locus fit.

§ 8. Sanctae quoque res, veluti muri et portae, quodammodo divini juris sunt.

§ 9. Quod autem divini juris est, id nullius in bonis est: id vero quod humani [juris est, plerumque alicujus in bonis est; potest autem et nullius in bonis esse; nam res hereditariae, antequam aliquis heres existat, nullius in bonis sunt]. . . . . ve domino. § 10. Hae autem, quae humani juris sunt, aut publicae sunt aut privatae. § 11. Quae publicae sunt nullius creduntur in bonis esse; ipsius enim universitatis esse creduntur: privatae sunt, quae singulorum sunt.

§ 10. *Sanctae quoque res, veluti muri et portae, quodammodo divini juris sunt*, et ideo nullius in bonis sunt. Ideo autem muros sanctos dicimus, quia poena capitis constituta est in eos qui aliquid in muros deliquerint. Ideo et legum eas partes quibus poenas constituimus adversus eos qui contra leges fecerint, sanctiones vocamus.

§ 65. Ergo ex his quae diximus apparet quaedam naturali jure alienari, qualia sunt ea quae traditione alienantur; quaedam civili, nam mancipationis et in jure cessionis et usucapionis jus proprium est civium Romanorum.

§ 11. Singulorum autem hominum multis modis res fiunt: quarundam enim rerum dominium nanciscimur jure naturali, quod, sicut diximus, appellatur jus gentium; quarundam jure civili. Commodius est itaque a vetustiore jure incipere: palam est autem vetustius esse jus naturale, quod cum ipso genere humano rerum natura prodidit. Civilia enim jura tunc esse coeperunt, cum et civitates condi, et magistratus creari et leges scribi coeperunt.

§ 66. Nec tamen ea tantum quae traditione nostra fiunt, naturali nobis ratione adquiruntur, sed etiam quae occupando ideo adquisierimus, quia antea nullius essent: qualia sunt omnia quae terra mari, coelo capiuntur. § 67. Itaque si feram bestiam, aut volucrem, aut piscem [ceperimus, jure gentium id quod ita captum fuerit, statim nostrum fit, et] eo usque nostrum esse intelligitur, donec nostra custodia coerceatur; cum vero custodiam nostram evaserit et in naturalem libertatem se receperit, rursus occupantis fit, quia nostra esse desiit. Naturalem autem libertatem recipere videtur, cum aut oculos nostros evaserit, aut licet in conspectu sit nostro, difficilis tamen ejus rei persecutio sit.

§ 12. Ferae igitur bestiae, volucres, et pisces, id est, omnia animalia quae in terra, mari, caelo nascuntur, simul atque ab aliquo capta fuerint, jure gentium statim illius esse incipiunt: quod enim ante nullius est, id naturali ratione occupanti conceditur. Nec interest, feras bestias et volucres utrum in suo fundo quis capiat, an in alieno. Plane qui in alienum fundum ingreditur venandi aut aucupandi gratia, potest a domino, si is providerit, prohiberi ne ingrediatur. Quidquid autem eorum ceperis, *eo usque* tuum *esse intelligitur, donec* tua *custodia coerceatur. Cum vero evaserit custodiam* tuam, *et in naturalem libertatem se receperit,* tuum *esse desinit, et rursus occupantis fit. Naturalem autem libertatem recipere* intelligitur, *cum vel oculos* tuos effugerit, vel ita sit *in conspectu* tuo, ut *difficilis sit ejus persecutio.* § 13. Illud quaesitum est, an si fera bestia ita vulnerata sit, ut capi possit, statim tua esse intelligatur. Quibusdam placuit statim tuam esse, et eo usque tuam videri donec eam persequaris. Quod si desieris persequi, desinere tuam esse et rursus fieri occupantis. Alii non aliter putaverunt tuam esse quam si eam ceperis. Sed posteriorem sententiam nos confirmamus, quia multa accidere solent, ut eam non capias. § 14. Apium quoque natura fera est. Itaque quae in arbore tua consederint, antequam a te alveo includantur, non magis tuae esse intelliguntur, quam volucres quae in tua arbore nidum fecerint. Ideoque si alius eas incluserit, is earum dominus erit. Favos quoque, si quos eae fecerint, quilibet eximere potest. Plane integra re, si provideris ingredientem in fundum tuum, poteris eum jure prohibere ne ingrediatur. Examen quoque quod ex alveo tuo evolaverit, eo usque tuum esse intelligitur, donec in conspectu tuo est nec difficilis ejus persecutio est; alioquin occupantis fit. § 15. Pavonum etiam et columbarum fera natura est: nec ad rem pertinet, quod ex consuetudine avolare et revolare solent; nam et apes idem faciunt, quarum constat feram esse naturam. Cervos quoque ita quidam mansuetos habent, ut in sylvas ire et redire soleant, quorum et ipsorum feram esse naturam nemo negat.

§ 68. In iis autem animalibus, quae ex consuetudine abire et redire solent, veluti columbis et apibus, item cervis qui in sylvas ire et redire solent, talem habemus regulam traditam, ut si revertendi animum habere desierint, etiam nostra esse desinant, et fiant occupantium. Revertendi autem animum videntur desinere habere, cum revertendi consuetudinem deseruerint.

In iis autem animalibus quae ex consuetudine abire et redire solent, talis regula comprobata est, ut eo usque tua esse intelligantur, donec animum revertendi habeant. Nam *si revertendi animum habere desierint, etiam* tua *esse desinunt, et fiunt occupantium. Revertendi autem animum videntur desinere habere, tunc cum revertendi consuetudinem deseruerint.*

§ 16. Gallinarum et anserum non est fera natura: idque ex eo possumus intelligere, quod aliae sunt gallinae quas feras vocamus, item alii anseres quos feros appellamus. Ideoque si anseres tui aut gallinae tuae aliquo casu turbati turbataeve evolaverint, licet conspectum tuum effugerint, quocumque tamen loco sint, tui tuaeve esse intelliguntur; et qui lucrandi animo ea animalia retinuerit, furtum committere intelligitur.

§ 69. Ea quoque quae ex hostibus capiuntur, naturali ratione nostra fiunt.

§ 17. *Item ea quae ex hostibus capimus*, jure gentium statim *nostra fiunt:* adeo quidem, ut et liberi homines in servitutem nostram deducantur, qui tamen si evaserint nostram potestatem et ad suos reversi fuerint, pristinum statum recipiunt. § 18. Item, lapilli, et gemmae, et caetera quae in litore inveniuntur, jure naturali, statim inventoris fiunt. § 19. Item, ea quae ex animalibus dominio tuo subjectis nata sunt, eodem jure tibi acquiruntur.

§ 70. Sed et id quod per alluvionem nobis adjicitur eodem jure nostrum fit. Per alluvionem autem ita videtur adjici quod ita paulatim flumen agro nostro adjicit, ut aestimare non possimus quantum quoquo momento temporis adjiciatur. Hoc est quod vulgo dicitur, per alluvionem id adjici videri quod ita paulatim adjicitur ut oculos nostros fallat. § 71. Itaque si flumen partem aliquam ex tuo praedio resciderit et ad meum praedium pertulerit, haec pars tua manet.

§ 20. Praeterea, *quod per alluvionem* agro tuo flumen *adjecit, jure* gentium tibi acquiritur. Est autem alluvio incrementum latens. *Per alluvionem autem id videtur adjici quod ita paulatim adjicitur, ut intelligere non possis quantum quoquo momento temporis adjiciatur.* § 21. *Quod si vis fluminis partem aliquam ex tuo praedio detraxerit et* vicini *praedio attulerit*, palam est eam tuam permanere. Plane, si longiore tempore fundo vicini haeserit, arboresque quas secum traxerit in eum fundum radices egerint, ex eo tempore videntur vicini fundo acquisitae esse.

§ 72. At si in medio flumine insula nata sit, haec eorum omnium communis est, qui ab utraque parte fluminis prope ripam praedia possident. Si vero non sit in medio

§ 22. *Insula* quae in mari nata est, quod raro accidit, occupantis fit: nullius enim esse creditur. At *in flumine nata*, quod frequenter accidit, si quidem mediam partem

flumine, ad eos pertinet qui, ab ea parte quae proxima est, juxta ripam praedia habent.

fluminis teneat, *communis est eorum qui ab utraque parte fluminis prope ripam praedia possident*, pro modo latitudinis cujusque fundi quae latitudo prope ripam sit. Quod si alteri parti proximior sit, eorum est tantum *qui ab ea parte* prope *ripam praedia* possident. Quod si aliqua parte divisum sit flumen, deinde infra unitum agrum alicujus in formam insulae redegerit, ejusdem permanet is ager cujus et fuerat. § 23. Quod si naturali alveo in universum derelicto, alia parte fluere coeperit: prior quidem alveus eorum est qui prope ripam ejus praedia possident, pro modo scilicet latitudinis cujusque agri, quae latitudo prope ripam sit. Novus autem alveus ejus juris esse incipit cujus et ipsum flumen, id est, publicus. Quod si post aliquod tempus ad priorem alveum reversum fuerit flumen, rursus novus alveus eorum esse incipit qui prope ripam ejus praedia possident. § 24. Alia sane causa est, si cujus totus ager inundatus fuerit; neque enim inundatio speciem fundi commutat, et ob id, si recesserit aqua, palam est eum fundum ejus manere cujus et fuit.

§ 79 In aliis quoque speciebus naturalis ratio requiritur: proinde si ex uvis, [aut olivis, aut spicis] meis vinum, aut oleum, aut frumentum feceris, quaeritur utrum meum sit id vinum aut oleum aut frumentum, an tuum. Item si ex auro aut argento meo vas aliquod feceris, vel ex tabulis meis navem, aut armarium, aut subsellium fabricaveris; item si ex lana mea vestimentum feceris, vel si ex vino et melle meo mulsum feceris, sive ex medicamentis meis emplastrum aut collyrium feceris, [quaeritur, utrum tuum sit id quod ex meo effeceris] an meum. Quidam materiam et substantiam spectandam esse putant, id est, ut cujus materia sit, illius et res quae facta sit videatur esse; idque maxime placuit Sabino et Cassio. Alii vero ejus rem esse putant qui fecerit; idque maxime diversae scholae auctoribus visum est; sed eum

§ 25. Cum ex aliena materia species aliqua facta sit ab aliquo, *quaeri* solent, quis eorum naturali ratione dominus sit, utrum is qui fecerit, an ille potius qui materiae dominus fuerit? ut ecce, *si* quis *ex* alienis *uvis, aut olivis, aut spicis, vinum, aut oleum, aut frumentum fecerit*; aut *ex* alieno *auro, vel argento*, vel aere *vas aliquod fecerit;* vel *ex* alieno *vino et melle mulsum miscuerit;* vel *ex medicamentis* alienis *emplastrum aut collyrium composuerit;* vel *ex* aliena *lana vestimentum fecerit;* vel *ex* alienis *tabulis navem, vel armarium, vel subsellium fabricaverit.* Et post multas Sabinianorum et Proculeianorum ambiguitates, placuit media sententia existimantium, si ea species ad materiam reduci possit, eum videri dominum esse qui materiae dominus fuerit; si non possit reduci, eum potius intelligi dominum qui fecerit; ut ecce: vas conflatum potest ad rudem massam aeris, vel argenti, vel auri reduci; vinum autem, aut oleum, aut frumentum: ad uvas, vel olivas, vel spicas reverti non potest; ac ne mulsum quidem ad vinum et mel resolvi potest. Quod si partim ex sua

quoque cujus materia et substantia fuerit, furti adversus eum qui subripuerit habere actionem; nec minus adversus eumdem condictionem ei competere, quia extincta res, licet vindicari non possit, condici tamen furibus et quibusdam aliis possessoribus possunt.

materia, partim ex aliena speciem aliquam fecerit quis, veluti ex suo vino et alieno melle mulsum miscuerit, aut ex suis et alienis medicamentis emplastrum aut collyrium, aut ex sua et aliena lana vestimentum fecerit, dubitandum non est, hoc casu, eum esse dominum qui fecerit; cum non solum operam suam dedit, sed et partem ejusdem materiae praestaverit.

§ 26. Si tamen alienam purpuram vestimento suo quis intexuit, licet pretiosior est purpura, accessionis vice cedit vestimento; et qui dominus fuit purpurae, adversus eum qui subripuit habet furti actionem et condictionem, sive ipse sit qui vestimentum fecit, sive alius; *nam extinctae res, licet vindicari non possint, condici tamen a furibus et a quibusdam aliis possessoribus possunt.* § 27. Si duorum materiae ex voluntate dominorum confusae sint, totum id corpus, quod ex confusione fit, utriusque commune est, veluti si qui vina sua confuderint, aut massas argenti vel auri conflaverint. Sed et si diversae materiae sint, et ob id propria species facta sit, forte ex vino et melle mulsum, aut ex auro et argento electrum, idem juris est; nam et eo casu communem esse speciem non dubitatur. Quod si fortuitu, et non voluntate dominorum, confusae fuerint, vel diversae materiae vel quae ejusdem generis sunt, idem juris esse placuit. § 28. Quod si frumentum Titii tuo frumento mixtum fuerit, si quidem ex voluntate vestra, commune erit, quia singula corpora, id est, singula grana quae cujusque propria fuerint, ex consensu vestro communicata sunt. Quod si casu id mixtum fuerit, vel Titius id miscuerit sine voluntate tua, non videtur commune esse, quia singula corpora in sua substantia durant, nec magis istis casibus commune fit frumentum, quam grex communis esse intelligitur, si pecora Titii tuis pecoribus mixta fuerint. Sed si ab alterutro vestrum id totum frumentum retineatur, in rem quidem actio pro modo frumenti cujusque competit, arbitrio autem judicis continetur, ut is aestimet quale cujusque frumentum fuerit.

§ 29. Cum in suo solo aliquis ex aliena materia aedificaverit, ipse dominus intelligitur aedificii, quia omne quod inaedificatur solo cedit. Nec tamen ideo is qui materiae dominus fuerat desinit ejus dominus esse; sed tantisper neque vindicare eam potest, neque ad exhibendum de ea re agere, propter legem Duodecim Tabularum, qua cavetur, ne quis tignum alienum aedibus suis injunctum eximere cogatur, sed duplum pro eo praestet, per actionem quae vocatur de tigno juncto (appellatione autem tigni omnis materia significatur ex qua aedificia fiunt): quod ideo provisum est, ne aedificia rescindi necesse sit. Sed si aliqua ex causa dirutum sit aedificium, poterit materiae dominus, si non fuerit duplum jam consecutus, tunc eam vindicare, et ad exhibendum de ea re agere.

§ 73. Praeterea id quod in solo nostro ab aliquo aedificatum est, quamvis ille suo nomine aedificaverit, jure naturali nostrum fit, quia superficies solo cedit.

§ 30. Ex diverso, si quis in alieno solo sua materia domum aedificaverit, illius fit domus cujus et solum est. Sed hoc casu materiae dominus proprietatem ejus amittit, quia voluntate ejus alienata intelligitur, utique si non ignorabat in alieno solo se aedificare; et ideo, licet diruta sit domus, vindicare materiam non poterit. Certe illud constat, si in possessione constituto aedificatore soli dominus petat domum suam esse, nec solvat pretium materiae et mercedes fabrorum, posse eum per exceptionem doli mali repelli; utique si bonae fidei possessor fuit qui aedificasset: nam scienti alienum esse solum, potest culpa objici, quod temere aedificaverit in eo solo, quod intelligeret alienum esse.

§ 74. Multoque magis id accidit et in planta quam quis in solo nostro posuerit, si modo radicibus terram complexa fuerit.

§ 31. Si Titius alienam plantam in suo solo posuerit, ipsius erit. Et ex diverso, si Titius suam plantam in Maevii solo posuerit, Maevii planta erit, si modo, utroque casu, radices egerit; antequam autem radices egerit, ejus permanet cujus et fuerat. Adeo autem, ex eo tempore quo radices egerit planta, proprietas ejus commutatur, ut si vicini arbor ita terram Titii presserit, ut in ejus fundum radices ageret, Titii effici arborem dicimus: ratio etenim non permittit, ut alterius arbor esse intelligatur quam cujus in fundum radices egisset. Et ideo prope confinium arbor posita, si etiam in vicini fundum radices egerit, communis fit.

§ 75. Idem contingit et in frumento, quod in solo nostro ab aliquo satum fuerit. § 76. Sed si ab eo petamus fructum vel aedificium, et impensas in aedificium, vel in seminaria, vel in sementem factas ei solvere nolimus, poterit nos per exceptionem doli mali repellere; utique si bonae fidei possessor fuerit.

§ 32. Qua ratione autem plantae quae terra coalescunt solo cedunt, eadem ratione, frumenta quoque quae sata sunt, solo cedere intelliguntur. Ceterum sicut is qui in alieno solo aedificaverit, *si ab eo* dominus *petat aedificium*, defendi potest *per exceptionem doli mali*, secundum ea quae diximus; ita ejusdem exceptionis auxilio tutus esse potest is qui in alienum fundum sua impensa bona fide conseruit.

§ 77. Eadem ratione probatum est, quod in chartulis sive membranis meis aliquis scripserit, licet aureis litteris, meum

§ 33. *Literae* quoque *licet aureae* sint, perinde *chartis membranisve cedunt*, acsi solo cedere solent ea quae inaedificantur aut inseruntur; ideoque si in chartis membranisve tuis carmen, vel historiam, vel

esse, quia litterae chartulis sive membranis cedunt. Itaque si ego eos libros easve membranas petam, nec impensam scripturae solvam, per exceptionem doli mali summoveri potero. § 78. Sed si in tabula mea aliquis pinxerit velut imaginem, contra probatur: magis enim dicitur tabulam picturae cedere. Cujus diversitatis vix idonea ratio redditur. Certe secundum hanc regulam, si me possidente petas imaginem tuam esse, nec solvas pretium tabulae, poteris per exceptionem doli mali summoveri. At si tu possideas, consequens est, ut utilis mihi actio adversum te dari debeat; quo casu, nisi solvam impensam picturae, poteris me per exceptionem doli mali repellere, utique si bona fide possessor fueris. Illud palam est, quod sive tu subripueris tabulam, sive alius, competit mihi furti actio.

orationem Titius scripserit, hujus corporis non Titius, sed tu dominus esse judiceris. Sed si a Titio petas tuos *libros*, tuasve *membranas nec impensas scripturae* solvere paratus sis, *poterit* se Titius defendere *per exceptionem doli mali*, utique si bona fide earum chartarum membranarumve possessionem nactus est. § 34. *Si* quis *in* aliena *tabula pinxerit*, quidam putant *tabulam picturae cedere;* aliis videtur picturam, qualiscumque sit, tabulae cedere. Sed nobis videtur melius esse tabulam picturae cedere: ridiculum est enim picturam Apellis vel Parrhasii in accessionem vilissimae tabulae cedere. *Unde si a domino tabulae imaginem possidente, is qui pinxit, eam petat, nec solvat pretium tabulae, poterit per exceptionem doli mali summoveri. At si is qui pinxit possideat, consequens est, ut utilis actio domino tabulae adversus eum detur, quo casu, si non solvat impensam picturae, poterit per exceptionem doli mali repelli, utique si bona fide possessor fuerit ille qui picturam imposuit. Illud enim palam est, quod, sive is qui pinxit subripuit tabulas, sive alius, competit domino tabularum furti actio.*

§ 35. Si quis a non domino, quem dominum esse crediderit, bona fide fundum emerit, vel ex donatione aliave qualibet justa causa aeque bona fide acceperit; naturali ratione placuit fructus quos percepit ejus esse pro cultura et cura. Et ideo si postea dominus supervenerit, et fundum vindicet, de fructibus ab eo consumptis agere non potest. Ei vero qui sciens alienum fundum possederit, non idem concessum est; itaque cum fundo etiam fructus, licet consumpti sint, cogitur restituere. § 36. Is ad quem ususfructus fundi pertinet, non aliter fructuum dominus efficietur, quam si eos ipse perceperit. Et ideo, licet maturis fructibus nondum tamen perceptis decesserit, ad heredem ejus non pertinent, sed domino proprietatis acquiruntur. Eadem fere et de colono dicuntur. § 37. In pecudum fructu etiam fetus est, sicut lac, et pilus et lana; itaque agni, et haedi, et vituli, et equuli, et suculi, statim naturali jure dominii sunt fructuarii. Partus vero ancillae in fructu non est, itaque ad dominum proprietatis pertinet: absurdum enim videbatur hominem in fructu esse, cum omnes fructus rerum natura gratia hominis comparaverit.

§ 38. Sed si gregis usumfructum quis habeat, in locum demortuorum capitum ex foetu fructuarius summittere debet (ut et Juliano visum est), et in vinearum demortuarum vel arborum locum alias debet substituere; recte enim colere debet et quasi bonus paterfamilias.

§ 39. Thesauros quos quis in loco suo invenerit divus Hadrianus, naturalem aequitatem secutus, ei concessit qui invenerit. Idemque statuit, si quis in sacro aut in religioso loco fortuitu casu invenerit. At si quis in alieno loco, non data ad hoc opera, sed fortuitu invenerit, dimidium inventori, dimidium domino soli concessit. Et convenienter, si quis in Caesaris loco invenerit, dimidium inventoris, dimidium Caesaris esse statuit. Cui conveniens est, ut si quis in fiscali loco vel publico vel civitatis invenerit, dimidium ipsius esse debeat, et dimidium fisci, vel civitatis.

§ 40. Per traditionem quoque jure naturali res nobis acquiruntur; nihil enim tam conveniens est naturali aequitati, quam voluntatem domini volentis rem suam in alium transferre ratam haberi: et ideo, cujuscumque generis sit corporalis res, tradi potest, et a domino tradita alienatur. Itaque stipendiaria quoque et tributaria praedia eodem modo alienantur. Vocantur autem stipendiaria et tributaria praedia quae in provinciis sunt, inter quae nec non et Italica praedia ex nostra constitutione nulla differentia est; sed si quidem ex causa donationis, aut dotis, aut qualibet alia ex causa tradantur, sine dubio transferuntur. § 41. Venditae vero res et traditae, non aliter emptori acquiruntur, quam si is venditori pretium solverit, vel alio modo ei satisfecerit, veluti expromissore aut pignore dato. Quod cavetur quidem ex lege Duodecim Tabularum, tamen recte dicitur et jure gentium, id est, jure naturali, id effici: sed si is qui vendidit fidem emptoris secutus fuerit, dicendum est statim rem emptoris fieri. § 42. Nihil autem interest, utrum ipse dominus tradat alicui rem suam an voluntate ejus alius. § 43. Qua ratione, si cui libera universorum negotiorum administratio a domino permissa fuerit, isque ex iis negotiis rem vendiderit et tradiderit, facit eam accipientis. § 44. Interdum etiam sine traditione nuda voluntas domini sufficit ad rem transferendam, veluti si rem quam tibi aliquis commodavit, aut locavit, aut apud te deposuit, vendiderit tibi, aut donaverit. Quamvis enim ex ea causa tibi eam non tradiderit, eo tamen ipso quod patitur tuam esse, statim acquiritur tibi proprietas, perinde ac si eo nomine tradita fuisset.

45. Item si quis merces in horreo depositas vendiderit, simul atque claves horrei tradiderit emptori, transfert proprietatem mercium ad emptorem. §. 46. Hoc amplius interdum et in incertam personam collocata voluntas domini transfert rei proprietatem; ut ecce, praetores vel consules, qui missilia jactant in vulgus, ignorant quid eorum quisque excepturus sit; et tamen, quia volunt quod quisque exceperit ejus esse, statim eum dominum efficiunt. § 47. Qua ratione verius esse videtur, ut si rem pro derelicto a domino habitam occupaverit quis, statim eum dominum effici. Pro derelicto autem habetur quod dominus ea mente abjecerit, ut id rerum suarum esse nollet, ideoque statim dominus esse desinit. § 48. Alia causa est earum rerum quae, in tempestate maris, levandae navis causa ejiciuntur: hae enim dominorum permanent, quia palam est eas non eo animo ejici, quod quis eas habere non vult, sed quo magis cum ipsa navi periculum maris effugiat: qua de causa si quis, eas fluctibus expulsas, vel etiam in ipso mari nactus, lucrandi animo abstulerit, furtum committit. Nec longe discedere videntur ab his quae de rheda currente non intelligentibus dominis cadunt.

Tit. ii. De rebus corporalibus et incorporalibus.

§ 12. Quaedam praeterea res corporales sunt, quaedam incorporales. § 13. [Corporales sunt] hae quae tangi possunt, veluti fundus, homo, vestis, aurum, argentum, et denique aliae res innumerabiles. § 14. Incorporales sunt quae tangi non possunt: qualia sunt ea quae in jure consistunt, sicut hereditas, ususfructus, obligationes quoquo modo contractae. Nec ad rem pertinet [quod in hereditate res corporales continentur nam] et fructus, qui ex fundo percipiuntur res corporales sunt, et quod ex aliqua obligatione nobis debetur etiam plerumque corporale est, veluti fundus, homo, pecunia: nam ipsum jus successionis, et ipsum jus utendi fruendi, et ipsum jus obligationis incorporale est. Eodem numero sunt jura praediorum urbanorum et rusticor[um, quae etiam servitutes vocantur] . . . . . .

Quaedam praeterea res corporales sunt, quaedam incorporales. § 1. *Corporales hae sunt, quae* sui natura *tangi possunt, veluti fundus, homo, vestis, aurum, argentum, et denique aliae res innumerabiles.* § 2. *Incorporales autem sunt quae tangi non possunt: qualia sunt ea quae in jure consistunt, sicut hereditas, ususfructus, obligationes quoquo modo contractae. Nec ad rem pertinet quod in hereditate res corporales continentur; nam et fructus, qui ex fundo percipiuntur, corporales sunt, et id quod ex aliqua obligatione nobis debetur, plerumque corporale est, veluti fundus, homo, pecunia; nam ipsum jus hereditatis, et ipsum jus utendi fruendi, et ipsum jus obligationis, incorporale est.* § 3. *Eodem numero sunt jura praediorum urbanorum et rusticorum, quae etiam servitutes vocantur.*

Tit. iii. De servitutibus.

Rusticorum praediorum jura sunt haec: iter, actus, via, aquaeductus. Iter est jus eundi, ambulandi hominis, non etiam jumentum agendi vel vehiculum. Actus est jus agendi vel jumentum vel vehiculum. Itaque qui iter habet, actum non habet; qui actum habet, et iter habet, eoque uti potest etiam sine jumento. Via est jus eundi et agendi et ambulandi: nam et iter et actum in se continet via. Aquaeductus est jus aquae ducendae per fundum alienum.

§ 14A. [Urbanorum praediorum jura sunt] altius tollendi ut officiant aedium luminibus vicini aedes, aut non extollendi, ne luminibus vicini officiatur. § 14B. Item fluminum et stillicidiorum idem jus, ut . . . . . . enim vel jus aquae ducendae . . . .

§ 1. Praediorum urbanorum servitutes sunt quae aedificiis inhaerent, ideo urbanorum praediorum dictae, quoniam aedificia omnia, urbana praedia appellamus, etsi in villa aedificata sint. Item praediorum urbanorum servitutes sunt hae: ut vicinus onera vicini sustineat; ut in parietem ejus liceat vicino tignum immittere; ut stillicidium vel flumen recipiat quis in aedes suas, vel in aream, vel in cloacam, vel non recipiat; et ne altius tollat quis aedes suas, ne luminibus vicini officiatur. § 2. In rusticorum praediorum servitutes quidam computari recte putant aquae haustum, pecoris ad aquam adpulsum, jus pascendi, calcis coquendae, arenae fodiendae.

§ 3. Ideo autem hae servitutes praediorum appellantur, quoniam sine praediis constitui non possunt. Nemo enim potest servitutem acquirere urbani vel rustici praedii, nisi qui habet praedium; nec quisquam debere, nisi qui habet praedium. § 4. Si quis velit vicino aliquod jus constituere, pactionibus atque stipulationibus id efficere debet. Potest etiam in testamento quis heredem suum damnare ne altius tollat aedes suas, ne luminibus aedium vicini officiat, vel ut patiatur eum tignum in parietem immittere, vel stillicidium habere; vel ut patiatur eum per fundum ire, agere, aquamve ex eo ducere.

Tit. iv. De usufructu.

Ususfructus est jus alienis rebus utendi fruendi, salva rerum substantia. Est enim jus in corpore, quo sublato, et ipsum tolli necesse est. § 1. Ususfructus a proprietate separationem recipit, idque pluribus modis accidit. Ut ecce, si quis alicui usumfructum legaverit; nam heres nudam habet proprietatem, legatarius usumfructum. Et contra, si fundum legaverit, deducto usufructu, legatarius nudam habet proprietatem, heres vero usumfructum.

Item alii usumfructum, alii, deducto eo, fundum legare potest. Sine testamento vero si quis velit alii usumfructum constituere, pactionibus et stipulationibus id efficere debet. Ne tamen in universum inutiles essent proprietates, semper abscedente usufructu, placuit certis modis extingui usumfructum et ad proprietatem reverti. § 2. Constituitur autem ususfructus non tantum in fundo et aedibus, verum etiam in servis, et jumentis ceterisque rebus, exceptis iis quae ipso usu consumuntur: nam hae res, neque naturali ratione, neque civili, recipiunt usumfructum: quo numero sunt vinum, oleum, frumentum, vestimenta: quibus proxima est pecunia numerata, namque in ipso usu assidua permutatione quodammodo extinguitur. Sed utilitatis causa, senatus censuit posse etiam earum rerum usumfructum constitui, ut tamen eo nomine heredi utiliter caveatur. Itaque si pecuniae ususfructus legatus sit, ita datur legatario ut ejus fiat, et legatarius satisdet heredi de tanta pecunia restituenda, si morietur aut capite minuetur. Ceterae quoque res ita traduntur legatario ut ejus fiant; sed aestimatis his, satisdatur, ut si morietur aut capite minuetur, tanta pecunia restituatur, quanti hae fuerint aestimatae. Ergo senatus non fecit quidem earum rerum usumfructum, nec enim poterat: sed per cautionem quasi usumfructum constituit. § 3. Finitur autem ususfructus morte usufructuarii, et duabus capitis deminutionibus, maxima et media, et non utendo per modum et tempus: quae omnia nostra statuit constitutio. Item finitur ususfructus, si domino proprietatis ab usufructuario cedatur (nam extraneo cedendo nihil agit); vel ex contrario si fructuarius proprietatem rei acquisierit, quae res consolidatio appellatur. Eo amplius constat, si aedes incendio consumptae fuerint, vel etiam terrae motu, aut vitio suo corruerint, extingui usumfructum, et ne areae quidem usumfructum deberi. § 4. Cum autem finitus fuerit totus ususfructus, revertitur scilicet ad proprietatem, et ex eo tempore nudae proprietatis dominus incipit plenam habere in re potestatem.

Tit. v. De usu et habitatione.

Iisdem istis modis quibus ususfructus constituitur, etiam nudus usus constitui solet; iisdemque illis modis finitur, quibus et ususfructus desinit. § 1. Minus autem scilicet juris in usu est quam in usufructu; namque is qui fundi nudum usum habet, nihil ulterius habere intelligitur quam ut oleribus, pomis, floribus, foeno, stramentis et lignis ad usum quotidianum utatur. In eo quoque fundo hactenus ei morari licet, ut neque domino fundi molestus sit, neque iis per quos opera rustica fiunt impedimento sit; nec ulli alii jus quod habet aut vendere aut locare aut gratis concedere potest, cum is qui usumfructum habet potest haec omnia facere. § 2. Item, is qui aedium usum habet, hactenus juris habere intelligitur, ut ipse tantum habitet, nec hoc jus ad alium transferre potest. Et vix receptum esse videtur, ut hospitem ei recipere liceat, et cum uxore sua liberisque suis, item libertis, nec non aliis liberis personis quibus non minus quam servis utitur, habitandi jus habeat, et convenienter si ad mulierem usus aedium pertineat, cum marito ei habitare liceat. § 3. Item, is ad quem servi usus pertinet, ipse tantum operis atque ministerio ejus uti potest; ad alium vero nullo modo jus suum transferre ei concessum est. Idem scilicet juris est et in jumento. § 4. Sed si pecoris vel ovium usus legatus fuerit, neque lacte neque agnis neque lana utetur usuarius, quia ea in fructu sunt. Plane ad stercorandum agrum suum pecoribus uti potest.

§ 5. Sed si cui habitatio legata, sive aliquo modo constituta sit, neque usus videtur, neque ususfructus, sed quasi proprium aliquod jus: quam habitationem habentibus, propter rerum utilitatem, secundum Marcelli sententiam, nostra decisione promulgata, permisimus non solum in ea degere, sed etiam aliis locare.

§ 6. Haec de servitutibus, et usufructu, et usu, et habitatione dixisse sufficiat. De hereditatibus autem et de obligationibus suis locis proponemus. Exposuimus summatim quibus modis jure gentium res acquiruntur, modo videamus quibus modis legitimo et civili jure acquiruntur.

§ 15. [Omnes res aut mancipi sunt aut nec mancipi. Mancipi sunt praedia in Italico solo, tam rustica, qualis est fundus, quam urbana, qualis domus; item servi, et quadrupedes quae dorso collove domantur, veluti boves, muli, equi, asini. Sed haec animalia nostri quidem praeceptores] statim ut nata sunt, mancipi esse putant: Nerva vero, Proculus et ceteri diversae scholae auctores non aliter ea mancipi esse putant, quam si domita sunt; et si propter nimiam feritatem domari non possunt, tunc videri mancipi esse incipere, cum ad eam aetatem pervenerint, qua domari solent. § 16. At ferae bestiae nec mancipi sunt, veluti, ursi, leones, item ea animalia quae fere . . . . . . bestiarum numero sunt, veluti elephanti et cameli; et ideo ad rem non pertinet, quod haec animalia etiam collo dorsove domari solent, quia ne mentio quidem eorum animalium illo tempore fecit, quo constituebatur, quasdam res mancipi esse, quasdam nec mancipi. § 17. Item fere omnia quae incorporalia sunt, nec mancipi sunt, exceptis servitutibus praediorum rusticorum, nam eas mancipi esse constat quamvis sint ex numero rerum incorporalium.

§ 18. Magna autem differentia est quae inter mancipi res existit et nec mancipi. § 19. Nam res nec mancipi ipsa traditione pleno jure alterius fiunt si modo corporales sunt et ob id recipiunt traditionem. § 20. Itaque si tibi vestem, vel aurum, vel argentum tradidero, sive ex venditionis causa, sive ex donationis, sive quavis alia ex causa, statim tua fit ea res si modo ego ejus dominus sim jure civili. § 21. In eadem causa sunt provincialia praedia, quorum alia stipendiaria, alia tributaria vocamus. Stipendiaria sunt ea, quae in iis provinciis sunt quae proprie populi Romani esse intelliguntur; tributaria sunt ea quae in iis provinciis sunt quae proprie Caesaris esse creduntur. § 22. Mancipi vero res sunt, quae per mancipationem ad alium transferuntur; unde etiam mancipi res sunt dictae. Quod autem valet [mancipatio, quae privatim fieri potest, idem valet et in jure cessio. § 23. Et] mancipatio quidem quemadmodum fiat, superiore commentario tradidimus. § 24. In jure cessio autem hoc modo fit. Apud magistratum populi Romani, velut praetorem, vel apud praesidem provinciae, is cui res in jure ceditur, rem tenens ita dicit: "Hunc ego hominem ex jure quiritium meum esse aio"; deinde, postquam hic vindicaverit, praetor interrogat eum qui cedit, an contra vindicet; quo negante aut tacente, tunc ei qui vindicaverit eam rem addicit. Idque legis actio vocatur, quae fieri potest etiam in provinciis apud praesides earum. § 25. Plerumque tamen et fere semper mancipationibus utimur: quod enim ipsi per nos praesentibus amicis agere possumus, hoc non interest neque est necesse cum majore difficultate apud praetorem aut apud praesidem provinciae quaerere. § 26. Quod si neque mancipata, neque in jure cessa sit res mancipi. . . . . . § 27. [In summa admonendi sumus nexum Italici soli proprium jus esse, provincialis soli nexum non esse: recipit enim nexus significationem solum non aliter quam si mancipi est, provinciale vero nec mancipi est]; enim vero provincia . . . . de mancipa . . . .

§ 28. Incorporales [res] traditionem non recipere manifestum est. § 29. Sed jura praediorum urbanorum in jure cedi possunt; rusticorum vero etiam mancipari possunt. § 30. Ususfructus in jure cessionem tantum recipit: nam dominus proprietatis alii usumfructum in jure cedere potest, ut ille usumfructum habeat, et ipse nudam proprietatem retineat. Ipse usufructuarius, in jure cedendo domino proprietatis usumfructum, efficit ut a se discedat et convertatur in proprietatem: alii vero in jure cedendo nihilominus jus suum retinet; creditur enim ea cessione nihil agi. § 31. Sed haec scilicet in Italicis praediis ita sunt, quia et ipsa praedia mancipationem et in jure cessionem recipiunt; alioquin in provincialibus praediis, sive quis usumfructum, sive jus eundi, agendi, aquamve ducendi, vel altius tollendi aedes, aut non tollendi, ne luminibus vicini officiatur, ceteraque similia jura constituere velit, pactionibus et stipulationibus id efficere potest: quia ne ipsa quidem praedia mancipationem aut in jure cessionem recipiunt. § 32. Sed cum ususfructus et hominum et ceterorum animalium constitui possit, intelligere debemus, horum usumfructum etiam in provinciis per in jure cessionem constitui posse. § 33. Quod autem diximus, usumfructum in jure cessionem tantum recipere, non est temere dictum, quasi etiam per mancipationem constitui possit eo, quod in mancipanda proprietate detrahi potest: non enim ipse ususfructus mancipatur, sed cum in mancipanda proprietate deducatur, eo fit ut apud alium ususfructus, apud alium proprietas sit. § 34. Hereditas quoque in jure cessionem tantum recipit. § 35. Nam si is, ad quem ab intestato, legitimo jure pertinet hereditas, in jure eam alii ante aditionem cedat, id est antequam heres extiterit, perinde fit heres is, cui in jure cesserit, ac si ipse per legem ad hereditatem vocatus esset: post obligationem vero si cesserit, nihilominus ipse heres permanet, et ob id a creditoribus tenebitur; debita vero pereunt, eoque modo debitores hereditarii lucrum faciunt; corpora vero ejus hereditatis perinde transeunt ad eum cui cessa est hereditas, ac si ei singula in jure cessa fuissent. § 36. Testamento autem scriptus heres, ante aditam quidem hereditatem, in jure cedendo eam alii nihil agit; postea vero quam adierit si cedat, eadem accidunt quae proxime diximus de eo ad quem ab intestato legitimo jure pertinet hereditas, si post obligationem in jure cedat. § 37. Idem et de necessariis heredibus diversae scholae auctores existimant, quod nihil videtur interesse utrum quis adeundo hereditatem fiat heres, an invitus statim existat; quod quale sit suo loco apparebit. Sed nostri praeceptores putant nihil agere necessarium heredem, cum in jure cedat hereditatem. § 38. Obligationes, quoquo modo contractae, nihil eorum [modorum] recipiunt. Nam quod mihi ab aliquo debetur, id si velim tibi deberi, nullo eorum modorum, quibus res corporales ad alium transferuntur, id efficere possum; sed opus est ut, jubente me, tu ab eo stipuleris: quae res efficit, ut a me liberetur et incipiat tibi teneri: quae dicitur novatio obligationis. § 39. Sine hac vero novatione non poteris tuo nomine agere; sed debes ex persona mea, quasi cognitor aut procurator meus, experiri.

§ 40. Sequitur ut admoneamus, apud peregrinos quidem unum esse dominium; nam aut dominus quisque est, aut dominus non intelligitur. Quo jure etiam populus Romanus olim utebatur; aut enim ex jure quiritium unusquisque dominus erat, aut non intelligebatur dominus; sed postea divisionem accepit dominium, ut alius possit esse ex jure quiritium dominus, alius in bonis habere. § 41. Nam si tibi rem mancipi neque mancipavero, neque in jure cessero, sed tantum tradidero, in bonis quidem tuis ea res efficitur, ex jure quiritium vero mea permanebit, donec tu eam possidendo usucapias: semel enim impleta usucapione, perinde pleno jure incipit, id est, et in bonis et ex jure quiritium tua res esse, ac si ea mancipata vel in jure cessa esset. § 42. Usucapio autem mobilium quidem rerum anno completur, fundi vero et aedium biennio; et ita lege xii tabularum cautum est.

§ 43. Caeterum ipsarum etiam earum rerum usucapio nobis competit, quae non a domino nobis traditae fuerint, sive mancipi sint eae res, sive nec mancipi, si modo eas bona fide acceperimus, cum crederemus, eum, qui tradiderit dominum esse. § 44. Quod ideo receptum videtur, ne rerum dominia diutius in incerto essent, cum sufficeret domino ad inquirendam rem suam anni aut biennii spatium, quod tempus ad usucapionem possessori tributum est.

§ 45. Sed aliquando, etiam si maxime quis bona fide alienam rem possideat, non

Tit. vi. De usucapionibus et longi temporis possessionibus.

Jure civili constitutum fuerat, ut qui bona fide ab eo qui dominus non erat, cum crediderit eum dominum esse, rem emerit, vel ex donatione aliave quavis justa causa acceperit: is eam rem, si mobilis erat, *anno* ubique, si immobilis, *biennio*, tantum in Italico solo, usucaperet, *ne rerum dominia in incerto essent.* Et cum hoc placitum erat, putantibus antiquioribus *dominis sufficere ad inquirendas res suas* praefata tempora; nobis melior sententia resedit, ne domini maturius suis rebus defraudentur, neque certo loco beneficium hoc concludatur, et ideo constitutionem super hoc promulgavimus, qua cautum est, ut res quidem mobiles per triennium usucapiantur, immobiles vero per longi temporis possessionem (id est, inter praesentes, decennio; inter absentes, viginti annis) usucapiantur, et his modis, non solum in Italia, sed etiam in omni terra quae nostro imperio gubernatur, dominia rerum justa causa possessionis praecedente acquirantur.

§ 1. *Sed aliquando etiam si maxime quis bona fide*

tamen illi usucapio procedit, velut si quis rem furtivam aut vi possessam possideat; nam furtivam lex xii tabularum usucapi prohibet, vi possessam lex Julia et Plautia. § 46. Item provincialia praedia usucapionem non recipiunt. § 47. [Item ante legem Claudiam si erant] res mulieris, quae in agnatorum tutela erat, res mancipi, usucapi non poterant, praeterquam si ab ipsa, tutore auctore, traditae essent; idque ita lege xii tabularum cautum erat. § 48. Item liberos homines et res sacras et religiosas usucapi non posse manifestum est.

rem possederit, non tamen illi usucapio ullo tempore *procedit, veluti si quis liberum hominem* vel *rem sacram, vel religiosam,* vel servum fugitivum *possideat.* § 2. *Furtivae* quoque *res,* et quae *vi possessae* sunt, nec si praedicto longo tempore bona fide possessae fuerint, usucapi possunt; *nam furtivarum rerum lex Duodecim Tabularum* et lex Atinia *inhibent usucapionem, vi possessarum, lex Julia et Plautia.*

§ 49. Quod ergo vulgo dicitur, furtivarum rerum et vi possessarum usucapionem per legem xii tabularum prohibitam esse, non eo pertinet, ut ne ipse fur, quive per vim possidet, usucapere possit (nam huic alia ratione usucapio non competit, quia scilicet mala fide possidet); sed nec ullus alius, quamquam ab eo bona fide emerit, usucapiendi jus habeat. § 50. Unde in rebus mobilibus non facile procedit, ut bonae fidei possessori usucapio competat, quia qui alienam rem vendidit et tradidit, furtum committit; idemque accidit, etiamsi ex alia causa tradatur. Sed tamen hoc aliquando aliter se habet: nam si heres rem defuncto commodatam aut locatam, vel apud eum depositam, existimans eam esse hereditariam, vendiderit aut donaverit, furtum non committit. Item si is ad quem ancillae ususfructus pertinet, partum etiam suum esse credens, vendiderit aut donaverit, furtum non committit; furtum enim sine affectu furandi non committitur. Aliis quoque modis accidere potest, ut quis, sine vitio

§ 3. *Quod autem dictum est, furtivarum et vi possessarum rerum usucapionem per leges prohibitam esse, non eo pertinet, ut ne ipse fur, quive per vim possidet, usucapere possit (nam his alia ratione usucapio non competit, quia scilicet mala fide possident), sed ne ullus alius, quamvis ab eis bona fide emerit,* vel ex alia causa acceperit, *usucapiendi jus habeat. Unde in rebus mobilibus non facile procedit, ut bonae fidei possessori usucapio competat. Nam qui sciens alienam rem vendidit, vel ex alia causa tradidit, furtum ejus committit.* § 4. *Sed tamen id aliquando aliter se habet: nam si heres rem defuncto commodatam, aut locatam, vel apud eum depositam existimans hereditariam esse,* bona fide accipienti *vendiderit, aut donaverit,* aut dotis nomine dederit, quin is qui acceperit usucapere possit dubium non est, quippe ea res in furti vitium non ceciderit, cum utique heres qui bona fide tamquam suam alienaverit, *furtum non committit.* § 5. *Item, si is ad quem ancillae ususfructus pertinet, partum suum esse credens, vendiderit, aut donaverit, furtum non committit: furtum enim sine affectu furandi non committitur.* § 6. *Aliis quoque modis accidere potest, ut quis sine vitio furti, rem alienam ad*

furti, rem alienam ad aliquem transferat et efficiat, ut a possessore usucapiatur. § 51. Fundi quoque alieni potest aliquis sine vi possessionem nancisci, quae vel ex negligentia domini vacet, vel quia dominus sine successore decesserit, vel longo tempore afuerit: nam si ad alium bona fide accipientem transtulerit, poterit usucapere possessor; et quamvis ipse, qui vacantem possessionem nactus est, intelligat alienum esse fundum, [tamen nihil hoc bonae fidei possessori] ad usucapionem nocet, cum improbata sit eorum sententia, qui putaverint, furtum fundi fieri posse.

aliquem transferat et efficiat, ut a possessore usucapiatur. § 7. Quod autem ad eas res quae solo continentur expeditius procedit, ut si *quis* loci vacantis *possessionem*, propter absentiam aut *negligentiam domini*, aut *quia sine successore decesserit, sine vi nanciscatur*, qui, quamvis ipse mala fide possidet (quia intelligit se alienum fundum occupasse), tamen si alii bona fide accipienti tradiderit, poterit ei longa possessione res adquiri, quia neque furtivum neque vi possessum acceperit. Abolita est enim quorundam veterum *sententia*, existimantium etiam *fundi* locive *furtum fieri.* Et eorum qui res soli possiderint, principalibus constitutionibus prospicitur, ne cui longa et indubitata possessio auferri debeat. § 8. Aliquando etiam furtiva vel vi possessa res usucapi potest, veluti si in domini potestatem reversa fuerit; tunc enim vitio rei purgato, procedit ejus usucapio. § 9. Res fisci nostri usucapi non potest, sed Papinianus scripsit, bonis vacantibus fisco nondum nuntiatis, bona fide emptorem sibi traditam rem ex his bonis usucapere posse; et ita divus Pius et divi Severus et Antoninus rescripserunt. § 10. Novissime sciendum est rem talem esse debere, ut in se non habeat vitium, ut a bona fide emptore usucapi possit, vel qui ex alia justa causa possidet.

§ 11. Error autem falsae causae usucapionem non parit; veluti si quis, cum non emerit, emisse se existimans, possideat, vel cum ei donatum non fuerit, quasi ex donatione possideat.

§ 52. Rursus ex contrario accidit ut, qui sciat alienam rem se possidere, usucapiat; veluti si rem hereditariam, cujus possessionem heres nondum nactus est, aliquis possederit; nam ei concessum est usucapere, si modo ea res est quae recipit usucapionem. Quae species possessionis et usucapionis pro herede vocatur. § 53. Et in tantum haec usucapio concessa est, ut et res, quae solo continentur, anno usucapiantur. § 54. Quare autem hoc casu etiam soli rerum annua constituta sit usucapio, illa ratio est, quod olim rerum hereditariarum possessione, [eae, sic]ut ipsae hereditates, usucapi credebantur, scilicet anno. Lex enim xii Tabularum soli quidem res biennio usucapi jussit, ceteras vero anno. Ergo hereditas in ceteris rebus videbatur esse, quia soli non est, quia neque corporalis est: et quamvis postea creditum sit ipsas hereditates usucapi non posse, tamen in omnibus rebus hereditariis, etiam quae solo teneantur, annua usucapio remansit. § 55. Quare autem omnino tam improba possessio et usucapio concessa sit, illa ratio est quod voluerunt veteres maturius hereditates adiri, ut essent qui sacra facerent, quorum illis temporibus summa observatio fuit, et ut creditores haberent, a quo suum consequerentur. § 56. Haec autem species possessionis et usucapionis etiam lucrativa vocatur; nam sciens quisque rem alienam lucrifacit. § 57. Sed hoc tempore etiam non est lucrativa, nam ex auctoritate . . . . . Hadriani senatus-consultum factum est, ut tales usucapiones revocarentur; et ideo potest heres ab eo, qui rem usucepit, hereditatem petendo, perinde eam rem consequi, atque si usucapta non esset. § 58. Et necessario tamen herede extante nihil, ipso jure, pro herede usucapi potest.

§ 59. Adhuc etiam ex aliis causis sciens quisque rem alienam usucapit; nam qui rem alicui fiduciae causa mancipio dederit, vel in jure cesserit, si eandem ipse possederit, potest usucapere, anno scilicet, etiam soli si sit: quae species usucapionis dicitur usureceptio, quia id quod aliquando habuimus, recipimus per usucapionem. § 60. Sed cum fiducia contrahitur, aut cum creditore pignoris jure, aut cum amico, quod tutius nostrae res apud eum essent, si quidem cum amico contracta sit fiducia, sane omnimodo competit usureceptio; si vero cum creditore, soluta quidem pecunia omnimodo competit, nondum vero soluta ita demum competit, si neque conduxerit eam rem a creditore debitor, neque precario rogaverit ut eam rem possidere sibi liceret. § 61. Item si rem obligatam sibi populus vendiderit, eamque dominus possederit, concessa est usureceptio; sed hoc casu praedium biennio usurecipitur. Et hoc est quod vulgo dicitur, ex praediatura possessionem usurecipi; nam qui mercatur a populo, praediator appellatur.

§ 12. Diutina possessio quae prodesse coeperat defuncto, et heredi et bonorum possessori continuatur, licet ipse sciat praedium alienum. Quod si ille initium justum non habuit, heredi et bonorum possessori, licet ignoranti, possessio non prodest. Quod nostra constitutio similiter et in usucapionibus observari constituit ut tempora continuentur. § 13. Inter venditorem quoque et emptorem conjungi tempora divi Severus et Antoninus rescripserunt.

§ 14. Edicto divi Marci, cavetur eum qui a fisco rem alienam emit, si post venditionem quinquennium praeteriérit, posse dominum rei per exceptionem repellere. Constitutio autem divae memoriae Zenonis bene prospexit iis qui a fisco per venditionem, vel donationem, vel alium titulum, aliquid accipiunt, ut ipsi quidem securi statim fiant, et victores existant, sive conveniantur, sive experiantur. Adversus sacratissimum autem aerarium usque ad quadriennium liceat intendere iis qui pro dominio vel hypotheca earum rerum, quae alienatae sunt, putaverint sibi quasdam competere actiones. Nostra autem divina constitutio, quam nuper promulgavimus, etiam de iis qui a nostra vel venerabilis Augustae domo aliquid acceperint, haec statuit quae in fiscalibus alienationibus praefata Zenoniana constitutione continentur.

Tit. vii. De donationibus.

Est et aliud genus acquisitionis, donatio. Donationum autem duo sunt genera: mortis causa, et non mortis causa. § 1. Mortis causa donatio est quae propter mortis fit suspicionem, cum quis ita donat, ut si quid humanitus ei contigisset, haberet is qui accepit, sin autem supervixisset, is qui donavit reciperet, vel si eum donationis poenituisset, aut prior decesserit is cui donatum sit. Hae mortis causa donationes ad exemplum legatorum redactae sunt per omnia: nam cum prudentibus ambiguum fuerat, utrum donationis an legati instar eam obtinere oporteret, et utriusque causae quaedam habebat insignia, et alii ad aliud genus eam retrahebant, a nobis constitutum est, ut per omnia fere legatis connumeretur, et sic procedat quemadmodum eam nostra formavit constitutio. Et in summa, mortis causa donatio est, cum magis se quis velit habere, quam eum cui donatur, magisque eum cui donat, quam heredem suum. Sic apud Homerum Telemachus donat Piraeo:

Πείραι', οὐ γάρ τ' ἴδμεν, ὅπως ἔσται τάδε ἔργα.
Εἴ κεν ἐμὲ μνηστῆρες ἀγήνορες ἐν μεγάροισι
Λάθρη κτείναντες, πατρώϊα πάντα δάσωνται,
Αὐτὸν ἔχοντά σε βούλομ' ἐπαυρέμεν, ἤ τινα τῶνδε.
Εἰ δέ κ' ἐγὼ τούτοισι φόνον καὶ κῆρα φυτεύσω,
Δὴ τότε μοι χαίροντι φέρειν πρὸς δώματα χαίρων.

§ 2. Aliae autem donationes sunt quae sine ulla mortis cogitatione fiunt, quas inter vivos appellamus, quae omnino non comparantur legatis; quae si fuerint perfectae, temere revocari non possunt. Perficiuntur autem cum donator suam voluntatem scriptis aut sine scriptis manifestaverit. Et ad exemplum venditionis, nostra constitutio eas etiam in se habere necessitatem traditionis voluit, ut etsi non tradantur, habeant plenissimum et perfectum robur, et traditionis necessitas incumbat donatori. Et cum retro principum dispositiones insinuari eas actis intervenientibus volebant, si majores ducentorum fuerant solidorum, nostra constitutio eam quantitatem usque ad quingentos solidos ampliavit, quam stare etiam sine insinuatione statuit; et quasdam donationes invenit, quae penitus insinuationem fieri minime desiderant, sed in se plenissimam habent firmitatem. Alia insuper multa ad uberiorem exitum donationum invenimus; quae omnia ex nostris constitutionibus quas super his exposuimus, colligenda sunt. Sciendum tamen est, quod etsi plenissimae sint donationes, tamen si ingrati existant homines in quos beneficium collatum est, donatoribus per nostram constitutionem licentiam praestitimus certis ex causis eas revocare: ne qui suas res in alios contulerunt, ab his quandam patiantur injuriam vel jacturam, secundum enumeratos in nostra constitutione modos.

§ 3. Est et aliud genus inter vivos donationum, quod veteribus quidem prudentibus penitus erat incognitum, postea autem a junioribus divis principibus introductum est; quod ante nuptias vocabatur, et tacitam in se conditionem habebat, ut tunc ratum esset, cum matrimonium esset insecutum. Ideoque ante nuptias appellabatur, quod ante matrimonium efficiebatur et nunquam post nuptias celebratas talis donatio procedebat. Sed primus quidem divus Justinus, pater noster, cum augeri dotem et post nuptias fuerat permissum, si quid tale evenerit, etiam ante nuptias donationem augeri, et constante matrimonio, sua constitutione permisit. Sed tamen nomen inconveniens remanebat, cum ante nuptias quidem vocabatur, post nuptias autem tale accipiebat incrementum. Sed nos, plenissimo fini tradere sanctiones cupientes et consequentia nomina rebus esse studentes, constituimus, ut tales donationes non augeantur tantum, sed et constante matrimonio initium accipiant, et non ante nuptias, sed propter nuptias vocentur, et dotibus in hoc exaequentur, ut quemadmodum dotes constante matrimonio non solum augentur, sed etiam fiunt; ita et istae donationes quae propter nuptias introductae sunt, non solum antecedant matrimonium, sed etiam eo contracto et augeantur et constituantur.

§ 4. Erat olim et alius modus civilis acquisitionis per jus accrescendi, quod est tale: si communem servum habens aliquis cum Titio, solus libertatem ei imposuit vel vindicta, vel testamento; eo casu pars ejus amittebatur, et socio accrescebat. Sed cum pessimum fuerat exemplo, et libertate servum defraudari, et ex ea humanioribus quidem dominis damnum inferri, saevarioribus autem lucrum accrescere; hoc quasi invidiae plenum pio remedio per nostram constitutionem mederi necessarium duximus; et invenimus viam per quam et manumissor, et socius ejus, et qui libertatem accepit, nostro fruantur beneficio, libertate cum effectu procedente (cujus favore et antiquos legislatores multa et contra communes regulas statuisse manifestissimum est), et eo qui eam imposuit suae liberalitatis stabilitate gaudente, et socio indemni conservato, pretiumque servi, secundum partem dominii, quod nos definivimus, accipiente.

Tit. viii. Quibus alienare licet vel non.

§ 62. Accidit aliquando, ut qui dominus sit, alienandae rei potestatem non habeat, et qui dominus non sit, alienare possit. § 63. Nam dotale praedium maritus, invita muliere, per legem Juliam prohibetur alienare, quamvis ipsius sit, vel mancipatum ei dotis causa, vel in jure cessum, vel usucaptum. Quod quidem jus utrum ad Italica tantum praedia, an etiam ad provincialia pertineat, dubitatur.

§ 64. Ex diverso agnatus furiosi curator rem furiosi alienare potest ex lege xii Tabularum: item procurator, [id est, cui libera administratio permissa est]; item creditor pignus ex pactione, quamvis ejus ea res non sit: sed hoc forsitan ideo videatur fieri, quod voluntate debitoris intelligitur pignus alienari, qui olim pactus est ut liceret

Accidit aliquando, ut qui dominus sit, alienare non possit; et contra, *qui dominus non sit, alienandae rei potestatem habeat. Nam dotale praedium maritus, invita muliere, per legem Juliam prohibetur alienare, quamvis ipsius sit, dotis causa ei datum.* Quod nos, legem Juliam corrigentes, in meliorem statum deduximus. Cum enim lex in soli tantummodo rebus locum habebat quae Italicae fuerant; et alienationes inhibebat quae invita muliere fiebant, hypothecas autem earum etiam volente; utrisque remedium imposuimus ut etiam in eas res quae in provinciali solo positae sunt, interdicta fiat alienatio vel obligatio, et neutrum eorum neque consentientibus mulieribus procedat, ne sexus muliebris fragilitas in perniciem substantiae earum converteretur.

§ 1. Contra autem, *creditor pignus ex pactione, quamvis ejus ea res non sit, alienare potest: sed hoc forsitan ideo videtur fieri, quod voluntate debitoris intelligitur pignus alienari, qui ab initio contractus pactus est, ut liceret creditori pignus vendere, si pecunia non solvatur.* Sed ne creditores jus suum persequi impedirentur, neque debitores temere suarum rerum dominium amittere videantur, nostra constitutione consultum est, et certus modus impositus est per quem

creditori pignus vendere, si pecunia non solvatur.

pignorum distractio possit procedere; cujus tenore utrique parti, creditorum et debitorum, satis abundeque provisum est.

De pupillis; an aliquid a se alienare possunt.

§ 80. Nunc admonendi sumus, neque feminam, neque pupillum sine tutoris auctoritate rem mancipi alienare posse; nec mancipi vero feminam quidem posse, pupillum non posse. § 81. Ideoque, si quando mulier mutuam pecuniam alicui sine tutoris auctoritate dederit, quia facit eam accipientis, cum scilicet certa pecunia res nec mancipi sit, contrahit obligationem. § 82. At si pupillus idem fecerit, quia [non facit accipientis sine tutoris auctoritate pecuniam,] nullam contrahit obligationem. Unde pupillus vindicare quidem nummos suos potest, sicubi extent, id est, [intendere suos ex jure quiritium esse; mala vero fide consumptos ab eo qui accepit] repetere potest, [quasi possideret. Unde] de pupillo quidem quaeritur, an nummos quos mutuos dedit, ab eo qui accepit [bona fide alienatos petere] possit, quoniam [is scilicet accipientis eos nummos facere videtur]. § 83. Sed ex contrario [res tam mancipi quam] nec mancipi mulieribus et pupillis sine tutoris auctoritate solvi possunt, quoniam meliorem conditionem suam facere iis etiam sine tutoris auctoritate concessum est. § 84. Itaque si debitor pecuniam pupillo solvat, facit quidem pecuniam pupilli, sed ipse non liberatur, quia nullam obligationem pupillus sine tutoris auctoritate dissolvere potest (quia nullius rei alienatio ei sine tutoris auctoritate concessa est). Sed tamen, si ex ea pecunia locupletior factus sit, et adhuc petat, per exceptionem doli mali summoveri

§ 2. *Nunc admonendi sumus, neque pupillum, neque* pupillam, ullam *rem sine tutoris auctoritate alienare posse. Ideoque si mutuam pecuniam alicui sine tutoris auctoritate dederit, non contrahit obligationem, quia pecuniam non facit accipientis; ideoque vindicare nummos possunt, sicubi extent.* Sed si nummi quos mutuo minor dederit, ab eo qui accepit bona fide consumpti sunt, condici possunt; si mala fide, ad exhibendum de his agi potest. At, ex contrario, omnes res pupillo et pupillae sine tutoris auctoritate recte dari possunt. Ideoque si debitor pupillo solvat, necessaria est tutoris auctoritas: alioquin non liberabitur. Sed etiam hoc evidentissima ratione statutum est in constitutione quam ad Caesarienses advocatos, ex suggestione Triboniani, viri eminentissimi, quaestoris sacri palatii nostri, promulgavimus: qua dispositum est, ita licere tutori vel curatori debitorem pupillarem solvere, ut prius sententia judicialis, sine omni damno celebrata, hoc permittat. Quo subsecuto, si et judex pronuntiaverit, et debitor solverit, sequatur hujusmodi solutionem plenissima securitas. Sin autem aliter quam disposuimus solutio facta fuerit, pecuniam autem salvam habeat pupillus, aut *ex ea locupletior sit, et adhuc* eandem summam *petat, per exceptionem doli mali summoveri poterit;* quodsi aut male consumpserit, aut furto amiserit, nihil proderit debitori doli mali exceptio, sed nihilominus damnabitur, quia te-

potest. § 85. Mulieri vero etiam sine tutoris auctoritate recte solvi potest; nam qui solvit, liberatur obligatione, quia res nec mancipi, ut proxime diximus, a se dimittere mulier etiam sine tutoris auctoritate potest: quamquam hoc ita est, si accipiat pecuniam; at si non accipiat, et habere se dicat, et per acceptilationem velit debitorem sine tutoris auctoritate liberare, non potest.

§ 86. Adquiritur autem nobis non solum per nosmetipsos, sed etiam per eos quos in potestate, manu, mancipiove habemus; item per eos servos in quibus usumfructum habemus; item per homines liberos et servos alienos quos bona fide possidemus: de quibus singulis diligenter dispiciamus.

mere, sine tutoris auctoritate, et non secundum nostram dispositionem solverit. Sed ex diverso, pupilli vel pupillae solvere sine tutore auctore non possunt, quia id quod solvunt non fit accipientis, cum scilicet *nullius rei alienatio* eis *sine tutoris auctoritate concessa est.*

Tit ix. Per quas personas nobis adquiritur.

Adquiritur nobis non solum per nosmetipsos, sed etiam per eos quos in potestate habemus; item per eos servos in quibus usumfructum habemus; item per homines liberos et servos alienos quos bona fide possidemus: de quibus singulis diligentius dispiciamus.

§ 1. *Igitur liberi nostri* utriusque sexus, *quos in potestate habemus*, olim quidem quidquid ad eos pervenerat, exceptis videlicet castrensibus peculiis, hoc parentibus suis adquirebant sine ulla distinctione. Et hoc ita parentum fiebat, ut esset eis licentia, quod per unum vel unam eorum adquisitum est, alii filio, vel extraneo donare vel vendere, vel quocumque modo voluerint, applicare. Quod nobis inhumanum visum est, et generali constitutione emissa et liberis pepercimus, et patribus debitum reservavimus. Sancitum etenim a nobis est, ut si quid ex re patris ei obveniat, hoc, secundum antiquam observationem, totum parenti adquirat (quae enim invidia est, quod ex patris occasione profectum est, hoc ad eum reverti?); quod autem ex alia causa sibi filiusfamilias adquisivit, hujus usumfructum quidem patri adquirat, dominium autem apud eum remaneat, ne quod ei ex suis laboribus, vel prospera fortuna accessit, hoc in alium perveniens, luctuosum ei procedat. § 2. Hoc quoque a nobis dispositum est et in ea specie, ubi parens emancipando liberum, ex rebus quae adquisitionem effugiunt, sibi partem tertiam retinere si voluerat, licentiam ex anterioribus constitutionibus habebat, quasi pro pretio quodammodo emancipationis, et inhumanum quiddam accidebat, ut filius rerum suarum ex hac emancipatione dominio pro parte defraudetur, et quod honoris ei ex emancipatione additum est, quod sui juris effectus est, hoc per rerum deminutionem decrescat. Ideoque statuimus, ut parens, pro tertia bonorum parte dominii quam retinere poterat, dimidiam, non dominii rerum, sed ususfructus, retineat: ita etenim et res intactae apud filium remanebunt, et pater ampliore summa fruetur, pro tertia dimidia potiturus.

§ 87. Igitur quod liberi nostri quos in potestate habemus, item quod servi nostri mancipio accipiunt, vel ex traditione nanciscuntur, sive quid stipulantur, vel ex aliaqualibet causa adquirant, id nobis adquiritur: ipse enim qui in potestate nostra est, nihil suum habere potest, et ideo si heres institutus sit, nisi nostro jussu, hereditatem adire non potest; et, si jubentibus nobis adierit, hereditatem nobis adquirit, perinde atque si nos ipsi heredes instituti essemus. Et convenienter scilicet etiam legatum per eos nobis adquiritur. § 88. Dum tamen sciamus, si alterius in bonis sit servus, alterius ex jure quiritium, ex omnibus causis ei solo per eum adquiri cujus in bonis est. § 89. Non solum autem proprietas, per eos quos in potestate habemus, adquiritur nobis, sed etiam possessio: cujus enim rei possessionem adepti fuerint, id nos possidere videmur; unde etiam per eos usucapio procedit.

§ 3. *Item vobis adquiritur quod servi vestri ex traditione nanciscuntur, sive quid stipulentur, vel ex qualibet alia causa adquirant:* hoc etenim vobis et ignorantibus et invitis obvenit. *Ipse enim servus qui in potestate alterius est, nihil suum habere potest, sed si heres institutus sit, non alias nisi jussu vestro hereditatem adire potest; et si jubentibus vobis adierit, vobis hereditas adquiritur, perinde ac si vos ipsi heredes instituti essetis: et convenienter scilicet legatum per eos vobis adquiritur. Non solum autem proprietas per eos quos in potestate habetis adquiritur vobis, sed etiam possessio: cujuscumque enim rei possessionem adepti fuerint, id vos possidere videmini; unde etiam per eos usucapio,* vel longi temporis possessio, *vobis accedit.*

§ 90. Per eas vero personas quas in manu mancipiove habemus, proprietas quidem adquiritur nobis ex omnibus causis, sicut per eos qui in potestate nostra sunt: an autem possessio adquiratur quaeri solet, quia ipsas non possidemus. § 91. De iis autem servis in quibus tantum usumfructum habemus, ita placuit, ut quidquid ex re nostra vel ex operis suis, adquirant, id nobis adquiratur; quod vero extra eas causas [persecuti sint], id ad dominum proprietatis pertineat: itaque si iste servus heres institutus sit, legatumve quod ei [aut] datum fuerit, non mihi, sed domino proprietatis adquiritur. § 92. Idem placet de eo qui a nobis bona fide possidetur, sive liber sit, sive alienus servus; quod enim placuit de usufruc-

§ 4. *De iis autem servis in quibus tantum usumfructum habetis, ita placuit, ut quidquid ex re vestra, vel ex operibus suis adquirant, id vobis adjiciatur; quod vero extra eas causas persecuti sint, id ad dominum proprietatis pertineat. Itaque si is servus heres institutus sit, legatumve quid ei, aut donatum fuerit,* non usufructuario, *sed domino proprietatis adquiritur. Idem placet et de eo qui a vobis bona fide possidetur, sive is liber sit, sive*

tuario, idem probatur etiam de bonae fidei possessore: itaque quod extra duas istas causas adquiritur, id vel ad ipsum pertinet, si liber est, vel ad dominum, si servus est. § 93. Sed sane bonae fidei possessor cum usuceperit servum, quia eo modo dominus fit, ex omni causa per eum sibi adquirere potest: usufructuarius vero usucapere non potest, primum quia non possidet, sed habet jus utendi et fruendi; deinde quia scit alienum servum esse. § 94. De illo quaeritur, an per eum servum in quo usumfructum habemus, possidere aliquam rem et usucapere possumus, quia ipsum non possidemus: per eum vero quem bona fide possidemus, sine dubio et possidere et usucapere possumus. Loquimur autem in utriusque persona secundum definitionem quam proxime exposuimus, id est, si quid ex re nostra vel ex operis suis adquirant, id nobis adquiritur. § 95. Ex his apparet, per liberos homines quos neque juri nostro subjectos habemus, neque bona fide possidemus, item per alienos servos in quibus neque usumfructum habemus, neque justam possessionem, nulla ex causa nobis adquiri posse. Et hoc est quod vulgo dicitur, per extraneam personam nobis adquiri non posse, tantum de possessione quaeritur, an per procuratorem nobis adquiratur.

alienus servus: quod enim placuit de usufructuario, idem placet et de bona fide possessore. Itaque quod extra duas istas causas adquiritur, id vel ad ipsum pertinet, si liber est, vel ad dominum, si servus est. Sed bonae fide possessor, cum usuceperit servum, quia eo modo dominus fit, ex omnibus causis per eum sibi adquirere potest: fructuarius vero usucapere non potest, primum, quia non possidet, sed habet jus utendi fruendi; deinde quia scit servum alienum esse. Non solum autem proprietas *per eos servos in quibus usumfructum habetis, vel quos bona fide possidetis,* vel per liberam personam quae bona fide vobis servit, adquiritur vobis, sed etiam possessio. *Loquimur autem in utriusque persona, secundum definitionem quam proxime exposuimus, id est, si* quam possessionem *ex re vestra, vel ex operis suis* adepti fuerint. § 5. *Ex his itaque apparet, per liberos homines, quos neque juri vestro subjectos habetis, neque bona fide possidetis; item per alienos servos, in quibus neque usumfructum habetis, neque justam possessionem, nulla ex causa vobis adquiri posse. Et hoc est quod dicitur, per extraneam personam nihil adquiri posse;* excepto eo, quod per liberam personam, veluti per procuratorem, placet non solum scientibus, sed etiam ignorantibus vobis adquiri possessionem, secundum divi Severi constitutionem, et per hanc possessionem etiam dominium, si dominus fuit qui tradidit, vel usucapionem, aut longi temporis praescriptionem, si dominus non sit.

§ 96. In summa sciendum est, iis qui in potestate, manu mancipiove sunt, nihil in jure cedi posse; cum enim istarum personarum nihil suum esse possit, conveniens est scilicet ut nihil per se in jure vindicare possint.

§ 97. [Hactenus] tantisper admonuisse sufficit, quemadmodum singulae res nobis adquirantur; nam legatorum

§ 6. *Hactenus tantisper admonuisse sufficit quemadmodum singulae res vobis adquirantur: nam legatorum jus, quo et ipso singulae res vobis adquiruntur* (item

jus, quo et ipso singulas res adquirimus, opportunius alio loco referemus. Videamus itaque nunc, quibus modis per universitatem res nobis adquirantur. § 98. Si cui [ergo] heredes facti sumus, sive cujus bonorum possessionem petierimus, sive cujus bona emerimus, sive quem adoptaverimus, sive quam in manum ut uxorem receperimus, ejus res ad nos transeunt.

§ 99. Ac prius de hereditatibus dispiciamus, quarum duplex conditio est : nam vel ex testamento, vel ab intestato ad nos pertinent.

§ 100. Et prius est, ut de his dispiciamus quae nobis ex testamento obveniunt.

fideicommissorum, ubi singulae res vobis relinquuntur). *opportunius* inferiore *loco referemus. Videamus itaque nunc, quibus modis per universitatem res adquiruntur. Si cui ergo heredes facti sitis, sive cujus bonorum possessionem petieritis*, vel *si quem* arrogaveritis, vel *si cujus bona* libertatum conservandarum causa vobis addicta fuerint, *ejus res* omnes *ad vos transeunt.*

Ac prius de hereditatibus dispiciamus, quarum duplex conditio est : nam vel ex testamento, vel ab intestato ad vos pertinent.

Et prius est, ut de his dispiciamus quae vobis ex testamento obveniunt : qua in re, necessarium est initium de ordinandis testamentis exponere.

§ 101. Testamentorum autem genera initio duo fuerunt. Nam aut calatis comitiis faciebant, quae comitia bis in anno testamentis faciendis destinata erant, aut in procinctu, id est, cum belli causa arma sumebant : procinctus est enim expeditus et armatus exercitus. Alterum itaque in pace et in otio faciebant, alterum in proelium exituri. § 102. Accessit deinde tertium genus testamenti, quod per aes et libram agitur. Qui neque calatis comitiis, neque in procinctu testamentum fecerat, is, si subito morte urguebatur, amico familiam suam, id est, patrimonium suum mancipio dabat, qui eum rogabat, quid, cuique post mortem suam dari vellet. Quod testamentum dicitur per aes et libram, scilicet quia per mancipationem peragitur. § 103. Sed illa quidem duo genera testamentorum in desuetudinem abierunt ; hoc vero solum, quod per aes et libram fit, in usu retentum est. Sed sane nunc aliter ordinatur, atque olim solebat : namque olim familiae emptor, id est,

Tit. x. De testamentis ordinandis.

Testamentum ex eo appellatur, quod testatio mentis est. § 1. Sed ut nihil antiquitatis penitus ignoretur, sciendum est olim quidem *duo genera testamentorum* in usu fuisse : quorum *altero in pace et in otio* utebantur, quod "*calatis comitiis*" appellabatur; *altero, cum in proelium exituri* essent, quod "*procinctum*" dicebatur. *Accessit deinde tertium genus testamentorum, quod dicebatur "per aes et libram", scilicet quia per mancipationem*, id est, imaginariam quandam venditionem agebatur, quinque testibus et libripende, civibus Romanis, puberibus, praesentibus, et eo qui familiae emptor dicebatur. *Sed illa quidem priora duo genera testamentorum* ex veteribus temporibus *in desuetudinem abierunt ; quod vero per aes et libram fiebat*, licet diutius permansit, attamen partim et hoc in usu esse desiit.

qui a testatore familiam accipiebat mancipio, heredis locum obtinebat, et ob id ei mandabat testator, quid cuique post mortem suam dari vellet; nunc vero alius heres testamento instituitur, a quo etiam legata relinquantur, alius dicis gratia, propter veteris juris imitationem, familiae emptor adhibetur.

§ 104. Eaque res ita agitur. Qui facit testamentum, adhibitis, sicut in ceteris mancipationibus, quinque testibus civibus Romanis puberibus et libripende, postquam tabulas testamenti scripserit, mancipat alicui dicis gratia familiam suam; in qua re his verbis familiae emptor utitur: "Familiam pecuniamque tuam endo mandatela tutela custodelaque mea esse aio, eaque, quo tu jure testamentum facere possis secundum legem publicam, hoc aere", et ut quidam adjiciunt "aeneaque libra, esto mihi empta". Deinde aere percutit libram, idque aes dat testatori, velut pretii loco. Deinde testator tabulas testamenti tenens ita dicit: "Haec ita uti in his tabulis cerisque scripta sunt, ita do, ita lego, ita testor, itaque vos, quirites, testimonium mihi perhibetote"; et hoc dicitur nuncupatio: nuncupare est enim palam nominare; et sane, quae testator specialiter in tabulis testamenti scripserit, ea videtur generali sermone nominare atque confirmare.

§ 2. Sed praedicta quidem nomina testamentorum ad jus civile referebantur; postea vero ex edicto praetoris alia forma faciendorum testamentorum introducta est: jure enim honorario nulla mancipatio desiderabatur, sed septem testium signa sufficiebant, cum jure civili signa testium non erant necessaria. § 3. Sed cum paulatim, tam ex usu hominum quam ex constitutionum emendationibus, coepit in unam consonantiam jus civile et praetorium jungi, constitutum est, ut uno eodemque tempore (quod jus civile quodammodo exigebat), septem testibus adhibitis, et subscriptione testium (quod ex constitutionibus inventum est), et (ex edicto praetoris) signacula testamentis imponerentur: ut hoc jus tripertitum esse videatur, ut testes quidem et eorum praesentia uno contextu, testamenti celebrandi gratia, a jure civili descendant, subscriptiones autem testatoris et testium, ex sacrarum constitutionum observatione adhibeantur, signacula autem et testium numerus ex edicto praetoris. § 4. Sed his omnibus ex nostra constitutione, propter testamentorum sinceritatem, ut nulla fraus adhibeatur, hoc additum est, ut per manum testatoris vel testium nomen heredis exprimatur, et omnia secundum illius constitutionis tenorem procedant.

§ 5. Possunt autem testes omnes et uno annulo signare testamentum. Quid enim si septem annuli una sculptura fuerint, secundum quod Papiniano visum est? Sed et alieno quoque annulo licet signare testamentum. § 6. Testes autem adhiberi possunt ii cum quibus testamenti factio est. Sed neque mulier, neque impubes, neque servus, neque mutus, neque surdus, neque furiosus, nec cui bonis interdictum est, nec is quem leges jubent improbum intestabilemque esse, possunt in numero testium adhiberi. § 7. Sed cum aliquis ex testibus testamenti quidem faciendi tempore liber existimabatur, postea vero servus apparuit, tam divus Hadrianus, Catonio Vero (quam postea divi Severus et Antoninus, rescripserunt), "subvenire se ex sua liberalitate testamento, ut sic habeatur, atque si, ut oportet, factum esset; cum eo tempore quo testamentum signaretur, omnium consensu hic testis liberorum loco fuerit, nec quisquam esset qui ei status quaestionem moveat". § 8. Pater, nec non is qui in potestate ejus est, item duo fratres qui in ejusdem patris potestate sunt, utrique testes in uno testamento fieri possunt; quia nihil nocet ex una domo plures testes alieno negotio adhiberi. § 9 *In testibus autem non debet esse qui in potestate testatoris est. Sed si filiusfamilias de castrensi peculio post missionem faciat testamentum, nec pater ejus recte testis adhibetur, nec is qui in potestate ejusdem patris est; reprobatum est enim in ea re domesticum testimonium.* § 10. Sed neque heres scriptus, neque is qui in potestate ejus est, neque pater ejus qui habet eum in potestate, neque fratres qui in ejusdem patris potestate sunt, testes adhiberi possunt: *quia totum hoc negotium quod agitur testamenti ordinandi gratia, creditur* hodie *inter* heredem *et testatorem agi.* Licet enim totum jus tale conturbatum fuerat, et veteres qui familiae emptorem et eos qui per potestatem ei coadunati fuerant, testamentariis testimoniis repellebant, heredi et iis qui conjuncti ei per potestatem fuerant, concedebant testimonia in testamentis praestare; licet ii qui id permittebant, *hoc jure minime abuti debere eos* suadebant, tamen nos, eandem observationem corrigentes, et quod ab illis suasum est in legis necessitatem transferentes, ad imitationem pristini familiae emptoris,

§ 105. In testibus autem non debet is esse, qui in potestate est aut familiae emptoris aut ipsius testatoris, propter veteris juris imitationem; quia totum hoc negotium, quod agitur testamenti ordinandi gratia, creditur inter familiae emptorem agi et testatorem: quippe olim, ut proxime diximus, is qui familiam testatoris mancipio accipiebat, heredis loco erat; itaque reprobatum est in ea re domesticum testimonium. § 106. Unde etiam si is qui in potestate patris est, familiae emptor adhibitus sit, pater ejus testis esse non potest; at ne is quidem qui in eadem potestate est, velut frater ejus. Sed si filiusfamilias ex castrensi peculio post missionem faciat testamentum, nec pater ejus recte testis adhibetur, nec is qui in potestate patris sit. § 107. De libripende eadem quae et de testibus dicta esse intelligemus ; nam et is testium numero est. § 108. Is vero qui in potestate heredis aut legatarii est, cujusve heres ipse aut legatarius in potestate est, quique in ejusdem potestate est, adeo testis et libripens adhiberi potest, ut ipse quoque heres aut legatarius jure adhibeatur. Sed tamen, quod ad heredem pertinet, quique in ejus potestate est, cujusve is in potestate erit, minime hoc jure uti debemus.

merito nec heredi qui imaginem vetustissimi familiae emptoris obtinet, nec aliis personis quae ei, ut dictum est, conjunctae sunt, licentiam concedimus sibi quodammodo testimonia praestare: ideoque nec ejusmodi veteres constitutiones nostro codici inseri permisimus. § 11. Legatariis autem et fideicommissariis, quia non juris successores sunt, et aliis personis eis conjunctis testimonium non denegamus : imo in quadam nostra constitutione et hoc specialiter concessimus, et multo magis iis qui in eorum potestate sunt, vel qui eos habent in potestate, hujusmodi licentiam damus.

§ 12. Nihil autem interest, testamentum in tabulis, an in chartis membranisve, vel in alia materia fiat. § 13. Sed et unum testamentum pluribus codicibus conficere quis potest, secundum obtinentem tamen observationem omnibus factis : quod interdum et necessarium est ; veluti si quis navigaturus et secum ferre et domi relinquere judiciorum suorum contestationem velit ; vel propter alias innumerabiles causas, quae humanis necessitatibus imminent. § 14. Sed haec quidem de testamentis quae in scriptis conficiuntur. Si quis autem voluerit sine scriptis ordinare jure civili testamentum, septem testibus adhibitis, et sua voluntate coram eis nuncupata, fiet hoc perfectissimum testamentum jure civili, firmumque constitutum.

De Testamentis militum.

§ 109. Sed haec diligens observatio in ordinandis testamentis militibus, propter nimiam imperitiam, constitutionibus principum remissa est; nam quamvis neque legitimum numerum testium adhibuerint, neque vendiderint familiam, neque nuncupaverint testamentum, recte nihilominus testantur. § 110. Praeterea permissum est iis et peregrinos et Latinos instituere heredes, vel iis legare ; cum alioquin peregrini quidem ratione civili prohibeantur capere hereditatem legataque, Latini vero per legem Juniam.

Tit. xi. De militari testamento.

Supradicta *diligens observatio in ordinandis testamentis militibus, propter nimiam imperitiam, constitutionibus principalibus remissa est; nam, quamvis ii neque legitimum numerum testium adhibuerint, neque* aliam testamentorum solemnitatem observaverint, *recte nihilominus testantur*, videlicet, cum in expeditionibus occupati sunt : quod merito nostra constitutio introduxit. Quoquo enim modo voluntas ejus suprema, sive scripta inveniatur sive sine scriptura, valet testamentum ex voluntate ejus. Illis autem temporibus, per quae citra expeditionum necessitatem in aliis locis vel in suis aedibus degunt, minime ad vindicandum tale

§ 111. Coelibes quoque, qui lege Julia hereditatem legataque capere vetantur, item orbi, id est, qui liberos non habent, quos lex [Papia plus quam semissem capere prohibet]. . . .

privilegium adjuvantur, sed testari quidem, etsi filiifamilias sunt, propter militiam conceduntur, jure tamen communi, eadem observatione et in eorum testamentis adhibenda, quam et in testamentis paganorum proxime exposuimus. § 1. Plane de militum testamentis divus Trajanus Statilio Severo ita rescripsit: "id privilegium quod militantibus datum est, ut quoquo modo facta ab iis testamenta rata sint, sic intelligi debet, ut utique prius constare debeat testamentum factum esse, quod et sine scriptura a non militantibus quoque fieri potest. Is ergo miles de cujus bonis apud te quaeritur, si convocatis ad hoc hominibus ut voluntatem suam testaretur, ita locutus est, ut declararet quem vellet sibi esse heredem et cui libertatem tribuere, potest videri sine scripto hoc modo esse testatus, et voluntas ejus rata habenda est. Ceterum, si (ut plerumque sermonibus fieri solet), dixit alicui:" ego te heredem facio, aut tibi bona mea relinquo, " non oportet hoc pro testamento observari. Nec ullorum magis interest, quam ipsorum quibus id privilegium datum est, ejusmodi exemplum non admitti. Alioquin non difficulter post mortem alicujus militis testes existerent, qui affirmarent se audisse dicentem aliquem relinquere se bona cui visum sit, et per hoc judicia vera subverterentur." § 2. Quinimo et mutus et surdus miles testamentum facere potest. § 3. Sed hactenus hoc illis a principalibus constitutionibus conceditur, quatenus militant et in castris degunt; post missionem vero veterani, vel extra castra si faciant adhuc militantes testamentum, communi omnium civium Romanorum jure facere debent. Et quod in castris fecerint testamentum, non communi jure, sed quomodo voluerint, post missionem intra annum tantum valebit. Quid ergo si intra annum quidem decesserit, conditio autem heredi adscripta post annum extiterit? an quasi militis testamentum valeat? et placet valere quasi militis. § 4. Sed et si quis ante militiam non jure fecit testamentum, et miles factus, et in expeditione degens, resignavit illud, et quaedam adjecit sive detraxit, vel alias manifesta est militis voluntas hoc valere volentis, dicendum est valere testamentum quasi ex nova militis voluntate. § 5. Denique et si in adrogationem datus fuerit miles, vel filiusfamilias emancipatus sit, testamentum ejus quasi militis ex nova voluntate valet, nec videtur capitis deminutione irritum fieri.

§ 6. Sciendum tamen est, quod ad exemplum castrensis peculii, tam anteriores leges quam principales constitutiones quibusdam quasi castrensia dederunt peculia, et quorum quibusdam permissum erat etiam in potestate degentibus testari: quod nostra constitutio, latius extendens, permisit omnibus in his tantummodo peculiis testari quidem, sed jure communi. Cujus constitutionis tenore perspecto licentia est nihil eorum quae ad praefatum jus pertinent, ignorare.

Tit. xii. Quibus non est permissum testamenta facere.

Non tamen omnibus licet facere testamentum. Statim enim ii qui alieno juri subjecti sunt, testamentum faciendi jus non habent, adeo quidem, ut quamvis parentes eis permiserint, nihilo magis jure testari possunt: exceptis iis quos antea enumeravimus, et praecipue militibus qui in potestate parentum sunt, quibus de eo quod in castris acquisierint, permissum est ex constitutionibus principum testamentum facere. Quod quidem jus, initio, tantum militantibus datum est, tam ex auctoritate divi Augusti, quam Nervae, necnon optimi Imperatoris Trajani; postea vero subscriptione divi Hadriani et etiam dimissis militia, id est veteranis, concessum est. Itaque si quod fecerint de castrensi peculio testamentum, pertinebit hoc ad eum quem heredem reliquerint. Si vero intestati decesserint, nullis liberis vel fratribus superstitibus, ad parentes eorum jure communi pertinebit. Ex hoc intelligere possumus, quod in castris adquisierit miles qui in potestate patris est, neque ipsum patrem adimere posse, neque patris creditores id vendere vel aliter inquietare, neque patre mortuo cum fratribus commune esse, sed scilicet proprium ejus esse id quod in castris adquisierit, quamquam jure civili omnium qui in potestate parentum sunt peculia, perinde in bonis parentum computantur, ac si servorum peculia in bonis dominorum numerantur. Exceptis videlicet iis quae ex sacris constitutionibus, et praecipue nostris, propter diversas causas non adquiruntur. Praeter hos igitur qui castrense peculium vel quasi castrense habent, si quis alius filiusfamilias testamentum fecerit, inutile est, licet suae potestatis factus decesserit.

§ 112. [Sed senatus divo Hadriano auctore, ut supra quoque significavimus, puberibus feminis] etiam sine coemptione testamentum facere permisit, si modo non minores es-

§ 1. Praeterea testamentum facere non possunt impuberes, quia nullum eorum animi judicium est; item furiosi, quia mente carent. Nec ad rem pertinet, si impubes postea pubes, aut furiosus postea compos mentis factus fuerit et decesserit. Furiosi autem, si per id tempus fecerint testamentum

sent annorum XII tutore auctore, scilicet ut quae tutela liberatae non essent, ita testari deberent. § 113. Videntur ergo melioris conditionis esse feminae, quam masculi: nam masculus minor annorum XIV testamentum facere non potest, etiamsi tutore auctore testamentum facere velit; femina vero post XII annum testamenti faciundi jus nanciscitur.

quo furor eorum intermissus est, jure testati esse videntur; certe eo quod ante furorem fecerint testamento valente: nam neque testamenta recte facta, neque aliud ullum negotium recte gestum, postea furor interveniens perimit. § 2. Item prodigus, cui bonorum suorum administratio interdicta est, testamentum facere non potest; sed id quod ante fecerit quam interdictio ei bonorum fiat, ratum est. § 3. Item mutus et surdus non semper testamentum facere possunt. Utique autem de eo surdo loquimur qui omnino non exaudit, non de eo qui tarde exaudit; nam et mutus is intelligitur qui eloqui nihil potest, non qui tarde loquitur. Saepe enim literati et eruditi homines variis casibus et audiendi et loquendi facultatem amittunt: unde nostra constitutio etiam his subvenit, ut, certis casibus et modis secundum normam ejus, possint testari, aliaque facere quae eis permissa sunt. Sed si quis post testamentum factum, adversa valetudine aut quolibet alio casu mutus aut surdus esse coeperit, ratum nihilominus ejus permanet testamentum. § 4. Caecus autem non potest facere testamentum, nisi per observationem quam lex divi Justini, patris nostri, introduxit. § 5. Ejus qui apud hostes est, testamentum quod ibi fecit non valet, quamvis redierit: sed quod, dum in civitate fuerat, fecit, sive redierit, valet jure postliminii, sive illic decesserit, valet ex lege Cornelia.

§ 114. Igitur si quaeramus an valeat testamentum, inprimis advertere debemus an is qui id fecerit, habuerit testamenti factionem; deinde si habuerit, requiremus, an secundum juris civilis regulam testatus sit; exceptis militibus, quibus propter nimiam imperitiam, ut diximus, quomodo velint, vel quomodo possint, permittitur testamenta facere.

Tit. xiii. De exheredatione liberorum.

§ 115. Non tamen, ut jure civili valeat testamentum, sufficit ea observatio quam supra exposuimus, de familiae venditione et de testibus et de nuncupationibus. § 116. Ante omnia requirendum est, an institutio heredis sollemni more facta sit; nam aliter facta institutione nihil proficit familiam testatoris ita venire, testesve ita adhibere, aut nuncupare testamentum, ut supra diximus. § 117. Sollemnis autem institutio haec est: "Titius heres

Non tamen, ut omnimodo *valeat testamentum, sufficit haec observatio quam supra exposuimus.*

esto". Sed et illa jam comprobata videtur: "Titium heredem esse jubeo". At illa non est comprobata: "Titium heredem esse volo". Set et illae a plerisque improbatae sunt: "Titium heredem instituo", item "Heredem facio".

§ 118. Observandum praeterea est, ut, si mulier, quae in tutela sit, faciat testamentum, tutoris auctoritate facere debeat: alioquin inutiliter jure civili testabitur. § 119. Praetor tamen, si septem signis testium signatum sit testamentum, scriptis heredibus secundum tabulas testamenti [bonorum possessionem] pollicetur; et si nemo sit ad quem ab intestato jure legitimo pertineat hereditas, velut frater eodem patre natus, aut patruus, aut fratris filius, ita poterunt scripti heredes retinere hereditatem. Nam idem juris est, et si alia ex [causa] testamentum non valeat, velut quod familia non venierit, aut nuncupationis verba testator locutus non sit. § 120. Sed videamus an, etiamsi frater aut patruus extent, potiores scriptis heredibus habeantur; rescripto enim imperatoris Antonini significatur, eos qui secundum tabulas testamenti non jure factas bonorum possessionem petierint, posse, adversus eos qui ab intestato vindicant hereditatem, defendere se per exceptionem doli mali. § 121. Quod sane quidem ad masculorum testamenta pertinere certum est, item ad feminarum, quae ideo non utiliter testatae sint, quod verbi gratia familiam non vendiderint, aut nuncupationis verba locutae non sint: an autem et ad ea testamenta feminarum, quae sine tutoris auctoritate fecerint, haec constitutio pertineat, videbimus. § 122. Loquimur autem de his scilicet feminis quae non in legitima parentium aut patronorum tutela sunt, sed de his quae alterius generis tutores habent, qui etiam inviti coguntur auctores fieri: alioquin parentem et patronum sine auctoritate ejus facto testamento, non summoveri palam est.

§ 123. Item, qui filium in potestate habet, curare debet, ut eum vel heredem instituat, vel nominatim exheredet; alioquin, si eum silentio praeterierit, inutiliter testabitur: adeo quidem, ut nostri praeceptores existiment, etiam si vivo patre filius defunctus sit, neminem heredem ex eo testamento existere posse, scilicet quia statim ab initio non constiterit institutio. Sed diversae scholae auctores, si quidem filius mortis patris tempore vivat, sane impedimento eum esse scriptis heredibus, et illum ab intestato heredem fieri confitentur: si vero ante mortem patris inter-

Sed qui filium in potestate habet, curare debet, ut eum heredem instituat, vel exheredem nominatim faciat; alioquin, si eum silentio praeterierit, inutiliter testabitur: adeo quidem, ut etsi vivo patre filius mortuus sit, nemo ex eo testamento heres existere possit, quia scilicet ab initio non constiterit tes-

ceptus sit, posse ex testamento hereditatem adiri putant, nullo jam filio impedimento; quia scilicet existimant [non] statim ab initio inutiliter fieri testamentum filio praeterito. § 124. Ceteras vero liberorum personas si praeterierit testator, valet testamentum, sed praeteritae istae personae heredibus in partem adcrescunt: si sui heredes sint, in virilem; si extranei, in dimidiam: id est, si quis tres verbi gratia filios heredes instituerit, et filiam praeterierit, filia adcrescendo pro quarta parte fit heres, et ea ratione id consequitur quod ab intestato patre mortuo habitura esset; at si extraneos ille heredes instituerit, et filiam praeterierit, filia adcrescendo ex dimidia parte fit heres. Quae de filia diximus, eadem et de nepote deque omnibus liberorum personis, seu masculini seu feminini sexus, dicta intelligimus. § 125. Quid ergo est? licet hae, secundum ea quae diximus, scriptis dimidiam partem modo heredibus detrahant, tamen praetor iis contra tabulas bonorum possessionem promittit, qua ratione extranei heredes a tota hereditate repelluntur, et efficiuntur sine re heredes; et hoc jure utebamur, quasi nihil inter feminas et masculos interesset. § 126. Sed nuper imperator Antoninus significavit rescripto suo, non plus nancisci feminas per bonorum possessionem, quam quod jure adcrescendi consequerentur. Quod in emancipatis [feminis similiter obtinet, scilicet ut quod] adcrescendi jure habiturae essent, si in potestate fuissent, id ipsum etiam per bonorum possessionem habeant. § 127. Sed si quidem filius a patre exheredetur, nominatim exheredari debet, alioquin non prodest eum exheredari. Nominatim autem exheredari videtur, sive ita exheredetur: "Titius filius meus exheres esto", sive ita: "Filius meus exheres esto", non adjecto proprio nomine. § 128. Caeterae vero liberorum personae vel feminini sexus vel masculini satis recte inter caeteros exheredantur, id est, •his verbis: "Caeteri omnes exheredes sunto". Quae verba semper post institutionem heredum adjici solent. Sed hoc ita est jure civili. § 129. Nam praetor omnes virilis sexus, liberorum personas, id est, nepotes quoque et pronepotes, [nominatim exheredari jubet, feminini vero inter caeteros: qui nisi fuerint ita exheredati, promittit iis contra tabulas bonorum possessionem.]

tamentum. Sed non ita de filiabus, vel aliis per virilem sexum descendentibus liberis utriusque sexus fuerat antiquitati observatum: sed si non fuerant heredes scripti scriptaeve, vel exheredati exheredataeve, testamentum quidem non infirmabatur, jus autem accrescendi eis ad certam portionem praestabatur. Sed nec nominatim eas personas exheredare parentibus necesse erat, sed licebat et inter ceteros hoc facere.

Nominatim autem quis exheredari videtur, sive ita exheredetur: "Titius filius meus exheres esto", sive ita: "Filius meus exheres esto", non adjecto proprio nomine, scilicet si alius filius non extet.

§ 130. Postumi quoque liberi vel heredes institui debent vel exheredari. § 131. Et in eo par omnium conditio [est, quod et in filio postumo et in quolibet ex caeteris liberis, sive feminini sexus, sive masculini, praeterito, valet quidem testamentum, sed postea agnatione postumi sive postumae rumpitur, et ea ratione totum infirmatur: ideoque si mulier ex qua postumus aut postuma sperabatur, abortum fecerit, nihil impedimento est scriptis heredibus ad hereditatem adeundam. § 132. Sed feminini quidem sexus personae vel nominatim vel inter caeteros exheredari solebant, dum tamen, si inter caeteros exheredentur, aliquid eis legetur, ne videantur per oblivionem praeteritae esse: masculos vero postumos, id est, filium et deinceps, placuit non aliter recte exheredari, nisi nominatim exheredentur, hoc scilicet modo: "Quicumque mihi filius genitus fuerit, exheres esto". § 133. Postumorum loco sunt et hi qui, in sui heredis locum succedendo, quasi agnascendo fiunt parentibus sui heredes, ut ecce: si filium et ex eo nepotem neptemve in potestate habeam, quia filius gradu praecedit, is solus jura sui heredis habet, quamvis nepos quoque et neptis ex eo in eadem potestate sint; sed si filius meus me vivo moriatur, aut qualibet ratione exeat de potestate mea, incipit nepos neptisve in ejus locum succedere, et eo modo jura suorum heredum quasi agnatione nanciscuntur.] § 134. Ne ergo eo modo rumpatur mihi [testamentum, sicut ipsum filium vel heredem instituere vel exheredare nominatim debeo, ne non jure faciam testamentum, ita et nepotem neptemve ex eo necesse est mihi vel heredem instituere vel exheredare, ne forte, me vivo filio mortuo,

§ 1. *Postumi quoque liberi vel heredes institui debent, vel exheredari. Et in eo par omnium conditio est, quod et in filio postumo, et in quolibet ex caeteris liberis, sive feminini sexus sive masculini, praeterito, valet quidem testamentum, sed postea agnatione postumi sive postumae rumpitur, et ea ratione totum infirmatur: ideoque si mulier, ex qua postumus aut postuma sperabatur, abortum fecerit, nihil impedimento est scriptis heredibus ad hereditatem adeundam. Sed feminini quidem sexus personae vel nominatim, vel inter caeteros exheredari solebant: dum tamen si inter caeteros exheredentur, aliquid eis legetur, ne videantur per oblivionem praeteritae esse. Masculos vero postumos, id est filium et deinceps, placuit non aliter recte exheredari, nisi nominatim exheredentur, hoc scilicet modo: "Quicumque mihi filius genitus fuerit, exheres esto".* § 2. *Postumorum autem loco sunt et hi qui, in sui heredis locum succedendo, quasi agnascendo fiunt parentibus sui heredes. Ut ecce: si quis filium et ex eo nepotem neptemve in potestate habeat, quia filius gradu praecedit, is solus jura sui heredis habet, quamvis nepos quoque et neptis ex eo in eadem potestate sint. Sed si filius ejus vivo eo moriatur, aut qualibet alia ratione exeat de potestate ejus, incipit nepos neptisve in ejus locum succedere, et eo modo jura suorum heredum quasi agnatione nanciscuntur. Ne ergo eo modo rumpatur* ejus *testamentum, sicut ipsum filium vel heredem instituere vel nominatim exheredare debet testator, ne non jure faciat testamentum, ita et nepotem neptemve ex filio necesse est ei vel heredem instituere vel exheredare, ne forte, vivo eo filio mortuo, succedendo in* succedendo in locum ejus nepos neptisve] quasi agnatione rumpat testamentum: idque lege Junia Velleia provisum est; in qua similis [postumorum] exheredationis modus notatur: ut virilis sexus nominatim, feminini vel nominatim vel inter caeteros exheredentur, dum tamen iis qui inter caeteros exheredantur, aliquid legetur.

§ 135. Mancipatos liberos jure civili neque heredes instituere, neque exheredare necesse est, quia non sunt sui heredes. Sed praetor omnes, tam feminini quam masculini sexus, si heredes non instituantur, exheredari jubet, virilis sexus nominatim, feminini vel nominatim vel inter "caeteros". Quod si neque heredes instituti fuerint, neque ita, ut supra diximus, exheredati, praetor promittit eis contra tabulas bonorum possessionem.

locum ejus nepos neptisve quasi agnatione rumpant testamentum. Idque lege Junia Velleia provisum est, in qua simul exheredationis modus ad similitudinem postumorum demonstratur.

3. *Emancipatos liberos jure civile neque heredes instituere, neque exheredare necesse est, quia non sunt sui heredes. Sed praetor omnes, tam feminini sexus quam masculini, si heredes non instituantur, exheredari jubet, virilis sexus nominatim, feminini vero et inter "caeteros". Quod si neque heredes instituti fuerint, neque ita, ut diximus, exheredati, promittit eis praetor contra tabulas testamenti bonorum possessionem.*

§ 135A. In potestate patris non sunt, cum eo civitate Romana donati sint, [si] nec in accipienda civitate Romana pater [petierit] statim a principe ut eos in potestate haberet, aut si cum petierit, non impetraverit; nam qui in potestatem patris ab imperatore rediguntur, nihil differunt ab heredibus suis.

§ 136. Adoptivi filii, quamdiu manent in adoptionem, naturalium loco sunt: emancipati vero a patre adoptivo neque jure civili, neque quod ad edictum praetoris pertinet, inter liberos numerantur. § 137. Qua ratione accidit, ut ex diverso, quod ad naturalem parentem pertinet, quamdiu quidem sint in adoptiva familia, extraneorum numero habeantur; si vero emancipati fuerint ab adoptivo patre, tunc incipiant in ea causa esse, qua futuri essent, si ab ipso naturali patre [emancipati] fuissent.

§ 4. *Adoptivi liberi, quamdiu* sunt in potestate patris adoptivi, ejusdem juris habentur cujus sunt justis nuptiis quaesiti: itaque heredes instituendi vel exheredandi sunt, secundum ea quae de naturalibus exposuimus. *Emancipati vero a patre adoptivo, neque jure civili, neque quod ad edictum praetoris attinet, inter liberos numerantur. Qua ratione accidit, ut ex diverso, quod ad naturalem parentem attinet, quamdiu quidem sint in adoptiva familia, extraneorum numero habeantur,* ut eos neque heredes instituere, neque exheredare necesse sit. *Cum vero emancipati fuerint ab adoptivo patre, tunc incipiunt in ea causa esse in qua futuri essent, si ab ipso naturali patre emancipati fuissent.*

§ 5. Sed haec quidem vetustas introducebat. Nostra vero constitutio nihil inter masculos et feminas in hoc jure interesse existimans, quia utraque persona in hominum procreatione similiter naturae officio fungitur, et lege antiqua Duodecim Tabularum omnes similiter ad successionem ab intestato vocabantur, quod et praetores postea secuti esse videntur, ideo simplex ac simile jus et in filiis et in filiabus et in ceteris descendentium per virilem sexum personis, non solum jam natis, sed etiam postumis, introduxit: ut omnes, sive sui, sive emancipati sint, aut heredes instituantur, aut nominatim exheredentur, et eundem habeant effectum circa testamenta parentum suorum infirmanda et hereditatem auferendam, quem filii sui vel emancipati habent, sive jam nati sint, sive adhuc in utero constituti postea nati sint. Circa adoptivos autem filios certam induximus divisionem quae in nostra constitutione, quam super adoptivis tulimus, continetur. § 6. Sed si in expeditione occupatus miles testamentum faciat, et liberos suos jam natos vel postumos nominatim non exheredaverit, sed silentio praeterierit, non ignorans an habeat liberos, silentium ejus pro exheredatione nominatim facta valere constitutionibus principum cautum est. § 7. Mater vel avus maternus necesse non habent liberos suos aut heredes instituere aut exheredare, sed possunt eos omittere. Nam silentium matris aut avi materni, ceterorumque per matrem ascendentium, tantum facit, quantum exheredatio patris. Neque enim matri filium, filiamve, neque avo materno nepotem neptemve ex filia, si eum eamve heredem non instituat, exheredare necesse est, sive de jure civili quaeramus, sive de edicto praetoris quo praeteritis liberis contra tabulas bonorum possessionem promittit. Sed aliud eis adminiculum servatur, quod paulo post vobis manifestum fiet.

§ 185. Sicut autem liberi homines, ita et servi, tam nostri quam alieni, heredes scribi possunt. § 186. Sed noster servus simul et liber et heres esse juberi debet, id est, hoc modo: "Stichus servus meus liber heresque esto", vel "Heres liberque esto". § 187. Nam si sine libertate heres institutus sit, etiamsi postea manumissus fuerit a domino, heres esse non potest, quia in-

Tit. xiv. De heredibus instituendis.

Heredes instituere permissum est tam liberos homines quam servos, et tam proprios quam alienos. Proprios autem servos, olim quidem secundum plurium sententias, non aliter quam cum libertate recte instituere licebat. Hodie vero etiam sine libertate ex nostra constitutione heredes eos instituere permissum est. Quod non per innovationem introduximus, sed quoniam et aequius erat, et Atilicino placuisse Paulus suis libris, quos tam ad Masurium Sabinum quam ad Plautium scripsit, refert. Proprius autem servus etiam is intelligitur, in quo nudam proprietatem testator habet, alio usumfructum habente. Est autem casus in quo nec cum libertate utiliter servus a domina heres insti-

stitutio in persona ejus non constitit; ideoque, licet alienatus sit, non potest jussu domini novi cernere hereditatem.

tuitur, ut constitutione divorum Severi et Antonini cavetur, cujus verba haec sunt: "Servum adulterio maculatum, non jure testamento manumissum ante sententiam ab ea muliere videri, quae rea fuerat ejusdem criminis postulata, rationis est. Quare sequitur, ut in eundem a domina collata heredis institutio nullius momenti habeatur". Alienus servus etiam is intelligitur, in quo usumfructum testator habet.

§ 188. Cum libertate vero heres institutus, si quidem in eadem causa duraverit, fit ex testamento liber et inde necessarius heres. Si vero ab ipso testatore manumissus fuerit, suo arbitrio hereditatem adire potest. Quod si alienatus sit, jussu novi domini adire hereditatem debet, qua ratione per eum dominus fit heres; nam ipse alienatus neque heres neque liber esse potest. § 189. Alienus quoque servus heres institutus, si in eadem causa duraverit, jussu domini hereditatem adire debet; si vero alienatus ab eo fuerit, aut vivo testatore, aut post mortem ejus antequam cernasset, debet jussu novi domini cernere. Si vero manumissus est, suo arbitrio adire hereditatem potest.

§ 1. Servus autem a domino suo *heres institutus, si quidem in eadem causa manserit, fit ex testamento liber heresque necessarius. Si vero a* vivo *testatore manumissus fuerit, suo arbitrio adire hereditatem potest:* quia non fit heres necessarius, cum utrumque ex domini testamento non consequitur. *Quod si alienatus fuerit, jussu novi domini adire hereditatem debet, et ea ratione per eum dominus fit heres; nam ipse alienatus, neque liber neque heres esse potest,* etiamsi cum libertate heres institutus fuerit; destitisse etenim a libertatis datione videtur dominus, qui eum alienavit. *Alienus quoque servus heres institutus, si in eadem causa duraverit, jussu domini adire hereditatem debet. Si vero alienatus ab eo fuerit, aut vivo testatore, aut post mortem ejus, antequam* adeat, *debet jussu novi domini* adire. *At si manumissus est* vivo testatore, vel mortuo antequam adeat, *suo arbitrio adire hereditatem potest.*

§ 190. Si autem servus alienus heres institutus est, vulgari cretione data, ita intelligitur dies cretionis cedere, si ipse servus scierit se heredem institutum esse, nec ullum impedimentum sit, quominus certiorem dominum faceret, ut illius jussu cernere possit.

§ 2. Servus autem alienus post domini mortem recte heres instituitur, quia et cum hereditariis servis est testamenti factio. Nondum enim adita hereditas, personae vicem sustinet, non heredis futuri, sed defuncti: cum etiam ejus qui in utero est, servus recte heres instituitur. § 3. Servus plurium, cum quibus testamenti factio est, ab extraneo institutus heres, unicuique dominorum cujus jussu adierit, pro portione dominii adquirit hereditatem.

§ 4. Et unum hominem, et plures in infinitum,

quot quis velit heredes facere, licet. § 5. Hereditas plerumque dividitur in duodecim uncias, quae assis appellatione continentur. Habent autem et hae partes propria nomina, ab uncia usque ad assem, ut puta haec: uncia, sextans, quadrans, triens, quincunx, semis, septunx, bes, dodrans, dextans, deunx, as. Non autem utique semper duodecim uncias esse oportet: nam tot unciae assem efficiunt, quot testator voluerit; et si unum tantum quis ex semisse verbi gratia heredem scripserit, totus as in semisse erit. Neque enim idem ex parte testatus, et ex parte intestatus decedere potest, nisi sit miles, cujus sola voluntas in testando spectatur. Et e contrario potest quis in quantascumque voluerit plurimas uncias suam hereditatem dividere. § 6. Si plures instituantur, ita demum partium distributio necessaria est, si nolit testator eos ex aequis partibus heredes esse: satis enim constat, nullis partibus nominatis, ex aequis partibus eos heredes esse. Partibus autem in quorundam personis expressis, si quis alius sine parte nominatus erit, si quidem aliqua pars assi deerit, ex ea parte heres fiet; et si plures sine parte scripti sunt, omnes in eandem partem concurrent. Si vero totus as completus sit, ii qui nominatim expressas partes habent, in partem dimidiam vocantur, et ille vel illi omnes in alteram dimidiam. Nec interest, primus, an medius, an novissimus sine parte heres scriptus sit: ea enim pars data intelligitur, quae vacat. § 7. Videamus, si pars aliqua vacet, nec tamen quisquam sine parte heres institutus sit, quid juris sit? veluti si tres ex quartis partibus heredes scripti sunt. Et constat vacantem partem singulis tacite pro hereditaria parte accedere, et perinde haberi ac si ex tertiis partibus heredes scripti essent; et ex diverso si plures in portionibus sint, tacite singulis decrescere, ut si, verbi gratia, quatuor ex tertiis partibus heredes scripti sint, perinde habeantur ac si unusquisque ex quarta parte scriptus fuisset. § 8. Si plures unciae quam duodecim distributae sint, is qui sine parte institutus sit quod dupondio deest habebit: idemque erit, si dupondius expletus sit. Quae omnes partes ad assem postea revocantur, quamvis sint plurium unciarum.

§ 9. Heres et pure et sub conditione institui potest. Ex certo tempore, aut ad certum tempus, non potest: veluti "post quinquennium quam moriar", vel "ex calendis illis", aut "usque ad calendas illas heres esto". Denique diem adjectum pro supervacuo haberi placet, et perinde esse ac si pure heres institutus esset. § 10. Impossibilis conditio in institutionibus et legatis, nec non in fideicommissis et libertatibus, pro non scripto habetur. § 11. Si plures conditiones institutioni adscriptae sunt, si quidem conjunctim, ut puta: "si illud et illud facta erint", omnibus parendum est; si separatim veluti: "si illud aut illud factum erit", cuilibet obtemperare satis est.

§ 12. Ii quos numquam testator vidit, heredes institui possunt, veluti si fratris filios peregrinatos, ignorans qui essent, heredes instituerit: ignorantia enim testantis inutilem institutionem non facit.

De substitutionibus.

§ 174. Interdum duos pluresve gradus heredum facimus, hoc modo: "Lucius Titius heres esto, cernitoque in diebus centum proximis, quibus scies poterisque: quodni ita creveris, exheres esto; tum Maevius heres esto, cernitoque in diebus centum," et reliqua; et deinceps, in quantum velimus, substituere possumus [et in novissimum subsidium vel necessarium heredem substituere]. § 175. Et licet nobis vel unum in unius locum substituere pluresve, et contra in plurium locum vel unum vel plures substituere. § 176. Primo itaque gradu scriptus heres hereditatem cernendo fit heres, et substitutus excluditur; non cernendo summovetur, etiamsi pro herede gerat, et in locum ejus substitutus succedit. Et deinceps si plures gradus sint, in singulis simili ratione idem contingit. § 177. Sed si cretio sine exheredatione sit data, id est, in haec verba: "Si non creverit, tum Publius Maevius heres esto," illud diversum invenitur, quia si prior omissa cretione pro herede gerat, substitutus in partem admittitur, et fiunt ambo ex aequis partibus heredes, quod si neque cernat neque pro herede gerat, tum sane in universo summovetur, et substitutus in totam hereditatem succedit. § 178. Sed Sabino quidem placuit, quamdiu cernere et eo modo heres fieri possit prior, etiamsi pro herede gesserit, non tamen admitti substitutum; cum vero cretio finita sit, tum pro herede gerendo admitti substitutum: aliis vero placuit, etiam superante cretione per se eum (pro herede gerendo) in partem substitutum admittere, et amplius ad cretionem reverti non posse.

Tiv. xv. De vulgari substitutione.

Potest autem quis in testamento suo *plures gradus heredum facere*, ut puta: "si ille heres non erit, ille heres esto": *et deinceps, in quantum velit testator, substituere potest, et novissimo loco in subsidium vel* servum *necessarium heredem* instituere. § 1. *Et plures in unius locum possunt substitui, vel unus in plurium*, vel singuli singulis, vel invicem ipsi qui heredes instituti sunt.

§ 2. Et si ex disparibus partibus heredes scriptos invicem substituerit, et nullam mentionem in substitutione habuerit partium, eas videtur partes in substitutione dedisse, quas in institutione expressit: et ita divus Pius rescripsit. § 3. Sed si instituto heredi, et coheredi suo substituto dato, alius substitutus fuerit, divi Severus et Antoninus, "sine distinctione," rescripserunt, "ad utramque partem substitutum admitti." § 4. Si servum alienum quis patremfamilias arbitratus, heredem scripserit, et si heres non esset, Maevium ei substituerit, isque servus jussu domini adierit hereditatem, Maevius in partem admittitur. Illa enim verba: "si heres non erit", in eo quidem quem alieno juri subjectum esse testator scit, sic accipiuntur: "si neque ipse heres erit, neque alium heredem effecerit": in eo vero quem patremfamilias arbitratur, illud significant: "si hereditatem sibi, eive cujus juri postea subjectus esse coeperit, non adquisierit." Idque Tiberius Caesar in persona Parthenii servi sui constituit.

Tit. xvi. De pupillari substitutione.

§ 179. Liberis nostris impuberibus quos in potestate habemus, non solum ita, ut supra diximus, substituere possumus, id est, ut si heredes non extiterint, alius nobis heres sit: sed eo amplius, ut, etiam si heredes nobis extiterint et adhuc impuberes mortui fuerint, sit iis aliquis heres, velut hoc modo: "Titius filius meus mihi heres esto; si filius meus mihi [heres non erit, sive heres] erit et prius moriatur quam in suam tutelam venerit, tunc Seius heres esto." § 180. Quo casu siquidem non extiterit heres filius, substitutus patri fit heres: si vero heres extiterit filius, et ante pubertatem decesserit, ipsi filio fit heres substitutus.

Liberis suis impuberibus quos in potestate quis habet, non solum ita, ut supra diximus, substituere potest, id est, ut si heredes ei non extiterint, alius ei sit heres; sed eo amplius, ut, et si heredes ei extiterint et adhuc impuberes mortui fuerint, sit iis aliquis heres. Veluti si quis dicat *hoc modo: "Titius filius meus mihi heres esto; si filius meus mihi heres non erit, sive heres erit et prius moriatur quam in suam tutelam venerit"* (id est, pubes factus sit), "*tunc Seius heres esto.*" *Quo casu siquidem non extiterit heres filius,* tunc *substitutus patri fit heres; si vero extiterit heres filius, et ante pubertatem decesserit, ipsi filio fit heres substitutus.* Nam moribus institutum est, ut, cum ejus aetatis filii sint in qua ipsi sibi testamentum facere non possunt, parentes eis faciant. § 1. Qua ratione excitati, etiam constitutionem posuimus in nostro codice, qua prospectum est, ut si mente captos habeant filios vel nepotes vel pronepotes cujuscumque sexus vel gradus, liceat eis, etsi puberes sint, ad exemplum pupillaris substitutionis certas personas substituere, sin autem resipuerint, eandem substitutionem infirmari, et hoc ad exemplum pupillaris substitutionis quae, postquam pupillus adoleverit, infirmatur. § 2. Igitur in pupillari substitutione secundum praefatum modum ordinata, *duo*

Quamobrem duo quodammodo sunt testamenta, aliud patris, aliud filii, tamquam si ipse filius sibi heredem instituisset; aut certe unum est testamentum duarum hereditatum.

§ 181. Ceterum, ne post obitum parentis periculo insidiarum subjectus videatur pupillus, in usu est vulgarem quidem substitutionem palam facere, id est, eo loco quo pupillum heredem instituimus: nam vulgaris substitutio ita vocat ad hereditatem substitutum, si omnino pupillus heres non extiterit; quod accidit cum vivo parente moritur, quo casu nullum substituti maleficium suspicari possumus, cum scilicet, etiam vivo testatore, omnia quae in testamento scripta sint, ignorentur: at illam autem substitutionem per quam, etiamsi heres extiterit pupillus et intra pubertatem decesserit, substitutum vocamus, separatim in inferioribus tabulis scribimus easque tabulas proprio lino propriaque cera consignamus; et in prioribus tabulis cavemus ne inferiores tabulae vivo filio et adhuc impubere aperiantur. Sed longe tutius est, utrumque genus substitutionis separatim in inferioribus tabulis consignari, quod, si ita consignatae vel separatae fuerint substitutiones, ut diximus, ex priore potest intelligi in altera quoque idem esse substitutus.

§ 182. Non solum autem heredibus institutis impuberibus liberis ita substituere possumus, ut si ante pubertatem mortui fuerint, sit is heres quem nos voluerimus, sed etiam exheredatis. Itaque eo casu, si quid pupillo ex hereditatibus legatisve aut donationibus propinquorum adquisitum fuerit, id omne ad substitutum pertinet. § 183. Quaecumque diximus de substitutione impuberum liberorum vel heredum institutorum vel exheredatorum, eadem etiam de postumis intellegemus.

quodammodo sunt testamenta, alterum patris, alterum filii, tamquam si ipse filius sibi heredem instituisset; aut certe unum est testamentum duarum causarum, id est duarum *hereditatum.*

§ 3. Sin autem quis ita formidolosus sit, ut timeret ne filius ejus, pupillus adhuc, ex eo quod palam substitutum accepit, *post obitum ejus periculo insidiarum subjiceretur, vulgarem quidem substitutionem palam facere,* et in primis quidem testamenti partibus ordinare debet; *illam autem substitutionem per quam, etsi heres extiterit pupillus et intra pubertatem decesserit, substitutus vocatur, separatim in inferioribus partibus scribere, eamque partem proprio lino propriaque cera consignare, et in priore parte testamenti cavere debet ne inferiores tabulae vivo filio et adhuc impubere aperiantur.* Illud palam est, non ideo minus valere substitutionem impuberis fiiii, quod in iisdem tabulis scripta sit quibus sibi quisque heredem instituisset, quamvis hoc pupillo periculosum sit.

§ 4. *Non solum autem heredibus institutis impuberibus liberis ita substituere parentes possunt, ut et si* heredes eis extiterint et *ante pubertatem mortui fuerint, sit* eis *heres is quem ipsi voluerint, sed etiam exheredatis. Itaque eo casu, si quid pupillo ex hereditatibus legatisve aut donationibus propinquorum* atque amicorum *adquisitum fuerit, id omne ad substitutum pertinet. Quaecumque diximus de substitutione impuberum liberorum vel heredum institutorum vel exheredatorum, eadem etiam de postumis intellegimus.*

§ 5. Liberis autem suis testamentum facere nemo potest, nisi et sibi faciat: nam pupillare testamentum pars et sequela est paterni testamenti, adeo ut si patris testamentum non valeat, nec filii quidem valebit. § 6. Vel singulis autem liberis, vel ei qui eorum novissimus impubes morietur, substitui potest: singulis quidem, si neminem eorum intestato decedere voluerit; novissimo, si jus legitimarum hereditatum integrum inter eos custodiri velit. § 7. Substituitur autem impuberi aut nominatim, veluti "Titius heres esto"; aut generaliter, ut "quisquis mihi heres erit": quibus verbis vocantur ex substitutione, impubere filio mortuo, qui et ei scripti sunt heredes et extiterunt, et pro qua parte heredes facti sunt. § 8. Masculo igitur usque ad quatuordecim annos substitui potest; feminae usque ad duodecim annos: et si hoc tempus excesserint, substitutio evanescit.

§ 184. Extraneo vero [vel puberi filio] heredi instituto ita substituere non possumus, ut, si heres extiterit et intra aliquod tempus decesserit, alius ei heres sit; sed hoc solum nobis permissum est, ut eum per fideicommissum obligemus, ut hereditatem nostram totam vel pro parte restituat; quod jus quale sit, suo loco trademus.

§ 9. *Extraneo vero, vel filio puberi heredi instituto, ita substituere nemo potest, ut, si heres extiterit et intra aliquod tempus decesserit, alius ei sit heres; sed hoc solum permissum est, ut eum per fideicommissum testator obliget alii hereditatem ejus vel totam vel pro parte restituere; quod jus quale sit, suo loco trademus.*

Tit. xvii. Quibus modis testamenta infirmantur.

§ 138. Si quis post factum testamentum adoptaverit sibi filium, aut per populum, eum qui sui juris est, aut per praetorem, eum qui in potestate parentis fuerit, omnimodo testamentum ejus rumpitur quasi agnatione sui heredis.

Testamentum jure factum usque eo valet, donec rumpatur, irritumve fiat. § 1. Rumpitur autem testamentum cum, in eodem statu manente testatore ipsius testamenti jus vitiatur. *Si quis* enim *post factum testamentum adoptaverit sibi filium*, per imperatorem, *eum qui sui juris est, aut per praetorem*, secundum nostram constitutionem, *eum qui in potestate parentis fuerit, testamentum ejus rumpitur*, *quasi agnatione sui heredis.*

§ 139. Idem juris est, si cui post factum testamentum vel uxor in manum conveniat, vel quae in manu fuit nubat: nam eo modo filiae loco esse incipit et quasi sua est. § 140. Nec prodest, sive haec, sive ille qui adoptatus est, in eo testamento sit institutus institutave; nam de exheredatione ejus supervacuum videtur quaerere, cum testamenti faciundi tempore suorum heredum numero non fuerit. § 141. Filius quoque, qui ex prima secundave mancipatione manumittitur, quia revertitur in potestatem patriam, rumpit ante factum testamentum, nec prodest si in eo testamento heres institutus vel exheredatus fuerit. § 142. Simile jus olim fuit in ejus persona cujus nomine ex senatus-consulto erroris causa probatur, quia forte ex peregrina vel latina, quae per errorem quasi civis Romana uxor ducta esset, natus esset; nam sive heres institutus esset a parente, sive exheredatus, sive vivo patre causa probatur, sive post mortem ejus, omnimodo quasi agnatione rumpebat testamentum. § 143. Nunc vero ex novo senatus-consulto quod auctore divo Hadriano factum est, si quidem vivo patre causa probatur, aeque ut olim omnimodo rumpit testamentum: si vero post mortem patris, praeteritus quidem rumpit testamentum, si vero heres in eo scriptus est vel exheredatus, non rumpit testamentum; ne scilicet diligenter facta testamenta rescinderentur eo tempore quo renovari non possent.

§ 144. Posteriore quoque testamento, quod jure factum est, superius rumpitur. Nec interest an extiterit aliquis ex eo heres, an non extiterit: hoc enim solum spectatur, an existere potuerit. Ideoque si quis ex posteriore testamento, quod jure factum est, aut noluerit heres esse, aut vivo testatore, aut post mortem ejus, antequam hereditatem adiret, decesserit, aut per cretionem exclusus fuerit, aut conditione sub qua heres institutus est defectus sit, aut propter coelibatum ex lege Julia summotus fuerit ab hereditate: quibus casibus paterfamilias intestatus moritur: nam et prius testamentum non valet, ruptum a posteriore, et posterius aeque nullas vires habet, cum ex eo nemo heres extiterit.

§ 2. *Posteriore quoque testamento, quod jure perfectum est, superius rumpitur. Nec interest an extiterit aliquis heres ex eo, an non extiterit: hoc enim solum spectatur, an aliquo casu existere potuerit. Ideoque si quis aut noluerit heres esse, aut vivo testatore, aut post mortem ejus antequam hereditatem adiret, decesserit, aut conditione sub qua heres institutus est defectus sit: in his casibus paterfamilias intestatus moritur: nam et prius testamentum non valet, ruptum a posteriore; et posterius aeque nullas vires habet, cum ex eo nemo heres extiterit.*

§ 3. Sed si quis priore testamento jure perfecto, posterius aeque jure fecerit, etiam si ex certis rebus in eo heredem instituerit, superius tamen testamentum sublatum esse divi Severus et Antoninus rescripserunt. Cujus constitutionis verba inseri jussimus, cum aliud quoque praeterea in ea constitutione expressum est. "Imperatores Severus et Antoninus, Cocceio Campano. Testamentum secundo loco factum, licet in eo certarum rerum heres scriptus sit, jure valere perinde ac si rerum mentio facta non esset, sed teneri heredem scriptum, ut contentus rebus sibi datis, aut suppleta quarta ex lege Falcidia, hereditatem restituat his qui in priore testamento scripti fuerant, propter inserta verba secundo testamento, quibus, ut valeret prius testamentum expressum est, dubitari non oportet." Et ruptum quidem testamentum hoc modo efficitur.

§ 145. Alio quoque modo testamenta jure facta infirmantur, velut, cum is qui fecerit testamentum capite deminutus sit. Quod quibus modis accidat, primo commentario relatum est. § 146. Hoc autem casu irrita fieri testamenta dicemus, cum alioquin et quae rumpuntur irrita fiant; [et quae statim ab initio non jure fiunt, irrita sunt; ut ea, quae jure facta, postea propter capitis deminutionem irrita fiunt], possunt nihilominus rupta dici. Sed quia sane commodius erat singulas causas singulis appellationibus distingui, ideo quaedam non jure fieri dicuntur, quaedam jure facta rumpi, vel irrita fieri.

§ 4. *Alio quoque modo testamenta jure facta infirmantur, veluti, cum is qui fecerit testamentum capite deminutus sit. Quod quibus modis accidat, primo* libro *retulimus.* § 5. *Hoc autem casu irrita fieri testamenta dicuntur, cum alioquin et quae rumpantur irrita fiunt; et quae statim ab initio non jure fiunt, irrita sunt; et ea quae jure facta sunt et postea propter capitis deminutionem irrita fiunt, possumus nihilominus rupta dicere. Sed quia sane commodius erat singulas causas singulis appellationibus distingui, ideo quaedam non jure facta dicuntur; quaedam jure facta rumpi, vel irrita fieri.*

§ 147. Non tamen per omnia inutilia sunt ea testamenta, quae vel ab initio non jure facta sunt, vel jure facta, postea irrita facta aut rupta sunt. Nam, si septem testium signis signata sint testamenta, potest scriptus heres secundum tabulas bonorum possessionem petere, si modo defunctus testator et civis Romanus et suae potestatis mortis tempore fuerit: nam, si ideo irritum fit testamentum, quod puta civitatem vel etiam libertatem testator amisit [aut quod cum] adoptionem se dedisset mortis tempore in adoptivi patris potestate fuit, non potest scriptus heres secundum tabulas bonorum possessionem petere.

§ 6. *Non tamen per omnia inutilia sunt ea testamenta, quae, ab initio jure facta,* propter capitis deminutionem *irrita facta sunt. Nam si septem testium signis signata sunt, potest scriptus heres secundum tabulas testamenti bonorum possessionem agnoscere, si modo defunctus et civis Romanus et suae potestatis mortis tempore fuerit: nam, si ideo irritum factum sit testamentum, quod civitatem vel etiam libertatem testator amisit, aut quia in adoptionem se dedit et mortis tempore in adoptivi patris potestate sit, non potest scriptus heres secundum tabulas bonorum possessionem petere.*

§ 148. [Sed si qui] secundum tabulas testamenti, quae aut statim ab initio non jure factae sint, aut jure factae postea ruptae vel irritae erunt, bonorum possessionem accipiunt, si modo possunt hereditatem obtinere, habebunt bonorum possessionem cum re; si vero ab iis avocari hereditas potest, habebunt bonorum possessionem sine re. § 149. Nam, si quis heres jure civili institutus sit vel ex primo vel ex posteriore testamento, vel ab intestato jure legitimo heres sit, is potest ab iis hereditatem avocare: si vero nemo sit alius jure civili heres, ipsi retinere hereditatem possunt, nec ullum jus adversus eos habent. . . . . [qui legi]timo jure deficiuntur, quali . . . . quoque notavimus. [Interdum tamen, quanquam testamento jure civili institutus, vel] legitimus quo[que heres sit,] potiores scripti habentur, [velut si ideo non jure] factum sit testamentum, aut quod familia non venierit, aut nuncupationis verba testator locutus non sit. § 150. [Alia causa est eorum, qui herede non extante bona possiderint, nec tamen a praetore bonorum possessionem acceperint; etiam hi possessores tamen res olim obtinebant ante legem Julium, qua] lege bona caduca fiunt et ad populum deferri jubentur, si defuncto nemo [successor extiterit]. § 151. Potest, ut jure facta testamenta [contraria voluntate] infirmentur. Apparet [autem] non posse [ex eo solo infirmari] testamentum, [quod postea] testator id noluerit valere, usque adeo, ut si linum ejus inciderit, nihilominus jure civili valeat; quin etiam si deleverit quoque aut obleverit tabulas testamenti non ideo protinus desinent valere [quae fuerant scripta], licet eorum probatio directa non sit. Quid ergo est? Si quis ab intestato bonorum possessionem petierit et is qui ex eo testamento heres est petat hereditatem [vincat quidem necesse est in hereditatis petitione, sed fiscus ei quasi indigno auferet hereditatem, ne ullo modo ad eum, quem testator heredem habere noluit], perveniat hereditas et ita rescripto imperatoris Antonini significatur.

§ 7. *Ex eo autem solo non potest infirmari testamentum, quod postea testator id noluit valere: usque adeo, ut,* etsi quis post factum prius testamentum posterius facere coeperit, et aut mortalitate praeventus, aut quid eum ejus rei poenituit, non perfecerit, divi Pertinacis oratione cautum sit, ne alias tabulae priores jure factae irritae fiant, nisi sequentes jure ordinatae et perfectae fuerint, nam imperfectum testamentum sine dubio nullum est. § 8. Eadem oratione expressit, "non admissurum se hereditatem ejus qui litis causa principem heredem reliquerit; neque tabulas non legitime factas, in quibus ipse ob eam causam heres institutus erat, probaturum: neque ex nuda voce heredis nomen admissurum, neque ex ulla scriptura cui juris auctoritas desit aliquid adepturum." Secundum haec divi quoque Severus et Antoninus saepissime rescripserunt: "Licet enim" inquiunt "legibus soluti simus, attamen legibus vivimus."

Tit. xviii. De inofficioso testamento.

Quia plerumque parentes sine causa liberos suos vel exheredant vel omittunt, inductum est, ut de inofficioso testamento agere possint liberi, qui queruntur aut inique se exheredatos, aut inique praeteritos: hoc colore, quasi non sanae mentis fuerint, cum testamentum ordinarent. Sed hoc dicitur non quasi vere furiosus sit; sed recte quidem fecerit testamentum, non autem ex officio pietatis: nam si vere furiosus sit, nullum est testamentum. § 1. Non tantum autem liberis permissum est parentum testamentum inofficiosum accusare, verum etiam parentibus liberorum. Soror autem et frater, turpibus personis scriptis heredibus, ex sacris constitutionibus praelati sunt: non ergo contra omnes heredes agere possunt. Ultra fratres igitur et sorores cognati nullo modo aut agere possunt, aut agentes vincere. § 2. Tam autem naturales liberi, quam secundum nostrae constitutionis divisionem adoptati, ita demum de inofficioso testamento agere possunt, si nullo alio jure ad bona defuncti venire possunt. Nam qui ad hereditatem totam vel partem ejus alio jure veniunt, de inofficioso agere non possunt. Postumi quoque qui nullo alio jure venire possunt, de inofficioso agere possunt. § 3. Sed haec ita accipienda sunt, si nihil eis penitus a testatoribus testamento relictum est: quod nostra constitutio ad verecundiam naturae introduxit. Sin vero quantacumque pars hereditatis vel res eis fuerit relicta, inofficiosi querela quiescente, id quod eis deest usque ad quartam legitimae partis repleatur, licet non fuerit adjectum, boni viri arbitratu debere eam compleri. § 4. Si tutor nomine pupilli cujus tutelam gerebat, ex testamento patris sui legatum acceperit, cum nihil erat ipsi tutori relictum a patre suo, nihilominus possit nomine suo de inofficioso patris testamento agere. § 5. Sed et si, e contrario, pupilli nomine cui nihil relictum fuerit, de inofficioso egerit, et superatus est, ipse tutor quod sibi in eodem testamento legatum relictum est non amittit. § 6. Igitur quartam quis debet habere, ut de inofficioso testamento agere non possit, sive jure hereditario, sive jure legati vel fideicommissi, vel si mortis causa ei quarta donata fuerit, vel inter vivos, in his tantummodo casibus, quorum nostra constitutio mentionem facit, vel aliis modis qui constitutionibus continentur. § 7. Quod autem de quarta diximus, ita intelligendum est, ut sive unus fuerit sive plures quibus agere de inofficioso testamento permittitur, una quarta eis dari possit, ut ea pro rata eis distribuatur, id est pro virili portione quarta.

§ 152. Heredes autem aut necessarii dicuntur, aut sui et necessarii, aut extranei.

§ 153. Necessarius heres est servus cum libertate heres institutus, ideo sic appellatus, quia, sive velit, sive nolit, omnimodo post mortem testatoris protinus liber et heres est. § 154. Unde qui facultates suas suspectas habet, solet servum primo aut secundo vel etiam ulteriore gradu liberum et heredem instituere, ut, si creditoribus satis non fiat, potius hujus heredis quam ipsius testatoris bona veneant, id est, ut ignominia, quae accedit ex venditione bonorum, hunc potius heredem, quam ipsum testatorem contingat; quamquam apud Fufidium Sabino placeat eximendum eum esse ignominia, quia non suo vitio, sed necessitate juris bonorum venditionem pateretur: sed alio jure utimur. § 155. Pro hoc tamen incommodo illud ei commodum praestatur, ut ea quae post mortem patroni sibi adquisierit, sive ante bonorum venditionem sive postea, ipsi reserventur. Et quamvis pro portione bona venierint, iterum ex hereditaria causa bona ejus non venient, nisi si quid ei ex hereditaria causa fuerit adquisitum, velut si latinum adquisierit, et locupletior factus sit; cum ceterorum hominum quorum bona venierint pro portione, si quid postea adquirant, etiam saepius eorum bona venire solent.

§ 156. Sui autem et necessarii heredes sunt velut filius filiave, nepos neptisve ex filio, deinceps caeteri, qui modo in potestate morientis fuerint. Sed uti nepos neptisve suus heres sit, non sufficit eum in potestate avi mortis tempore fuisse, sed opus est, ut pater quoque ejus, vivo patre suo, desierit suus heres esse, aut morte interceptus, aut qualibet ratione liberatus potestate: tum enim nepos neptisme in locum sui patris succedunt. § 157. Sed sui quidem heredes ideo appellantur,

Tit. xix. De heredum qualitate et differentia.

Heredes autem aut necessarii dicuntur, aut sui et necessarii, aut extranei.

§ 1. *Necessarius heres est servus heres institutus, ideo sic appellatus, quia, sive velit, sive nolit, omnimodo post mortem testatoris protinus liber et necessarius heres fit. Unde qui facultates suas suspectas habet, solet servum suum primo aut secundo vel etiam ulteriore gradu heredem instituere, ut, si creditoribus satis non fiat, potius ejus heredis bona quam ipsius testatoris* a creditoribus possideantur, vel distrahantur vel inter eos dividantur. *Pro hoc tamen incommodo illud ei commodum praestatur, ut ea, quae post mortem patroni sui sibi adquisierit, ipsi reserventur; et quamvis* non sufficiant bona defuncti creditoribus, *iterum ex ea causa res ejus* quas sibi adquisierit, non veneunt.

§ 2. *Sui autem et necessarii heredes sunt veluti filius filiave, nepos neptisve ex filio, et deinceps caeteri liberi qui modo in potestate morientis fuerint. Sed ut nepos neptisve sui heredes sint, non sufficit eum* eamve *in potestate avi mortis tempore fuisse, sed opus est, ut pater ejus, vivo patre suo, desierit suus heres esse, aut morte interceptus, aut qualibet alia ratione liberatus potestate: tunc enim nepos neptisve in locum patris sui succedit. Sed sui quidem heredes ideo appellantur, quia domestici heredes*

quia domestici heredes sunt, et vivo quoque parente quodammodo domini existimantur. Unde etiam, si quis intestatus mortuus sit, prima causa est in successione liberorum. Necessarii vero ideo dicuntur, quia omnimodo, sive velint, sive nolint, tam ab intestato, quam ex testamento heredes fiunt. § 158. Sed his praetor permittit abstinere se ab hereditate, ut potius parentis bona veneant. § 159. Idem juris est et in uxoris persona quae in manu est, quia filiae loco est, et in nuru quae in manu filii est, quia neptis loco est. § 160. Quin etiam similiter abstinendi potestatem facit praetor etiam ei qui in causa mancipii est, id est mancipato, cum liber et heres institutus sit; cum necessarius, non etiam suus heres sit, tamquam servus.

§ 161. Caeteri qui testatoris juri subjecti non sunt, extranei heredes appellantur. Itaque liberi quoque nostri qui in potestate nostra non sunt, heredes a nobis instituti, sicut extranei videntur. Qua de causa et qui a matre heredes instituuntur, eodem numero sunt, quia feminae liberos in potestate non habent. Servi quoque, qui cum libertate heredes instituti sunt et postea a domino manumissi, eodem numero habentur.

sunt, et vivo quoque patre quodammodo domini existimantur. Unde etiam, si quis intestatus mortuus sit, prima causa est in successione liberorum. Necessarii vero ideo dicuntur, quia omnimodo, sive velint, sive nolint, tam ab intestato quam ex testamento heredes fiunt. Sed his praetor permittit volentibus *abstinere se ab hereditate, ut potius parentis* quam ipsorum *bona* similiter a creditoribus possideantur.

§ 3. *Caeteri qui testatoris juri subjecti non sunt, extranei heredes appellantur. Itaque liberi quoque nostri qui in potestate nostra non sunt, heredes a nobis instituti, extranei heredes videntur. Qua de causa et qui heredes a matre instituuntur, eodem numero sunt, quia feminae in potestate liberos non habent. Servus quoque* a domino *heres institutus, et post* testamentum factum ab eo *manumissus, eodem numero habetur.* § 4. In extraneis heredibus illud observatur, ut sit cum eis testamenti factio, sive ipsi heredes instituantur, sive hi qui in potestate eorum sunt. Et id duobus temporibus inspicitur: testamenti quidem facti, ut constiterit institutio; mortis vero testatoris, ut effectum habeat. Hoc amplius, et cum adierit hereditatem, esse debet cum eo testamenti factio, sive pure sive sub conditione heres institutus sit, nam jus heredis eo vel maxime tempore inspiciendum est, quo adquirit hereditatem. Medio autem tempore, inter factum testamentum et mortem testatoris, vel conditionem institutionis existentem, mutatio juris heredi non nocet, quia, ut diximus, tria tempora inspicimus. Testamenti autem factionem non solum is habere videtur qui testamentum facere potest; sed etiam qui ex alieno testamento vel ipse capere potest vel alii adquirere, licet non possit facere testamentum.

Et ideo furiosus, et mutus, et postumus, et infans, et filiusfamilias, et servus alienus, testamenti factionem habere dicuntur: licet enim testamentum facere non possint, attamen ex testamento vel sibi vel alii adquirere possunt.

§ 162. Extraneis autem heredibus deliberandi potestas data est de adeunda hereditate, vel non adeunda. § 163. Sed sive is cui abstinendi potestas est, immiscuerit se bonis hereditariis, sive is cui de adeunda hereditate deliberare licet, adierit, postea relinquendae hereditatis facultatem non habet, nisi si minor sit annorum xxv: nam hujus aetatis hominibus, sicut in caeteris omnibus causis, deceptis, ita etiam si temere damnosam hereditatem susceperint, praetor succurrit. Scio quidem divum Hadrianum etiam majori xxv annorum veniam dedisse, cum post aditam hereditatem grande aes alienum, quod aditae hereditatis tempore latebat, apparuisset.

§ 5. *Extraneis autem heredibus deliberandi potestas est de adeunda hereditate, vel non adeunda. Sed sive is cui abstinendi potestas est, immiscuerit se bonis hereditariis, sive* extraneus *cui de adeunda hereditate deliberare licet, adierit, postea relinquendae hereditatis facultatem non habet, nisi minor sit annis vigintiquinque: nam hujus aetatis hominibus, sicut in caeteris omnibus causis, deceptis, ita et si temere damnosam hereditatem susceperint, praetor succurrit.* § 6. *Sciendum tamen est divum Hadrianum etiam majori vigintiquinque annis veniam dedisse, cum post aditam hereditatem grande aes alienum, quod aditae hereditatis tempore latebat, emersisset.* Sed hoc quidem divus Hadrianus speciali beneficio cuidam praestitit; divus autem Gordianus postea in militibus tantummodo hoc extendit. Sed nostra benevolentia commune omnibus subjectis imperio nostro hoc praestitit beneficium, et constitutionem tam aequissimam quam nobilem scripsit, cujus tenorem si observaverint homines, licet eis et adire hereditatem, et in tantum teneri in quantum valere bona hereditatis, contigerit; ut ex hac causa neque deliberationis auxilium eis fiat necessarium, nisi, omissa observatione nostrae constitutionis, et deliberandum existimaverint et sese veteri gravamini aditionis supponere maluerint.

§ 164. Extraneis heredibus solet cretio dari, id est, finis deliberandi, ut intra certum tempus vel adeant hereditatem, vel, si non adeant, temporis fine summoveantur. Ideo autem cretio appellatur, quia cernere est quasi decernere et constituere. § 165. Cum ergo ita scriptum sit: "Heres Titius esto": adjicere debemus; "cernitoque in centum diebus proxumis, quibus scies poterisque; quodni ita creveris, exheres esto". § 166. Et quia ita heres institutus est, si velit heres esse, debebit intra diem cretionis cernere, id est, haec verba dicere: "Quod me Titium Publius Maevius testamento suo heredem instituit, eam hereditatem adeo cernoque". Quod si ita non creverit, finito tempore cretionis, excluditur; nec quicquam proficit, si pro herede gerat, id est, si rebus hereditariis tamquam heres utatur. § 167. At is qui sine cretione heres institutus sit, aut qui ab intestato legitimo jure ad hereditatem vocatur, potest aut cernendo, aut pro herede gerendo, vel etiam nuda voluntate suscipiendae hereditatis heres fieri; eique liberum est, quocumque tempore voluerit, adire hereditatem: sed solet praetor, postulantibus hereditariis creditoribus, tempus constituere, intra quod, si velit, adeat hereditatem; sin minus, ut liceat creditoribus bona defuncti vendere. § 168. At sicut is qui cum cretione heres institutus, nisi creverit hereditatem, non fit heres, ita non aliter excluditur, quam si non creverit intra id tempus quo cretio finita sit; itaque, licet ante diem cretionis constituerit hereditatem non adire, tamen paenitentia actus, superante die cretionis, cernendo heres esse potest. § 169. At is, qui sine cretione heres institutus est, quique ab intestato per legem vocatur, sicut voluntate nuda heres fit, ita etiam contraria destinatione statim ab hereditate repellitur. § 170. Omnis autem cretio certo tempore constringitur. In quam rem tolerabile tempus visum est centum dierum. Potest tamen nihilominus jure civili aut longius aut brevius tempus dari: longius tamen interdum praetor coarctat. § 171. Et quamvis omnis cretio certis diebus constringatur, tamen alia cretio vulgaris vocatur, alia certorum dierum: vulgaris illa, quam supra exposuimus, id est, in qua adjiciuntur haec verba: "quibus sciet poteritque"; certorum dierum, in qua, detractis his verbis, caetera scribuntur. § 172. Quarum cretionum magna differentia est. Nam, vulgari cretione data, nulli dies computantur, nisi quibus scierit quisque se heredem esse institutum, et possit cernere. Certorum vero dierum cretione data, etiam nescienti se heredem institutum esse, numerantur dies continui; item ei quoque qui

§ 7. Item extraneus heres, testamento *institutus, aut ab intestato ad legitimam hereditatem vocatus, potest aut pro herede gerendo, vel etiam nuda voluntate suscipiendae hereditatis, heres fieri.* Pro herede autem gerere quis videtur, si rebus hereditariis tamquam heres utatur, vel vendendo res hereditarias, aut praedia colendo locandove, et quoquo modo, si voluntatem suam declaret vel re vel verbis de adeunda hereditate, dummodo sciat eum in cujus bonis pro herede gerit testatum intestatumve obiisse, et se ei heredem esse. Pro herede enim gerere est pro domino gerere: veteres enim heredes pro dominis appellabant.

Sicut autem nuda voluntate extraneus *heres fit, ita et contraria destinatione statim ab hereditate repellitur.* Eum qui mutus vel surdus natus est, vel postea factus, nihil prohibet pro herede gerere et adquirere sibi hereditatem, si tamen intelligit quod agitur.

aliqua ex causa cernere prohibetur, et eo amplius ei qui sub conditione heres institutus est, tempus numeratur [continuum]: § 173. unde continua haec cretio vocatur. Sed quia tamen dura est haec cretio, altera magis in usu habetur: unde etiam vulgaris dicta est.

§ 191. Post haec videamus de legatis: quae pars juris extra propositam quidem materiam videtur; nam loquimur de iis juris figuris quibus per universitatem res nobis adquiruntur; sed, cum omnimodo de testamentis, deque heredibus qui testamento instituuntur, locuti sumus, non sine causa sequenti loco poterat haec juris materia tractari.

Tit. xx. De legatis.

Post haec videamus de legatis: quae pars juris extra propositam quidem materiam videtur; nam loquimur de iis juris figuris quibus per universitatem res nobis adquiruntur; sed, cum omnino de testamentis, deque heredibus qui testamento instituuntur, locuti sumus, non sine causa sequenti loco potest haec juris materia tractari.

§ 1. Legatum itaque est donatio quaedam a defuncto relicta.

De legatis.

§ 192. Legatorum utique genera sunt quattuor: aut enim per vindicationem legamus, aut per damnationem, aut sinendi modo, aut per praeceptionem.

§ 193. Per vindicationem hoc modo legamus: "Lucio Titio", verbi gratia, "hominem Stichum do lego". Sed et si alterutrum verbum positum sit, veluti: "do" aut "lego" aeque per vindicationem legatum est. Item, ut magis visum est, si ita legatum fuerit: "Sumito", vel ita: "Sibi habeto", vel ita: "Capito", aeque per vindicationem legatum est. § 194. Ideo autem per vindicationem legatum appellatur, quia post aditam hereditatem statim ex jure quiritium [res] legatarii fit; et si eam rem legatarius vel ab herede, vel ab alio quocumque qui eam possidet, petat, vindicare debet, id est, intendere eam rem suam ex jure quiritium esse. § 195. In eo solo dissentiunt prudentes, quod Sabinus quidem et Cassius, caeterique nostri praeceptores, quod ita legatum sit, statim post aditam hereditatem putant fieri legatarii, etiamsi ignoret sibi legatum esse dimissum, et posteaquam scierit etiam spretum legatum perinde esse atque si legatum non esset: Nerva vero et Proculus, caeterique illius scholae auctores, non aliter putant rem legatarii fieri, quam si voluerit eam ad se pertinere. Sed hodie ex divi Pii Antonini constitutione hoc magis jure uti videmur quod Proculo placuit; nam cum legatus fuisset latinus per vindicationem coloniae: "Deliberent", inquit, "decuriones, an ad se velint pertinere, perinde ac si uni legatus esset".

§ 196. Hae autem solae res per vindicationem legantur recte, quae ex jure quiritium ipsius testatoris sunt. Sed eas quidem res quae pondere, numero, mensura constant, placuit sufficere, si mortis tempore sint ex jure quiritium testatoris, veluti vinum, oleum, frumentum, pecuniam numeratam. Caeteras res vero placuit utroque tempore testatoris ex jure quiritium esse debere, id est, et quo faceret testamentum et quo moreretur: alioquin inutile est legatum. § 197. Sed sane hoc ita est jure civili: postea vero auctore Nerone Caesare senatus-consultum factum est, quo cautum est ut, si eam rem quisque legaverit quae ejus numquam fuerit, perinde utile sit legatum atque si optimo jure relictum esset. Optimum autem jus est per damnationem legatum; quo genere etiam aliena res legari potest, sicut inferius apparebit. § 198. Sed si quis rem suam legaverit, deinde post testamentum factum eam alienaverit, plerique putant, non solum jure civili inutile esse legatum, sed ne ex senatus-consulto confirmari. Quod ideo dictum est, quia, etiamsi per damnationem aliquis rem suam legaverit, eamque postea alienaverit, plerique putant, licet ipso jure debeatur legatum, tamen legatarium petentem posse per exceptionem doli mali repelli, quasi contra voluntatem defuncti petat. § 199. Illud constat, si duobus pluribusve per vindicationem eadem res legata sit, sive conjunctim, sive disjunctim, et omnes veniant ad legatum, partes ad singulos pertinere, et deficientis portionem collegatario adcrescere. Conjunctim autem ita legatur: "Titio et Seio hominem Stichum do lego"; disjunctim ita: "Lucio Titio hominem Stichum do lego. Seio eundem hominem do lego." § 200. Illud quaeritur, quod sub conditione per vindicationem legatum est, pendente conditione cujus esset. Nostri praeceptores heredis esse putant exemplo statu liberi, id est, ejus servi qui testamento sub aliqua conditione liber esse jussus est, quem constat interea heredis servum esse. Sed diversae scholae auctores putant nullius interim eam rem esse; quod multo magis dicunt de eo quod sine conditione pure legatum est, antequam legatarius admittat legatum.

§ 201. Per damnationem hoc modo legamus: "Heres meus Stichum servum meum dare damnas esto"; sed et si "dato" scriptum sit, per damnationem legatum est. § 202. Eoque genere legati etiam aliena res legari potest, ita ut heres redimere et praestare aut aestimationem ejus dare debeat. § 203. Ea quoque res quae in rerum natura non est, si modo futura est, per damnationem legari potest, velut: "fructus, qui in illo fundo nati erunt", aut, "quod ex illa ancilla natum erit". § 204. Quod autem ita legatum est, post aditam hereditatem, etiamsi pure legatum est, non, ut per vindicationem legatum, continuo legatario adquiritur, sed nihilominus heredis est; et ideo legatarius in personam agere debet, id est, intendere heredem sibi dare oportere: et tum heres [rem], si mancipi sit, mancipio dare, aut in jure cedere, possessionemque tradere debet; si nec mancipi sit, sufficit si tradiderit. Nam si mancipi rem tantam tradiderit, nec mancipaverit, usucapione [demum completa] pleno jure fit legatarii: completur autem usucapio, sicut alio quoque loco diximus, mobilium quidem rerum anno, earum vero quae solo tenentur, biennio. § 205. Est et illa differentia hujus legati quod si eadem res duobus pluribusve per damnationem legata sit, si quidem conjunctim, plane singulis partes debentur, sicut in illo [quoque est, si ve]ro disjunctim, singulis solida res debetur, ut scilicet heres alteri rem, alteri aestimationem ejus praestare debeat. Et in conjunctis, deficientis portio non ad collegatarium pertinet, sed in hereditate remanet.

§ 206. Quod autem diximus, deficientis portionem in per damnationem quidem legato in hereditate retineri, in per vindicationem vero collegatario adcrescere, admonendi sumus ante legem Papiam jure civili ita fuisse: post legem vero Papiam deficientis portio caduca fit, et ad eos pertinet qui in eo testamento liberos habent. § 207. Et quamvis prima causa sit, in caducis vindicandis, heredum liberos habentium, deinde, si heredes liberos non habeant, legatariorum liberos habentium, tamen ipsa lege Papia significatur ut collegatarius conjunctus, si liberos habeat, potior sit heredibus, etiamsi liberos habebunt. § 208. Sed plerisque placuit, quantum ad hoc jus quod lege Papia conjunctis constituitur, nihil interesse, utrum per vindicationem, an per damnationem legatum sit.

§ 209. Sinendi modo ita legamus: "Heres meus damnas esto sinere Lucium Titium hominem Stichum sumere sibique habere." § 210. Quod genus legati plus quidem habet quam per vindicationem legatum, minus autem quam per damnationem. Nam eo modo non solum suam rem testator utiliter legare potest, sed etiam heredis sui: cum alioquin per vindicationem nisi suam rem legare non potest; per damnationem autem cujuslibet extranei rem legare potest. § 211. Sed si quidem mortis testatoris tempore res, vel ipsius testatoris sit vel heredis, plane utile legatum est, etiamsi testamenti faciendi tempore neutrius fuerit. § 212. Quod si post mortem testatoris ea res heredis esse coeperit, quaeritur an utile sit legatum. Et plerique putant inutile esse: quid ergo est? Licet aliquis eam rem legaverit, quae neque ejus unquam fuerit, neque postea heredis ejus unquam esse coeperit, ex senatus-consulto Neroniano perinde videtur ac si per damnationem relicta esset. § 213. Sicut autem per damnationem legata res non statim post aditam hereditatem legatarii efficitur, sed manet heredis eo usque, donec is heres tradendo, vel mancipando, vel in jure cedendo legatarii eam fecerit; ita et in sinendi modo legato juris est: et ideo hujus quoque legati nomine in personam actio est, "Quidquid heredem ex testamento dare facere oportet." § 214. Sunt tamen qui putant, ex hoc legato non videri obligatum heredem ut mancipet, aut in jure cedat, aut tradat, sed sufficere, ut legatarium rem sumere patiatur; quia nihil ultra ei testator imperaverit quam ut sinat, id est patiatur, legatarium rem sibi habere. § 215. Major illa dissensio in hoc legato intervenit, si eandem rem duobus pluribusve disjunctim legasti: quidam putant utrisque solidum deberi, sicut per [damn]ationem: nonnulli occupantis esse meliorem conditionem aestimant; quia, cum in eo genere legati damnetur heres patientiam praestare ut legatarius rem habeat, sequitur ut, si priori patientiam praestiterit, et is rem sumpserit, securus sit adversus eum qui postea legatum petierit, quia neque habet rem ut patiatur eam ab eo sumi, neque dolo malo fecit quominus eam rem haberet.

§ 216. Per praeceptionem hoc modo legamus: "Lucius Titius hominem Stichum praecipito." § 217. Sed nostri quidem praeceptores nulli alii eo modo legari posse putant, nisi ei qui aliqua ex parte heres scriptus esset: praecipere enim esse praecipuum sumere; quod tantum in ejus persona procedit, qui aliqua ex parte heres institutus est, quod is extra portionem hereditatis praecipuum legatum habiturus sit. § 218. Ideoque, si extraneo legatum fuerit, inutile est legatum, adeo ut Sabinus existimaverit, ne quidem ex senatus-consulto Neroniano posse convalescere: nam "eo", inquit, "senatus-consulto ea tantum confirmantur, quae verborum vitio jure civili non valent, non quae propter ipsam personam legatarii non deberentur." Sed Juliano et Sexto placuit, etiam hoc casu ex senatus-consulto confirmari legatum; nam ex verbis etiam hoc casu accidere, ut jure civili inutile sit legatum inde manifestum est, quod eidem aliis verbis recte legetur, tunc autem vitio personae legatum non valere, cum ei legatum sit cui nullo modo legari possit, velut peregrino cum quo testamenti factio non sit, quo plane casu senatus-consulto locus non est. § 219. Item nostri praeceptores, quod ita legatum est, nulla ratione putant posse consequi eum cui ita fuerit legatum, praeterquam judicio familae erciscundae: officio enim judicis id contineri, ut ei, quod per praeceptionem legatum est, adjudicetur. § 220. Unde intelligimus, nihil aliud secundum nostrorum praeceptorum opinionem per praeceptionem legari posse, nisi quod testatoris sit: nulla enim alia res quam hereditaria deducitur in hoc judicium. Itaque, si non suam rem eo modo testator legaverit, jure quidem civili inutile erit legatum, sed ex senatus-consulto confirmabitur. Aliquo tamen casu etiam alienam rem per praeceptionem legari posse fatentur, veluti si quis eam rem legaverit, quam creditori fiduciae causa mancipio dederit; nam officio judicis coheredes cogi posse existimant solutam pecuniam solvere eam rem, ut possit praecipere is cui ita legatum sit. § 221. Sed diversae scholae auctores putant etiam extraneo per praeceptionem legari posse, perinde ac si ita scribatur: "Titius hominem Stichum capito," supervacuo adjecta "prae" syllaba; ideoqûe per vindicationem eam rem legatam videri: quae sententia dicitur divi Hadriani constitutione confirmata esse. § 222. Secundum hanc igitur opinionem, si ea res ex jure quiritium defuncti fuerit, [paret] posse a legatario vindicari, sive is unus ex heredibus sit, sive extraneus; quodsi in bonis tantum testatoris fuerit, extraneo quidem ex senatus-consulto utile erit legatum, heredi vero familiae erciscundae judicio, judicis officio praestabitur; quod si nullo jure fuerit testatoris, tam heredi quam extraneo ex senatus-consulto utile erit. § 223. Sive tamen heredibus, secundum nostrorum opinionem, sive etiam extraneis, secundum illorum opinionem, duobus pluribusve eadem res conjunctim aut disjunctim legata fuerit, singuli partes habere debent.

cf. Gai., § 192.

§ 2. Sed olim quidem erant *legatorum genera quattuor: per vindicationem, per damnationem, sinendi modo, per praeceptionem;* et certa quaedam verba cuique generi legatorum adsignata erant, per quae singula genera legatorum significabantur. Sed ex constitutionibus divorum principum solemnitas hujusmodi verborum penitus sublata est. Nostra autem constitutio quam cum magna fecimus lucubratione, defunctorum voluntates validiores esse cupientes, et non verbis, sed voluntatibus eorum faventes, disposuit, ut omnibus legatis una sit natura, et quibuscumque verbis aliquid derelictum sit, liceat legatariis id persequi, non solum per actiones personales, sed etiam per in rem, et per hyphothecariam : cujus constitutionis perpensum modum ex ipsius tenore perfectissime accipere possibile est. § 3. Sed non usque ad eam constitutionem standum esse existimavimus. Cum enim antiquitatem invenimus legata quidem stricte concludentem, fideicommissis autem, quae ex voluntate magis descendebant defunctorum, pinguiorem naturam indulgentem : necessarium esse duximus omnia legata fideicommissis exaequare, ut nulla sit inter ea differentia : sed, quod deest legatis, hoc repleatur ex natura fideicommissorum, et, si quid amplius est in legatis, per hoc crescat fideicommissi natura. Sed, ne in primis legum cunabulis, permixte de his exponendo, studiosis adolescentibus, quandam introducamus difficultatem, operae pretium esse duximus, interim separatim prius de legatis, et postea de fideicommissis tractare, ut natura utriusque juris cognita, facile possint permixtionem eorum eruditi subtilioribus auribus accipere.

§ 4. Non solum autem testatoris vel heredis *res*,

cf. Gai., § 202.

sed *et aliena legari potest : ita ut heres* cogatur *redimere* eam *et praestare*, vel, si non potest redimere, *aestimationem ejus dare*. Sed si talis res sit cujus non est commercium nec aestimatio ejus debetur, sicuti, si campum Martium, vel basilicas, vel templa, vel quae publico usui destinata sunt, legaverit : nam nullius momenti legatum est. Quod autem diximus alienam rem posse legari, ita intelligendum est, si defunctus sciebat alienam rem esse, non et si ignorabat : forsitan enim, si scisset alienam, non legasset. Et ita divus Pius rescripsit, "et verius esse ; ipsum qui agit, id est legatarium, probare oportere, scisse alienam rem legare defunctum ; non heredem probare oportere, ignorasse alienam : quia semper necessitas probandi incumbit illi qui agit." § 5. Sed et si rem obligatam creditori aliquis legaverit, necesse habet heres luere. Et hoc quoque casu idem placet quod in re aliena, ut ita demum luere necesse habet heres, si sciebat defunctus rem obligatam esse : et ita divi Severus et Antoninus rescripserunt. Si tamen defunctus voluit legatarium luere, et hoc expressit, non debet heres eam luere. § 6. Si res aliena legata fuerit, et ejus vivo testatore legatarius dominus factus fuerit : si quidem ex causa emptionis, ex testamento actione pretium consequi potest ; si vero ex causa lucrativa, veluti ex donatione, vel ex alia simili causa, agere non potest. Nam traditum est "duas lucrativas causas in eundem hominem et in eandem rem concurrere non posse." Hac ratione, si ex duobus testamentis eadem res eidem debeatur, interest utrum

rem an aestimationem ex testamento consecutus est: nam si rem, agere non potest, quia habet eam ex causa
cf. Gai., § 203. lucrativa; si aestimationem, agere potest. § 7. *Ea quoque res quae in rerum natura non est, si modo futura est,* recte *legatur, veluti fructus qui in illo fundo nati erunt, aut quod ex illa ancilla natum erit.*
cf. Gai., § 199. § 8. *Si eadem res duobus legata sit, sive conjunctim, sive disjunctim;* si ambo *perveniant ad legatum,* scinditur inter eos legatum; si alter deficiat, quia aut spreverit legatum, aut vivo testatore decesserit, aut alio quolibet modo defecerit, totum ad collegatarium pertinet. *Conjunctim autem legatur,* veluti si quis dicat: "*Titio et Seio hominem Stichum do lego;*" *disjunctim ita:* "*Titio hominem Stichum do lego, Seio* Stichum *do lego.*" Sed et si expresserit, "*Eundem hominem* Stichum," aeque disjunctim legatum intelligitur. § 9. Si cui fundus alienus legatus fuerit, et emerit proprietatem detracto usufructu, et usufructus ad eum pervenerit, et postea ex testamento agat: recte eum agere et fundum petere Julianus ait, quia ususfructus in petitione servitutis locum obtinet; sed officio judicis contineri ut, deducto usufructu, jubeat aestimationem praestari. § 10. Sed si rem legatarii quis ei legaverit, inutile legatum est, quia, quod proprium est ipsius, amplius ejus fieri non potest; et, licet alienaverit eam, non debetur nec ipsa, nec aestimatio ejus. § 11. Si quis rem suam quasi alienam legaverit, valet legatum: nam plus valet quod in veritate est, quam quod in opinione. Sed et si legatarii putavit, valere constat, quia exitum voluntas de-
cf. Gai., § 198. functi potest habere. § 12. *Si rem suam legaverit testator, posteaque eam alienaverit,* Celsus existimat, si non adimendi animo vendidit, nihilominus deberi, idque divi Severus et Antoninus rescripserunt. Iidem rescripserunt eum qui, post testamentum factum, praedia quae legata erant pignori dedit, ademisse legatum non videri, et ideo legatarium cum herede agere posse, ut praedia a creditore luantur. Si vero quis partem rei legatae alienaverit, pars quae non est alienata omnimodo debetur, pars autem alienata ita debetur, si non adimendi animo alienata sit. § 13. Si quis debitori suo liberationem legaverit, legatum utile est; et neque ab ipso debitore, neque ab herede ejus potest heres petere, neque ab alio qui heredis loco est, sed et potest a debitore conveniri, ut liberet eum. Potest autem quis vel ad tempus jubere ne heres petat. § 14. Ex contrario, si debitor creditori suo quod debet legaverit, inutile est legatum si nihil plus est in legato quam in debito, quia nihil amplius

habet per legatum. Quod si in diem vel sub conditione debitum ei pure legaverit, utile est legatum propter repraesentationem. Quod si vivo testatore dies venerit, aut conditio extiterit, Papinianus scripsit, utile esse nihilominus legatum quia semel constitit. Quod et verum est: non enim placuit sententia existimantium extinctum esse legatum, quia in eam causam pervenit a qua incipere non potest. § 15. Sed si uxori maritus dotem legaverit, valet legatum, quia plenius est legatum quam de dote actio. Sed si quam non acceperit dotem legaverit, divi Severus et Antoninus rescripserunt, si quidem simpliciter legaverit, inutile esse legatum; si vero certa pecunia, vel certum corpus, aut instrumentum dotis in praelegando demonstrata sunt, valere legatum. § 16. Si res legata sine facto heredis perierit, legatario decedit. Et si servus alienus legatus, sine facto heredis manumissus fuerit, non tenetur heres. Si vero heredis servus legatus fuerit, et ipse eum manumiserit, teneri eum Julianus scripsit, nec interest scierit, an ignoraverit a se legatum esse. Sed et si alii donaverit servum, et is, cui donatus est, eum manumiserit, tenetur heres, quamvis ignoraverit a se eum legatum esse. § 17. Si quis ancillas cum suis natis legaverit, etiamsi ancillae mortuae fuerint, partus legato cedunt. Idem est, et si ordinarii servi cum vicariis legati fuerint, et, licet mortui sint ordinarii, tamen vicarii legato cedunt. Sed si servus cum peculio fuerit legatus, mortuo servo, vel manumisso, vel alienato, et peculii legatum extinguitur. Idem est, si fundus instructus vel cum instrumento legatus fuerit: nam fundo alienato et instrumenti legatum extinguitur. § 18. Si grex legatus fuerit, posteaque ad unam ovem pervenerit, quod superfuerit vindicari potest. Grege autem legato, etiam eas oves, quae post testamentum factum gregi adjiciuntur, legato cedere, Julianus ait: esse enim gregis unum corpus, ex distantibus capitibus, sicuti aedium unum corpus est, ex cohaerentibus lapidibus. § 19. Aedibus denique legatis, columnas et marmora, quae post testamentum factum adjecta sunt, legato cedere. § 20. Si peculium legatum fuerit, sine dubio quidquid peculio accedit vel decedit vivo testatore, legatarii lucro vel damno est. Quod si post mortem testatoris, ante aditam hereditatem, servus adquisierit, Julianus ait, si quidem ipsi manumisso peculium legatum fuerit, omne quod ante aditam hereditatem adquisitum est legatario cedere, quia dies hujus legati ab adita hereditate cedit; sed si extraneo peculium legatum fuerit, non cedere ea legato, nisi ex rebus peculiaribus auctum fuerit. Peculium autem, nisi legatum fuerit, manumisso non debetur, quamvis, si vivus manumiserit, sufficit, si non adimatur; et ita divi Severus et Antoninus rescripserunt. Iidem rescripserunt, peculio legato, non videri id relictum, ut petitionem habeat pecuniae quam in rationes dominicas impendit. Iidem rescripserunt, peculium videri legatum, cum rationibus redditis liber esse jussus est, et ex eo reliquas inferre. § 21. Tam autem corporales res quam incorporales legari possunt. Et ideo, et quod defuncto debetur, potest alicui legari, ut actiones suas heres legatario praestet, nisi exegerit vivus testator pecuniam: nam hoc casu legatum extinguitur. Sed et tale legatum valet: "damnas esto heres, domum illius reficere", vel "illum aere alieno liberare." § 22. Si generaliter servus vel alia res legetur, electio legatarii est, nisi aliud testator dixerit. § 23. Optionis legatum, id est ubi testator ex servis suis vel aliis rebus optare legatarium jusserat, habebat in se conditionem, et ideo, nisi ipse legatarius vivus optaverat, ad heredem legatum non transmittebat. Sed ex constitutione nostra, et hoc ad meliorem statum reformatum est, et data est licentia et heredi legatarii optare, licet vivus legatarius hoc non fecit. Et, diligentiore tractatu habito, et hoc in nostra constitutione additum est, ut sive plures legatarii existant, quibus optio relicta est, et dissentiant in corpore eligendo, sive unius legatarii plures heredes, et inter se circa optandum dissentiant, alio aliud corpus eligere cupiente, ne pereat legatum (quod plerique prudentium contra benevolentiam introducebant), fortunam esse hujus optionis judicem, et sorte esse hoc dirimendum, ut, ad quem sors perveniat, illius sententia in optione praecellat.

§ 24. Legari autem illis solis potest cum quibus testamenti factio est.

§ 238. Incertae personae legatum inutiliter relinquitur. Incerta autem videtur persona, quam per incertam opinionem animo suo testator subjicit, velut cum ita legatum sit: "Qui primus ad funus meum venerit, ei heres meus x millia dato." Idem juris est, si generaliter omnibus legaverit: "Quicumque ad funus meum venerit." In eadem causa est quod ita relinquitur: "Quicumque filio meo in matrimonium filiam suam collocave-

§ 25. *Incertis vero personis* neque *legata*, neque fideicommissa olim relinqui concessum erat: nam nec miles quidem incertae personae poterat relinquere, ut divus Hadrianus rescripsit. *Incerta autem persona videbatur, quam incerta opinione animo suo testator subjiciebat, veluti si* quis *ita* dicat: "*Quicumque filio meo in matrimonium filiam suam collocaverit, ei heres meus illum fundum dato.*" *Illud quoque quod* his *relinquebatur,* "*Qui post testamentum* scriptum primi *consules de-*

rit, ei heres meus x millia dato." Illud quoque in eadem causa est quod ita relinquitur: "Qui post testamentum consules designati erunt," nam aeque incertis personis legari videtur. Et denique aliae multae hujusmodi species sunt. Sub certa vero demonstratione incertae personae recte legatur, veluti: "Ex cognatis meis, qui nunc sunt, qui primus ad funus meum venerit, ei x millia heres meus dato." § 239. Libertas quoque non videtur incertae personae dari posse, quia lex Fusia Caninia jubet nominatim servos liberari.

§ 241. Postumo quoque alieno inutiliter legatur: est autem alienus postumus, qui natus inter suos heredes testatori futurus non est; ideoque ex emancipato quoque filio conceptus nepos extraneus postumus est; item qui in utero est ejus, quae in jure civili non intellegitur uxor, extraneus postumus patri intellegitur.

§ 240. Tutor quoque certus dari debet.

§ 242. Ac ne heres quidem potest institui postumus alienus; est enim incerta persona. § 243. Cetera vero quae supra diximus, ad legata proprie pertinent; quamquam non immerito quibusdam placeat, poenae nomine heredem institui non posse; nihil enim interest, utrum legatum dare jubeatur heres, si fecerit aliquid aut non fecerit, an coheres ei adjiciatur; quia tam coheredis adjectione quam legati datione compellitur, ut aliquid contra propositum suum faciat aut non faciat.

signati erunt," *aeque incertae personae legari* videbatur: *et denique multae aliae hujusmodi species sunt. Libertas quoque non* videbatur *posse incertae personae dari, quia* placebat *nominatim servos liberari.* Tutor quoque certus dari debebat. *Sub certa vero demonstratione,* id est, ex certis personis incertae *personae, recte* legabatur, *veluti:* "*Ex cognatis meis, qui nunc sunt,* si *quis* filiam meam uxorem duxerit, *ei heres meus* illam rem *dato.*" Incertis autem personis legata vel fideicommissa relicta et per errorem soluta repeti non posse, sacris constitutionibus cautum erat.

§ 26. *Postumo quoque alieno inutiliter* legabatur: *est autem alienus postumus qui natus inter suos heredes testatoris futurus non est; ideoque ex emancipato filio conceptus nepos extraneus* erat *postumus* avo. § 27. Sed nec hujusmodi species penitus est sine justa emendatione derelicta, cum in nostro codice constitutio posita est per quam et huic parti medevimus, non solum in hereditatibus, sed etiam in legatis et fideicommissis; quod evidenter ex ipsius constitutionis lectione clarescit. *Tutor* autem *nec* per nostram constitutionem *incertus dari debet,* quia certo judicio debet quis pro tutela suae posteritati cavere. § 28. Postumus autem alienus heres institui et antea poterat, et nunc potest, nisi in utero ejus sit quae jure nostro uxor esse non potest. § 29. Si quis in nomine, cognomine, praenomine legatarii erraverit testator, si de persona constat, nihilominus valet legatum; idemque in heredibus servatur, et recte: nomina enim significandorum hominum gratia reperta sunt, qui si quolibet alio modo intelligantur, nihil interest. § 30. Huic proxima est illa juris regula, falsa demonstratione legatum non perimi, veluti si quis ita legaverit: "Stichum servum meum vernam do lego": licet enim non verna, sed emptus sit, de servo tamen constat, utile est legatum. Et convenienter, si ita demonstraverit: "Stichum servum, quem a Seio emi", sitque ab alio emptus, utile est legatum, si de servo constat. § 31. Longe magis legato falsa causa non nocet, veluti cum ita quis dixerit: "Titio, quia, absente me, negotia mea curavit, Stichum do lego"; vel ita: "Titio, quia patrocinio ejus capitali crimine liberatus sum, Stichum do lego": licet enim neque negotia testatoris unquam gessit Titius, neque patrocinio ejus liberatus est, legatum tamen valet. Sed si conditionaliter enuntiata fuerit causa, aliud juris est, veluti hoc modo: "Titio, si negotia mea curaverit, fundum do lego."

§ 244. An ei, qui in potestate sit ejus, quem heredem instituimus recte legemus, quaeritur. Servius recte legari putat, sed evanescere legatum, si, quo tempore dies legatorum cedere solet, adhuc in potestate sit: ideoque, sive pure legatum sit et vivo testatore in potestate heredis esse desierit, sive sub conditione et ante conditionem id acciderit, deberi legatum. Sabinus et Cassius sub conditione recte legari, pure non recte, putant; licet enim vivo testatore possit desinere in potestate heredis esse, ideo tamen inutile legatum intelligi oportere, quia, quod nullas vires habiturum foret, si statim post testamentum factum decessisset testator, hoc ideo valere, quia vitam longius traxerit, absurdum esset. Diversae scholae auctores nec sub conditione recte legari [putant], quia quos in potestate habemus, eis non magis sub conditione quam pure debere possumus. § 245. Ex diverso constat, ab eo qui in potestate tua est, herede instituto, recte tibi legari: sed si tu per eum heres extiteris, evanescere legatum, quia ipse tibi legatum debere non possis; si vero filius emancipatus, aut servus manumissus erit, vel in alium translatus, et ipse heres extiterit, aut alium fecerit, deberi legatum.

§ 32. *An* servo *heredis recte legamus, quaeritur.* Et constat *pure* inutiliter *legari;* nec quidquam proficere, si *vivo testatore* de *potestate heredis* exierit, *quia, quod* inutile *foret* legatum, *si statim post factum testamentum decessisset testator, hoc* non debet ideo *valere, quia* diutius testator *vixerit. Sub conditione vero recte legatur,* ut requiramus an, quo tempore dies legati cedit, in potestate heredis non sit. § 33. *Ex diverso, herede instituto servo,* quin domino *recte* etiam sine conditione *legetur,* non dubitatur. Nam et si statim post factum testamentum decesserit testator, non tamen apud eum qui heres sit dies legati cedere intelligitur, cum hereditas a legato separata sit, et possit per eum servum alius heres effici, si prius quam jussu domini adeat, in alterius potestatem translatus sit, vel *manumissus ipse heres* efficitur: quibus casibus utile est legatum; quodsi in eadem causa permanserit, et jussu legatarii adierit, *evanescit legatum.*

De inutiliter relictis legatis.

§ 229. Ante heredis institutionem inutiliter legatur, scilicet quia testamenta vim ex institutione heredis accipiunt, et ob id velut caput et fundamentum intelligitur totius testamenti heredis institutio. § 230. Pari ratione nec libertas ante heredis institutionem dari potest. § 231. Nostri praeceptores nec tutorem eo loco dari posse existimant: sed Labeo et Proculus tutorem posse dari, quod nihil ex hereditate erogatur tutoris datione.

§ 232. Post mortem quoque heredis inutiliter legatur; id est hoc modo: "Cum heres meus mortuus erit, do lego", aut "dato". Ita autem recte legatur: "Cum heres morietur": quia non post mortem heredis relinquitur, sed ultimo vitae ejus tempore. Rursum ita non potest legari: "Pridie quam heres meus morietur"; quod non pretiosa ratione receptum videtur. § 233. Eadem et de libertatibus dicta intelligemus. § 234. Tutor vero an post mortem heredis dari possit quaerentibus eadem forsitan poterit esse quaestio, quae de eo agitatur qui ante heredum institutionem datur.

§ 34. *Ante heredis institutionem inutiliter* antea legabatur, *scilicet quia testamenta vim ex institutione heredum accipiunt, et ob id veluti caput atque fundamentum intelligitur totius testamenti heredis institutio. Pari ratione nec libertas ante heredis institutionem dari* poterat. Sed quia incivile esse putavimus, ordinem quidem scripturae sequi (quod et ipsi antiquitati vituperandum fuerat visum), sperni autem testatoris voluntatem: per nostram constitutionem et hoc vitium emendavimus, ut liceat, et ante heredis institutionem, et inter medias heredum institutiones, legatum relinquere, et multo magis libertatem, cujus usus favorabilior est.

§ 35. *Post mortem quoque heredis* aut legatarii simili modo *inutiliter* legabatur: veluti si quis ita dicat, "*Cum heres meus mortuus erit, do lego*"; item: "*Pridie quam heres* aut legatarius *morietur*". Sed simili modo et hoc correximus, firmitatem hujusmodi legatis ad fideicommissorum similitudinem praestantes, ne vel in hoc casu deterior causa legatorum quam fideicommissorum inveniatur.

De poenae causa relictis legatis.

§ 235. Poenae quoque nomine inutiliter legatur. Poenae autem nomine legari videtur, quod coercendi heredis causa relinquitur, quo magis heres aliquid faciat aut non faciat; veluti quod ita legatur: "Si heres meus filiam suam Titio in matrimonium collocaverit, x millia Seio dato"; vel ita: "Si filiam Titio in matrimonium non collocaverit, x millia Titio dato". Sed etiam si heres, verbi gratia,

§ 36. *Poenae quoque nomine inutiliter* legabatur et adimebatur vel transferebatur. *Poenae autem nomine legari videtur quod coercendi heredis causa relinquitur, quo magis is aliquid faciat, aut non faciat: veluti* si quis ita scripserit. "*Heres meus, si filiam suam in matrimonium Titio collocaverit*" (vel ex diverso, "*si non collocaverit*"), "*dato decem* aureos *Seio*"; aut si *ita* scripserit: "Heres meus, intra biennium monumentum sibi non fecerit, x Titio dari" jusserit, poenae nomine legatum videtur. Denique ex ipsa definitione multas similes species proprias fingere possumus. § 236. Nec libertas quidem poenae nomine dari potest, quamvis de ea re fuerit quaesitum. § 237. De tutore vero nihil possumus quaerere, quia non potest datione tutoris heres compelli quidquam facere aut non facere; ideo quando etiam poenae nomine tutor datus fuerit, magis sub conditione quam poenae nomine datus videbitur.

si servum Stichum alienaverit" (vel ex diverso, "si non alienaverit"), "Titio decem aureos dato". Et in tantum haec regula observabatur, ut perquam pluribus principalibus constitutionibus significetur, nec principem quidem agnoscere, quod ei poenae nomine legatum sit. Nec ex militis quidem testamento talia legata valebant, quamvis aliae militum voluntates in ordinandis testamentis valde observantur. Quin etiam *nec libertatem poenae nomine dari posse* placebat; eo amplius nec heredem poenae nomine adjici posse Sabinus existimabat, veluti si quis ita dicat: "Titius heres esto, si Titius filiam suam Seio in matrimonium collocaverit, Seius quoque heres esto": nihil enim intererat, qua ratione Titius coerceatur, utrum legati datione, an coheredis adjectione. Sed hujusmodi scrupulositas nobis non placuit, et generaliter ea quae relinquuntur, licet poenae nomine fuerint relicta, vel adempta, vel in alios translata, nihil distare a ceteris legatis constituimus vel in dando, vel in adimendo, vel in transferendo; exceptis his videlicet, quae impossibilia sunt, vel legibus interdicta, aut alias probrosa: hujusmodi enim testatorum dispositiones valere secta temporum meorum non patitur.

Tit. xxi. De ademptione et translatione legatorum.

Ademptio legatorum, sive eodem testamento adimantur legata, sive codicillis, firma est, sive contrariis verbis fiat ademptio, veluti si quod ita quis legaverit "do lego": ita adimatur "non do, non lego": sive non contrariis, id est, aliis quibuscumque verbis. § 1. Transferri quoque legatum ab alio ad alium potest, veluti si quis ita dixerit: "Hominem Stichum quem Titio legavi, Seio do lego"; sive in eodem testamento, sive in codicillis hoc fecerit. Quo casu simul Titio adimi videtur, et Seio dari.

Ad legem Falcidiam.

§ 224. Sed olim quidem licebat totum patrimonium legatis atque libertatibus erogare, nec quicquam heredi relinquere praeterquam inane nomen heredis; idque lex xii Tabularum permittere videbatur, qua cavetur, ut quod quisque de re sua testatus esset, id ratum haberetur

Tit. xxii. De lege Falcidia.

Superest ut de lege Falcidia dispiciamus, qua modus novissime legatis impositus est. Cum enim *olim lege Duodecim Tabularum* libera erat legandi potestas, ut liceret vel *totum patri-*

his verbis: "uti legassit suae rei, ita jus esto." Quare qui scripti heredes erant, ab hereditate se abstinebant; et idcirco plerique intestati moriebantur. § 225. Itaque lata est lex Furia, qua, exceptis personis quibusdam, caeteris plus mille assibus legatorum nomine mortisve causa capere permissum non est. Sed etiam haec lex non perfecit quod voluit: qui enim verbi gratia quinque millium aeris patrimonium habebat, poterat quinque hominibus singulis millenos asses legando totum patrimonium erogare. § 226. Ideo postea lata est lex Voconia, qua cautum est, ne cui plus legatorum nomine mortisve causa capere liceret, quam heredes caperent. Ex qua lege plane quidem aliquid utique heredes habere videbantur, sed tamen fere vitium simile nascebatur; nam in multas legatariorum personas distributo patrimonio, poterat adeo heredi minimum relinquere testator, ut non expediret heredi, hujus lucri gratia, totius hereditatis onera sustinere. § 227. Lata est itaque lex Falcidia, qua cautum est, ne plus legare liceat quam dodrantem: itaque necesse est ut heres quartam partem hereditatis habeat; et hoc nunc jure utimur. § 228. In libertatibus quoque dandis nimiam licentiam compescuit lex Fusia Caninia, sicut in primo commentario retulimus.

monium legatis erogare (quippe ea lege ita cautum esset: "*uti legassit suae rei, ita jus esto*"), visum est hanc legandi licentiam coarctare. Idque ipsorum testatorum gratia provisum est, ob *id* quod *plerumque intestati moriebantur*, recusantibus *scriptis heredibus* pro nullo aut minimo lucro *hereditates* adire. Et cum super hoc tam *lex Furia* quam *lex Voconia latae sunt*, quarum neutra sufficiens ad rei consummationem videbatur, novissime *lata est lex Falcidia, qua cavetur, ne plus legare liceat quam dodrantem* totorum bonorum, id *est*, ut sive unus *heres* institutus esset, sive plures, apud eum eosve *pars quarta* remaneret.

§ 1. Et cum quaesitum esset, duobus heredibus institutis, veluti Titio et Seio, si Titii pars aut tota exhausta sit legatis quae nominatim ab eo data sunt, aut supra modum onerata, a Seio vero aut nulla relicta sint legata, aut quae partem ejus duntaxat in partem dimidiam minuunt, an, quia is quartam partem totius hereditatis aut amplius habet, Titio nihil ex legatis quae ab eo relicta sunt, retinere liceret? placuit, ut quartam partem suae partis salvam habeat: etenim in singulis heredibus ratio legis Falcidiae ponenda est. § 2. Quantitas autem patrimonii, ad quam ratio legis Falcidiae redigitur, mortis tempore spectatur. Itaque si, verbi gratia, is qui centum aureorum patrimonium in bonis habebat, centum aureos legaverit, nihil legatariis prodest, si ante aditam hereditatem per servos hereditarios aut ex partu ancillarum hereditariarum aut ex fetu pecorum tantum accesserit hereditati, ut centum (aureis) legatorum nomine erogatis heres quartam (partem hereditatis) habiturus sit; sed necesse est, ut nihilominus quarta pars legatis detrahatur. Ex diverso, si septuaginta quinque legaverit, et ante aditam hereditatem in tantum decreverint bona, incendiis forte aut naufragiis aut morte servorum, ut non amplius quam septuaginta quinque (aureorum substantia) vel etiam minus relinquatur, solida legata debentur. Nec ea res damnosa est heredi, cui liberum est non adire hereditatem: quae res efficit, ut necesse sit legatariis, ne destituto testamento nihil consequantur, cum herede in portionem pacisci. § 3. Cum autem ratio legis Falcidiae ponitur, ante deducitur aes alienum; item funeris impensa et pretia servorum manumissorum: tunc deinde in reliquo ita ratio habetur, ut ex eo quarta pars apud heredes remaneat, tres vero partes inter legatarios distribuantur, pro rata scilicet portione ejus quod cuique eorum legatum fuerit. Itaque si fingamus quadringentos aureos legatos esse, et patrimonii quantitatem ex qua legata erogari oportet quadringentorum esse, quarta pars singulis legatariis detrahi debet. Quod si trecentos quinquaginta legatos fingamus, octava debet detrahi. Quod si quingentos legaverit, initio quinta, deinde quarta detrahi debet: ante enim detrahendum est quod extra bonorum quantitatem est, deinde quod ex bonis apud heredem remanere oportet.

Tit. xxiii. De fideicommissariis hereditatibus.

GAI.	JUST.
§ 246. Nunc transeamus ad fideicommissa. § 247. Et prius de hereditatibus videamus.	*Nunc transeamus ad fideicommissa. Et prius de hereditatibus* fideicommissariis *videamus.*

§ 1. Sciendum itaque est omnia fideicommissa primis temporibus infirma esse, quia nemo invitus cogebatur praestare id de quo rogatus erat. Quibus enim non poterant hereditatem vel legata relinquere, si relinquebant, fidei committebant eorum qui capere ex testamento poterant; et ideo fideicommissa appellata sunt, quia nullo vinculo juris, sed tantum pudore eorum qui rogabantur, continebantur. Postea divus Augustus, semel iterumque gratia personarum motus, vel quia per ipsius salutem rogatus quis diceretur, aut ob insignem quorundam perfidiam, jussit consulibus auctoritatem suam interponere. Quod, quia justum videbatur et populare erat, paulatim conversum est in assiduam jurisdictionem; tantusque eorum favor factus est, ut paulatim etiam praetor proprius crearetur qui de fideicommissis jus diceret, quem fideicommissarium appellabant.

§ 248. In primis igitur sciendum est, opus esse ut aliquis heres recto jure instituatur, ejusque fidei committatur ut eam hereditatem alii restituat: alioquin inutile est testamentum in quo nemo recto jure heres instituitur. § 250. Cum igitur scripserimus: "Lucius Titius heres esto", possumus adjicere: "Rogo te, Luci Titi, petoque a te, ut cum primum possis hereditatem meam adire, Gaio Seio reddas restituas". Possumus autem et de parte restituenda rogare; et liberum est vel sub conditione, vel pure relinquere fideicommissa, vel ex die certa. § 251. Restituta autem hereditate, is qui restituit nihilominus heres permanet; is vero qui recipit hereditatem, aliquando heredis loco est, aliquando legatarii.

§ 2. *In primis igitur sciendum est, opus esse ut aliquis recto jure* testamento *heres instituatur, ejusque fidei committatur, ut eam hereditatem alii restituat: alioquin inutile est testamentum in quo nemo heres instituitur. Cum igitur* aliquis *scripserit: "Lucius Titius heres esto": poterit adjicere: "Rogo te, Luci Titi, ut cum primum possis hereditatem meam adire*, eam *Gaio Seio reddas restituas". Potest autem* quisque *et de parte restituenda* heredem *rogare; et liberum est vel pure vel sub conditione relinquere fideicommissum, vel ex die certo.* § 3. *Restituta autem hereditate, is quidem qui restituit, nihilominus heres permanet; is vero qui recipit hereditatem, aliquando heredis, aliquando legatarii loco* habebatur.

§ 252. Olim autem neque heredis loco erat, nec legatarii, sed potius emptoris. Tunc enim in usu erat, ei cui restituebatur hereditas, nummo uno eam hereditatem dicis causa venire; et quae stipulationes inter [venditorem hereditatis et emptorem interponi solent, eaedem interponebantur inter] heredem et eum cui restituebatur hereditas, id est, hoc modo: heres quidem stipulabatur ab eo cui restituebatur hereditas, ut quidquid hereditario nomine [dedisset, sive cujus rei nomine] condemnatus fuisset, sive quid alias bona fide dedisset, eo nomine indemnis esset, et omnino si quis cum eo hereditario nomine ageret, ut recte defenderetur; ille vero qui recipiebat hereditatem, invicem stipulabatur, ut si quid ex hereditate ad heredem pervenisset, id sibi restitueretur; ut etiam pateretur eum hereditarias actiones procuratorio aut cognitorio nomine exequi.

§ 253. Sed post[ea Neronis] temporibus, Trebellio Maximo et Annaeo Seneca consulibus, senatus-consultum factum est, quo cautum est, ut, si cui hereditas ex fideicommissaria causa restituta sit, actiones quae jure civili heredi et in heredem competerent, ei et in eum darentur cui ex fideicommisso restituta esset hereditas. Post quod senatus-consultum desierunt illae cautiones in usu ha-

§ 4. *Et in Neronis quidem temporibus, Trebellio Maximo et Annaeo Seneca consulibus, senatus-consultum factum est, quo cautum est, ut, si cui hereditas ex fideicommissaria causa restituta sit*, omnes *actiones quae jure civili heredi et in heredem competerent, ei et in eum darentur cui ex fideicommisso restituta esset hereditas. Post quod senatus-consultum praetor utiles actiones ei et in eum qui recepit hereditatem,*

beri; praetor enim utiles actiones ei et in eum qui recipit hereditatem, quasi heredi et in heredem, dare coepit, [formul]aeque in [hunc casum in] edicto proponuntur. § 254. Sed rursus, quia heredes scripti, cum aut totam hereditatem, aut pene totam plerumque restituere rogabantur, adire hereditatem ob nullum aut minimum lucrum recusabant, atque ob id extinguebantur fideicommissa, postea [Vespasiani Augusti tempore, consule] Pegaso et Pusione senatus censuit, ut ei, qui rogatus est hereditatem restituere, perinde liceret quartam partem retinere, atque e lege Falcidia in legatis retinendis conceditur. Ex singulis quoque rebus quae per fideicommissum relinquuntur, eadem retentio permissa est. Per quod senatus-consultum ipse [heres] onera hereditaria sustinet; ille autem qui ex fideicommisso reliquam partem hereditatis recipit, legatarii partiarii loco est, id est, ejus legatarii cui pars bonorum legatur; quae species legati partitio vocatur, quia cum herede legatarius partitur hereditatem. Unde effectum est ut, quae solent stipulationes inter heredem et partiarium legatarium interponi, eaedem interponantur inter eum qui ex fideicommissaria causa recipit hereditatem, et heredem, id est, ut et lucrum et damnum hereditarium pro rata parte inter eos commune sit. § 255. Ergo si quidem non plus quam dodrantem hereditatis scriptus heres rogatus sit restituere, tum ex Trebelliano senatus-consulto restituitur hereditas, et in utrumque actiones hereditariae pro rata parte dantur: in heredem quidem jure civili, in eum vero qui recipit hereditatem ex senatus-consulto Trebelliano: quamquam heres, etiam pro ea parte quam restituit, heres permanet, eique et in eum solidae actiones competunt; sed non ulterius

quasi heredi et in heredem dare coepit. § 5. *Sed quia heredes scripti, cum aut totam hereditatem aut pene totam plerumque restituere rogabantur, adire hereditatem ob nullum aut minimum lucrum recusabant, atque ob id extinguebantur fideicommissa, postea Vespasiani Augusti temporibus, Pegaso et Pusione consulibus, senatus censuit, ut ei, qui rogatus esset hereditatem restituere, perinde liceret quartam partem retinere, atque lege Falcidia ex legatis retinere conceditur. Ex singulis quoque rebus quae per fideicommissum relinquuntur, eadem retentio permissa est. Post quod senatus-consultum, ipse heres onera hereditaria sustinebat; ille autem qui ex fideicommisso recepit partem hereditatis, legatarii partiarii loco* erat, *id est, ejus legatarii cui pars bonorum* legabatur. *Quae species legati partitio* vocabatur, *quia cum herede legatarius* partiebatur *hereditatem. Unde quae* solebant *stipulationes inter heredem et partiarium legatarium interponi, eaedem* interponebantur *inter eum qui ex fideicommisso recepit hereditatem, et heredem: id est, ut et lucrum et damnum hereditarium pro rata parte inter eos commune sit.* § 6. *Ergo si quidem non plus quam dodrantem hereditatis scriptus heres rogatus sit restituere, tunc ex Trebelliano senatus-consulto* restituebatur *hereditas et in utrumque actiones hereditariae, pro rata parte* dabantur; *in heredem quidem jure civili; in eum vero qui* recipiebat *hereditatem, ex senatus-consulto Trebelliano,* tamquam in heredem. *At si plus quam dodrantem vel etiam totam hereditatem restituere rogatus sit, locus erat Pegasiano senatus-consulto,* et heres *qui semel adierit hereditatem, si modo sua voluntate*

oneratur, nec ulterius illi dantur actiones, quam apud eum commodum hereditatis remanet. § 256. At si quis plus quam dodrantem, vel etiam totam hereditatem restituere rogatus sit, locus est Pegasiano senatus-consulto. § 257. Sed is qui semel adierit hereditatem, si modo sua voluntate adierit, sive retinuerit quartam partem, sive noluerit retinere, ipse universa onera hereditaria sustinet: sed quarta quidem retenta, quasi partis et pro parte stipulationes interponi debent, tamquam inter partiarium legatarium et heredem; si vero totam hereditatem restituerit, ad exemplum emptae et venditae hereditatis stipulationes interponendae sunt. § 258. Sed si recuset scriptus heres adire hereditatem, ob id quod dicat eam sibi suspectam esse quasi damnosam, cavetur Pegasiano senatus-consulto, ut, desiderante eo cui restituere rogatus est, jussu praetoris adeat et restituat, perindeque ei et in eum qui receperit [hereditatem] actiones dentur, ac juris est ex senatus-consulto Trebelliano. Quo casu nullis stipulationibus opus est, quia simul et huic qui restituit securitas datur, et actiones hereditariae ei et in eum transferuntur qui receperit hereditatem.

adierit, sive retinuerit quartam partem, sive noluerit retinere, ipse universa onera hereditaria sustinebat. *Sed quarta quidem retenta, quasi partis et pro parte stipulationes* interponebantur, *tamquam inter partiarium legatarium et heredem; si vero totam hereditatem restituerit, emptae et venditae hereditatis stipulationes* interponebantur. *Sed si recuset scriptus heres adire hereditatem, ob id quod dicat eam sibi suspectam esse quasi damnosam, cavetur Pegasiano senatus-consulto, ut desiderante eo cui restituere rogatus est, jussu praetoris adeat et restituat hereditatem, perindeque ei et in eum qui recepit hereditatem actiones dentur, ac juris est ex Trebelliano senatus-consulto. Quo casu nullis stipulationibus opus est, quia simul et huic qui restituit securitas datur, et actiones hereditariae ei et in eum transferuntur qui recepit hereditatem,* utroque senatus-consulto in hac specie concurrente.

§ 7. Sed quia stipulationes ex senatus-consulto Pegasiano descendentes et ipsi antiquitati displicuerunt, et quibusdam casibus captiosas eas homo excelsi ingenii Papinianus appellat, et nobis in legibus magis simplicitas quam difficultas placet: ideo, omnibus nobis suggestis tam similitudinibus quam differentiis utriusque senatus-consulti, placuit, exploso senatus-consulto Pegasiano quod postea supervenit, omnem auctoritatem Trebelliano senatus-consulto praestare, ut ex eo fideicommissariae hereditates restituantur, sive habeat heres ex voluntate testatoris quartam, sive plus, sive minus, sive penitus nihil; ut tunc, quando vel nihil, vel minus quartae apud eum remanet, liceat ei vel quartam, vel quod deest ex nostra auctoritate retinere, vel repetere solutum, quasi ex Trebelliano senatus-consulto, pro rata portione actionibus tam in heredem quam in fideicommissarium competentibus. Si vero totam hereditatem sponte restituerit, omnes hereditariae actiones fideicommissario et adversus eum competunt. Sed etiam id quod praecipuum Pegasiani senatus-consulti fuerat, ut quando recusabat heres scriptus sibi datam hereditatem adire, necessitas ei imponeretur totam hereditatem volenti fideicommissario restituere, et omnes ad eum et contra eum transire actiones; et hoc transponimus ad senatus-consultum Trebellianum, ut ex hoc solo et necessitas heredi imponatur, si ipso, nolente adire, fideicommissarius desiderat restitui sibi hereditatem, nullo nec damno nec commodo apud heredem manente.

§ 259. Nihil autem interest utrum aliquis ex asse heres institutus aut totam hereditatem aut pro parte restituere rogetur, an ex parte heres institutus aut totam eam partem aut partis partem restituere rogetur; nam et hoc casu de quarta parte ejus partis ratio ex Pegasiano senatus-consulto haberi solet.

§ 8. *Nihil autem interest utrum aliquis ex asse heres institutus, aut totam hereditatem aut pro parte restituere rogatur, an ex parte heres institutus, aut totam eam partem, aut partis partem restituere rogatur: nam et hoc casu* eadem observari praecipimus, quae in totius hereditatis restitutione diximus. § 9. Si quis una aliqua re deducta sive praecepta quae quartam continet, veluti fundo vel alia re, rogatus sit restituere hereditatem, simili modo ex Trebelliano senatus-consulto restitutio fiat, perinde ac si quarta parte retenta rogatus esset reliquam hereditatem restituere. Sed illud interest, quod altero casu, id est cum deducta sive praecepta aliqua re restituitur hereditas, in solidum ex eo senatus-consulto actiones transferuntur; et res quae remanet apud heredem, sine ullo onere hereditario apud eum remanet, quasi ex legato ei acquisita. Altero vero casu, id est cum quarta parte retenta rogatus est heres restituere hereditatem et restituit, scinduntur actiones, et pro dodrante quidem transferuntur ad fideicommissarium; pro quadrante remaneant apud heredem. Quin etiam, licet una re aliqua deducta aut praecepta restituere aliquis hereditatem rogatus est, qua maxima pars hereditatis contineatur, aeque in solidum transferuntur actiones, et secum deliberare debet is cui restituitur hereditas, an expediat sibi restitui. Eadem scilicet interveniunt, et si duabus pluribusve deductis praeceptisve rebus restituere hereditatem rogatus sit. Sed et si certa summa deducta praeceptave, quae quartam vel etiam maximam partem hereditatis continet, rogatus sit aliquis hereditatem restituere, idem juris est. Quae diximus de eo qui ex asse heres institutus est, eadem transferimus et ad eum qui ex parte heres scriptus est.

§ 10. Praeterea intestatus quoque moriturus potest rogare eum ad quem bona sua vel legitimo jure vel honorario pertinere intelligit, ut hereditatem suam totam partemve ejus, aut rem aliquam, veluti fundum, hominem, pecuniam, alicui restituat: cum alioquin legata, nisi ex testamento, non valeant. § 11. Eum quoque cui aliquid restituitur potest rogare, ut id rursum alii, aut totum aut pro parte, vel etiam aliquid aliud restituat. § 12. Et quia prima fideicommissorum cunabula a fide heredum pendent, et tam nomen quam substantiam acceperunt, et ideo divus Augustus ad necessitatem juris ea detraxit; nuper et nos, eundem principem superare contendentes, ex facto quod Tribonianus, vir excelsus, quaestor sacri palatii, suggessit, constitutionem fecimus per quam disposuimus: si testator fidei heredis sui commisit, ut vel hereditatem vel speciale fideicommissum restituat, et neque ex scriptura, neque ex quinque testium numero, qui in fideicommissis legitimus esse noscitur, res possit manifestari, sed vel pauciores quam quinque vel nemo penitus testis intervenerit; tunc, sive pater heredis sive alius quicumque sit qui fidem heredis elegerit et ab eo aliquid restitui voluerit, si heres perfidia tentus adimplere fidem recusat, negando rem ita esse subsecutam, si fideicommissarius jusjurandum ei detulerit, cum prius ipse de calumnia juraverit, necesse eum habere, vel jusjurandum subire quod nihil tale a testatore audiverit, vel recusantem ad fideicommissi vel universitatis vel specialis solutionem coartari, ne depereat ultima voluntas testatoris fidei heredis commissa. Eadem observari censuimus etsi a legatario vel fideicommissario aliquid similiter relictum sit. Quod si is a quo relictum dicitur confiteatur quidem aliquid a se relictum esse, sed ad legis subtilitatem decurrat, omnimodo cogendus est solvere.

Tit. xxiv. De singulis rebus per fideicommissum relictis.

§ 260. Potest autem quisque etiam res singulas per fideicommissum relinquere, velut fundum, hominem, vestem, argentum, pecuniam; et vel ipsum heredem rogare ut alicui restituat, vel legatarium, quamvis a legatario legari non possit. § 261. Item potest non solum propria testatoris res per fideicommissum relinqui, sed etiam heredis, aut legatarii, aut cujuslibet

Potest autem quis etiam singulas res per fideicommissum relinquere, veluti fundum, hominem, vestem, argentum, pecuniam numeratam; *et vel ipsum heredem rogare, ut alicui restituat, vel legatarium, quamvis a legatario legari non possit.* § 1. *Potest autem non solum proprias testator res per fideicommissum relinquere, sed et heredis, aut legatarii,* aut fideicom-

alterius. Itaque et legatarius non solum de ea re rogari potest, ut eam alicui restituat, quae ei legata sit, sed etiam de alia, sive ipsius legatarii, sive aliena sit. Sed hoc solum observandum est, ne plus quisquam rogetur aliis restituere, quam ipse ex testamento ceperit; nam quod amplius est inutiliter relinquitur. § 262. Cum autem aliena res per fideicommissum relinquitur, necesse est ei qui rogatus est, aut ipsam redimere et praestare, aut aestimationem ejus solvere; sicuti juris est, si per damnationem aliena res legata sit. Sunt tamen qui putant, si rem per fideicommissum relictam dominus non vendat, extingui fideicommissum; sed aliam esse causam per damnationem legati.

missarii, *aut cujuslibet alterius. Itaque et legatarius* et fideicommissarius *non solum de ea re rogari potest, ut eam alicui restituat, quae ei relicta sit, sed etiam de alia, sive ipsius, sive aliena sit. Hoc solum observandum est, ne plus quisquam rogetur alicui restituere, quam ipse ex testamento ceperit; nam quod amplius est inutiliter relinquitur. Cum autem aliena res per fideicommissum relinquitur, necesse est ei qui rogatus est, aut ipsam redimere et praestare, aut aestimationem ejus solvere.*

§ 263. Libertas quoque servo per fideicommissum dari potest, ut vel heres rogetur manumittere, vel legatarius. § 264. [Nec interest utrum de suo proprio] servo testator roget, an de eo qui ipsius heredis, aut legatarii, vel etiam extranei sit. § 265. Itaque et alienus servus redimi et manumitti debet. Quod si dominus eum non vendat, sane extinguitur fideicommissaria libertas, quia hoc casu pretii computatio nulla intervenit. § 266. Qui autem ex fideicommisso manumittitur, non testatoris fit libertus, etiamsi testatoris servus fuerit, sed ejus qui manumittit. § 267. At qui directo testamento liber esse jubetur, velut hoc modo: "Stichus servus liber esto", vel hoc: "Stichum servum meum liberum esse jubeo", is [ipsius testa]toris fit libertus. Nec alius ullus directo ex testamento libertatem habere potest, quam qui utroque tempore testatoris ex jure

§ 2. *Libertas quoque servo per fideicommissum dari potest, ut heres eum rogetur manumittere, vel legatarius*, vel fideicommissarius. *Nec interest utrum de suo proprio servo testator roget, an de eo qui ipsius heredis, aut legatarii, vel etiam extranei sit. Itaque et alienus servus redimi et manumitti debet. Quod si dominus eum non vendat,* si modo nihil ex judicio ejus qui reliquit libertatem perceperit, non statim *extinguitur fideicommissaria libertas*, sed differtur, quia possit tempore procedente, ubicumque occasio redimendi servi fuerit, praestari libertas. *Qui autem ex causa fideicommissi manumittitur, non testatoris fit libertus, etiamsi testatoris servus sit, sed ejus qui manumittit. At is qui directo testamento liber esse jubetur, ipsius testatoris libertus fit,* qui etiam orcinus appellatur. *Nec alius ullus directo ex testamento libertatem habere potest, quam qui utroque tempore testatoris fuerit, et quo faceret testamentum, et quo moreretur.* Directa autem libertas tunc dari videtur, cum non ab alio

[quiritium fuerit et quo faceret] testamentum, et quo moreretur.

servum manumitti rogat, sed velut ex suo testamento libertatem ei competere vult.

§ 249. Verba autem utilia fideicommissorum haec recte maxime in usu esse videntur: "Peto," "rogo," "volo", "fideicommitto"; quae perinde firma singula sunt, atque si omnia in unum congesta sint.

§ 3. *Verba autem fideicommissorum haec maxime in usu habentur: "Peto", "rogo", "volo",* "mando", "*fidei* tuae *committo*"; *quae perinde singula firma sunt, atque si omnia in unum congesta essent.*

§ 268. Multum autem differunt ea, quae per fideicommissum legantur, ab his quae directo jure relinquuntur. § 269. Nam ecce per fideicommissum etiam [nutu] hereditas relinqui potest: cum alioquin legatum nisi testamento facto inutile sit. § 270. Item intestatus moriturus potest, ab eo ad quem bona ejus pertinent, fideicommissum alicui relinquere: cum alioquin ab eo legari non possit. § 270A. [Item legatum codicillis] relictum non aliter valet, quam si a testatore confirmati fuerint, id est, nisi in testamento caverit testator, ut quidquid in codicillis scripserit, id ratum sit: fideicommissum vero etiam non confirmatis codicillis relinqui potest. § 271. Item a legatario legari non potest: sed fideicommissum relinqui potest. Quin etiam ab eo quoque cui per fideicommissum relinquimus, rursus alii per fideicommissum relinquere possumus. § 272. Item servo alieno directo libertas dari non potest: sed per fideicommissum potest. § 273. Item codicillis nemo heres institui potest, neque exheredari, quamvis testamento confirmati sint: at is, qui testamento heres institutus est, potest codicillis rogari ut eam hereditatem alii totam vel ex parte restituat, quamvis testamento codicilli confirmati non sint. § 274. Item mulier, quae ab eo, qui centum millia aeris census est, per legem Voconiam, heres institui non potest, tamen fideicommisso relictam sibi hereditatem capere potest. § 275. Latini quoque, qui hereditates legataque directo jure lege Junia capere prohibentur, ex fideicommisso capere possunt. § 276. Item, cum senatus-consulto prohibitum sit proprium servum minorem annis xxx liberum et heredem instituere, plerisque placet posse nos jubere liberum esse cum annorum xxx erit, et rogare ut tunc illi restituatur hereditas. § 277. Item quamvis non post mortem ejus, qui nobis heres extiterit, alium in locum ejus heredem instituere, [testamento possimus], tamen possumus eum rogare ut, cum moriatur, alii eam hereditatem totam vel ex parte restituat; et quia post mortem quoque heredis fideicommissum dari potest, idem efficere possumus etiamsi ita scripserimus:

"Cum Titius heres meus mortuus erit, volo hereditatem meam ad Publium Maevium pertinere". Utroque autem modo, tam hoc quam illo, Titium heredem suum obligatum relinquit de fideicommisso restituendo. § 278. Praeterea legata per formulam petimus: fideicommissum vero Romae quidem apud consulem vel apud praetorem, qui praecipue de fideicommissis jus dicit, persequimur; in provinciis vero apud praesidem provinciae. § 279. Item de fideicommissis semper in urbe jus dicitur: de legatis vero, cum res aguntur. § 280. Fideicommissorum usurae et fructus debentur, si modo moram solutionis fecerit qui fideicommissum debebit: legatorum vero usurae non debentur; idque rescripto divi Hadriani significatur. Scio tamen Juliano placuisse, in eo legato quod sinendi modo relinquitur, idem juris esse quod in fideicommissis; quam sententiam etiam his temporibus magis obtinere video. § 281. Item legata graece scripta non valent: fideicommissa vero valent. § 282. Item si legatum per damnationem relictum heres infitietur, in duplum cum eo agitur: fideicommissi vero nomine semper in simplum persecutio est. § 283. Item quod quisque ex fideicommisso plus debito per errorem solverit, repetere potest: at id quod ex causa falsa per damnationem legati plus debito solutum sit, repeti non potest. Idem scilicet juris est de eo legato quod non debitum, vel ex hac, vel ex illa causa, per errorem solutum fuerit.

§ 284. Erant etiam aliae differentiae, quae nunc non sunt. § 285. Ut ecce peregrini poterant fideicommissa capere: et fere haec fuit origo fideicommissorum. Sed postea id prohibitum est; et nunc ex oratione divi Hadriani senatus-consultum factum est, ut ea fideicommissa fisco vindicarentur. § 286. Coelibes quoque, qui per legem Juliam alienas hereditates legataque capere prohibentur, olim fideicommissa videbantur capere posse. Item orbi, qui per legem Papiam, ob id quod liberos non habent, dimidias partes hereditatum legatorumque perdunt, olim solida fideicommissa videbantur capere posse. Sed postea senatus-consulto Pegasiano perinde fideicommissa quoque ac legata hereditatesque capere posse prohibiti sunt; eaque translata sunt ad eos qui testamento liberos habent, aut, si nullus liberos habebit, ad populum, sicuti juris est in legatis et in hereditatibus quae eadem aut simili ex cau[sa caduca fiunt]. § 287. Item olim incertae personae, vel postumo alieno per fideicommissum relinqui poterat, quamvis neque heres institui, neque legari ei possit. Sed senatus-consulto quod auctore divo Hadriano factum est, idem in fideicommissis, quod in legatis hereditatibusque, constitutum est. § 288. Item poenae nomine jam non dubitatur, nec per fideicommissum quidem relinqui posse. § 289. Sed quamvis in multis juris partibus longe latior causa sit fideicommissorum quam eorum quae directo relinquuntur, in quibusdam tantumdem valeant, tamen tutor non aliter testamento dari potest quam directo, veluti hoc modo : "Liberis meis Titius tutor esto", vel ita : "Liberis meis Titium tutorem do" : per fideicommissum vero dari non potest.

Tit. xxv. De codicillis.

Ante Augusti tempora constat codicillorum jus in usu non fuisse, sed primus Lucius Lentulus, ex cujus persona etiam fideicommissa coeperunt, codicillos introduxit. Nam cum decederet in Africa, scripsit codicillos testamento confirmatos, quibus ab Augusto petiit per fideicommissum, ut faceret aliquid ; et cum divus Augustus voluntatem ejus implesset, deinceps reliqui, auctoritatem ejus secuti, fideicommissa praestabant, et filia Lentuli legata quae jure non debebat solvit. Dicitur autem Augustus convocasse prudentes, inter quos Trebatium quoque, cujus tunc auctoritas maxima erat, et quaesisse, an posset hoc recipi, nec absonans a juris ratione codicillorum usus esset ; et Trebatium suasisse Augusto, quod diceret utilissimum et necessarium hoc civibus esse, propter magnas et longas peregrinationes quae apud veteres fuissent, ubi, si quis testamentum facere non posset, tamen codicillos posset. Post quae tempora, cum et Labeo codicillos fecisset, jam nemini dubium erat, quin codicilli jure optimo admitterentur.

§ 1. Non tantum autem testamento facto potest quis codicillos facere, sed et intestatus quis decedens fideicommittere codicillis potest. Sed cum ante testamentum factum codicilli facti erant, Papinianus ait non aliter vires habere, quam si speciali postea voluntate confirmentur. Sed divi Severus et Antoninus rescripserunt, ex iis codicillis qui testamentum praecedunt, posse fideicommissum peti, si appareat eum qui postea testamentum fecerat, a voluntate quam codicillis expresserat, non recessisse. § 2. Codicillis autem hereditas neque dari neque adimi potest, ne confundatur jus testamentorum et codicillorum, et ideo nec exheredatio scribi. Directo autem hereditas codicillis neque dari neque adimi potest, nam per fideicommissum hereditas codicillis jure relinquitur. Nec conditionem heredi instituto codicillis adjicere neque substituere directo potest. § 3. Codicillos autem etiam plures quis facere potest, et nullam sollemnitatem ordinationis desiderant.

INSTITUTIONUM

GAII COMMENTARIUS III. JUSTINIANI LIBER III.

Tit i. De hereditatibus quae ab intestato deferuntur.

Intestatus decedit, qui aut omnino testamentum non fecit, aut non jure fecit; aut id quod fecerat ruptum irritumve factum est, aut nemo ex eo heres extitit.

§ 1. [Intestatorum autem hereditates lege xii Tabularum primum ad suos heredes pertinent. § 2. Sui autem heredes existimantur ut et supra diximus liberi qui in potestate morientis fuerint, veluti filius filiave, nepos neptisve ex filio, pronepos proneptisve ex nepote filio nato prognatus prognatave: nec interest utrum naturales sint liberi, an adoptivi.

§ 1. *Intestatorum autem hereditates ex lege Duodecim Tabularum primum ad suos heredes pertinent.* § 2. *Sui autem heredes existimantur, ut et supra diximus, qui in potestate morientis fuerint: veluti filius filiave, nepos neptisve ex filio, pronepos proneptisve ex nepote filio nato prognatus prognatave: nec interest utrum naturales sint liberi, an adoptivi.* Quibus connumerari necesse est etiam eos qui ex legitimis quidem matrimoniis non sunt progeniti, curiis tamen civitatum dati, secundum divalium constitutionum quae super his positae sunt tenorem, heredum suorum jura nanciscuntur. Nec non eos quos nostrae amplexae sunt constitutiones, per quas jussimus, si quis mulierem in suo contubernio copulaverit, non ab initio affectione maritali, eam tamen cum qua poterat habere conjugium, et ex ea liberos sustulerit, postea vero affectione procedente etiam nuptialia instrumenta cum ea fecerit, filiosque vel filias habuerit, non solum eos liberos qui post dotem editi sunt, justos et in potestate patris esse, sed etiam anteriores, qui et eis qui postea nati sunt occasionem legitimi nominis praestiterunt. Quod obtinere censuimus, etiamsi non progeniti fuerint post dotale instrumentum confectum liberi, vel etiam nati ab hac luce subtracti fuerint.

Ita demum tamen nepos neptisve et pronepos proneptisve suorum heredum numero sunt, si praecedens persona desierit in potestate

Ita demum tamen nepos neptisve, pronepos proneptisve, suorum heredum numero sunt, si praecedens persona desierit in potestate paren-

parentis esse, sive morte id acciderit, sive alia ratione, veluti emancipatione. Nam si per id tempus quo quis moritur, filius in potestate ejus sit, nepos ex eo suus heres esse non potest. Idem et in caeteris deinceps liberorum personis dictum intellegemus. § 3. Uxor quoque quae in manu viri est, ei sua heres est, quia filiae loco est; item nurus quae in filii manu est, nam et haec neptis loco est. Sed ita demum erit sua heres, si filius cujus in manu erit, cum pater moritur, in potestate ejus non sit. Idemque dicemus et de ea quae in nepotis manu matrimonii causa sit, quia proneptis loco est. § 4. Postumi quoque, qui, si vivo parente nati essent, in potestate ejus futuri forent, sui heredes sunt. § 5. Idem juris est de his quorum nomine, ex lege Aelia Sentia vel ex senatus-consulto, post] mortem patris causa probatur; nam et hi, vivo patre causa probata, in potestate ejus futuri essent. § 6. Quod etiam de eo filio, qui ex prima secundave mancipatione, post mortem patris, manumittitur, intelligemus.

tis esse, sive morte id acciderit, sive alia ratione, veluti emancipatione. Nam si per id tempus quo quis moreretur, filius in potestate ejus sit, nepos ex eo suus heres esse non potest. Idque et in caeteris deinceps liberorum personis dictum intellegimus.

Postumi quoque, qui, si vivo parente nati essent, in potestate futuri forent, sui heredes sunt. § 3. Sui autem etiam ignorantes fiunt heredes, et licet furiosi sint, heredes possunt existere: quia quibus ex causis ignorantibus adquiritur nobis, ex his causis et furiosis adquiri potest, et statim a morte parentis quasi continuatur dominium: et ideo nec tutoris auctoritate opus est pupillis, cum etiam ignorantibus adquiritur suis heredibus hereditas: nec curatoris consensu adquiritur furioso, sed ipso jure. § 4. Interdum autem, licet in potestate mortis tempore suus heres non fuerit, tamen suus heres parenti efficitur, veluti si ab hostibus quis reversus fuerit post mortem patris: jus enim postliminii hoc facit. § 5. Per contrarium autem evenit ut, licet quis in familia defuncti sit mortis tempore, tamen suus heres non fiat: veluti si post mortem suam pater judicatus fuerit perduellionis reus, ac per hoc memoria ejus damnata fuerit: suum enim heredem habere non potest, cum fiscus ei succedit. Sed potest dici ipso jure esse suum heredem, sed desinere.

§ 7. Cum igitur filius filiave, et ex altero filio nepotes neptesve extant, pariter ad hereditatem vocantur; nec qui gradu proximior est ulteriorem excludit: aequum enim videbatur, nepotes neptesve in patris sui locum portionemque succedere. Pari ratione et si nepos neptisve sit ex filio et ex nepote pronepos pro-

§ 6. *Cum filius filiave, et ex altero filio nepos neptisve extant, pariter ad hereditatem vocantur; nec qui gradu proximior est, ulteriorem excludit: aequum enim esse videtur, nepotes neptesve in patris sui locum succedere. Pari ratione, et si nepos neptisve sit ex filio, et ex nepote pronepos* neptisve, simul omnes vocantur ad hereditatem. § 8. Et quia placebat, nepotes neptesve, item pronepotes proneptesve in parentis sui locum succedere, conveniens esse visum est, non in capita, sed in stirpes hereditates dividi, ita ut filius partem dimidiam hereditatis ferat, et ex altero filio duo pluresve nepotes alteram dimidiam; item si ex duobus filiis nepotes extent, et ex altero filio unus forte vel duo, ex altero tres aut quattuor, ad unum aut ad duos dimidia pars pertineat, et ad tres aut quattuor altera dimidia.

proneptisve, simul vocantur. Et quia placuit nepotes neptesque, item pronepotes et proneptes in parentis sui locum succedere, conveniens esse visum est, non in capita, sed in stirpes hereditatem dividi: ut filius partem dimidiam hereditatis habeat, et ex altero filio duo pluresve nepotes alteram dimidiam. Item, si ex duobus filiis nepotes extant, et altero unus forte aut duo, ex altero tres aut quattuor, ad unum aut ad duos dimidia pars pertinet, ad tres aut ad quattuor altera dimidia.

§ 7. Cum autem quaeritur an quis suus heres existere possit, eo tempore quaerendum est quo certum est aliquem sine testamento decessisse, quod accidit et destituto testamento. Hac ratione, si filius exheredatus fuerit et extraneus heres institutus: et filio mortuo postea certum fuerit heredem institutum ex testamento non fieri heredem, aut quia noluit esse heres, aut quia non potuit, nepos avo suus heres existet; quia, quo tempore certum est intestatum decessisse patremfamilias, solus invenitur nepos, et hoc certum est. § 8. Et licet post mortem avi natus sit, tamen avo vivo conceptus, mortuo patre ejus, posteaque deserto avi testamento, suus heres efficitur. Plane, si et conceptus et natus fuerit post mortem avi, mortuo patre suo, desertoque postea avi testamento, suus heres avo non existit, quia nullo jure cognationis patrem sui patris tetigit. Sic nec ille est inter liberos avi quem filius emancipatus adoptaverat. Hi autem, cum non sint quantum ad hereditatem liberi, neque bonorum possessionem petere possunt quasi proximi cognati.—Haec de suis heredibus.

§ 9. Emancipati autem liberi jure civili nihil juris habent: neque enim sui heredes sunt, quia in potestate parentis esse desierunt, neque alio ullo jure per legem Duodecim Tabularum vocantur. Sed praetor, naturali aequitate motus, dat eis bonorum possessionem "unde liberi", perinde ac si in potestate parentis mortis tempore fuissent; sive soli sint, sive cum suis heredibus concurrant. Itaque, duobus liberis extantibus, emancipato et qui mortis tempore in potestate fuerit, sane quidem is qui in potestate fuerit, solus jure civili heres est, id est solus suus heres est; sed, cum emancipatus beneficio praetoris in partem admittitur, evenit, ut suus heres pro parte heres fiat. § 10. At hi qui emancipati a parente in adoptionem se dederunt, non admittuntur ad bona naturalis patris quasi liberi: si modo, cum is moreretur, in adoptiva familia sint. Nam vivo eo emancipati ab adoptivo patre, perinde admittuntur ad bona naturalis patris, ac si emancipati ab ipso essent, nec unquam in adoptiva familia fuissent. Et convenienter, quod ad adoptivum patrem pertinet, extraneorum loco esse incipiunt. Post mortem vero naturalis patris emancipati ab adoptivo, et quantum ad hunc, aeque extraneorum loco fiunt, et quantum ad naturalis parentis bona pertinet, nihilo magis liberorum gradum nanciscuntur: quod ideo sic placuit, quia iniquum erat esse in potestate patris adoptivi, ad quos bona naturalis patris pertinerent, utrum ad liberos ejus, an ad agnatos. § 11. Minus ergo juris habent adoptivi quam naturales: namque naturales emancipati beneficio praetoris gradum liberorum retinent, licet jure civili perdunt; adoptivi vero emancipati, et jure civili perdunt gradum liberorum, et a praetore non adjuvantur, et recte: naturalia enim jura civilis ratio perimere non potest; nec quia desinunt sui heredes esse, desinere possunt filii filiaeve, aut nepotes neptesve esse. Adoptivi vero emancipati extraneorum loco incipiunt esse, quia jus nomenque filii filiaeve, quod per adoptionem consecuti sunt, alia civili ratione, id est emancipatione perdunt. § 12. Eadem haec observantur et in ea bonorum possessione, quam contra tabulas testamenti parentis liberis praeteritis, id est, neque heredibus institutis, neque ut oportet exheredatis, praetor pollicetur. Nam eos quidem qui in potestate parentis mortis tempore fuerint et emancipatos, vocat praetor ad eam bonorum possessionem; eos vero, qui in adoptiva familia fuerint per hoc tempus quo naturalis parens moreretur, repellit. Item, adoptivos liberos emancipatos ab adoptivo patre, sicut ab intestato, ita longe minus contra tabulas testamenti ad bona ejus admittit; quia desinunt in liberorum numero esse. § 13. Admonendi tamen sumus, eos qui in adoptiva familia sunt, quive post mortem naturalis parentis ab adoptivo patre emancipati fuerint, intestato parente naturali mortuo, licet ea parte edicti qua liberi ad bonorum possessionem vocantur, non admittantur, alia tamen parte vocari, id est, qua cognati defuncti vocantur. Ex qua parte ita admittuntur, si neque sui heredes liberi, neque emancipati obstent, neque agnatus quidem ullus interveniat: ante enim praetor liberos vocat tam suos heredes quam emancipatos, deinde legitimos heredes, deinde proximos cognatos. § 14. Sed ea omnia antiquitati quidem placuerunt: aliquam autem emendationem a nostra constitutione acceperunt, quam super his personis posuimus, quae a patribus suis naturalibus in adoptionem aliis dantur. Invenimus etenim nonnullos casus, in quibus filii et naturalium parentum successionem propter adoptionem amittebant, et, adoptione facile per emancipationem soluta, ad neutrius patris successionem vocabantur. Hoc solito more corrigentes, constitutionem scripsimus per quam definivimus, quando parens naturalis filium suum adoptandum alii dederit, integra omnia jura ita servari atque si in patris naturalis potestate permansisset, nec penitus adoptio fuisset subsecuta : nisi in hoc tantummodo casu, ut possit ab intestato ad patris adoptivi venire successionem. Testamento autem ab eo facto, neque jure civili neque praetorio aliquid ex hereditate ejus persequi potest, neque contra tabulas bonorum possessione agnita, neque inofficiosi querela instituta, cum nec necessitas patri adoptivo imponitur vel heredem eum instituere vel exheredatum facere, utpote nullo naturali vinculo copulatum; neque si ex Sabiniano senatus-consulto ex tribus maribus fuerit adoptatus : nam et in hujusmodi casu neque quarta ei servatur, neque ulla actio ad ejus persecutionem ei competit. Nostra autem constitutione exceptus est is, quem parens naturalis adoptandum susceperit : utroque enim jure, tam naturali quam legitimo, in hanc personam concurrente, pristina jura tali adoptioni servavimus, quemadmodum si paterfamilias sese dederit arrogandum. Quae specialiter et singulatim ex praefatae constitutionis tenore possunt colligi.

§ 15. Item vetustas, ex masculis progenitos plus diligens, solos nepotes vel neptes qui quaeve ex virili sexu descendunt ad suorum vocabat successionem, et juri agnatorum eos anteponebat; nepotes autem qui ex filiabus nati sunt, et pronepotes ex neptibus, cognatorum loco numerans, post agnatorum lineam eos vocabat, tam in avi vel proavi materni, quam in aviae vel proaviae, sive paternae sive maternae, successionem. Divi autem principes non passi sunt talem contra naturam injuriam sine competenti emendatione relinquere : sed cum nepotis et pronepotis nomen commune est utrisque qui tam ex masculis quam ex feminis descendunt, ideo eundem gradum et ordinem successionis eis donaverunt. Sed ut aliquid amplius sit eis qui non solum naturae, sed etiam veteris juris suffragio muniuntur, portionem nepotum vel neptum vel deinceps, de quibus supra diximus, paulo minuendam esse existimaverunt, ut minus tertiam partem acciperent, quam mater eorum vel avia fuerat acceptura, vel pater eorum vel avus paternus sive maternus, quando femina mortua sit cujus de hereditate agitur, iisque, licet soli sint, adeuntibus, agnatos minime vocabant. Et quemadmodum lex Duodecim Tabularum, filio mortuo, nepotes vel neptes, pronepotes vel proneptes in locum patris sui ad successionem avi vocat: ita et principalis dispositio in locum matris suae vel aviae eos cum jam designata partis tertiae deminutione vocat. § 16. Sed nos, cum adhuc dubitatio manebat inter agnatos et memoratos nepotes, partem quartam defuncti substantiae agnatis sibi vindicantibus ex cujusdam constitutionis auctoritate: memoratam quidem constitutionem a nostro codice segregavimus, neque inseri eam ex Theodosiano codice in eo concessimus. Nostra autem constitutione promulgata, toti juri ejus derogatum est; et sanximus, talibus nepotibus ex filia vel pronepotibus ex nepte et deinceps superstitibus, agnatos nullam partem mortui successionis sibi vindicare: ne hi qui ex transversa linea veniunt, potiores iis habeantur qui recto jure descendunt. Quam constitutionem nostram obtinere secundum sui vigorem et tempora et nunc sancimus: ita tamen, ut quemadmodum inter filios et nepotes ex filio antiquitas statuit, non in capita, sed in stirpes dividi hereditatem, similiter nos inter filios et nepotes ex filia distributionem fieri jubemus, vel inter omnes nepotes et neptes et alias deinceps personas: ut utraque progenies matris suae vel patris, aviae vel avi portionem sine ulla deminutione consequantur: ut si forte unus vel duo ex una parte, ex altera tres aut quattuor extent, unus aut duo dimidiam, alteri tres aut quattuor alteram dimidiam hereditatis habeant.

Tit. ii. De legitima agnatorum successione.

§ 9. Si nullus sit suorum heredum, tunc hereditas pertinet ex eadem lege XII tabularum ad agnatos. § 10. Vocantur autem agnati, qui legitima cognatione juncti sunt: legitima autem cognatio est ea quae per virilis sexus personas [conjungitur. Itaque eodem patre] nati fratres agnati [sibi sunt, qui etiam consanguinei] vocantur, nec requiritur an etiam matrem eandem habuerint.

Si nemo suus heres, vel eorum quos inter suos heredes praetor vel constitutiones vocant, extat, et qui successionem quoquo modo amplectatur: tunc ex lege Duodecim Tabularum ad agnatum proximum hereditas pertinet. § 1. Sunt *autem agnati*, ut primo quoque libro tradidimus, cognati *per virilis sexus personas cognatione juncti*, quasi a patre cognati. *Itaque eodem patre nati fratres, agnati sibi sunt, qui et consanguinei vocantur, nec requiritur an etiam eandem matrem habue-*

Item patruus fratris filio, et invicem is illi agnatus est. Eodem numero sunt fratres patrueles inter se, id est, qui ex duobus fratribus progenerati sunt, quos plerique consobrinos vocant. Qua ratione scilicet etiam ad plures gradus agnationis pervenire poterimus. § 11. Non tamen omnibus simul agnatis dat lex XII Tabularum hereditatem, sed his qui tum, cum certum est aliquem intestatum decessisse, proximo gradu sunt. § 12. Nec in eo jure successio est: ideoque si agnatus proximus hereditatem omiserit, vel antequam adierit, decesserit, sequentibus nihil juris ex lege competit. § 13. Ideo autem non mortis tempore quis [proximus] sit requirimus, sed eo tempore quo certum fuerit aliquem intestatum decessisse, quia si quis [testamento] facto decesserit, melius esse visum est tunc ex iis requiri proximum, cum certum esse coeperit neminem ex eo testamento fore heredem.

§ 14. Quod ad feminas tamen attinet, in hoc jure aliud in ipsarum hereditatibus capiendis placuit, aliud in caeterorum bonis ab his capiendis: nam feminarum quidem hereditates perinde ad nos agnationis jure redeunt, atque masculorum: nostrae vero hereditates ad feminas ultra consanguineorum gradum non pertinent. Itaque soror fratri sororive legitima heres est; amita vero et fratris filia legitima heres esse [non potest. Sororis autem nobis loco est] etiam mater aut noverca, quae per in manum conventionem apud patrem nostrum jura filiae nancta est.

rint. Item patruus fratris filio, et invicem is illi agnatus est. Eodem numero sunt fratres patrueles, id est, qui ex duobus fratribus procreati sunt, qui etiam consobrini vocantur. Qua ratione etiam ad plures gradus agnationis pervenire poterimus. Ii quoque qui post mortem patris nascuntur, jura consanguinitatis nanciscuntur. *Non tamen omnibus simul agnatis dat lex hereditatem; sed his qui tunc proximiore gradu sunt, cum certum esse coeperit aliquem intestatum decessisse.* § 2. Per adoptionem quoque agnationis jus consistit, veluti inter filios naturales, èt eos quos pater eorum adoptavit; nec dubium est quin improprie consanguinei appellentur. Item, si quis ex caeteris agnatis tuis, veluti frater, aut patruus, aut denique is qui longiore gradu est, aliquem adoptaverit, agnatos inter suos esse non dubitatur.

§ 3. Caeterum inter masculos quidem agnationis jure hereditas, etiam longissimo gradu, ultro citroque capitur. Quod ad feminas vero, ita placebat, ut ipsae consanguinitatis jure tantum capiant hereditatem, si sorores sint, ulterius non capiant: masculi vero ad earum hereditates, etiamsi longissimo gradu sint, admittantur. Qua de causa, fratris tui aut patrui tui filiae, vel amitae tuae hereditas ad te pertinet, tua vero ad illas non pertinebat. Quod ideo ita constitutum erat, quia commodius videbatur ita jura constitui, ut plerumque hereditates ad masculos confluerent. Sed quia sane iniquum erat in universum eas quasi extraneas repelli, praetor eas ad bonorum possessionem admittit ea parte qua proximitatis nomine bonorum possessionem pollicetur: ex qua parte ita scilicet admittuntur, si neque agnatus ullus, nec proximior cognatus interveniat. Et haec quidem lex Duodecim Tabularum nullo modo introduxit, sed simplicitatem legibus amicam amplexa, simili modo omnes agnatos, sive masculos sive feminas, cujuscumque gradus, ad similitudinem suorum, invicem ad successionem vocabat. Media autem jurisprudentia, quae erat lege quidem Duodecim Tabularum junior, imperiali autem dispositione anterior, subtilitate quadam excogitata praefatam differentiam inducebat, et penitus eas a successione agnatorum repellebat, omni alia successione incognita, donec praetores paulatim asperitatem juris civilis corrigentes, sive quod deerat implentes, humano proposito alium ordinem suis edictis addiderunt, et cognationis linea proximitatis nomine introducta, per bonorum possessionem eas adjuvabant, et pollicebantur his bonorum possessionem quae "Unde cognati" appellatur. Nos vero, legem Duodecim Tabularum sequentes, et ejus vestigia in hac parte conservantes, laudamus quidem praetores suae humanitatis, non tamen eos in plenum causae mederi invenimus: quare etenim, uno eodemque gradu naturali concurrente, et agnationis titulis tam in masculis quam in feminis aequa lance constitutis, masculis quidem dabatur ad successionem venire omnium agnatorum, ex agnatis autem mulieribus nullis penitus, nisi soli sorori, ad agnatorum successionem patebat aditus? Ideo in plenum omnia reducentes et ad jus Duodecim Tabularum eandem dispositionem exaequantes, nostra constitutione sanximus: omnes legitimas personas, id est per virilem sexum descendentes, sive masculini sive feminini generis sint, simili modo ad jura successionis legitimae ab intestato vocari secundum sui gradus praerogativam; nec ideo excludendas, quia consanguinitatis jura, sicuti germanae, non habent.

§ 15. Si ei qui defunctus erit sit frater et alterius fratris filius, sicut ex superioribus intelligitur, frater prior est, quia gradu praecedit; sed alia facta est juris interpretatio inter suos heredes. § 16. Quod si defuncti nullus frater extet, sed sint liberi fratrum, ad omnes quidem hereditas pertinet: sed quaesitum est, si dispari forte numero sint nati, velut ex uno unus vel duo, ex altero tres vel quattuor, utrum in stirpes dividenda sit hereditas, sicut inter suos heredes juris est, an potius in capita. Jam dudum tamen placuit, in capita dividendam esse heredi-

§ 4. Hoc etiam addendum nostrae constitutioni existimavimus, ut transferatur unus tantummodo gradus a jure cognationis in legitimam successionem: ut non solum fratris filius et filia, secundum quod jam definivimus, ad successionem patrui sui vocentur, sed etiam germanae consanguineae vel sororis uterinae filius et filia soli, et non deinceps personae, una cum his ad jura avunculi sui perveniant, et mortuo eo qui patruus quidem est fratris sui filiis, avunculus autem sororis suae soboli, simili modo ab utroque latere succedant, tamquam si omnes ex masculis descendentes legitimo jure veniant, scilicet ubi frater et soror superstites non

tatem: itaque, quotquot erunt ab utraque parte personae, in tot portiones hereditas dividetur, ita ut singuli singulas portiones ferant.

sunt. His etenim personis praecedentibus, et successionem admittentibus, caeteri gradus remanent penitus semoti, videlicet hereditate non in stirpes, sed in capita dividenda.

§ 5. Si plures sint gradus agnatorum, aperte lex Duodecim Tabularum proximum vocat: itaque si, verbi gratia, sit frater defuncti, et alterius fratris filius, aut patruus, frater potior habetur. Et quamvis, singulari numero usa, lex proximum vocet: tamen dubium non est quin, etsi plures sint ejusdem gradus, omnes admittantur: nam et proprie proximus ex pluribus gradibus intelligitur, et tamen dubium non est quin, licet unus sit gradus agnatorum, pertineat ad eos hereditas. § 6. Proximus autem, si quidem nullo testamento facto quisque decesserit, per hoc tempus requiritur quo mortuus est is cujus de hereditate quaeritur. Quod si facto testamento quisquam decesserit, per hoc tempus requiritur, quo certum esse coeperit nullum ex testamento heredem extaturum: tunc enim proprie quisque intelligitur intestatus decessisse. Quod quidem aliquando longo tempore declaratur; in quo spatio temporis saepe accidit ut, proximiore mortuo, proximus esse incipiat, qui moriente testatore non erat proximus. § 7. Placebat autem in eo genere percipiendarum hereditatum successionem non esse: id est, ut quamvis proximus qui, secundum ea quae diximus, vocatur ad hereditatem, aut spreverit hereditatem, aut antequam adeat decesserit, nihilo magis legitimo jure sequentes admittuntur. Quod iterum praetores, imperfecto jure corrigentes, non in totum sine adminiculo relinquebant, sed ex cognatorum ordine eos vocabant, utpote agnationis jure eis recluso. Sed nos nihil deesse perfectissimo juri cupientes, nostra constitutione, quam de jure patronatus, humanitate suggerente, protulimus, sanximus successionem in agnatorum hereditatibus non esse eis denegandam, cum satis absurdum erat, quod cognatis a praetore apertum est, hoc agnatis esse reclusum, maxime cum in onere quidem tutelarum et primo gradu deficiente sequens succedit, et quod in onere obtinebat, non erat in lucro permissum.

§ 8. Ad legitimam successionem nihilominus vocatur etiam parens qui, contracta fiducia, filium vel filiam, nepotem vel neptem, ac deinceps, emancipat. Quod ex nostra constitutione omnimodo inducitur, ut emancipationes liberorum semper videantur contracta fiducia fieri; cum apud antiquos non aliter hoc obtinebat, nisi specialiter contracta fiducia parens manumisisset.

§ 17. Si nullus agnatus sit, eadem lex xii Tabularum gentiles ad hereditatem vocat. Qui sint autem gentiles, primo commentario rettulimus; et cum illic admonuerimus totum gentilitium jus in desuetudinem abisse, supervacuum est hoc quoque loco de ea re curiosius tractare.

Tit. iii. De senatus-consulto Tertulliano.

Lex Duodecim Tabularum ita stricto jure utebatur, et praeponebat masculorum progeniem, et eos qui per feminini sexus necessitudinem sibi junguntur adeo expellebat, ut ne quidem inter matrem et filium filiamve ultro citroque hereditatis capiendae jus daret, nisi quod praetores ex proximitate cognatorum eas personas ad successionem, bonorum possessione "unde cognati" accommodata, vocabant. § 1. Sed hae juris angustiae postea emendatae sunt. Et primus quidem divus Claudius matri, ad solatium liberorum amissorum, legitimam eorum detulit hereditatem. § 2. Postea autem senatus-consulto Tertulliano, quod divi Hadriani temporibus factum est, plenissime de tristi successione matri, non etiam aviae, deferenda cautum est: ut mater ingenua trium liberorum jus habens, libertina quattuor, ad bona filiorum filiarumve admittatur intestato mortuorum, licet in potestate parentis sit: ut scilicet, cum alieno juri subjecta est, jussu ejus adeat cujus juri subjecta est. § 3. Praeferuntur autem matri liberi defuncti qui sui sunt, quive suorum loco sunt, sive primi gradus, sive ulterioris. Sed et filiae suae mortuae filius vel filia opponitur ex constitutionibus matri defunctae, id est aviae suae. Pater quoque utriusque, non etiam avus vel proavus, matri anteponitur, scilicet cum inter eos solos de hereditate agitur. Frater autem consanguineus tam filii quam filiae excludebat matrem; soror autem consanguinea pariter cum matre admittebatur: sed si fuerat frater et soror consanguinei, et mater liberis honorata, frater quidem matrem excludebat, communis autem erat hereditas ex aequis partibus fratri et sorori. § 4. Sed nos constitutione, quam in codice nostro nomine decorato posuimus, matri subveniendum esse existimavimus, respicientes ad naturam et puerperium et periculum et saepe mortem ex hoc casu matribus illatam. Ideoque impium esse credidimus casum fortuitum in ejus admitti detrimentum: si enim ingenua ter, vel libertina quater non pepererit, immerito defraudabatur successione suorum liberorum: quid enim peccavit, si non plures, sed paucos pepererit? Et dedimus jus legitimum plenum matribus, sive ingenuis sive libertinis, etsi non ter enixae fuerint vel quater, sed eum tantum vel eam qui quaeve morte intercepti sunt, ut et sic vocentur in liberorum suorum legitimam successionem. § 5. Sed cum antea constitutiones, jura legitimae successionis perscrutantes, partim matrem adjuvabant, partim eam praegravabant, et non in solidum eam vocabant, sed in quibusdam casibus, tertiam partem ei abstrahentes, certis legitimis dabant personis, in aliis autem contrarium faciebant: nobis visum est recta et simplici via matrem omnibus legitimis personis anteponi, et sine ulla deminutione filiorum suorum successionem accipere, excepta fratris et sororis persona, sive consanguinei sint sive sola cognationis jura habentes, ut quemadmodum eam toti alii ordini legitimo praeposuimus, ita omnes fratres et sorores, sive legitimi sint sive non, ad capiendas hereditates simul vocemus: ita tamen ut, si quidem solae sorores agnatae vel cognatae, et mater defuncti vel defunctae supersint, dimidiam quidem mater, alteram vero dimidiam partem omnes sorores habeant, si vero matre superstite et fratre vel fratribus solis, vel etiam cum sororibus, sive legitima sive sola cognationis jura habentibus, intestatus quis vel intestata moriatur, in capita distribuatur ejus hereditas.

§ 6. Sed quemadmodum nos matribus prospeximus, ita eas oportet suae soboli consulere: scituris eis, quod si tutores liberis non petierint, vel in locum remoti vel excusati intra annum petere neglexerint, ab eorum impuberum morientium successione merito repellentur.

§ 7. Licet autem vulgo quaesitus sit filius filiave, potest tamen ad bona ejus mater ex Tertulliano senatus-consulto admitti.

Tit. iv. De senatus-consulto Orphitiano.

Per contrarium autem, ut liberi ad bona matrum intestatarum admittantur, senatus-consulto Orphitiano, Orphito et Rufo Consulibus, effectum est, quod latum est divi Marci temporibus; et data est tam filio quam filiae legitima hereditas, etiamsi alieno juri subjecti sunt, et praeferuntur et consanguineis et agnatis defunctae matris. § 1. Sed cum ex hoc senatus-consulto nepotes ad aviae successionem legitimo jure non vocabantur, postea hoc constitutionibus principalibus emendatum est, ut ad similitudinem filiorum filiarumque et nepotes et neptes vocentur. § 2. Sciendum est autem hujusmodi successiones, quae a Tertulliano et Orphitiano senatus-consultis deferuntur, capitis deminutione non perimi, propter illam regulam qua novae hereditates legitimae capitis deminutione non pereunt, sed illae solae quae ex lege Duodecim Tabularum deferuntur. § 3. Novissime sciendum est, etiam illos liberos qui vulgo quaesiti sunt, ad matris hereditatem ex hoc senatus-consulto admitti.

§ 4. Si ex pluribus legitimis heredibus quidam omiserint hereditatem, vel morte vel alia causa impediti fuerint, quo minus adeant: reliquis qui adierint, adcrescit illorum portio, et licet ante decesserint, ad heredes tamen eorum pertinet.

Tit. v. De successione cognatorum.

§ 18. Hactenus lege xii Tabularum finitae sunt intestatorum hereditates: quod jus quemadmodum strictum fuerit, palam est intelligere. § 19. Statim enim emancipati liberi nullum jus in hereditatem parentis ex ea lege habent, cum desierint sui heredes esse. § 20. Idem juris est, si ideo liberi non sint in potestate patris, quia sint cum eo civitate Romana donati, nec ab imperatore in potestatem redacti fuerint. § 21. Item agnati capite deminuti non admittuntur ex ea lege ad hereditatem, quia nomen agnationis capitis deminutione perimitur. § 22. Item proximo agnato non adeunte hereditatem, nihilo magis sequens jure legitimo admittitur. § 23. Item feminae agnatae, quaecumque consanguineorum gradum excedunt, nihil juris ex lege habent. § 24. Similiter non admittuntur cognati, qui per feminini sexus personas necessitudine junguntur; adeo quidem, ut nec inter matrem et filium filiamve ultro citroque hereditatis capiendae jus competat, praeterquam si per in manum conventionem consanguinitatis jura inter eos constiterint.

§ 25. Sed hae juris iniquitates edicto praetoris emendatae sunt. § 26. Nam eos omnes qui legitimo jure deficiuntur, vocat ad hereditatem perinde ac si in potestate parentis mortis tempore fuissent, sive soli sint, sive etiam sui heredes, id est, qui in potestate patris fuerunt, concurrant. § 27. Agnatos autem capite deminutos non secundo gradu post suos heredes vocat, id est, non eo gradu vocat quo per legem vocarentur, si capite minuti non essent; sed tertio proximitatis nomine; licet enim capitis deminutione jus legitimum perdiderint, certe cognationis jura retinent. Itaque si quis alius sit qui integrum

Post suos heredes eosque quos inter suos heredes praetor et constitutiones vocant, et post legitimos quorum numero sunt agnati, et ii quos in locum agnatorum tam supradicta senatus-consulta quam nostra erexit constitutio, proximos cognatos praetor vocat. § 1. Qua parte, naturalis cognatio spectatur; nam agnati capite deminuti, quique ex his progeniti sunt, ex lege Duodecim Tabularum inter legitimos non habentur, sed a praetore tertio ordine vocantur, exceptis solis tantummodo fratre et sorore emancipatis, non etiam liberis eorum,

jus agnationis habebit, is potior erit, etiamsi longiore gradu fuerit. § 28. Idem juris est, ut quidam putant, in ejus agnati persona qui, proximo agnato omittente hereditatem, nihilo magis jure legitimo admittitur. Sed sunt qui putant hunc eodem gradu a praetore vocari quo etiam per legem agnatis hereditas datur. § 29. Feminae certe agnatae, quae consanguineorum gradum excedunt, tertio gradu vocantur, id est, si neque suus heres, neque agnatus ullus erit. § 30. Eodem gradu vocantur etiam eae personae quae per feminini sexus personas copulatae sunt. § 31. Liberi quoque qui in adoptiva familia sunt, ad naturalium parentum hereditatem hoc eodem gradu vocantur.

quos lex Anastasiana cum fratribus integri juris constitutis vocat quidem ad legitimam fratris hereditatem, sive sororis; non aequis tamen partibus, sed cum aliqua deminutione quam facile est ex ipsius constitutionis verbis colligere: aliis vero agnatis inferioris gradus, licet capitis deminutionem passi non sunt, tamen eos anteponit, et procul dubio cognatis. § 2. Hos etiam qui per feminini sexus personas ex transverso cognatione junguntur, tertio gradu, proximitatis nomine, praetor ad successionem vocat. § 3. *Liberi quoque, qui in adoptiva familia sunt, ad naturalium parentum hereditatem hoc eodem gradu vocantur.* § 4. Vulgo quaesitos nullum habere agnatum manifestum est; cum agnatio a patre, cognatio a matre sit; hi autem nullum patrem habere intelliguntur. Eadem ratione nec inter se quidem possunt videri consanguinei esse, quia consanguinitatis jus species est agnationis: tantum igitur cognati sunt sibi, sicut ex matre cognati. Itaque omnibus istis ea parte competit bonorum possessio, qua proximitatis nomine cognati vocantur. § 5. Hoc loco et illud necessario admonendi sumus: agnationis quidem jure admitti aliquem ad hereditatem, etsi decimo gradu sit, sive de lege Duodecim Tabularum quaeramus, sive de edicto quo praetor legitimis heredibus daturum se bonorum possessionem pollicetur. Proximitatis vero nomine iis solis praetor promittit bonorum possessionem, qui usque ad sextum gradum cognationis sunt, et ex septimo, a sobrino sobrinaque nato nataeve.

§ 35. Caeterum saepe quibusdam ita datur bonorum possessio, ut is cui data sit, [non tamen ideo] obtineat hereditatem; quae bonorum possessio dicitur sine re. § 36. Nam si, verbi gratia, jure facto testamento, heres institutus creverit hereditatem, sed bonorum possessionem secundum tabulas testamenti petere noluerit, contentus eo, quod jure civili heres sit, nihilominus ii qui nullo facto testamento ad intestati bona vocantur, possunt petere bonorum possessionem: sed sine re ad eos pertinet, cum testamento scriptus heres evincere hereditatem possit. § 37. Idem juris est si, intestato aliquo mortuo, suus heres noluerit petere bonorum possessionem, contentus [legitimo jure: nam] et agnato competit quidem bonorum possessio, sed sine re, quia evinci hereditas aper[te ab] suo herede potest. Et illud convenienter [invenitur], si ad agnatum jure civili pertinet hereditas, et is adierit hereditatem, sed bonorum possessionem petere noluerit, etsi quis ex proximis cognatus petierit, sine re habebit bonorum possessionem propter eandem rationem. § 38. Sunt et alii quidam similes casus, quorum aliquos superiore commentario tradidimus.

Tit. vi. De gradibus cognationum.

Hoc loco necessarium est exponere, quemadmodum gradus cognationis numerentur. Qua in re in primis admonendi sumus cognationem aliam supra numerari, aliam infra, aliam ex transverso quae etiam a latere dicitur. Superior cognatio est parentum: inferior, liberorum; ex transverso, fratrum sororumve, eorumque qui quaeve ex his progenerantur, et convenienter patrui, amitae, avunculi, materterae. Et superior quidem et inferior cognatio a primo gradu incipit; at ea quae ex transverso numeratur, a secundo. § 1. Primo gradu est: supra, pater, mater; infra, filius, filia. § 2. Secundo: supra, avus, avia; infra, nepos, neptis; ex transverso, frater, soror. § 3. Tertio: supra, proavus, proavia: infra, pronepos, proneptis; ex transverso, fratris sororisque filius, filia, et convenienter patruus, amita, avunculus, matertera. Patruus est patris frater qui graece *πάτρως* vocatur. Avunculus est matris frater qui apud graecos proprie *μήτρως* appellatur: et promiscue *θεῖος* dicitur. Amita est patris soror; matertera vero, matris soror: utraque *θεία*, vel, apud quosdam, *τηθὶς* appellatur. § 4. Quarto gradu: supra, abavus, abavia; infra, abnepos, abneptis; ex transverso, fratris sororisque nepos, neptis, et convenienter patruus magnus, amita magna, id est, avi frater et soror, item avunculus magnus, matertera magna, id est, aviae frater et soror; consobrinus, consobrina, id est, qui quaeve ex fratribus aut sororibus progenerantur. Sed quidam recte consobrinos eos proprie putant dici qui ex duabus sororibus progenerantur, quasi consororinos: eas vero qui ex duobus fratribus progenerantur, proprie fratres patrueles vocari: si autem ex duobus fratribus filiae nascuntur, sorores patrueles appellari; et eos qui ex fratre et sorore propagantur, amitinos proprie dici: amitae tuae filii consobrinum te appellant, tu illos amitinos. § 5. Quinto: supra, atavus, atavia; infra, adnepos, adneptis; ex transverso, fratris sororisque pronepos, proneptis, et convenienter propatruus, proamita, id est, proavi frater et soror, proavunculus, promatertera, id est, proaviae frater et soror; item fratris patruelis, sororis patruelis, consobrini, consobrinae, amitini, amitinae filius, filia propius sobrino, sobrina: hi sunt patrui magni, amitae magnae, avunculi magni, materterae magnae filius, filia. § 6. Sexto gradu: supra, tritavus, tritavia; infra, trinepos, trineptis; ex transverso, fratris sororisque abnepos, abneptis; et convenienter abpatruus, abamita, id est, abavi frater et soror, abavunculus, abmatertera, id est, abaviae frater et soror; item sobrini sobrinaeque, id est, qui quaeve ex fratribus vel sororibus patruelibus, vel consobrinis, vel amitinis progenerantur. § 7. Hactenus ostendisse sufficiet, quemadmodum gradus cognationis numerentur. Namque ex his palam est intelligere, quemadmodum ulteriores quoque gradus numerare debeamus: quippe semper generata quaeque persona gradum adjiciat, ut longe facilius sit respondere quoto quisque gradu sit, quam propria cognationis appellatione quemquam denotare.

§ 8. Agnationis quoque gradus eodem modo numerantur. § 9. Sed cum magis veritas oculata fide quam per aures animis hominum infigitur, ideo necessarium duximus, post narrationem graduum, etiam eos praesenti libro inscribi, quatenus possint et auribus et oculorum inspectione adolescentes perfectissimam graduum doctrinam adipisci.

§ 10. Illud certum est ad serviles cognationes illam partem edicti, qua proximitatis nomine bonorum possessio promittitur, non pertinere: nam nec ulla antiqua lege talis cognatio computabatur. Sed nostra constitutione, quam pro jure patronatus fecimus (quod jus usque ad nostra tempora satis obscurum atque nube plenum et undique confusum fuerat), et hoc humanitate suggerente concessimus, ut si quis in servili consortio constitutus liberum vel liberos habuerit, sive ex libera sive ex servilis conditionis muliere, vel contra serva mulier ex libero vel servo habuerit liberos cujuscumque sexus, et ad libertatem his pervenientibus, et ii qui ex servili ventre nati sunt, libertatem meruerint, vel, dum mulieres liberae erant, ipsi in servitutem eos habuerint, et postea ad libertatem pervenerint, ut hi omnes ad successionem vel patris vel matris veniant, patronatus jure in hac parte sopito: hos enim liberos non solum in suorum parentum successionem, sed etiam alterum in alterius mutuam successionem vocavimus, ex illa lege specialiter eos vocantes, sive soli inveniantur qui in servitute nati et postea manumissi sunt, sive una cum aliis qui post libertatem parentum concepti sunt, sive ex eodem

					VI. Tritavus.	VI. Tritavia.					
				VI. Abpatruus. Abamita.	V. Atavus.	V. Atavia.	VI. Abavunculus. Abmatertera.				
			VI. Propatrui, proamitae filius, filia.	V. Propatruus. Proamita.	IV. Abavus.	IV. Abavia.	V. Proavunculus. Promatertera.	VI. Proavunculi, promaterterae. filius, filia.			
		VI. Sobrinus. Sobrina.	V. Propior sobrinus, sobrina.	IV. Patruus magnus. Amita magna,	III. Proavus.	III. Proavia.	IV. Avunculus magnus. Matertera magna.	V. Propior sobrinus, sobrina.	VI. Sobrinus. Sobrina.		
	VI. Fratris et sororis patruelis, amitini, amitinae nepos, neptis.	V. Fratris et sororis patruelis, amitini, amitinae filius, filia.	IV. Frater et soror patruelis, amitinus, amitina.	III. Patruus. Amita.	II. Avus.	II. Avia.	III. Avunculus. Matertera.	IV. Frater consobrinus. Soror consobrina.	V. Fratris consobrini, sororis consobrinae filius, filia.	VI. Fratris consobrini, sororis consobrinae nepos, neptis.	
VI. Fratris abnepos, abneptis.	V. Fratris pronepos, proneptis.	IV. Fratris nepos, neptis.	III. Fratris filius, filia.	II. Frater.	I. Pater.	I. Mater	II. Soror.	III. Sororis filius, filia.	IV. Sororis nepos, neptis.	V. Sororis pronepos, proneptis.	VI. Sororis abnepos, abneptis.
					I. Filius.	I. Filia.					
					II. Nepos.	II. Neptis.					
					III. Pronepos.	III. Proneptis.					
					IV. Abnepos.	IV. Abneptis.					
					V. Adnepos.	V. Adneptis.					
					VI. Trinepos.	VI. Trineptis.					

patre vel ex eadem matre, sive ex aliis nuptiis, ad similitudinem eorum qui ex justis nuptiis procreati sunt.

§ 11. Repetitis itaque omnibus quae jam tradidimus, apparet non semper eos qui parem gradum cognationis obtinent, pariter vocari; eoque amplius, nec eum quidem qui proximior sit cognatus, semper potiorem esse. Cum enim prima causa sit suorum heredum, et eorum quos inter suos heredes jam enumeravimus, apparet pronepotem vel abnepotem defuncti potiorem esse quam fratrem aut patrem matremque defuncti: cum alioquin pater quidem et mater, ut supra quoque tradidimus, primum gradum cognationis obtineant, frater vero secundum, pronepos autem tertio gradu sit cognatus, et abnepos quarto; nec interest, in potestate morientis fuerit, an non, quod vel emancipatus vel ex emancipato, aut ex feminino sexu propagatus est. § 12. Amotis quoque suis heredibus, quosque inter suos heredes vocari diximus, agnatus, qui integrum jus agnationis habet, etiamsi longissimo gradu sit, plerumque potior habetur quam proximior cognatus: nam patrui nepos vel pronepos avunculo vel materterae praefertur. Totiens igitur dicimus, aut potiorem haberi eum qui proximiorem gradum cognationis obtinet, aut pariter vocari eos qui cognati sunt, quotiens neque suorum heredum jure, quique inter suos heredes sunt, neque agnationis jure, aliquis praeferri debeat, secundum ea quae tradidimus: exceptis fratre et sorore emancipatis, qui ad successionem fratrum vel sororum vocantur, qui, etsi capite deminuti sunt, tamen praeferuntur caeteris ulterioris gradus agnatis.

Tit. vii. De successione libertorum.

§ 39. Nunc de libertorum bonis videamus. § 40. Olim itaque licebat liberto patronum suum impune testamento praeterire: nam ita demum lex XII Tabularum ad hereditatem liberti vocabat patronum, si intestatus mortuus esset libertus, nullo suo herede relicto. Itaque intestato quoque mortuo liberto, si is suum heredem reliquerat, nihil in bonis ejus patrono juris erat. Et si quidem ex naturalibus liberis aliquem suum heredem reliquisset, nulla videbatur esse querela; si vero vel adoptivus filius filiave, vel uxor quae in manu

Nunc de libertorum bonis videamus. Olim itaque licebat liberto patronum suum impune testamento praeterire: nam ita demum lex Duodecim Tabularum ad hereditatem liberti vocabat patronum, si intestatus mortuus esset libertus, nullo suo herede relicto. Itaque intestato quoque mortuo liberto, si is suum heredem reliquisset, nihil in bonis ejus patrono juris erat. Et si quidem ex naturalibus liberis aliquem suum heredem reliquisset, nulla videbatur querela; si vero adoptivus filius esset, aperte iniquum erat nihil

esset, sua heres esset, aperte iniquum erat nihil juris patrono superesse. § 41. Qua de causa postea praetoris edicto haec juris iniquitas emendata est. Sive enim faciat testamentum libertus, jubetur ita testari ut patrono suo partem dimidiam bonorum suorum relinquat; et, si aut nihil aut minus quam partem dimidiam reliqueret, datur patrono contra tabulas testamenti partis dimidiae bonorum possessio. Si vero intestatus moriatur, suo herede relicto adoptivo filio, vel uxore quae in manu ipsius esset, vel nuru quae in manu filii ejus fuerit, datur aeque patrono adversus hos suos heredes partis dimidiae bonorum possessio. Prosunt autem liberto ad excludendum patronum naturales liberi, non solum quos in potestate mortis tempore habet, sed etiam emancipati et in adoptionem dati, si modo aliqua ex parte heredes scripti [sint, aut praeteriti con]tra tabulas testamenti bonorum possessionem ex edicto petierint; nam exheredati nullo modo repellunt patronum. § 42. Postea lege Papia aucta sunt jura patronorum quod ad locupletiores libertos pertinet. Cautum est enim ea lege, ut ex bonis ejus qui sestertiorum [nummorum centum millium plurisve] patrimonium reliquerit, et pauciores quam tres liberos habebit, sive is testamento facto, sive intestato mortuus erit, virilis pars patrono debeatur. Itaque cum unum filium unamve filiam heredem reliquerit libertus, perinde pars dimidia patrono debetur, ac si sine ullo filio filiave moreretur: cum vero duos duasve heredes reliquerit, tertia pars debetur; si tres reliquat, repellitur patronus.

juris patrono superesse. § 1. *Qua de causa postea praetoris edicto haec juris iniquitas emendata est. Sive enim faciebat testamentum libertus, jubebatur ita testari ut patrono partem dimidiam bonorum suorum relinqueret; et, si aut nihil aut minus partis dimidiae reliquerat, dabatur patrono contra tabulas testamenti partis dimidiae bonorum possessio; si vero intestatus* moriebatur, *suo herede relicto filio adoptivo,* dabatur *aeque patrono contra hunc suum heredem partis dimidiae bonorum possessio. Prodesse autem liberto* solebant *ad excludendum patronum naturales liberi, non solum quos in potestate mortis tempore* habebat, *sed etiam emancipati et in adoptionem dati: si modo ex aliqua parte heredes scripti* erant, *aut praeteriti contra tabulas bonorum possessionem ex edicto petierant; nam exheredati nullo modo repellebant patronum.* § 2. *Postea lege Papia adaucta sunt jura patronorum qui locupletiores libertos* habebant. *Cautum est enim, ut ex bonis ejus qui sestertiorum centum millium patrimonium reliquerit, et pauciores quam tres liberos* habebat, *sive is testamento facto, sive intestato mortuus* erat, *virilis pars patrono* deberetur. *Itaque, cum unum quidem filium filiamve heredem reliquerit libertus, perinde pars dimidia patrono* debebatur, *ac si is sine ullo filio filiave* decessisset: *cum duos duasve heredes* reliquerat, *tertia pars* debebatur *patrono; si tres* reliquerat, repellebatur *patronus.*

§ 43. In bonis libertinarum nullam injuriam antiquo jure patiebantur patroni; cum enim hae in patronorum legitima tutela essent, non aliter scilicet testamentum facere poterant, quam patrono auctore. Itaque, sive auctor ad testamentum faciendum factus [erat, aut de se queri debebat, quod sibi nihil relictum erat, aut ipsum ex testamento, si heres factus erat seque]batur hereditas; si vero auctor ei factus non erat, aut intestata liberta moriebatur [quia suos heredes femina habere non potest ad patronum] pertinebat, nec queri ullus heres [poterat quod non] posset patronum a bonis [libertae invitum] repellere. § 44. Sed postea lex Papia, cum quattuor liberorum jure libertinas tutela patronorum liberaret, et eo modo concederet eis etiam sine tutoris auctoritate [condere testamenta prospexit], ut pro numero liberorum [quos liberta mortis tempore] habuerit, virilis pars patrono debeatur, eique ex bonis ejus, quae omnia . . . . . ideo juris . . . . . . ad patronum pertinet.

§ 45. Quae diximus de patrono, eadem intelligemus et de filio patroni, item de nepote ex filio, pronepote [ex nepote] filio nato prognato. § 46. Filia vero patroni, item [neptis] ex filio et proneptis ex nepote filio nato prognata, olim quidem [habuit idem jus quod ex] lege XII Tabularum patrono datum est, praetor autem vocat tantum masculini sexus patronorum liberos ad bonorum possessionem : illa vero ut contra tabulas testamenti liberti aut ab intestato contra filium adoptivum, vel uxorem nurumve, quae in manu fuerit, bonorum possessionem petat, trium liberorum jure lege Papia consequitur : aliter hoc jus non habet. § 47. Sed ut ex bonis libertae testatae quattuor liberos habentis virilis pars ei debetur, ne liberorum quidem jure consequitur, ut quidam putant. Sed tamen intestata liberta mortua, verba legis Papiae faciunt, ut ei virilis pars debeatur: si vero testamento facto mortua sit liberta, tale jus ei datur, quale datum est contra tabulas testamenti liberti [patronorum liberis] id est, quale et virilis sexus patronorum liberi contra tabulas testamenti liberti habent, quamvis parum diligenter ea pars legis scripta sit. § 48. Ex his apparet, extraneos heredes patronorum longe remotos esse ab omni eo jure, quod vel in intestatorum bonis, vel contra tabulas testamenti patrono competit.

§ 49. Patronae olim ante legem Papiam hoc solum jus habebant in bonis libertorum, quod etiam patronis ex lege XII Tabularum datum est. Nec enim, ut contra tabulas testamenti ingrati liberti vel ab intestato contra filium adoptivum vel uxorem nurumve bonorum possessionem partis dimidiae peterent, praetor similiter ut de patrono liberisque ejus curabat. § 50. Sed lex Papia duobus liberis honoratae ingenuae patronae, libertinae tribus, eadem fere jura dedit, quae ex edicto praetoris patroni habent; trium vero liberorum jure honoratae ingenuae patronae ea jura dedit quae per eandem legem patrono data sunt: libertinae autem patronae non idem juris praestitit. § 51. Quod autem ad libertinarum bona pertinet, si quidem intestatae decesserint, nihil novi patronae liberis honoratae lex Papia praestat. Itaque si neque ipsa patrona, neque liberta capite deminuta sit, ex lege XII Tabularum ad eam hereditas pertinet, et excluduntur libertae liberi; quod juris est etiam si liberis honorata non sit patrona: numquam enim, sicut supra diximus, feminae suum heredem habere possunt. si vero vel hujus vel illius capitis deminutio interveniat, rursus liberi libertae excludunt patronam; quia, legitimo jure capitis deminutione perempto, evenit ut liberi libertae cognationis jure potiores habeantur. § 52. Cum autem testamento facto moritur liberta, ea quidem patrona quae liberis honorata non est, nihil juris habet contra libertae testamentum: ei vero quae liberis honorata sit, hoc jus tribuitur per legem Papiam, quod habet ex edicto patronus contra tabulas liberti.

§ 53 Eadem lex patronae filio liberis honorato omnia fere patronae jura dedit; sed in hujus persona etiam unius filii filiaeve jus sufficit.

§ 54. Hactenus omnia [manumissionum] jura quasi per indicem tetigisse satis est: alioquin diligentior interpretatio propriis commentariis exposita est.

§ 55. Sequitur ut de bonis Latinorum libertinorum dispiciamus. § 56. Quae pars juris ut manifestior fiat, admonendi sumus, id, quod alio loco diximus, eos qui nunc Latini Juniani dicuntur, olim ex jure quiritium servos fuisse, sed auxilio praetoris in libertatis forma servari solitos; unde etiam res eorum peculii jure ad patronos pertinere solita est: postea vero per legem Juniam eos omnes quos praetor in libertatem tuebatur, liberos esse coepisse, et appellatos esse Latinos Junianos: Latinos ideo, quia lex eos liberos perinde esse voluit, atque si essent cives Romani ingenui qui, ex urbe Roma in Latinas colonias deducti, Latini coloniarii esse coeperunt: Junianos ideo, quia per legem Juniam liberi facti sunt, etiamsi non essent cives Romani. Legis itaque Juniae lator, cum intelligerit futurum ut ea fictione res Latinorum defunctorum ad patronos pertinere desinerent, quia [scilicet] neque ut servi decederent, ut possent jure peculii res eorum ad patronos pertinere, neque liberi Latini hominis bona possent manumissionis jure ad patronos pertinere, necessarium existimavit, ne beneficium istis datum in injuriam patronorum converteretur, cavere ut bona eorum perinde ad manumissores pertinerent, ac si lex lata non esset. Itaque jure quodammodo peculii bona Latinorum ad manumissores ea lege pertinent. § 57. Unde accidit, ut longe differant ea jura, quae in bonis Latinorum ex lege Junia constituta sunt, ab his quae in hereditate civium Romanorum libertorum observantur. § 58. Nam civis Romani liberti hereditas ad extraneos heredes patroni nullo modo pertinet: ad filium autem patroni nepotesque ex filio et pronepotes ex nepote [filio nato] prognatos omnimodo pertinet, etiamsi a parente fuerint exheredati: Latinorum autem bona, tamquam peculia servorum, etiam ad extraneos heredes pertinent, et ad liberos manumissoris exheredatos non pertinent. § 59. Item [civis Romani liberti] hereditas ad duos pluresve patronos aequaliter pertinet, licet dispar in eo servo dominium habuerint: bona vero Latinorum pro ea parte pertinent, pro qua parte quisque eorum dominus fuerit. § 60. Item in hereditate civis Romani liberti patronus alterius patroni filium excludit, et filius patroni alterius patroni nepotem repellit: bona autem Latinorum et ad ipsum patronum et ad alterius patroni heredem simul pertinent, pro qua parte ad ipsum manumissorem pertinerent. § 61. Item si unius patroni tres forte liberi sunt et alterius unus, hereditas civis Romani liberti in capita dividitur, id est, tres fratres tres portiones ferunt, et unus quartam: bona vero Latinorum pro ea parte ad successores pertinent, pro qua parte ad ipsum manumissorem pertinerent. § 62. Item si alter ex iis patronis suam partem in hereditate civis Romani liberti spernat, vel ante moriatur quam cernat, tota hereditas ad alterum pertinet: bona autem Latini pro parte decedentis patroni caduca fiunt et ad populum pertinent.

§ 63. Postea Lupo et Largo Consulibus senatus censuit, ut bona Latinorum primum ad eum pertinerent qui eos liberasset; deinde ad liberos eorum non nominatim exheredatos, uti quisque proximus esset; tunc antiquo jure ad heredes eorum qui liberassent pertinerent. § 64. Quo senatus-consulto quidam id actum esse putant, ut in bonis Latinorum eodem jure utamur, quo utimur in hereditate civium Romanorum libertinorum; idque maxime Pegaso placuit. Quae sententia aperte falsa est. Nam civis Romani liberti hereditas nunquam ad extraneos patroni heredes pertinet: bona autem Latinorum etiam ex hoc ipso senatus-consulto, non obstantibus liberis manumissoris, etiam ad extraneos heredes pertinent. Item in hereditate civis Romani liberti liberis manumissoris nulla exheredatio nocet: in bonis Latinorum nocere nominatim factam exheredationem ipso senatus-consulto significatur. Verius est ergo hoc solum eo senatus-consulto actum esse, ut manumissoris liberi qui nominatim exheredati non sint, praeferantur extraneis heredibus. § 65. Itaque emancipatus filius patroni praeteritus, quamvis contra tabulas testamenti parentis sui bonorum possessionem non petierit, tamen extraneis heredibus in bonis Latinorum potior habetur. § 66. Item filia caeterique sui heredes licet jure civili inter caeteros exheredati sint et ab omni hereditate patris sui summoveantur, tamen in bonis Latinorum, nisi nominatim a parente fuerint exheredati, potiores erunt extraneis heredibus. § 67. Item ad liberos qui ab hereditate parentis se abstinuerunt, [tamen nihilominus] bona Latinorum pertinent [ex ea] hereditate, quia exheredati nullo modo dici possunt, non magis quam qui testamento silentio praeteriti sunt. § 68. Ex iis omnibus satis illud apparet, si is qui Latinum fecerit . . . . . § 69. Item illud quoque constare videtur, si solos liberos ex disparibus partibus patronus [heredes reliquerit rectius existimare, qui Latinum pro hereditariis partibus pu]tant ad eos pertinere; quia, nullo interveniente extraneo herede, senatus-consulto locus non est ei. § 70. Sed, si cum liberis suis etiam extraneum heredem patronus reliquerit, Caelius Sabinus ait, tota bona pro virilibus partibus ad liberos defuncti pertinere, quia, cum extraneus heres intervenit, non habet lex Junia locum, sed senatus-consultum: Javolenus autem ait, tantum eam partem ex senatus-consulto liberos patroni pro virilibus partibus habituros esse, quam extranei heredes ante senatus-consultum lege Junia habituri essent; reliquas vero partes pro hereditariis partibus ad eos pertinere. § 71. Item quaeritur, an hoc senatus-consultum ad eos patroni liberos pertineat, qui ex filia nepteve procreantur, id est, ut nepos meus ex filia potior sit in bonis Latini mei, quam extraneus heres; item an ad maternos Latinos hoc senatus-consultum pertineat, quaeritur, id est, ut in bonis Latini materni potior sit patronae filius, quam heres extraneus matris. Cassio placuit, utroque casu locum esse senatus-consulto. Sed hujus sententiam plerique improbant, quia senatus de his liberis patronarum nihil sentiat, qui aliam familiam sequerentur; idque ex eo apparet, quod nominatim exheredatos summoveat: nam videtur de his sentire, qui exheredari a parente solent, si heredes non instituantur; neque autem matri filium filiamve, neque avo materno nepotem neptemve, si eum eamve heredem non instituat, exheredare necesse est, sive de jure civili quaeramus, sive de edicto praetoris, quo praeteritis liberis contra tabulas testamenti bonorum possessio promittitur.

§ 72. Aliquando tamen civis Romanus libertus tamquam Latinus moritur, veluti si Latinus salvo jure patroni ab imperatore jus quiritium consecutus fuerit: nam ita divus Trajanus constituit, si Latinus invito vel ignorante patrono jus quiritium ab imperatore consecutus sit. Quibus casibus, dum vivit, iste libertus, caeteris civibus Romanis libertis similis est, et justos liberos procreat; moritur autem Latini jure, nec ei liberi ejus heredes esse possunt; et in hoc tantum habet testamenti factionem, ut patronum heredem instituat, eique, si heres esse noluerit, alium substituere possit. § 73. Et, quia hac constitutione videbatur effectum ut ne umquam isti homines tamquam cives Romani morerentur, quamvis eo jure postea usi essent, quo vel ex lege Aelia Sentia vel ex senatus-consulto cives Romani essent, divus Hadrianus, iniquitate rei motus, auctor fuit senatus-consulti faciundi, ut qui ignorante vel recusante patrono ab imperatore jus quiritium consecuti essent, si eo jure postea usi essent, quo ex lege Aelia Sentia vel ex senatus-consulto, si Latini mansissent, civitatem Romanam consequerentur, perinde ipsi haberentur, ac si lege Aelia Sentia vel senatus-consulto ad civitatem Romanam pervenissent.

§ 74. Eorum autem quos lex Aelia Sentia dedititiorum numero facit, bona modo quasi civium Romanorum libertorum, modo quasi Latinorum ad patronos pertinent. § 75. Nam eorum bona qui, si in aliquo vitio non essent, manumissi cives Romani futuri essent, quasi civium Romanorum patronis eadem lege tribuuntur. Non tamen ut habent etiam testamenti factionem; nam id plerisque placuit, nec immerito: nam incredible videbatur, pessimae conditionis hominibus voluisse legis latorem testamenti faciendi jus concedere. § 76. Eorum vero bona qui, si non in aliquo vitio essent manumissi, futuri Latini essent, perinde tribuuntur patronis, ac si Latini decessissent. Nec me praeterit, non satis in ea re legislatorem voluntatem suam verbis expressisse.

§ 3. Sed nostra constitutio, quam pro omnium notione graeca lingua compendioso tractatu habito composuimus, ita hujusmodi causas definivit: ut, si quidem libertus vel liberta minores centenariis sint, id est, minus centum aureis habeant substantiam (sic enim legis Papiae summam interpretati sumus, ut pro mille sestertiis unus aureus computetur), nullum locum habeat patronus in eorum successionem, si tamen testamentum fecerint. Sin autem intestati decesserint nullo liberorum relicto, tunc patronatus jus quod erat ex lege Duodecim Tabularum, integrum reservavit. Cum vero majores centenariis sint, si heredes vel bonorum possessores liberos habeant, sive unum, sive plures, cujuscumque sexus vel gradus, ad eos successionem parentum deduximus, patronis omnibus modis una cum sua progenie semotis. Sin autem sine liberis decesserint, si quidem intestati, ad omnem hereditatem patronos patronasque vocavimus; si vero testamentum quidem fecerint, patronos autem vel patronas praeterierint, cum nullos liberos haberent, vel habentes eos exheredaverint, vel mater sive avus maternus eos praeterierit, ita ut non possint argui inofficiosa eorum testamenta: tunc ex nostra constitutione, per bonorum possessionem contra tabulas, non dimidiam, ut antea, sed tertiam partem bonorum liberti consequantur, vel quod deest eis ex constitutione nostra repleatur, si quando minus tertia parte bonorum suorum libertus vel liberta eis reliquerint, ita sine onere, ut nec liberis liberti libertaeve ex ea parte legata vel fideicommissa praestentur, sed ad coheredes hoc onus redundaret; multis aliis casibus a nobis in praefata constitutione congregatis, quos necessarios esse ad hujusmodi juris dispositionem perspeximus: ut tam patroni patronaeque, quam liberi eorum, nec non qui ex transverso latere veniunt usque ad quintum gradum, ad successionem libertorum vocentur, sicut ex ea constitutione intelligendum est: ut, si ejusdem patroni vel patronae, vel duorum duarum pluriumve liberi sint, qui proximior est, ad liberti seu libertae vocetur successionem, et in capita, non in stirpes, dividatur successio: eodem modo et in iis qui ex transverso latere veniunt, servando pene enim consonantia jura ingenuitatis et libertinitatis in successionibus fecimus. § 4. Sed haec de iis libertinis hodie dicenda sunt, qui in civitatem Romanam pervenerunt, cum nec sunt alii liberti, simul et dedititiis et Latinis sublatis, cum Latinorum legitimae successiones nullae penitus erant, qui licet ut liberi vitam suam peragebant, attamen in ipso ultimo spiritu simul animam atque libertatem amittebant, et quasi servorum ita bona eorum jure quodammodo peculii ex lege Junia manumissores detinebant. Postea vero senatus-consulto Largiano cautum fuerat, ut liberi manumissoris non nominatim exheredati facti extraneis heredibus eorum in bonis Latinorum praeponerentur. Quibus supervenit etiam divi Trajani edictum, quod eundem hominem, si invito vel ignorante patrono ad civitatem venire ex beneficio principis festinavit, faciebat vivum quidem civem Romanum, Latinum autem morientem. Sed nostra constitutione, propter hujusmodi conditionum vices et alias difficultates, cum ipsis Latinis etiam legem Juniam et senatus-consultum Largianum et edictum divi Trajani in perpetuum deleri censuimus, ut omnes liberti civitate Romana fruantur, et mirabili modo, quibusdam adjectionibus, ipsas vias quae in Latinitatem ducebant ad civitatem Romanam capiendam transposuimus.

Tit. viii. De adsignatione libertorum.

In summa, quod ad bona libertorum, admonendi sumus censuisse senatum, ut quamvis ad omnes patroni liberos qui ejusdem gradus sunt, aequaliter bona libertorum pertineant, tamen liceret parenti uni ex liberis adsignare libertum, ut post mortem ejus solus is patronus habeatur cui adsignatus est, et caeteri liberi qui ipsi quoque ad eadem bona, nulla adsignatione interveniente, pariter admitterentur, nihil juris in his bonis habeant. Sed ita demum pristinum jus recipiunt, si is cui adsignatus est decesserit nullis liberis relictis. § 1. Nec tantum libertum, sed etiam libertam, et non tantum filio nepotive, sed etiam filiae neptive adsignare permittitur. § 2. Datur autem haec adsignandi facultas ei qui duos pluresve liberos in potestate habebit, ut eis quos in potestate habet, adsignare ei libertum libertamve liceat. Unde quaerebatur, si eum cui adsignaverit postea emancipaverit, num evanescat adsignatio? Sed placuit evanescere, quod et Juliano et aliis plerisque visum est. § 3. Nec interest testamento quis adsignet, an sine testamento; sed etiam quibuscumque verbis hoc patronis permittitur facere, ex ipso senatus-consulto, quod Claudianis temporibus factum est, Suillo Rufo et Osterio Scapula consulibus.

Tit. ix. De bonorum possessionibus.

Jus bonorum possessionis introductum est a praetore, emendandi veteris juris gratia. Nec solum in intestatorum hereditatibus vetus jus eo modo praetor emendavit, sicut supra dictum est, sed in eorum quoque qui testamento facto decesserint. Nam si alienus postumus heres fuerit institutus, quamvis hereditatem jure civili adire non poterat: cum institutio non valebat, honorario tamen jure bonorum possessor efficiebatur, videlicet cum a praetore adjuvabatur: sed et is a nostra constitutione hodie recte heres instituitur, quasi et jure civili non incognitus.

§ 34. [Aliquando tamen neque emendandi, neque impugnandi veteris juris, sed magis confirmandi gratia, praetor pollicetur bonorum possessionem; nam illis quoque qui recte facto testamento heredes instituti sunt, dat secundum tabulas bonorum possessionem; item ab in]testato heredes suos et agnatos ad bonorum possessionem vocat. Quibus casibus beneficium ejus in eo solo videtur aliquam utilitatem habere, ut is qui ita bonorum possessionem petit, interdicto, cujus principium est, "Quorum bonorum," uti possit: cujus interdicti quae sit utilitas, suo loco proponemus: alioquin, remota quoque bonorum possessione ad eos hereditas pertinet jure civili.

§ 1. *Aliquando tamen neque emendandi neque impugnandi veteris juris, sed magis confirmandi gratia, pollicetur bonorum possessionem; nam illis quoque qui recte facto testamento heredes instituti sunt, dat secundum tabulas bonorum possessionem: item ab intestato heredes suos et agnatos ad bonorum possessionem vocat. Sed et remota quoque bonorum possessione ad eos hereditas pertinet jure civili.*

§ 32. Quos autem praetor vocat ad hereditatem, hi heredes ipso quidem jure non fiunt; nam praetor heredes facere [non potest: per legem enim tantum vel similem juris institutionem heredes fiunt,] veluti per senatus-consultum et constitutionem principalem: sed [cum eisdem praetor dat bonorum possessionem,] loco heredum constituuntur.

§ 33. [Adhuc autem etiam] alios complures gradus fecit [praetor in bonorum possessionibus dandis, dum id agebat ne quis sine successore moreretur]: de quibus in his commentariis consulto [non agimus] cum hoc jus totum propriis commentariis explicaverimus: hoc solum admonuisse sufficit.

§ 2. *Quos autem praetor* solus *vocat ad hereditatem, heredes quidem ipso jure non fiunt; nam praetor heredem facere non potest: per legem enim tantum vel similem juris constitutionem heredes fiunt, veluti per senatus-consulta et constitutiones principales; sed cum eis praetor dat bonorum possessionem, loco heredum constituuntur,* et vocantur bonorum possessores. *Adhuc autem et alios complures gradus praetor fecit in bonorum possessionibus dandis, dum id agebat ne quis sine successore moriatur:* nam angustissimis finibus constitutum per legem Duodecim Tabularum jus percipiendarum hereditatum praetor ex bono et aequo dilatavit.

§ 3. Sunt autem bonorum possessiones ex testamento quidem hae: prima, quae praeteritis liberis datur, vocaturque "contra tabulas"; secunda, quam omnibus jure scriptis heredibus praetor pollicetur, ideoque vocatur "secundum tabulas". Et cum de testamentis prius locutus est, ad intestatos transitum fecit; et primo loco, suis heredibus et iis qui ex edicto praetoris inter suos heredes connumerantur, dat bonorum possessionem, quae vocatur "unde liberi". Secundo, legitimis heredibus. Tertio, decem personis quas extraneo manumissori praeferebat. Sunt autem decem personae hae: pater, mater, avus, avia, tam paterni quam materni; item filius, filia, nepos, neptis, tam ex filio quam ex filia; frater, soror, sive consanguinei sive uterini. Quarto, cognatis proximis. Quinto, "tum quem ex familia". Sexto, patrono et patronae, liberisque eorum et parentibus. Septimo, viro et uxori. Octavo, cognatis manumissoris. § 4. Sed eas quidem praetoria introduxit jurisdictio: a nobis tamen nihil incuriosum praetermissum est, sed nostris constitutionibus omnia corrigentes, "contra tabulas" quidem et "secundum tabulas" bonorum possessiones admissimus, utpote necessarias constitutas, nec non ab intestato "unde liberi" et "unde legitimi" bonorum possessiones. Quae autem in praetoris edicto quinto loco posita fuerat, id est "unde decem personae", eam pio proposito et compendioso sermone supervacuam ostendimus: cum enim praefata bonorum possessio decem personas praeponebat extraneo manumissori, nostra constitutio quam de emancipatione liberorum facimus, omnibus parentibus eisdemque manumissoribus contracta fiducia manumissionem facere. dedit, ut ipsa manumissio eorum hoc in se habeat privilegium et supervacua fiat praedicta bonorum possessio. Sublata igitur praefata quinta bonorum possessione, in gradum ejus sextam antea bonorum possessionem induximus, et quintam fecimus, quam praetor proximis cognatis pollicetur. § 5. Cumque antea fuerat septimo loco bonorum possessio "tum quem ex familia", et octavo "unde liberi patroni patronaeque et parentes eorum", utramque per constitutionem nostram quam de jure patronatus fecimus, penitus vacuavimus. Cum enim ad similitudinem successionis ingenuorum, libertinorum successiones posuimus, quas usque ad quintum tantummodo gradum coarctavimus, ut sit aliqua inter ingenuos et libertos differentia, sufficit eis tam "contra tabulas" bonorum possessio, quam "unde legitimi" et "unde cognati", ex quibus possunt sua jura vindicare, omni scrupulositate et inextricabili errore duarum istarum bonorum possessionum resoluto. § 6. Aliam vero bonorum possessionem, quae "unde vir et uxor" appellatur, et nono loco inter veteres bonorum possessiones posita fuerat, et in suo vigore servavimus, et altiore loco, id est sexto, eam posuimus: decima veteri bonorum possessione, quae erat "unde cognati manumissoris", propter causas enarratas merito sublata, ut sex tantummodo bonorum possessiones ordinariae permaneant, suo vigore pollentes. § 7. Septima eas secuta, quam optima ratione praetores introduxerunt. Novissime enim promittitur edicto iis etiam bonorum possessio, quibus ut detur lege, vel senatus-consulto, vel constitutione comprehensum est, quam neque bonorum possessionibus quae ab intestato veniunt, neque iis quae ex testamento sunt, praetor stabili jure connumeravit, sed quasi ultimum extraordinarium auxilium, prout res exigit, accommodavit, scilicet iis qui ex legibus, senatus-consultis, constitutionibusve principum ex novo jure, vel ex testamento, vel ab intestato veniunt. § 8. Cum igitur plures species successionum praetor introduxisset, easque per ordinem disposuisset, et in unaquaque specie successionis saepe plures extent dispari gradu personae: ne actiones creditorum differentur, sed haberent quos convenirent, et ne facile in possessionem bonorum defuncti mitterentur, et eo modo sibi consulerent, ideo petendae bonorum possessioni certum tempus praefinivit. Liberis itaque et parentibus, tam naturalibus quam adoptivis, in petenda bonorum possessione anni spatium, caeteris centum dierum dedit. § 9. Et si intra hoc tempus aliquis bonorum possessionem non petierit, ejusdem gradus personis adcrescit; vel si nemo sit, deinceps, caeteris perinde bonorum possessionem ex successorio edicto pollicetur, acsi is qui praecedebat ex eo numero non esset. Si quis itaque delatam sibi bonorum possessionem repudiaverit, non quousque tempus bonorum possessioni praefinitum excesserit expectatur, sed statim caeteri ex eodem edicto admittuntur. § 10. In petenda autem bonorum possessione, dies utiles singuli considerantur. Sed bene anteriores principes et huic causae providerunt, ne quis pro petenda bonorum possessione curet, sed quocumque modo si admittentis eam indicium intra statuta tamen tempora ostenderit, plenum habeat earum beneficium.

§ 77. Videamus autem et de ea successione quae nobis ex emptione bonorum competit. § 78. Bona autem veneunt aut vivorum aut mortuorum. Vivorum, velut eorum qui fraudationis causa latitant, nec absentes defenduntur; item eorum qui ex lege Julia bonis cedunt; item judicatorum post tempus quod eis, partim lege XII Tabularum, partim edicto praetoris, ad expediendam pecuniam tribuitur. Mortuorum bona veneunt, veluti eorum quibus certum est neque heredes, neque bonorum possessores, neque ullum alium justum successorem existere. § 79. Si quidem vivi bona veneant, jubet ea praetor per dies continuos XXX possideri et proscribi; si vero mortui, post dies XV, postea jubentur convenire creditores, et ex eo numero magistrum creare, id est, eum per quem bona veneant. Idque si vivi bona veneant, in diebus . . . . fieri jubet, si mortui, ... diebus; itaque vivi bona . . . . . mortui vero . . . . . [die] emptori addici jubet. Qua re autem tardius viventium bonorum venditionem compleri jubetur, illa ratio est, quia de vivis curandum erat, ne facile bonorum venditiones paterentur.

§ 80. Neque autem bonorum possesso[rum, neque bonorum emptorum res] pleno jure fiunt, sed in bonis efficiuntur; ex jure quiritium autem ita demum adquiruntur, si ii usuceperunt. Interdum quidem bonorum emptoribus ne usu quidem capio contingit, veluti si per eos in possessione sit bonorum emptor . . . . . § 81. Item quae debita sunt ei cujus fuerunt bona, aut ipse debuit, neque bonorum possessori, neque bonorum emptori ipso jure debentur [aut ipse debet et] ideo de omnibus rebus [utilibus actionibus et conveniuntur et experiuntur, quas] in sequenti commentario proponemus.

§ 82. Sunt autem etiam alterius generis successiones, quae neque lege XII Tabularum neque praetoris edicto, sed eo jure quod consensu receptum est, introductae sunt. § 83. Ecce enim, cum paterfamilias se in adoptionem dedit, mulierve in manum convenit, omnes eorum res incorporales et corporales, quaeque eis debitae sunt, patri adoptivo coemptionatorive adquiruntur, exceptis iis quae per capitis deminutionem pereunt, quales sunt ususfructus, operarum obligatio libertorum quae per jusjurandum contracta est, [et quae continentur] legitimo judicio.

Tit. x. De adquisitione per adrogationem.

Est et alterius generis per universitatem *successio, quae neque lege Duodecim Tabularum neque praetoris edicto, sed eo jure quod consensu receptum est, introducta est.* § 1. *Ecce enim, cum paterfamilias sese in* adrogationem *dat, omnes res ejus corporales et incorporales quaeque ei debitae sunt,* adrogatori ante quidem pleno jure adquirebantur, *exceptis iis quae per capitis deminutionem pereunt, quales sunt operarum obligationes* et jus agnationis. Usus etenim et *ususfructus,* licet his antea connumerabantur, attamen capitis deminutione minima, eos tolli nostra prohibuit constitutio. § 2. Nunc autem nos eandem adquisitionem quae per adrogationem fiebat coarctavimus ad similitudinem naturalium parentum: nihil etenim aliud nisi tantummodo ususfructus, tam naturalibus patribus quam adoptivis, per filiosfamilias adquiritur in iis rebus quae extrinsecus filiis obveniunt, dominio eis integro servato; mortuo autem filio adrogato in adoptiva familia, etiam dominium ejus ad adrogatorem transit, nisi supersint aliae personae quae ex constitutione nostra patrem, in iis quae adquiri non possunt, antecedunt.

§ 84. Ex diverso quod is debuit [qui se in] adoptionem dedit, quaeque in manum convenit, non transit ad coemptionatorem, aut ad patrem adoptivum, nisi hereditarium aes alienum fuerit;

§ 3. Sed *ex diverso,* pro eo *quod is debuit qui se in adoptionem dedit,* ipso quidem

etenim, quia ipse pater adoptivus aut coemptionator heres fit, directo tenetur jure, is enim ipse qui se adoptandum dedit, quaeve in manum convenit, desinit esse heres. De eo vero quod proprio nomine eae personae debuerint, licet neque pater adoptivus teneatur, neque coemptionator, neque ipse quidem qui se in adoptionem dedit, aut quae in manum convenit, maneat obligatus obligatave, quia scilicet per capitis deminutionem liberentur, tamen in eum eamve utilis actio datur, rescissa capitis deminutione: et, si adversus hanc actionem non defendantur, quae bona eorum futura fuissent, si se alieno juri non subjecissent, universa vendere creditoribus praetor permittit.

jure adrogator non *tenetur*, sed nomine filii convenietur, et si noluerit eum defendere, *permittitur creditoribus* per competentes nostros magistratus, bona quae eorum cum usufructu futura fuissent, *si se alieno juri non subjecissent*, possidere et legitimo modo ea disponere.

---

§ 85. . . . . . ad legitimam hereditatem vocatus sit, antequam cernat, aut pro herede gerat, alii in jure cedat, pleno jure fit ille heres, cui cessa est hereditas [perinde ac si ipse per] legem ad hereditatem vocaretur. Quod si, posteaquam heres extiterit, cesserit, adhuc heres manet, et ob id a creditoribus ipse tenebitur: sed res corporales transferet, perinde ac si singulas in jure cessisset; debita vero pereunt, eoque modo debitores hereditarii lucrum faciunt. § 86. Idem juris est, si testamento scriptus heres, posteaquam heres extiterit, in jure cesserit hereditatem; ante aditam vero hereditatem cedendo, nihil agit. § 87. Suus autem et necessarius heres an aliquid agat in jure cedendo, quaeritur. Nostri praeceptores nihil eos agere existimant: diversae scholae auctores idem éos agere putant, quod caeteri post aditam hereditatem; nihil enim interest, utrum aliquis cernendo aut pro herede gerendo heres fiat, an juris necessitate hereditati adstringatur.

Tit. xi. De eo cui libertatis causa bona addicuntur.

Accessit novus casus successionis ex constitutione divi Marci. Nam si ii qui libertatem acceperunt a domino in testamento ex quo non aditur hereditas, velint bona sibi addici, libertatum conservandarum causa, audiuntur. § 1. Et ita rescripto divi Marci ad Popilium Rufum continetur. Verba rescripti ita se habent: "Si Virginio Valenti, qui testamento suo libertatem quibusdam adscripsit, nemine successore ab intestato existente, in ea causa bona ejus esse coeperunt, ut veniri debeant: is cujus de ea re notio est, aditus, rationem desiderii tui habebit, ut libertatum, tam earum quae directo, quam earum quae per speciem fideicommissi relictae sunt, tuendarum gratia addicantur tibi, si idonee creditoribus caveris de solido quod cuique debetur solvendo. Et ii quidem quibus directa libertas data est, perinde liberi erunt, acsi hereditas adita esset; ii autem quos heres rogatus est manumittere, a te libertatem consequentur, ita ut, si non alia conditione velis bona tibi addici, quam ut etiam qui directo libertatem acceperunt, tui liberti fiant: nam huic etiam voluntati tuae, si ii quorum de statu agitur consentiant, auctoritatem nostram accommodavimus. Et ne hujus rescriptionis nostrae emolumentum alia ratione irritum fiat, si fiscus bona agnoscere voluerit, et ii qui rebus nostris attendunt, scient commodo pecuniario praeferendam libertatis causam, et ita bona cogenda, ut libertas iis salva sit qui eam adipisci potuerunt, si hereditas ex testamento adita esset." § 2. Hoc rescripto subventum est et libertatibus, et defunctis, ne bona eorum a creditoribus possideantur et veneant. Certe si fuerint hac de causa bona addicta, cessat bonorum venditio: extitit enim defuncti defensor, et quidem idoneus, qui de solido creditoribus cavet. § 3. In primis hoc rescriptum totiens locum habet, quotiens testamento libertates datae sunt. Quid ergo si quis intestatus decedens codicillis libertate dederit, neque adita sit ab intestato hereditas? Favor constitutionis debebit locum habere. Certe, si testatus decedat, et codicillis dederit libertatem, competere eam nemini dubium est. § 4. Tunc constitutioni locum esse verba ostendunt, cum nemo successor ab intestato existat: ergo quamdiu incertum erit, utrum existat an non, cessabit constitutio; si certum esse coeperit neminem extare, tunc erit constitutioni locus. § 5. Si is qui in integrum restitui potest, abstinuerit se ab hereditate, quamvis potest in integrum restitui, potest admitti constitutio et addictio bonorum fieri. Quid ergo si, post addictionem libertatum conservandarum causa factam, in integrum sit restitutus? Utique non erit dicendum revocari libertates, quae semel competierunt. § 6. Haec constitutio libertatum tuendarum causa introducta est: ergo si libertates nullae sint datae, cessat constitutio. Quid ergo, si vivus dederit libertates, vel mortis causa, et ne de hoc quaeratur, utrum in fraudem creditorum, an non, factum sit, idcirco velint sibi addici bona, an audiendi sunt? Et magis est, ut audiri debeant, etsi deficiant verba constitutionis. § 7. Sed cum multas divisiones ejusmodi constitutioni deesse perspeximus, lata est a nobis plenissima constitutio, in quam multae species collatae sunt, quibus jus hujusmodi successionis plenissimum est effectum, quas ex ipsa lectione constitutionis potest quis cognoscere.

Tit. xii. De successionibus sublatis, quae fiebant per bonorum venditionem et ex senatus-consulto Claudiano.

Erant ante praedictam successionem olim et aliae per universitatem successiones. Qualis fuerat bonorum emptio quae de bonis debitoris vendendis per multas ambages fuerat introducta, et tunc locum habebat quando judicia ordinaria in usu fuerunt. Sed cum extraordinariis judiciis posteritas usa est, ideo cum ipsis ordinariis judiciis etiam bonorum venditiones expiraverunt, et tantummodo creditoribus datur officio judicis bona possidere, et prout eis utile visum fuerit, ea disponere, quod ex latioribus Digestorum libris perfectius apparebit. § 1. Erat et ex senatus-consulto Claudiano miserabilis per universitatem adquisitio, cum libera mulier, servili amore bacchata, ipsam libertatem per senatus-consultum amittebat, et cum libertate substantiam: quod indignum nostris temporibus esse existimantes, et a nostra civitate deleri, et non inseri nostris Digestis concessimus.

Tit. xiii. De obligationibus.

§ 88. [Nunc transeamus] ad obligationes. Quarum summa divisio in duas species deducitur: omnis enim obligatio vel ex contractu nascitur vel ex delicto.

§ 89. Et prius videamus de his quae ex contractu nascuntur. Harum quattuor genera sunt: aut enim re contrahitur obligatio, aut verbis, aut litteris, aut consensu.

Nunc transeamus ad obligationes. Obligatio est juris vinculum, quo necessitate adstringimur alicujus solvendae rei, secundum nostrae civitatis jura. § 1. Omnium autem obligationum *summa divisio in duo* genera *deducitur:* namque aut civiles sunt, aut praetoriae. Civiles sunt, quae aut legibus constitutae aut certe jure civili comprobatae sunt. Praetoriae sunt, quas praetor ex sua jurisdictione constituit, quae etiam honorariae vocantur. § 2. Sequens divisio in quattuor species deducitur: aut enim *ex contractu* sunt, aut quasi ex contractu, aut ex maleficio, aut quasi ex maleficio. *Prius* est, ut *de his quae ex contractu* sunt dispiciamus. *Harum* aeque *quattuor* species *sunt: aut enim re contrahuntur, aut verbis, aut litteris, aut consensu.* De quibus singulis dispiciamus.

Tit. xiv. Quibus modis re contrahitur obligatio.

§ 90. Re contrahitur obligatio, velut mutui datione. [Mutui autem datio] proprie in his fere rebus contingit, quae pondere, numero, mensura constant: qualis est pecunia numerata, vinum, oleum, frumen-

Re contrahitur obligatio, veluti mutui datione. Mutui autem datio in his rebus consistit quae pondere, numero mensurave constant, veluti vino, oleo, frumento, pecunia numerata, aere, argento,

tum, aes, argentum, aurum, quas res aut numerando, aut metiendo, aut pendendo in hoc damus, ut accipientium fiant, et quandoque nobis non eadem, sed aliae ejusdem naturae reddantur: unde etiam mutuum appellatum est, quia quod ita tibi a me datum est, ex meo tuum fiat. § 91. Is quoque qui non debitum accepit ab eo qui per errorem solvit, re obligatur: nam perinde ei condici potest, "si paret eum dare oportere", ac si mutuum accepisset. Unde quidam putant, pupillum aut mulierem, cui sine [tutoris auctoritate] non debitum per errorem datum est, non teneri condictione, non magis quam mutui datione. Sed haec species obligationis non videtur ex contractu consistere, quia is qui solvendi animo dat, magis distrahere vult negotium, quam contrahere.

auro; quas res aut numerando, aut metiendo, aut pendendo in hoc damus, ut accipientium fiant, et quandoque nobis non eaedem res, sed aliae ejusdem naturae et qualitatis *reddantur: unde etiam mutuum appellatum est, quia ita a me tibi datur, ut ex meo tuum fiat.* Et ex eo contractu nascitur actio quae vocatur condictio. § 1. *Is quoque qui non debitum accepit ab eo qui per errorem solvit, re obligatur,* daturque agenti contra eum propter repetitionem condictitia actio. *Nam perinde ei condici potest "si paret eum dare oportere", ac si mutuum accepisset. Unde pupillus,* si ei *sine tutoris auctoritate non debitum per errorem datum est, non tenebitur* indebiti *condictione non magis quam mutui datione. Sed haec species obligationis non videtur ex contractu consistere,* cum *is qui solvendi animo dat, magis distrahere voluit negotium quam contrahere.*

§ 2. Item is cui res aliqua utenda datur, id est commodatur, re obligatur, et tenetur commodati actione. Sed is ab eo qui mutuum accepit, longe distat: namque non ita res datur, ut ejus fiat; et ob id de ea re ipsa restituenda tenetur. Et is quidem qui mutuum accepit, si quolibet fortuitu casu quod accepit amiserit, veluti incendio, ruina, naufragio, aut latronum hostiumve incursu, nihilominus obligatus permanet. At is qui utendum accepit, sane quidem exactam diligentiam custodiendae rei praestare jubetur, nec sufficit ei tantam diligentiam adhibuisse, quantam in suis rebus adhibere solitus est, si modo alius diligentior poterit eam rem custodire; sed propter majorem vim majoresve casus non tenetur, si modo non hujus ipsius culpa is casus intervenerit: alioquin, si id quod tibi commodatum est peregre tecum ferre malueris, et, vel incursu hostium praedonumve, vel naufragio, amiseris, dubium non est, quin de restituenda ea re tenearis. Commodata autem res tunc proprie intelligitur, si, nulla mercede accepta vel constituta, res tibi utenda data est; alioquin, mercede interveniente, locatus tibi usus rei videtur, gratuitum enim debet esse commodatum.

§ 3. Praeterea et is apud quem res aliqua deponitur re obligatur, et actione depositi, quia et ipse de ea re quam accepit restituenda tenetur. Sed is ex eo solo tenetur, si quid dolo commiserit, culpae autem nomine, id est desidiae atque negligentiae, non tenetur: itaque securus est, qui parum diligenter custoditam rem furto amiserit, quia qui negligenti amico rem custodiendam tradidit, suae facilitati id imputare debet.

§ 4. Creditor quoque qui pignus accepit re obligatur, quia et ipse de ea re quam accepit restituenda tenetur actione pigneratitia. Sed quia pignus utriusque gratia datur, et debitoris, quo magis ei pecunia crederetur, et creditoris, quo magis ei in tuto sit creditum, placuit sufficere, quod ad eam rem custodiendam exactam diligentiam adhiberet: quam si praestiterit, et aliquo fortuitu casu rem amiserit, securum esse, nec impediri creditum petere.

§ 92. Verbis obligatio fit ex interrogatione et responsione, veluti: "dari spondes? spondeo"; "dabis? dabo"; "promittis? promitto"; "fide promittis? fide promitto"; "fide jubes? fide jubeo"; "facies? faciam". § 93. Sed haec quidem verborum obligatio: "dari spondes? spondeo", propria civium Romanorum est, caeterae vero juris gentium sunt; itaque inter omnes homines, sive cives Romanos sive peregrinos, valent; et quamvis ad graecam vocem expressae fuerint, velut hoc modo: ["δώσεις; δώσω" "ὁμολογεῖς; ὁμολογῶ" "πίστει κελεύεις; πίστει κελεύω" "ποιήσεις; ποιήσω"]; etiam haec tamen inter cives Romanos valent, si modo graeci sermonis intellectum habeant. Et e contrario quamvis latine enuntientur, tamen etiam inter peregrinos valent, si modo latini sermonis intellectum habeant. At illa verborum obligatio: "dari spondes? spondeo", adeo propria civium Romanorum est, ut ne quidem in graecum sermonem per interpretationem proprie transferri possit; quamvis dicatur a graeca voce figurata esse. § 94. Unde [quod] dicitur uno casu hoc verbo peregrinum quoque obligari posse, videlicet si imperator noster principem alicujus peregrini populi de pace ita interroget: "Pacem futuram spon-

Tit. xv. De verborum obligatione.

Verbis obligatio contrahitur *ex interrogatione et responsione*, cum quid dari fierive nobis stipulamur; ex qua duae proficiscuntur actiones, tam condictio si certa sit stipulatio, quam ex stipulatu, si incerta. Quae hoc nomine inde utitur, quia stipulum apud veteres firmum appellabatur, forte a stipite descendens.

§ 1. In hac re olim talia verba tradita fuerunt: "*spondes? spondeo*"; "*promittis? promitto*"; "*fide promittis? fide promitto*"; "*fide jubes? fide jubeo*"; "*dabis? dabo*"; "*facies? faciam*". Utrum autem latina an graeca, vel qua alia lingua stipulatio concipiatur, nihil interest, scilicet si uterque stipulantium intellectum hujus linguae habeat; nec necesse est eadem lingua utrumque uti, sed sufficit congruenter ad interrogatum respondere; quin etiam duo graeci latina lingua obligationem contrahere possunt.

des"? vel ipse eodem modo interrogetur, nimium subtiliter dictum est; quia, si quid adversus pactionem fiat, non ex stipulatu agitur, sed jure belli res vindicatur. § 95. Illud dubitari potest, si quis ...... et debitores mulieri simplicius dum ...... doti dicant ..... obligatio contrahi non potest. § 96. Et ideo, si quis alius [pro muliere dotem viro promiserit, com]muni jure obligari debet, scilicet, ut stipulata promittatur. Item uno loco ...... obligatio ... an ... jurejurando homines obligentur: utique cum quaeritur de jure Romanorum; nam apud peregrinos quid juris sit, singularum civitatium jura requirentes, aliud intelligere poterimus.

Sed haec sollemnia verba olim quidem in usu fuerunt; postea autem Leoniana constitutio lata est, quae sollemnitate verborum sublata, sensum et consonantem intellectum ab utraque parte solum desiderat, licet quibuscumque verbis expressus est.

§ 2. Omnis stipulatio aut pure, aut in diem, aut sub conditione fit. Pure, veluti: "quinque aureos dare spondes?" idque confestim peti potest. In diem, cum adjecto die quo pecunia solvatur, stipulatio fit, veluti: "decem aureos primis calendis Martiis dare spondes?" Id autem quod in diem stipulamur, statim quidem debetur; sed peti priusquam dies venerit non potest. Ac ne eo quidem ipso die in quem stipulatio facta est peti potest, quia totus is dies arbitrio solventis tribui debet; neque enim certum est eo die in quem promissum est, datum non esse, priusquam is praeterierit. § 3. At si ita stipuleris: "decem aureos annuos, quoad vivam, dare spondes?" et pure facta obligatio intelligitur, et perpetuatur, quia ad tempus deberi non potest; sed heres petendo pacti exceptione submovebitur. § 4. Sub conditione stipulatio fit, cum in aliquem casum differtur obligatio, ut si aliquid factum fuerit aut non fuerit, stipulatio committatur, veluti: "si Titius consul fuerit factus, quinque aureos dare spondes?" Si quis ita stipuletur: "si in Capitolium non ascendero, dare spondes?" perinde erit, ac si stipulatus esset, cum morietur, sibi dari. Ex conditionali stipulatione tantum spes est debitum iri, eamque ipsam spem in heredem transmittimus, si priusquam conditio existat, mors nobis contigerit. § 5. Loca etiam inseri stipulationi solent, veluti: "Carthagine dare spondes?" Quae stipulatio, licet pure fieri videatur, tamen re ipsa habet tempus injectum, quo promissor utatur ad pecuniam Carthagine dandam. Et ideo si quis Romae ita stipuletur: "hodie Carthagine dare spondes?" inutilis erit stipulatio, cum impossibilis sit repromissio. § 6. Conditiones quae ad praeteritum vel ad praesens tempus referuntur, aut statim infirmant obligationem, aut omnino non differunt: veluti "si Titius consul fuit", vel "si Maevius vivit, dare spondes?" Nam si ea ita non sunt, nihil valet stipulatio; sin autem ita se habent, statim valet; quae enim per rerum naturam certa sunt, non morantur obligationem, licet apud nos incerta sint.

§ 7. Non solum res in stipulatum deduci possunt, sed etiam facta, ut si stipulemur aliquid fieri vel non fieri. Et in hujusmodi stipulationibus optimum erit poenam subjicere, ne quantitas stipulationis in incerto sit, ac necesse sit actori probare, quid ejus intersit. Itaque si quis, ut fiat aliquid, stipuletur, ita adjici poena debet: "si ita factum non erit, tunc poenae nomine decem aureos dare spondes?" Sed si quaedam fieri, quaedam non fieri, una eademque conceptione stipuletur, clausula erit hujusmodi adjicienda: "si adversus ea factum erit, sive quid ita factum non erit, tunc poenae nomine decem aureos dare spondes?"

Tit. xvi. De duobus reis stipulandi et promittendi.

Et stipulandi et promittendi duo pluresve rei fieri possunt. Stipulandi ita si, post omnium interrogationem, promissor respondeat: "spondeo", ut puta, cum duobus separatim stipulantibus, ita promissor respondeat: "utrique vestrum dare spondeo." Nam si prius Titio spoponderit, deinde, alio interrogante, spondeat, alia atque alia erit obligatio, nec creduntur duo rei stipulandi esse. Duo pluresve rei promittendi ita fiunt: "Maevi, quinque aureos dare spondes? Sei, eosdem quinque aureos dare spondes?" si respondent singuli separatim: "spondeo." § 1. Ex hujusmodi obligationibus, et stipulantibus solidum singulis debetur, et promittentes singuli in solidum tenentur. In utraque tamen obligatione una res vertitur, et vel alter debitum accipiendo, vel alter solvendo, omnium perimit obligationem et omnes liberat. § 2. Ex duobus reis promittendi alius pure, alius in diem, vel sub conditione obligari potest; nec impedimento erit dies, aut conditio, quo minus ab eo qui pure obligatus est petatur.

Tit. xvii. De stipulatione servorum.

Servus ex persona domini jus stipulandi habet. Sed hereditas in plerisque personae defuncti vicem sustinet: ideoque quod servus hereditarius ante aditam hereditatem stipulatur, adquirit hereditati, ac per hoc etiam heredi postea facto adquiritur. § 1. Sive autem domino, sive sibi, sive conservo suo, sive impersonaliter servus stipuletur, domino adquirit. Idem juris est, et in liberis qui in potestate patris sunt, ex quibus causis adquirere possunt. § 2. Sed cum factum in stipulatione continebitur, omnimodo persona stipulantis continetur, veluti si servus stipuletur, ut sibi ire, agere liceat. Ipse enim tantum prohiberi non debet, non etiam dominus ejus. § 3. Servus communis, stipulando, unicuique dominorum pro portione dominii adquirit, nisi unius eorum jussu, aut nominatim cui eorum stipulatus est; tunc enim ei soli adquiritur. Quod servus communis stipulatur, si alteri ex dominis adquiri non potest, solidum alteri adquiritur, veluti si res quam dari stipulatus est unius domini sit.

Tit. xviii. De divisione stipulationum.

Stipulationum aliae sunt judiciales, aliae praetoriae, aliae conventionales, aliae communes, tam praetoriae, quam judiciales. § 1. Judiciales sunt dumtaxat, quae a mero judicis officio proficiscuntur: veluti de dolo cautio, vel de persequendo servo qui in fuga est, restituendove pretio. § 2. Praetoriae sunt, quae a mero praetoris officio proficiscuntur, veluti damni infecti, vel legatorum. Praetorias autem stipulationes sic exaudiri oportet, ut in his contineantur etiam aedilitiae; nam et hae ab jurisdictione veniunt. § 3. Conventionales sunt, quae ex conventione utriusque partis concipiuntur, hoc est, neque jussu judicis, neque jussu praetoris, sed ex conventione contrahentium. Quarum totidem genera sunt, quot, pene dixerim, rerum contrahendarum. § 4. Communes sunt stipulationes, veluti rem salvam fore pupilli; nam et praetor jubet rem salvam fore pupillo caveri, et interdum judex, si aliter expediri haec res non potest; vel de rato stipulatio.

§ 97. Si id quod dari stipulamur, tale sit ut dari non possit, inutilis est stipulatio: velut si quis hominem liberum, quem servum esse credebat, aut mortuum,

Tit. xix. De inutilibus stipulationibus.

Omnis res quae dominio nostro subjicitur in stipulationem deduci potest, sive illa mobilis, sive soli sit. § 1. *At si quis rem quae in rerum natura non est, aut esse non potest, dari stipulatus fuerit, veluti:* Stichum qui *mortuus sit, quem vivere credebat, aut hippocentaurum* qui esse non possit, *inutilis erit stipulatio.* § 2. Idem juris est, si rem *sacram* aut *religiosam quam humani juris esse*

quem vivum esse credebat, aut locum sacrum vel religiosum, quem putabat humani juris esse dari stipuletur. § 97A. [Item si quis rem quae in rerum natura non est aut esse non potest, velut hippocentaurum, sibi dari stipuletur] aeque inutilis est stipulatio.

credebat, vel publicam quae usibus populi perpetuo exposita sit, ut forum vel theatrum, vel *liberum hominem quem servum esse credebat*, vel cujus commercium non habuerit, vel *rem suam dari quis stipuletur*, nec in pendente erit stipulatio ob id, quod publica res in privatum deduci, et ex libero servus fieri potest, et commercium adipisci stipulator potest, et res stipulatoris esse desinere potest: sed protinus inutilis est. Item contra, licet initio utiliter res in stipulatum deducta sit, si postea in earum qua causa de quibus supra dictum est, sine facto promissoris devenerit, extinguitur stipulatio. Ac ne statim ab initio talis stipulatio valebit: "Lucium Titium, cum servus erit, dare spondes?" et similia; quia quae, natura sui, dominio nostro exempta sunt, in obligationem deduci nullo modo possunt.

§ 3. Si quis alium daturum facturumve quid spoponderit, non obligabitur, veluti si spondeat Titium quinque aureos daturum. Quod si effecturum se, ut Titius daret, spoponderit, obligatur.

§ 103. Praeterea inutilis est stipulatio, si ei dari stipulemur, cujus juri subjecti non sumus: unde illud quaesitum est, si quis sibi et ei, cujus juri subjectus non est, dari stipuletur, in quantum valeat stipulatio. Nostri praeceptores putant in universum valere, et perinde ei soli qui stipulatus sit, solidum deberi, atque si extranei nomen non adjecisset. Sed diversae scholae auctores dimidium ei deberi existimant, pro altera vero parte inutilem esse stipulationem. Alia causa est . . . dari spondes . . . solidum deberi et me.

§ 4. Si quis alii quam cujus juri subjectus sit stipuletur, nihil agit. Plane solutio etiam in extranei personam conferri potest (veluti si quis ita stipuletur: "mihi aut Seio dare spondes?") ut obligatio quidem stipulatori adquiratur, solvi tamen Seio etiam invito eo recte possit, ut liberatio ipso jure contingat, sed ille adversus Seium habeat mandati actionem. Quod si quis sibi et alii cujus juri subjectus non sit, dari decem aureos stipulatus est, valebit quidem stipulatio; sed utrum totum debeatur quod in stipulationem deductum est, an vero pars dimidia, dubitatum est; sed placet non plus quam partem dimidiam ei adquiri. Ei qui tuo juri subjectus est si stipulatus sis, tibi adquiris, quia vox tua tanquam filii sit, sicuti filii vox tamquam tua intelligitur in iis rebus quae tibi adquiri possunt.

§ 102. Adhuc inutilis est stipulatio, si quis ad id quod interrogatus erit, non responderit: veluti si sestertia decem a te dari stipuler, et tu sestertia quinque

§ 5. Praeterea *inutilis est stipulatio, si quis ad ea* quae *interrogatus erit, non respondeat: veluti, si decem* aureos *a te dari stipuletur, tu quinque promittas*, vel contra; *aut si ille pure stipuletur, tu sub conditione promittas*, vel contra; si modo scilicet id exprimas, id est, si cui sub conditione vel in diem stipulanti tu respondeas: "praesenti die spondeo." Nam

promittas; aut si ego pure stipuler, tu sub conditione promittas.

si hoc solum respondeas: "promitto", breviter videris in eandem diem aut conditionem spopondisse; neque enim necesse est in respondendo eadem omnia repeti, quae stipulator expresserit.

§ 104. Item inutilis est stipulatio si ab eo stipuler, qui juri meo subjectus est, vel si is a me stipuletur. Servus quidem et qui in mancipio est et [filia familias], et quae in manu est non solum ipsi cujus juri subjecti subjectaeve sunt, obligari non possunt, sed ne alii quidem ulli.

§ 105. Mutum neque stipulari neque promittere posse palam est; idem etiam in surdo receptum est: quia et is, qui stipulatur, verba promittentis, et qui promittit, verba stipulantis exaudire debet. § 106. Furiosus nullum negotium gerere potest, quia non intelligit quid agat. § 107. Pupillus omne negotium recte gerit, ita tamen ut tutor, sicubi tutoris auctoritas necessaria sit, adhibeatur, velut si ipse obligetur; nam alium sibi obligare etiam sine tutoris auctoritate potest. § 108. Item juris est in feminis quae in tutela sunt. § 109. Sed quod diximus de pupillo utique de eo verum est qui jam aliquem intellectum habet: nam infans et qui infanti proximus est, non multum a furioso differt, quia hujus aetatis pupilli nullum intellectum habent; sed in his pupillis propter utilitatem benignior juris interpretatio facta est.

§ 6. *Item inutilis est stipulatio, si ab eo stipuleris qui juri tuo subjectus est, vel si is a te stipuletur. Sed servus quidem, non solum* domino suo *obligari non potest, sed ne alii quidem ulli;* filii vero familias aliis obligari possunt.

§ 7. *Mutum neque stipulari neque promittere posse palam est. Quod et in surdo receptum est; quia et is qui stipulatur verba promittentis, et is qui promittit, verba stipulantis, audire debet.* Unde apparet, non de eo nos loqui qui tardius exaudit, sed de eo qui omnino non audit. § 8. *Furiosus nullum negotium gerere potest, quia non intelligit quid agit.* § 9. *Pupillus omne negotium recte gerit; ita tamen ut, sicubi tutoris auctoritas necessaria sit, adhibeatur tutor, veluti si ipse obligetur; nam alium sibi obligare etiam sine tutoris auctoritate potest.* § 10. *Sed quod diximus de pupillis, utique de iis verum est qui jam aliquem intellectum habent: nam infans et qui infanti proximus est, non multum a furioso distant, quia hujus aetatis pupilli nullum intellectum habent; sed in proximis infanti, propter utilitatem eorum, benignior juris interpretatio facta est,* ut idem juris habeant quod pubertati proximi. Sed qui in parentis potestate est impubes, nec auctore quidem patre obligatur.

§ 98. Item si quis sub ea conditione stipuletur, quae existere non potest, veluti si digito caelum tetigerit, inutilis est stipulatio. Sed legatum sub impossibili conditione relictum nostri praeceptores perinde deberi putant, acsi sine conditione relictum esset; diversae scholae auctores nihilominus legatum inutile existimant quam stipulationem; et sane vix idonea diversitatis ratio reddi

§ 11. Si impossibilis conditio obligationibus adjiciatur, nihil valet stipulatio. Impossibilis autem conditio habetur, cui natura impedimento est, quo minus existat, veluti si quis ita dixerit: "Si *digito caelum* attigero, dare spondes?" At si ita stipuletur: "Si digito caelum

potest. § 99. Praeterea inutilis est stipulatio, si quis, ignorans rem suam esse, dari sibi eam stipuletur; quippe quod alicujus est, id ei dari non potest.

non attigero, dare spondes?" pure facta obligatio intelligitur, ideoque statim petere potest.

§ 12. Item verborum obligatio inter absentes concepta inutilis est. Sed cum hoc materiam litium contentiosis hominibus praestabat, forte post tempus tales allegationes opponentibus, et non praesentes esse vel se vel adversarios suos contendentibus: ideo nostra constitutio propter celeritatem dirimendarum litium introducta est, quod ad Caesarienses advocatos scripsimus: per quam disposuimus tales scripturas quae praesto esse partes indicant, omnimodo esse credendas, nisi ipse qui talibus utitur improbis allegationibus, manifestissimis probationibus vel per scripturam vel per testes idoneos approbaverit, in ipso toto die quo conficiebatur instrumentum, sese vel adversarium suum in aliis locis esse.

§ 100. Denique inutilis est talis stipulatio, si quis ita dari stipuletur: "post mortem meam dari spondes?" vel ita: [" post mortem tuam dari spondes?" valet autem, si quis ita dari stipuletur: "cum moriar, dari spondes?" vel ita]: "cum morieris, dari spondes?" id est, ut in novissimum vitae tempus stipulatoris aut promissoris obligatio conferatur. Nam inelegans visum est, ab heredis persona incipere obligationem. Rursus ita stipulari non possumus: "pridie quam moriar," aut: "pridie quam morieris, dari spondes?" quia non potest aliter intelligi pridie quam aliquis morietur, quam si mors secuta sit; rursus, morte secuta, in praeteritum reducitur] stipulatio, et quodammodo talis est: "heredi meo dari spondes?" quae sane inutilis est. § 101. Quaecumque de morte diximus, eadem et de capitis deminutione dicta intelligemus.

§ 13. *Post mortem* suam *dari* sibi nemo stipulari poterat, non magis quam post mortem ejus a quo stipulabatur. Ac ne is qui in alicujus potestate est, post mortem ejus stipulari poterat, quia patris vel domini voce loqui videtur. Sed et si quis ita stipuletur: "*pridie quam moriar*," *vel* "*pridie quam morieris dari?*" inutilis erat stipulatio. Sed cum (ut jam dictum est) ex consensu contrahentium stipulationes valent, placuit nobis etiam in hunc juris articulum necessariam inducere emendationem, ut sive post mortem, sive pridie quam morietur stipulator sive promissor, stipulatio concepta est, valeat stipulatio.

§ 14. Item, si quis ita stipulatus erat "Si navis ex Asia venerit, hodie dare spondes?" inutilis erat stipulatio, quia praepostere concepta est. Sed cum Leo, inclytae recordationis, in dotibus eandem stipulationem quae praepostera nuncupatur, non esse rejiciendam existimavit, nobis placuit et huic perfectum robur accommodare, ut non solum in dotibus, sed etiam in omnibus valeat hujusmodi conceptio stipulationis. § 15. Ita autem concepta stipulatio, veluti si Titius dicat: "Cum moriar, dare spondes?" vel "cum morieris", et apud veteres utilis erat, et nunc valet. § 16. Item post mortem alterius recte stipulamur. § 17. Si scriptum fuerit in instrumento promisisse aliquem, perinde habetur, atque si interrogatione praecedente responsum sit. § 18. Quotiens plures res una stipulatione comprehenduntur, si quidem promissor simpliciter respondeat: "dare spondeo", propter omnes tenetur; si vero unam ex his, vel quasdam daturum se responderit, obligatio in iis pro quibus spoponderit contrahitur. Ex pluribus enim stipulationibus una vel quaedam videntur esse perfectae: singulas enim res stipulari et ad singulas respondere debemus. § 19. Alteri stipulari (ut supra dictum est) nemo potest: inventae sunt enim hujusmodi obligationes ad hoc, ut unusquisque sibi adquirat quod sua interest; ceterum ut alii detur, nihil interest stipulatoris. Plane si quis velit hoc facere, poenam stipulari conveniet, ut nisi ita factum sit, ut comprehensum est, committatur poenae stipulatio etiam ei cujus nihil interest: poenam enim cum stipulatur quis, non illud inspicitur, quid intersit ejus, sed quae sit quantitas in conditione stipulationis. Ergo si quis stipuletur Titio, dari, nihil agit, sed si addiderit poenam: "Nisi dederis, tot aureos dare spondes?" tunc committitur stipulatio. § 20. Sed et si quis stipuletur alii, cum ejus interesset, placuit stipulationem valere. Nam si is qui pupilli tutelam administrare coeperat, cessit administratione contutori suo, et stipulatus est rem pupilli salvam fore, quoniam interest stipulatoris fieri quod stipulatus est, cum obligatus futurus esset pupillo, si male res gesserit, tenet obligatio. Ergo et si quis procuratori suo dari stipulatus sit, stipulatio vires habebit. Et si creditori suo dari quis stipulatus sit, quod sua interest, ne forte vel poena committatur, vel praedia distrahantur quae pignori data erant, valet stipulatio. § 21. Versa vice, qui alium facturum promisit videtur in ea esse causa, ut non teneatur, nisi poenam ipse promiserit. § 22. Item nemo rem suam futuram in eum casum quo sua sit utiliter stipulatur. § 23. Si de alia re stipulator senserit, de alia promissor, perinde nulla contrahitur obligatio, ac si ad interrogatum responsum non esset; veluti, si hominem Stichum a te quis stipulatus fuerit, tu de Pamphilo senseris, quem Stichum vocari credideris. § 24. Quod turpi ex causa promissum est, veluti si quis homicidium vel sacrilegium se facturum promittat, non valet.

§ 25. Cum quis sub aliqua conditione fuerit stipulatus, licet ante conditionem decesserit, postea existente conditione, heres ejus agere potest. Idem est et ex promissoris parte. § 26. Qui hoc anno aut hoc mense dari stipulatus est, nisi omnibus partibus anni vel mensis praeteritis, non recte petet. § 27. Si fundum dari stipuleris vel hominem, non poteris continuo agere, nisi tantum spatium praeterierit quo traditio fieri possit.

§ 110. Possumus tamen ad id, quod stipulamur, alium adhibere, qui idem stipuletur: quem vulgo adstipulatorem vocamus. § 111. Sed huic perinde actio competit, perindeque ei recte solvitur ac nobis; sed quidquid consecutus erit, mandati judicio nobis restituere cogetur. § 112. Caeterum potest etiam aliis verbis uti adstipulator, quam quibus nos usi sumus. Itaque si verbi gratia ego ita stipulatus sim: "dari spondes?" ille sic adstipulari potest: "idem fide tua promittis?" vel "idem fide jubes?" vel contra. § 113. Idem minus adstipulari potest, plus non potest. Itaque si ego sestertia decem stipulatus sum, ille sestertia quinque stipulari potest; contra vero plus non potest. Item si ego pure stipulatus sim, ille sub conditione stipulari potest; contra vero non potest. Non solum autem in quantitate, sed etiam in tempore minus et plus intelligitur: plus est enim statim aliquid dare, minus est post tempus dare. § 114. In hoc autem jure quaedam singulari jure observantur. Nam adstipulatoris heres non habet actionem. Item servus adstipulando nihil agit, quamvis ex caeteris omnibus causis stipulatione domino adquirat. Idem de eo qui in mancipio est, magis placuit; nam et is servi loco est. Is autem, qui in potestate patris est, agit aliquid; sed parenti non adquirit, quamvis ex omnibus caeteris causis stipulando ei adquirat: ac ne ipsi quidem aliter actio competit, quam si sine capitis deminutione exierit e potestate parentis, veluti morte ejus, aut quod ipse flamen Dialis inauguratus est. Eadem de filia-familias, et quae in manu est, dicta intelligemus.

Tit. xx. De fidejussoribus.

§ 115. Pro eo quoque qui promittit, solent alii obligari: quorum alios sponsores, alios fidepromissores, alios fidejussores appellamus. § 116. Sponsor ita interrogatur: "idem dari spondes?" fidepromissor: "idem fide promittis?" fidejussor ita: "idem fide tua esse jubes?" Videbimus de his autem quo proprio nomine possint

Pro eo qui promittit solent alii obligari, qui fidejussores appellantur, quos homines accipere solent, dum curant, ut diligentius sibi cautum sit.

appellari, qui ita interrogantur: "idem dabis?" "idem promittis?" "idem facies?" § 117. Sponsores quidem et fidepromissores et fidejussores saepe solemus accipere, dum curamus, ut diligentius nobis cautum sit: adstipulatorem vero fere tunc solum adhibemus, cum ita stipulamur ut aliquid post mortem nostram detur, [quod cum] stipulando nihil agimus, adhibetur autem adstipulator, ut is post mortem nostram agat: qui si quid fuerit consecutus, de restituendo eo mandati judicio heredi meo tenetur.

§ 118. Sponsoris vero et fidepromissoris similis conditio est, fidejussoris valde dissimilis. § 119. Nam illi quidem nullis obligationibus accedere possunt nisi verborum, quamvis interdum ipse quidem [qui quid] promiserit, non fuerit obligatus, veluti si [mulier] aut pupillus sine tutoris auctoritate, aut quilibet post mortem suam dari promiserit; at illud quaeritur, si servus aut peregrinus spoponderit, an pro eo sponsor aut fidepromissor obligetur. Fidejussor vero omnibus obligationibus, id est, sive re, sive verbis, sive litteris, sive consensu contractae fuerint obligationes, adjici potest; ac ne illud quidem interest, utrum civilis an naturalis obligatio sit, cui adjiciatur; adeo quidem ut pro servo quoque obligetur, sive extraneus sit, qui a servo fidejussorem accipiat, sive dominus in id quod sibi debeatur. § 120. Praeterea sponsoris et fidepromissoris heres non tenetur, nisi si de peregrino fidepromissore quaeramus, et alio jure civitas ejus utatur: fidejussoris autem etiam heres tenetur. § 121. Item sponsor et fidepromissor lege Furia biennio liberantur; et quotquot erunt numero eo tempore quo pecunia peti potest, in tot partes deducitur inter eos obligatio, et singuli viriles partes solvere tenentur. Fidejussores vero perpetuo tenentur; et quotquot erunt numero, singuli in solidum obligantur. Itaque liberum est creditori a quo velit solidum petere. Sed nunc ex epistola divi Hadriani compellitur creditor a singulis qui modo solvendo sint, partes petere. Eo igitur distat haec epistola a lege Furia, quod, si quis ex sponsoribus aut fidepromissoribus solvendo non sit, hoc quoque onus ad caeterorum [partes] pertinet. Sed cum lex Furia tantum in Italia locum

§ 1. *In omnibus autem obligationibus adsumi possunt, id est, sive re, sive verbis, sive litteris, sive consensu contractae fuerint. At ne illud quidem interest, utrum civilis an naturalis sit obligatio cui adjiciatur fidejussor; adeo quidem, ut pro servo quoque obligetur, sive extraneus sit qui fidejussorem a servo accipiat, sive ipse dominus in id quod sibi naturaliter debetur.* § 2. *Fidejussor* non tantum ipse obligatur, sed etiam *heredem* obligatum relinquit. § 3. Fidejussor et praecedere obligationem et sequi potest. § 4. Si plures sint *fidejussores, quotquot erunt numero, singuli, in solidum tenentur. Itaque liberum est creditori a quo velit solidum petere. Sed ex epistola divi Hadriani compellitur creditor a singulis, qui modo solvendo sint* litis contestatae tempore, *partes petere.*

habeat, evenit, ut in caeteris provinciis sponsores quoque et fidepromissores perinde ac fidejussores in perpetuum teneantur, et singuli in solidum obligentur, nisi ex epistola divi Hadriani hi quoque adjuventur in parte. § 122. Praeterea inter sponsores et fidepromissores lex Apuleia quandam societatem introduxit; nam, si quis horum plus sua portione solverit, de eo, quod amplius dederit, adversus caeteros actiones constituit; quae lex ante legem Furiam lata est, quo tempore in solidum obligabantur: unde quaeritur, an post legem Furiam adhuc legis Apuleiae beneficium supersit. Et utique extra Italiam superest; nam lex quidem Furia tantum in Italia valet, Apuleia vero etiam in caeteris provinciis: sed an etiam in Italia supersit, valde quaeritur. Ad [fidejussores autem lex] Apuleia non pertinet. Itaque si creditor ab uno totum consecutus fuerit, hujus solius detrimentum erit, scilicet si is pro quo fidejussit solvendo non sit. Sed, ut ex supradictis apparet, is a quo creditor totum petit, poterit ex epistola divi Hadriani desiderare ut pro parte in se detur actio. § 123. Praeterea lege Cicereia cautum est, ut is, qui sponsores aut fidepromissores accipiat, praedicat palam et declaret, et de qua re satis accipiat, et quot sponsores aut fidepromissores in eam obligationem accepturus sit; et, nisi praedixerit, permittitur sponsoribus et fidepromissoribus intra diem XXX praejudicium postulare, quo quaeratur an ex ea lege praedictum sit; et, si judicatum fuerit praedictum non esse, liberantur. Qua lege fidejussorum mentio nulla fit; sed in usu est, etiam si fidejussores accipiamus, praedicere.

§ 124. Sed beneficium legis Corneliae omnibus commune est. Qua lege idem pro eodem, apud eundem, eodem anno, vetatur in ampliorem summam obligari creditae pecuniae, quam in XX millium; et quamvis [sponsor vel fidepromissor in] ampliorem pecuniam, velut in sestertium C millia [se obligaverit, non tamen tenebitur]. Pecuniam autem creditam dicimus non solum eam quam credendi causa damus, sed omnem quam tunc, cum contrahitur obligatio, certum est debitum iri, id est, [quae] sine ulla conditione deducitur in obligationem: itaque etiam ea pecunia quam in diem certum dari stipulamur, eodem numero est, quia certum est eam debitum iri, licet post tempus petatur. Appellatione autem pecuniae omnes res in ea lege significantur: itaque si vinum vel fru-

Ideoque, si quis ex fidejussoribus eo tempore *solvendo non sit, hoc caeteros onerat. Sed et si ab uno fidejussore creditor totum consecutus fuerit, hujus solius detrimentum erit, si is pro quo fidejussit solvendo non sit:* et sibi imputare debet, cum *potuerit* adjuvari *ex epistola divi Hadriani, et desiderare ut pro parte in se detur actio.*

mentum, et si fundum vel hominem stipulemur, haec lex observanda est. § 125. Ex quibusdam tamen causis permittit ea lex in infinitum satis accipere, veluti si dotis nomine, vel ejus quod ex testamento tibi debeatur, aut jussu judicis satis accipiatur; et adhuc lege vicesima hereditatum cavetur, ut ad eas satisdationes, quae ex ea lege proponuntur, lex Cornelia non pertineat.

§ 126. In eo quoque jure par conditio est omnium sponsorum, fidepromissorum, fidejussorum, quod ita obligari non possint ut plus debeant quam debet is pro quo obligantur: at ex diverso, ut minus debeant, obligari possunt, sicut in adstipulatoris persona diximus nam ut adstipulatoris, ita et horum obligatio accessio est principalis obligationis, nec plus in accessione esse potest quam in principali re. § 127. In eo quoque par omnium causa est, quod, si quid pro reo solverit, ejus recuperandi causa habet cum eo mandati judicium; et hoc amplius sponsores ex lege Publilia propriam habent actionem in duplum, quae appellatur depensi.

§ 5. *Fidejussores ita obligari non possunt, ut plus debeant quam debet is pro quo obligantur:* nam eorum *obligatio accessio est principalis obligationis, nec plus in accessione esse potest quam in principali re. At ex diverso, ut minus debeant, obligari possunt. Itaque si* reus decem aureos promiserit, fidejussor in quinque recte obligatur; *contra vero* obligari non potest. *Item si* ille *pure* promiserit, fidejussor *sub conditione* promittere *potest; contra vero non potest: non solum enim in quantitate, sed etiam in tempore minus et plus intelligitur: plus est enim statim aliquid dare; minus est post tempus dare.* § 6. *Si quid autem fidejussor pro reo solverit, ejus recuperandi causa habet cum eo mandati judicium.*

§ 7. Graece fidejussor ita accipitur: τῇ ἐμῇ πίστει κελεύω, λέγω, θέλω, sive βούλομαι; sed et si φημὶ dixerit, pro eo erit ac si dixerit λέγω. § 8. In stipulationibus fidejussorum sciendum est generaliter hoc accipi, ut quodcumque scriptum sit quasi actum, videatur etiam actum: ideoque constat, si quis se scripserit fidejussisse, videri omnia sollemniter acta.

Tit. xxi. De litterarum obligatione.

§ 128. Litteris obligatio fit, veluti in nominibus transcriptitiis. Fit autem nomen transcriptitium duplici modo, vel a re in personam, vel a persona in personam. § 129. [A re in personam trans]criptio fit, veluti si id quod tu ex emptionis causa, aut conductionis, aut societatis mihi debeas, id expensum tibi tulero. § 130. A persona in personam transcriptio fit, veluti si id quod mihi Titius debet, tibi id expensum tulero, id est, si Titius te delegaverit mihi. § 131. Alia causa est eorum nominum quae arcaria vocantur: in his enim rei, non litterarum, obligatio consistit: quippe non aliter valet, quam si numerata sit pecunia; numeratio autem pecuniae rei, [non litterarum] facit obligationem. Qua de causa recte dicemus, arcaria nomina nullam facere obligationem, sed obligationis factae testimonium praebere. § 132. Unde etiam proprie dicitur, arcariis nominibus peregrinos obligari, quia non ipso nomine, sed numeratione pecuniae obligantur: quod genus obligationis juris gentium est: § 133. transcriptitiis vero nominibus an obligentur peregrini merito quaeritur, quia quo fiat juris civilis est talis obligatio: quod Nervae placuit: Sabino autem et Cassio visum est, si a re in personam fiat nomen transcriptitium, etiam peregrinos obligari; si vero a persona in personam, non obligari. § 134. Praeterea litterarum obligatio fieri videtur chirographis et syngraphis, id est, si quis debere se aut daturum se scribat, ita scilicet, si eo nomine stipulatio non fiat. Quod genus obligationis proprium peregrinorum est.

Olim scriptura fiebat obligatio, quae nominibus fieri dicebatur; quae nomina hodie non sunt in usu. Plane si quis debere se scripserit quod ei numeratum non est, de pecunia minime numerata post multum temporis exceptionem opponere non potest: hoc enim saepissime constitutum est. Sic fit, ut et hodie, dum queri non potest, scriptura obligetur; et ex ea nascitur condictio, cessante scilicet verborum obligatione. Multum autem tempus in hac exceptione antea quidem ex principalibus constitutionibus usque ad quinquennium procedebat: sed ne creditores diutius possint suis pecuniis forsitan defraudari, per constitutionem nostram tempus coarctatum est, ut ultra biennii metas hujusmodi exceptio minime extendatur.

Tit. xxii. De consensu obligatione.

§ 135. Consensu fiunt obligationes in emptionibus et venditionibus, locationibus conductionibus, societatibus, mandatis. § 136. Ideo autem istis modis consensu dicimus obligationes contrahi, quia neque verborum, neque scripturae ulla proprietas desideratur, sed sufficit eos qui negotium gerunt, consensisse. Unde inter absentes quoque talia negotia contrahuntur, veluti per epistolam, aut per internuntium: cum alioquin verborum obligatio inter ab-

Consensu fiunt obligationes in emptionibus venditionibus, locationibus conductionibus, societatibus, mandatis. Ideo autem istis modis consensu dicitur obligatio contrahi, quia neque scriptura neque praesentia omnimodo opus est, ac nec dari quidquam necesse est, ut substantiam capiat obligatio; *sed sufficit eos qui negotium gerunt consentire. Unde inter absentes quoque talia negotia contrahuntur, veluti per epistolam aut per nuntium. Item in his contractibus*

sentes fieri non possit. § 137. Item in his contractibus alter alteri obligatur de eo quod alterum alteri ex bono et aequo praestare oportet: cum alioquin in verborum obligationibus alius stipuletur, alius promittat, et in nominibus alius expensum ferendo obliget, alius obligetur. § 138. Sed absenti expensum ferri potest, etsi verborum obligatio cum absente contrahi non possit.

alter alteri obligatur in id quod alterum alteri ex bono et aequo praestare oportet, cum alioquin in verborum obligationibus alius stipuletur, alius promittat.

Tit. xxiii. De emptione et venditione.

§ 139. [Emptio venditio contrahitur] cum de pretio convenerit, quamvis nondum pretium numeratum sit, ac ne arrha quidem data fuerit; nam quod arrhae nomine datur, argumentum est emptionis et venditionis contractae.

Emptio et venditio contrahitur simul atque de pretio convenerit, quamvis nondum pretium numeratum sit, ac ne arrha quidem data fuerit: nam quod arrhae nomine datur argumentum est emptionis et venditionis contractae. Sed haec quidem de emptionibus et venditionibus quae sine scriptura consistunt, obtinere oportet: nam nihil a nobis in hujusmodi venditionibus innovatum est. In his autem quae scriptura conficiuntur, non aliter perfectam esse emptionem et venditionem constituimus, nisi et instrumenta emptionis fuerint conscripta, vel manu propria contrahentium, vel ab alio quidem scripta, a contrahentibus autem subscripta, et, si per tabelliones fiant, nisi et completiones acceperint, et fuerint partibus absoluta. Donec enim aliquid ex his deest, et poenitentiae locus est, et potest emptor vel venditor sine poena recedere ab emptione. Ita tamen impune eis recedere concedimus, nisi jam arrharum nomine aliquid fuerit datum: hoc etenim subsecuto, sive in scriptis sive sine scriptis venditio celebrata est, is qui recusat adimplere contractum, si quidem emptor est, perdit quod dedit, si vero venditor, duplum restituere compellitur, licet super arrhis nihil expressum est.

§ 140. Pretium autem certum esse debet: nam alioquin si ita inter eos convenerit, ut quanti Titius rem aestimaverit, tanti sit empta, Labeo negavit, ullam vim hoc negotium habere; cujus opinionem Cassius probat: Ofilius et eam emptionem et venditionem

§ 1. *Pretium autem* constitui oportet: nam nulla emptio sine pretio esse potest. Sed et *certum* pretium *esse debet: alioquin, si ita inter aliquos convenerit, ut quanti Titius rem aestimaverit, tanti sit empta*, inter veteres satis abundeque hoc dubitabatur, sive constat venditio, sive non. Sed nostra decisio ita hoc constituit; ut quotiens sic composita sit venditio: "Quanti ille aestimaverit", sub hac conditione stare contractus: ut, si quidem ipse qui nominatus est pretium defi-

[esse existimavit], cujus opinionem Proculus secutus est.

nierit, omnimodo secundum ejus aestimationem et pretium persolvatur, et res tradatur, ut venditio ad effectum perducatur, emptore quidem ex empto actione, venditore autem ex vendito agente. Sin autem ille qui nominatus est, vel noluerit vel non potuerit pretium definire, tunc pro nihilo esse venditionem, quasi nullo pretio statuto. Quod jus, cum in venditionibus nobis placuit, non est absurdum et in locationibus et conductionibus trahere.

§ 141. Item pretium in numerata pecunia consistere debet; nam in caeteris rebus an pretium esse possit, veluti homo, aut toga, aut fundus alterius rei [pretium esse possit], valde quaeritur. Nostri praeceptores putant, etiam in alia re posse consistere pretium; unde illud est quod vulgo putant, per permutationem rerum emptionem et venditionem contrahi, eamque speciem emptionis et venditionis vetustissimam esse; argumentoque utuntur graeco poeta Homero, qui aliqua parte sic ait:

§ 2. *Item pretium in numerata pecunia consistere debet; nam in caeteris rebus an pretium esse possit, veluti homo aut fundus aut toga alterius rei pretium esse possit, valde* quaerebatur. Sabinus et Cassius *etiam in alia re putant posse pretium consistere*: *unde illud est quod vulgo* dicebatur *per permutationem rerum emptionem et venditionem contrahi, eamque speciem emptionis venditionisque vetustissimam esse; argumentoque utebantur graeco poeta Homero, qui aliqua parte* exercitum Achivorum vinum sibi comparasse ait, permutatis quibusdam rebus, his verbis:

ἔνθεν ἄρ' οἰνίζοντο καρηκομόωντες Ἀχαιοί,
ἄλλοι μὲν χαλκῷ, ἄλλοι δ' αἴθωνι σιδήρῳ,
ἄλλοι δὲ ῥινοῖς, ἄλλοι δ' αὐτοῖσι βόεσσι,
ἄλλοι δ' ἀνδραπόδεσσι.

et reliqua: diversae scholae auctores dissentiunt, aliudque esse existimant permutationem rerum, aliud emptionem et venditionem: alioquin non [posse] rem expediri, permutatis rebus, quae videatur res venisse, et quae pretii nomine data esse; sed rursus utramque videri et venisse et utramque pretii nomine datam esse absurdum videri. Sed ait Caelius Sabinus, si rem tibi venalem habenti, veluti fundum, accesserim, et pretii nomine hominem forte dederim, fundum quidem videri venisse, hominem autem pretii nomine datum esse.

Diversae scholae auctores contra sentiebant, *aliudque esse* existimabant *permutationem rerum, aliud emptionem et venditionem: alioquin non posse rem expediri, permutatis rebus, quae videatur res venisse et quae pretii nomine data esse; nam utramque videri et venisse et pretii nomine datam esse, rationem non pati.* Sed Proculi sententia dicentis, permutationem propriam esse speciem contractus a venditione separatam, merito praevaluit, cum et ipsa aliis Homericis versibus adjuvatur, et validioribus rationibus argumentatur. Quod et anteriores divi principes admiserunt, et in nostris Digestis latius significatur. § 3. Cum autem emptio et venditio contracta sit (quod effici diximus simul atque de pretio convenerit, cum sine scriptura res agitur): periculum rei venditae statim ad emptorem pertinet, tametsi adhuc ea res emptori tradita non sit. Itaque si homo mortuus sit, vel aliqua parte corporis laesus fuerit, aut aedes totae vel aliqua ex parte incendio consumptae fuerint, aut fundus vi fluminis totus vel aliqua ex parte ablatus sit, sive etiam inundatione aquae aut arboribus turbine dejectis longe minor aut deterior esse coeperit: emptoris damnum est, cui necesse est, licet rem non fuerit nactus, pretium solvere. Quidquid enim sine dolo et culpa venditoris accidit, in eo venditor securus est. Sed et si post emptionem fundo aliquid per alluvionem accessit, ad emptoris commodum pertinet: nam et commodum ejus esse debet cujus periculum est. Quodsi fugerit homo qui veniit, aut subreptus fuerit, ita ut neque dolus neque culpa venditoris interveniat, animadvertendum erit, an custodiam ejus usque ad traditionem venditor susceperit; sane enim, si suscepit, ad ipsius periculum is casus pertinet; si non suscepit, securus erit. Idem et in caeteris animalibus caeterisque rebus intelligimus. Utique tamen vindicationem rei et condictionem exhibere debebit emptori; quia sane qui rem nondum emptori tradidit, adhuc ipse dominus est. Idem est etiam de furti et de damni injuriae actione. § 4. Emptio tam sub conditione, quam pure contrahi potest. Sub conditione, veluti: "si Stichus intra certum diem tibi placuerit, erit tibi emptus aureis tot." § 5. Loca sacra vel religiosa, item publica (veluti forum, basilicam) frustra quis sciens emit, quae tamen si pro privatis vel profanis deceptus a venditore emerit, habebit actionem ex empto, quod non habere ei liceat, ut consequatur quod sua interest deceptum non esse. Idem juris est, si hominem liberum pro servo emerit.

§ 142. Locatio autem et conductio similibus regulis constituitur: nisi enim merces certa statuta sit, non videtur locatio et conductio contrahi. § 143. Unde si alieno arbitrio merces permissa sit, veluti quanti Titius aestimaverit, quaeritur an locatio et

Tit. xxiv. De locatione et conductione.

Locatio et conductio proxima est emptioni et venditioni, iisdemque juris regulis consistit. Nam ut emptio et venditio ita contrahitur, si de pretio convenerit, sic etiam locatio et conductio ita contrahi intelligitur, si merces constituta sit; et competit locatori quidem locati actio, conductori vero conducti. § 1. Et quae supra diximus, si alieno arbitrio pretium permissum fuerit, eadem et de locatione et conductione dicta esse intelligamus, *si alieno arbitrio merces permissa*

conductio contrahatur. Qua de causa si fulloni polienda curandave, sarcinatori sarcienda vestimenta dederim, nulla statim mercede constituta, postea tantum daturus quanti inter nos convenerit, quaeritur an locatio et conductio contrahatur. § 144. Vel si rem tibi utendam dederim, et invicem aliam rem utendam acceperim, quaeritur an locatio et conductio contrahatur.

fuerit. Qua de causa si fulloni polienda curandave, aut sarcinatori sarcienda vestimenta quis dederit, nulla statim mercede constituta, sed postea tantum daturus quantum inter eos convenerit, non proprie *locatio et conductio contrahi* intelligitur, sed eo nomine actio praescriptis verbis datur. § 2. Praeterea, sicut vulgo quaerebatur, an permutatis rebus emptio et venditio contrahitur, ita quaeri solebat de locatione et conductione, si forte rem aliquam tibi utendam sive fruendam quis dederit, et invicem a te aliam rem utendam sive fruendam acceperit. Et placuit non esse locationem et conductionem, sed proprium genus esse contractus. Veluti si, cum unum bovem quis haberet et vicinus ejus unum, placuerit inter eos, ut per denos dies invicem boves commodarent ut opus facerent, et apud alterum bos periit, neque locati neque conducti, neque commodati competit actio, quia non fuit gratuitum commodatum, verum praescriptis verbis agendum est.

§ 145. Adeo autem emptio et venditio et locatio et conductio familiaritatem aliquam inter se habere videntur, ut in quibusdam causis quaeri soleat, utrum emptio et venditio contrahatur, an locatio et conductio: veluti si qua res in perpetuum locata sit, quod evenit in praediis municipum, quae ea lege locantur, ut, quamdiu id vectigal praestetur, neque ipsi conductori, neque heredi ejus praedium auferatur; sed magis placuit locationem conductionemque esse.

§ 3. *Adeo autem familiaritatem aliquam inter se habere videntur emptio et venditio, item locatio et conductio, ut in quibusdam causis quaeri soleat, utrum emptio et venditio contrahatur, an locatio et conductio; ut ecce de praediis quae perpetuo* quibusdam fruenda traduntur, id est, ut *quamdiu* pensio sive reditus pro his domino *praestetur, neque ipsi conductori neque heredi ejus,* cuive conductor heresve ejus id praedium vendiderit aut donaverit, aut dotis nomine dederit, aliove quoquo modo alienaverit, auferre liceat. Sed talis contractus, quia inter veteres dubitabatur, et a quibusdam locatio, a quibusdam venditio existimabatur: lex Zenoniana lata est quae emphyteuseos contractui propriam statuit naturam, neque ad locationem neque ad venditionem inclinantem, sed suis pactionibus fulciendam, et si quidem aliquid pactum fuerit, hoc ita obtinere, ac si natura talis esset contractus; sin autem nihil de periculo rei fuerit pactum, tunc si quidem totius rei interitus accesserit, ad dominum super hoc redundare periculum, sin particularis, ad emphyteuticarium hujusmodi damnum venire. Quo jure utimur.

§ 146. Item si gladiatores ea lege tibi tradiderim, ut in singulos, qui integri exierint, pro sudore denarii xx mihi darentur, in eos vero singulos, qui occisi aut debilitati fuerint, denarii mille: quaeritur utrum emptio et venditio, an locatio et conductio contrahatur. Et magis placuit, eorum qui integri exierint, locationem et conductionem contractam videri, et eorum qui occisi aut debilitati sunt, emptionem et venditionem esse: idque ex accidentibus apparet, tamquam sub conditione facta cujusque venditione an locatione; jam enim non dubitatur, quin sub conditione res veniri et locari possint. § 147. Item quaeritur, si cum aurifice mihi convenerit, ut is ex auro suo certi ponderis certaeque formae annulos mihi faceret, et acciperet verbi gratia denarios CC, utrum emptio et venditio, an locatio et conductio contrahatur. Cassius ait, materiae quidem emptionem venditionem contrahi, operarum autem locationem et conductionem. Sed plerisque placuit, emptionem et venditionem contrahi. Atqui, si meum aurum ei dederim [et de] mercede pro opera constituta, convenerit locationem conductionem contrahi.

§ 4. *Item quaeritur, si cum aurifice Titius convenerit, ut is ex auro suo certi ponderis certaeque formae annulos ei faceret, et acceperet verbi gratia* aureos decem, *utrum emptio et venditio an locatio et conductio contrahi videatur. Cassius ait, materiae quidem emptionem et venditionem contrahi, operae autem locationem et conductionem; sed placuit tantum emptionem et venditionem contrahi. Quod si* suum *aurum Titius dederit, mercede pro opera constituta,* dubium non est *quin locatio et conductio sit.*

§ 5. Conductor omnia secundum legem conductionis facere debet, et si quid in lege praetermissum fuerit, id ex bono et aequo debet praestare. Qui pro usu aut vestimentorum, aut argenti, aut jumenti, mercedem aut dedit aut promisit, ab eo custodia talis desideratur qualem diligentissimus paterfamilias suis rebus adhibet: quam si praestiterit, et aliquo casu rem amiserit, de restituenda ea non tenebitur.

§ 6. Mortuo conductore intra tempora conductionis, heres ejus eodem jure in conductione succedit.

Tit. xxv. De societate.

§ 148. Societatem coire solemus aut totorum bonorum, aut unius alicujus negotii, veluti mancipiorum emendorum aut vendendorum.

Societatem coire solemus aut totorum bonorum, quam graeci specialiter κοινοπραξίαν appellant; *aut unius alicujus negotiationis, veluti mancipiorum emendorum vendendorumque,* aut olei, vini, frumenti emendi vendendique. § 1. Et quidem si nihil de partibus lucri et damni nominatim convenerit, aequales scilicet partes et in lucro et in damno spectantur. Quod si expressae fuerint partes, hae servari debent: nec enim umquam dubium fuit, quin valeat conventio, si duo inter se pacti sunt, ut ad unum quidem duae partes et lucri et damni pertineant, ad alium tertia.

§ 149. Magna autem quaestio fuit, an ita coiri possit societas, ut quis majorem partem lucretur, minorem damni praestet. Quod Quintus Mucius etiam [contra naturam societatis esse censuit; sed Servius Sulpicius, cujus] etiam praevaluit sententia, adeo ita coiri posse societatem existimavit, ut dixerit, illo quoque modo coiri posse, ut quis nihil omnino damni praestet, sed lucri partem capiat, si modo opera ejus tam pretiosa videatur, ut aequum sit eum cum hac pactione in societatem admitti. Nam et ita posse coiri societatem constat, ut unus pecuniam conferat, alter non conferat, et tamen lucrum inter eos commune sit; saepe enim opera alicujus pro pecunia valet. § 150. Et illud certum est, si de partibus lucri et damni nihil inter eos convenerit, tamen aequis ex partibus commodum et incommodum inter eos commune esse. Sed si in altero partes expressae fuerint, velut in lucro, in altero vero omissae, in eo quoque quod omissum est, similes partes erunt.

§ 2. De illa sane conventione quaesitum est, si Titius et Seius inter se pacti sunt, ut ad Titium lucri duae partes pertineant, damni tertia, ad Seium duae partes damni, lucri tertia, an rata debeat haberi conventio? *Quintus Mucius contra naturam societatis* talem pactionem esse existimavit, et ob id non esse ratam habendam. *Servius Sulpicius, cujus sententia praevaluit,* contra sensit, quia saepe quorundam ita *pretiosa est opera* in societate, ut eos justum sit meliore conditione *in societatem admitti: nam et ita coiri posse societatem* non dubitatur, *ut alter pecuniam conferat, alter non conferat, et tamen lucrum inter eos commune sit, quia saepe opera alicujus pro pecunia valet.* Et adeo contra Quinti Mucii sententiam obtinuit, ut illud quoque constiterit posse convenire, ut quis lucri partem ferat, damno non teneatur, quod et ipsum Servius convenienter sibi existimavit: quod tamen ita intelligi oportet, ut si in aliqua re lucrum, in aliqua damnum, allatum sit, compensatione facta, solum quod superest intelligatur lucri esse. § 3. Illud expeditum est, *si* in una causa *pars fuerit expressa, veluti* in solo *lucro* vel in solo damno, *in altera vero omissa: in eo quoque quod praetermissum est, eandem partem servari.*

§ 151. Manet autem societas eousque donec in eodem sensu perseverant; at cum aliquis renuntiaverit societati, societas solvitur. Sed plane, si quis in hoc renuntiaverit societati, ut obveniens aliquod lucrum solus habeat, veluti si mihi totorum bonorum socius, cum ab aliquo herés esset relictus, in hoc renuntiaverit societati, ut hereditatem solus lucrifaceret, cogetur hoc lucrum communicare; si quid vero aliud lucrifecerit, quod non captaverit, ad ipsum solum pertinet: mihi vero quidquid omnino post renuntiatam socie-

§ 4. *Manet autem societas eousque donec in eodem consensu perseveraverint; at cum aliquis renuntiaverit societati, solvitur societas. Sed plane, si quis* callide *in hoc renuntiaverit societati, ut obveniens aliquod lucrum solus habeat, veluti si totorum bonorum socius, cum ab aliquo heres esset relictus, in hoc renuntiaverit societati, ut hereditatem solus lucrifaceret, cogetur hoc lucrum communicare; si quid vero aliud lucrifaceret quod non captaverit, ad ipsum solum pertinet.* Ei *vero* cui renuntiatum est, *quidquid omnino*

tatem adquiritur, soli conceditur. § 152. Solvitur adhuc societas etiam morte socii; quia qui societatem contrahit, certam personam sibi eligit. § 153. Dicitur etiam capitis deminutione solvi societatem, quia civili ratione capitis deminutio morti coaequatur; sed si adhuc consentiant in societatem, nova videtur incipere societas. § 154. Item si cujus ex sociis bona publice aut privatim venierint, solvitur societas. Sed haec quoque societas de qua loquimur [denuo] consensu contrahitur nudo; juris gentium est, itaque inter omnes homines naturali ratione consistit.

post renuntiatam societatem adquiritur, soli conceditur. § 5. *Solvitur adhuc societas etiam morte socii, quia qui societatem contrahit, certam personam sibi elegit.* Sed et si consensu plurium societas contracta sit, morte unius socii solvitur, etsi plures supersint, nisi in coeunda societate aliter convenerit. § 6. Item si alicujus rei contracta societas sit, et finis negotio impositus est, finitur societas. § 7. Publicatione quoque distrahi societatem manifestum est, scilicet si universa bona socii publicentur: nam, cum in ejus locum alius succedat, pro mortuo habetur. § 8. *Item si quis ex sociis* mole debiti praegravatus *bonis* suis cesserit, et ideo propter publica aut privata debita substantia ejus *veneat, solvitur societas. Sed hoc casu, si adhuc consentiant in societatem, nova videtur incipere societas.*

§ 9. Socius socio utrum eo nomine tantum teneatur pro socio actione, si quid dolo commiserit, sicut is qui deponi apud se passus est, an etiam culpae, id est desidiae atque negligentiae nomine, quaesitum est: praevaluit tamen etiam culpae nomine teneri eum. Culpa autem non ad exactissimam diligentiam dirigenda est: sufficit enim talem diligentiam in communibus rebus adhibere socium, qualem suis rebus adhibere solet. Nam qui parum diligentem socium sibi assumpsit, de se queri debet.

Tit. XXVI. De mandato.

§ 155. Mandatum consistit, sive nostra gratia mandemus sive aliena. Itaque sive ut mea negotia geras, sive ut alterius mandaverim, contrahitur mandati obligatio, et invicem alter alteri tenebimur in id quod vel me tibi vel te mihi bona fide [paret] praestare oportere. § 156. Nam si tua gratia tibi mandem, supervacuum est mandatum; quod enim tu tua gratia facturus sis, id de tua sententia, non ex meo mandatu facere videberis:

Mandatum contrahitur quinque modis, sive sua tantum gratia aliquis tibi mandet, sive sua et tua, sive aliena tantum, sive sua et aliena, sive tua et aliena. At si tua tantum gratia tibi mandatum sit, supervacuum est mandatum, et ob id nulla ex eo obligatio, nec mandati inter vos actio nascitur.

§ 1. Mandantis tantum gratia intervenit mandatum: veluti, si quis tibi mandet, ut negotia ejus gereres, vel ut fundum ei emeres, vel ut pro eo sponderes. § 2. Tua et mandantis: veluti, si mandet tibi, ut pecuniam sub usuris crederes ei qui in rem ipsius mutuaretur, aut si, volente te agere cum eo ex fidejussoria causa, tibi mandet, ut cum reo agas periculo mandantis : vel ut ipsius periculo stipuleris ab eo quem tibi deleget in id quod tibi debuerat. § 3. Aliena autem causa intervenit mandatum, veluti, si tibi mandet, ut Titii negotia gereres, vel ut Titio fundum emeres, vel ut pro Titio sponderes. § 4. Sua et aliena, veluti, si de communibus suis et Titii negotiis gerendis tibi mandet, vel ut sibi et Titio fundum emeres, vel ut pro eo et Titio sponderes. § 5. Tua et aliena, veluti, si tibi mandet, ut Titio sub usuris crederes. Quod si ut sine usuris crederes, aliena tantum gratia intercedit mandatum. § 6. Tua gratia intervenit mandatum, veluti, si tibi mandet, ut pecunias tuas potius in emptiones praediorum colloces quam foeneres, vel ex diverso, ut foeneres potius quam in emptiones praediorum colloces. Cujus generis mandatum, magis consilium quam mandatum est, et ob id non est obligatorium : quia nemo ex consilio obligatur, etiamsi non expediat ei cui dabitur, cum liberum cuique sit apud se explorare, an expediat consilium.

itaque si otiosam pecuniam domi tuae habentem hortatus fuerim ut eam foenerares, quamvis eam ei mutuam dederis a quo servare non potueris, non tamen habebis mecum mandati actionem. Item et si hortatus sim ut rem aliquam emeres, quamvis non expedierit tibi eam emisse, non tamen mandati tibi tenebor. Et adeo haec ita sunt, ut quaeratur an mandati teneatur, qui mandavit tibi ut Titio pecuniam foenerares : Servius negavit; [sed] sequimur Sabini opinionem consentientis, quod non aliter credidisses, quam si tibi mandatum esset.

Itaque si otiosam pecuniam domi te habentem hortatus fuerit aliquis, ut rem aliquam emeres, vel eam crederes, quamvis non expediat tibi eam emisse vel credidisse, non tamen tibi mandati tenetur. Et adeo haec ita sunt, ut quaesitum sit, an mandati teneatur, qui mandavit tibi ut Titio pecuniam foenerares: sed obtinuit Sabini sententia, obligatorium esse in hoc casu mandatum, quia non aliter Titio credidisses, quam si tibi mandatum esset.

§ 157. Illud constat, si quis de ea re mandet, quae contra bonos mores est, non contrahi obligationem, veluti si tibi mandem, ut Titio furtum aut injuriam facias.

§ 7. *Illud quoque mandatum non est obligatorium, quod contra bonos mores est; veluti, si Titius de furto aut de damno faciendo, aut de injuria facienda tibi mandet.* Licet enim poenam istius facti nomine praestiteris, non tamen ullam habes adversus Titium actionem.

§ 161. Cum autem is, cui recte mandaverim, egressus fuerit mandatum, ego quidem eatenus cum eo habeo mandati actionem, quatenus mea interest, implesse eum mandatum, si modo implere potuerit : at ille mecum agere non

§ 8. *Is* qui exequitur mandatum, non debet excedere fines mandati. Ut ecce, si quis usque ad *centum* aureos *mandaverit tibi, ut fundum emeres*, vel ut pro Titio sponderes, neque pluris emere debes, neque in ampliorem pecuniam fidejubere :

potest. Itaque si mandaverim tibi ut verbi gratia fundum mihi sestertiis C [millibus] emeres, tu sestertiis CL [millibus] emeris, non habebis mecum mandati actionem, etiamsi tanti velis mihi dare fundum, quanti emendum tibi mandassem: idque maxime Sabino et Cassio placuit. Quod si minoris emeris, habebis mecum scilicet actionem, quia qui mandat ut C millibus emeretur, is utique mandare intelligitur, uti minoris, si posset, emeretur.

alioquin *non habebis cum eo mandati actionem:* adeo quidem, ut *Sabino et Cassio placuerit, etiam si* usque ad centum aureos cum eo agere volueris inutiliter te acturum; diversae scholae auctores recte usque ad centum aureos te acturum existimant: quae sententia sane benignior est. *Quod si minoris emeris, habebis scilicet cum eo actionem, quoniam qui mandat, ut sibi centum* aureorum fundus *emeretur, is utique mandasse intelligitur, ut minoris, si posset, emeretur.*

§ 158. Item si quis post mortem meam faciendum mandet, inutile mandatum est, quia generaliter placuit ab heredis persona obligationem incipere non posse.

§ 159. Sed recte quoque [contractum] mandatum, si, dum adhuc integra res sit, revocatum fuerit, evanescit. § 160. Item, si adhuc integro mandato mors alterutrius alicujus interveniat, id est, vel ejus qui mandaverit, vel ejus qui mandatum susceperit, solvitur mandatum. Sed utilitatis causa receptum est ut, si mortuo eo qui mihi mandaverit, ignorans eum decessisse, executus fuerim mandatum, posse me agere mandati actione: alioquin justa et probabilis ignorantia damnum mihi adferet. Et huic simile est quod plerisque placuit, si debitor meus manumisso dispensatori meo per ignorantiam solverit, liberari eum: cum alioquin stricta juris ratione non posset liberari, quod alii solvisset, quam cui solvere deberet.

§ 9. *Recte quoque mandatum contractum, si, dum adhuc integra res sit, revocatum fuerit, evanescit.* § 10. *Item, si adhuc integro mandato mors alterutrius interveniat, id est, vel ejus qui mandaverit, vel ejus qui mandatum susceperit, solvitur mandatum. Sed utilitatis causa receptum est, ut si mortuo eo qui tibi mandaverit, tu, ignorans eum decessisse, executus fueris mandatum, posse te agere mandati actione: alioquin justa et probabilis ignorantia damnum tibi adferet. Et huic simile est quod placuit, si debitores, manumisso dispensatore Titii, per ignorantiam liberto solverint, liberari eos: cum alioquin stricta juris ratione non possent liberari, quia alii solvissent quam cui solvere debuerint.*

§ 11. Mandatum non suscipere cuilibet liberum est: susceptum autem consummandum est, aut quamprimum renuntiandum, ut per semetipsum aut per alium eandem rem mandator exequatur. Nam nisi ita renuntiatus, ut integra causa mandatori reservetur eandem rem explicandi, nihilominus mandati actio locum habet, nisi justa causa intercessit, aut non renuntiandi, aut intempestive renuntiandi.

§ 12. Mandatum et in diem differri, et sub conditione fieri potest.

§ 162. In summa sciendum [est, quotiens faciendum] aliquid gratis dederim, quo nomine, si mercedem statuissem, locatio et conductio contraheretur, mandati esse actionem: veluti si fulloni polienda curandave vestimenta, aut sarcinatori sarcienda [dederim.]

§ 13. *In summa sciendum est* mandatum, nisi gratuitum sit, in aliam formam negotii cadere: nam *mercede constituta* incipit *locatio et conductio* esse. Et, ut generaliter dixerimus: quibus casibus sine mercede suscepto officio mandati aut depositi contrahitur negotium, iis casibus interveniente mercede locatio et conductio contrahi intelligitur. Et ideo si *fulloni polienda curandave vestimenta quis dederit, aut sarcinatori sarcienda*, nulla mercede constituta neque promissa, *mandati competit actio.*

Tit. xxvii. De obligationibus quasi ex contractu.

Post genera contractuum enumerata, dispiciamus etiam de iis obligationibus, quae non proprie quidem ex contractu nasci intelliguntur, sed tamen, quia non ex maleficio substantiam capiunt, quasi ex contractu nasci videntur. § 1. Igitur cum quis absentis negotia gesserit, ultro citroque inter eos nascuntur actiones, quae appellantur negotiorum gestorum: sed domino quidem rei gestae adversus eum qui gessit directa competit actio; negotiorum autem gestori, contraria. Quas ex nullo contractu proprie nasci manifestum est: quippe ita nascuntur istae actiones, si sine mandato quisque alienis negotiis gerendis se obtulerit; ex qua causa ii quorum negotia gesta fuerint, etiam ignorantes obligantur. Idque utilitatis causa receptum est, ne absentium qui subita festinatione coacti, nulli demandata negotiorum suorum administratione, peregre profecti essent, desererentur negotia: quae sane nemo curaturus esset, si de eo quod quis impendisset, nullam habiturus esset actionem. Sicut autem is qui utiliter gesserit negotia habet obligatum dominum negotiorum: ita et contra iste quoque tenetur, ut administrationis rationem reddat. Quo casu ad exactissimam quisque diligentiam compellitur reddere rationem: nec sufficit talem diligentiam adhibuisse qualem suis rebus adhibere soleret, si modo alius diligentior commodius administraturus esset negotia. § 2. Tutores quoque, qui tutelae judicio tenentur, non proprie ex contractu obligati intelliguntur (nullum enim negotium inter tutorem et pupillum contrahitur); sed quia sane non ex maleficio tenentur, quasi ex contractu teneri videntur. Et hoc autem casu mutae sunt actiones: non tantum enim pupillus cum tutore habet tutelae actionem; sed, ex contrario, tutor cum pupillo habet contrariam tutelae, si vel impenderit aliquid in rem pupilli, vel pro eo fuerit obligatus, aut rem suam creditoribus ejus obligaverit. § 3. Item, si inter aliquos communis sit res sine societate, veluti quod pariter eis legata donatave esset, et alter eorum alteri ideo teneatur communi dividundo judicio, quod solus fructus ex ea re perceperit, aut quod socius ejus solus in eam rem necessarias impensas fecerit : non intelligitur proprie ex contractu obligatus esse (quippe nihil inter se contraxerunt) ; sed quia non ex maleficio tenetur, quasi ex contractu teneri videtur. § 4. Idem juris est de eo qui coheredi suo familiae erciscundae judicio ex his causis obligatus est. § 5. Heres quoque legatorum nomine non proprie ex contractu obligatus intelligitur (neque enim cum herede, neque cum defuncto, ullum negotium legatarius gessisse proprie dici potest): et tamen, quia ex maleficio non est obligatus heres, quasi ex contractu debere intelligitur. § 6. Item is cui quis per errorem non debitum solvit, quasi ex contractu debere videtur. Adeo enim non intelligitur proprie ex contractu obligatus, ut si certiorem rationem sequamur, magis (ut supra diximus) ex distractu, quam ex contractu possit dici obligatus esse ; nam qui solvendi animo pecuniam dat, in hoc dare videtur ut distrahat potius negotium quam contrahat. Sed tamen perinde is qui accepit obligatur, acsi mutuum illi daretur, et ideo condictione tenetur. § 7. Ex quibusdam tamen causis repeti non potest quod per errorem non debitum solutum sit. Sic namque definierunt veteres, ex quibus causis inficiando lis crescit, ex iis causis non debitum solutum repeti non posse : veluti ex lege Aquilia, item ex legato. Quod veteres quidem in iis legatis locum habere voluerunt, quae certa constituta, per damnationem cuicumque fuerant legata : nostra autem constitutio, cum unam naturam omnibus legatis et fideicommissis indulsit, hujusmodi augmentum in omnibus legatis et fideicommissis extendi voluit ; sed non omnibus legatariis praebuit, sed tantummodo in iis legatis et fideicommissis quae sacrosanctis ecclesiis caeterisque venerabilibus locis, quae religionis vel pietatis intuitu honorificantur, derelicta sunt. Quae, si indebita solvantur, non repetuntur.

Tit. xxviii. Per quas personas nobis obligatio adquiritur.

§ 163. Expositis generibus obligationum, quae ex contractu nascuntur, admonendi sumus adquiri

Expositis generibus obligationum, quae ex contractu, vel quasi ex contractu *nascuntur, ad-*

nobis non solum per nosmetipsos, sed etiam per eas personas quae in nostra potestate, manu, mancipiove sunt.

monendi sumus adquiri nobis, non solum per nosmetipsos, sed etiam per eas personas quae in nostra potestate sunt: veluti per servos et filios nostros; ut tamen, quod per servos quidem nobis adquiritur, totum nostrum fiat, quod autem per liberos quos in potestate habemus ex obligatione fuerit adquisitum, hoc dividatur secundum imaginem rerum proprietatis et ususfructus quam nostra discrevit constitutio; ut quod ab actione commodum perveniat, hujus usumfructum quidem habeat pater, proprietas autem filio servetur, scilicet patre actionem movente secundum novellae nostrae constitutionis divisionem.

§ 164. Per liberos quoque homines et alienos servos quos bona fide possidemus, adquiritur nobis; sed tantum ex duabus causis, id est, si quid ex operis suis, vel ex re nostra adquirant. § 165. Per eum quoque servum in quo usumfructum habemus, similiter ex duabus istis causis nobis adquiritur. § 166. Sed qui nudum jus quiritium in servo habet, licet dominus sit, minus tamen juris in ea re habere intelligitur, quam usufructuarius et bonae fidei possessor; nam placet ex nulla causa ei adquiri posse, adeo ut, etsi nominatim ei dari stipulatus fuerit servus, mancipiove nomine ejus acceperit, [quid] quidam existiment nihil ei adquiri.

§ 1. Item *per liberos homines et alienos servos quos bona fide possidemus adquiritur nobis, sed tantum ex duabus causis, id est, si quid ex operibus suis vel ex re nostra adquirant.* § 2. *Per eum quoque servum in quo usumfructum* vel usum *habemus similiter ex duabus istis causis nobis adquiritur.*

§ 167. Communem servum pro dominica parte dominis adquirere certum est, excepto eo, quod uni nominatim stipulando, aut mancipio accipiendo, illi soli adquirit, veluti cum ita stipuletur: "Titio domino meo dari spondes?" aut cum ita mancipio accipiat: "hanc rem ex jure quiritium Lucii Titii domini mei esse aio, eaque ei empta esto hoc aere aeneaque libra." § 167A. Illud quaeritur, [an], tamquam domini nomen adjectum domini [illius unius] efficit, idem faciat unius ex dominis jussum intercedens. Nostri praeceptores, perinde ei, qui jusserit, soli adquiri existimant, atque si nominatim ei soli stipulatus esset servus, mancipiove accepisset. Diversae scholae auctores perinde utrique adquiri putant ac si nullius jussum intervenisset.

§ 3. *Communem servum pro dominica parte dominis adquirere certum est, excepto eo, quod uni nominatim stipulando, aut* per traditionem *accipiendo, illi soli adquirit, veluti cum ita stipulatur: "Titio domino meo dare spondes?"* sed si *unius domini* jussu servus fuerit stipulatus, licet antea dubitabatur, tamen post nostram decisionem res expedita est, ut illi tantum *adquirat qui* hoc ei facere *jussit*, ut supra dictum est.

Tit. xxix. Quibus modis obligatio tollitur.

§ 168. Tollitur autem obligatio praecipue solutione ejus quod debetur. Unde quaeritur, si quis consentiente creditore aliud pro alio solverit, utrum ipso jure liberetur, quod nostris praeceptoribus placet, an ipso jure maneat obligatus, sed adversus petentem exceptione doli mali defendi debeat, quod diversae scholae auctoribus visum est.

Tollitur autem omnis *obligatio solutione ejus quod debetur;* vel *si quis, consentiente creditore, aliud pro alio solverit.* Nec tamen interest quis solvat, utrum ipse qui debet, an alius pro eo: liberatur enim et alio solvente, sive sciente debitore sive ignorante vel invito, solutio fiat. Item si reus solverit, etiam ii qui pro eo intervenerunt liberantur. Idem, ex contrario contingit, si fidejussor solverit: non enim solus ipse liberatur, sed etiam reus.

§ 169. Item per acceptilationem tollitur obligatio. Acceptilatio autem est veluti imaginaria solutio. Quod enim ex verborum obligatione tibi debeam, id si velis mihi remittere, poterit sic fieri, ut patiaris haec verba me dicere: "quod ego tibi promisi, habesne acceptum?" et tu respondeas: "habeo". § 170. Quo genere, ut diximus, [proprie quidem eae tantum obligationes solvuntur, quae ex verbis consistunt,] non etiam caeterae: consentaneum enim visum est, verbis factam obligationem posse aliis verbis dissolvi. Sed et id quod ex alia causa debeatur, potest in stipulationem deduci et per acceptilationem .... [dissolvi]. § 171. Imaginaria solutione tamen mulier sine tutoris auctoritate acceptum facere non potest; cum alioquin solvi ei sine tutoris auctoritate possit. § 172. Item quod debetur, pro parte, recte solvitur: an autem in partem acceptum fieri possit, quaesitum est.

§ 1. *Item per acceptilationem tollitur obligatio. Est autem acceptilatio imaginaria solutio. Quod enim ex verborum obligatione Titio debetur, id si velit Titius remittere, poterit sic fieri, ut patiatur haec verba debitorem dicere: "quod ego tibi promisi, habesne acceptum?" et Titius respondeat. "habeo."* Sed et graece potest acceptum fieri, dummodo sic fiat ut latinis verbis solet: ἔχεις λαβὼν δηνάρια τόσα; ἔχω λαβών. *Quo genere, (ut diximus) tantum eae obligationes solvuntur quae ex verbis consistunt, non etiam caeterae: consentaneum enim visum est, verbis factam obligationem posse aliis verbis dissolvi. Sed et id quod ex alia causa debetur, potest in stipulationem deduci et per acceptilationem dissolvi.* Sicut autem *quod debetur, pro parte recte solvitur,* ita *in partem debiti acceptilatio fieri potest.* § 2. Est prodita stipulatio quae vulgo Aquiliana appellatur, per quam stipulationem contingit, ut omnium rerum obligatio in stipulatum deducatur, et ea per acceptilationem tollatur. Stipulatio enim Aquiliana novat omnes obligationes, et a Gallo Aquilio ita composita est: "Quidquid te mihi ex quacumque causa dare, facere oportet, oportebit, praesens in diemve; quarumque rerum mihi tecum actio, quaeque adversus te petitio, vel adversus te persecutio est, eritve, quodve tu meum habes, tenes, possidesve, dolove malo fecisti quominus possideas: quanti quaeque earum rerum res erit, tantam pecuniam dari stipulatus est Aulus Agerius, spopondit Numerius Negidius." Item ex diverso Numerius Negidius interrogavit Aulum Agerium: "Quidquid tibi hodierno die per Aquilianam stipulationem spopondi, id omne habesne acceptum?" respondit Aulus Agerius: "Habeo acceptumque tuli."

§ 173. Est etiam alia species imaginariae solutionis per aes et libram. Quod et ipsum genus certis in causis receptum est, veluti si quid eo nomine debeatur, quod per aes et libram gestum sit, sive etiam ex testamento quid vel ex judicati causa debitum sit. § 174. [Eaque res ita fit]: adhibentur non minus quam quinque testes et libripens: deinde is qui liberatur, ita oportet loquatur: "Quod ego tibi tot millibus condemnatus sum me eo nomine recte solvo liberoque hoc aere aeneaque libra; hanc tibi libram primam postremam expendo [secundum] legem publicam": deinde asse percutit libram, eumque dat ei a quo liberatum [se esse vult], veluti solvendi causa. § 175. Similiter legatarius heredem eodem modo liberat de legato quod per damnationem relictum est ut tamen scilicet, sicut judicatus condemnatum se esse significat, ita heres [testamento] dare damnatum esse dicat. De eo tamen tantum potest heres eo modo liberari, quod pondere, numero constet; et ita, si certum sit, quidam et de eo quod mensura constat idem existimant.

§ 176. Praeterea novatione tollitur obligatio, veluti si quod tu mihi debeas, a Titio dari stipulatus sim. Nam interventu novae personae nova nascitur obligatio, et prima tollitur translata in posteriorem: adeo ut interdum, licet posterior stipulatio inutilis sit, tamen prima novationis jure tollatur, veluti si quod mihi debes, a Titio post mortem ejus vel a muliere pupillove sine tutoris auctoritate stipulatus fuero. Quo casu rem amitto; nam et prior debitor liberatur, et posterior obligatio nulla est. Non idem juris est si a servo stipulatus fuero; nam tunc [prior] perinde adhuc obligatus

§ 3. *Praeterea novatione tollitur obligatio: veluti si id quod tu Seio debeas, a Titio dari stipulatus sit. Nam interventu novae personae nova nascitur obligatio, et prima tollitur translata in posteriorem: adeo ut interdum, licet posterior stipulatio inutilis sit, tamen prima novationis jure tollatur; veluti si id quod tu Titio debebas, a pupillo sine tutoris auctoritate stipulatus fuerit. Quo casu res amittitur; nam et prior debitor liberatur, et posterior obligatio nulla est. Non idem juris est, si a servo quis stipulatus fuerit; nam tunc prior perinde obligatus* tenetur, ac si postea a nullo stipulatus fuissem. § 177. Sed si eadem persona sit a qua postea stipuler, ita demum novatio fit, si quid in posteriore stipulatione novi sit, forte si conditio, vel dies, aut sponsor adjiciatur aut detrahatur. § 178. Sed quae de sponsore dixi, non constat; nam diversae scholae auctoribus placuit, nihil ad novationem proficere sponsoris adjectionem aut detractationem. § 179. Quod autem diximus, si conditio adjiciatur, novationem fieri, sic intelligi [oportet,] ut ita dicamus factam novationem, si conditio extiterit: alioquin, si defecerit, durat prior obligatio. Sed videamus, num is, qui eo nomine agat, doli mali aut pacti conventi exceptione possit summoveri, quia videtur inter eos id actum, ut ita ea res peteretur, si posterioris stipulationis extiterit conditio. Servius tamen Sulpicius existimavit statim et pendente conditione novationem fieri, et, si defecerit conditio, ex neutra causa agi posse, eoque modo rem perire. Qui consequenter et illud respondit, si quis id quod sibi Lucius Titius deberet, a servo fuerit stipulatus, novationem fieri, et rem perire; quia cum servo agi non posset. Sed in utroque casu alio jure utimur: nec magis his casibus novatio fit, quam si id quod tu mihi debeas, a peregrino, cum quo sponsi communio non est, "spondes" verbo stipulatus sim.

manet, ac si postea nullus stipulatus fuisset. Sed si eadem persona sit a qua postea stipuleris, ita demum novatio fit, si quid in posteriore stipulatione novi sit, forte si conditio aut dies aut fidejussor *adjiciatur aut detrahatur. Quod autem diximus, si conditio adjiciatur, novationem fieri, sic intelligi oportet, ut ita dicamus factam novationem, si conditio extiterit; alioquin, si defecerit, durat prior obligatio.* Sed cum hoc quidem inter veteres constabat, tunc fieri novationem cum novandi animo in secundam obligationem itum fuerat; per hoc autem dubium erat quando novandi animo videretur hoc fieri, et quasdam de hoc praesumptiones alii in aliis casibus introducebant: ideo nostra processit constitutio, quae apertissime definivit tunc solum fieri novationem, quotiens hoc ipsum inter contrahentes expressum fuerit, quod propter novationem prioris obligationis convenerunt; alioquin manere et pristinam obligationem, et secundam ei accedere, ut maneat ex utraque causa obligatio secundum nostrae constitutionis definitiones, quas licet ex ipsius lectione apertius cognoscere.

§ 4. Hoc amplius: eae obligationes quae consensu contrahuntur, contraria voluntate dissolvuntur. Nam si Titius et Seius inter se consenserint, ut fundum Tusculanum emptum Seius haberet centum aureorum, deinde re nondum secuta, id est, neque pretio soluto neque fundo tradito, placuerit inter eos, ut discederetur ab ea emptione et venditione, invicem liberantur. Idem est et in conductione et locatione, et in omnibus contractibus qui ex consensu descendunt, sicut jam dictum est.

§ 180. Tollitur adhuc obligatio litis contestatione, si modo legitimo judicio fuerit actum. Nam tunc obligatio quidem principalis dissolvitur, incipit autem teneri reus litis contestatione: sed, si condemnatus sit, sublata litis contestatione, incipit ex causa judicati teneri. Et hoc est quod apud veteres scriptum est: "Ante litem contestatam dare debitorem oportere, post litem contestatam condemnari oportere, post condemnationem judicatum facere oportere." § 181. Unde fit, ut, si legitimo judicio debitum petiero, postea de eo ipso jure agere non possim, quia inutiliter intendo "dari mihi oportere"; quia litis contestatione dari oportere desiit: aliter atque si imperio continenti judicio egerim; tunc enim nihilominus obligatio durat, et ideo ipso jure postea agere possum; sed debeo per exceptionem rei judicatae vel in judicium deductae summoveri. Quae autem legitima sint judicia, et quae imperio contineantur, sequenti commentario referemus.

JUSTINIANI INSTITUTIONUM LIBER IV.

Tit. i. De obligationibus quae ex delicto nascuntur.

§ 182. Transeamus nunc ad obligationes quae ex delicto nascuntur: veluti si quis furtum fecerit, bona rapuerit, damnum dederit, injuriam commiserit; quarum omnium rerum uno genere consistit obligatio, cum ex contractu obligationes in quattuor genera deducantur, sicut supra exposuimus.

Cum expositum sit, superiore libro, de obligationibus ex contractu et quasi ex contractu, sequitur ut de obligationibus ex maleficio dispiciamus. Sed illae quidem, ut suo loco tradidimus, in quattuor genera dividuntur: hae vero unius generis sunt, nam omnes ex re nascuntur, id est, ex ipso maleficio, veluti ex furto, aut rapina, aut damno, aut injuria.

§ 1. Furtum est contrectatio rei fraudulosa, vel ipsius rei, vel etiam usus ejus possessionisve; quod lege naturali prohibitum est admittere. § 2. Furtum autem vel a furvo, id est nigro, dictum est, quod clam et obscure fit et plerumque nocte; vel a fraude; vel a ferendo, id est, auferendo; vel a graeco sermone, qui φῶρας appellant fures. Imo etiam graeci ἀπὸ τοῦ φέρειν φῶρας dixerunt.

§ 183. Furtorum autem genera Servius Sulpicius et Masurius Sabinus quattuor esse dixerunt, manifestum et nec manifestum, conceptum et oblatum: Labeo duo, manifestum, nec manifestum; nam conceptum et oblatum species potius actionis esse furto cohaerentes, quam genera furtorum; quod

§ 3. *Furtorum autem genera duo sunt: manifestum et nec manifestum. Nam conceptum et oblatum species potius actionis sunt furto cohaerentes quam genera furtorum, sicut in-*

sane verius videtur, sicut inferius apparebit. § 184. Manifestum furtum quidam id esse dixerunt, quod dum fit, deprehenditur. Alii vero ulterius, quod eo loco deprehenditur, ubi fit: velut si in oliveto olivarum, in vineto uvarum furtum factum sit, quamdiu in eo oliveto aut vineto fur sit; aut si in domo furtum factum sit, quamdiu in ea domo fur sit. Alii adhuc ulterius, eo usque manifestum furtum esse dixerunt, donec perferretur eo quo perferre fur destinasset. Alii adhuc ulterius, quandoque eam rem fur tenens visus fuerit; quae sententia non obtinuit. Sed et illorum sententia qui existimaverunt, donec perferretur eo quo fur destinasset, deprehensum furtum manifestum esse, ideo non videtur [posse] probari, quod magnam recepit dubitationem, utrum unius diei, an etiam plurium dierum spatio id determinandum sit: quod eo pertinet, quia saepe in aliis civitatibus subreptae res sunt, in alias civitates vel in alias provincias destinat fures perferre. Ex duabus itaque superioribus opinionibus alterutra approbatur: magis tamen plerique posteriorem probant. § 185. Nec manifestum furtum quid sit, ex iis, quae diximus, intelligitur: nam quod manifestum furtum non est, id nec manifestum est. § 186. Conceptum furtum dicitur, cum apud aliquem, testibus praesentibus, furtiva res quaesita et inventa est: nam in eum propria actio constituta est, quamvis fur non sit, quae appellatur concepti. § 187. Oblatum furtum dicitur, cum res furtiva tibi ab aliquo oblata sit, eaque apud te concepta sit; utique si ea mente data tibi fuerit, ut apud te potius quam apud eum qui dederit conciperetur. Nam tibi, apud quem concepta est, propria adversus eum qui obtulit, quamvis fur non sit, constituta est actio, quae appellatur oblati. § 188. Est etiam prohibiti furti actio adversus eum qui furtum quaerere volentem prohibuerit.

ferius apparebit. Manifestus fur est quem graeci ἐπ' αὐτοφώρῳ appellant; nec solum is qui in ipso furto *deprehenditur*, sed etiam is *qui eo loco deprehenditur* quo *fit, veluti* qui *in domo furtum* fecit, et nondum egressus januam deprehensus fuerit, vel qui in *oliveto olivarum aut in vineto uvarum* furtum fecit, *quamdiu in oliveto aut in vineto fur* deprehensus *sit;* imo *ulterius furtum manifestum* extendendum est, quamdiu *eam rem fur tenens visus* vel deprehensus *fuerit*, sive in publico sive in privato, vel a domino vel ab alio, antequam *eo* pervenirit *quo perferre* ac deponere rem *destinasset*. Sed si pertulerit quo destinavit, tametsi deprehendatur cum re furtiva, non est manifestus fur. *Nec manifestum furtum quid sit, ex iis quae diximus intelligitur: nam quod manifestum non est, id scilicet nec manifestum est.* § 4. *Conceptum furtum dicitur, cum apud aliquem, testibus praesentibus, furtiva res quaesita et inventa sit: nam in eum propria actio constituta est, quamvis fur non sit, quae appellatur concepti. Oblatum furtum dicitur, cum res furtiva ab aliquo tibi oblata sit, eaque apud te concepta sit; utique si ea mente tibi data fuerit, ut apud te potius quam apud eum qui dederit conciperetur. Nam tibi, apud quem concepta sit, propria adversus eum qui obtulit, quamvis fur non sit, constituta est actio, quae appellatur oblati. Est etiam prohibiti furti actio adversus eum qui furtum quaerere* testibus praesentibus *volentem pro-*

hibuerit. Praeterea poena constituitur edicto praetoris, per actionem furti non exhibiti, adversus eum qui furtivam rem apud se quaesitam et inventam non exhibuit. Sed hae actiones, id est, concepti et oblati, et furti prohibiti, nec non furti non exhibiti, in desuetudinem abierunt. Cum enim requisitio rei furtivae hodie secundum veterem observationem non fit, merito ex consequentia etiam praefatae actiones ab usu communi recesserunt, cum manifestissimum est, quod omnes qui scientes rem furtivam susceperint et celaverint furti nec manifesti obnoxii sunt.

§ 5. *Poena manifesti furti quadrupli est, tam ex servi quam ex liberi persona; nec manifesti, dupli.*

§ 189. Poena manifesti furti ex lege XII Tabularum capitalis erat. Nam liber verberatus addicebatur ei cui furtum fecerat; utrum autem servus efficeretur ex addictione, an adjudicati loco constitueretur, veteres quaerebant. Servum aeque verberatum e saxo dejiciebant. Sed postea improbata est asperitas poenae, et tam ex servi persona, quam ex liberi, quadupli actio praetoris edicto constituta est. § 190. Nec manifesti furti poena per legem XII Tabularum dupli irrogatur; eamque etiam praetor conservat. § 191. Concepti et oblati poena ex lege xii Tabularum tripli est; quae similiter a praetore servatur. § 192. Prohibiti actio quadrupli est ex edicto praetoris introducta. Lex autem eo nomine nullam poenam constituit: hoc solum praecepit, ut qui quaerere velit, nudus quaerat, linteo cinctus, lancem habens; qui si quid invenerit, jubet id lex furtum manifestum esse. § 193. Quid sit autem linteum, quaesitum est; sed verius est, consuti genus esse quo necessariae partes tegerentur. Quare lex tota ridicula est. Nam qui vestitum quaerere prohibet, is etiam nudum quaerere prohibiturus est, eo magis quod ita quaesita res inventa majori poenae subjiciatur. Deinde quod lancem sive ideo haberi jubeatur ut manibus occupatis nihil subjiciatur, sive ideo ut quod invenerit ibi imponat, neutrum eorum procedit, si id quod quaeratur ejus magnitudinis aut naturae sit, ut neque subjici neque ibi imponi possit. Certe non dubitatur, cujuscumque materiae sit ea lanx, satis legi fieri. § 194. Propter hoc tamen quod lex ex ea causa manifestum furtum esse jubet, sunt qui scribunt furtum manifestum aut lege [esse] aut natura: lege, id ipsum de quo loquimur; natura, illud, de quo superius exposuimus. Sed verius est, natura tantum manifestum furtum intelligi: neque enim lex facere potest, ut qui manifestus fur non sit, manifestus sit, non magis quam ut qui omnino fur non sit, fur sit, et qui adulter aut homicida non sit, adulter vel homicida sit: at illud sane lex facere potest, ut perinde aliquis poena teneatur atque si furtum, vel adulterium, vel homicidium admisisset, quamvis nihil eorum admiserit.

§ 195. Furtum autem fit, non solum cum quis intercipiendi causa rem alienam amovet, sed generaliter cum quis rem alienam invito domino contractat. § 196. Itaque, si quis re, quae apud eum deposita sit, utatur, furtum committit; et si quis utendam rem acceperit, eamque in alium usum transtulerit, furti obligatur: veluti si quis argentum utendum acceperit, [quod] quasi amicos ad coenam invitaturus, et id peregre secum tulerit, aut si quis equum gestandi gratia commodatum longius [quam quo] rogaverit eum, aliquo duxerit; quod veteres scripserunt de eo qui in aciem perduxisset. § 197. Placuit tamen eos qui rebus commodatis aliter uterentur quam utendas accepissent, ita furtum committere, si intelligant id se invito domino facere, eumque, si intellexisset, non permissurum; at si permissurum credant, extra furti crimen videri: optima sane distinctione, quia furtum sine dolo malo non committitur. § 198. Sed etsi credat aliquis invito domino se rem contrectare, domino autem volente id fiat, dicitur furtum non fieri. Unde illud quaesitum est, cum Titius servum meum sollicitaverit ut quasdam res mihi subriperet et ad eum perferret, et servus id ad me pertulerit, ego, dum volo Titium in ipso delicto deprehendere, permiserim servo quasdam res ad eum perferre, utrum furti, an servi corrupti judicio teneatur Titius mihi, an neutro? Responsum, neutro eum teneri: furti, ideo quod non invito me res contrectaret, servi corrupti, ideo quod deterior servus factus non est.

§ 6. *Furtum autem fit, non solum cum quis intercipiendi causa rem alienam amovet, sed generaliter cum quis alienam rem invito domino contrectat. Itaque, sive* creditor pignore, sive is *apud* quem res *deposita* est, ea *re utatur, sive* is qui *rem utendam accepit, in alium usum eam transferat* quam cujus gratia ei data est, *furtum committit. Veluti, si quis argentum utendum acceperit, quasi amicos ad coenam invitaturus, et id peregre secum tulerit, aut si quis equum gestandi causa commodatum sibi longius aliquo duxerit; quod veteres scripserunt de eo qui in aciem equum perduxisset.* § 7. *Placuit tamen eos qui rebus commodatis aliter uterentur quam utendas acceperint, ita furtum committere, si intelligant id se invito domino facere, eumque, si intellexisset, non permissurum; at si permissurum credant, extra crimen videri: optima sane distinctione, quia furtum* sine affectu furandi *non committitur.* § 8. *Sed etsi credat aliquis invito domino se rem* commodatam sibi *contrectare domino autem volente id fiat, dicitur furtum non fieri. Unde illud quaesitum est: cum Titius servum Maevii sollicitaverit ut quasdam res domino subriperet et ad eum perferret, et servus id ad Maevium pertulerit, Maevius, dum vult Titium in ipso delicto deprehendere, permiserit servo quasdam res ad eum perferre, utrum furti, an servi corrupti judicio teneatur Titius, an neutro?* Et cum nobis super hac dubitatione suggestum est, et antiquorum prudentium super hoc altercationes perspeximus, quibusdam neque furti neque servi corrupti actionem praestantibus, quibusdam furti tantummmodo: nos hujusmodi calliditati obviam euntes, per nostram decisionem sanximus, non solum furti actionem, sed etiam servi corrupti contra eum dari: licet enim is servus deterior a sollicitatore minime factus est, et ideo non concurrant regulae quae servi corrupti actionem introducerent, tamen consilium corruptoris ad pernitiem probitatis servi introductum est, ut sit ei poenalis actio imposita, tamquam si re ipsa fuisset servus corruptus; ne ex hujusmodi impunitate et in alium servum qui facile possit corrumpi, tale facinus a quibusdam perpetretur.

§ 199. Interdum autem etiam liberorum hominum furtum fit, veluti si quis liberorum nostrorum, qui in potestate nostra sunt, sive etiam uxor, quae in manu nostra sit, sive etiam judicatus vel auctoratus meus subreptus fuerit. § 200. Aliquando etiam suae rei quisque furtum committit, veluti si debitor rem quam creditori pignori dedit, subtraxerit vel etiam bonae fidei possessori rem meam possidenti subripuerim: unde placuit eum, qui servum suum, quem alius bona fide possidebat, ad se reversum celaverit, furtum committere. § 201. Rursus ex diverso, interdum alienas res occupare et usucapere concessum est, nec creditur furtum fieri, veluti res hereditarias, quarum heres non est nactus possessionem nisi necessarius heres esset; nam necessario herede extante placuit nihil pro herede usucapi posse. Item debitor rem quam fiduciae causa creditori mancipaverit aut in jure cesserit, [interdum secundum] ea quae in superiore commentario rettulimus, sine furto possidere et usucapere potest.

§ 9. *Interdum etiam liberorum hominum furtum fit: veluti, si quis liberorum nostrorum, qui in potestate nostra sunt subreptus fuerit.* § 10. *Aliquando etiam suae rei quisque furtum committit: veluti, si debitor rem quam creditori pignoris causa dedit, subtraxerit.*

§ 202. Interdum furti tenetur, cum ipse furtum non fecerit, qualis est, cujus ope consilio furtum factum est: in quo numero est, qui nummos tibi excussit, ut eos alius surriperet, vel obstitit tibi, ut alius surriperet, aut oves aut boves tuas fugavit, ut alius eas exciperet; et hoc veteres scripserunt de eo, qui panno rubro fugavit armentum; sed, quamvis per lasciviam, et non data opera ut furtum committeretur, factum sit, videbimus an utilis actio de [ea re] dari debeatur, cum per legem Aquiliam quoque, de damno latam, etiam culpa puniatur.

§ 11. *Interdum furti tenetur cum ipse furtum non fecerit, qualis est, cujus ope et consilio furtum factum est: in quo numero est, qui tibi nummos excussit, ut alios eos raperet, aut obstitit tibi, ut alius rem tuam exciperet, vel oves aut boves tuas fugaverit, ut alius eas exciperet; et hoc veteres scripserunt de eo, qui panno rubro fugavit armentum. Sed si quid eorum per lasciviam, et non data opera ut furtum admitteretur, factum est,* in factum *actio dari debet.* At ubi ope Maevii Titius furtum fecerit, ambo furti tenentur. Ope et consilio ejus quoque furtum admitti videtur, qui scalas forte fenestris supposuit, aut ipsas fenestras vel ostium effregit, ut alius furtum faceret, quive ferramenta ad effringendum, aut scalas, ut fenestris supponerentur commodaverit, sciens cujus gratia commodaverit. Certe qui nullam opem ad furtum faciendum adhibuit, sed tantum consilium dedit, atque hortatus est ad furtum faciendum, non tenetur furti. § 12. Hi qui in parentum vel dominorum potestate sunt, si rem eis subripiant, furtum quidem illis faciunt, et res in furtivam causam cadit (nec ob id ab ullo usucapi potest, antequam in domini potestatem revertatur), sed furti actio non nascitur, quia nec ex alia ulla causa potest inter eos actio nasci: si vero ope et consilio alterius furtum factum fuerit, quia utique furtum committitur, convenienter ille furti tenetur, quia verum est ope et consilio ejus furtum factum esse.

GAI.	JUST.
§ 203. Furti autem actio ei competit cujus interest rem salvam esse, licet dominus non sit: itaque nec domino aliter competit, quam si ejus intersit rem non perire. § 204. Unde constat creditorem de pignore subrepto furti agere posse; adeo quidem ut, quamvis ipse dominus, id est, ipse debitor eam rem subripuerit, nihilominus creditori competat actio furti. § 205. Item si fullo polienda curandave, aut sarcinator sarcienda vestimenta mercede certa acceperit, eaque furto amiserit, ipse furti habet actionem, non dominus; quia domini nihil interest ea non perisse, cum judicio locati a fullone aut sarcinatore suum consequi possit, si modo is fullo aut sarcinator repraesentandae pecuniae sufficiat; nam si solvendo non est, tunc quia ab eo dominus suum consequi non potest, ipsi furti actio competit, quia hoc casu ipsius interest rem salvam esse. § 206 Quae de fullone aut sarcinatore diximus, eadem transferemus et ad eum cui rem commodavimus: nam, ut	§ 13. *Furti autem actio ei competit cujus interest rem salvam esse, licet dominus non sit: itaque nec domino aliter competit, quam si ejus intersit rem non perire.* § 14. *Unde constat creditorem de pignore subrepto furti agere posse,* etiamsi idoneum debitorem habeat, quia expedit ei pignori potius incumbere quam in personam agere: *adeo quidem, ut quamvis ipse debitor eam rem subripuerit, nihilominus creditori competit actio furti.* § 15. *Item si fullo polienda curandave, aut sarcinator sarcienda vestimenta mercede certa acceperit, eaque furto amiserit, ipse furti habet actionem, non dominus; quia domini nihil interest eam rem non perisse, cum judicio locati a fullone aut sarcinatore rem suam persequi potest.* Sed et bonae fidei emptori subrepta re quam emerit, quamvis dominus non sit, omnimodo competit furti actio, quemadmodum et creditori. Fulloni vero et sarcinatori non aliter furti competere placuit, quam si solvendo sint, hoc est, si domino rei aestimationem solvere possint; *nam si solvendo non sint, tunc, quia ab eis suum dominus consequi non possit, ipsi domino furti actio competit, quia hoc casu ipsius interest rem salvam esse.* Idem est, etsi in partem solvendo sint fullo aut sarcinator. § 16. *Quae de fullone et*

illi mercedem capiendo custodiam praestant, ita hic quoque utendi commodum percipiendo similiter necesse habet custodiam praestare.

sarcinatore diximus, eadem et ad eum, cui commodata res est, transferenda veteres existimabant: *nam ut ille fullo mercedem accipiendo custodiam praestat, ita is quoque qui commodum utendi percipit similiter necesse habet custodiam praestare.* Sed nostra providentia etiam hoc in decisionibus nostris emendavit, ut in domini sit voluntate, sive commodati actionem adversus eum qui rem commodatam accepit movere desiderat, sive furti adversus eum qui rem subripuit, et alterutra earum electa, dominum non posse ex poenitentia ad alteram venire actionem. Sed si quidem furem elegerit, illum qui rem utendam accepit, penitus liberari. Sin autem commodator veniat adversus eum qui rem utendam accepit: ipsi quidem nullo modo competere posse adversus furem furti actionem, eum autem qui pro re commodata convenitur, posse adversus furem furti habere actionem; ita tamen, si dominus, sciens rem esse subreptam, adversus eum cui res commodata fuit pervenit; sin autem nescius, et dubitans rem non esse apud eum, commodati actionem instituit, postea autem re comperta voluit remittere quidem commodati actionem, ad furti autem pervenire, tunc licentia ei concedatur, et adversus furem venire, nullo obstaculo ei opponendo, quoniam incertus constitutus movit adversus eum qui rem utendam accepit commodati actionem (nisi domino ab eo satisfactum est: tunc etenim omnimodo furem a domino quidem furti actione liberari, suppositum autem esse ei qui pro re sibi commodata domino satisfecit), cum manifestissimum est, etiamsi ab initio dominus actionem commodati instituit, ignarus rem esse subreptam, postea autem hoc ei cognito adversus furem transivit, omnimodo liberari eum qui rem commodatam accepit, quemcumque causae exitum dominus adversus furem habuerit: eadem definitione obtinente, sive in partem sive in solidum solvendo sit is qui rem commodatam accepit.

§ 207. Sed is, apud quem res deposita est, custodiam non praestat, tantumque in eo obnoxius est, si quid ipse dolo [malo] fecerit: qua de [causa,] si res ei subrepta fuerit, quia restituendae ejus nomine depositi non tenetur, nec ob id ejus interest rem salvam esse: furti itaque agere non potest; sed ea actio domino competit.

§ 17. *Sed is, apud quem res deposita est custodiam non praestat, sed tantum in eo obnoxius est, si quid ipso dolo malo fecerit: qua de causa, si res ei subrepta fuerit, quia restituendae ejus nomine depositi non tenetur, nec ob id ejus interest rem salvam esse, furti agere non potest, sed furti actio domino competit.*

§ 208. In summa sciendum est, quaesitum esse, an impubes rem alienam amovendo furtum faciat. Plerisque placet, quia furtum ex affectu consistit, ita demum obligari eo crimine impuberem, si proximus pubertati sit, et ob id intelligat se delinquere.

§ 18. *In summa sciendum est, quaesitum esse, an impubes, rem alienam amovendo, furtum faciat. Et placet quia furtum ex affectu consistit, ita demum obligari eo crimine impuberem, si proximus pubertati sit, et ob id intelligat se delinquere.*

§ 19. Furti actio, sive dupli sive quadrupli, tantum ad poenae persecutionem pertinet: nam ipsius rei persecutionem extrinsecus habet dominus, quam aut vindicando aut condicendo potest auferre. Sed vindicatio quidem adversus possessorem est, sive fur ipse possidet, sive alius quilibet; condictio autem adversus ipsum furem heredemve ejus, licet non possideat, competit.

Tit. ii. De vi bonorum raptorum.

§ 209. Qui res alienas rapit, tenetur [quidem] etiam furti: quis enim magis alienam rem invito domino contrectat, quam qui [vi] rapit? itaque recte dictum est, eum improbum furem esse; sed propriam actionem ejus delicti nomine praetor introduxit, quae appellatur vi bonorum raptorum; et est intra annum quadrupli actio, post annum simpli. Quae actio utilis est, etsi quis unam rem, licet minimam, rapuerit.

Qui res alienas rapit, tenetur quidem etiam furti: quis enim magis alienam rem invito domino contrectat, quam qui vi rapit? Ideoque recte dictum est, eum improbum furem esse; sed tamen propriam actionem ejus delicti nomine praetor introduxit, quae appellatur vi bonorum raptorum; et est intra annum quadrupli, post annum simpli. Quae actio utilis est, etiam si quis unam rem, licet minimam, rapuerit. Quadruplum autem non totum poena est, et extra poenam rei persecutio, sicut in actione furti manifesti diximus: sed in quadruplo inest et rei persecutio, ut poena tripli sit, sive comprehendatur raptor in ipso delicto, sive non. Ridiculum enim esset levioris conditionis esse eum qui vi rapit, quam qui clam amovet. § 1. Quia tamen ita competit haec actio, si dolo malo quisque rapuerit, qui, aliquo errore inductus, rem suam esse existimans, et imprudens juris, eo animo rapuit, quasi domino liceat rem suam etiam per vim auferre a possessoribus, absolvi debet. Cui scilicet conveniens est, nec furti teneri eum qui eodem hoc animo rapuit. Sed ne, dum talia excogitentur, inveniatur via per quam raptores impune suam exerceant avaritiam, melius divalibus constitutionibus pro hac parte prospectum est, ut nemini liceat vi rapere rem mobilem vel se moventem, licet suam eandem rem existimet; sed si quis contra statuta fecerit, rei quidem suae dominio cadere, sin autem aliena sit, post restitutionem ejus, etiam aestimationem ejusdem rei praestare. Quod non solum in mobilibus rebus quae rapi possunt, constitutiones obtinere censuerunt, sed etiam in invasionibus quae circa res soli fiunt, ut ex hac causa omni rapina homines abstineant. § 2. Sane in hac actione non utique expectatur rem in bonis actoris esse; nam sive in bonis sit, sive non sit, si tamen ex bonis sit, locum haec actio habebit. Quare sive locata, sive commodata, sive pignerata, sive etiam deposita sit apud Titium, sic, ut intersit ejus eam rem non auferri, veluti si in re deposita culpam quoque promisit, sive bona fide possideat, sive usumfructum in ea quis habeat, vel quod aliud jus, ut intersit ejus non rapi, dicendum est competere ei hanc actionem, ut non dominium accipiat, sed illud solum quod ex bonis ejus qui rapinam passus est, id est, quod ex substantia ejus ablatum esse proponatur. Et generaliter dicendum est, ex quibus causis furti actio competit in re clam facta, ex iisdem causis omnes habere hanc actionem.

§ 210. Damni injuriae actio constituitur per legem Aquiliam: cujus primo capite cautum est ut, si quis hominem alienum, alienamve quadrupedem quae pecudum numero sit, injuria occiderit, quanti ea res in eo anno plurimi fuerit, tantum domino dare damnetur.

Tit. iii. De lege Aquilia.

Damni injuriae actio constituitur per legem Aquiliam: cujus primo capite cautum est ut, si quis hominem alienum, alienamve quadrupedem quae pecudum numero sit, injuria occiderit, quanti ea res in eo anno plurimi fuerit, tantum domino dare damnetur. § 1. Quod autem non praecise de quadrupede, sed de ea tantum quae pecudum numero est, cavetur, eo pertinet, ut neque de feris bestiis, neque de canibus cautum esse intelligamus, sed de iis tantum quae gregatim proprie pasci dicuntur: quales sunt equi, muli, asini, boves, oves, caprae. De suibus quoque idem placuit; nam et sues pecudum appellatione continentur, quia et hi gregatim pascuntur; sic denique et Homerus in Odyssea ait, sicut Aelius Marcianus in suis institutionibus refert:

δῆεις τόν γε σύεσσι παρήμενον· αἱ δὲ νέμονται
πὰρ Κόρακος πέτρῃ, ἐπί τε κρήνῃ Ἀρεθούσῃ.

§ 211. Injuria autem occidere intelligitur, cujus dolo aut culpa id acciderit, nec ulla alia lege damnum, quod sine injuria datur, reprehenditur: itaque impunitus est

§ 2. *Injuria autem occidere intelligitur* qui nullo jure occidit. Itaque qui latronem occidit, non tenetur, utique si aliter periculum effugere non potest. § 3. Ac ne

qui, sine culpa et dolo malo, casu quodam damnum committit.

is quidem hac lege tenetur, qui casu occidit, si modo culpa ejus nulla inveniatur; nam alioquin non minus ex dolo quam ex culpa quisque hac lege tenetur. § 4. Itaque si quis, dum jaculis ludit vel exercitatur, transeuntem servum tuum trajecerit, distinguitur. Nam, si id a milite quidem in campo, eoque ubi solitum est exercitari, admissum est, nulla culpa ejus intelligitur; si alius tale quid admiserit, culpae reus est. Idem juris est et de milite, si is in alio loco quam qui exercitandis militibus destinatus est, id admisit. § 5. Item si putator, ex arbore dejecto ramo, servum tuum transeuntem occiderit, si prope viam publicam aut vicinalem id factum est, neque praeclamavit, ut casus evitari possit, culpae reus est; si praeclamavit, neque ille curavit cavere, extra culpam est putator. Aeque extra culpam esse intelligitur, si seorsum a via forte, vel in medio fundo caedebat, licet non praeclamavit, quia eo loco nulli extraneo jus fuerat versandi. § 6. Praeterea si medicus qui servum tuum secuit, dereliquerit curationem, atque ob id mortuus fuerit servus, culpae reus est. § 7. Imperitia quoque culpae annumeratur, veluti si medicus ideo servum tuum occiderit, quod eum male secuerit, aut perperam ei medicamentum dederit. § 8. Impetu quoque mularum, quas mulio propter imperitiam retinere non potuerit, si servus tuus oppressus fuerit, culpae reus est mulio. Sed et si propter infirmitatem retinere eas non potuerit, cum alius firmior retinere potuisset, aeque culpae tenetur. Eadem placuerunt de eo quoque qui, cum equo veheretur, impetum ejus aut propter infirmitatem aut propter imperitiam suam retinere non potuerit.

§ 214. Quod autem additum est in hac lege: "quanti in eo anno plurimi ea res fuerit," illud efficit ut, si claudum, puta, aut luscum servum occiderit, qui in eo anno integer fuerit, ita aestimatio fiat; quo fit, ut quis plus interdum consequatur, quam ei damnum datum est.

§ 9. His autem verbis, *legis*, "*quanti in eo anno plurimi fuerit*", illa sententia exprimitur, ut si quis hominem tuum qui hodie *claudus* aut mancus aut *luscus* erit, *occiderit, qui in eo anno integer* aut pretiosus *fuerit*, non tanti teneatur quanti is hodie erit, sed quanti in eo anno plurimi fuerit. Qua ratione creditum est poenalem esse hujus legis actionem, quia non solum tanti quisque obligatur quantum damni dederit, sed aliquando longe pluris: ideoque constat in heredem eam actionem non transire, quae transitura fuisset, si ultra damnum numquam lis aestimaretur.

§ 212. Nec solum corpus [interempti servi] in actione hujus legis aestimatur, sed si in eo servo occiso plus dominus capiat damni quam

§ 10. Illud non ex verbis legis, sed ex interpretatione placuit, non solum perempti corporis aestimationem

pretium servi sit, id quoque aestimatur: veluti si servus meus ab aliquo heres institutus, antequam jussu meo hereditatem cerneret, occisus fuerit; non enim tantum ipsius pretium aestimatur, sed etiam hereditatis amissae quantitas. Item si ex gemellis, vel ex comoedis, vel ex symphoniacis unus occisus fuerit, non solum occisi fit aestimatio, sed eo amplius id quoque computatur quod caeteri, qui supersunt, depretiati sunt. Idem juris est etiam, si quis ex pari mularum unam, vel etiam ex quadrigis equorum unum occiderit. § 213. Cujus autem servus occisus est, is liberum arbitrium habet, vel capitali crimine reum facere eum qui occiderit, vel hac lege damnum persequi.

habendam esse, secundum ea quae diximus, sed eo amplius quidquid praeterea perempto eo corpore damni vobis allatum fuerit, veluti si servum tuum heredem ab aliquo institutum antea quis occiderit, quam is jussu tuo adiret; nam hereditatis quoque amissae rationem esse habendam constat. *Item si ex pari mularum unam, vel ex quadriga equorum unum occiderit, vel ex comoedis unus servus fuerit occisus: non solum occisi fit aestimatio, sed eo amplius id quoque computatur quanto depretiati sunt qui supersunt.* § 11. *Liberum autem est ei cujus servus occisus fuerit* et judicio privato *legis Aquiliae damnum persequi, et capitalis criminis eum reum facere.*

§ 215. Capite secundo [adversus] adstipulatorem, qui pecuniam in fraudem stipulatoris acceptam fecerit, quanti ea res esset, tanti actio constituitur. § 216. Qua et ipsa parte legis damni nomine actionem introduci manifestum est; sed id caveri non fuit necessarium, cum actio mandati ad eam rem sufficeret; nisi quod ea lege adversus infitiantem in duplum agitur.

§ 12. Caput secundum legis Aquiliae in usu non est.

§ 217. Capite tertio de omni caetero damno cavetur. Itaque, si quis servum, vel eam quadrupedem quae pecudum numero [est, vulneraverit, sive eam quadrupedem, quae pecudum numero non est], velut canem, aut feram bestiam, velut ursum, leonem, vulneraverit vel occiderit, ex hoc capite actio constituitur. In caeteris quoque animalibus, item in omnibus rebus quae anima carent, damnum injuria datum hac parte vindicatur. Si quid enim ustum, aut ruptum, aut fractum fuerit, actio hoc capite constituitur; quamquam potuerit sola rupti appellatio in omnes istas causas sufficere: "ruptum" [enim intelligitur, quod quoquo modo corruptum] est. Unde non solum usta, aut fracta, sed etiam scissa et collisa et effusa

§ 13. *Capite tertio de omni caetero damno cavetur. Itaque, si quis servum, vel eam quadrupedem quae pecudum numero est, vulneraverit, sive eam quadrupedem quae pecudum numero non est, veluti canem aut feram bestiam, vulneraverit aut occiderit, hoc capite actio constituitur. In caeteris quoque omnibus animalibus, item in omnibus rebus quae anima carent, damnum injuria datum hac parte vindicatur. Si quid enim ustum, aut ruptum, aut fractum fuerit, actio ex hoc capite constituitur; quamquam potuerit sola rupti appellatio in omnes istas causas sufficere: "ruptum" enim intelligitur, quod quoquo modo corruptum est. Unde non solum usta, aut fracta, sed etiam scissa, et collisa, et effusa,* et quoquo modo vitiata aut peremptа atque deteriora facta hoc verbo continentur.

§ 218. Hoc tamen capite non quanti in eo anno, sed quanti in diebus triginta proximis ea res fuerit, obligatur is qui damnum dederit. Ac ne "plurimi" quidem verbum adjicitur: et ideo quidam putaverunt, liberum esse judici arbitrium, ad id tempus ex diebus triginta aestimationem redigere, quo plurimi res fuit, vel ad id quo minoris fuit. Sed Sabino placuit, perinde habendum, ac si etiam hac parte "plurimi" verbum adjectum esset: nam legis latorem contentum fuisse, [quod prima parte eo verbo usus esset.] § 219. Caeterum placuit, ita demum ex ista lege actionem esse, si quis corpore suo damnum dederit, itaque alio modo damno dato, utiles actiones dantur: veluti si quis alienum hominem aut pecudem incluserit et fame necaverit, aut jumentum tam vehementer egerit, ut rumperetur; item si quis alieno servo persuaserit, ut in arborem ascenderet vel in puteum descenderet, et is ascendendo aut descendendo ceciderit, et aut mortuus fuerit, aut aliqua parte corporis laesus sit: item si quis alienum servum de ponte aut ripa in flumen projecerit, et is suffocatus fuerit, quamvis hic corpore suo damnum dedisse, eo quod projecerit, non difficiliter intelligi potest.

et quoquo modo perempta atque deteriora facta, hoc verbo continentur; denique responsum est, si quis in alienum vinum aut oleum id immiserit quo naturalis bonitas vini vel olei corrumperetur, ex hac parte legis eum teneri. § 14. Illud palam est, sicut ex primo capite ita demum quisque tenetur, si dolo aut culpa ejus homo aut quadrupes occisus occisave fuerit, ita ex hoc capite, ex dolo aut culpa de caetero damno quemque teneri. *Hoc tamen capite, non quanti in eo anno, sed quanti in diebus triginta proximis res fuerit, obligatur is qui damnum dederit.* § 15. *Ac ne "plurimi" quidem verbum adjicitur. Sed Sabino* recte *placuit, perinde habendam aestimationem, ac si etiam hac parte "plurimi" verbum adjectum fuisset; nam plebem Romanam quae, Aquilio tribuno rogante, hanc legem tulit, contentam fuisse quod prima parte eo verbo usa est.* § 16. *Caeterum, placuit ita demum ex hac lege actionem esse, si quis* praecipue *corpore suo damnum dederit; ideoque in eum qui alio modo damnum dederit, utiles actiones dari solent: veluti, si quis hominem alienum aut pecus ita incluserit, ut fame necaretur, aut jumentum tam vehementer egerit, ut rumperetur,* aut pecus in tantum exagitaverit, ut praecipitaretur: aut *si quis alieno servo persuaserit, ut in arborem ascenderet, vel in puteum descenderet, et is ascendendo vel descendendo, aut mortuus aut aliqua parte corporis laesus fuerit,* utilis actio in eum datur. Sed *si quis alienum servum de ponte aut ripa in flumen dejecerit, et is suffocatus fuerit, eo quod projecerit, corpore suo damnum dedisse non difficiliter intelligi poterit:* ideoque ipsa lege Aquilia tenetur. Sed si non corpore damnum fuerit datum, neque corpus laesum fuerit, sed alio modo damnum alicui contigerit, cum non sufficit, neque directa neque utilis Aquilia, placuit eum qui obnoxius fuerit in factum actione teneri: veluti, si quis misericordia ductus alienum servum compeditum solverit, ut fugeret.

Tit. iv. De injuriis.

Generaliter injuria dicitur omne quod non jure fit; specialiter alias contumelia, quae a contemnendo dicta est, quam graeci ὕβριν appellant, alias culpa, quam graeci ἀδίκημα dicunt, sicut in lege Aquilia damnum injuriae accipitur, alias iniquitas et injustitia, quam graeci ἀδικίαν vocant. Cum enim praetor vel judex non jure contra quem pronuntiat, injuriam accepisse dicitur.

§ 220. Injuria autem committitur, non solum cum quis pugno, puta, aut fuste percussus, vel etiam verberatus erit, sed et si cui convicium factum fuerit, sive quis bona alicujus quasi debitoris, sciens eum nihil sibi debere, sibi proscripserit, sive quis ad infamiam alicujus libellum aut carmen scripserit, sive quis matremfamilias aut praetextatum adsectatus fuerit, et denique aliis pluribus modis. § 221. Sed pati injuriam videmur non solum per nosmet ipsos, sed etiam per liberos nostros quos in potestate habemus; item per uxores nostras cum in manu nostra sint. Itaque si veluti filiae meae, quae Titio nupta est, injuriam feceris, non solum filiae nomine tecum agi injuriarum potest, verum etiam meo quoque et Titii nomine.

§ 1. *Injuria autem committitur non solum cum quis pugno puta aut fustibus caesus vel etiam verberatus erit, sed etiam si cui convicium factum fuerit, sive cujus bona quasi debitoris, possessa* fuerint ab eo qui intelligebat *nihil eum sibi debere, vel si quis ad infamiam alicujus libellum aut carmen scripserit,* composuerit, ediderit, dolove malo fecerit quo quid eorum fieret, *sive quis matremfamilias aut praetextatum* praetextatamve *adsectatus fuerit,* sive cujus *pudicitia* attentata esse dicetur; *et denique aliis pluribus modis* admitti injuriam manifestum est. § 2. *Patitur autem quis injuriam non solum per semetipsum, sed etiam per liberos suos quos in potestate habet; item per uxorem suam,* id enim magis praevaluit. *Itaque si filiae alicujus quae Titio nupta est, injuriam feceris, non solum filiae nomine tecum injuriarum agi potest, sed etiam patris quoque et mariti nomine.* Contra autem, si viro injuria facta sit, uxor injuriarum agere non potest: defendi enim uxores a viris, non viros ab uxoribus, aequum est. Sed et socer, nurus nomine cujus vir in potestate est, injuriarum agere potest.

§ 222. Servo autem ipsi quidem nulla injuria intelligitur fieri, sed domino per eum fieri videtur: non tamen iisdem modis quibus etiam per liberos nostros vel uxores injuriam pati videmur, sed ita cum quid atrocius commissum fuerit, quod aperte contumeliam domini respiciat, et in hunc casum formula

§ 3. *Servis autem ipsis quidem nulla injuria fieri intelligitur, sed domino per eos fieri videtur: non tamen iisdem modis quibus etiam per liberos et uxores, sed ita cum quid atrocius commissum fuerit, et quod aperte ad contumeliam domini respicit, veluti si quis alienum servum*

proponitur veluti "si quis alienum servum verberaverit"; at si qui servo convicium fecerit, vel pugno eum percusserit, non proponitur ulla formula, nec temere petenti datur.

verberaverit; et in hunc casum actio *proponitur. At si quis servo convicium fecerit, vel pugno eum percusserit, nulla in eum* actio *domino competit.* § 4. Si communi servo injuria facta sit, aequum est, non pro ea parte qua dominus quisque est, aestimationem injuriae fieri, sed ex dominorum persona, quia ipsis fit injuria. § 5. Quod si ususfructus in servo Titii est, proprietas Maevii est, magis Maevio injuria fieri intelligitur. § 6. Sed si libero qui tibi bona fide servit, injuria facta sit, nulla tibi actio dabitur, sed suo nomine is experiri poterit; nisi in contumeliam tuam pulsatus sit, tunc enim competit et tibi injuriarum actio. Idem ergo est et in servo alieno bona fide tibi serviente, ut totiens admittatur injuriarum actio, quotiens in tuam contumeliam injuria ei facta sit.

§ 223. Poena autem injuriarum ex lege XII Tabularum propter membrum quidem ruptum talio erat; propter os vero fractum aut collisum trecentorum assium poena erat [videlicet] si libero os fractum erat; at si servo, CL: propter caeteras vero injurias XXV assium poena erat constituta; et videbantur illis temporibus, in magna [omnium] paupertate, satis idoneae istae pecuniae. § 224. Sed nunc alio jure utimur; permittitur enim nobis a praetore ipsis injuriam aestimare; et judex vel tanti condemnat, quanti nos aestimaverimus, vel minoris, prout ei visum fuerit. Sed cum atrocem injuriam praetor aestimare soleat, si simul constituerit, quantae pecuniae eo nomine fieri debeat vadimonium, hac ipsa quantitate taxamur formula, et judex, quamvis possit vel minoris damnare, plerumque tamen propter ipsius praetoris auctoritatem non audet minuere condemnationem.

§ 7. *Poena autem injuriarum, ex lege Duodecim Tabularum, propter membrum quidem ruptum talio erat; propter os vero fractum* nummariae *poenae erant constitutae,* quasi *in magna* veterum *paupertate. Sed* postea *praetores permittebant ipsis qui injuriam* passi sunt, eam *aestimare; ut judex vel tanti* reum *condemnet, quanti* injuriam passus *aestimaverit, vel minoris, prout ei visum fuerit.* Sed poena quidem injuriae quae ex lege Duodecim Tabularum introducta est, in desuetudinem abiit; quam autem praetores introduxerunt, quae etiam "honoraria" appellatur, in judiciis frequentatur. Nam secundum gradum dignitatis vitaeque honestatem crescit aut minuitur aestimatio injuriae: qui gradus condemnationis et in servili persona non immerito servatur, ut aliud in servo actore, aliud in medii actus homine, aliud in vilissimo vel compedito constituatur. § 8. Sed et lex Cornelia de injuriis loquitur et injuriarum actionem introduxit, quae competit ob eam rem, quod se pulsatum quis verberatumve, domumve suam vi introitam esse dicat. Domum autem accipimus, sive in propria domo quis habitat, sive in conducta, vel gratis, sive hospitio receptus sit.

§ 225. Atrox autem injuria aestimatur vel ex facto, velut si quis ab aliquo vulneratus, aut verberatus, fustibusve caesus fuerit; vel ex loco, velut si cui in theatro aut in foro injuria facta sit; vel ex persona, velut si magistratus injuriam passus fuerit, vel senatoribus ab humili persona facta sit injuria.

§ 9. *Atrox injuria aestimatur vel ex facto, veluti si quis ab aliquo vulneratus fuerit, vel fustibus caesus; vel ex loco, veluti si cui in theatro, vel in foro*, vel in conspectu praetoris, *injuria facta sit; vel ex persona, veluti si magistratus injuriam passus fuerit, vel si senatori ab humili persona injuria facta sit*, aut parenti patronove fiat a liberis vel libertis (aliter enim senatoris et parentis patronique, aliter extranei et humilis personae injuria aestimatur); nonnumquam et locus vulneris atrocem injuriam facit, veluti si in oculo quis percussus sit. Parvi autem refert, utrum patrifamilias, an filiofamilias talis injuria facta sit: nam et haec atrox aestimabitur.

§ 10. In summa sciendum est, de omni injuria eum qui passus est posse vel criminaliter agere, vel civiliter. Et si quidem civiliter agatur, aestimatione facta, secundum quod dictum est, poena imponitur. Sin autem criminaliter, officio judicis extraordinaria poena reo irrogatur: hoc videlicet observando, quod Zenoniana constitutio introduxit, ut viri illustres, quique supra eos sunt, et per procuratorem possint actionem injuriarum criminaliter vel persequi vel suscipere, secundum ejus tenorem qui ex ipsa manifestius apparebit.

§ 11. Non solum autem is injuriarum tenetur qui fecit injuriam, id est, qui percussit; verum ille quoque continebitur qui dolo fecit, vel qui curavit, ut cui mala pugno percuteretur. § 12. Haec actio dissimulatione aboletur; et ideo si quis injuriam dereliquerit, hoc est, statim ut passus ad animum suum non revocaverit, postea ex poenitentia remissam injuriam non poterit recolere.

Tit. v. De obligationibus quae quasi ex delicto nascuntur.

Si judex litem suam fecerit, non proprie ex maleficio obligatus videtur. Sed quia neque ex maleficio neque ex contractu obligatus est, et utique peccasse aliquid intelligitur, licet per imprudentiam, ideo videtur quasi ex maleficio teneri: et in quantum de ea re aequum religioni judicantis videbitur, poenam sustinebit. § 1. Item, is ex cujus coenaculo, vel proprio ipsius, vel conducto, vel in quo gratis habitabat, dejectum effusumve aliquid est, ita ut alicui noceretur quasi ex maleficio obligatus intelligitur: ideo autem non proprie ex maleficio obligatus intelligitur, quia plerumque ob alterius culpam tenetur, aut servi aut liberi. Cui similis est is qui, ea parte qua vulgo iter fieri solet, id positum aut suspensum habet, quod potest, si ceciderit, alicui nocere: quo casu poena decem aureorum constituta est. De eo vero quod dejectum effusumve est, dupli, quanti damnum datum sit, constituta est actio. Ob hominem vero liberum occisum, quinquaginta aureorum poena constituitur; si vero vivat, nocitumque ei esse dicatur, quantum ob eam rem aequum judici videtur, actio datur: judex enim computare debet mercedes medicis praestitas, caeteraque impendia quae in curatione facta sunt, praeterea operarum quibus caruit aut cariturus est, ob id quod inutilis factus est. § 2. Si filiusfamilias seorsum a patre habitaverit, et quid ex coenaculo ejus dejectum effusumve sit, sive quid positum suspensumve habuerit, cujus casus periculosus est: Juliano placuit in patrem nullam esse actionem, sed cum ipso filio agendum. Quod et in filiofamilias judice observandum est, qui litem suam fecerit. § 3. Item exercitor navis, aut cauponae, aut stabuli, de damno aut furto, quod in navi aut in caupona aut in stabulo factum erit, quasi ex maleficio teneri videtur, si modo ipsius nullum est maleficium, sed alicujus eorum quorum opera navem aut cauponam aut stabulum exerceret: cum enim, neque ex contractu sit adversus eum constituta haec actio, et aliquatenus culpae reus est, quod opera malorum hominum uteretur, ideo quasi ex maleficio teneri videtur. In his autem casibus in factum actio competit, quae heredi quidem datur, adversus heredem autem non competit.

GAII INSTITUTIONUM COMMENTARIUS IV.

§ 1. [Superest ut de actionibus loquamur.

Et si quaeramus], quot genera actionum sint, verius videtur duo esse: in rem et in personam; nam qui quattuor esse dixerunt ex sponsionum generibus, non animadverterunt quasdam species actionum inter genera se rettulisse. § 2. In

Tit. vi. De actionibus.

Superest ut de actionibus loquamur. Actio autem nihil aliud est quam jus persequendi in judicio quod sibi debetur.

§ 1. Omnium actionum quibus inter aliquos apud judices arbitrosve de quacumque re quaeritur, summa divisio in *duo genera* deducitur: aut enim *in rem* sunt, aut *in personam*. Namque agit unusquisque, aut cum eo, qui ei obligatus est vel ex con-

personam actio est, quotiens cum aliquo agimus, qui nobis vel ex contractu, vel ex delicto obligatus est, id est, cum intendimus dare, facere, praestare oportere. § 3. In rem actio est, cum aut corporalem rem intendimus nostram esse, aut jus aliquod nobis competere, velut utendi, aut utendi fruendi, eundi, agendi aquamve ducendi, vel altius tollendi, prospiciendive. Item actio ex diverso adversario [contraria nihilominus etiam actio est in rem, quamquam] est negativa.

tractu vel ex maleficio, quo casu proditae *actiones in personam* sunt, per quas *intendit* adversarium ei *dare facere oportere*, et aliis quibusdam modis: aut cum eo agit qui nullo jure ei obligatus est, movet tamen alicui de aliqua re controversiam, quo casu proditae *actiones in rem* sunt, veluti, *si rem corporalem* possideat quis, quam Titius suam esse affirmet, et possessor dominum se esse dicat; nam si Titius suam esse intendat, in rem actio est. § 2. Aeque si agat jus sibi esse fundo forte vel aedibus *utendi fruendi*, vel per fundum vicini *eundi agendi*, vel ex fundo vicini *aquam ducendi*, in rem actio est. Ejusdem generis est actio de jure praediorum urbanorum: veluti si agat jus sibi esse *altius* aedes suas *tollendi, prospiciendive*, vel projiciendi aliquid, vel immittendi tignum in vicini aedes. Contra quoque de usufructu et de servitutibus praediorum rusticorum, item praediorum urbanorum invicem quoque proditae sunt actiones, ut si quis intendat jus non esse adversario utendi fruendi, eundi agendi, aquamve ducendi, item altius tollendi, prospiciendi, projiciendi, immittendi, istae quoque actiones in rem sunt, sed *negativae*. Quod genus actionis in controversiis rerum corporalium proditum non est; nam in his is agit qui non possidet: ei vero qui possidet, non est actio prodita per quam neget rem auctoris esse. Sane hoc uno casu, qui possidet nihilominus actoris partes obtinet, sicut in latioribus Digestorum libris opportunius apparebit.

§ 3. *Sed istae quidem actiones* quarum mentionem habuimus, et si quae sunt similes, ex legitimis et civilibus causis descendunt. Aliae autem sunt quas praetor ex sua jurisdictione comparatas habet, tam in rem quam in personam, quas et ipsas necessarium est exemplis ostendere. Ecce plerumque ita permittitur in rem agere, ut vel actor diceret se quasi usucepisse quod non usuceperit, vel, ex diverso, possessorem diceret adversarium suum non usucepisse quod usuceperit. § 4. Namque si cui ex justa causa res aliqua tradita fuerit, veluti ex causa emptionis aut donationis, aut dotis, aut legatorum, necdum ejus rei dominus effectus est, si ejus rei casu possessionem amiserit, nullam habet directam in rem actionem ad eam rem persequendam; quippe ita proditae sunt jure civili actiones, ut quis dominium suum vindicet. Sed quia sane durum erat eo casu deficere actionem, inventa est a praetore actio, in qua dicit is qui possessionem amisit, eam rem se usucepisse et ita vindicat suam esse. Quae actio Publiciana appellatur, quoniam primum a Publicio praetore in edicto proposita est. § 5. Rursus ex diverso, si quis, cum reipublicae causa abesset vel in hostium potestate esset, rem ejus qui in civitate esset usuceperit, permittitur domino, si possessor reipublicae causa abesse desierit, tunc intra annum, rescissa usucapione, eam petere, id est ita petere, ut dicat possessorem usu non cepisse, et ob id suam rem esse. Quod genus actionis quibusdam at aliis, simili aequitate motus, praetor accommodat, sicut ex latiore Digestorum seu Pandectarum volumine intelligere licet. § 6. Item, si quis in fraudem creditorum rem suam alicui tradiderit, bonis ejus a creditoribus ex sententia praesidis possessis, permittitur ipsis creditoribus, rescissa traditione, eam rem petere, id est, dicere eam rem traditam non esse, et ob id in bonis debitoris mansisse. § 7. Item Serviana, et quasi Serviana, (quae etiam hypothecaria vocatur), ex ipsius praetoris jurisdictione substantiam capiunt. Serviana autem experitur quis de rebus coloni, quae, pignoris jure, pro mercedibus fundi ei tenentur; quasi Serviana autem, qua creditores pignora hypothecasve persequuntur. Inter pignus autem et hypothecam, quantum ad actionem hypothecariam attinet, nihil interest; nam de qua re inter creditorem et debitorem convenerit, ut sit pro debito obligata, utraque hac appellatione continetur; sed in aliis differentia est: nam pignoris appellatione eam proprie rem contineri dicimus, quae simul etiam traditur creditori, maxime si mobilis sit; at eam quae sine traditione nuda conventione tenetur, proprie hypothecae appellatione contineri dicimus. § 8. In personam quoque actiones ex sua jurisdictione propositas habet praetor; veluti de pecunia constituta, cui similis videbatur receptitia: sed ex nostra constitutione, cum et si quid plenius habebat, hoc in actionem pecuniae constitutae transfusum est, ea quasi supervacua jussa est cum sua auctoritate a nostris legibus recedere. Item praetor proposuit de peculio servorum filiorumque familias, et ex qua quaeritur an actor juraverit, et alias complures. § 9. De pecunia autem constituta cum omnibus agitur, quicumque vel pro se vel pro alio soluturum se constituerit, nulla scilicet stipulatione interposita. Nam alioquin, si stipulanti promiserit, jure civili tenetur. § 10. Actiones autem de peculio ideo adversus patrem dominumve comparavit praetor, quia licet ex contractu filiorum servorumve ipso jure non teneantur, aequum tamen est peculio tenus, quod veluti patrimonium est filiorum filiarumque, item servorum, condemnari eos. § 11. Item si quis, postulante adversario, juraverit deberi sibi pecuniam quam peteret, neque ei solvatur, justissime accommodat ei talem actionem per quam non illud quaeritur, an ei pecunia debeatur, sed an juraverit. § 12. Poenales quoque actiones bene multas ex sua jurisdictione introduxit: veluti, adversus eum qui quid ex albo ejus corrupisset; et in eum qui patronum vel parentem in jus vocasset, cum id non impetrasset; item adversus eum qui vi exemerit eum qui in jus vocaretur, cujusve dolo alius exemerit; et alias innumerabiles. § 13. Praejudiciales actiones in rem esse videntur: quales sunt per quas quaeritur, an aliquis liber vel libertus sit, vel de partu agnoscendo. Ex quibus fere una illa legitimam causam habet, per quam quaeritur, an aliquis liber sit; caeterae ex ipsius praetoris jurisdictione substantiam capiunt.

§ 4. Sic itaque discretis actionibus certum est, non posse nos rem nostram ab alio ita petere: "si paret eum dare oportere:" nec enim quod nostrum est, nobis dari potest, cum solum id dari nobis intelligatur quod ita datur, ut nostrum fiat; nec res quae est nostra, nostra amplius fieri potest. Plane odio furum, quo magis pluribus actionibus teneantur, effectum est ut, extra poenam dupli aut quadrupli, rei recipiendae nomine fures ex hac actione etiam teneantur: "si paret eos dare oportere", quamvis sit etiam adversus eos haec actio qua "rem nostram esse", petimus. § 5. Appellantur autem in rem quidem actiones, vindicationes; in personam vero actiones, quibus dari fierive oportere intendimus, condictiones.

§ 14. *Sic itaque discretis actionibus certum est, non posse actorem rem suam ita ab aliquo petere: "si paret eum dare oportere:" nec enim quod actoris est, id ei dari oportet, quia scilicet dari cuiquam id intelligitur, quod ita datur, ut ejus fiat; nec res quae jam actoris est, magis ejus fieri potest. Plane odio furum, quo magis pluribus actionibus teneantur, effectum est ut, extra poenam dupli aut quadrupli, rei recipiendae nomine fures etiam hac actione teneantur: "si paret eos dare oportere", quamvis sit adversus eos etiam haec in rem actio, per quam rem suam quis esse petit.* § 15. *Appellamus autem in rem quidem actiones, vindicationes; in personam vero actiones, quibus dare facere oportere intenditur, condictiones. Condicere enim est denuntiare prisca lingua; nunc vero* abusive *dicimus, condictionem actionem in personam esse qua actor intendit dari sibi oportere: nulla enim hoc tempore eo nomine denuntiatio fit.*

cf. Gai., § 18.

§ 6. Agimus autem interdum ut rem tantum consequamur, interdum ut poenam tantum, alias ut rem et poe-

§ 16. Sequens illa divisio est, quod quaedam actiones rei persequendae gratia comparatae sunt, quaedam poenae persequendae, quaedam mixtae

nam. § 7. Rem tantum persequimur, velut actionibus quibus ex contractu agimus.

§ 8. Poenam tantum consequimur, velut actione furti, et injuriarum, et, secundum quorundam opinionem, actione vi bonorum raptorum; nam ipsius rei et vindicatio et condictio nobis competit. § 9. Rem vero et poenam persequimur, velut ex his causis ex quibus adversus infitiantem in duplum agimus: quod accidit per actionem judicati, depensi, damni injuriae lege Aquilia, aut legatorum nomine quae per damnationem certa relicta sunt.

sunt. § 17. Rei persequendae causa comparatae sunt omnes in rem actiones. Earum vero actionum quae in personam sunt, eae quidem quae ex contractu nascuntur, fere omnes rei persequendae causa comparatae videntur: veluti quibus mutuam pecuniam vel in stipulatum deductam petit actor, itemque commodati, depositi, mandati, pro socio, ex empto vendito, locato conducto. Plane si depositi agatur eo nomine, quod tumultus, incendii, ruinae, naufragii causa depositum sit, in duplum actionem praetor reddit: si modo cum ipso apud quem depositum sit, aut cum herede ejus ex dolo ipsius agetur; quo casu mixta est actio. § 18. Ex maleficiis vero proditae actiones, aliae tantum poenae persequendae causa comparatae sunt, aliae tam poenae quam rei persequendae, et ob id mixtae sunt. *Poenam tantum persequitur quis actione furti*: sive enim manifesti agatur quadrupli, sive nec manifesti dupli, de sola poena agitur: nam ipsam rem propria actione persequitur quis, id est, suam esse petens, sive fur ipse eam rem possideat, sive alius quilibet; eo amplius, adversus furem etiam condictio est rei. § 19. *Vi autem bonorum raptorum* actio mixta est, quia in quadruplum rei persecutio continetur: poena autem tripli est. Sed et legis Aquiliae actio de damno injuriae mixta est, non solum si *adversus infitiantem in duplum agatur*, sed interdum et si in simplum quisque agit: veluti si quis hominem claudum aut luscum occiderit, qui in eo anno integer et magni pretii fuerit: tanti enim damnatur quanti is homo in eo anno plurimi fuerit, secundum jam traditam divisionem. Item mixta est actio contra eos qui relicta sacrosanctis ecclesiis vel aliis venerabilibus locis, legati vel fideicommissi nomine dare distulerint usque adeo, ut etiam in judicium vocarentur: tunc enim et ipsam rem vel pecuniam quae relicta est dare compelluntur, et aliud tantum pro poena, et ideo in duplum ejus fit condemnatio.

§ 20. Quaedam actiones mixtam causam obtinere videntur, tam in rem, quam in personam. Qualis est familiae erciscundae actio, quae competit coheredibus de dividenda hereditate; item communi dividundo, quae inter eos redditur inter quos aliquid commune est, ut id dividatur; item finium regundorum, quae inter eos agitur qui confines agros habent. In quibus tribus judiciis permittitur judici, rem alicui ex litigatoribus ex bono et aequo adjudicare, et si unius pars praegravari videbitur, eum invicem certa pecunia alteri condemnare.

§ 21. Omnes autem actiones vel in simplum conceptae sunt, vel in duplum, vel in triplum, vel in quadruplum; ulterius autem nulla actio extenditur. § 22. In simplum agitur: veluti ex stipulatione, ex mutui datione, ex empto vendito, locato conducto, mandato, et denique ex aliis compluribus causis. § 23. In duplum agimus: veluti furti nec manifesti, damni injuriae ex lege Aquilia, depositi ex quibusdam casibus. Item servi corrupti, quae competit in eum cujus hortatu consiliove servus alienus fugerit, aut contumax adversus dominum factus est, aut luxuriose vivere coeperit, aut denique quolibet modo deterior factus sit: in qua actione etiam earum rerum quas fugiendo servus abstulit aestimatio deducitur. Item ex legato quod venerabilibus locis relictum est, secundum ea quae supra diximus. § 24. Tripli vero, cum quidam majorem verae aestimationis quantitatem in libello conventionis inseruit, ut ex hac causa viatores, id est executores litium, ampliorem summam sportularum nomine exegerint: tunc enim id quod propter eorum causam damnum passus fuerit reus, in triplum ab actore consequetur, ut in hoc triplo et simplum, in quo damnum passus est, connumeretur. Quod nostra constitutio induxit, quae in nostro codice fulget, ex qua dubio procul est ex lege condictitiam emanare. § 25. Quadrupli, veluti furti manifesti, item de eo quod metus causa factum sit, deque ea pecunia quae in hoc data sit, ut is cui datur, calumniae causa negotium alicui faceret vel non faceret. Item ex lege condictitia ex nostra constitutione oritur, in quadruplum condemnationem imponens iis executoribus litium, qui contra constitutionis normam a reis quidquam exegerint. § 26. Sed furti quidem nec manifesti actio, et servi corrupti, a caeteris, de quibus simul locuti sumus, eo differunt, quod hae actiones omnimodo dupli sunt; at illae, id est, damni injuriae ex lege Aquilia, et interdum depositi, infitiatione duplicantur, in confitentem autem in simplum dantur; sed illa quae de iis competit quae relicta venerabilibus locis sunt non solum infitiatione duplicatur, sed etiam si distulerit relicti solutionem usque quo jussu magistratuum nostrorum conveniatur, in confitentem vero, ante quam jussu magistratuum conveniatur solventem, simpli redditur. § 27. Item actio de eo quod metus causa factum sit, a caeteris de quibus simul locuti sumus eo differt, quod ejus natura tacite continetur, ut qui judicis jussu ipsam rem actori restituat, absolvatur; quod in caeteris casibus non ita est, sed omnimodo quisque in quadruplum condemnatur, quod est et in furti manifesti actione.

§ 10. Quaedam praeterea sunt actiones quae ad legis actionem exprimuntur, quaedam sua vi ac potestate constant. Quod ut manifestum fiat, opus est ut prius de legis actionibus loquamur.

§ 11. Actiones quas in usu veteres habuerunt, legis actiones appellabantur, vel ideo quod legibus proditae erant, quia tunc edicta praetoris, quibus complures actiones introductae sunt, nondum in usu habebantur; vel ideo quod ipsarum legum verbis accommodatae erant, et ideo immutabiles perinde atque leges observabantur. Unde eum, qui de vitibus succisis ita egisset, ut in actione vites nominaret, reperimus perdidisse [causam] quia debuisset "arbores" nominare, eo, quod lex XII Tabularum, ex qua de vitibus succisis actio competeret, generaliter de arboribus succisis loqueretur.

§ 12. Lege autem agebatur modis quinque: sacramento, per judicis postulationem, per condictionem, per manus injectionem, per pignoris capionem.

§ 13. Sacramenti actio generalis erat: de quibus enim rebus ut aliter ageretur lege cautum non erat, de his sacramento agebatur. Eaque actio perinde periculosa erat falsi [convictis] atque hoc tempore periculosa est actio certae creditae pecuniae, propter sponsionem, qua periclitatur reus si temere neget, et restipulationem, qua periclitatur actor si non debitum petat: nam qui victus erat, summam sacramenti praestabat poenae nomine; eaque in publicum cedebat, praedesque eo nomine praetori dabantur, non ut nunc sponsionis et restipulationis poena lucro cedit creditori aut debitori, ut qui vicerit. § 14. Poena autem sacramenti aut quingenaria erat, aut quinquagenaria. Nam de rebus mille aeris plurisve quingentis assibus, de minoris vero quinquaginta assibus sacramento contendebatur; nam ita lege XII Tabularum cautum erat. At si de libertate hominis controversia erat, etsi pretiosissimus homo esset, tamen ut quinquaginta assibus sacramento contenderetur, eadem lege cautum est, favore scilicet libertatis ne satisdatione onerarentur adsertatores. § 15. . . . . ad judicem accipiendum venirent. Postea vero reversis dabatur. Ut autem die trigesimo judex daretur per legem Pinariam factum est; ante eam autem legem statim dabatur judex. Illud ex superioribus intellegimus, si de re minoris quam mille aeris agebatur, quinquagenario sacramento, non quingenario eos contendere solitos fuisse. Postea tamen quam judex datus esset, comperendinum diem, ut ad judicem venirent, denuntiabant. Deinde cum ad judicem venerant, antequam apud eum causam perorarent, solebant breviter ei, et quasi per indicem, rem exponere: quae dicebatur causae collectio, quasi causae suae in breve coactio. § 16. Si in rem agebatur, mobilia quidem et moventia, quae modo in jus adferri adducive possent, in jure vindicabantur ad hunc modum. Qui vindicabat festucam tenebat; deinde ipsam rem adprehendebat, veluti hominem, et ita dicebat: "hunc ego hominem ex jure quiritium meum esse aio secundum suam causam sicut dixi: ecce tibi vindictam imposui": et simul homini festucam imponebat. Adversarius eadem similiter dicebat et faciebat. Cum uterque vindicasset, praetor dicebat: "mittite ambo hominem". Illi mittebant. Qui prior vindicaverat, dicebat: "postulo anne dicas qua ex causa vindicaveris". Ille respondebat: "jus feci sicut vindictam imposui". Deinde qui prior vindicaverat, dicebat: "quando tu injuria vindicavisti, quingentis aeris sacramento te provoco". Adversarius quoque dicebat similiter. [Quod si de re minoris quam mille aeris agebatur] quinquaginta asses sacramentum nominabant. Deinde eadem sequebantur quae cum in personam ageretur. Postea praetor secundum alterum eorum vindicias dicebat, id est, interim aliquem possessorem constituebat, eumque jubebat praedes adversario dare litis et vindiciarum, id est, rei et fructuum: alios autem praedes ipse praetor ab utroque accipiebat sacramenti [nomine], quando id in publicum cedebat. Festuca autem utebantur quasi hastae loco, signo quodam justi dominii, quod maxime sua esse credebant quae ex hostibus cepissent: unde in centumviralibus judiciis hasta praeponitur. § 17. Si qua res talis erat, ut sine incommodo non posset in jus adferri vel adduci, velut si columna [aut navis] aut grex alicujus pecoris esset, pars aliqua inde sumebatur; deinde in eam partem, quasi in totam rem praesentem, fiebat vindicatio. Itaque ex grege vel una ovis aut capra in jus adducebatur, vel etiam pilus inde sumebatur et in jus adferebatur; ex nave vero et columna aliqua pars defringebatur. Similiter si de fundo, vel de aedibus, sive de hereditate controversia erat, pars aliqua inde sumebatur et in jus adferebatur, et in eam partem perinde atque in totam rem praesentem fiebat vindicatio: velut ex fundo gleba sumebatur, et ex aedibus tegula, et si de hereditate controversia erat, aeque . . . . . .

§ 18. . . . . . . die XXX ad judicem capiendum praesto esse de[bebant; con]dicere autem denuntiare est prisca lingua. Itaque haec quidem actio proprie condictio vocabatur: nam auctor adversario denuntiabat, ut ad judicem capiendum die XXX adesset. Nunc vero non proprie condictionem dicimus actionem in personam qua intendimus dari nobis oportere; nulla enim hoc tempore eo nomine denuntiatio fit. § 19. Haec autem legis actio constituta est per legem Siliam et Calpurniam: lege quidem Silia certae pecuniae, lege vero Calpurnia de omni certa re. § 20. Qua re autem haec actio desiderata sit, cum de eo, quod nobis dari oportet, potuerimus aut sacramento, aut per judicis postulationem agere, valde quaeritur.

§ 21. Per manus injectionem aeque de his rebus agebatur, de quibus ut ita ageretur, lege aliqua cautum est, velut judicati lege XII Tabularum. Quae actio talis erat. Qui agebat sic dicebat: "quod tu mihi judicatus—sive damnatus—es sestertium X millia, quae dolo malo non solvisti, ob eam rem ego tibi sestertium X millium judicati manus injicio"; et simul aliquam partem corporis ejus prendebat. Nec licebat judicato manum sibi depellere, et pro se lege agere; sed vindicem dabat, qui pro se causam agere solebat: qui vindicem non dabat, domum ducebatur ab actore et vinciebatur. § 22. Postea quaedam leges ex quibusdam causis pro judicato manus injectionem in quosdam dederunt: sicut lex Publilia in eum pro quo sponsor dependisset, si in sex mensibus proximis quam pro eo depensum esset, non solvisset sponsori pecuniam; item lex Furia de sponsu adversus eum qui a sponsore plus quam virilem partem exegisset: denique complures aliae leges in multis causis talem actionem dederunt. § 23. Sed aliae leges ex quibusdam causis constituerunt quasdam actiones per manus injectionem, sed puram, id est, non pro judicato: velut lege Furia testamentaria adversus eum qui legatorum nomine mortisve causa plus mille assibus cepisset, cum ea lege non esset exceptus ut ei plus capere liceret; item lege Marcia adversus foeneratores, ut, si usuras exegissent, de his reddendis per manus injectionem cum eis ageretur. § 24. Ex quibus legibus, et si quae aliae similes essent, cum agebatur, manum sibi depellere et pro se lege agere licebat. Nam et actor in ipsa legis actione non adjiciebat hoc verbum "pro judicato", sed nominata causa ex qua agebat, ita dicebat: "ob eam rem ego tibi manum injicio"; cum hi, quibus pro judicato actio data erat, nominata causa ex qua agebant, ita inferebant: "ob eam rem ego tibi pro judicato manum injicio". Nec me praeterit, in form[ul]a legis Furiae testamentariae "pro judicato" verbum inseri, cum in ipsa lege non sit: quod videtur nulla ratione factum. § 25. Sed postea lege Vallia (?) excepto judicato et eo, pro quo depensum est, caeteris omnibus, cum quibus per manus injectionem agebatur, permissum est sibi manum depellere et pro se agere. Itaque judicatus et is pro quo depensum est, etiam post hanc legem, vindicem dare debebant, et, nisi darent, domum ducebantur; idque, quamdiu legis actiones in usu erant, semper ita observabantur: unde nostris temporibus is cum quo judicati depensive agitur, judicatum solvi satisdare cogitur.

§ 26. Per pignoris capionem lege agebatur de quibusdam rebus moribus [de quibusdam] lege. § 27. Introducta est moribus aeris militaris. Nam propter stipendium licebat militi ab eo qui [id] distribuebat, nisi daret, pignus capere. Dicebatur autem ea pecunia quae stipendii nomine dabatur aes militare. Item propter eam pecuniam licebat pignus capere ex qua equus emendus erat, quae pecunia dicebatur aes equestre. Item propter eam pecuniam ex qua hordeum equis erat comparandum, quae pecunia dicebatur aes hordiarium. § 28. Lege autem introducta est pignoris capio, velut lege XII Tabularum adversus eum qui hostiam emisset, nec pretium redderet; item adversus eum qui mercedem non redderet pro eo jumento quod quis ideo locasset, ut inde pecunia accepta, in dapem, id est, in sacrificium impenderet. Item lege censoria data est pignoris capio publicanis vectigalium publicorum populi Romani adversus eos qui aliqua lege iis vectigalia deberent. § 29. Ex omnibus autem istis causis certis verbis pignus capiebatur; et ob id plerisque placebat hanc quoque actionem legis actionem esse; quibusdam autem [haud] placebat, primum quod pignoris capio extra jus peragebatur, id est, non apud praetorem, plerumque etiam absente adversario, cum alioquin caeteris actionibus non aliter uti possent quam apud praetorem, praesente adversario; praeterea quod nefasto quoque die, id est, quo non licebat lege agere, pignus capi poterat.

§ 30. Sed istae omnes legis actiones paulatim in odium venerunt; namque ex nimia subtilitate veterum, qui tunc jura condiderunt, eo res perducta est, ut qui minimum errasset, litem perderet. Itaque per legem Æbutiam et duas Julias sublatae sunt istae legis actiones; effectumque est ut per concepta verba, id est, per formulas litigaremus. § 31. Tantum ex duabus causis permissum est lege agere: damni infecti, et si centumvirale judicium futurum est. Sane quotienscumque ad centumviros itur, ante lege agitur sacramento apud praetorem urbanum vel peregrinum praetorem, damni vero infecti nemo vult lege agere, sed potius stipulatione, quae in edicto proposita est, obligat adversarium suum, idque et commodius jus et plenius est. Per pignoris . . . . . . apparet. § 32. Contra in ea formula, quae publicano proponitur, talis fictio est, ut, quanta pecunia olim, si pignus captum esset, id pignus is, a quo captum erat, luere deberet, tantam pecuniam condemnetur. § 33. Nulla autem formula ad condictionis fictionem exprimitur, sive enim pecuniam sive rem aliquam certam debitam nobis petamus, eam ipsam "dari nobis oportere" intendimus; neque ullam adjungimus condictionis fictionem. Itaque simul intellegimus, eas formulas quibus pecuniam aut rem aliquam nobis "dare oportere" intendimus, sua vi ac potestate valere. Ejusdem naturae sunt actiones commodati, fiduciae, negotiorum gestorum, et aliae innumerabiles.

§ 34. Habemus adhuc alterius generis fictiones in quibusdam formulis, velut cum is, qui ex edicto bonorum possessionem petit, ficto se herede agit. Cum enim praetorio jure is, non legitimo succedat in locum defuncti, non habet directas actiones, et neque id quod defuncti fuit, potest intendere suum esse ex jure quiritium, neque id quod ei debebatur, potest intendere dari sibi oportere: itaque ficto se herede, intendit, velut hoc modo: "judex esto. Si Aulus Agerius," id est, ipse actor, "Lucio Titio heres esset, tum si paret fundum de quo agitur ex jure quiritium ejus esse oporteret"; vel si in personam agatur, praeposita similiter fictione, illa ita subjicitur: "tum si paret Numerium Negidium Aulo Agerio sestertium X millia dare oportere". § 35. Similiter et bonorum emptor ficto se herede agit. Sed interdum et alio modo agere solet; nam ex persona ejus cujus bona emerit, sumpta intentione, convertit condemnationem in suam personam, id est, ut, quod illius esset, vel illi dare oporteret, eo nomine adversarius huic condemnetur, quae species actionis appellatur Rutiliana, quia a praetore Publio Rutilio, qui etiam bonorum venditionem introduxisse dicitur, comparata est. Superior autem species actionis, qua ficto se herede bonorum emptor agit, Serviana vocatur. § 36. Ejusdem generis est, quae Publiciana vocatur. Datur autem haec actio ei, qui ex justa causa traditam sibi rem nondum usucepit, eamque amissa possessione petit. Nam, quia non potest eam "ex jure quiritium suam esse" intendere, fingitur rem usucepisse, et ita quasi ex jure quiritium dominus factus esset, intendit velut hoc modo: "judex esto. Si quem hominem Aulus Agerius emit, et is ei traditus est, anno possedisset, tum si eum hominem, de quo agitur ejus ex jure quiritium esse oporteret", et reliqua. § 37. Item civitas Romana peregrino fingitur, si eo nomine agat, aut cum eo agatur, quo nomine nostris legibus actio constituta est, si modo justum sit, eam actionem etiam ad peregrinum extendi: velut si furtum faciat peregrinus, et cum eo agatur, formula ita concipitur: "judex esto. Si paret [a Dinone Hermaei filio L. Titio furtum factum esse" aut "si paret ope] consiliove Dinonis Hermaei filii furtum factum esse paterae aureae, quam ob rem eum, si civis romanus esset, pro fure damnum decidere oporteret", et reliqua. Item si peregrinus furti agat, civitas ei Romana fingitur. Similiter si ex lege Aquilia peregrinus damni injuriae agat, aut cum eo agatur, ficta civitate Romana judicium datur. § 38. Praeterea aliquando fingimus adversarium nostrum capite deminutum non esse. Nam si ex contractu nobis obligatus obligatave sit, et capite deminutus deminutave fuerit, velut mulier per coemptionem, masculus per adrogationem, desinit jure civili debere nobis, nec directo intendi potest sibi dare eum eamve oportere; sed, ne in potestate ejus sit jus nostrum corrumpere, introducta est contra eum eamve actio utilis, rescissa capitis deminutione, id est, in qua fingitur capite deminutus deminutave non esse.

§ 39. Partes autem formularum [praecipue] hae sunt: demonstratio, intentio, adjudicatio, condemnatio. § 40. Demonstratio est ea pars formulae quae ideo inseritur, ut demonstretur res de qua agitur, velut haec pars formulae: "Quod Aulus Agerius Numerio Negidio hominem—vendidit"; item haec: "Quod Aulus Agerius apud Numerium Negidium hominem—deposuit". § 41. Intentio est ea pars formulae qua actor desiderium suum concludit, velut haec pars formulae: "Si paret Numerium Negidium Aulo Agerio sestertium X millia dare oportere"; item haec: "Quidquid paret Numerium Negidium Aulo Agerio dare facere oportere;" item haec: "Si paret hominem—ex jure quiritium Auli Agerii esse". § 42. Adjudicatio est ea pars formulae qua permittitur judici rem alicui ex litigatoribus adjudicare: velut si inter coheredes familiae erciscundae agatur, aut inter socios communi dividundo, aut inter vicinos finium regundorum; nam illic ita est: "Quantum adjudicari oportet, judex Titio adjudicato". § 43. Condemnatio est ea pars formulae qua judici condemnandi absolvendive potestas permittitur, velut haec pars formulae: "Judex Numerium Negidium Aulo Agerio sestertium—condemna: si non paret, absolve";

item haec: "Judex Numerium Negidium Aulo Agerio duntaxat x millia condemna : si non paret, absolvito"; item haec: "Judex Numerium Negidium Aulo Agerio x millia condemnato", et reliqua, ut non adjiciatur "duntaxat". § 44. Non tamen istae omnes partes simul [in omnibus formulis] inveniuntur, sed quaedam inveniuntur, quaedam non inveniuntur. Certe intentio aliquando sola invenitur, sicut in praejudicialibus formulis, qualis est qua quaeritur aliquis libertus sit, vel quanta dos sit, et aliae complures. Demonstratio autem et adjudicatio et condemnatio nunquam solae inveniuntur, nihil enim omnino [demonstratio] sine intentione vel condemnatione valet; item condemnatio sine demonstratione vel intentione vel adjudicatio [sine demonstratione et intentione et condemnatio]ne nullas vires habet, et ob id nunquam solae inveniuntur.

§ 45. Sed eas quidem formulas in quibus de jure quaeritur, in jus conceptas vocamus: quales sunt quibus intendimus "nostrum esse" aliquid "ex jure quiritium", vel "nobis dare oportere", aut "pro fure damnum decidere oportere"; in quibus juris civilis intentio est. § 46. Caeteras vero in factum conceptas vocamus, id est, in quibus nulla talis intentio concepta est, sed initio formulae nominato eo quod factum est, adjiciuntur ea verba per quae judici damnandi absolvendive potestas datur: qualis est formula qua utitur patronus contra libertum, qui eum contra edictum praetoris in jus vocavit; nam in ea ita est: "recuperatores sunto. Si paret illum patronum ab illo patroni liberto contra edictum illius praetoris in jus vocatum esse, recuperatores illum libertum illi patrono sestertium x millia condemnate; si non paret, absolvite". Caeterae quoque formulae quae sub titulo, de in jus vocando, propositae sunt, in factum conceptae sunt, velut adversus eum qui in jus vocatus neque venerit, neque vindicem dederit; item contra eum qui vi exemerit eum qui in jus vocaretur; et denique innumerabiles ejusmodi aliae formulae in albo proponuntur. § 47. Sed ex quibusdam causis praetor et in jus et in factum conceptas formulas proponit, veluti depositi et commodati. Illa enim formula quae ita concepta est: "judex esto: quod Aulus Agerius apud Numerium Negidium mensam argenteam deposuit, qua de re agitur, quidquid ob eam rem Numerium Negidium Aulo Agerio dare facere oportet, ex fide bona, ejus idem judex, Numerium Negidium Aulo Agerio condemnato, nisi restituat: si non paret, absolvito", in jus concepta est. At illa formula quae ita concepta est: "judex esto. Si paret Aulum Agerium apud Numerium Negidium mensam argenteam deposuisse, eamque dolo malo Numerii Negidii Aulo Agerio redditam non esse, quanti ea res erit, tanta pecunia judex Numerium Negidium Aulo Agerio condemnato : si non paret, absolvito", in factum concepta est. Similes etiam commodati formulae sunt.

§ 48. Omnium autem formularum quae condemnationem habent, ad pecuniariam aestimationem condemnatio [nunc] concepta est. Itaque etsi corpus aliquod petamus, velut fundum, hominem, vestem, aurum, argentum, judex non ipsa re condemnat eum cum quo actum est, sicut olim fieri solebat, [at] aestimata re pecunia eum condemnat. § 49. Condemnatio autem vel certae pecuniae in formula ponitur, vel incertae. § 50. Certae pecuniae velut in ea formula qua certam pecuniam petimus ; nam illic ima parte formulae ita est : "Judex Numerium Negidium Aulo Agerio sestertium x millia condemna : si non paret, absolve." § 51. Incertae vero pecuniae condemnatio duplicem significationem habet. Est enim una cum aliqua praefinitione, quae vulgo dicitur cum taxatione, velut si incertum aliquid petamus ; nam illic ima parte formulae ita est : "Judex Numerium Negidium Aulo Agerio duntaxat x millia condemna : si non paret, absolve". [Condemnatio] vero incerta est etiam infinita, velut si rem aliquam a possidente nostram esse petamus, id est, si in rem agamus, vel [si agamus] ad exhibendum ; nam illic ita est : "Quanti ea res erit, tanta pecunia judex Numerium Negidium eidem [Aulo Agerio] condemna : si non paret, absolve." § 52. Quid ergo est ? judex si condemnet, certa pecunia condemnare debet, etsi certa pecunia in condemnatione posita non sit. Debet autem judex attendere ut cum certae pecuniae condemnatio posita sit, neque majoris, neque minoris summa posita condemnet : alioquin litem suam facit. Item si taxatio posita sit, ne pluris condemnet quam taxatio posita, alias enim similiter litem suam facit ; minoris autem damnare ei permissum est . . . . .

§ 61. [In bonae fidei judiciis libera potestas permitti videtur judici, ex bono et aequo aestimandi quantum actori restitui debeat : in quo et illud] continetur, ut habita ratione ejus quod invicem actorem ex eadem causa praestare oporteret, in reliquum eum cum quo actum est, condemnare debeat. § 62. Sunt au-

§ 28. Actionum autem quaedam bonae fidei sunt, quaedam stricti juris. *Bonae fidei sunt hae : ex empto vendito, locato conducto, negotiorum gestorum, mandati, depositi, pro socio, tutelae, commodati*, pigneratitia, familiae erciscundae, communi dividundo, praescriptis verbis quae de aestimato proponitur, et ea quae ex permutatione competit, et hereditatis petitio.

tem bonae fidei judicia haec: ex empto vendito, locato conducto, negotiorum gestorum, mandati, depositi, fiduciae, pro socio, tutelae, commodati. § 63. [Datur] libertas tamen judici nullam omnino invicem compensationis rationem habere, neque [enim] in parte formulae verbis praecipitur; sed quia id bonae fidei judicio conveniens videtur, ideo officio ejus contineri creditur. § 64. Alia causa est illius actionis qua argentarius experitur: nam is cogitur cum compensatione agere, et ea compensatio verbis formulae exprimitur, adeo quidem, ut statim, ab initio compensatione facta, minus intendit sibi dare oportere. Ecce enim si sestertium x millia debeat Titio, atque ei xx millia debeantur, sic intendit: "si paret Titium sibi x millia dare oportere amplius quam ipse Titio debet."

Quamvis enim usque adhuc incertum erat, sive inter bonae fidei judicia connumeranda sit hereditatis petitio, sive non, nostra tamen constitutio aperte eam esse bonae fidei disposuit. § 29. Fuerat antea et rei uxoriae actio una ex bonae fidei judiciis: sed cum pleniorem esse ex stipulatu actionem invenientes, omne jus quod res uxoria ante habebat, cum multis divisionibus in actionem ex stipulatu quae de dotibus exigendis proponitur, transtulimus: merito, rei uxoriae actione sublata, ex stipulatu quae pro ea introducta est, naturam bonae fidei judicii tantum in exactione dotis meruit, ut bonae fidei sit. Sed et tacitam ei dedimus hypothecam: praeferri autem aliis creditoribus in hypothecis tunc censuimus, cum ipsa mulier [de dote sua experiatur, cujus solius providentia hoc induximus. § 30. *In bonae fidei autem judiciis libera potestas permitti videtur judici ex bono et aequo aestimandi, quantum actori restitui debeat. In quo et illud continetur ut, si quid invicem actorem praestare oporteat, eo compensato, in reliquum is cum quo actum est condemnari debeat.* Sed et in strictis judiciis ex rescripto divi Marci, opposita, doli mali exceptione, compensatio inducebatur. Sed nostra constitutio eas compensationes, quae jure aperto nituntur, latius introduxit, ut actiones ipso jure minuant, sive in rem, sive in personam, sive alias quascumque, excepta sola depositi actione, cui aliquid compensationis nomine opponi satis impium esse credidimus, ne sub praetextu compensationis depositarum rerum quis exactione defraudetur.

§ 65. Item de[fraudatoris utique nomine] bonorum emptor cum deductione agere jubetur, id est, ut in hoc solum adversarius ejus condemnetur, quod superest, deducto eo, quod invicem ei bonorum emptor defraudatoris nomine debet. § 66. Inter compensationem autem, quae argentario opponitur, et deductionem, quae objicitur bonorum emptori, illa differentia est, quod in compensationem hoc solum vocatur, quod ejusdem generis et naturae est, veluti ut pecunia cum pecunia compensatur, triticum cum tritico, vinum cum vino: adeo ut quibusdam placeat, non omnimodo vinum cum vino, aut triticum cum tritico compensandum, sed ita si ejusdem naturae qualitatisque sit; in deductionem autem vocatur et quod non est ejusdem generis; itaque si a Titio pecuniam petat bonorum emptor, et invicem frumentum aut vinum Titio debeat, deducto [a bonorum emptore] quanti id erit, in reliquum experitur. § 67. Item vocatur in deductionem et id, quod in diem debetur: compensatur autem hoc solum quod praesenti die debetur. § 68. Praeterea compensationis quidem ratio in intentione ponitur; quo fit ut, si facta compensatione plus nummo uno intendat argentarius, causa cadat et ob id rem perdat: deductio vero ad condemnationem ponitur, quo loco plus petenti periculum non intervenit; utique bonorum emptore agente, qui, licet de certa pecunia agat, incertam tamen condemnationem concipit.

§ 31. Praeterea, quasdam actiones arbitrarias, id est, ex arbitrio judicis pendentes, appellamus, in quibus, nisi arbitrio judicis is cum quo agitur actori satisfaciat, veluti rem restituat, vel exhibeat, vel solvat, vel ex noxali causa servum dedat, condemnari debeat. Sed istae actiones tam in rem quam in personam inveniuntur: in rem, veluti Publiciana, Serviana de rebus coloni, quasi Serviana quae etiam hypothecaria vocatur; in personam, veluti quibus de eo agitur quod aut metus causa aut dolo malo factum est, item cum id quod certo loco promissum est petitur. Ad exhibendum quoque actio ex arbitrio judicis pendet. In his enim actionibus et caeteris similibus permittitur judici ex bono et aequo, secundum cujusque rei de qua actum est naturam, aestimare quemadmodum actori satisfieri oporteat.

§ 32. Curare autem debet judex, ut omnimodo, quantum possibile ei sit, certae pecuniae vel rei sententiam ferat, etiamsi de incerta quantitate apud eum actum est.

§ 53. Si quis intentione plus complexus fuerit, causa cadit, id est, rem perdit; nec a praetore in integrum restituitur, exceptis quibusdam casibus in quibus non patitur . . . . . [Plus autem quattuor] modis petitur: re, tempore, loco, causa. Re velut [si quis pro decem] millibus quae ei debentur, viginti millia petierit, aut si cujus ex parte res est, totam eam aut majore ex parte suam esse intenderit; [tempore, veluti si quis ante diem vel ante conditionem

§ 33. *Si quis* agens, *in intentione* sua *plus complexus fuerit* quam ad eum pertineret, *causa* cadebat, *id est*, *rem* amittebat, *nec* facile *in integrum a praetore* restituebatur, nisi minor erat vigintiquinque annis, huic enim, sicut in aliis causis causa cognita succurrebatur, si lapsus juventute fuerat, ita et in hac causa succurri solitum erat. Sane, si tam magna causa justi erroris interveniebat, ut etiam constantissimus quisque labi posset, etiam majori vigintiquinque

impletam petierit, loco, velut si quis quod certo loco] dari promissum est, id [alio loco sine commemoratione] ejus loci petat, velut si [is, qui stipulatus fuerit: "Ephesi] dare spondes"? domi Romae [pure intenderit: si paret dare mihi oportere, vel etiam si Romae intenderit: si paret Ephesi] dare mihi oportere, plus enim petere intelligitur [quia utilitas solvendi utroque modo promissori adimitur; utique tamen qui stipulatus fuerit: "Ephesi dare spondes?" Ephesi] recte potest pure, petere id est vel non adjecto loco.

§ 53A. Causa plus petitur, velut si quis in intentione tollat electionem debitoris, quam is habet obligationis jure; velut si quis ita stipulatus sit: "Sestertium x millia aut hominem Stichum dare spondes?" deinde alterutrum [merum] ex his petat; nam quamvis petat quod minus est, plus tamen petere videtur, quia potest adversarius interdum facilius id praestare quod non petitur. Similiter si quis genus stipulatus sit, deinde speciem petat; velut si quis purpuram stipulatus sit generaliter, deinde tyriam specialiter petat, quin etiam licet vilissimam petat, idem juris est, propter eam rationem, quam proxime diximus. Idem juris est, si quis generaliter hominem stipulatus sit, deinde nominatim aliquem petat, velut Stichum, quamvis vilissimum. Itaque sicut ipsa stipulatio concepta est, ita et intentio formulae concipi debet.

annis succurrebatur: veluti, si quis totum legatum petierit, post deinde prolati fuerint codicilli quibus aut pars legati adempta sit, aut quibusdam aliis legata data sint, quae efficiebant, ut plus petiisse videretur petitor quam dodrantem, atque ideo lege Falcidia legata minuebantur.

Plus autem quattuor modis petitur: re, tempore, loco, causa. Re: veluti si quis, pro decem aureis *qui ei debebantur, viginti petierit, aut si is cujus ex parte res est, totam eam, vel majore ex parte, suam esse intenderit. Tempore: veluti si quis ante diem vel ante conditionem petierit;* qua ratione enim qui tardius solvit quam solvere deberet, minus solvere intelligitur, eadem ratione qui praemature petit, plus petere videtur. *Loco plus petitur; veluti cum quis id quod certo loco sibi stipulatus est, alio loco petit sine commemoratione illius loci* in quo sibi dari stipulatus fuerit; *verbi gratia, si is qui ita stipulatus fuerit: "Ephesi dare spondes?" Romae pure intendat dari sibi oportere.* Ideo *autem plus petere intelligitur,* quia *utilitatem quam habuit promissor si Ephesi solveret, adimit ei pura intentione;* propter quam causam alio loco petenti arbitraria actio proponitur, in qua scilicet ratio habetur utilitatis quae promissori competitura fuisset, si illo loco solveret. Quae utilitas plerumque in mercibus maxima invenitur, veluti vino, oleo, frumento, quae per singulas regiones diversa habent pretia: sed et pecuniae numeratae non in omnibus regionibus sub iisdem usuris foenerantur. *Si quis tamen Ephesi petat, id est eo loco petat quo ut sibi detur stipulatus est, pura actione recte agit:* idque etiam praetor monstrat, scilicet quia utilitas solvendi salva est promissori. Huic autem qui loco plus petere intelligitur, proximus est is qui *causa plus petit: ut ecce, si quis ita a te stipulatus sit: "Hominem Stichum aut decem* aureos *dare spondes?"*

deinde alterutrum petat, veluti hominem tantum, aut decem aureos *tantum.* Ideo autem plus petere intelligitur, quia in eo genere stipulationis promissoris est electio, utrum pecuniam an hominem solvere malit: qui igitur pecuniam tantum, vel hominem tantum sibi dari oportere intendit, eripit electionem adversario, et eo modo suam quidem conditionem meliorem facit, adversarii vero sui deteriorem. Qua de causa, talis in ea re prodita est actio, ut quis intendat hominem Stichum aut aureos decem sibi dari oportere, id est, ut eodem modo peteret quo sibi stipulatus est. Praeterea, *si quis generaliter hominem stipulatus sit;* et specialiter *Stichum petat,* aut generaliter vinum stipulatus, specialiter campanum petat, aut *generaliter purpuram* stipulatus sit, *deinde specialiter tyriam petat,* plus petere intelligitur; quia electionem adversario tollit, cui stipulationis jure liberum fuit aliud solvere quam quod peteretur. Quin etiam, licet *vilissimum* sit quod quis petat, nihilominus plus petere intelligitur; quia saepe accidit ut promissori *facilius* sit illud solvere *quod* majoris pretii est. Sed haec quidem antea in usu fuerant; postea autem lex Zenoniana et nostra rem coercuit. Et si quidem tempore plus fuerit petitum, quid statui oportet, Zenonis divae memoriae loquitur constitutio; sin autem quantitate vel alio modo plus fuerit petitum, omne si quod forte damnum ut in sportulis, ex hac causa acciderit, ei contra quem plus petitum fuerit, commissa tripli condemnatione, sicut supra diximus, puniatur.

§ 54. Illud satis apparet, in incertis formulis plus peti non posse, quia, cum certa quantitas non petatur, sed "quidquid adversarium dare facere oportere" intendatur, nemo potest plus intendere. Idem juris est, et si in rem incertae partis actio data sit; velut talis "quantam partem paret in eo fundo, quo de agitur actoris esse": quod genus actionis in paucissimis causis dari solet.

§ 55. Item palam est, si quis aliud pro alio intenderit, nihil eum periclitari, eumque ex integro agere posse, quia nihil ante videtur egisse, velut si is qui hominem Stichum petere deberet, Erotem petierit; aut si quis ex testamento dari sibi oportere intenderit, cui ex stipulatu debebatur; aut si cognitor aut procurator intenderit "sibi" dari oportere. § 56. Sed plus quidem intendere, sicut supra diximus, periculosum est: minus autem intendere licet; sed de reliquo intra ejusdem praeturam agere non permittitur; nam qui ita agit, per exceptionem excluditur, quae exceptio appellatur litis dividuae. § 57.

§ 34. Si minus in intentione complexus fuerit actor quam ad eum pertineret, veluti si, cum ei decem deberentur, quinque sibi dari oportere intenderit, aut si, cum totus fundus ejus esset,

At si in condemnatione plus positum sit quam oportet, actoris periculum nullum est, sed [reus] quia iniquam formulam acceperit, in integrum restituitur, ut minuatur condemnatio. Sin vero minus positum fuerit quam oportet, hoc solum consequitur actor quod posuit: nam tota quidem res in judicium deducitur, constringitur autem condemnationis fine, quem judex egredi non potest. Nec ex ea parte praetor in integrum restituit: facilius enim reis praetor succurrit quam actoribus. Loquimur autem exceptis minoribus xxv annorum; nam hujus aetatis hominibus in omnibus rebus lapsis praetor succurrit. § 58. Si in demonstratione plus aut minus positum sit, nihil in judicium deducitur, et ideo res in integro manet: et hoc est quod dicitur, falsa demonstratione rem non perimi. § 59. Sed sunt qui putent minus recte comprehendi, ut qui forte Stichum et Erotem emerit, recte videatur ita demonstrare: "Quod ego de te hominem Erotem emi", et si velit, de Sticho alia formula idem agat, quia verum est eum qui duos emerit, singulos quoque emisse. Sed si is qui unum emerit, de duobus egerit, falsum demonstrat. Idem et in aliis actionibus est, velut commodati et depositi, idque ita maxime Labeoni visum esse . . . . auctor est. § 60. Sed nos apud quosdam scriptum invenimus, in actione depositi, et denique in caeteris omnibus, ex quibus damnatus unusquisque ignominia notatur, eum, qui plus quam oporteret demonstraverit, litem perdere: velut si quis, una re deposita, duas pluresve deposuisse demonstraverit; aut si is, cui pugno mala percussa est, in actione injuriarum etiam aliam partem corporis percussam sibi demonstraverit. Quod an debeamus credere varius esse diligentius requiremus. Certe cum duae sint depositi formulae, alia in jus concepta, alia in factum, sicut supra quoque notavimus, et in ea quidem formula quae in jus concepta est, initio res de qua agitur demonstratorio modo designetur, deinde inferatur juris intentio his verbis: "quidquid ob eam rem illum mihi dare facere oportet"; in ea vero quae in factum concepta est, statim initio intentionis alio modo res de qua agitur designetur his verbis: "si paret illum apud illum rem illam deposuisse", dubitare non debemus, quin, si quis, in formula quae in factum composita est, plures res designaverit quam deposuerit, litem perdat, quia in intentione plus posuisse videtur . . . . .

partem dimidiam suam esse petierit, sine periculo agit: in reliquum enim nihilominus judex adversarium in eodem judicio ei condemnat, ex constitutione divae memoriae Zenonis. § 35. *Si quis aliud pro alio intenderit, nihil eum periclitari* placet, sed in eodem judicio, cognita veritate, errorem suum corrigere ei permittimus, *veluti si is qui hominem Stichum petere deberet, Erotem petierit, aut si quis ex testamento sibi dari oportere intenderit, quod ex stipulatu debetur.*

§ 36. Sunt praeterea quaedam actiones quibus non solidum quod debetur nobis persequimur, sed modo solidum consequimur, modo minus: ut ecce, si in peculium filii servive agamus. Nam si non minus in peculio sit quam persequimur, in solidum pater dominusve condemnatur: si vero minus inveniatur, eatenus condemnat judex quatenus in peculio sit. Quemadmodum autem peculium intelligi debeat, suo ordine proponemus. § 37. Item, si de dote judicio mulier agat, placet eatenus maritum condemnari debere quatenus facere possit, id est, quatenus facultates ejus patiuntur. Itaque, si dotis quantitati concurrant facultates ejus, in solidum damnatur; si minus, in tantum quantum facere potest. Propter retentionem quoque dotis repetitio minuitur; nam ob impensas in res dotales factas marito retentio concessa est, quia ipso jure necessariis sumptibus dos minuitur, sicut ex latioribus Digestorum libris cognoscere liceat. § 38. Sed et si quis cum parente suo patronove agat, item si socius cum socio judicio societatis agat, non plus actor consequitur quam adversarius ejus facere potest. Idem est, si quis ex donatione sua conveniatur. § 39. *Compensationes quoque oppositae plerumque efficiunt, ut minus quisque consequatur, quam ei debebatur: namque ex bono et aequo, habita ratione ejus, quod invicem actorem ex eadem causa praestare oporteret, judex in reliquum eum cum quo actum est condemnat,* sicut jam dictum est. § 40. Eum quoque qui creditoribus suis bonis cessit, si postea aliquid adquisierit quod idoneum emolumentum habeat, ex integro in id quod facere potest creditores cum eo experiuntur: inhumanum enim erat spoliatum fortunis suis in solidum damnari.

Tit. vii. Quod cum eo qui in aliena potestate est negotium gestum esse dicitur.

§ 69. Quia tamen superius mentionem habuimus de actione, qua in peculium filiorumfamilias servorumque agatur, opus est ut de hac actione et de caeteris, quae eorumdem nomine in parentes dominosve dari solent, diligentius admoneamus.

Quia tamen superius mentionem habuimus de actione, qua in peculium filiorumfamilias servorumve agitur, opus est, ut de hac actione et de caeteris, quae eorundem nomine in parentes dominosve dari solent, diligentius admoneamus. Et quia, sive cum servis negotium gestum sit, sive cum iis qui in potestate parentis sunt, his fere eadem jura servantur, ne verbosa fiat disputatio, dirigamus sermonem in personam servi dominique, idem intellecturi de liberis quoque et parentibus quorum in potestate sunt. Nam si quid in his proprie observatur, separatim ostendemus.

§ 70. In primis itaque si jussu patris dominive negotium gestum erit, in solidum praetor actionem in patrem dominumve comparavit, et recte; quia, qui ita negotium gerit, magis patris dominive, quam filii servive fidem sequitur. § 71. Eadem ratione comparavit duas alias actiones, exercitoriam et institoriam. Tunc autem exercitoria locum habet, cum pater dominusve filium servumve magistrum navis praeposuerit, et quid cum eo, ejus rei gratia cui praepositus fuit, negotium gestum erit. Cum enim ea quoque res ex voluntate patris dominive contrahi videatur, aequissimum esse visum est, in solidum actionem dari. Quin etiam, licet extraneum quis quemvis magistrum navis praeposuerit, sive servum, sive liberum, tamen ea praetoria actio in eum redditur. Ideo autem exercitoria actio appellatur, quia exercitor vocatur is, ad quem quotidianus navis quaestus pervenit. Institoria vero formula tum locum habet, cum quis tabernae aut cuilibet negotiationi filium servumve aut quemlibet extraneum, sive servum, sive liberum, praeposuerit, et quid cum eo, ejus rei gratia cui praepositus est, contractum fuerit. Ideo autem institoria vocatur, quia qui tabernae praeponitur, institor appellatur. Quae et ipsa formula in solidum est.

§ 1. *Si igitur jussu domini* cum servo *negotium gestum erit, in solidum praetor* adversus *dominum actionem* pollicetur, scilicet *quia qui ita* contrahit *fidem domini sequi* videtur. § 2. *Eadem ratione praetor duas alias in solidum actiones pollicetur, quarum altera exercitoria, altera institoria appellatur. Exercitoria tunc locum habet, cum quis servum suum magistrum navis praeposuerit, et quid cum eo ejus rei gratia cui praepositus erit* contractum *fuerit. Ideo autem exercitoria vocatur, quia exercitor appellatur is ad quem quotidianus navis quaestus* pertinet. *Institoria tunc locum habet, cum quis tabernae forte aut cuilibet negotiationi servum praeposuerit, et quid cum eo ejus rei causa cui praepositus erit contractum fuerit. Ideo autem institoria appellatur, quia qui negotiationibus praeponuntur institores vocantur.* Istas tamen duas *actiones praetor reddit, etsi liberum quis* hominem aut alienum *servum navi* aut tabernae aut cuilibet negotiationi *praeposuerit:* scilicet, quia eadem aequitatis ratio etiam eo casu interveniebat.

§ 72. Praeterea tributoria quoque actio in patrem dominumve constituta est, cum filius servusve in peculiari aliquo pretio merceve sciente patre dominove negotiatur. Nam si quid eo ejus rei gratia cum eo contractum fuerit, ita praetor jus dicit, ut quidquid in his mercibus [erit, quodque inde receptum erit, id inter patrem dominumve, si quid ei debebitur, et caeteros creditores pro rata portione distri-

§ 3. Introduxit et aliam actionem praetor, quae *tributoria vocatur.* Namque si servus *in peculiari merce sciente domino negotietur, et quid cum eo ejus rei causa contractum erit, ita praetor jus dicit ut, quidquid in his mercibus erit, quodque inde receptum erit, id inter dominum, si quid ei debebitur, et caeteros creditores pro rata portione distribuatur; et quia ipsi domino distributionem permittit, si quis ex credi-*

buatur; et quia ipsi patri dominove distributionem permittit, si quis ex creditoribus queratur, quasi minus ei tributum sit quam oportuerit, hanc ei actionem accommodat, quae tributoria appellatur.

toribus queratur, quasi minus ei tributum sit quam oportuerit, hanc ei actionem accommodat, quae tributoria appellatur.

§ 73. Praeterea introducta est actio de peculio, deque eo quod in rem patris dominive versum erit, ut, quamvis sine voluntate patris dominive negotium gestum erit, tamen, sive quid in rem ejus versum fuerit, id totum praestare debeat, sive quid non sit in rem ejus versum, id eatenus praestare debeat quatenus peculium patitur. In rem autem patris dominive versum intelligitur, quidquid necessario in rem ejus impenderit filius servusve: veluti si mutuatus pecuniam creditoribus ejus solverit, aut aedificio ruentia fulserit, aut familiae frumentum emerit, vel etiam fundum aut quamlibet aliam rem necessariam mercatus erit. Itaque, si ex decem, ut puta, sestertiis quae servus tuus a Titio mutua accepit, creditori tuo quinque sestertia solverit, reliqua vero quinque quolibet modo consumpserit, pro quinque quidem in solidum damnari debes, pro caeteris vero quinque eatenus, quatenus in peculio sit. Ex quo scilicet apparet, si tota decem sestertia in rem tuam versa fuerint, tota decem sestertia Titium consequi posse. Licet enim una est actio qua de peculio, deque eo quod in rem patris dominive versum sit, agitur, tamen duas habet condemnationes. Itaque judex, apud quem ea actione agitur, ante dispicere solet, an in rem patris dominive versum sit; nec aliter ad peculii aestimationem transit, quam si aut nihil in rem patris dominive versum esse intelligatur, aut non totum. Cum autem quaeritur, quantum in peculio sit, ante de]ducitur quod patri dominove, quique in potestate

§ 4. *Praeterea introducta est actio de peculio, deque eo, quod in rem domini versum erit: ut quamvis sine voluntate domini negotium gestum erit, tamen sive quid in rem ejus versum fuerit, id totum praestare debeat, sive quid non sit in rem ejus versum, id eatenus praestare debeat quatenus peculiam patitur. In rem autem domini versum intellegitur quidquid necessario in rem ejus impenderit servus; veluti si mutuatus pecuniam creditoribus ejus solverit, aut aedificia ruentia fulserit, aut familiae frumentum emerit, vel etiam fundum aut quamlibet aliam rem necessariam mercatus erit. Itaque, si ex decem, ut puta,* aureis *quos servus tuus a Titio mutuos accepit, creditori tuo quinque* aureos *solverit, reliquos vero quinque quolibet modo consumpserit, pro quinque quidem in solidum damnari debes; pro caeteris vero quinque, eatenus, quatenus in peculio sit. Ex quo scilicet apparet, si toti decem* aurei *in rem tuam versi fuerint, totos decem* aureos *Titium consequi posse. Licet enim una est actio qua de peculio, deque eo quod in rem domini versum sit agitur, tamen duas habet condemnationes. Itaque judex, apud quem de ea actione agitur, ante dispicere solet, an in rem domini versum sit, nec aliter ad peculii aestimationem transit, quam si aut nihil in rem domini versum intellegatur, aut non totum. Cum autem quaeritur, quantum in peculio sit, ante deducitur quidquid servus domino, quive in potestate ejus sit, debet; et quod superest, id solum peculium intellegitur. Aliquando tamen id, quod ei debet*

ejus sit, a filio servove debetur, et quod superest, hoc solum peculium esse intellegitur. Aliquando tamen id quod ei debet filius servusve qui in potestate patris dominive sit, non deducitur ex peculio, velut si is cui debet, in hujus ipsius peculio sit.

§ 74. Caeterum dubium non est, quin et is, qui jussu patris dominive contraxit, cuique exercitoria vel institoria, formula competit, de peculio aut de in rem verso agere possit; sed nemo tam stultus erit, ut qui aliqua illarum actionum sine dubio solidum consequi possit, vel in difficultatem se deducat probandi habere peculium eum, cum quo contraxerit exque eo peculio posse sibi satis fieri, vel id quod persequitur in rem patris dominive versum esse. Is quoque cui tributoria actio competit, de peculio vel de in rem verso agere potest, sed huic sane plerumque expedit hac potius actione uti quam tributoria; nam in tributoria ejus solius peculii ratio habetur, quod in his mercibus est, in quibus negotiatur filius servusve, quodque inde receptum erit: at in actione peculii, totius;—et potest quisque tertia forte, aut quarta, vel etiam minore parte peculii negotiari, maximam vero partem peculii in aliis rebus habere;—longe magis, si potest approbari id quod contraxit in rem patris dominive versum esse, ad hanc actionem transire debet; nam, ut supra diximus, eadem formula et de peculio et de in rem verso agitur.

servus qui in potestate domini sit, non deducitur ex peculio: veluti si is in hujus ipsius peculio sit quod eo pertinet, ut, si quid vicario suo servus debeat, id ex peculio ejus non deducatur.

§ 5. *Caeterum dubium non est, quin is quoque, qui jussi domini contraxerit, cuique institoria, vel exercitoria actio competit, de peculio deque eo quod in rem* domini *versum est, agere possit; sed erit stultissimus,* si omissa *actione,* qua facillime *solidum* ex contractu *consequi possit, se ad difficultatem perducat probandi in rem domini versum esse, vel habere servum peculium, et tantum habere ut solidum sibi solvi possit. Is quoque, cui tributoria actio competit, aeque de peculio et in rem verso agere potest, sed sane* huic modo tributoria expedit agere, modo de peculio et de in rem verso. Tributoria ideo expedit agere, quia in ea domini conditio praecipua non est, id est, quod domino debetur non deducitur, sed ejusdem juris est dominus cujus et caeteri creditores: *at in actione de peculio,* ante deducitur quod domino debetur, et in id quod reliquum est, creditori dominus condemnatur. Rursus de peculio ideo expedit agere, quod in hac actione *totius peculii ratio habetur, at in tributoria* ejus tantum *quod negotiatur, et potest quisque tertia forte parte peculii aut quarta, vel etiam minima negotiari, majorem autem partem in praediis* et mancipiis aut foenebri pecunia habere. Prout ergo expedit, ita quisque vel hanc actionem vel illam eligere debet: certe, qui potest probare in rem domini versum esse, de in rem verso agere debet.

§ 6. Quae diximus de servo et domino, eadem intelligimus et de filio et filia aut nepote et nepte, et patre avove in cujus potestate sunt. § 7. Illud proprie servatur in eorum persona, quod senatus-consultum Macedonianum prohibuit mutuas pecunias dari eis qui in parentis erunt potestate; et ei qui crediderit denegatur actio, tam adversus ipsum filium filiamve, nepotem neptemve (sive adhuc in potestate sint, sive morte parentis, vel emancipatione suae potestatis esse coeperint), quam adversus patrem avumve, sive habeat eos adhuc in potestate, sive emancipaverit. Quae ideo senatus prospexit, quia saepe onerati aere alieno creditarum pecuniarum quas in luxuriam consumebant, vitae parentum insidiabantur.—§ 8. Illud in summa admonendi sumus, id quod jussu patris dominive contractum fuerit, quodque in rem ejus versum erit, directo quoque posse a patre dominove condici, tamquam si principaliter cum ipso negotium gestum esset. Ei quoque qui vel exercitoria vel institoria actione tenetur, directo posse condici placet, quia hujus quoque jussu contractum intellegitur.

Tit. viii. De noxalibus actionibus.

§ 75. Ex maleficiis filiorumfamilias servorumve, veluti si furtum fecerint, aut injuriam commiserint, noxales actiones proditae sunt, uti liceret patri dominove aut litis aestimationem sufferre, aut noxae dedere: erat enim iniquum, nequitiam eorum ultra ipsorum corpora parentibus dominisve damnosam esse.

Ex maleficiis servorum, veluti si furtum fecerint, aut bona rapuerint, aut damnum dederint, aut *injuriam commiserint, noxales actiones proditae sunt, quibus domino* damnato *permittitur, aut litis aestimationem sufferre, aut hominem noxae dedere.* § 1. Noxa autem est corpus quod nocuit, id est, servus; noxia ipsum maleficium, veluti furtum, damnum, rapina, injuria. § 2. Summa autem ratione permissum est noxae deditione defungi; *namque erat iniquum nequitiam eorum ultra ipsorum corpora dominis damnosam esse.* § 3. Dominus noxali judicio servi sui nomine conventus, servum actori noxae dedendo liberatur; nec minus perpetuum ejus dominium a domino transfertur: si autem damnum ei cui deditus est servus resarcierit quaesita pecunia, auxilio praetoris invito domino manumittetur.

§ 76. Constitutae sunt autem noxales actiones aut legibus, aut edicto pretoris: legibus, velut furti lege XII Tabularum, damni injuriae velut lege Aquilia; edicto praetoris, velut injuriarum et vi bonorum raptorum. § 77. Omnes autem noxales actiones capita sequuntur: nam si filius tuus servusve noxam commiserit, quamdiu in tua potes-

§ 4. *Sunt autem constitutae noxales actiones aut legibus aut edicto praetoris: legibus, veluti furti lege Duodecim Tabularum, damni injuriae lege Aquilia; edicto praetoris, veluti injuriarum et vi bonorum raptorum.* § 5. *Omnis autem noxalis actio caput sequitur. Nam si servus tuus noxiam commiserit, quamdiu*

tate est, tecum est actio; si in alterius potestatem pervenerit, cum illo incipit actio esse; si sui juris coeperit esse, directa actio cum ipso est, et noxae deditio extinguitur. Ex diverso quoque directa actio noxalis esse incipit; nam si paterfamilias noxam commiserit, et is se in adrogationem tibi dederit, aut servus tuus esse coeperit, (quod quibusdam casibus accidere primo commentario tradidimus), incipit tecum noxalis actio esse, quae ante directa fuit. § 78. Sed si filius patri, aut servus domino noxam commiserit, nulla actio nascitur, nulla enim omnino inter me et eum qui in potestate mea est obligatio nascitur. Ideoque, etsi in alienam potestatem pervenerit, aut sui juris esse coeperit, neque cum ipso, neque cum eo, cujus nunc in potestate est, agi potest. Unde quaeritur, si alienus servus filiusve noxam commiserit mihi, et is postea in mea esse coeperit potestate, utrum intercidat actio, an quiescat. Nostri praeceptores intercidere putant, quia in eum casum deducta sit, in quo [omnino] consistere non potuerit; ideoque, licet exierit e mea potestate, agere me non posse. Diversae scholae auctores, quamdiu in mea potestate sit, quiescere actionem putant, [quando]que ipse mecum agere non possum, cum, vero exierit e mea potestate, tunc eam resuscitari. § 79. Cum autem filius familias ex noxali causa mancipio datur, diversae scholae auctores putant ter eum mancipio dari debere, quia lege XII Tabularum cautum sit, [ne aliter filius e potestate patris] exeat, quam si ter fuerit mancipatus, Sabinus et Cassius caeterique nostrae scholae auctores, sufficere unam mancipationem crediderunt et illas tres legis XII Tabularum ad voluntarias mancipationes pertinere.

§ 80. Haec ita de his personis quae in potestate sunt, sive ex contractu, sive ex maleficio earum instituta actio est, quod vero ad eas personas quae in manu mancipiove sunt, ita jus dicitur, ut, cum [judicio legitimo e contrac]tu earum ageretur, nisi ab eo cujus

in tua potestate est, tecum est actio: si in alterius potestatem pervenerit, cum illo incipit actio esse, at si manumissus fuerit, directo ipse tenetur, et extinguitur noxae deditio. Ex diverso quoque directa actio noxalis esse incipit: nam si liber homo *noxiam commiserit, et is servus tuus esse coeperit, (quod quibusdam casibus effici primo* libro *tradidimus); incipit tecum esse noxalis actio, quae ante directa fuisset.* § 6. *Si servus domino noxiam commiserit, nulla actio nascitur: namque inter dominum et eum qui in ejus potestate est nulla obligatio nasci potest; ideoque, etsi in alienam potestatem servus pervenerit, aut manumissus fuerit, neque cum ipso, neque cum eo cujus nunc in potestate sit, agi potest. Unde, si alienus servus noxiam tibi commiserit, et is postea in potestate tua esse coeperit, intercidit actio, quia in eum casum deducta sit, in quo consistere non potuit; ideoque licet exierit de tua potestate, agere non potes,* quemadmodum si dominus in servum suum aliquid commiserit, nec si manumissus vel alienatus fuerit servus, ullam actionem contra dominum habere potest.

juri subjectae sunt in solidum defendantur, bona, quae earum futura forent, si ei juri subjectae non essent, veneunt, rescissa capitis deminutione, sed cum imperio continenti judicio. . . . § 81. . . . . ergo est? etiam sic, de qua re modo diximus, quamquam non permissum fuerit ei, mortuos homines dedere, tamen et si quis eum dederit, qui fato suo vita decesserit, aeque liberatur.

§ 7. Sed veteres quidem haec et in filiisfamilias masculis et feminis admiserunt. Nova autem hominum conversatio hujusmodi asperitatem recte respuendam esse existimavit, et ab usu communi haec penitus recessit. Quis enim patiatur filium suum et maxime filiam in noxam alii dare, ut pene per corpus pater magis quam filius periclitetur, cum in filiabus etiam pudicitiae favor hoc bene excludit? Et ideo placuit in servos tantummodo noxales actiones esse proponendas, cum apud veteres legum commentatores invenimus saepius dictum, ipsos filiosfamilias pro suis delictis posse conveniri.

Tit. ix. Si quadrupes pauperiem fecisse dicatur.

Animalium nomine quae ratione carent, si quidem lascivia aut fervore aut feritate pauperiem fecerint, noxalis actio lege Duodecim Tabularum prodita est. Quae animalia, si noxae dedantur, proficiunt reo ad liberationem, quia ita lex Duodecim Tabularum scripta est: ut puta, si equus calcitrosus calce percusserit, aut bos cornu petere solitus petierit. Haec autem actio in iis quae contra naturam moventur locum habet; caeterum si genitalis sit feritas, cessat. Denique si ursus fugit a domino, et sic nocuit, non potest quondam dominus conveniri, quia desinit dominus esse, ubi fera evasit. Pauperies autem est damnum sine injuria facientis datum; nec enim potest animal injuriam fecisse dici, quod sensu caret. Haec quod ad noxalem actionem pertinet.

§ 1. Caeterum sciendum est aedilitio edicto prohiberi nos canem, verrem, aprum, ursum, leonem, ibi habere qua vulgo iter fit; et si adversus ea factum erit, et nocitum homini libero esse dicetur, quod bonum et aequum judici videtur, tanti dominus condemnetur, caeterarum rerum, quanti damnum datum sit, dupli. Praeter has autem aedilitias actiones, et de pauperie locum habebit. Nunquam enim actiones, praesertim poenales, de eadem re concurrentes, alia aliam consumit.

§ 82. Nunc admonendi sumus, agere nos aut nostro nomine, aut alieno: alieno, veluti cognitorio, procuratorio, tutorio, curatorio; cum olim alieno nomine agere non liceret proprie, quam ex certis causis. § 83. Cognitor autem certis verbis in litem coram adversario substituitur. Nam actor sic cognitorem dat: "quod ego a te", verbi gratia, "fundum peto, in eam rem Lucium Titium tibi cognitorem do"; adversarius ita: "quia tu a me fundum petis, in eam rem tibi Publium Maevium cognitorem do." Potest, ut actor ita dicat: "quod ego tecum agere volo, in eam rem cognitorem do"; adversarius ita: "quia tu mecum agere vis, in eam rem cognitorem do." Nec interest, praesens an absens cognitor detur: sed si absens datus fuerit, cognitor ita erit, si cognoverit et susceperit officium cognitoris.

§ 84. Procurator vero nullis certis verbis in litem substituitur; sed ex solo mandato, et absente et ignorante adversario, constituitur. Quin etiam sunt qui putant, eum quoque procuratorem videri, cui non sit mandatum, si modo bona fide accedat ad negotium, et caveat, ratam rem dominum habiturum; quamquam et ille, cui mandatur, plerumque satis dare debet, quia saepe mandatum initio litis in obscuro est, et postea apud judicem ostenditur.

§ 85. Tutores autem et curatores quemadmodum constituantur, primo commentario rettulimus.

§ 86. Qui autem alieno nomine agit, intentionem quidem ex persona domini sumit, condemnationem autem in suam personam convertit. Nam si, verbi gratia, Lucius Titius pro Publio Maevio agat, ita formula concipitur: "si paret Numerium Negidium Publio Maevio sestertium x millia dare oportere, judex Numerium Negidium Lucio Titio sestertium x millia con-

Tit. x. De iis per quos agere possumus.

Nunc admonendi sumus, agere posse quemlibet, aut suo nomine, aut alieno: alieno, veluti procuratorio, tutorio, curatorio; cum olim in usu fuisset, alterius nomine agere non posse, nisi pro populo, pro libertate, pro tutela. Praeterea lege Hostilia permissum erat furti agere eorum nomine qui apud hostes essent, aut reipublicae causa abessent, qui quaeve in eorum cujus tutela essent. Et quia hoc non minimam incommoditatem habebat, quod alieno nomine neque agere neque excipere actionem licebat, coeperunt homines per procuratores litigare: nam et morbus et aetas et necessaria peregrinatio, itemque aliae multae causae, saepe hominibus impedimento sunt, quominus rem suam ipsi exequi possint.

§ 1. *Procurator,* neque *certis verbis,* neque praesente *adversario,* immo plerumque *ignorante* eo *constituitur:* cuicumque enim permiseris rem tuam agere aut defendere, is tuus procurator intelligitur.

§ 2. *Tutores et curatores quemadmodum constituantur, primo* libro expositum est.

demna; si non paret, absolve." In rem quoque si agat, intendit "Publii Maevii rem esse ex jure quiritium", et condemnationem in suam personam convertit. § 87. Ab adversarii quoque parte si interveniat aliquis cum quo actio constituitur, intenditur "dominum dare oportere"; condemnatio autem in ejus personam convertitur qui judicium accepit. Sed cum in rem agitur, nihil in intentione facit ejus persona cum quo agitur, sive suo nomine, sive alieno aliquis judicio interveniat; tantum enim intenditur "rem actoris esse".

88. Videamus nunc quibus ex causis is, cum quo agitur, vel hic qui agit, cogatur satisdare. § 89. Igitur si, verbi gratia, in rem tecum agam, satis mihi dare debes: aequum enim visum est te eo quod interea tibi rem, quae an ad te pertineat dubium est, possidere conceditur, cum satisdatione mihi cavere, ut, si victus sis, neque ipsam rem restituas, nec litis aestimationem sufferas, sit mihi potestas aut tecum agendi, aut cum sponsoribus tuis. § 90. Multoque magis debes satisdare mihi, si alieno nomine judicium accipias. § 91. Caeterum cum in rem actio duplex sit, aut enim per formulam petitoriam agitur, aut per sponsionem: si quidem per formulam petitoriam agitur, illa stipulatio locum habet, quae appellatur "judicatum solvi": si vero per sponsionem, illa quae appellatur "pro praede litis et vindiciarum". § 92. Petitoria autem formula haec est, qua actor intendit rem suam esse. § 93. Per sponsionem vero hoc modo agimus. Provocamus adversarium tali sponsione: "si homo, quo de agitur, ex jure quiritium meus est, sestertios xxv dare spondes?" Deinde formulam edimus, qua intendimus, sponsionis summam nobis dari oportere; qua formula ita demum vincimus, si probaverimus rem nostram esse. § 94. Non tamen haec summa sponsionis exigitur; non enim poenalis est, sed praejudicialis, et propter hoc solum fit ut per eam de re judicetur; unde etiam is, cum quo agitur, non restipulatur; ideo autem appellata est "pro praede litis vindiciarum" stipulatio, quia in locum praedium successit, quod olim,

Tit. xi. De satisdationibus.

Satisdationum modus alius antiquitati placuit; alium novitas per usum amplexa est.

Olim enim, *si in rem* agebatur, *satisdare* possessor compellebatur, ut *si victus, nec rem ipsam restitueret nec litis aestimationem, potestas* esset petitori *aut cum eo agendi, aut cum* fidejussoribus ejus. Quae satisdatio appellatur "judicatum solvi". Unde autem sic appellatur, facile est intelligere; namque stipulatur quis, ut solvatur sibi quod fuerit judicatum. *Multo magis is*, qui in rem actione conveniebatur, *satisdare* cogebatur, *si alieno nomine judicium* accipiebat.

cum lege agebatur, pro lite et vindiciis, id est, pro re et fructibus, a possessore petitori dabantur praedes. § 95. Caeterum, si apud centumviros agitur, summam sponsionis non per formulam petimus, sed per legis actionem: sacramento majore provocato; eaque sponsio sestertiorum CXXV nummorum [fieri solet] propter legem Crepeream. § 96. Ipse autem qui in rem agit, si suo nomine agit, satis non dat. § 97. Ac nec si per cognitorem quidem agatur, ulla satisdatio vel ab ipso, vel a domino desideratur; cum enim certis et quasi solemnibus verbis in locum domini substituatur cognitor, merito domini loco habetur. § 98. Procurator vero si agat, satisdare jubetur "ratam rem dominum habiturum": periculum enim est, ne iterum dominus de eadem re experiatur; quod periculum jam non intervenit, si per cognitorem actum fuerit; quia de qua re quisque per cognitorem egerit, de ea non magis amplius actionem habet, quam si ipse egerit. § 99. Tutores et curatores, eodem modo quo et procuratores, satisdare debere verba edicti faciunt; sed aliquando illis satisdatio remittitur. § 100. Haec ita si in rem agatur. Si vero in personam, ab actoris quidem parte quando satisdari debeat quaerentes, eadem reperiemus quae diximus in actione qua in rem agitur. § 101. Ab ejus vero parte, cum quo agitur, si quidem alieno nomine aliquis interveniat, omnimodo satisdari debet, quia nemo alienae rei sine satisdatione defensor idoneus intellegitur. Sed si quidem cum cognitore agatur, dominus satisdare jubetur; si vero cum procuratore, ipse procurator. Idem et de tutore et de curatore juris est. § 102. Quod si proprio nomine aliquis judicium accipiat in personam, certis ex causis satisdari solet, quas ipse praetor significat. Quarum satisdationum duplex causa est; nam [ita praetoris edicto cautum est, ut] aut propter genus actionis satisdaretur, aut propter personam, quia suspecta sit: propter genus actionis, velut judicati, depensive, aut cum de moribus mulieris agatur: propter personam, velut si cum eo

Ipse autem qui in rem agebat, *si suo nomine petebat, satisdare non* cogebatur.

Procurator vero, si in rem agebat, *satisdare* jubebatur "*ratam rem dominum habiturum*"*: periculum enim* erat, *ne iterum dominus de eadem re experiatur.*

Tutores et curatores, eodem modo quo et procuratores, satisdare debere verba edicti faciebant; *sed aliquando* his agentibus *satisdatio remittebatur. Haec ita* erant, *si in rem agebatur.* § 1. *Si vero in personam: ab actoris quidem parte eadem* obtinebant, *quae diximus in actione qua in rem agitur. Ab ejus vero parte cum quo agitur, si quidem alieno nomine aliquis interveniret, omnimodò satisdaret, quia nemo defensor in aliena re sine satisdatione idoneus esse creditur. Quod si proprio nomine aliquis judicium accipiebat in personam,* "judicatum solvi" satisdare non cogebatur.

agitur, qui decoxerit, cujusve bona a creditoribus possessa proscriptave sint, sive cum eo herede agatur, quem praetor suspectum aestimaverit.

§ 2. Sed haec hodie aliter observantur. Sive enim quis in rem actione convenitur, sive in personam suo nomine: nullam satisdationem pro litis aestimatione dare compellitur, sed pro sua tantum persona, quod in judicio permaneat usque ad terminum litis, vel committitur suae promissioni cum jurejurando (quam juratoriam cautionem vocant), vel nudam promissionem, vel satisdationem pro qualitate personae suae dare compellitur. § 3. Sin autem per procuratorem lis vel infertur vel suscipitur: in actoris quidem persona, si non mandatum actis insinuatum est, vel praesens dominus litis in judicio procuratoris sui personam confirmaverit, ratam rem dominum habiturum satisdationem procurator dare compellitur; eodem observando, et si tutor vel curator, vel aliae tales personae quae alienarum rerum gubernationem receperunt, litem quibusdam per alium inferunt. § 4. Si vero aliquis convenitur: si quidem praesens procuratorem dare paratus est, potest vel ipse in judicium venire, et sui procuratoris personam per "judicatum solvi" satisdationis sollemnes stipulationes firmare, vel extra judicium satisdationem exponere, per quam ipse sui procuratoris fidejussor existat pro omnibus "judicatum solvi" satisdationis clausulis. Ubi et de hypotheca suarum rerum convenire compellitur, sive in judicio promiserit, sive extra judicium caverit, ut tam ipse quam heredes ejus obligentur; alia insuper cautela, vel satisdatione, propter personam ipsius exponenda, quod tempore sententiae recitandae in judicio invenietur, vel si non venerit, omnia dabit fidejussor quae condemnatione continentur, nisi fuerit provocatum. § 5. Si vero reus praesto ex quacumque causa non fuerit, et alius velit defensionem ejus subire, nulla differentia inter actiones in rem vel in personam introducenda, potest hoc facere: ita tamen, ut satisdationem "judicatum solvi" pro litis aestimatione praestet. Nemo enim secundum veterem regulam (ut jam dictum est) alienae rei sine satisdatione defensor idoneus intelligitur. § 6. Quae omnia apertius et perfectissime a quotidiano judiciorum usu in ipsis rerum documentis apparent. § 7. Quam formam non solum in hac regia urbe, sed etiam in omnibus nostris provinciis, etsi propter imperitiam forte aliter celebrantur, obtinere censemus, cum necesse est omnes provincias, caput omnium nostrarum civitatum, id est hanc regiam urbem ejusque observantiam sequi.

§ 103. Omnia autem judicia aut legitimo jure consistunt, aut imperio continentur. § 104. Legitima sunt judicia, quae in urbe Roma, vel intra primum urbis Romae milliarium, inter omnes cives Romanos, sub uno judice accipiuntur ; eaque lege Julia judiciaria, nisi in anno et sex mensibus judicata fuerint, expirant : et hoc est, quod vulgo dicitur, lege Julia litem anno et sex mensibus mori. § 105. Imperio vero continentur recuperatoria, et quae sub uno judice accipiuntur, interveniente peregrini persona judicis aut litigatoris. In ea causa sunt quaecumque extra primum urbis Romae milliarium, tam inter cives Romanos quam inter peregrinos, accipiuntur. Ideo autem imperio contineri judicia dicuntur, quia tamdiu valent, quamdiu is qui ea praecepit, imperium habebit. § 106. Et si quidem imperio continenti judicio peractum fuerit, sive in rem, sive in personam, sive ea formula quae in factum concepta est, sive ea, quae in jus habet intentionem, postea nihilominus ipso jure de eadem re agi potest, et ideo necessaria est exceptio rei judicatae vel judicium deductae. § 107. At ubi legitimo judicio in personam actum sit, ea formula, quae juris civilis habet intentionem, postea ipso jure de eadem re agi non potest, et ob id exceptio supervacua est. Si vero vel in rem, vel in factum actum fuerit, ipso jure nihilominus postea agi potest, et ob id exceptio necessaria est rei judicatae vel in judicium deductae. § 108. Alia causa fuit olim legis actionum ; nam qua de re actum semel erat, de ea postea ipso jure agi non poterat, nec omnino ita ut nunc usus erat illis temporibus exceptionum. § 109. Caeterum potest ex lege quidem esse judicium, sed legitimum non esse ; et contra ex lege non esse, sed legitimum esse : nam si, verbi gratia, ex lege Aquilia, vel Ollinia, vel Furia, in provinciis agatur, imperio continebitur judicium ; idemque juris est et si Romae apud recuperatores agamus, vel apud unum judicem interveniente peregrini persona. Et ex diverso, si ex ea causa, ex qua nobis edicto praetoris datur actio, Romae sub uno judice inter omnes cives Romanos accipiatur judicium, legitimum est.

Tit. xii. De perpetuis et temporalibus actionibus et quae ad heredes et in heredes transeunt.

§ 110. Quo loco admonendi sumus, eas quidem actiones, quae ex lege senatusve-consultis proficiscuntur, perpetuo solere	*Hoc loco admonendi sumus, eas quidem actiones quae ex lege, senatusve-consulto* sive ex sacris constitutionibus *proficiscuntur, perpetuo solere* antiquitus competere, donec sacrae constitutiones tam in rem quam in per-

praetorem accommodare, eas vero, quae ex propria ipsius jurisdictione pendent, plerumque intra annum dare. § 111. Aliquando tamen etiam praetor perpetuo dat velut quibus mitatur jus legitimum; quales sunt eae, quas bonorum possessoribus caeterisque qui heredis loco sunt accommodat. Furti quoque manifesti actio, quamvis ex ipsius praetoris jurisdictione proficiscatur, perpetuo datur, et merito, cum pro capitali poena pecuniaria constituta est.

sonalibus actionibus certos fines dederunt: *eas vero quae ex propria* praetoris *jurisdictione pendent, plerumque intra annum* vivere, nam et ipsius praetoris intra annum erat imperium. *Aliquando tamen et in perpetuum extenduntur*, id est usque ad finem ex constitutionibus introductum; *quales sunt eae quas bonorum possessori, caeterisque qui heredis loco sunt, accommodat. Furti quoque manifesti actio, quamvis ex ipsius praetoris jurisdictione proficiscatur, tamen perpetuo datur:* absurdum enim esse existimavit anno eam terminari.

§ 112. Non omnes autem actiones quae in aliquem aut ipso jure competunt, aut a praetore dantur, etiam in heredem aeque competunt, aut dari solent. Est enim certissima juris regula, ex maleficiis poenales actiones in heredem nec competere, nec dari solere, velut furti, vi bonorum raptorum, injuriarum, damni injuriae. Sed heredibus quidem hujusmodi actiones competunt, nec denegantur, excepta injuriarum actione, et si qua alia similis inveniatur actio. § 113. Aliquando tamen etiam ex contractu actio neque heredi, neque in heredem competit: nam adstipulatoris heres non habet actionem, et sponsoris et fidepromissoris heres non tenetur.

§ 1. *Non omnes autem actiones, quae in aliquem aut ipso jure competunt, aut a praetore dantur, et in heredem aeque competunt aut dari solent. Est enim certissima juris regula, ex maleficiis poenales actiones in heredem non competere: veluti furti, vi bonorum raptorum, injuriarum, damni injuriae. Sed heredibus hujusmodi actiones competunt, nec denegantur, excepta injuriarum actione, et si qua alia similis inveniatur. Aliquando tamen etiam ex contractu actio contra heredem non competit*, cum testator dolose versatus sit et ad heredem ejus nihil ex eo dolo pervenerit. Poenales autem actiones, quas supra diximus, si ab ipsis principalibus personis fuerint contestatae, et heredibus dantur, et contra heredes transeunt.

§ 114. Superest ut dispiciamus, si ante rem judicatam is, cum quo agitur, post acceptum judicium, satisfaciat actori, quid officio judicis conveniat, utrum absolvere, an ideo potius damnare, quia judicii accipiendi tempore in ea causa fuerit ut damnari debeatur. Nostri praeceptores absolvere eum debere existimant; nec interest cujus generis fiat judicium: et hoc est quod vulgo dicitur Sabino et Cassio placere "omnia judicia esse absolutoria". [Diversae scholae auctoribus de stricti juris judiciis contra placet,] de bonae

§ 2. *Superest ut admoneamus quod, si ante rem judicatam, is cum quo actum est satisfaciat actori, officio judicis convenit eum absolvere*, licet *judicii accipiendi tempore in ea causa fuisset, ut damnari debeat; et hoc est quod*

fidei judiciis autem idem sentiunt quia in ejusmodi judiciis liberum est officium judicis; tantumdem etiam de in rem actionibus putant, quia . . . .

ante *vulgo dicebatur*, "*omnia judicia absolutoria esse*".

Tit. xiii. De exceptionibus.

§ 115. Sequitur ut de exceptionibus dispiciamus. § 116. Comparatae sunt autem exceptiones defendendorum eorum gratia cum quibus agitur: saepe enim accidit ut quis jure civili teneatur, sed iniquum sit, eum judicio condemnari: velut si stipulatus sim abs te pecuniam tamquam credendi causa numeraturus, nec numeraverim; nam eam pecuniam a te peti posse certum est, dare enim te oportet, cum ex stipulatu tenearis: sed quia iniquum est, te eo nomine condemnari, placet per exceptionem doli mali te defendi debere. Item si pactus fuero tecum ne id, quod mihi debeas a te petam, nihilominus id ipsum a te petere possum "dare mihi oportere", quia obligatio pacto convento non tollitur; sed placet debere me petentem per exceptionem pacti conventi repelli. § 117. In his quoque actionibus, quae in personam non sunt, exceptiones locum habent: velut si metu me coegeris, aut dolo malo induxeris, ut tibi rem aliquam mancipi darem mancipio; si enim eam rem a me petas, da-

Sequitur ut de exceptionibus dispiciamus. Comparatae sunt autem exceptiones defendendorum eorum gratia, cum quibus agitur: saepe enim accidit ut, licet ipsa persecutio qua actor experitur, justa sit, tamen iniqua sit adversus eum cum quo agitur. § 1. Verbi gratia, si metu coactus, aut dolo inductus, aut errore lapsus, stipulanti Titio promisisti, quod non debueras promittere, palam est jure civili te obligatum esse: et actio, qua intenditur dare te oportere, efficax est; sed iniquum est te condemnari, ideoque datur tibi exceptio metus causa, aut doli mali, aut in factum composita, ad impugnandam actionem. § 2. *Idem juris est, si quis quasi credendi causa pecuniam stipulatus fuerit, neque numeravit. Nam eam pecuniam a te petere posse eum certum est; dare enim te oportet, cum ex stipulatu tenearis: sed quia iniquum est eo nomine te condemnari, placet per exceptionem* pecuniae non numeratae *te defendi debere*, cujus tempora nos, secundum quod jam superioribus libris scriptum est constitutione nostra coarctavimus. § 3. Praeterea debitor, si pactus fuerit, cum creditore ne a se peteretur, nihilominus obligatus manet, quia pacto convento obligationes non omnimodo dissolvuntur: qua de causa, efficax est adversus eum actio qua actor intendit, "si paret eum dare oportere"; sed quia iniquum est contra pactionem eum damnari, defenditur *per exceptionem pacti conventi.* § 4. Aeque si debitor, deferente creditore, juraverit nihil se dare oportere, adhuc obligatus permanet: sed quia iniquum est de perjurio quaeri, defenditur per exceptionem jurisjurandi. *In iis quoque actionibus* quibus in rem agitur, aeque necessariae sunt exceptiones: veluti, si, petitore deferente, possessor juraverit eam rem suam esse, et nihilominus eandem rem petitor vindicet. Licet enim verum sit quod intendit, id est, rem ejus esse, iniquum est tamen possessorem condemnari. § 5. Item, si judicio tecum actum fuerit, sive in rem, sive in personam, nihilominus obligatio durat, et ideo ipso jure

tur mihi exceptio, per quam, si metus causam te fecisse vel dolo malo arguero, repelleris. Item, si fundum litigiosum sciens a non possidente emeris, eumque a possidente petas, opponitur tibi exceptio, per quam omnimodo summoveris. § 118. Exceptiones autem alias in edicto praetor habet propositas, alias causa cognita accommodat; quae omnes vel ex legibus, vel ex his quae legis vicem obtinent, substantiam capiunt, vel ex jurisdictione praetoris proditae sunt.

§ 119. Omnes autem exceptiones in contrarium concipiuntur, quam adfirmat is, cum quo agitur. Nam, si, verbi gratia, reus dolo malo aliquid actorem facere dicat, quod forte pecuniam petit, quam non numeravit, sic exceptio concipitur: "Si in ea re nihil dolo malo ab Aulo Agerio factum sit, neque fiat." Item, si dicat contra pactionem pecunia peti, ita concipitur exceptio: "Si inter Aulum Agerium et Numerium Negidium non convenerit, ne ea pecunia peteretur." Et denique in caeteris causis similiter concipi solet: ideo scilicet, quia omnis exceptio objicitur quidem a reo, sed ita formulae inseritur, ut conditionalem faciat condemnationem, id est, ne aliter judex eum, cum quo agitur condemnet, quam si nihil in ea re, qua de agitur, dolo malo actoris factum sit; item ne aliter judex eum condemnet, quam si nullum pactum conventum de non petenda pecunia factum fuerit.

§ 120. Dicuntur autem exceptiones aut peremptoriae, aut dilatoriae. § 121. Peremptoriae sunt quae perpetuo valent, nec evitari possunt: velut, quod metus causa, aut dolo malo, aut quod contra legem senatusve consultum factum est, aut quod res judicata est vel in judicium deducta est; item pacti conventi quo pactum est ne omnino pecunia peteretur. § 122. Dilatoriae sunt exceptiones quae ad tempus nocent: veluti illius pacti conventi quod factum est, verbi gratia, ne intra quinquennium peteretur; finito enim eo tempore non habet locum exceptio. Cui similis exceptio est litis dividuae et rei residuae: nam, si quis partem rei petierit, et

postea de eadem re adversus te agi potest; sed debes per exceptionem rei judicatae adjuvari. § 6. Haec exempli causa retulisse sufficiet. Alioquin, quam ex multis variisque causis exceptiones necessariae sint, ex latioribus Digestorum seu Pandectarum libris intelligi potest. § 7. *Quarum quaedam ex legibus vel ex iis, quae legis vicem obtinent, vel ex ipsius praetoris jurisdictione substantiam capiunt.*

§ 8. *Appellantur autem exceptiones*, aliae perpetuae et *peremptoriae*, aliae temporales et *dilatoriae*. § 9. Perpetuae et *peremptoriae sunt quae* semper agentibus obstant, et semper rem de qua agitur perimunt: qualis est exceptio *doli mali*, et *quod metus causa factum est*, et *pacti conventi* cum ita convenerit *ne omnino pecunia peteretur*. § 10. Temporales atque *dilatoriae sunt quae ad tempus nocent*, et temporis dilationem tribuunt:

intra ejusdem praeturam reliquam partem petat, hac exceptione summovetur, quae appellatur litis dividuae. Item, si is, qui cum eodem plures [ob easdem res] lites habebat, de quibusdam egerit, de quibusdam distulerit, si intra ejusdem praeturam de his, quae ita distulerit, agat, per hanc exceptionem, quae appellatur rei residuae summovetur. § 123. Observandum est autem ei, cui dilatoria objicitur exceptio, ut differat actionem; alioquin, si objecta exceptione egerit, rem perdit; nec enim, post illud tempus, quo integra re eam evitare poterat, adhuc ei potestas agendi superest, [nam cum res] in judicium deducta esset, per exceptionem perempta est.

qualis est *pacti conventi*, cum ita convenerit *ne intra* certum tempus *ageretur*, veluti *intra quinquennium;* nam *finito eo tempore, non* impeditur actor rem exequi. Ergo ii quibus intra certum tempus agere volentibus *objicitur exceptio* aut pacti conventi aut alia similis, *differre* debent *actionem* et post tempus agere: ideo enim et dilatoriae istae exceptiones appellantur. *Alioquin*, si intra tempus *egerint, objectaque* sit *exceptio*, neque eo judicio quidquam consequerentur propter exceptionem; *nec post tempus* olim agere poterant, cum temere rem in judicium deducebant et consumebant, qua ratione rem amittebant. Hodie autem non ita stricte haec procedere volumus, sed eum qui ante tempus pactionis vel obligationis, litem inferre ausus est, Zenonianae constitutioni subjacere censemus, quam sacratissimus legislator de iis qui tempore plus petierint protulit, ut et inducias quas ipse actor sponte indulserit, vel natura actionis continet, contempserit, in duplum habeant ii qui talem injuriam passi sunt, et post eas finitas non aliter litem suscipiant, nisi omnes expensas litis antea acceperint, ut actores tali poena perterriti tempora litium doceantur observare.

§ 124. Non solum autem ex tempore, sed etiam ex persona dilatoriae exceptiones intelleguntur, quales sunt cognitoriae, veluti si is, qui per edictum cognitorem dare non potest, per cognitorem agat, vel dandi quidem cognitoris jus habeat, sed eum det cui non licet cognituram suscipere: nam si objiciatur exceptio cognitoria, si ipse talis erat ut ei non liceat cognitorem dare, ipse agere potest, si ut cognitori non liceat cognituram suscipere, per alium cognitorem aut per semetipsum liberam habet agendi potestatem. Potest autem tam hoc quam illo modo evitare exceptionem; quod si dissimulaverit [eam et] per cognitorem egerit, rem perdit. § 125. Semper

§ 11. Praeterea *etiam ex persona dilatoriae* sunt *exceptiones; quales sunt* procuratoriae *veluti si* per militem aut mulierem agere quis velit: nam militibus nec pro patre, vel matre, vel uxore, nec ex sacro rescripto, procuratorio nomine experiri conceditur; suis vero negotiis superesse sine offensa disciplinae possunt. Eas vero exceptiones quae olim procuratoribus propter infamiam vel dantis vel ipsius procuratoris opponebantur, cum in judiciis frequentari nullo modo perspeximus, conquiescere sancimus: ne dum de his altercatur, ipsius negotii disceptatio proteletur.

autem peremptoria quidem exceptione si reus per errorem non fuerit usus, in integrum restituitur adjiciendae exceptionis gratia; dilatoria vero si non fuerit usus, an in integrum restituatur, quaeritur.

§ 126. Interdum evenit ut exceptio, quae prima facie justa videatur, inique noceat actori. Quod cum accidat, alia adjectione opus est adjuvandi actoris gratia, quae adjectio replicatio vocatur, quia per eam replicatur atque resolvitur vis exceptionis. Nam, si, verbi gratia, pactus sim tecum, ne pecuniam, quam mihi debes a te peterem, deinde postea in contrarium pacti sumus, id est, ut petere mihi liceat, et, si agam tecum, excipias tu ut ita demum mihi condemneris, "si non convenerit ne eam pecuniam peterem", nocet mihi exceptio pacti conventi; namque nihilominus hoc verum manet, etiamsi postea in contrarium pacti simus: sed quia iniquum est me excludi exceptione, replicatio mihi datur ex posteriore pacto, hoc modo: "si non postea convenit ut mihi eam pecuniam petere liceret". Item, si argentarius pretium rei, quae in auctionem venierit, persequatur, objicitur ei exceptio, ut ita demum emptor damnetur, "si ei res quam emerit, tradita est"; quae est justa exceptio: sed si in auctione praedictum est, ne ante res emptori traderetur, quam si pretium solverit, replicatione tali argentarius adjuvatur: "aut si praedictum est, ne aliter emptori res traderetur, quam si pretium emptor solverit".

§ 127. Interdum autem evenit, ut rursus replicatio, quae prima facie justa sit, inique reo noceat: quod cum accidat, adjectione opus est, adjuvandi rei gratia, quae duplicatio vocatur. § 128. Et, si rursus ea prima facie justa videatur, sed propter aliquam causam inique actori noceat, rursus adjectione opus est, qua actor adjuvetur, quae dicitur triplicatio. § 129. Quarum omnium adjectionum usum interdum etiam ulterius, quam diximus, varietas negotiorum introduxit.

Tit. xiv. De replicationibus.

Interdum evenit ut exceptio, quae prima facie justa videatur, inique noceat. Quod cum accidit, alia allegatione opus est adjuvandi actoris gratia, quae replicatio vocatur, quia per eam replicatur, atque resolvitur vis exceptionis. Veluti cum *pactus est aliquis cum debitore suo ne ab eo pecuniam petat, deinde postea in contrarium pacti sunt, id est, ut petere creditori liceat; si agat creditor, et excipiat debitor, ut ita demum condemnetur, "si non convenerit ne eam pecuniam creditor petat", nocet ei exceptio. Convenit enim ita: namque nihilominus hoc verum manet, licet postea in contrarium pacti sint. Sed quia iniquum est creditorem excludi, replicatio ei dabitur ex posteriore pacto convento.*

§ 1. *Rursus interdum evenit ut replicatio, quae prima facie justa sit, inique noceat. Quod cum accidit, alia allegatione opus est adjuvandi rei gratia, quae duplicatio vocatur.* § 2. *Et si rursus ea prima facie justa videatur, sed propter aliquam causam inique actori noceat, rursus alia allegatione opus est, qua actor adjuvetur, quae dicitur triplicatio.* § 3. *Quarum omnium* exceptionum *usum, interdum ulterius quam diximus, varietas negotiorum introduxit*; quas omnes apertius ex latiore Digestorum volumine facile est cognoscere.

§ 4. Exceptiones autem quibus debitor defenditur plerumque accommodari solent etiam fidejussoribus ejus, et recte: quia quod ab iis petitur, id ab ipso debitore peti videtur, quia mandati judicio redditurus est eis quod ii pro eo solverint. Qua ratione, etsi de non petenda pecunia pactus quis cum reo fuerit, placuit perinde succurrendum esse per exceptionem pacti conventi illis quoque qui pro eo obligati essent, ac si cum ipsis pactus esset ne ab eis ea pecunia peteretur. Sane quaedam exceptiones non solent his accommodari. Ecce enim debitor, si bonis suis cesserit, et cum eo creditor experiatur, defenditur per exceptionem, "nisi bonis cesserit": sed haec exceptio fidejussoribus non datur, scilicet ideo, quia qui alios pro debitore obligat, hoc maxime prospicit, ut, cum facultatibus lapsus fuerit debitor, possit ab iis quos pro eo obligavit suum consequi.

§ 130. Videamus etiam de praescriptionibus, quae receptae sunt pro actore. § 131. Saepe enim ex una eademque obligatione aliquid jam praestari oportet, aliquid in futura praestatione est; velut cum in singulos annos vel menses certam pecuniam stipulati fuerimus: nam finitis quibusdam annis aut mensibus, hujus quidem temporis pecuniam praestari oportet, futurorum autem annorum sane quidem obligatio contracta intellegitur, praestatio vero adhuc nulla est. Si ergo velimus id quidem, quod praestari oportet, petere, et in judicium deducere, futuram vero obligationis praestationem in incerto relinquere, necesse est ut cum hac praescriptione agamus: "ea res agatur cujus rei dies fuit"; alioquin, si sine hac praescriptione egerimus, ea scilicet formula, qua incertum petimus, cujus intentio his verbis concepta est: "quidquid paret Numerium Negidium Aulo Agerio dare facere oportere", totam obligationem, id est, etiam futuram, in hoc judicium deducimus, et quae ante tempus obliga[tio consumpta est litis contestatione non] est postea permissa [revocari in judicium]. Item, si, verbi gratia, ex empto agamus, ut nobis fundus mancipio detur, debemus hoc modo praescribere: "ea res agatur, de fundo mancipando", ut postea, si velimus vacuam possessionem nobis tradi, ... totius illius juris obligatio illa incerta actione: "quidquid ob eam rem Numerium Negidium Aulo Agerio dare facere oportet", litis contestatione consumitur, ut postea nobis agere volentibus de vacua possessione tradenda nulla supersit actio. § 132.

Praescriptiones vero appellatas esse ab eo quod ante formulas praescribuntur, plus quam manifestum est.

§ 133. Sed his quidem temporibus, sicut supra quoque notavimus, omnes praescriptiones ab actore proficiscuntur. Olim autem quaedam etiam pro reo opponebantur; qualis illa erat praescriptio: "ea res agatur: si praejudicium hereditati non fiat," quae nunc in speciem exceptionis deducta est, et locum habet cum petitor hereditatis alio genere judicii praejudicium hereditati faciat, velut cum singulas res petat; est enim iniquum [per singulas res disceptationem fieri de tota hereditate] . . . § 134. . . intentione formulae det[erminatur] is cui dari oportet; et sane domino dari oportet, quod servus stipulatur; at in praescriptione de facto, quaeritur, quod secundum naturalem significationem verum esse debet. § 135. Quaecumque autem diximus de servis, eadem de caeteris quoque personis, quae nostro juri subjectae sunt, dicta intellegemus. § 136. Item admonendi sumus, si cum ipso agamus qui incertum promiserit, ita nobis formulam esse propositam, ut praescriptio inserta sit formulae loco demonstrationis, hoc modo: "Judex esto. Quod Aulus Agerius de Numerio Negidio incertum stipulatus est, cujus rei dies fuit, quidquid ob eam rem Numerium Negidium Aulo Agerio dare facere oportet," et reliqua. § 137. At si cum sponsore aut fidejussore agatur, praescribi solet, in persona quidem sponsoris hoc modo: "ea res agatur, quod Aulus Agerius de Lucio Titio incertum stipulatus est, quo nomine Numerius Negidius sponsor est, cujus rei dies fuit;" in persona vero fidejussoris ita: "ea res agatur, quod Numerius Negidius pro Titio incertum fide sua esse jussit, cujus rei dies fuit;" deinde formula subjicitur.

Tit. xv. De interdictis.

§ 138. Superest ut de interdictis dispiciamus. § 139. Certis igitur ex causis praetor aut proconsul principaliter auctoritatem suam finiendis controversiis proponit: quod tum maxime facit cum de possessione aut quasi possessione inter aliquos contenditur; et in summa aut jubet aliquid fieri aut fieri prohibet.	*Sequitur ut dispiciamus de interdictis,* seu actionibus quae pro his exercentur. Erant autem interdicta formae *atque conceptiones verborum quibus praetor aut* jubebat *aliquid fieri, aut fieri* prohibebat: *quod tunc maxime* faciebat, *cum de possessione aut quasi-possessione inter aliquos* contendebatur.

Formulae autem et verborum conceptiones quibus in ea re utitur interdicta aut decreta vocantur; § 140. decreta, cum fieri aliquid jubet, velut cum praecipit ut aliquid exhibeatur aut restituatur; interdicta vero, cum prohibet fieri, velut cum praecipit: "ne sine vitio de [altero] possidenti vis fiat, neve in loco sacro aliquid fiat. Unde omnia interdicta aut restitutoria, aut exhibitoria, aut prohibitoria vocantur. § 141. Nec tamen, cum quid jusserit fieri, aut fieri prohibuerit, statim peractum est negotium, sed ad judicem recuperatoresve itur, et ibi editis formulis quaeritur, an aliquid adversus praetoris edictum factum sit, vel an factum non sit quod is fieri jusserit. Et modo cum poena agitur, modo sine poena: cum poena, velut cum per sponsionem agitur; sine poena, velut cum arbiter petitur. Et quidem ex prohibitoriis interdictis semper per sponsionem agi solet; ex restitutoriis vero vel exhibitoriis, modo per sponsionem, modo per formulam agitur quae arbitraria vocatur.

§ 142. Principalis igitur divisio in eo est, quod aut prohibitoria sunt interdicta, aut restitutoria, aut exhibitoria.

§ 1. Summa autem *divisio interdictorum haec est, quod aut prohibitoria sunt, aut restitutoria, aut exhibitoria.* Prohibitoria sunt, quibus praetor vetat aliquid fieri: veluti vim sine vitio possidenti, vel mortuum inferenti quo ei jus erat inferendi, vel in loco sacro aedificari, vel in flumine publico ripave ejus aliquid fieri quo pejus navigetur. Restitutoria sunt, quibus restitui aliquid jubet: veluti, bonorum possessori possessionem eorum quae quis pro herede aut pro possessore possidet ex ea hereditate, aut cum jubet ei qui vi possessione fundi dejectus sit, restitui possessionem. Exhibitoria sunt per quae jubet exhiberi: veluti eum cujus de libertate agitur, aut libertum cui patronus operas indicere velit, aut parenti liberos qui in potestate ejus sunt. Sunt tamen qui putant proprie interdicta ea vocari quae prohibitoria sunt, quia interdicere est denuntiare et prohibere; restitutoria autem et exhibitoria, proprie decreta vocari: sed tamen obtinuit omnia interdicta appellari, quia "inter duos dicuntur".

§ 143. Sequens in eo est divisio, quod vel adipiscendae possessionis causa comparata sunt, vel retinendae, vel recuperandae.

—§ 2. *Sequens divisio interdictorum haec est, quod quaedam adipiscendae possessionis causa comparata sunt, quaedam retinendae, quaedam recuperandae.*

§ 144. Adipiscendae possessionis causa interdictum accommodatur bonorum possessori, cujus principium est "Quorum bonorum"; ejusque vis et potestas haec est, ut quod quisque ex his bonis, quorum possessio alicui data est, si pro herede aut pro possessore possi-

§ 3. *Adipiscendae possessionis causa interdictum accommodatur bonorum possessori, quod appellatur "quorum bonorum": ejusque vis et potestas haec est, ut, quod ex iis bonis quisque, quorum possessio alicui data est, pro herede aut pro possessore possideat, id ei, cui*

deret, [possederit] id ei cui bonorum possessio data est, restituatur. Pro herede autem possidere videtur tam is, qui heres est, quam is, qui putat se heredem esse. Pro possessore is possidet qui sine causa aliquam rem hereditariam, vel etiam totam hereditatem, sciens ad se non pertinere, possidet. Ideo autem adipiscendae possessionis vocatur, quod ei tantum utile est, qui nunc primum conatur adipisci rei possessionem ; itaque, si quis adeptus possessionem eam amiserit, desinit ei id interdictum utile esse. § 145. Bonorum quoque emptori similiter proponitur interdictum, quod quidam possessorium vocant. § 146. Item ei, qui publice bona emerit, ejusdem conditionis interdictum proponitur quod appellatur sectorium, quod sectores vocantur, qui publice bona mercantur. § 147. Interdictum quoque quod appellatur Salvianum, adipiscendae possessionis causa comparatum est, eoque utitur dominus fundi de rebus coloni, quas is pro mercedibus fundi pignori futuras pepigisset.

§ 148. Retinendae possessionis causa solet interdictum reddi, cum ab utraque parte de proprietate alicujus rei controversia est, et ante quaeritur, uter ex litigatoribus possidere, et uter petere debeat : cujus rei gratia comparata sunt "uti possidetis" et "utrubi". § 149. Et quidem "uti possidetis" interdictum de fundi vel aedium possessoriis [controversiis] redditur, "utrubi" vero de rerum mobilium possessione. § 150. Et si quidem de fundo vel aedibus interdicitur, eum potiorem esse praetor jubet qui, eo tempore quo interdictum redditur, nec vi, nec clam, nec precario ab adversario possideat; si vero de re mobili, eum potiorem esse jubet, qui majore parte ejus anni nec vi, nec clam, nec precario ab adversario possederit ; idque

bonorum possessio data est, restituere debeat. Pro herede autem possidere videtur, qui putat se heredem esse. Pro possessore is possidet, qui nullo jure rem hereditariam vel etiam totam hereditatem, sciens ad se non pertinere, possidet. Ideo autem adipiscendae possessionis vocatur interdictum, quia ei tantum utile est, qui nunc primum conatur adipisci rei possessionem : itaque, si quis adeptus possessionem amiserit eam, hoc interdictum ei inutile est.

Interdictum quoque quod appellatur Salvianum, adipiscendae possessionis causa comparatum est, eoque utitur dominus fundi de rebus coloni, quas is pro mercedibus fundi pignori futuras pepigisset.

§ 4. *Retinendae possessionis causa comparata sunt interdicta "uti possidetis" et "utrubi", cum ab utraque parte de proprietate alicujus rei controversia sit, et ante quaeritur, uter ex litigatoribus possidere, et uter petere debeat.* Namque nisi ante exploratum fuerit utrius eorum possessio sit, non potest petitoria actio institui, quia et civilis et naturalis ratio facit, ut alius possideat, alius a possidente petat. Et quia longe commodius est possidere potius quam petere, ideo plerumque et fere semper ingens existit contentio de ipsa possessione. Commodum autem possidendi in eo est quod, etiamsi ejus res non sit qui possidet, si modo actor non potuerit suam esse probare, remanet suo loco possessio ; propter quam causam, cum obscura sunt

satis ipsis verbis interdictorum significatur. § 151. Sed in "utrubi" interdicto non solum sua cuique possessio prodest, sed etiam alterius quam justum est ei accedere: velut ejus cui heres extiterit, ejusque a quo emerit, vel ex donatione aut dotis nomine acceperit. Itaque si nostrae possessioni juncta alterius justa possessio exsuperat adversarii possessionem nos eo interdicto vincimus. Nullam autem propriam possessionem habenti accessio temporis nec datur, nec dari potest; nam ei, quod nullum est, nihil accedere potest. Sed et si vitiosam habeat possessionem, id est, aut vi, aut clam, aut precario ab adversario adquisitam, non datur; nam accessio non sua ei nihil prodest. § 152. Annus autem retrorsus numeratur; itaque si tu, verbi gratia, octo mensibus possederis prioribus, et ego septem posterioribus, ego potior ero quod trium priorum mensium possessio nihil tibi in hoc interdicto prodest, quod alterius anni possessio est. § 153. Possidere autem videmur, non solum si ipsi possideamus, sed etiam si nostro nomine aliquis in possessione sit, licet is nostro juri subjectus non sit, qualis est colonus et inquilinus. Per eos quoque apud quos deposuerimus, aut quibus commodaverimus, aut quibus gratuitam habitationem tribuerimus, ipsi possidere videmur; et hoc est quod vulgo dicitur, retineri possessionem posse per quemlibet, qui nostro nomine sit in possessione. Quin etiam plerique putant, animo quoque retineri possessionem, [quamvis neque ipsi in possessione simus ne]que nostro nomine alius, si tamen non relinquendae possessionis animo, sed postea reversuri, inde discesserimus. Adipisci vero possessionem per quos possimus, secundo commentario rettulimus;

utriusque jura, contra petitorem judicari solet. Sed *interdicto quidem "uti possidetis" de fundi vel aedium possessione* contenditur, "*utrubi*" *vero* interdicto *de rerum mobilium possessione:* quorum vis ac potestas plurimam inter se differentiam apud veteres habebat; nam uti possidetis interdicto is vincebat *qui interdicti tempore possidebat*, si modo *nec vi, nec clam, nec precario* nactus fuerat *ab adversario* possessionem, etiamsi alium vi expulerat, aut clam abripuerat alienam possessionem, aut precario rogaverat aliquem ut sibi possidere liceret; utrubi *vero interdicto* is vincebat *qui majore parte ejus anni nec vi, nec clam, nec precario ab adversario* possidebat. Hodie tamen aliter observatur: nam utriusque interdicti potestas, quantum ad possessionem pertinet, exaequata est, ut ille vincat, et in re soli et in re mobili, qui possessionem nec vi, nec clam, nec precario ab adversario litis contestationis tempore detinet. § 5. *Possidere autem videtur* quisque, *non solum si ipse possideat, sed et si* ejus *nomine aliquis in possessione sit, licet is* ejus *juri subjectus non sit, qualis est colonus et inquilinus. Per eos quoque apud quos deposuerit quis, aut quibus commodaverit, ipse possidere videtur; et hoc est, quod dicitur, retinere possessionem posse aliquem per quemlibet qui ejus nomine sit in possessione. Quin etiam animo quoque retineri possessionem placet,* id est, ut, quamvis neque ipse sit in possessione, neque ejus nomine alius, tamen, si non relinquendae *possessionis animo,* sed postea *reversurus* inde *discesserit, retinere possessionem videatur. Adipisci vero possessionem per quos aliquis potest, secundo* libro *exposuimus; nec ulla dubitatio est, quin animo*

nec ulla dubitatio est, quin animo possessionem adipisci non possimus.

§ 154. Recuperandae possessionis causa solet interdictum dari, si quis ex possessione vi dejectus sit; nam ei proponitur interdictum cujus principium est: "Unde tu illum vi dejecisti;" per quod is, qui vi dejecit, cogitur ei restituere rei possessionem, si modo is qui dejectus est, nec vi, nec clam, nec precario possideret ab altero; cum, qui a me vi, aut clam, aut precario possideret, [impune a me] dejici [potest]. § 155. Interdum tamen et si cum vi dejecerim, qui a me vi, aut clam, aut precario possederit, cogor ei restituere possessionem, velut si armis eum vi dejecerim: nam propter atrocitatem delicti in tantum patior actionem, ut omnimodo debeam ei restituere possessionem. Armorum autem appellatione non solum scuta et gladios et galeas significari intellegimus, sed et fustes et lapides.

§ 156. Tertia divisio interdictorum in hoc est, quod aut simplicia sunt, aut duplicia: § 157. Simplicia velut in quibus alter actor, alter reus est: qualia sunt omnia restitutoria aut exhibitoria; namque actor est, qui desiderat aut exhiberi aut restitui, reus is est, a quo desideratur ut exhibeat, aut restituat. § 158. Prohibitoriorum autem interdictorum alia duplicia, alia simplicia sunt. § 159. Simplicia sunt, velut, quibus prohibet praetor in loco sacro, aut in flumine publico ripave ejus aliquid facere eum; nam actor est, qui desiderat, ne quid fiat, reus, is, qui aliquid facere conatur. § 160. Duplicia sunt, velut "uti possidetis" interdictum et "utrubi". Ideo autem duplicia vocantur, quia par utriusque litigatoris in his conditio

solo possessionem adipisci nemo possit.

§ 6. *Recuperandae possessionis causa solet interdici, si quis ex possessione fundi vel aedium vi dejectus fuerit. Nam ei proponitur interdictum "unde vi" per quod is qui dejecit cogitur ei restituere possessionem, licet is ab eo qui vi dejecit, vi, vel clam, vel precario possidebat.* Sed ex sacris constitutionibus, ut supra diximus, si quis rem per vim occupaverit, si quidem in bonis ejus est, dominio ejus privatur, si aliena, post ejus restitutionem etiam aestimationem rei dare vim passo compellitur. Qui autem aliquem de possessione per vim dejecerit, tenetur lege Julia de vi privata, aut de vi publica; sed de vi privata, si sine armis vim fecerit, sin autem cum armis eum de possessione expulerit, de vi publica. *Armorum autem appellatione non solum scuta et gladios et galeas significari intellegimus, sed et fustes et lapides.*

§ 7. *Tertia divisio interdictorum haec est, quod aut simplicia sunt, aut duplicia. Simplicia sunt, veluti in quibus alter actor, alter reus est: qualia sunt omnia restitutoria aut exhibitoria; namque actor est qui desiderat aut exhiberi aut restitui, reus is est a quo desideratur, ut restituat aut exhibeat. Prohibitoriorum autem interdictorum alia simplicia sunt, alia duplicia. Simplicia sunt, veluti cum prohibet praetor in loco sacro, vel in flumine publico ripave ejus aliquid fieri: nam actor est, qui desiderat, ne quid fiat; reus, qui aliquid facere conatur. Duplicia sunt, veluti "uti possidetis" interdictum et "utrubi". Ideo autem "duplicia" vocantur, quia par utriusque litigatoris in his conditio est, nec quisquam*

est, nec quisquam praecipue reus vel actor intellegitur, sed unusquisque tam rei quam actoris partes sustinet; quippe praetor pari sermone cum utroque loquitur; nam summa conceptio eorum interdictorum haec est: "uti nunc possidetis, quominus ita possideatis vim fieri veto;" item alterius: "utrubi hic homo, de quo agitur, apud quem majore parte hujus anni fuit, quominus is eum ducat vim fieri veto."

praecipue reus vel actor intellegitur, sed unusquisque tam rei quam actoris partes sustinet.

§ 161. Expositis generibus interdictorum, sequitur, ut de ordine et de exitu eorum dispiciamus; et incipiamus a simplicibus. § 162. Si igitur restitutorium vel exhibitorium interdictum redditur, velut ut restituatur ei possessio, qui vi dejectus est, aut ut exhibeatur libertus, cui patronus operas indicere vellet, modo sine periculo res ad exitum perducitur, modo cum periculo. § 163. Namque, si arbitrum postulaverit is, cum quo agitur, accipit formulam, quae appellatur arbitraria: ut judicis arbitrio, si quid restitui vel exhiberi debeat, id sine periculo exhibeat aut restituat, et ita absolvatur; quod si nec restituat, neque exhibeat, quanti ea res est, condemnatur. Sed etiam actor quoque sine poena experitur cum eo, quem neque exhibere, neque restituere quicquam oportere [paret] praeterquam si calumniae judicium ei oppositum fuerit decimae partis; quamquam Proculo pla[cuit non esse permitten]dum calumniae judicio uti ei, qui arbitrum postulaverit, quasi hoc ipso confessus videatur restituere se vel exhibere debere; sed alio jure utimur, et recte: plus enim est modestiore via litiget arbitrum quisque petit, quam quia convictus sit. § 164. Caeterum observare debet is, qui vult arbitrum petere ut statim petat, antequam a praetore discedat: sero enim petentibus non indulgetur. § 165. Itaque si arbitrum non petierit, sed tacitus de jure exierit, cum periculo res ad exitum perducitur, nam actor provocat adversarium sponsione [quod] contra edictum praetoris non exhibuerit aut non restituerit; ille autem adversus sponsionem adversarii restipulatur. Deinde actor quidem sponsionis formulam edit adversario; ille huic invicem restipulationis. Sed actor sponsionibus aliis committit etiam aliud judicium de re restituenda vel exhibenda, ut, si is sponsione vicerit, nisi ei res exhibeatur aut restituatur . . . . . . fructus licitando is tantisper in possessione constituitur, si modo adversario suo fructuaria stipulatione caverit cujus vis ac potestas haec est, ut si contra eum . . . . . . fuerit eam summam adversario solvat. § 166. Haec autem licendi contentio fructus licitatio vocatur scilicet, quia

§ 8. *De ordine et* veteri *exitu interdictorum* supervacuum est hodie dicere: nam quotiens extra ordinem jus dicitur (qualia sunt hodie omnia judicia), non est necesse reddi interdictum, sed perinde judicatur sine interdictis, atque si utilis actio ex causa interdicti reddita fuisset.

. . . . . postea alter alterum sponsione provocat "ni adversus edictum praetoris possidenti sibi vis facta est" et invicem ambo restipulantur adversus sponsionem . . . . . . una inter eos sponsio, itemque restipulatio . . . . . . ad eam fit . . . . . . judex apud quem de ea re agitur, illud scilicet requirit [primum] quod praetor interdicto complexus est, id est, uter eorum eum fundum easve aedes, per id tempus, quo interdictum redditur, nec vi, nec clam, nec precario possideret. Cum judex id exploraverit, et forte secundum me judicatum sit, adversarium mihi et sponsionis et restipulationis summas, quas cum eo feci, condemnat, et convenienter me sponsionis et restipulationis, quae mecum factae sunt, absolvit; et hoc amplius, si apud adversarium meum possessio est, quand[o quidem] is fructus licitatione vicit, nisi restituat mihi possessionem, Cascelliano sive secutorio judicio condemnatur. § 167. Ergo is qui fructus licitatione vicit, si non probaverit ad se pertinere possessionem, sponsionis et restipulationis et fructus licitationis summam poenae nomine solvere, et praeterea possessionem restituere jubetur; et hoc amplius fructus, quos interea percepit, reddet: summa enim fructus licitationis non pretium est fructuum, sed poenae nomine solvitur, quod quis alienam possessionem per hoc tempus retinere et facultatem fruendi nancisci conatus est. § 168. Ille autem, qui fructus licitatione victus est, si non probaverit ad se pertinere possessionem, tantum sponsionis et restipulationis summam poenae nomine debet. § 169. Admonendi tamen sumus, liberum esse ei, qui fructus licitatione victus fuerit, omissa fructuaria stipulatione, sicut Cascelliano sive secutorio judicio de possessione recuperanda experitur, [sic etiam] de fructus licitatione agere: in quam rem proprium judicium comparatum est, quod appellatur fructuarium, quo nomine actor judicatum solvi satis accipiat. Dicitur autem et hoc judicium secutorium, quod sequitur sponsionis victoriam, sed non aeque Cascellianum vocatur. § 170. Sed quia nonnulli, interdicto reddito, caetera ex interdicto facere nolebant, atque ob id non poterat res expediri, praetor in eam rem prospexit et comparavit interdicta quae secundaria appellamus, quod secundo loco redduntur, quorum [vis ac potestas] haec est, ut qui caetera ex interdicto non faciat, velut qui vim non faciat aut fructus non liceatur, aut qui fructus licitationis satis non det aut qui sponsiones [restipulationes]ve non faciat sponsionumve judicia non accipiat, si possideat, ut restituat adversario possessionem, [si non possideat ut vim] illi possidenti non faciat. Itaque etsi alias potuerit interdicto "uti possidetis" vincere, si caetera ex interdicto [facere voluisset] tamen per interdictum secundarium V . . . . . secundarium . . . . . quamvis hanc opinionem . . . . . Sabinus et Cassius secuti fuerint . . . . pecuniaria poena, modo jurisjurandi religione coerceatur.

§ 171. Eaque praetor praecipue ideo . . . . adversus infitiantes ex quibusdam causis dupli actio constituitur, velut si judicati, aut depensi, aut damni injuriae, aut legatorum per damnationem relictorum nomine agitur. Ex quibusdam causis sponsionem facere permittitur, velut de pecunia certa credita et pecunia constituta; sed certae quidem creditae pecuniae tertiae partis, constitutae vero pecuniae partis dimidiae. § 172. Quod si neque sponsionis, neque dupli actionis periculum ei, cum quo agitur injungatur, ac ne statim quidem ab initio pluris quam simpli sit actio, permittit praetor jusjurandum exigere "non calumniae causa infitias ire": unde, quamvis heredes, vel qui heredum loco habentur, [simplotenus] obligati sint, item feminae pupillique quamvis eximantur periculo sponsionis, jubet tamen eos jurare. § 173. Statim autem ab initio pluris quam simpli actio est, velut furti manifesti quadrupli, nec manifesti dupli, concepti et oblati tripli, nam ex his causis et aliis quibusdam, sive quis neget sive fateatur, pluris quam simpli est actio.

Tit. xvi. De poena temere litigantium.

Nunc admonendi sumus, magnum curam egisse eos qui jura sustinebant, *ne facile homines ad litigandum procederent;* quod et nobis studio est. Idque eo maxime fieri potest, quod temeritas tam agentium, quam eorum cum quibus ageretur, *modo pecuniaria poena, modo jurisjurandi religione,* modo infamiae metu *coercetur.* § 1. Ecce enim jusjurandum omnibus qui conveniuntur ex nostra constitutione defertur: nam reus non aliter suis allegationibus utitur, nisi prius juraverit, quod putans sese bona instantia uti ad contradicendum pervenit. *At adversus infitiantes ex quibusdam causis dupli* vel tripli *actio constituitur: veluti si damni injuriae, aut legatorum* locis venerabilibus relictorum nomine agetur. *Statim autem ab initio pluris quam simpli est actio: veluti, furti manifesti quadrupli; nec manifesti dupli: nam ex his causis et aliis quibusdam, sive quis neget, sive fateatur, pluris quam simpli est actio.*

§ 174. Actoris quoque calumnia coercetur modo calumniae judicio, modo contrario, modo jurejurando, modo restipulatione. § 175. Et quidem calumniae judicium adversus omnes actiones locum habet, et est decimae partis rei; sed adversus adsertorem tertiae partis est. § 176. Sed liberum est autem ei, cum quo agitur, aut calumniae judicium opponere, aut jusjurandum exigere "non calumniae causa agere". § 177. Contrarium autem judicium certis ex causis constituitur: velut si injuriarum agatur, et si cum muliere eo nomine agatur, quod dicatur

Item actoris quoque calumnia coercetur: nam etiam actor pro calumnia jurare cogitur ex nostra constitutione. Utriusque etiam partis advocati jusjurandum subeunt, quod alia nostra constitu-

ventris nomine in possessionem missa, dolo malo ad alium possessionem transtulisse; et si quis eo nomine agat, quod dicat se, a praetore in possessionem missum, ab alio quo admissum non esse. Sed adversus injuriarum quidem actionem decimae partis datur; adversus vero duas istas, quintae. § 178. Severior autem coercitio est per contrarium judicium: nam in calumniae judicio decimae [sive quintae] partis nemo damnatur, nisi qui intellegit non recte se agere, sed vexandi adversarii gratia actionem instituit, potiusque ex judicis errore vel iniquitate victoriam sperat, quam ex causae veritate; contrario vero judicio omnimodo damnatur actor, is causam non tenuerit, licet falsa opinione inductus crediderit se recte agere. § 179. Utique autem ex quibus [quis] causis contrario judicio agere potest, etiam calumniae judicium locum habet: sed alterutro tamen judicio agere permittitur. Qua ratione, si jusjurandum de calumnia exactum fuerit, quemadmodum calumniae judicium non datur, ita et contrarium dari non debet. § 180. Restipulationis quoque poena ex certis causis fieri solet; et quemadmodum contrario judicio omnimodo condemnatur actor, si causam non tenuerit, nec requiritur, an scierit non recte se agere, ita etiam restipulationis poena omnimodo damnatur actor. § 181. [Sane si ab actore ea re]stipulationis poena petatur, ei neque calumniae judicium opponitur, neque jurisjurandi religio injungitur: nam contrarium judicium in his causis locum non habere palam est.

tione comprehensum est. Haec autem omnia pro veteris calumniae actione introducta sunt, quae in desuetudinem abiit, quia in partem decimam litis actores mulctabat, quod nunquam factum esse invenimus; sed pro his introductum est et praefatum jusjurandum, et ut improbus litigator etiam damnum et impensas litis inferre adversario suo cogatur.

§ 182. Quibusdam judiciis damnati ignominiosi fiunt, velut furti, vi bonorum raptorum, injuriarum, pro socio, fiduciae, tutelae, mandati, depositi. Sed furti, aut vi bonorum raptorum, aut injuriarum non solum damnati notantur ignominia, sed etiam pacti: ut in edicto praetoris scriptum est, et recte: plurimum enim interest, utrum ex delicto aliquis, an ex contractu debitor sit. Item illa parte edicti id ipsum nominatim expre[ssum est, ut pactus igno]miniosus [habeatur] qua prohibetur [pro aliis] postulare, procurator dari, procuratorem adhibere cognitoremve, vel cognitorio nomine judicio intervenire . . . .

§ 2. Ex *quibusdam judiciis damnati ignominiosi fiunt: veluti furti, vi bonorum raptorum, injuriarum,* de dolo, *item tutelae, mandati, depositi,* directis non contrariis actionibus; *item pro socio,* quae ab utraque parte directa est; et ob id quilibet ex sociis eo judicio damnatus ignominia notatur. *Sed furti quidem, aut vi bonorum raptorum, aut injuriarum, aut de dolo, non solum damnati notantur ignominia, sed etiam pacti, et recte: plurimum enim interest utrum ex delicto aliquis, an ex contractu debitor sit.*

§ 183. In summa sciendum est, eum, qui. . . oportere et eum, qui vocatus est. . . Quasdem [tamen personas] sine permissu praetoris in jus vocare non licet velut parentes et patronos patronorumque liberos et parentes patroni patronaeve, et in eum, qui adversus ea egerit, poena consi[tituitur].

§ 3. Omnium autem actionum instituendarum principium ab ea parte edicti proficiscitur qua praetor edicit de in jus vocando: utique enim in primis adversarius in jus vocandus est, id est, ad eum vocandus est qui jus dicturus sit. Qua parte praetor parentibus et patronis, item liberis parentibusque patronorum et patronarum hunc praestat honorem, ut non aliter liceat liberis libertisque eos in jus vocare, quam si id ab ipso praetore postulaverint et impetraverint; et si quis aliter vocaverit, in eum poenam solidorum quinquaginta constituit.

§ 184. Cum autem in jus vocatus fuerit adversarius, neque eo die finiri potuerit negotium, vadimonium ei faciendum est, ut promittat se certo die sisti. § 185. Fiunt autem vadimonia quibusdam ex causis pura, id est, sine satisdatione; quibusdam, cum satisdatione; quibusdam, jurejurando; quibusdam, recuperatoribus suppositis, id est, ut qui non steterit, protinus a recuperatoribus in summam vadimonii condemnetur: eaque singula diligenter praetoris edicto significantur. § 186. Et siquidem judicati depensive agetur, tanti fit vadimonium, quanti ea res erit; si vero ex caeteris causis, quanti actor juraverit non calumniae causa postulare sibi vadimonium promitti. nec tamen [pluris quam partis dimidiae, nec plu]ribus quam sestertium C millibus fit vadimonium: itaque si centum millium res erit, nec judicati depensive agetur, non plus quam sestertium quinquaginta millibus fit vadimonium. § 187. Quas autem personas sine permissu praetoris impune in jus vocare non possumus, easdem ne vadimonio [quidem] invitas obligare possumus, praeterquam si praetor aditus permittat.

Tit. xvii. De officio judicis.

Superest ut de officio judicis dispiciamus. Et quidem in primis illud observare debet judex, ne aliter judicet quam quod legibus, aut constitutionibus, aut moribus proditum est. § 1. Ideo si noxali judicio addictus est, observare debet ut, si condemnandus videbitur dominus, ita debeat condemnare: "Publium Maevium Lucio Titio decem aureis condemno, aut noxam dedere". § 2. Et si in rem actum sit, sive contra petitorem judicaverit, absolvere debet possessorem, sive contra possessorem, jubere eum debet, ut rem ipsam restituat cum fructibus. Sed si in praesenti neget se possessor restituere posse, et sine frustratione videbitur tempus restituendi causa petere, indulgendum est ei, ut tamen de litis aestimatione caveat cum fidejussore, si intra tempus quod ei datum est non restituisset. Et si hereditas petita sit, eadem circa fructus interveniunt quae diximus intervenire in singularum rerum petitione. Illorum autem fructuum quos culpa sua possessor non perceperit in utraque actione eadem ratio pene habetur, si praedo fuerit. Si vero bona fide possessor fuerit, non habetur ratio consumptorum, neque non perceptorum; post inchoatam autem petitionem etiam illorum ratio habetur qui culpa possessoris percepti non sunt, vel percepti consumpti sunt. § 3. Si ad exhibendum actum fuerit, non sufficit, si exhibeat rem is cum quo actum est, sed opus est, ut etiam causam rei debeat exhibere, id est ut eam causam habeat actor quam habiturus esset, si cum primum ad exhibendum egisset, exhibita res fuisset. Ideoque si inter moras usucapta sit res a possessore, nihilominus condemnatur. Praeterea fructus medii temporis, id est, ejus quod post acceptum ad exhibendum judicium ante rem judicatam intercessit, rationem habere debet judex. Quod si neget is cum quo ad exhibendum actum est, in praesenti exhibere se posse, et tempus exhibendi causa petat, idque sine frustratione postulare videatur, dari ei debet: ut tamen caveat se restiturum; quod si neque statim jussu judicis rem exhibeat, neque postea exhibiturum se caveat, condemnandus sit in id quod actoris intererat ab initio rem exhibitam esse. § 4. Si familiae erciscundae judicio actum sit, singulas res singulis heredibus adjudicare debet, et si in alterius persona praegravare videatur adjudicatio, debet hunc invicem coheredi certa pecunia, sicut jam dictum est, condemnare. Eo quoque nomine coheredi quisque suo condemnandus est, quod solus fructus hereditarii fundi percepit, aut rem hereditariam corruperit aut consumpserit, quae quidem similiter inter plures quoque quam duos coheredes subsequuntur. § 5. Eadem interveniunt, et si communi dividundo de pluribus rebus actum fuerit. Quod si de una re, veluti de fundo, si quidem iste fundus commode regionibus divisionem recipiat, partes ejus singulis adjudicare debet, et si unius pars praegravare videbitur, is invicem certa pecunia alteri condemnandus est; quod si commode dividi non possit, veluti si homo forte aut mulus erit de quo actum sit, tunc uni totus adjudicandus est, et is invicem alteri certa pecunia condemnandus. § 6. Si finium regundorum actum fuerit, dispicere debet judex an necessaria sit adjudicatio: quae sane uno casu necessaria est, si evidentioribus finibus distingui agros commodius sit, quam olim fuissent distincti: nam tunc necesse est ex alterius agro partem aliquam alterius agri domino adjudicari; quo casu conveniens est, ut is alteri certa pecunia debeat condemnari. Eo quoque nomine damnandus est quisque hoc judicio, quod forte circa fines malitiose aliquid commisit, verbi gratia, quia lapides finales furatus est aut arbores finales cecedit. Contumaciae quoque nomine quisque eo judicio condemnatur, veluti si quis jubente judice metiri agros passus non fuerit. § 7. Quod autem istis judiciis alicui adjudicatum sit, id statim ejus fit cui adjudicatum est.

Tit. xviii. De publicis judiciis.

Publica judicia neque per actiones ordinantur, nec omnino quidquam simile habent cum caeteris judiciis de quibus locuti sumus, magnaque diversitas est eorum et instituendis et in exercendis. § 1. Publica autem dicta sunt, quod cuivis ex populo executio eorum plerumque datur. § 2. Publicorum judiciorum quaedam capitalia sunt, quaedam non capitalia. Capitalia dicimus quae ultimo supplicio afficiunt, vel aquae et ignis interdictione, vel deportatione, vel metallo; caetera, si quam infamiam irrogant cum damno pecuniario, haec publica quidem sunt, non tamen capitalia.

§ 3. Publica autem judicia sunt haec: Lex Julia majestatis, quae in eos qui contra imperatorem vel rempublicam aliquid moliti sunt, suum vigorem extendit. Hujus poena animae amissionem sustinet, et memoria rei etiam post mortem damnatur. § 4. Item lex Julia de adulteriis coercendis, quae non solum temeratores alienarum nuptiarum gladio punit, sed etiam eos qui cum masculis nefandam libidinem exercere audent. Sed eadem lege Julia etiam stupri flagitium punitur, cum quis sine vi vel virginem vel viduam honeste viventem stupraverit. Poenam autem eadem lex irrogat peccatoribus: si honesti sunt, publicationem partis dimidiae bonorum, si humiles, corporis coercitionem cum relegatione. § 5. Item lex Cornelia de sicariis, quae homicidas ultore ferro persequitur, vel eos qui hominis occidendi causa cum telo ambulant. Telum autem, ut Gaius noster in interpretatione legis Duodecim Tabularum scriptum reliquit, vulgo quidem id appellatur quod ab arcu mittitur, sed et omne significatur quod manu cujusdam mittitur: sequitur ergo, ut lapis et lignum et ferrum hoc nomine contineatur; dictumque ab eo, quod in longinquum mittitur, a graeca voce figuratum, ἀπὸ τοῦ τηλοῦ; et hanc significationem invenire possumus et in graeco nomine: nam quod nos telum appellamus, illi βέλος appellant ἀπὸ τοῦ βάλλεσθαι. Admonet nos Xenophon, nam ita scripsit: καὶ τὰ βέλη ὁμοῦ ἐφέρετο, λόγχαι, τοξεύματα, σφενδόναι, πλεῖστοι δὲ καὶ λίθοι. Sicarii autem appellantur a sica, quod significat ferreum cultrum. Eadem lege et venefici capite damnantur, qui artibus odiosis, tam venenis vel susurris magicis, homines occiderint, vel mala medicamenta publice vendiderint. § 6. Alia deinde lex asperrimum crimen nova poena persequitur, quae Pompeia de parricidiis vocatur: qua cavetur ut, si quis parentis aut filii, aut omnino affectionis ejus quae nuncupatione parricidii continetur, fata properaverit; sive clam, sive palam id ausus fuerit, nec non is cujus dolo malo id factum est, vel conscius criminis existit, licet extraneus sit, poena parricidii puniatur, et neque gladio, neque ignibus, neque ulla alia sollemni poena subjiciatur, sed insutus culeo cum cane et gallo gallinaceo et vipera et simia, et inter eas ferales angustias comprehensus, secundum quod regionis qualitas tulerit, vel in vicinum mare vel in amnem projiciatur, ut omnium elementorum usu vivus carere incipiat, et ei caelum superstiti, et terra mortuo auferatur. Si quis autem alias cognatione vel affinitate conjunctas personas necaverit, poenam legis Corneliae de sicariis sustinebit. § 7. Item lex Cornelia de falsis, quae etiam testamentaria vocatur, poenam irrogat ei qui testamentum vel aliud instrumentum falsum scripserit, signaverit, recitaverit, subjecerit, quive signum adulterinum fecerit, sculpserit, expresserit sciens dolo malo. Ejusque legis poena in servos ultimum supplicium est, quod etiam in lege de sicariis et veneficis servatur; in liberos vero deportatio. § 8. Item lex Julia de vi publica seu privata adversus eos exoritur qui vim vel armatam vel sine armis commiserint. Sed si quidem armata vis arguatur, deportatio ei ex lege Julia de vi publica irrogatur; si vero sine armis, in tertiam partem bonorum publicatio imponitur. Sin autem per vim raptus virginis, vel viduae, vel sanctimonialis, vel aliae fuerit perpetratus, tunc et peccatores, et ii qui opem flagitio dederunt capite puniuntur, secundum nostrae constitutionis definitionem ex qua hoc apertius est scire. § 9. Lex Julia peculatus eos punit, qui pecuniam, vel rem publicam, vel sacram, vel religiosam furati fuerint. Sed si quidem ipsi judices tempore administrationis publicas pecunias subtraxerunt, capitali animadversione puniantur, et non solum hi, sed etiam qui ministerium eis ad hoc adhibuerint, vel qui subtractas ab his scientes susceperint; alii vero qui in hanc legem inciderint poenae deportationis subjugantur. § 10. Est et inter publica judicia lex Fabia de plagiariis, quae interdum capitis poenam ex sacris constitutionibus irrogat, interdum leviorem. § 11. Sunt praeterea publica judicia lex Julia de ambitu, et lex Julia repetundarum, et lex Julia de annona, et lex Julia de residuis, quae de certis capitulis loquuntur, et animae quidem amissionem non irrogant, aliis autem poenis eos subjiciunt qui praecepta earum neglexerint.

§ 12. Sed de publicis judiciis haec exposuimus, ut vobis possibile sit summo digito, et quasi per indicem, ea tetigisse: alioquin diligentior eorum scientia vobis ex latioribus Digestorum seu Pandectarum libris, Deo propitio, adventura est.

THE INSTITUTES OF GAIUS AND JUSTINIAN,

TRANSLATED BY

T. LAMBERT MEARS, M.A., LL.D. (LOND.),

OF THE INNER TEMPLE, BARRISTER-AT-LAW.

THE

INSTITUTES OF JUSTINIAN.

PREAMBLE.

IN THE NAME OF OUR LORD JESUS CHRIST.

THE EMPEROR CAESAR FLAVIAN JUSTINIAN,
THE CONQUEROR OF THE ALEMANIANS,
GOTHS, FRANKS, GERMANS, ANTIANS,
ALANIANS, VANDALS, AND AFRICANS,
THE PIOUS, HAPPY, GLORIOUS,
VICTORIOUS, AND TRIUMPHANT,
EVER AUGUST,

TO THE YOUTH DESIROUS OF STUDYING THE LAWS,
GREETING.

OUR Imperial Majesty should not only shine by force of arms, but be armed by the force of laws, so that the state may be rightly directed in peace as in war, and the Roman Emperor, ever victorious over his enemies in the field as well as over the transgressors of his ordinances, may be equally renowned for the rigid maintenance of law as for success in war.

§ 1. With unwearied watchfulness and anxious forethought we have, by the blessing of God, pursued this double path. Barbarian nations, subjected to our yoke, acknowledge our warlike powers, Africa and numberless other provinces, brought by divine providence, after a long interval, again under the Roman dominion, attest our victories and have been added to our empire, moreover all people are governed by the laws promulgated and drawn up by ourselves. § 2. The Imperial constitutions, hitherto in confusion, have been reduced by us to lucid harmony, after which we turned our attention to the countless volumes of the ancient jurisconsults, and plunging as it were into the depths of the sea, we have, with the favour of heaven, already completed this work previously deemed insurmountable. § 3. No sooner had we, with the blessing of God, accomplished this task than we called to our counsels our eminent Tribonian, master and ex-quæstor of our palace, as well as our illustrious professors of law Theophilus and Dorotheus (of all of whose capacity, legal knowledge, and fidelity we have already had many proofs), and we specially commanded them to draw up under our authority and direction these Institutes, in order that you may no longer become acquainted with the elements of law through antiquated channels, but imbibe them by the light of the Imperial Majesty, and with neither your ears nor your minds burdened with useless or erroneous matter, you may be instructed in that only which actually obtains, so that, whereas formerly the most diligent could scarcely after four years' study commence reading the imperial constitutions, you may now approach them at the outset, for you are held worthy of the honour and happiness of having the beginning and the end of your studies in law proceed from the mouth of the Emperor. § 4. When therefore, through the labours of the same most excellent Tribonian and other illustrious and talented men, we had compiled the fifty books of the Digest or Pandects, in which the whole of the ancient law has been collected, we ordered the above mentioned Institutes to be arranged in four books, to include the first elements of the whole science of law. § 5. Herein are set forth with brevity both that which formerly obtained and that which becoming subsequently obscured by disuse has been re-established by our imperial solicitude. § 6. This work, compiled from all the ancient institutes, and especially from the Institutes of our Gaius, and from his Commentaries on daily matters, and from other sources, has been submitted to us by the before-mentioned learned men, and we have read and considered it, and have given it all the force of our constitutions.

§ 7. Receive therefore, and study with eager alacrity, these our laws, and show such a mastery of them as shall encourage you to indulge in the cheering hope that when your legal studies are completed you may be able to govern such portions of our empire as may be entrusted to you.

Given at Constantinople on the eleventh day before the calends of December, in the third Consulate of our Emperor Justinian ever August, (22 November, A.D. 533).

INSTITUTES

OF

GAIUS, COMMENTARY I. JUSTINIAN, BOOK I.

Title i. Of Justice and of Law.

Justice is the continual desire of always rendering to each one that which is his due.

§ 1. Jurisprudence is the knowledge of things divine and human; the science of that which is lawful and unlawful.

§ 2. Now passing from these general propositions to the study of the laws of the Romans, we think it will be best to commence with a simple and brief exposition, leaving a more careful and accurate examination to a subsequent period; for if at the very outset we overload with a multitude of various details the youthful and untrained mind of the student, one of two things will result, either we shall drive him to abandon his studies or we shall slowly drag him (with great labour to himself and at the risk of giving rise to that diffidence in his own powers which so often turns the student aside) towards that same point to which he might have been readily conducted without weariness or distrust.

§ 3. The maxims of the law are: to live honestly, to hurt no one, to render to each his due.

§ 4. Law consists of two parts: public and private. Public law relates to the constitution of the state; private law is concerned with individual interests. Let us now discuss the subject of private law, which is drawn from three sources, viz.: from the precepts due to natural law, the law of nations, and the civil law.

Title. ii. Of Natural Law, the Law of Nations, and the Civil Law.

Natural law is that which nature teaches to all animals, for it is not peculiar to the human race, but is common to all animals which are produced in the air, on the earth, or in the sea. Hence comes the union of male and female, which we call marriage; hence the procreation and education of their young, for we see, in fact, that the other animals besides man act in conformity with this law as if they were acquainted with it.

Of the Law of Nations and the Civil Law.

§ I. All communities of men governed by laws and customs, partly use their own particular law and partly that common to all men, for that law which each particular community establishes for itself, is peculiar to that community and is called the civil law, as being the peculiar law of that community; but that which natural reason establishes between all men is equally maintained by all communities, and is called the law of nations, as being that law which is used by all nations. In this way the Romans use partly their own peculiar law, partly that common to all men. How these distinctions affect our subject we will discuss as occasion arises.

§ I. Civil law may be distinguished from the law of nations thus: all communities of men governed by laws and customs partly use their own particular law and partly that common to all men, for that law which each particular community establishes for itself, is peculiar to that community and is called the civil law, as being the peculiar law of that community; but that which natural reason establishes between all men, is equally maintained by all communities, and is called the law of nations, as being that law which is used by all nations. In this way the Romans use partly their own peculiar law, partly that common to all men. How these distinctions affect the subject we will discuss as occasion arises.

§ 2. The civil law derives its name from each particular community, as, for instance, from the Athenians, for it would not be an erroneous expression to call the laws of Solon or Draco the civil law of the Athenians. So we call the law which is used by the Roman people the civil law of the Romans, or that of the Quirites, as being used by the Quirites; for the Romans were called Quirites from Quirinus. But whenever we do not add the name of the community to which the law belongs, we intend to be understood as referring to our own law; just as when we speak of the poet without any addition, the name understood amongst the Greeks would be that of the famous Homer, with us Virgil. On the other hand, the law of nations is common to the whole human race, for mankind, from the necessities of human life and the demands of the occasion, have established certain laws for themselves, for wars have arisen, followed by captivity and slavery, which are contrary to natural law, as at the outset, and by natural law all men were born free. And it is through this law of nations that almost all our contracts have been introduced, as the contract of sale, hire, partnership, deposit, loan, and innumerable others.

§ 2. The laws of the Romans consist of laws, ordinances of the plebeians, decrees of the senate, the constitutions of the emperors, the edicts of those who have the right of declaring the law, and of the answers of the learned in the law.

§ 3. Our law, like that of the Greeks, is written or unwritten. Written law consists of laws, ordinances of the plebeians, decrees of the senate, constitutions of the emperors, edicts of magistrates, and of the answers of the learned in the law.

§ 3. A law is that which the people orders and establishes. An ordinance of the plebeians is that which the plebeians order and establish. Now the plebeians differ from the people in that by the term people the whole of the citizens are comprehended, including the patricians; but under the term plebeians the remainder of the citizens, without the patricians, are referred to; hence formerly the patricians contended that they were not bound by ordinances of the plebeians, for that they were made without their concurrence; but afterwards the Hortensian law was passed, enacting that ordinances of the plebeians should bind the whole people, and in this way they became equal to laws.

§ 4. A law is that which was enacted by the Roman people on the proposition of a senatorial magistrate, such as a consul. An ordinance of the plebeians is that which was enacted by the plebeians on the proposition of a plebeian magistrate, such as a tribune. The plebeians differ from the people as the species from its genus; for, under the term people, the whole of the citizens are comprehended, including the patricians and the senators, but the expression plebeians only includes the citizens remaining after deducting the patricians and the senators, though, after the passing of the Hortensian law, ordinances of the plebeians acquired the same force as laws.

§ 4. A decree of the senate is that which the senate orders and establishes, and it has the force of a law, although this has been doubted.

§ 5. A decree of the senate is that which the senate orders and establishes; for when the Roman people had increased to such an extent that it was a matter of difficulty to convoke them all for the purpose of sanctioning laws, it seemed expedient that the senate should be consulted instead of the people.

§ 5. A constitution of the emperor is that which the emperor establishes by decree, edict, or rescript, and it has never been doubted that this has the force of

§ 6. The will of the emperor has also the force of law; for by the royal law which is passed to confer authority on him, the people yield up to him all its authority

a law, since the emperor himself receives his authority by a law.

and power. Whatever, therefore, the emperor directs by rescript, or decrees by a judgment, or ordai- by edict, is admitted to be law; and these are wh·.. are called constitutions. Of these obviously some are personal, and are not to be drawn into precedents, since such is not the intention of the emperor; for that which he has granted to anyone as a reward for merit, or that which he has inflicted as a punishment, or that which he has given by way of assistance in an extraordinary case, does not apply beyond the particular individual. But other constitutions, being general, are undoubtedly binding on all.

§ 6. The right of declaring the law is vested in the magistrates of the Roman people, and this right is exercised to its greatest extent in the edicts of the two prætors, viz., the urban prætor and the prætor for aliens, whose equivalent jurisdiction in the provinces is exercised by the respective governors. A similar right is exercised in the edicts of the curule ædiles, whose jurisdiction the quæstors have in the provinces assigned to the Roman people; for quæstors are never sent into the provinces assigned to the emperor, and on that account no publication of this last-mentioned edict takes place in such provinces.

§ 7. The edicts of the prætors also carry no slight authority. These we are accustomed to include under the term honorary law, because those who bear honours, that is, the magistrates, have given rise to this description of law. The curule ædiles also used to publish an edict relative to certain matters, and this edict forms a portion of the honorary law.

§ 7. The answers of the learned in the law are the decisions and opinions of those who are authorised to settle points of law, and their unanimous decision has the force of a law, though, if they disagree, it is lawful for the judge to follow that decision which he thinks best, as is laid down in a rescript of the late Emperor Hadrian.

§ 8. The answers of the learned in the law are the decisions and opinions of those who were authorised to settle points of law, for it was formerly provided that there should be public interpreters of the law, to whom the power of expounding the law was given by the emperor, and who were called juris-consults. The unanimous decisions and opinions of these persons had such weight that it was settled by a constitution that the judge should not be at liberty to decide otherwise.

§ 9. The unwritten law is that which usage has approved; for daily customs, approved by those in the habit of using them, resemble laws.

§ 10. It does not seem unreasonable that the civil law should have been divided into two branches, for the origin of the distinction appears to have been derived from the institutions of two states, viz., that of Athens and Lacedæmon; for in these states it was usual for the Lacedemonians rather to commit to memory that which they observed as law, whilst, on the other hand, the Athenians followed those rules which were set down in writing in their laws.

§ 11. The natural laws commonly observed by all nations and established by divine wisdom, always remain fixed and immutable, but those laws which each community establishes for itself are liable to frequent change, either by the tacit consent of the people or in consequence of subsequent legislation.

Of the Division of Law.

§ 8. All our law relates either to persons, things, or actions, and first let us treat of persons.

§ 12. All our law relates either to persons, things, or actions, and first let us treat of persons, for it will avail little to know the law if we do not know the persons for whom the law was established.

Of the Condition of Men.

§ 9. The principal division of the law of persons is this, that all men are either free or slaves.

Title iii. Of the law of Persons.

The principal division of the law of persons is this, that all men are either free or slaves.

§ 1. Freedom, in consequence of which persons are said to be free, consists in the natural capacity to do that which each one pleases, except in so far as restrained by force or law.

§ 2. Slavery, on the other hand, is an institution due to the law of nations, by which one person is subjected to the power of another, contrary to nature.

§ 3. Such persons are called "servi" from "servare", because generals do not usually kill their captives, but order them to be sold, and thus preserve them. They are also called "mancipia", because they are taken from the enemy by the hand.

§ 4. Moreover, slaves are either born so or become so. They are born so when they are the offspring of our female slaves; they become so either by the law of nations, that is, as the result of captivity, or by the civil law, as when a free person above the age of twenty has allowed himself to be sold in order that he may share the price paid for him.

§ 10. Again, as to free men, some are freeborn, others are freedmen.

§ 5. In the condition of slaves there are no distinctions; but amongst free persons there are many, for they are either freeborn or freedmen.

Title iv. Of the freeborn.

§ II. The freeborn are those who have been born free.

The freeborn is one who, from the moment of his birth, is free, whether the issue of the marriage of two freeborn persons, or of two freed-persons, or of one freed-person, and one freeborn. So also, though the father were a slave, still, if the mother was free, the child would be freeborn, just as is the case where the mother is free but the father uncertain, since the child is the result of promiscuous intercourse. Moreover, it is sufficient if the mother is free at the time the child is born, although conceived in slavery; and, on the other hand, if the mother was free when she conceived, but was a slave when the child was born, it is settled that the child is born free, for the calamity which has befallen the mother ought not to be visited on the child in her womb. Hence the question arose, if a female slave was manumitted whilst pregnant, and her child was born after she had been again reduced to slavery, would the child be born free or a slave? Marcellus inclines to the view that the child would be free, because it is sufficient to the unborn child to have had a free mother in the intermediate time; and this view we hold to be correct.

§ I. When a person has been born free, his position is not affected by the fact of his having been in slavery and afterwards manumitted, for it has been repeatedly decided that manumission cannot affect the rights of birth.

Title v. Of freed-persons.

Freed-persons are those who have been manumitted from lawful slavery.

Freed-persons are those who have been manumitted from lawful slavery.

Manumission is the giving of liberty, for so long as a person is in slavery, he is under the hand and under the power of another, and when manumitted he is freed from this power. This matter arises out of the law of nations, for since by natural law all were born free; manumission could not be known, as slavery itself was unknown. But after that slavery had, through the law of nations, invaded the rights of the freeborn, the boon of manumission followed. And whereas we were all called by the one common name of men, by the law of nations three classes of men came into existence, viz., the free, and, in opposition to them, slaves; and, thirdly, freed persons, who had ceased to be slaves. § 1. Manumission is effected in various ways; either in the sacred churches, according to the imperial constitutions, or by the process of fictitious vindication, or in the presence of friends, or by letter, or by testament, or by any other expression of a man's last wishes. And liberty may be also conferred on a slave in many other ways, by virtue of our own or earlier constitutions.

§ 12. Again there are three classes of freed-persons, for they are either Roman citizens or Latins, or fall under the head of surrendered persons. We shall treat of each of these classes separately, and begin with the last named.

Of surrendered persons and of the Ælian Sentian Law.

§ 13. By the Ælian Sentian Law, it is enacted that slaves, who have been by way of punishment put in chains by their masters, or branded by them, or, on suspicion of some wrongful act, subjected to torture, and convicted of the crime, or who have been delivered over to fight with swords, or with wild beasts, or thrown into a gladiatorial school, or prison; and afterwards manumitted by the same or by another master, shall become free persons of the same class as surrendered aliens.

Of surrendered aliens.

§ 14. The term surrendered aliens applies to those who, formerly having taken up arms, fought against the Roman people, but when conquered, surrendered themselves.

§ 15. Therefore we say of slaves who have been subject to degradation of the above-mentioned description, that in whatever way, and at whatever age they may have been manumitted, and although they have been in the full power of their masters, they can never become Roman citizens or Latins, but in all respects are to be regarded as belonging to the class of surrendered persons. § 16. But if a slave has incurred no such serious stain, he may by manumission sometimes become a Roman citizen, sometimes a Latin. § 17. For he in whose person the three following requisites unite, viz., that he is over thirty years of age, that he is the property of his master by the law of the quirites, and that he is manumitted in a regular and statutory mode, that is, by the process of fictitious vindication, or at the census, or by testament, such an one thereby becomes a Roman citizen, but, if any one of these requisites is wanting, he will be a Latin.

Of manumission and of proving a case for citizenship.

§ 18. The requirement as to the age of the slave was introduced by the Ælian Sentian law, for that law only allows slaves manumitted under thirty years of age to become Roman citizens if they have been freed by the process of fictitious vindication after a lawful ground of manumission has been approved by the council. § 19. A lawful ground of manumission is, for example, when anyone manumits before the council a son or daughter, or brother or sister by blood, or foster child, or his preceptor, or a male slave about to be made his procurator, or a female slave for the purpose of marrying her.

Of the Recuperators.

§ 20. This council is composed in the city of Rome of five senators and five knights, Romans of the age of puberty; in the provinces of twenty recuperators who are Roman citizens, and their meeting for this purpose is held on the last day of the assizes; but at Rome the manumission takes place before the council on certain fixed days.

Slaves who are more than thirty years of age may be manumitted at any time, so that manumission may even take place when the prætor or pro-consul is on his way to the baths or to the theatre. § 21. So a slave under thirty years of age may by manumission become a Roman citizen if he has been made free and appointed heir by the testament of an insolvent master . . . . (twenty-four lines illegible). . . . . § 22. . . . . those who are thus manumitted are called Latin Junians: Latins because they are assimilated to Latin colonists, and Junians because they have received liberty through the Junian law, although formerly regarded as slaves. § 23. But the Junian law does not allow them to make a will, nor to take anything by the testament of another, nor can they be appointed tutors by testament. § 24. Though in saying that they cannot take by testament, we must be understood to mean that they cannot take directly by way of inheritance or of legacy; for they may take by way of bequest in trust. § 25. Whereas those classed amongst surrendered persons cannot in any way acquire by testament any more than an alien, nor, according to the better opinion* can they make a testament. § 26. Hence those classed as surrendered persons enjoy the lowest form of liberty,

§ 2. Slaves may be manumitted by their masters at any time; so that the manumission may even take place when the prætor or proconsul, or governor of a province, is on his way to the baths or the theatre.

* *post*, iii, § 75.

and cannot attain to the Roman citizenship by virtue of any law, decree of the senate, or imperial constitution. § 27. And further, they are forbidden to dwell in the city of Rome, or within a hundred miles of the city; and on violation of this rule they and their property are ordered to be publicly sold, with a proviso that they shall not serve as slaves in the city of Rome, or within a hundred miles of it, and that they shall never be manumitted; and if they shall have been manumitted, then they are ordered to be slaves of the Roman people; and all these points are included under the Ælian Sentian law.

Of the means by which Latins become Roman citizens.

§ 28. Latins may obtain the Roman citizenship in various ways. § 29. For it is directly enacted by the Ælian Sentian law, that slaves manumitted under thirty years of age, and made Latins, if they have married wives who are either Roman citizens or Latin colonists, or of the same condition as themselves; and if they have solemnly declared this fact in the presence of not less than seven Roman citizens over the age of puberty, and if they have also begotten a son, then, when this child has attained to the age of one year, this law gives them the right to go before the prætor (or in the provinces the governor), and prove that according to the terms of the Ælian Sentian law they have married, and that there is issue of this marriage a son a year old; and if he before whom the matter is brought shall have declared it to be as asserted, then both the Latin himself and his wife (if she be of the same condition as himself), and their son (if he also be of the same condition) are ordered to be Roman citizens. § 30. The reason why we have added in respect of the son the words, "if he be of the same condition", is because, if the wife of the Latin be a Roman citizen, her offspring will be by birth a Roman citizen in virtue of a recent decree of the senate, passed in the reign of the late Emperor Hadrian. § 31. Although the Ælian Sentian law only accorded this mode of becoming Roman citizens to slaves manumitted, and made Latins under thirty years of age, yet afterwards, by a decree of the senate, passed in the consulship of Pegasus and Pusio, the same right was conferred on slaves manumitted and made Latins when over thirty years of age. § 32. Again, if the Latin shall have died before proving that he has a son a year old, the mother may do so, and in this way she may herself become a Roman citizen, and . . . . (eight lines illegible) . . . . that is, they become Roman citizens if they have served six years at Rome in the night-watch; and a subsequent decree of the senate is said to have conferred the citizenship after the completion of three years of such military service. Moreover, by the Claudian edict, Latins became entitled to enjoy the law of the quirites if they had built a sea-going vessel capable of stowing a cargo of not less than ten thousand measures of corn, and for six years that vessel, or one substituted for it, has been employed carrying cargoes of corn to Rome. § 33. Moreover, in the reign of Nero, the Senate conceded quiritarian rights to the Latin who, possessing a patrimony of more than two hundred thousand sesterces, built a house in the city of Rome, in the building of which he had expended not less than one half of his patrimony. § 34. Finally, Trajan decreed that a Latin should enjoy quiritarian rights who carried on for three years the business of a corn-miller, using a mill in which not less than one hundred measures of corn were ground daily. § 35. . . . . . (fourteen lines illegible). . . . . . But if a slave, owned as part of a person's goods, and also by the law of the quirites, be manumitted, it is to be understood that he may become a Latin, and then in the same way acquire quiritarian rights.

§ 3. There existed formerly a threefold division of freedmen. For those who were manumitted sometimes obtained the legally complete, and greatest degree of liberty, and became Roman citizens; sometimes a lesser degree of liberty, and became Latins under the Junian-Norbana law; and sometimes a liberty of still lower degree, and fell, by the Ælian Sentian law, under the class of surrendered persons. But this lowest class, that of surrendered persons, has long since disappeared, and the name of Latins is not often met with; and therefore in our benevolence, which induces us to increase and improve everything, we have corrected this matter in two constitutions, and brought things back to their original condition; for in the primitive infancy of the city of Rome there was but one simple liberty, that is, the same as that possessed by the manumittor himself, except that of course the person manumitted was a freed-person, whilst the manumittor was free-born. We have abolished the class of surrendered persons by a constitution published among our decisions, by which, at the suggestion of our excellent quæstor Tribonian, we have settled the disputed points arising out of the ancient law, and by another constitution, which shines among the imperial ordinances, and which was suggested to us by the same quæstor, we have amended the law as to Latin Junians and as to all that relates to them. We now grant Roman citizenship to all freed men, making no distinction (as used to be the case) in the age of the slave, or the kind of ownership possessed by the manumittor, or the mode of manumission; and we have introduced many new methods by which liberty may be conferred on slaves, together with Roman citizenship, which now-a-days always accompanies it.

Title vi. Of those who cannot manumit and the reasons why.

§ 36. The right of manumitting is not, however, open to everyone. § 37. For he who manumits in fraud of the rights of his creditors or patron, does not attain his end, because the Ælian Sentian law puts an obstacle in the way of the gift of freedom.

The right of manumitting is not, however, open to everyone, for he who manumits in fraud of his creditors does not attain his end, because the Ælian Sentian law puts an obstacle in the way of the gift of freedom. § I. But an insolvent master may by will institute his slave as his heir, at the same time giving him his liberty, so that the slave becomes free and his only and necessary heir, provided that no other person becomes heir under the same testament, either because no other person was instituted heir, or because he who was instituted, for some reason or other, fails to become heir. This was established by the before-mentioned Ælian Sentian law, and on good grounds, for it was greatly to be desired that provision should be made to meet the case of needy men who would not be likely to find any other heir, and who should therefore be able to make a slave their necessary heir, who would meet the claims of their creditors; or in default of his so doing, the creditors would have it in their power to sell the property belonging to the inheritance in the name of the slave, and, in this way, no stigma would attach to the memory of the deceased. § 2. The law is the same, although the slave has been instituted heir without giving him his freedom, for our constitution, in quite a new spirit of humanity, establishes the principle, not only in the case of an insolvent master, but generally, that the mere fact of the institution implies the gift of liberty. For it is not very likely that a testator, on the ground that he had omitted to mention the gift of freedom, would wish the person selected by him as his heir to remain a slave, and that he himself should have no heir. § 3. A person is held to manumit in fraud of his creditors, who is insolvent at the time of the manumission, or who ceases to be solvent in consequence of the gift of liberty. It seems, however, to be now settled, that although the property may prove insufficient to meet the claims of his creditors, the gift of liberty is not invalidated unless there was a fraudulent intention on the part of the manumittor, for men often count on their property being of greater value than it really is. Therefore we hold the gift of liberty only invalidated when creditors are defrauded in both ways, that is, both by the intention of the manumittor, and in fact, by the property proving insufficient to meet the claims of the creditors.

§ 38. By the same law, a master under the age of twenty is not allowed to manumit, except by the process of fictitious vindication, and on a lawful ground, approved by the council. § 39. Lawful grounds for manumission are, for example, to manumit father or mother, preceptor or foster-brother; but those grounds which we have stated above* in respect of a slave less than thirty years of age, may be also applied to the present case, and so, on the other hand, the grounds specified in relation to a master under twenty, may be extended to the case of a slave under thirty.

* *ante*, § 19.

§ 4. By the same Ælian Sentian law, a master under the age of twenty is not allowed to manumit, except by the process of fictitious vindication, and on a lawful ground approved by the council. § 5. Lawful grounds for manumission are, for example, to manumit father or mother, son or daughter, brother or sister by blood, preceptor, nurse, foster-father, foster-child, or foster-brother; or a slave to make him his procurator, or a female slave for the purpose of marrying her, provided the marriage be performed within six months, unless prevented by some lawful cause; and provided that the slave who is to be made a procurator, be not manumitted under the age of seventeen years. § 6. But the ground stated for manumisssion having been once approved, cannot, whether true or false, be withdrawn.

§ 40. A certain limit being thus imposed by the Ælian Sentian law on the power of manumission to masters under twenty, it follows that, although he who has completed his fourteenth year may make a will, and in that will appoint an heir and bequeath legacies,

§ 7. A certain limit being thus imposed by the Ælian Sentian law on the power of manumission to masters under twenty, it followed that, although he who had completed his fourteenth year might make a will, and in that will appoint an heir, and bequeath lega-

yet if he be under twenty, he cannot give liberty to a slave. § 41. And even though a master under twenty only intends to make a Latin, still he ought to prove a satisfactory ground to the council, after which he may manumit in the presence of friends.

cies, yet if under twenty he could not give liberty to a slave. It seemed an untenable position that he to whom the power was given to will respecting his entire property, should not be able to give liberty to one single slave, wherefore we have conceded the right to such a person to dispose by his last will as he pleases of his slaves, just as he can do in respect of other matters, and to give such slaves their liberty. But as liberty is of inestimable value, and on this account persons under twenty were prohibited from giving liberty to a slave, we adopt something of a middle course, and only permit those persons under twenty to confer freedom on slaves by testament who have completed their seventeenth year and entered on their eighteenth year. For since, according to the ancient practice, persons at this age were permitted to plead even for others, why should not their judgment be deemed sufficiently matured also in respect of such a matter as the giving of liberty to their own slaves?

§ 42. Again by the Fusian Caninian law, a certain limit is imposed in respect of the power of manumitting slaves by testament. § 43. For he who has more than two and not more than ten slaves, may manumit up to half the number; and he who has more than ten and not more than thirty, may manumit up to one-third of the number; but he who has more than thirty and not more than one hundred, may manumit up to one-fourth part; and lastly, he who has more than a hundred and not more than five hundred, may not manumit more than the fifth part; and no greater number are counted, as the law provides that it shall not be lawful for anyone to manumit more than one hundred slaves; on the other hand, if a person possesses but one or two slaves this law will not touch

Title vii. Of the repeal of the Fusian Caninian law.

By the Fusian Caninian law, a limit was imposed on the manumission of slaves by testament; but we have thought it expedient to repeal this law, as being based to some extent on an odious principle, since it seems contrary to the dictates of humanity to give persons during their life the power to manumit all their slaves, if there is no special reason to prevent them, and to deprive the dying of the power of doing the same.

him, and therefore, his power of manumission is unrestrained. § 44. Nor does this law affect those who manumit otherwise than by testament; and, therefore, it is lawful for those who manumit by the process of fictitious vindication, or at the census or among friends, to free all their slaves, provided no other obstacle to their freedom existed. § 45. But what we have said respecting the number of slaves that may be manumitted by testament, is to be understood in this sense, that out of the number from which a half, a third, a fourth, or a fifth may be freed, that number at least may be freed under the higher number which would have been lawful under the lower; and this was the intention of the law, for it would be truly absurd that the master of ten slaves should be permitted to enfranchise five, because he has the right to manumit up to one-half, whilst the owner of twelve slaves should not be permitted to manumit more than four; but, that those who have over ten and not . . . (twenty-four lines illegible) . . . § 46. For, if in a testament, freedom be given to slaves whose names are written in a circle, then, since no order of manumission can be discovered, none will be free, because the Fusian Caninian law renders inoperative that which is done for the purpose of evading the law. There are also special decrees of the Senate rendering inoperative other attempted infringements of this law.

§ 47. Finally, it is to be observed that the provision of the Ælian Sentian law, rendering freedoms in fraud of creditors void, applies also to aliens; for, the Senate has so determined on the authority of the Emperor Hadrian, but the other provisions of this law do not refer to them.

§ 48. We now come to another division of the law of persons; for some persons are free from the power of others, and some are subject to the power of others. § 49. Again, of those persons who are subject to the power of others, some are in the power of their ascendants, others in that of their masters, others in that of their husbands, others are freemen in

Title viii. Of those who are free from power, and of those who are in the power of others.

We now come to another division of the law of persons; for some persons are free from the power of others, and others are subject to the power of others. Of those, again, who are subject to the power of others, some are in the power of ascendants, others in that of masters. Let us now con-

a state of bondage. § 50. Let us now consider the position of those who are subject to the power of others; for, if we have ascertained who these are, we shall at the same time understand who are free from the power of others.

§ 51. And first, let us treat of those who are in the power of ascendants or masters.

§ 52. Now, slaves are in the power of their masters, which kind of power is due to the law of nations; for, it will be found that, amongst nearly all nations masters have the power of life and death over their slaves; and also that whatever is acquired by the slave is acquired for the master. § 53. But, at the present day, it is not lawful for Roman citizens, or any other persons under the dominion of the Roman people, to punish their slaves with excessive severity and without grounds; for, by a constitution of the most sacred Emperor Antonine, he who, without lawful excuse, kills his own slave, is not less liable than he who has killed the slave of another. The excessive severity of masters is also restrained by a constitution of the same emperor. For, when consulted by certain governors of provinces respecting slaves flying for refuge to the temples of the gods, or to the statues of the emperors, he decided that, if the severity of the masters should appear to have been excessive, they should be forced to sell their slaves: and both these rules are good, for we ought not to make a bad use of our right, and it is on this principle that prodigals are restrained from managing their own property.

sider the position of those who are subject to the power of others; for, if we have ascertained who these are, we shall at the same time understand who are free from the power of others.

And first let us treat of those who are in the power of masters.

§ 1. Slaves are in the power of their masters, which kind of power is due to the law of nations; for, it will be found that, amongst nearly all nations masters have the power of life and death over their slaves; and also that whatever is acquired by the slave is acquired for the master. § 2. But, at the present day, it is not lawful for any of our subjects to punish their slaves with excessive severity and without a ground recognised by law; for, by a constitution of the late Emperor Antonine, he who, without lawful excuse, kills his own slave, is not less liable to be punished than he who has killed the slave of another. The excessive severity of masters is also restrained by a constitution of the same emperor. For, when consulted by certain governors of provinces respecting slaves flying for refuge, either to sacred edifices or to the statues of the emperors, he decided that, if the severity of the masters should appear to have been excessive, they should be forced to sell their slaves on reasonable terms, and that the price should be paid over to them; and this decision is just, as the welfare of the State demands that no one should make a bad use of his own property. The terms of the rescript which was addressed to Ælius Marcianus are as follows:—

"The power of masters over their slaves ought not to be impaired, nor should any man be deprived of his right, but it is in the interests of the masters that assistance should not be denied to those who on good grounds plead against cruelty, starvation, or other intolerable wrong. Examine, therefore, into the complaints of those slaves who have fled from the househould of Julius Sabinus to the statue of the emperor; and should you find that they have been more harshly dealt with than seems right, or subjected to wanton outrage, order them to be sold in such a way, that they may not return again under the power of their master; and if the said Sabinus should attempt to evade this my constitution, he will find out how severe will be the punishment."

§ 54. But since amongst Roman citizens ownership consists of two kinds, for a slave may be held as part of a person's goods, or by the law of the quirites, or in both rights; nevertheless we consider a slave to be in the power of his master if he is held by him as part of his goods, even though he be not his master by the law of the quirites, for he who has merely quiritarian rights over his slave, is not considered to have him in his power.

Title ix. Of paternal power.

§ 55. Likewise our children begotten in lawful marriage are in our power, and this kind of right is peculiar to the Roman people; for there are scarcely any other men possessing such a power over their children as we have, and this fact is referred to thus in the edict of the late Emperor Hadrian, which he issued respecting those who sought from him, both for themselves and their children, the Roman citizenship: "Nor does it escape me that the Galatian race regard children as in the power of their ascendants."

Our children begotten in lawful marriage are in our power. § 1. Now the marriage tie, or matrimony, is the union of a man and woman entraining the obligation to live in inseparable communion. § 2. The power which we have over our children is peculiar to Roman citizens; for there are no other men possessing such a power over their children as we have.

§ 3. Therefore the child born to you and your wife is in your power. So also is the child born to your son and to his wife, that is your grandson or granddaughter; and your great-grandson and great-granddaughter and other descendants are equally in your power. But a child born of your daughter is not in your power, but in the power of his father.

Title x. Of marriage.

§ 56. Roman citizens contract lawful marriages, if they have married Roman citizens, or even Latins or aliens, with whom they have

Roman citizens contract lawful marriages between themselves when they unite in conformity with the law, the males having attained the

the right of intermarriage; and since this right so operates as to make the children of the same condition as their father, it follows that they become not only Roman citizens, but also that they are in the power of their father. § 57. Hence, after due enquiry, it has been customary by imperial constitutions to grant the right of intermarriage to certain classes of veterans with those Latins or aliens whom they have first married after obtaining their discharge, and the children born from these marriages are both Roman citizens and are in the power of their ascendants.

§ 58. It is however to be observed that it is not lawful to marry any woman we please, for from certain marriages we are bound to abstain.

§ 59. Marriage cannot be contracted between persons standing to each other in the relation of ascendant and descendant, for no right of intermarriage exists between them; as for example, between father and daughter, mother and son, grandfather and granddaughter; and if such persons do unite they are considered to have contracted a wicked and incestuous marriage, and this is carried so far that ascendants and descendants, who are only so by adoption, cannot intermarry; and even after the adoption has been dissolved, the rule still holds; therefore I cannot marry a woman who has been in the position of daughter or granddaughter by adoption to me, although I have emancipated her.

§ 60. Similar remarks apply to the case of marriage between persons connected by collateral ties,

age of puberty, and the females the age when they are fit to be married, whether they are heads of families or only subject members; but if the latter, they must have the consent of the ascendant in whose power they are. For both natural reason and the law require this consent; so much so, indeed, that this authorization ought to precede the marriage. Hence the question arose whether the daughter of a lunatic could be married, or the son of a lunatic marry? and as opinions differed as to the son, a decision of ours has been published permitting a son, in the same way as the daughter, of a lunatic to marry, without the intervention of the father, in a mode pointed out by our constitution.

§ 1. Hence it is not lawful to marry any woman without distinction, for from certain marriages we are bound to abstain.

Marriage cannot be contracted between persons standing to each other in the relation of ascendant and descendant, as between father and daughter, grandfather and granddaughter, mother and son, grandmother and grandson, and so on; and if such persons do unite, they are considered to have contracted a wicked and incestuous marriage; and this is carried so far, that ascendants and descendants, who are only so by adoption, cannot intermarry; and even after the adoption has been dissolved, the rule still holds, and therefore you cannot marry a woman who has been either your daughter or granddaughter by adoption, although you have emancipated her.

§ 2. Similar remarks apply to the case of marriage between persons connected by collateral ties, but not to the same extent. § 61. Of course a brother and sister are forbidden to marry, whether they are the children of the same father and mother, or of one of the two only. But if a woman becomes my sister by adoption, so long as the link by adoption continues, there can be no marriage between us; when, however, the adoption is destroyed by emancipation, I can make her my wife; and so, if I have myself been emancipated, no impediment will exist to the marriage.

but not to the same extent. Of course a brother and sister are forbidden to marry, whether they are the children of the same father and mother, or of one of the two only. But if a woman becomes your sister by adoption, so long as the link by adoption continues, there can be no marriage between you: when, however, the adoption is destroyed by emancipation, you can make her your wife, and so, if you yourself have been emancipated, no impediment will exist to the marriage. Hence it is clear that if a man wishes to adopt his son-in-law he should first emancipate his daughter, and if he wishes to adopt his daughter-in-law he should first emancipate his son.

§ 62. A man may marry his brother's daughter, a rule first established when Claudius had married his brother's daughter Agrippina, but it is not lawful to marry a sister's daughter, and this is laid down in the imperial constitutions; so also marriage is prohibited with a paternal or maternal aunt.

§ 3. A man may not marry his brother's or sister's daughter, nor their granddaughter, although she is four degrees removed, for if we may not marry the daughter of any person, neither may we marry the granddaughter; but there would seem to be no impediment to marrying the daughter of a woman whom your father has adopted, for she is neither civilly nor naturally related to you. § 4. The children of two brothers, or of two sisters, or of a brother and sister, may unite in marriage. § 5. Again, a man may not marry his paternal aunt, even though only so by adoption; nor his maternal aunt, because they are held to occupy the position of ascendants, and on this ground it is also clear that the prohibition extends to marrying a paternal or maternal great-aunt.

§ 63. The same prohibition extends to marrying a person formerly standing in the position of mother-in-law or daughter-in-law, or step-daughter or step-mother; and we have said "former", as, if the marriage still exists which is the ground of the affinity, another reason prevents the marriage, because the same woman cannot at

§. 6. Relationship by marriage is also a ground for abstaining from certain marriages; for example, a man may not marry his step-daughter or his daughter-in-law, for they both stand in the position of daughters to him; but this is of course to be understood as referring to one who has been a daughter-in-law or step-daughter: for it she be

the same time have two husbands, nor can the same man have two wives.

still your daughter-in-law, that is, if she be still married to your son, there is another reason why you cannot marry her, viz., that she cannot be the wife of two persons at once. And so if she be still your step-daughter, that is, if her mother is still married to you, you cannot marry her, because it is not lawful to have two wives at the same time. § 7. Again, a man may not marry his mother-in-law nor his step-mother, because they stand in the position of a mother, which rule also can only operate when the relationship by affinity is dissolved; for if she be still your step-mother, that is, if she be still married to your father, she could not be married to you too, as the general rule would apply which forbids a woman to have two husbands at the same time; so, if she be still your mother-in-law, that is, if her daughter is still married to you, you cannot marry her, because you cannot have two wives at the same time. § 8. The son of a husband by a different wife, and the daughter of a wife by a different husband, or vice versâ, may lawfully marry although they have a brother or sister born in the subsequent marriage. § 9. Your divorced wife's daughter by a second husband is not your step-daughter, but Julian lays down that such marriages should be abstained from, for a woman betrothed to a son is not a daughter-in-law, nor is a woman betrothed to a father a step-mother; and yet it is more expedient and more in accordance with law to abstain from such a marriage. § 10. It is undoubted that the relationship between slaves forms an impediment to marriage, if father and daughter or brother and sister have been manumitted. § 11. There are other persons, also, between whom, for various reasons, marriage is prohibited, and these reasons have been collected from the ancient law, and by our permission enumerated in the books of the Digests or Pandects.

§ 64. Therefore, if any one has contracted a wicked and incestuous marriage, he is held to have neither wife nor children; and hence it arises, that the issue of such a union are considered as having a mother but no father, and, on that account, are not in his power, and, therefore, are like those whose mother has conceived them in promiscuous intercourse; for these last are held to have no father, since

§ 12. If any persons unite in opposition to the rules we have stated, then no husband or wife, marriage ceremony, or marriage, or dowry, is recognised, and, hence, the issue of such a union are not in the power of the father, but such children are, as far as relates to the paternal power, in the same position as children conceived by the mother in promiscuous intercourse; for these last are held to

it is uncertain who he is, and hence it is usual to call them "spurious" children, either from the Greek word signifying children conceived, as it were, "scattered", or because they are children, as it were, without a father.

have no father, since it is uncertain who he is, and hence it is usual to call them spurious children, either from the Greek word signifying children conceived, as it were, "scattered", or because they are children, as it were, without a father. It follows, therefore, that on the dissolution of such a union there can be no demand for the return of the dowry; and persons who contract prohibited marriages are further liable to other penalties enumerated in the imperial constitutions.

§ 65. But it sometimes happens that children who at their birth were not in the power of their ascendants are brought under it afterwards. § 66. For example, if a Latin, in accordance with the Ælian Sentian law, has married and begotten a son, whether the child is a Latin because his mother is a Latin woman, or a Roman citizen because his mother is such, he will not be in the power of his father; but when, subsequently, the father has proved his case,* the Roman citizenship is acquired, and, at the same time, he commences to have his son in his power.

* *ante*, § 29.

§. 13. But it sometimes happens that children who at their birth were not in the power of their ascendants are brought under it afterwards. Such is the case with one who, being a natural son, and subsequently enrolled in the local senate, falls into the power of his father. So, again, as to one born of a free woman, with whom marriage was in no way prohibited by law, but with whom the father only cohabited, and who subsequently falls into the power of his father, in consequence of deeds settling a dowry having been drawn up in accordance with the provisions of our constitution. And this constitution confers the same right in respect of any other children who may be subsequently born of the same marriage.

§ 67. So also, if a Roman citizen has married a Latin or an alien, under the impression that she was a Roman citizen, and has had a son by her, this son is not in his father's power, because the son is not even a Roman citizen, but is either a Latin or an alien, that is, he is of whatever condition his mother is, for no one attains to the condition of the father unless the right of intermarriage existed between father and mother; but, in accordance with the decree of the senate, he is at liberty to prove a case of error, and in this way both wife and son obtain the Roman citizenship: and from that time the son falls into the power of the father. The law is the same if, through ignorance, he has married a woman belonging to the class of surrendered persons, except that the wife does not become a Roman citizen. § 68. In the same way, if a Roman woman be, through a mistake, married to an alien, supposing him to be a Roman citizen, she may prove a case of error, and then both the son and the husband attain to the Roman citizenship, and the son at the same time falls into the power of the father. The same rule holds if she be married to an alien, supposing him to be a Latin in accordance with the Ælian Sentian law; for this case is by a decree of the senate specially provided for. The same rule to some extent holds if she be married, in accordance with the Ælian Sentian law, to a man in the class of surrendered persons, supposing him to be a Roman or a Latin, except that he, who is classed amongst surrendered persons, remains in that condition; and therefore the son, although he becomes a Roman citizen, does not fall into the power of the father. § 69. In the same way, if a Latin woman be married to an alien, whom she thought was a Latin, she may, under the decree of the senate, after the birth of a son, prove a case of error; by which means they will all become Roman citizens, and the son at the same time falls into the power of the father. § 70. The same rule is now established in the case of a Latin having married, in accordance with the Ælian Sentian law, an alien, supposing her to be a Latin or a Roman citizen. § 71. Further, if a Roman citizen, supposing himself to be a Latin, has married a Latin woman, he may, after the birth of a son, prove a case of error just as if he had married in accordance with the Ælian Sentian law. Similarly, the decree of the senate allows a Roman citizen who believed himself to be an alien, and had married an alien, upon the birth of a son, to prove a case of error; after which the foreign wife becomes a Roman citizen, and the son not only attains to the Roman citizenship but falls into the power of the father. § 72. All that we have said as to a son is to be understood as applying equally to the case of a daughter; § 73. and, as far as concerns the proof of the case of error, it is immaterial what age the son or daughter may be . . . (two lines illegible) . . . unless the son or daughter be less than a year old, the proof of the case does not lie, and I am not unmindful that it has been so settled by a certain rescript of Hadrian . . . . (two lines illegible) . . . § 74. If an alien had married a Roman citizen . . . (two lines illegible)

. . . this favour was specially conferred on him, but when the alien had married a Roman citizen and, after the birth of a son, had attained in some other way the Roman citizenship, then the question was raised whether he could prove a case of error, and the Emperor Antonine, in a rescript, decided that he could, just as if he had remained an alien; from which we gather that the alien could prove a case of error. § 75. From what we have said it appears that whether a Roman citizen marries a foreign woman, or an alien marries a Roman citizen, the child born will be an alien, but if such a marriage has been contracted by mistake, it seems the blot may be removed in the way we have pointed out above; if, however, there is no ground for a case of error, but he, knowing the true state of his condition, has married, then no relief can be had. § 76. We are speaking however, of those only between whom the right of intermarriage does not exist; for otherwise, if a Roman citizen has married an alien, with whom he has the right of intermarriage, then, as we have also stated above, a lawful marriage is contracted, and therefore he who is the issue of such a marriage will be a Roman citizen and fall into the power of the father. § 77. And so if a Roman woman be married to an alien, with whom the right of intermarriage exists, the son, though indeed an alien, will still be the legitimate son of the father, just as if the mother had been an alien; but now-a-days, by virtue of a decree of the senate passed in the reign of the late Emperor Hadrian, even though the right of intermarriage did not exist between the Roman woman and the alien, still the child who is born is the legitimate son of his father. § 78. But as to what we said, that on a marriage being contracted between a Roman woman and an alien the son born is an alien . . . (nine lines partly illegible, but to the effect that the Minician law set aside the ordinary rule founded on the law of nations, that where there was no right of intermarriage the child followed the condition of the mother) . . . § 79. And so it comes to this that . . . (three lines illegible, but? to the effect that the Minician law only applies to) actual foreigners (? and not to) those whom we call Latins; but relates to those other Latins who have their own distinct people and rights of citizenship and who were reckoned amongst the number of aliens. § 80. By a similiar principle, in the opposite case, the child of a Latin and a Roman woman, (whether the marriage be contracted in accordance with the Ælian

Sentian law or otherwise), is born a Roman citizen; yet some have thought that, where the marriage was contracted in accordance with the Ælian Sentian law, the child would be born a Latin, because it seemed that in this case the right of intermarriage between them resulted from the Ælian Sentian and the Junian law, and the right of intermarriage always involves that the child follows the condition of the father; but, that the child born in a marriage otherwise contracted follows, by the law of nations, the condition of the mother, and would, therefore, be a Roman citizen; but this is due to the decree of the senate, passed in the reign of the late Emperor Hadrian, by which it was settled that in either case a child born to a Latin and Roman woman, should be a Roman citizen. § 81. Consistently with these principles, the same decree of the senate, passed in the reign of the late Emperor Hadrian, lays down that a child born to a Latin and an alien woman, or conversely to an alien and a Latin woman, follows the condition of the mother. § 82. From this it also follows that the child of a female slave and a free man is, according to the law of nations, born a slave; and, on the other hand, that the child of a free woman and a slave is born free. § 83. But we must be careful to note where any law, or that which is equivalent to a law, has altered the rule of the law of nations. § 84. Thus, for example, by force of the Claudian decree of the senate, a Roman woman who cohabits with the slave of another, and has the master's consent, remains herself, by virtue of the agreement, free; but the child born is a slave, for what had been agreed upon between the woman and the master of this slave was by this decree of the senate made binding; but subsequently the late emperor Hadrian, moved by the injustice and inconsistency of the law, restored the rule of the law of nations, that, when the woman herself remains free, the child born shall also be free. § 85. On the other hand, by the . . . . . law the children of a female slave and a free man may be born free, for by that law it is provided that if any one has cohabited with another's slave, supposing her to be a free woman and male children are born, they shall be free; but female children belong to the owner of the mother. But also in this case, the late Emperor Vespasian, moved by the inconsistency of the law, restored the rule of the law of nations, that in any case, even if males are born, they are the slaves of him to whom the mother belongs. § 86. But that part of the same law was left untouched, by which the children of a free woman and another person's slave, whom she knew to be a slave, are born slaves. Hence, in a country where no such law exists, the children born would, according to the law of nations, follow the condition of the mother.

§ 87. It is perfectly obvious that in those cases where the child follows the condition of the mother, and not of the father, there the child is not in the power of the father, even though the father be a Roman citizen; and, hence, as we have pointed out above,* in certain cases where an unlawful marriage has been by mistake contracted, the senate intervenes and strikes out the defective point connected with the marriage, and in that way it usually happens that the son falls into the power of the father. § 88. But if a female slave, who has cohabited with a Roman citizen, and then, after having been manumitted and become a Roman citizen, gives birth to a child, although the child is a Roman citizen like his father, still he is not in the power of the father, because he was not conceived during a cohabitation recognised in law, and no decree of the senate has placed such cohabitation in a position as if it were lawful.

* *ante*, §§ 67, etc.

§ 89. But the received opinion that, if a female slave has cohabited with a Roman citizen, the child born after her manumission is free, rests on natural reason; for the status of children illegitimately conceived is decided at the moment of their birth, and so if they are the offspring of a free woman they are free, nor is it material by whom, whilst a slave, the mother conceived them. But the status of those who are legitimately conceived is decided at the time of conception. § 90. Therefore, if a Roman citizen, whilst pregnant, be interdicted from fire and water, and having become by that means an alien, then gives birth to a child, in the opinion of many, a distinction is to be drawn, viz., that if the conception took place during a lawful marriage, the child will be a Roman citizen, but if the result of promiscuous intercourse, the child will be an alien. § 91. In the same way, if a pregnant Roman woman is reduced to slavery, in accordance with the Claudian decree of the senate, because she has persisted in cohabiting with a slave against the will and in spite of the warning of that slave's master,† in the opinion of many, a distinction is to be made; and they hold that, if she conceived during a lawful marriage, the child is a Roman citizen, but if the result of promiscuous intercourse, the child when born is the

† cf. § 160.

slave of him whose slave the mother would become. § 92. If an alien conceives in promiscuous intercourse, the child born after she becomes a Roman citizen, will be a Roman citizen; but if when the father is an alien, and the connection consistent with the law and with the customs of aliens, then it seems in accordance with a decree of the senate, passed in the reign of the late Emperor Hadrian, that she will give birth to a Roman citizen if the Roman citizenship be given to the child's father. § 93. If an alien applies for the grant of the Roman citizenship for himself and his children, the children will not fall into his power unless the emperor has brought them into it; and this is only done when, after due enquiry, it is considered that this will be advantageous to the children, and this enquiry is conducted with very great care and circumspection where the interests of children under the age of puberty and absentees are involved, as is laid down by an edict of the late Emperor Hadrian. § 94. So also if the Roman citizenship be bestowed on a man and his pregnant wife, the child will be born, as I have stated above,* a Roman citizen, but will not be in the power of the father, as was determined in a special decision of the late Emperor Hadrian; for this reason, a man who is aware of his wife's pregnancy whilst he is applying to the emperor for the bestowal of the citizenship on himself and his wife, should make it a part of his petition that when the child is born it may fall into his power. § 95. The case is different with those who, by the Latian right, attain to the Roman citizenship with their children; for the children of such persons fall into their power. § 96. This right has also been conferred on certain foreign communities, either by the people of Rome, or by the senate, or by the emperor . . . . and is either that of the greater or lesser Latian right. It is the greater Latian right, when those who are selected as local senators, as well as he who holds office or a magistracy, acquire the Roman citizenship; but it is the lesser Latian right, when those alone who actually hold office or a magistracy, acquire the Roman citizenship, as is laid down in many imperial rescripts.

* *ante*, § 92.

Title xi. Of adoption.

§ 97. Not only are our actual children, as we have stated, in our power, but those also whom we adopt.

Not only are our actual children, as we have stated, in our power, but those also whom we adopt.

§ 98. Now adoption takes place in two modes; either by authority of the people, or by that of a magistrate, as for example, that of the prætor. § 99. We adopt by authority of the people those persons who are free from power, and this mode of adoption is called arrogation, because he who adopts is asked, that is, the question is formally put to him, whether he wishes that he whom he is about to adopt should become his lawful son; he who is being adopted is asked whether he consents thereto, and the people are asked whether they ordain that this shall be done. We adopt by the authority of the magistrate those who are in the power of their ascendants, whether they stand in the first degree, as a son and a daughter, or in an inferior degree, as grandson or granddaughter, great-grandson or great granddaughter.

§ 1. Now adoption takes place in two ways, either by imperial rescript or by the authority of a magistrate. We adopt by imperial authority persons of either sex who are free from power; and this mode adoption is called arrogation. We adopt by the authority of the magistrate those persons of either sex who are in the power of their ascendants, whether in the first degree, as a son and a daughter, or in an inferior degree, as grandson, granddaughter, or great grandson, great granddaughter.

§ 100. The adoption sanctioned by the people takes place only in Rome, but the other kind may also be carried out in the provinces, and usually before the governors. § 101. And the opinion has prevailed that women may not be adopted by the authority of the people; but before the prætor, or, in the provinces, the pro-consul or legate, it has been the custom to adopt women also.

§ 2. But at the present day, in virtue of our constitution, when a son in power is given in adoption by his actual father to a person not an ascendant, the power of the actual father is in no wise dissolved; and no such right passes to the adopting father, nor does the adopted son fall into his power, although we have given the adopted son rights of succession to the adopting father in the event of the latter's intestacy. But if the actual father should give his son in adoption, not to a stranger, but to the son's maternal grandfather; or if the actual father has himself been emancipated, and he gives the son in adoption to the son's paternal grandfather, or to the son's paternal or maternal great grandfather, then, as the rights of nature and adoption are united in one person, the power of the adopting father, based as it is on a natural tie and bound by a lawful adoption, is preserved undiminished, so that the adopted son is not only in the family, but also in the power of his adopting father.

§ 102. The adoption of a person under the age of puberty before the people has been at times prohibited, at times permitted; now, according to an epistle of the Emperor Antonine addressed to

§ 3. When any one under the age of puberty is arrogated by imperial rescript, the arrogation is only allowed after enquiry, and the reason assigned for the arrogation is looked into, to see whether

the chief priests, it is permitted under certain conditions if there are good grounds assigned for the adoption. But a person of any age may be adopted before the prætor, or, in the provinces, before the pro-consul or legate.

it is honourable and advantageous for the pupil. And the arrogation is always made under certain conditions, that is, the arrogator is obliged to find security who will be responsible to a public person, viz., a notary, "that if the pupil should die under the age of puberty, the arrogator will restore all the property to those who would have been the pupils' successors had no adoption taken place." So also the arrogator cannot emancipate those whom he has arrogated until an enquiry has been made, and good grounds ascertained for the emancipation, and then the arrogator must restore all their property to them; and further, if the adoptor shall, on his decease, disinherit the adopted child, or in his lifetime emancipate him on grounds not recognised in law, he is obliged to leave him the fourth part of all his goods, in addition, that is, to what the son brought him at the time of arrogation, or the benefit of which he afterwards acquired through him.

§ 106. Whether a younger can adopt an older person is a doubtful question applying to both kinds of adoption.

§ 4. It is not lawful for a younger person to adopt an older; for adoption imitates the order of nature; and it would be an absurdity for the son to be older than the father; and therefore he who wishes either to arrogate or adopt a son, should be the elder by the full term of puberty, that is by eighteen years; § 5. but it is lawful for a person to adopt another in the position of grandson or great grandson, granddaughter or great granddaughter, or any other descendant, although he has no son; § 6. and a man is at liberty to adopt the son of another as his grandson, or the grandson of another as his son; § 7. but if a man adopts a person to stand in the position of grandson, as if he were a descendant of a son already adopted, or of an actual son in his power, then the consent of that son should first be obtained, in order that the son may not have given him, against his will, an heir who would at law succeed him as a co-owner of his patrimony. But, on the other hand, if a grandfather gives his grandson by a son in adoption, it is not necessary that the son should consent.

§ 105. Again, whether a person has adopted another before the people, or the prætor, or the governor of a province, he may again give

§ 8. An adopted or arrogated person is assimilated in many respects to the offspring of a lawful marriage; and therefore, if anyone adopts another by imperial rescript, or, if the person is not a descendant, before the prætor, or the governor of

the same person to another in adoption. § 103. It is a rule common to both modes of adoption, that persons who cannot procreate, as being impotent, may adopt. § 104. On the other hand, women cannot in any way adopt because they have not even their own actual children in their power.

a province, he may give the same person in adoption to another; § 9. but it is a rule common to both modes of adoption, that persons who cannot procreate, such as those born impotent, may adopt, but that persons who have been made impotent cannot. § 10. Women also cannot adopt: for they have not even their own actual children in their power; but permission to adopt may be accorded to them by the Emperor, as a solace for the loss of their own children.

§ 107. There is this peculiarity about the adoption which takes place before the people, that if the person who gives himself in arrogation has children in his power not only is he himself subjected to the power of the arrogator, but his children also fall into the same power in the position of grandchildren.

§ 11. There is this peculiarity about the adoption which takes place by rescript of the Emperor, that if the person who gives himself in arrogation has children in his power not only is he himself subjected to the power of the arrogator, but his children also fall into the same power in the position of grandchildren. Hence the late Emperor Augustus did not adopt Tiberius until Tiberius had adopted Germanicus, in order that directly the adoption had taken place Germanicus might become the grandson of Augustus.

§ 12. The ancient authorities refer to a statement of Cato which correctly lays down that slaves when adopted by their masters are thereby made free. Guided by this opinion, we have decided by a constitution that a slave to whom his master in a public document gives the title of son is thereby made free, although this does not suffice to give him the rights of a son.

§ 108. Now let us consider the position of those persons who are in marital power, which is a right peculiar to Roman citizens. § 109. But, though persons of both sexes may be in power, women only are subject to marital power. § 110. Formerly they might fall under this marital power in one of three ways, viz., by use, by the ceremony of the spelt cake, and by fictitious purchase. § 111. Use brought a woman under the marital power when she continued as a married woman to occupy her husband's house for a whole year without interruption, for she was then, as it were, acquired by uninterrupted user through one year's possession, passing into her husband's family and filling the place of a daughter. And, therefore, the Twelve Tables provided that if she was unwilling to fall in this way under the marital power of her husband, she should absent herself three nights every year,* and thus the acquisition by use of each year would be interrupted. But these regulations have been abolished, partly by legislation and partly by disuse. § 112. Marital power results from the ceremony of the spelt cake by way of a kind of sacrificial offering to Jupiter Farreus in which spelt cake is used, and hence the ceremony is also called marriage by the spelt cake. Besides this, many other things are done and observances gone through, with a set form of solemn words, in the presence of ten witnesses, for the purpose of carrying out this form of proceeding; and this right is practised, even in our times; for, the greater flamens, that is, the priests of Jupiter, Mars, and Quirinus, as also the sacrificial priests, unless they are the issue of a marriage by the spelt cake ceremony, cannot be selected, nor can they hold office unless their own marriage was contracted in the same way. § 113. Women fall under the marital power through a fictitious purchase, made by means of the process of formal conveyance, that is, a kind of imaginary sale, in which, in the presence of not less than five witnesses, Roman citizens, above the age of puberty, and a scale bearer, the husband buys the woman, who falls into his marital power. § 114. But a woman may go through the fictitious purchase, not only with her husband, but also with a stranger, and hence it is said that the fictitious purchase may be made either for a matrimonial or fiduciary purpose; for the woman who goes through the forms of a fictitious purchase with her husband, in order that she may stand related to him as a daughter, is said to have gone through the ceremony for a matrimonial purpose, whereas she who goes through the fictitious purchase with her husband, or with a stranger for some other object, is said to have gone through the fictitious purchase for a fiduciary purpose, as, for example, to escape from guardianship. § 115. And this is effected thus: If a woman desires to set aside her present guardians in favour of others, she goes through the forms of the fictitious purchase by the authority of those guardians, and then she is again formally sold by the fictitious purchaser to him whom she wishes to have as guardian, and being released from power by the process of fictitious vindication by this last person, he becomes her guardian, and is called a fiduciary guardian, as will appear below.† § 115A. Formerly, a fiduciary fictitious purchase was resorted to for the

* tab. vi, 4.

† see § 195A.

purpose of making a testament. For, at that time, with the exception of certain persons, women had not the right of making a testament unless they had gone through the fictitious purchase, and had been again formally sold, and afterwards released from power. But, in the reign of the late Emperor Hadrian, the senate dispensed with the necessity of going through the fictitious purchase . . . (two lines illegible). § 115B. But, though the woman has gone through a fictitious purchase with her husband for a fiduciary purpose, nevertheless, she, from that time, occupies the place of a daughter, for no matter what may be the reason which has brought the wife under the marital power of her husband, it is settled that her rights which then commence are those of a daughter.

§ 116. We have now to point out what free persons are in a state of bondage. § 117. All children, then, whether male or female, who are in the power of their ascendant, may be sold by the very same formal process by which slaves are sold. § 118. The same rule holds as to those persons who are under marital power; for women may be sold by their fictitious purchasers by the same formal process used in the case of children when sold by their ascendant; and this is so true that, although only a woman who is married to him, can be in the position of a daughter to a fictitious purchaser, yet even she who is not married to him, and who, therefore, is not in the position of a daughter to him, may yet be sold by him. § 118A. These formal sales are usually only gone through by ascendants and fictitious purchasers when they desire to release the persons so sold from their power, as will appear more clearly further on. § 119. Now, the process of formal conveyance is, as we have already stated,* a kind of imaginary sale, and is a right peculiar to Roman citizens. The ceremony is conducted thus:—In the presence of not less than five witnesses, Roman citizens above the age of puberty, with another person possessing similar qualifications, holding a copper scale, and therefore called the scale bearer; he who is receiving the thing into bondage, holding it, says: "I assert that this (e. g.) slave is mine, by the law of the quirites, and he has been bought by me by means of this piece of copper and copper scale". He then strikes the scale with the piece of copper and gives the piece of copper by way of price to him from whom he receives the thing into bondage. § 120. In this way both slaves and free persons are sold,

* *ante*, § 113.

as also those animals which fall within the class of things requiring a formal transfer,* in which number are included oxen, horses, mules, asses. In the same way it is customary to sell such urban and rural estates as are comprised amongst the class of things requiring a formal transfer, as in the case of Italian estates. § 121. The sale of estates differs from the sale of other things in this only, that slaves and free persons, as well as animals that are included under the class of things requiring a formal transfer, cannot be sold unless they are present; and, therefore, it is necessary that he who receives by way of formal transfer should take hold of the thing itself which is given him in this solemn mode, and hence, also, it is called "mancipatio", because the thing is taken by the hand. But estates, though at a distance, may be conveyed in this way. § 122. The piece of copper and the scale form part of the ceremonial used, because formerly only copper money was used, and there were pound, two-pound, half-pound, and quarter-pound pieces, but no gold or silver money, as may be seen by reference to the Twelve Tables; and the value of this money did not consist in its number, but in its weight, as, for example, the pound pieces were one pound in weight, and the two-pound pieces then weighed two pounds, whence comes the term "dupondius" . . . . which stands for two pounds, and this name is still retained in use. The half-pound and the quarter-pound pieces had also a fixed weight; that is, they were of their proportional weight of a pound. . . . . Hence money was not counted but weighed, and hence those slaves to whom money matters were entrusted were called weighers-out, and are still so called. § 123. If it be asked in what consists the difference between the fictitious purchase of a woman, and the process of formal sale, it is that she who goes through the forms of the fictitious purchase is not reduced into a servile condition, but those persons of either sex who are subjected to the process of formal sale by their ascendants and by fictitious purchasers, are held to occupy the position of slaves; so that they can neither take an inheritance nor a legacy from him who has them in this state of bondage, unless they are ordered by the same testament to be free, just as in the case of slaves. And the reason of this difference is obvious, since they are received into this bondage by their ascendants and by fictitious purchasers with the same words as slaves, which is not the case in the form of fictitious purchase of a woman.

* *post*, ii, § 15, etc.

Title xii. Of the means by which persons are released from the power of others.

§ 124. Let us now see by what means persons in the power of others may be released from the authority to which they are subject. § 125. And first let us consider the case of those who are in the power of their ascendants or masters. § 126. Though how slaves are freed from power may be gathered from what we have already explained above* respecting the manumission of slaves.

§ 127. Those who are in the power of an ascendant become free from power at his death. But this statement is subject to this qualification, that though when a father dies, his sons and daughters undoubtedly become free from power, yet when a grandfather dies, his grandsons and granddaughters do not always become free from power, but only if, after their grandfather's death they do not fall into the power of their father. Therefore, if their father is living at their grandfather's death, and was in the power of his father, then, on the grandfather's death, they fall into the power of their own father; but if at the time their grandfather dies, their father is either already dead, or has passed out of the power of his father, then, as they cannot fall into his power, they become free from power.

§ 128. But since he, who, by the Cornelian law, on account of some crime, is interdicted from fire and water, loses the Roman citizenship, it follows that the children of a person thus removed from the number of Roman citizens cease to be in his power, just as if he were dead, for it would be an

Let us now see by what means persons in the power of others may be released from the authority to which they are subject, though how slaves are freed from power may be gathered from what we have explained above† respecting the manumission of slaves.

* *ante*, § 13. † *ante*, tit. v.

Those who are in the power of an ascendant become free from power at his death. But this statement is subject to this qualification, that though when a father dies, his sons and daughters undoubtedly become free from power, yet when a grandfather dies, his grandsons and granddaughters do not always become free from power, but only if, after their grandfather's death they do not fall into the power of their father. Therefore, if their father is living at their grandfather's death, and was in the power of his father, then, on the grandfather's death, they fall into the power of their own father; but if at the time their grandfather dies, their father is either already dead or has passed out of the power of his father, then, as they cannot fall into his power, they become free from power.

§ 1. But since he who on account of some crime undergoes banishment to an island loses the Roman citizenship, it follows that the children of a person thus removed from the number of Roman citizens, cease to be in his power just as if he were dead. On similar grounds, if he, who is in the

inconsistency that a man in the condition of an alien should have a Roman citizen in his power. On similar grounds, if he, who is in the power of an ascendant, be interdicted from fire and water, he ceases to be in the power of the ascendant, for it would be equally inconsistent that a man in the condition of an alien should be in the power of a Roman citizen ascendant.

power of an ascendant, be banished to an island, he ceases to be in the power of the ascendant. But, if through the clemency of the emperor, such persons are completely restored to their rights, they recover again their former condition. § 2. But fathers merely undergoing a term of exile to an island retain their children in their power, and, conversely, children undergoing a term of exile remain in the power of their ascendants. § 3. A man who is made a slave of punishment, ceases to have his children in his power. Persons become slaves of punishment who are condemned to the mines, or exposed to wild beasts. § 4. A son, though he become a soldier, a senator, or a consul, still remains in the power of his father, for neither military service nor consular dignity can free the son from power. But, by our constitution, the supreme dignity of the patriciate frees the son from the power of his father immediately the imperial patent is conferred, for who could endure that any father should be able by emancipation to release his son from the thraldom of his power, and yet the Imperial Majesty should not be able to withdraw from the power of another one selected to rank as a father.

§ 129. But if the ascendant should be taken prisoner by the enemy, although by that means he becomes the slave of the enemy, his rights in respect of his children remain in suspense on account of the law as to the resumption of rights; for those who have been taken by the enemy, if they return, recover all their former rights; and, therefore, he, on his return, will have his children in his power, but, if he should die in captivity, the children will be free from power, but whether they are free from power from the time when their ascendant died in captivity, or from the time when he was taken prisoner, is open to doubt. Similarly, if a son or a grandson is taken prisoner, the power of the ascendant, by reason of

§ 5. If an ascendant should be taken prisoner by the enemy, although he become the slave of the enemy, his rights in respect of his children remain in suspense on account of the law as to the resumption of rights; for those who have been taken by the enemy, if they return, recover all their former rights; and, therefore, when returned, he will have his children in his power, for the doctrine, as to the recovery of rights, assumes that the captive has never been absent. If, however, the father dies in captivity, the son is held to be free from power from the time when his father was taken prisoner. Similarly, if a son or a grandson is taken prisoner, the power of the ascendant, by reason of this law as to the resumption of rights, is held

this law as to the resumption of rights, is held in suspense. § 130. Moreover, male children are free from the power of their father when consecrated as priests of Jupiter, and female children when chosen as vestal virgins. § 131. Formerly, too, at the time when the Roman people sent out colonies into districts occupied by Latins, those who, by order of their ascendant, entered their name as a member of the Latin colony ceased to be in the power of the ascendant, because they had made themselves citizens of another community.

§ 132. Further, by emancipation children cease to be in the power of their ascendants. A son, indeed, requires three formal sales; but other children, whether male or female, are released from the power of ascendants by one formal sale. For the Twelve Tables speaks of the three formal sales only in relation to the person of a son in these words: "If a father has three times sold his son, let the son be free from the father"; and this transaction is conducted in the following way: the father sells his son to some person who releases him from power by the process of fictitious vindication, by which means the son falls again into the power of the father, who sells his son again, either to the same person or to others, but usually to the same person; and this person again releases the son from power by the process of fictitious vindication, and then when the son is again brought into the power of

in suspense. The term "postliminium" is derived from "post" and "limen", and, therefore, we may correctly say that he who, being taken prisoner, afterwards reaches our frontier, is returned again across the threshold. For, just as thresholds form, as it were, the boundaries of houses, so the ancients have intended that the boundary of the empire should be regarded as a threshold, and hence "limes" is so called as being a kind of end and termination, from which "postliminium" gets its name, because he is returned again across that threshold from which he had been lost. He, who having been taken prisoner, is, on the enemy being overthrown, recovered, is deemed to return by "postliminium".

§ 6. Further, by emancipation children cease to be in the power of their ascendants, but this emancipation formerly proceeded, either by adopting the process of the ancient law, which consisted of imaginary sales, with intermediate manumissions, or by imperial rescript; but we, in our forethought, have reformed this matter by a constitution, so that the old fictitious process being done away with ascendants go at once before the competent judges or magistrates, and free from their power their sons or daughters, grandsons or granddaughters, or other descendants. And then, according to the praetorian edict, the ascendant has the same rights in respect of the property of the manumitted son or daughter, grandson, or granddaughter, as the patron has over the property of his freed-man. And, further, if the son or daughter or other descendant emancipated be under the age of puberty, the

his father, the latter sells him a third time, either to the same person or to another, but usually to the same person, and by this last sale the son ceases to be in the power of the father, although he is not yet released from power, but in the condition of a person in a state of bondage.

§ 133. It is further to be remarked that he who has in his power a son, and by that son a grandson, is at liberty to emancipate the son, and retain in his power the grandson; and, conversely, he can release from his power the grandson or granddaughter and retain his son, or he may make them all free from power. Similar remarks apply to the case of a great-grandson, or a great-granddaughter.

§ 134. Again, ascendants cease also to have in their power such of their descendants as they have given in adoption, and in the case of a son so given in adoption, three sales and two intervening releases from power are gone through, just as are usual when a father releases him from power, in order that he may become his own master. After this is done, he is either resold to the father and formally claimed from him by the adoptor before the praetor as his son; when, the father not in turn claiming him, the son is adjudged by the praetor to the claimant; or he is not resold to the father, but he who is adopting the son formally claims him whilst in the process of the third sale; but it is more convenient for the son to be resold to the father. For other descendants, however, whether of the male or female sex, one formal sale suffices, and they may or may not be resold to the ascendant. The same method is commonly observed in the provinces before the president of the province. § 135. The child conceived from a son who has been sold once or twice, although born

ascendant, as the result of the emancipation, acquires the tutorship.

§ 7. It is further to be remarked that he who has in his power a son, and by that son a grandson or granddaughter, is at liberty to emancipate his son, and retain in his power the grandson or granddaughter; and, conversely, he can release from his power the grandson or granddaughter, and retain his son, or he may make them all free from power. Similar remarks apply to the case of a great-grandson or great-granddaughter.

§ 8. But, if a father gives in adoption the son whom he has in his power to the son's actual grandfather or great-grandfather, in conformity with our constitutions enacted on this subject, that is, if he declares his intention in a formal document, before a competent judge, in the presence of the adoptor and adopted, and without the dissent of the latter, then the power of the actual father is dissolved, and the child passes into the power in the adopting ascendant, in respect of whom, as we have already stated,* the adoption works its full effect. § 9. It should, however, be known that if your daughter-in-law has conceived by your son, and afterwards, during the daughter-in-law's preg-

* *ante*, tit. xi, § 2.

after the third sale of the father, is nevertheless in the power of the grandfather, and may be sold by him, or given in adoption; but a child conceived from a son whilst that son is in the state of bondage, resulting from the third sale, is not born in the power of the grandfather, and though Labeo is of opinion that the child is under the same bondage as that under which the father lies, still this rule is followed, viz., that so long as the father of the child is in the state of bondage the rights of the child are in suspense, and if the father be emancipated the child falls into the father's power; but if the father died whilst in the state of bondage, the child becomes free from power. The same remarks apply . . . . (three lines illegible), . . . as we have stated* above, three sales take place in the case of a son, one suffices for a grandson.

nancy, you emancipate your son, or give him in adoption, the child, when born, will be in your power; but, if the child is conceived subsequently to the emancipation or adoption, he becomes subject to the power of his emancipated father, or his adopting grandfather. § 10. Children, actual or adopted, have scarcely any means of compelling an ascendant to release them from his power.

* *ante*, § 132, 134.

§ 136. Women, although under marital power, are not released from the power of their ascendant unless they have gone through the forms of the fictitious purchase. This is confirmed by a decree of the Senate respecting the wife of a priest of Jupiter, passed in the consulship of Maximus and Tubero, in which it is laid down that the wife is under the marital power only so far as regards the sacred offices, but in respect of other matters, she is regarded just as if she had not come under the marital power. But women who have gone through the forms of the fictitious purchase are released by a formal sale from the power of their ascendant, and it matters little whether they be under the marital power of their husband, or of that of a stranger, although only those stand in the position of daughters who are under the marital power of their husbands.

§ 137. . . . . . (three lines illegible) . . . . then they cease to be under the marital power; and if, after that formal sale they should be manumitted, they become free from power . . . . . (two lines illegible) . . . . she can no more compel him than a daughter can her father, for a daughter cannot in any way compel the father, even though she be an adopted daughter; but the wife, after receiving a letter of divorce, can compel her husband to free her from the marital power, just as if she had never been married to him.

§ 138. Since those who are in this state of bondage

are looked upon as occupying the position of slaves, they become free from power when manumitted by the process of fictitious vindication, or at the census, or by testament. § 139. Nor does the Ælian Sentian law apply to the case, and therefore no inquiry need be made as to the age of the manumittor, or that of him who is manumitted; nor is a further inquiry needed as to whether the manumittor have a patron or creditor; nor does the limit as to number, imposed by the Fusian Caninian law,* apply to this class of persons. § 140. Wherefore, also, a person can obtain his freedom at the census against the will of the person in whose bondage he is, except when the father has placed him in this state of bondage on condition that he be resold to him. For the father is held then, in some sort, to reserve his own power, from the fact that he takes him back into his bondage. And so it is said, he cannot obtain his liberty at the census against the will of him in whose bondage he is, when the father, by way of surrendering him for damage he has caused† has placed him in the bondage of the complainant; for example, if the father has handed him over to be placed in the bondage of the plaintiff, because the father has been condemned for a theft committed by the son, for the plaintiff has the son in lieu of money compensation . . . . § 141. Finally, it is to be observed, that it is not lawful to offer any indignity to those whom we have in our bondage, otherwise we are liable to an action for outrage,‡ indeed, men are not kept long in this state, but, for form's sake, are usually so only for a moment, unless they have been formally surrendered by their ascendant on account of damage caused by them.

* *ante*, § 42-46.

† see *post*, iv, § 75, 79.

‡ *post*, iii, § 223, 224.

Title xiii. Of tutorship.

§ 142. Let us now pass to another division: for of those free persons who are not in the power of their ascendants, or of their husbands, or not in bondage, some are either under a tutor or under a curator, and some are not under either. Let us, therefore, see who are under a tutor, and who are under a curator, and we shall then understand the position of those who are not under either.

§ 143. And first let us treat of those who are in tutorship.

Let us now pass to another division: for of those who are not in power, some are either under a tutor or under a curator, and some are not under either. Let us, therefore, see who are under a tutor and who are under a curator, and we shall then understand the position of those who are not under either.

And first let us treat of those who are in tutorship.

§ 1. Now, tutorship, according to the definition of Servius, is the power and authority over a free person, given and permitted by the civil law, in order to protect him, who, on account of his youth, is unable to protect himself. § 2. And tutors are those who have this power and authority, taking the name from this fact itself; for they are called "tutors" as being "tuitores" (protectors) and defenders; just as "æditui" are so called, because they have the care of "ædes" (temples).

§ 144. Ascendants may appoint tutors by testament, to those children who are in their power, though if males, only whilst under the age of puberty, but females may be above the age of puberty, for the ancients wished that women, even of full age, should, on account of their weakness of intellect,* be kept in guardianship. § 145. And, therefore, if a tutor has been appointed by testament to a son and to a daughter, and both have attained to the age of puberty, the son, indeed, ceases to be under the tutor, but the daughter, nevertheless, remains under tutorship; for women are liberated from guardianship only by having the rights resulting from the birth of children,† according to the Julian and Papia-Poppæan law. We are speaking, however, with the exception of the vestal virgins, whom, even the ancients, in honour of their priestly office, wished to be free; and, therefore, also it is so provided by the Twelve Tables. § 146. But we can only appoint tutors by testament to grandsons and granddaughters, if, after our death, they do not by law fall into the power of their father. Therefore, if my son is in my power at the time of my death, my grandsons by that son cannot have a tutor appointed them by my testament, although they were in my power, because, at my death, they will be in the power of their father.

§ 3. Ascendants may appoint tutors by testament to those children, under the age of puberty, whom they have in their power, a rule applying equally to both sons and daughters; but ascendants can only appoint tutors by testament to their grandsons and granddaughters, if, after their death, they will not fall into the power of their father; and, therefore, if your son is in your power at the time of your death, your grandsons by that son cannot have a tutor appointed them by your testament, although they were in your power, because, at your death, they fall into the power of their father.

§ 147. As, for many other purposes, posthumous children are held to be already born, so also in this case it has been thought right that the power of appointing tutors by testament should extend not less in respect of posthumous children than to those already born; provided only in this case, that, if the posthumous children had been

§ 4. As, for many other purposes, posthumous children are held to be already born, so also in this case it has been thought right that the power of appointing tutors by testament should extend not less in respect of posthumous children than to those already born, provided only that, if the posthumous children had been born in the

* *post*, § 190. † *post*, § 194.

born in our lifetime, they would have been in our power. We may also institute them our heirs, though it is not allowable to institute as our heirs the posthumous children of strangers.

lifetime of their ascendants, they would have been in their power and their heirs, as being co-owners of the patrimony. § 5. But if a father by testament appoints a tutor to his emancipated son, the appointment is to be confirmed by order of the governor of the province in any case, that is, without inquiry.

§ 148. A tutor may be appointed to a wife under marital power, just as if she were a daughter, and to a daughter-in-law under the marital power of a son, just as if she were a granddaughter. § 149. A tutor is properly appointed in these terms: "I give Lucius Titius to my children as tutor"; and if it be thus written: "To my children", or "to my wife, Titius be tutor", the appointment is considered valid. § 150. But in respect of the wife under marital power, it is customary to permit the selection of a tutor, that is, she may acquire the right to choose a tutor for herself by this form of words: "I give to my wife Titia the choice of a tutor", in which case the wife is at liberty to select a tutor for everything or only for one or two matters. § 151. But the power of selection may be unlimited or restricted. § 152. The power of unlimited selection is usually given in the form set out above; but the limited power is usually thus given: "I give to my wife Titia the right of only once selecting her tutor", or, "I give it only twice". § 153. These two forms of selection differ much from each other, for she who has the power of unlimited selection may choose a tutor once, twice, three times, or oftener; but she who has a limited right only, if the power of selection is only for once, cannot exercise it more than once, if only for twice, she has no power of selecting more than twice. § 154. Tutors given by testament are called "dativi", but those who are appointed after the exercise of the right of selection are called "optivi".

Title xiv. Of those who can be appointed tutors by testament.

Not only a head of a family but also a son in power may be appointed tutor. § 1. A man may also lawfully by testament appoint as a tutor his own slave, at the same time giving him his liberty. But it is to be noted that, if he be appointed tutor without any reference to the gift of liberty, he is deemed to have impliedly received the direct gift of liberty, and may therefore lawfully act as tutor; though, if he has been appointed tutor in consequence of the testator having made a mistake in supposing him to be free, that is another matter. The unconditional appointment of another's slave as tutor is invalid, but the appointment is effectual if worded thus: "when he shall be free"; but the appointment of one's own slave as tutor in this way would be invalid. § 2. An insane person, or a person under the age of twenty-five years, appointed tutor by testament, will be able to act when the first shall have become of sound mind or the other completed his twenty-fifth year.

§ 3. There is no doubt that a tutor may be appointed up to a certain time, or from a certain time, or conditionally, and the appointment may precede the institution of the heir. § 4. But a tutor cannot be appointed for a particular matter or purpose, because he is appointed to the person, and not in respect of a matter or purpose.

§ 5. If anyone appoint a tutor to his daughters or sons, the appointment is held to apply also to his posthumous daughter or son, because, under the term "sons" or "daughters", is included a posthumous son or daughter. But if there are grandsons, would the appointment of tutors to sons include them? The answer is that, if the word "children" has been used, the appointment applies to them also, but they will not be included under the term "sons". But if the appointment is to posthumous descendants, the term obviously includes posthumous sons and all other children.

Title xv. Of the tutorship by law of agnates.

§ 155. By the Twelve Tables, agnates become the tutors by law of those to whom no tutor has been appointed by testament. § 156. Agnates are connected by cognation through persons of the male sex, that is, cognates on the father's side, as, for example, a brother sprung from the same father, the brother's son or his grandson by that son, so also a paternal uncle, and his son and his grandson by that son; but those who are connected by cognation

By the Twelve Tables, agnates become the tutors by law of those to whom no tutor has been appointed by testament. § 1. Agnates are connected by cognation through persons of the male sex, that is, cognates on the father's side, as, for example, a brother sprung from the same father, the brother's son, or his grandson by that son, so also a paternal uncle, and his son, and his grandson by that son; but those who are connected by cognation, through per-

through persons of the female sex are not agnates, but merely, by natural law, cognates, therefore there exists no agnation, but only cognation between a maternal uncle and a sister's son; so again the son of a paternal aunt or of a maternal aunt, is not related to me by agnation but by cognation, and of course, conversely, I am related to him in the same way, for children follow the family of their father, not that of their mother.

sons of the female sex, are not agnates, but merely, by natural law, cognates. And therefore the son of your paternal aunt is not your agnate but cognate, and of course, conversely, you will be connected with him in the same way, for children follow the family of their father, not that of their mother.

§ 157. In former times, according to the Twelve Tables, women had their agnates for tutors, but afterwards the Claudian law was passed abolishing this kind of tutorship so far as it related to women; and therefore a male, under the age of puberty, may have his brother over the age of puberty, or his paternal uncle for tutor; but women cannot have such a person for tutor.

§ 158. The tie of agnation is destroyed by a change of status; but the tie of cognation is not so altered, for although a rule of the civil law may destroy civil rights, it cannot do so in the case of natural rights.

§ 2. The rule calling agnates to the tutorship on intestacy, does not merely apply to the case of a person, who might have appointed a tutor, not having made any testament at all, but also includes the case of a person dying intestate, so far as regards the tutorship, which case would be held to arise if he who was appointed tutor died in the lifetime of the testator.

§ 3. The tie of agnation is ordinarily destroyed by all kinds of change of status, for agnation is a term of law; but the tie of cognation is not altered by all these modes, for, although a rule of the civil law may destroy civil rights, it cannot do so in the case of natural rights.

§ 159. The term "Capitis deminutio" indicates a change of one's former legal position, and this change has three gradations, viz., the greatest, the lesser (called by some the intermediate), and the least.

§ 160. It is a case of the greatest change of legal position when a person loses at the same time both citizenship and liberty, as happens to him who fails to deliver an account of his property to the cen-

Title xvi. Of changes in status.

The term "Capitis deminutio" indicates a change of one's former status, and this change has three gradations, viz., the greatest, the lesser (called by some the intermediate), and the least.

§ 1. It is a case of the greatest change of status, when a person at the same time loses both citizenship and liberty, as happens to those who, by the terribleness of their sentence, are made slaves of

sor after having received due notice to do so, according to a rule . . . (two lines illegible) . . . who contrary to that law have domiciled themselves in the city of Rome. Similarly, in the case of women, who, in accordance with the Claudian decree of the senate, have been made the slaves of the masters with whose slaves they persisted in cohabiting in spite of the master's wishes and warnings.

§ 161. It is a case of lesser (or intermediate) change of legal position when citizenship is lost, but freedom retained, as happens to him who is interdicted† from fire and water.

§ 162. It is a case of the least change of legal position when both citizenship and liberty are retained, but the status of the person undergoes a change, as happens in the case of those who are adopted, also of those who go through the form of a fictitious purchase, as well as of those who are given in bondage, and of those who are manumitted after a formal sale, so that as often as any one is formally sold, in order that he may be manumitted, so often does he suffer a change of legal position. § 163. Not only is the right of agnation destroyed by the greatest and the intermediate change, but also by the least; and, therefore, if a father should emancipate one of two children, then, on his death, neither of them can, by right of agnation, be tutor to the other.

† *ante*, § 128.

punishment),* as also to freedmen, condemned to slavery for ingratitude towards their patrons; as also to those who have suffered themselves to be sold for the purpose of sharing the price.

* *ante*, tit. xii, § 3.

§ 2. It is a case of lesser or (intermediate) change of status when citizenship is lost, but freedom retained, as happens to him who is interdicted from fire and water, or suffers banishment‡ to an island.

§ 3. It is a case of the least change of status when both citizenship and liberty are retained, but the status of the person undergoes a change, as happens to those who have been free from power, and then become subject to the power of another, and so, on the other hand, if a son is emancipated by the father he suffers a change of status. § 4. A slave, however, when manumitted does not suffer a change of status, because he never had the status implied by "caput". § 5. Those whose rank, rather than their status, is changed, do not suffer a change of status; and, therefore, it is well settled that exclusion from the Senate does not involve a change of status.

§ 6. When it is said, that the right of cognation remains in spite of a change of status, this is to be understood as referring only to the least change. For, if a person incurs the greatest change, the tie of cognation is dissolved, as, for example, by the slavery of a cognate; nor does he recover the cognation if he be manumitted. So, too, the tie of cognation is dissolved if a person suffers banishment** to an island.

‡ *ante*, tit. xii, § 1. ** *ante*, § 2.

§ 164. But when the tutorship falls to the agnates it does not belong to them all at the same time, but only to those in the nearest degree.

§ 7. But when the tutorship falls to the agnates it does not belong to them all at the same time, but only to those in the nearer degree, and if there are many in the same degree, then to all in that degree.

Title xvii. Of the tutorship by law of patrons.

§ 165. According to the same law of the Twelve Tables, the tutorship of freed-women and of freed-men under the age of puberty, belongs to the patrons, and the patrons' children. This tutorship is called "by law", not because the above law contains any express provision on the subject, but because it has been adopted by a deduction from the law, just as if it had been introduced by its very terms. For, since the law had provided that the inheritances of freed-men and freed-women, dying intestate, should fall to the patrons, or to the patrons' children, the ancients concluded that the law intended the tutorship also to fall to them, because it had directed that the same agnates, whom it called to the inheritance, should also be tutors.

According to the same law of the Twelve Tables, the tutorship of freed-men and of freed-women belongs to the patrons, and the patrons' children, and this tutorship is called "by law", not because the above law contains any express provision on the subject, but because it has been adopted by a deduction from the law, just as if it had been introduced by its very terms. For, since the law had provided that the inheritances of freed-men and freed-women, dying intestate, should fall to the patrons and the patrons' children, the ancients concluded that the law intended the tutorship also to fall to them, because the same agnates, whom it called to the inheritance it had directed, should be also tutors; for, in most cases, where the benefit of the succession is, there ought also to be the burden of the tutorship. We say "in most cases", because, if a slave, under the age of puberty, be manumitted by a female, she is called to the inheritance, although another person is tutor.

Title xviii. Of the tutorship by law of ascendants.

By analogy to the tutorship of patrons, there is another kind also called "by law"; for, if a person emancipate, under the age of puberty, his son, daughter, grandson, or granddaughter, by that son, or any other descendant, he will be their tutor by law.

§ 166. By analogy to the tutorship of patrons, other tutorships are recognised which are called fiduciary, that is, tutorships which fall to us because we have manumitted a free person who was formally sold to us by an ascendant or a fictitious purchaser. § 167. But the tutorship of male or female Latins, under the age of puberty, does not, in all cases, belong to those who have manumitted these freed-persons, but to those whose property they were by the law of the quirites before their manumission. Hence, if a female slave belongs to you by the law of the quirites, but is mine as being part of my goods, and she has been manumitted by me only, and not also by you, she can become a Latin, and her property belongs to me, but the tutorship falls to you by the provisions of the Junian law. And, therefore, if she be made a Latin by him who owns her, both as part of his goods and by the law of the quirites, then her property and the tutorship belong to the same person.

§ 168. Agnates and patrons, and those who have manumitted free persons, are allowed to transfer the tutorship of women to a third person by the process of judicial surrender;* but the tutorship of pupils cannot be so transferred, because this is not held to be burdensome, since it terminates at the time of puberty. § 169. He to whom the tutorship is transferred is called the tutor by surrender. § 170. And after his death, or change of legal position, the tutorship reverts to the tutor who transferred it, and if he who transferred it dies, or suffers a change of legal position, the tutorship departs from the tutor by surrender, and reverts to the person who, in respect of the tutorship, stands in the next degree to him who transferred it. § 171. But, as far as relates to agnates, no question can now arise as to the tutorship by surrender, since the Claudian law has abolished the tutorship of agnates† over women. § 172. And, according to some, the fiduciary tutors have not the right of transferring the tutorship, since they have voluntarily subjected themselves to the burden. But although this may be held to be so, yet the

Title xix. Of the fiduciary tutorship.

There is another kind of tutorship called fiduciary; for if an ascendant manumits, under the age of puberty, a son, a daughter, a grandson, or a granddaughter, or any other descendant, a tutorship by law of them arises, and on the ascendant's death, if he leave male children, these become the fiduciary tutors of their own sons, or brother, or sister, or other manumitted descendant of the deceased. But when a patron, who is a tutor by law, dies, his children also become tutors by law, for the son of the deceased, if he should not have been emancipated in the lifetime of the father, becomes, after his death, free from power, and would not fall into the power of his brothers, and therefore also not under their tutorship; but a freed-man, if he had remained a slave, would also, after the death of the master, be the slave of his master's children. These children, however, are not called to be tutors unless of full age, a rule which, by our constitution, applies generally to all tutorships and curatorships.

* *post*, ii, § 24. † *ante*, § 157.

rule ought not to apply to the case of an ascendant, who has placed his daughter, or granddaughter, or great granddaughter, in a state of bondage to another, on condition that she be resold to him, and has manumitted her after such re-sale, since he also is regarded as a tutor by law: and not less respect should be extended to him than to patrons.

§ 173. Moreover, women are permitted by a decree of the senate to apply for another in the place of an absent tutor, and, on the application being granted, the former tutor ceases to be such, and it is immaterial how long the tutor has been absent. § 174. But to this there is an exception, for freed-women cannot apply for a tutor in the place of an absent patron. § 175. And we regard that ascendant, as occupying the place of the patron, who has acquired the tutorship by law, in that he has manumitted a daughter, granddaughter, or great granddaughter resold to himself; but his children are reckoned as occupying the place of fiduciary tutors, although the children of a patron acquire the same tutorship as that which their father had. § 176. Sometimes an application for a substitute is allowed even in the case of an absent patron, as, for example, for the purpose of entering upon an inheritance. § 177. The senate has similarly decided in the case of a pupil who is the son of the patron. § 178. Also, by the Julian law concerning marriages, application is permitted to be made to the urban prætor for a substitute for the purpose of settling the dowry where the woman is under a tutorship by law to a pupil. § 179. The son of a patron, even under the age of puberty, becomes the tutor of the freed-woman, although he cannot in any matter give the requisite authority, since he himself is not allowed to do anything without the authority of his tutor. § 180. Again, if a woman is under the tutorship by law of an insane or dumb person, she can, by the decree of the senate, apply for another tutor for the purpose of settling the dowry. § 181. In all these cases it is clear that the tutorship is preserved for the patron and the son of the patron. § 182. Moreover, the senate has decided that, if the tutor of a male or female pupil be removed from the tutorship on suspicion, or excused on lawful grounds, and another tutor appointed in his place, then, on this being done, the former tutor loses his tutorship. § 183. These matters are similarly carried out at Rome and in the provinces, except that at Rome the application for a tutor is made to the urban prætor or to the prætor for aliens, and in the provinces to the governor.

Title xx. Of the Atilian and Julia-Titian tutors.

§ 185. Where a person has no tutor, one, called an Atilian tutor, is, under the provisions of the Atilian law, given him, at Rome by the urban prætor, and a majority of the tribunes of the plebeians; but, in the provinces, the tutor is appointed by the governor under the provisions of the Julia-Titian law. § 186. And, therefore, in cases where a tutor has been appointed by testament, subject to a condition, or from a certain time, another tutor may be given until the condition is fulfilled, or the time arrives. So, again, if a tutor has been given unconditionally, yet, for so long as there is no heir in existence, another tutor must be applied for, under the provisions of these laws, who ceases to be tutor as soon as the tutor under the testament enters upon his duties. § 187. And when a tutor has been taken prisoner by the enemy, another tutor should be applied for, under the provisions of these laws, who ceases to be tutor, if the captive tutor returns; for, on his return, he resumes the tutorship, by the law as to the resumption of rights on return.

Where a person had no tutor, one used to be, under the provisions of the Atilian law, given him, at Rome by the urban prætor, and a majority of the tribunes of the plebeians, but, in the provinces, the tutor was appointed by the governor under the provisions of the Julia-Titian law. § 1. And, where a tutor had been appointed by testament, subject to a condition, or from a certain time, so long as the condition was unfulfilled, or the time not arrived, a tutor could be given under the provisions of these laws. So, again, if a tutor had been given unconditionally, yet, for so long as no heir existed under the testament, a tutor had to be applied for under the provisions of these laws, but his office ceased when the condition was accomplished, the time arrived, or the heir existed. § 2. And when a tutor was taken prisoner by the enemy, another tutor was applied for, under the provisions of these same laws, whose office ceased, if the first tutor returned from captivity; for, on his return, he resumed the tutorship, by the law as to the resumption of rights on return.

§ 3. But tutors ceased to be applied for under these laws after tutors to pupils of either sex were appointed, in the first instance, by the consuls, after inquiry, and then by the prætors under imperial constitutions. For the above-mentioned laws contained no provisions as to requiring security from the tutors, that the property would be kept intact for the benefit of the pupil, or for compelling the tutors to perform the duties of their office. § 4. Under our present practice, tutors are appointed at Rome by the prefect of the city, or the prætor, according to his jurisdiction, and in the provinces, by the governor after inquiry; or, on his order by a magistrate, if the property of the pupil is of no great amount.

§ 5. We, however, by a constitution, have removed the difficulties arising from these distinctions, and have directed that, without waiting for the order of the governor, if the property of the pupil or adult does not exceed five hundred solidi, tutors or curators may be appointed by the defensors of the city, acting in conjunction with the bishop of the place, or other public functionary, that is, by the magistrates, or, in the city of Alexandria, by the administrator of justice; and security, to the amount required by law, must be given in accordance with the terms of the same constitution, that is to say, at the risk of those who receive it.

§ 188. From the above it appears how many species of tutorship there are, but if we inquire into how many kinds these species may be reduced, the discussion will prove a long one; for, on this matter, much difference of opinion formerly existed. We have carefully worked out this subject, both in our commentary on the edict, and in those books which we have based on the works of Quintus Mucius, and need only now observe, that some, like Quintus Mucius, have said that there are five kinds; whilst others, like Servius Sulpicius, say there are three; others, like Labeo, that there are two; whilst others are of opinion that there are as many kinds as there are species.

§ 189. Persons under the age of puberty are, by the law of every community, placed in tutorship; because it is agreeable to natural reason that he, who is not of full age, should receive guidance under the tutorship of another, and there is scarcely any state in which it is not lawful for the ascendants to appoint, by testament, a tutor to their children under the age of puberty; although, as we have said above,* only Roman citizens appear to have their children in their power. § 190. But there seems scarcely any sufficient reason for inclining to the view that women of full age should be under guardianship; for the argument commonly accepted,† viz., that women, on account of their weakness of intellect, are often deceived, and that therefore it is proper to subject them to the authority of a guardian, seems more plausible than true; for women who are of full age transact their own business, and in certain matters the tutor interposes his authority only for form's sake, and is often compelled by the prætor to give the requisite authorisation against his will.

* *ante*, § 55.

† *ante*, § 144.

§ 6. It is agreeable to natural law that persons under the age of puberty should be under tutorship, so that he who is not of full age may receive guidance under the tutorship of another.

§ 191. Hence, a woman has no action against her tutor arising out of the tutorship, but tutors who transact the business of their male or female pupils are liable to render an account to them after they have attained the age of puberty by an action for the purpose arising out of the tutor's administration. § 192. The tutorships by law of patrons and of ascendants, are not mere formal rights, for these tutors cannot be compelled to authorise the making of a will, or the alienating of things requiring a formal transfer, or incurring obligations, unless there is urgent necessity for the alienation of the thing requiring a formal transfer, or for incurring the obligation, for these matters are regulated in the interests of the tutors themselves, inasmuch as the property of women dying intestate passes to them, and therefore these rules prevent their being excluded by testament from the inheritance, or the inheritance reaching them diminished in value by the alienation of the more valuable part, or by being loaded with debts. § 193. Among foreign nations women are not under tutorship as they are with us, but still they are usually in an analogous position; as, for example, under the Bithynian law, a contract made by a woman must be sanctioned by her husband, or son of the age of puberty.

§ 7. And as, therefore, tutors manage the affairs of their male or female pupils, they are liable to render an account, by an action for the purpose arising out of the tutor's administration, when their pupils attain the age of puberty.

Title xxi. Of the authority of tutors.

The authority of a tutor is in certain cases essential, in certain other cases not, as, for example, if a person stipulate that something be given him, the authorisation of the tutor is not requisite, but if pupils make a promise to others it is requisite, for it is held that a pupil may, without the authorisation of his tutor, make his condition better, but not worse. And, therefore, in all matters out of which mutual obligations arise, as in sales, hirings, commissions, and deposits, if the authorisation of the tutor has not been interposed, the persons who contract with pupils are indeed bound, but the pupils are not bound towards them. § 1. And pupils cannot, without the authorisation of their tutor, enter on an inheritance, apply for the possession of goods, or take an inheritance by way of bequest in trust, even though to do so would involve a profit, and could not be attended with any loss. § 2. Moreover, it is the duty of the tutor to give his authorisation in person whilst the matter is in progress, if he considers it advantageous to his pupil, for if given afterwards, or by letter, his authorisation is of no effect.

§ 184. Formerly, when the actions of the law* were in use another tutor would also be given, when an action became necessary between a tutor and a woman or pupil, for, since the tutor could not give the requisite authority in conducting his own affair, another was appointed, by whose authority the action could be carried on, and he was called a prætorian tutor, because he was given by the urban prætor, but some think that, after the abolition of these actions, this mode of giving tutors fell into disuse, whilst others are of opinion that this is still the proper method of proceeding in the case of an action resulting from the civil law.†

§ 3. When the necessity for an action between tutor and pupil arises, as the tutor cannot give his authorisation in a matter concerning himself, a curator (not as formerly a prætorian tutor), is appointed, by whose intervention the action is carried on, and on its conclusion, he ceases to be curator.

* *post*, iv, § 11.

† *post*, iv, § 104.

Title xxii. Of the extinction of the tutorship.

§ 194. Freeborn women are released from tutorship on the ground of having three children, but freed-women, under the tutorship by law of a patron or of his children, must have four children to be able to claim the same exemption; whilst women who have tutors of other kinds, as, for example, Atilian or fiduciary, are released on the ground of having three children. § 195. But a freed-woman may have a tutor of another kind in many ways, as, for example, if she has been manumitted by a woman, for then she must, according to the Atilian law, or if in a province, according to the Julian and Titian law apply for a tutor, since the tutorship cannot be held by the female patron. § 195A. And so, if she be manumitted by a male, and after having, by his authority, gone through the forms of a fictitious purchase, she has then been resold and manumitted, she ceases to be under her patron's tutorship, and commences to have for a tutor him by whom she was manumitted, and who is called a fiduciary tutor.‡ Again, if her patron or his son has given himself in adoption, the freed-woman must apply for a tutor in accordance with the Atilian or Julia-Titian law; so also, in accordance with the same laws, a freed-woman should apply for a tutor, on the decease of a patron, who has not left any male descendant in his family.

‡ *ante*, § 115.

§ 196. But males are freed from tutorship when they have attained

Male and female pupils are freed from tutorship when they attain the age of puberty. Now Sabinus and Cassius, and the rest of our authorities, considered him only to have attained the age of puberty who showed this to be the case by his physical development, that is, who was capable of generating; but that as to those who could not attain to puberty, such as impotent persons, that age was to be accepted at which puberty is usually attained. But the founders of the opposite school think that puberty is a matter to be determined by computing the years, that is, they consider him to have attained to puberty who has completed fourteen years . . . (twenty-four lines illegible) . . . .

the age of puberty. Now the ancients were disposed to judge of puberty in males, not only by their years, but also by their physical development. But our imperial majesty, conformably with the purity of our time, has thought it proper that what seemed, even to the ancients, to be indecent in the case of females, namely, an inspection of the physical development, should be extended to the case of males also; and therefore, by a sacred constitution duly promulgated, we have settled that puberty in males should be considered to commence immediately on the completion of their fourteenth year; whilst, as to females, we have left undisturbed the excellent rule derived from the ancients, by which they are considered capable of marriage on the completion of their twelfth year. § 1. The tutorship is also at an end, if the pupil, while still under the age of puberty, is arrogated, or suffers banishment, or is reduced to slavery, or is taken prisoner by the enemy. § 2. And if a tutor is appointed by testament until a condition is fulfilled, he ceases to be tutor on the accomplishment of the condition. § 3. Tutorship ends also by the death either of tutors or pupils. § 4. And every kind of tutorship terminates by a change of status of the tutor, involving the loss of liberty or citizenship; but the least change of status of the tutor, arising, for example, when he has given himself in adoption, causes a destruction of the tutorship by law, but does not affect the other kinds. All kinds of tutorship are put an end to by any change of status of a male or female pupil, even by the least. § 5. Again, tutors appointed by testament to hold office for a certain time, give up their tutorship on the expiration of the time. § 6. Tutors also, in accordance with what will be found stated below,* cease to be such when they are removed from the tutorship on suspicion, or excuse themselves on good grounds and give up the burden of the tutorship.

**post* tit. xxv and xxvi

Title xxiii. Of curators.

§ 197. . . . has arrived at the age at which he can protect his own property, a rule observed

Males arrived at puberty, and females of a marriageable age, receive curators until they have com-

among foreign nations, as we have indicated above.*

* *ante*, § 189.

§ 198. For the same reasons curators are given in the provinces by the governor.

pleted their twenty-fifth year; for although they have attained the age of puberty, they are still of an age which makes them unfit to look after their own affairs. § 1. Curators are appointed by the same magistrates by whom tutors are given; but a curator cannot be appointed by testament, but if so given the appointment may be confirmed by a decree of the prætor or governor of a province. § 2. Persons between the ages of fourteen and twenty-five do not receive curators against their will, except for a law suit, for a curator may be appointed for a special matter. § 3. Lunatics and prodigals, although over twenty-five years of age, are placed under agnate curators by the Twelve Tables, though usually curators are appointed to them, after inquiry at Rome, by the prefect of the city or the prætor, and in the provinces by the governor. § 4. Idiots and deaf and dumb persons, and those subject to a perpetual malady, since they are unequal to the task of managing their own affairs, have curators placed over them. § 5. Sometimes even pupils receive curators, as, for instance, when the tutor by law is unfit, for a person who already has a tutor cannot have another given him. So, also, if a tutor appointed by testament, or by the prætor or governor of a province, is unfit to administer the affairs of his pupil, and yet is not acting fraudulently, it is usual to associate a curator with him. So again curators are appointed to supply the place of tutors excused, not altogether, but for a time only.

§ 6. If a tutor be prevented by illness or other unavoidable necessity from administering the affairs of his pupil, and the pupil is absent or an infant, the prætor or the governor of the province will appoint by decree, at the tutor's risk, anyone whom the tutor selects to act as agent.

Title xxiv. Of the security to be given by tutors and curators.

§ 199. In order to prevent the property of pupils, and of those persons placed under curators, being wasted or diminished by tutors or curators, the prætor takes care that both tutors and curators give security against this contingency.

In order to prevent the property of male or female pupils, and of those persons, whether male or female, placed under curators, being wasted or diminished by tutors or curators, the prætor takes care that both tutors and curators

§ 200. But this rule is not without exception. For tutors appointed by testament are not required to find security, because their fidelity and diligence have been approved by the testator himself; and those curators to whom the curatorship does not fall by virtue of a law, but who are given either by the consul, the prætor, or the governor of the province, are not usually called upon to find security, because sufficiently fit persons are selected.

give security against this contingency. But this rule is not without exception, for tutors appointed by testament are not required to find security, because their fidelity and diligence have been approved by the testator himself. So, also, in the case of tutors and curators appointed after inquiry, because proper persons are chosen.

§ 1. But if two or more have been appointed by testament, or after inquiry, one of them may by tendering security for the safety of the property of the pupil, or youth over fourteen, obtain the preference over his co-tutor or co-curator so as to alone administer the property, or compel his co-tutor or co-curator to tender security, if he wishes to obtain the preference and administer solely. Therefore, he cannot himself demand security from his co-tutor or co-curator; but he must tender it in order to put his co-tutor or co-curator to his election, whether to take or to find security. If none of them tender security, then, if one of them has been designated by the testator to manage the property, he should be the person to manage it; but if no one has been designated, then he should administer who is selected by a majority of the tutors, as is provided by the prætorian edict, and if the tutors disagree as to him or those who should act, then the prætor must interfere; and in the same way, when several are appointed after inquiry, the majority may select one to administer.

§ 2. It is, however, to be noted that not only are tutors and curators responsible for due administration of the property of pupils and adults and others,* but that there is against those who receive the security a subsidiary action, which furnishes them with a final source of protection. This subsidiary action is given against those who have wholly omitted to take security from tutors or curators, or have taken insufficient; and this action, according to the opinions of the jurisconsults, as well as in accordance with the imperial constitutions, lies also against their heirs. § 3. By the same constitutions, it is also expressly laid down that, where tutors and curators fail to give security, they may be compelled to do so by seizure of their property by way of pledge. § 4. The prefect of the city, the

* *ante*, tit. xxiii, § 3, 4.

prætor, the governor of a province, and others having the right of appointing tutors, are not liable to this action, but only those upon whom the duty usually falls of demanding security.

Title xxv. Of the grounds of exemption available to tutors and curators.

Both tutors and curators are excused on various grounds; the most usual being that of having children, whether in power or emancipated. For, if anyone has at Rome three children living, in Italy four, or in the provinces five, he may be excused from tutorship or curatorship, as in the analogous case of other offices; for it is held that both tutorships and curatorships are public offices. Adopted children do not count, though those given in adoption are reckoned in favour of their actual father. Grandchildren by a son are counted, as they may stand in the place of their father; but grandchildren by a daughter do not count. Only those children who are living can be reckoned as the ground of exemption from the office of tutor or curator, not those who are dead; but a doubt has been raised as to those lost in war, and it is settled that those only may be counted who die on the field of battle, for those who fall fighting for their country are considered to live eternally in glory. § 1. The late Emperor Marcus also declared by rescript, in his volume of the half-year's decrees, that he who was engaged in the treasury should, so as long as he was so occupied, be excused from being tutor or curator. § 2. Persons absent on the service of the State are excused from being tutors or curators; but if they were already tutors or curators, and afterwards are absent on the public service, they are excused so long as they are absent, and in the meantime a curator is appointed in their place, and, on their return they must again take upon them the burden of the tutorship; nor have they a year's grace, as stated by Papinian, in the fifth book of his answers, for this period only applies to their liability to be called to new tutorships. § 3. By a rescript of the late Emperor Marcus, all persons holding office may excuse themselves; but if they have undertaken the tutorship, they cannot abandon it. § 4. No tutor or curator can excuse himself by alleging that he has a lawsuit pending with the pupil or adult, unless the dispute be concerning the whole of the property or inheritance. § 5. Three unsought tutorships or curatorships are grounds for an excuse, so long as they are being administered, but the tutorship of several pupils, as, for example, of brothers, or the curatorship of their property, counts as one tutorship only. § 6. Poverty also may be tendered as an excuse, where the person excusing himself can successfully show that he is unequal to the burden imposed upon him, as laid down, not only by the divine brothers, but also separately by the late Emperor Marcus. § 7. Ill-health also, on account of which a man is unable to attend to his own affairs, may serve as a ground of excuse. § 8. So, too, a person unable to read should be excused, according to a rescript of the late Emperor Antoninus Pius, although untutored persons may be equal to the administration of business. § 9. So, also, if through enmity a father appoint any one by testament as tutor, this in itself will form a ground for an excuse; just as, on the other hand, they who have promised the father of the pupils that they would undertake the tutorship, cannot be excused. § 10. That the tutor was unknown to the father of a pupil is not of itself a sufficient excuse, according to a rescript of the divine brothers. § 11. Deadly enmity existing between the father of the pupil or adult, and the tutor, if no reconciliation has intervened, is usually considered as a ground of exemption from a tutorship or curatorship. § 12. So, too, if a person has had his status called in question by the father of the pupil, he is to be excused from the tutorship. § 13. Persons above seventy years of age may be excused from being tutors or curators. Persons under the age of twenty-five were formerly excused; but, by our constitution, they are now prohibited from aspiring to the tutorship or curatorship, so that an excuse is now unnecessary. This constitution provides that neither pupils nor youths under twenty-five are to be called to a tutelage by law, for it is irrational that those who are known to stand in need of the assistance of others in managing their own affairs, and who are themselves under other guidance, should undertake the tutorship or curatorship of others. § 14. The same remark applies to a soldier, for, though willing, they are not allowed to undertake the burden of a tutorship. § 15. Grammarians, rhetoricians, and physicians at Rome, and those who exercise such professions in their own country, and are included in the authorised number, are exempted from being tutors or curators.

§ 16. If a person wishes to excuse himself, and having several grounds of exemption, fails in the proof of some, he is not precluded from making use of the others within the prescribed time. Those who wish to excuse themselves do not do so by way of appeal, but whatever kind of tutors they may be, that is, however they may have been appointed, they must offer their excuses within fifty consecutive days after they knew of their appointment as tutors, if they are within the hundredth milestone from the place where they were appointed, but if they reside beyond the hundredth milestone, the calculation is made at the rate of one day for each twenty miles and thirty days over; but the time is, as Scævola said, to be so calculated as never to be less than fifty days. § 17. When the tutor is appointed he is considered as such for the whole patrimony. § 18. He who has filled the office of tutor to a person cannot be compelled against his will to act as curator to the same; so much so, that although the head of the family who appointed the tutor by testament, should have added that he made the same person curator, yet the late Emperors Severus and Antoninus decided by rescript that the person so appointed could not be compelled to act as curator against his will. § 19. The same emperors have decided by rescript, that a husband appointed as curator to his wife may excuse himself from the office, even although he may have intermeddled in the matter. § 20. If, however, a person has succeeded by false allegations in getting himself relieved of a tutorship he is not to be released of the responsibilities attaching to the office.

Title xxvi. Of suspected tutors or curators.

It is to be observed that the proceeding by way of accusation on suspicion is derived from the Twelve Tables. § 1. The power of removing suspected tutors is vested at Rome in the prætor; in the provinces in their governors or in the legate of the proconsul. § 2. We have shown who can take cognisance of a case of suspicion; let us now see who may be the objects of suspicion, and in fact all tutors may be so, whether testamentary or otherwise, so that even a tutor by law may be accused. But what is to be said of a patron? He, too, may be accused; but we must remember that his reputation must be spared, although he may be removed on suspicion. § 3. The next point to consider is who may bring the accusation of suspicion. Now, it must be understood that an accusation of this sort is quasi-public, that is, it is open to all. Nay, more, even women, by a rescript of the late Emperors Severus and Antoninus, are allowed to be accusers, though only those who are impelled to do so by feelings of affection, as, for example, in the case of a mother, a nurse, or a grandmother, or a sister; and, further, the prætor suffers any other woman to bring the accusation whom he perceives to be actuated by a lively affection, and who, without overstepping the modesty of her sex, is urged by this affection not to permit the mischief to be incurred by the pupils. § 4. Persons under the age of puberty cannot bring an accusation of suspicion against their tutors; but, according to the rescript of the late Emperors Severus and Antoninus, those who have attained the age of puberty may, under the advice of their relatives, accuse their curators. § 5. According to Julianus a tutor, though solvent, is considered as the object of suspicion who manages the tutorship unfaithfully. The same Julianus also writes, and a constitution has been drawn in accordance with his opinion, that a tutor may be removed on suspicion before he has entered on his duties. § 6. A suspected person removed on the ground of fraud is infamous, but not so if for negligence. § 7. If a person is accused on suspicion, so long as the inquiry lasts, administration by him, is, according to Papinian, interdicted. § 8. But if, after the inquiry has been entered upon, the tutor or curator dies, the accusation drops. § 9. If a tutor fail to be in attendance, so that proper provision may be decreed for the maintenance of the pupil, it is provided by a rescript of the late Emperors Severus and Antoninus, that the pupil is to be put into possession of the property of the tutor, and that a curator having been appointed, those things, which would become deteriorated by delay, are to be sold. Therefore, he who does not see to proper maintenance may be removed on suspicion. § 10. But, if he appear and assert that, on account of the pupil's want of means, no maintenance can be decreed, and this statement is false, he is to be handed over to the prefect of the city for punishment, just as he is handed over who has acquired a tutorship by bribery. § 11. So a freed-man proved to have acted fraudulently whilst tutor to the son or grandson of his patron, is to be handed over to the prefect of the city for punishment. § 12. Lastly, it is to be understood that those who fraudulently administer a tutorship or curatorship, although they offer security, are to be removed. For the tender of security does not affect the malevolent purpose of the tutor, but only serves to give him a longer period for damaging the property. § 13. We consider him to be the object of suspicion who so conducts himself as to give rise to suspicion, but a tutor or curator, though he be poor, if he is nevertheless faithful and diligent, is not to be removed on the ground of suspicion.

INSTITUTES

OF

GAIUS, COMMENTARY II.	JUSTINIAN, BOOK II.
	Title i. Of the division of things.
§ 1. In the preceding commentary we have dealt with the law of persons; now let us treat of things. These are either subject to private ownership, or are deemed incapable of being so subject. § 2. Hence, a leading division of things is into two classes, viz., those subject to divine law, and those subject to human law.	In the preceding book we have dealt with the law of persons; now let us treat of things. These are either subject to private ownership, or are deemed incapable of being so subject. For some things are by the law of nature common to all; some are public; some belong to corporations, and some cannot be claimed by anyone, but most things are the property of individuals, by whom they are acquired in various ways, as will appear hereafter.

§ 1. According to the law of nature, the following are common to all, viz., the air, running water, the sea, and consequently the shores of the sea. Hence, no one is forbidden to approach the sea-shore, provided he does not interfere with the country houses, monuments, and buildings which he may find there, because these, unlike the sea, are private property. § 2. But all rivers and ports are public; and, therefore, the right of fishing in a port and in rivers is common to all. § 3. The shore of the sea extends up to the point reached by the highest winter tide. § 4. The use of the river banks is by the law of nations public, just as is the use of the river itself. Therefore, anyone is as much at liberty to moor his vessel to the bank, to bind ropes to the trees growing there, and to discharge any part of his cargo there, as he is to navigate the river itself. But the ownership of these banks is in those to whom the adjoining lands belong, and for this reason, the trees that are growing there also belong to the same persons. § 5. The use of the sea-shore, is also, by the law of nations, public, just as is that of the sea itself; and, hence, any person is at liberty to erect a hut there for shelter, as he is to dry his nets there, or haul them out of the sea; but the ownership of the shore is to be deemed incapable of being claimed by anyone, and to be subject to the same rules as apply to the sea itself, and to the earth or sand beneath it. § 6. Corporate property, not belonging to individuals, includes, for instance, such things as are found in cities, as theatres, racecourses, and other similar places, and in fact all things which are the common property of the whole city.

§ 3. Subject to divine law are, for example, sacred and religious things. § 4. Sacred things are those consecrated to the gods. Religious things, those abandoned to departed spirits. § 5. But a thing is only accounted sacred when it is made so by the authority of the Roman people, as by virtue of a law, or a decree of the senate.

§ 7. Things sacred, religious, and sanctioned, belong to no one; for that which is subject to divine law cannot be included in the property of anyone. § 8. Sacred things are those duly consecrated to God by the pontiffs, as sacred buildings and offerings, properly dedicated to the service of God, and these latter we have forbidden by a constitution to be alienated or pledged, except for the purpose of ransoming captives. If anyone consecrates a building by his own authority, it is not sacred, but profane. But the ground on which a sacred edifice has once been built, even after the destruction of the building, still continues to be sacred, as Papinian lays down.

§ 6. But a religious thing may be so made of our own freewill, as, by interring a dead body in our ground, provided only the burial of the corpse is a matter incumbent upon us. § 7. But on provincial soil, according to the general opinion, the ground cannot be made religious, because the ownership of that land is in the Roman people or in the emperor, and we would seem to have but the mere possession and enjoyment of it. Still, although it be not strictly religious, it is treated as such, just as that which in the provinces is not consecrated by the authority of the Roman people is not properly sacred, still it is so accounted.

§ 9. Anyone may make of his own freewill a place religious by interring a dead body in his own ground, but he may not inter a dead body in land held in common and undefiled against the wish of his co-owner. But in a sepulchre held in common any one co-owner may inter, even against the wishes of the rest. So, if the use and enjoyment is in another, it is held that the owner cannot, without that other person's consent, make the place religious. But a dead body may be interred in a place belonging to another with the latter's consent; and, even if the owner only ratifies the act after the dead body has been interred, still the place will have become religious

§ 8. Sanctioned things also, such as walls and gates, are, in a certain way, subject to divine law.

§ 9. And that which is subject to divine law cannot form part of the property of any one; but that which is subject to human law is generally the property of some one, though this need not be the case; for things belonging to an inheritance are not included in the property of anyone until an heir exists. . . . (five lines illegible). . .

§ 10. Sanctioned things also, such as walls and gates, are, in a certain way, subject to divine law, and therefore form no part of the property of anyone. Walls are said to be sanctioned, because any offence in respect of them is declared to be the subject of a capital penalty. So those parts of laws, by which punishments are established against those who transgress the laws, we term sanctions.

§ 10. Things which are subject to human law are either public or private. § 11. Those which are public are held not to be the property of any one, for they are looked upon as belonging to the whole community. Private things are those which are the property of individuals.

§ 65. Therefore, from what we have said,* it appears that certain things can be alienated by natural law, such are those which are alienated by delivery; other things are alienated through the civil law, for the law relating to formal sales, to surrenders in Court and to acquisition by use, is peculiar to Roman citizens.

* see § 62 to 64 below.

§ 11. Things become the property of individuals in many ways; of some we acquire the ownership by natural law, which, as we have said, is called the law of nations; of other things we acquire the ownership by the civil law. It will be more convenient to begin with the more ancient law, and it is manifest that the law of nature is the more ancient, because it arose in the nature of things with mankind themselves, for civil law could but then begin when States began to be founded, magistrates to be appointed, and laws to be written.

§ 66. But not only are those things which become ours by delivery, acquired by natural right, but also those which we have acquired by occupation, because previously they were the property of no one. Such are all things that are captured on land, in the sea, and in the air. § 67. Hence, if we have caught a wild beast, or bird, or fish, it, so soon as caught, immediately becomes ours by the law of nations, and is deemed to be ours so long as it is retained in our control. But when it has es-

§ 12. Wild beasts, birds, and fishes, that is, all animals which are produced on land, in the sea, or in the air, so soon as they are caught by anyone, immediately become his by the law of nations; for, that which previously had no owner by natural reason passes to the first occupant. And it is immaterial whether a man take the wild beasts or birds upon his own ground, or on that of another, though, clearly, if anyone enters the ground of another for the purpose of hunting or snaring birds, he may, if his intention is foreseen, be forbidden by the owner to enter. Whatever

caped our control, and has recovered its natural freedom, it again becomes the property of the first occupant, because it has ceased to be with us. It is held to regain its natural freedom, either when it has escaped out of our sight, or, although still in sight, the pursuit of it would be difficult.

animals of this nature you capture are looked upon as yours, so long as they are under your control; but when they have escaped and recovered their natural liberty, they cease to be yours, and again become the property of the first occupant. An animal is held to have recovered its natural liberty when it has escaped out of your sight, or if, although still in sight, the pursuit of it would be difficult. § 13. The question has arisen whether, if a wild animal has been so wounded that it could be caught, it is to be deemed to be immediately your property. Some have held that it does so become yours, and that it continues to be yours so long as you continue to pursue it, but that if you cease to pursue it, it then ceases to be yours, and again can become the property of the first occupant. Others have thought that it does not become yours until you have caught it. We decide in favour of the latter opinion, because many things may happen to prevent your capturing it. § 14. Bees also are by their nature wild. Therefore, bees settling upon your tree are not held to be yours until you have hived them, any more than the birds which have built their nests on your tree. Hence, if another person hive them, he will be the owner of them. Anyone, too, is a liberty to take the honeycombs these bees may have made. But, clearly, if before anything has been done you see a person coming upon your land, you may lawfully forbid his entering. A swarm which has flown from your hive is held to be yours so long as you can see it, and pursuit is not difficult, otherwise it becomes the property of the first occupant. § 15. Peacocks, too, and pigeons are by nature wild, and it is immaterial that they are in the habit of flying away and returning, for bees do the same, and of these it is agreed that they are by nature wild. Some persons have deer tamed in such a way that they go into the woods and return again; yet no one denies that deer are by nature wild.

§ 68. In respect of those animals in the habit of going and returning, such as pigeons, and bees, and deer, which are in the habit of going into and returning out of the woods, we have the rule handed down that, when they have lost the intention of returning, they cease to

In respect of those animals in the habit of going and returning, the approved rule is, that they are held to be yours as long as they have the intention of returning; for, if they should cease to have this intention, they cease to be yours, and become the property of the first

be ours, and become the property of the first occupant; and they are deemed to have lost the intention when they have ceased to have a habit of returning.

occupant; and these animals are deemed to have ceased to have the intention of returning when they have ceased to have a habit of returning.

§ 16. Fowls and geese are not by nature wild, which may be gathered from the fact that there are other kinds of fowls and geese which we term wild. And, therefore, if your geese or your fowls should have become from some cause frightened, and have escaped, they are still held to be yours wherever they may be, although you may have lost sight of them; and whoever would retain these animals with the intention of profit is held to be guilty of theft.

§ 69. Those things which are captured from the enemy become ours by natural reason.

§ 17. So those things which we capture from the enemy immediately become ours by the law of nations, so that even free men may be thus reduced into our slavery; but if they should escape from us, and return to their own people, they regain their former condition. § 18. So precious stones, gems, and other things which are found upon the sea-shore, immediately become, by natural law, the property of the finder. § 19. So the offspring of those animals of which you are owner are acquired for you as the result of the same law.

§ 70. Moreover, the alluvial deposit which is added to our land becomes ours by the same right. Now that is considered as added by alluvial deposit which the river adds, little by little, to our land, so that we cannot estimate the quantity added at any moment of time. This is what is commonly meant by saying that that is to be held to be added by alluvial deposit which is added so gradually that its addition is not perceptible to our senses. § 71. Hence, if a river has swept off some portion of your land, and carried it to my land, the portion so carried off still remains yours.

§ 20. Moreover, the alluvial deposit which is added by a river to your land becomes yours by the law of nations. Now alluvion is an imperceptible increase, and that is considered as added by alluvial deposit which is added so gradually that you cannot detect how much is added at any one moment of time. § 21. But if the force of the current should sweep off a portion from your land, and carry it to that of your neighbour, it clearly still remains yours. If, however, it continues for a long time adhering to your neighbour's land, and the trees which it carried off with it take root in his ground, from that time the land and the trees are deemed to have become acquired by your neighbour's estate.

§ 72. But if an island is formed in the middle of a river, it is com-

§ 22. When an island is formed in the sea, which rarely happens,

mon to all who own the land on either bank of the river. But if it be not in the middle of the river it belongs to those who own the land on that bank which is nearest to it.

it becomes the property of the first occupant, for it is held previously to belong to no one. But if formed in a river, which frequently happens, and the island occupies the middle of the stream, it belongs in common to those who own the lands along the banks on each side of the river, in proportion to the length of each one's estate along the bank. But if the island is nearer to one side, then it belongs only to those who own land along that bank. If a river becomes divided, and lower down is united again, so that some person's land is reduced to the form of an island, the land still remains his whose it was. § 23. But if a river, entirely forsaking its natural bed, begins to flow over another part, the former bed belongs to those who possess the land along the old banks in proportion to the length of each one's land along the banks. The new bed becomes subject to the same rules as apply to the river itself, that is, it becomes public. And if, after a time, the river returns to its former bed, the new bed again becomes the property of those who own the land along what were the banks. § 24. The case is quite different if the whole of a person's land is inundated; for the inundation does not alter the character of the land, and, therefore, if the waters recede, it is clear that the land remains his whose it was.

§ 79. In other classes of cases, also, the rule of nature is sought; thus, if you have made wine, oil, or corn, out of my grapes, olives, or ears of corn, the question arises whether that wine, oil, or corn, is mine or yours; again, if you have made some vessel out of my gold or silver, or have constructed a ship or a chest, or a bench with my planks, or if you have made a garment out of my wool, or a sweet drink out of my wine and honey, or a plaster or balsam out of my drugs, the question arises whether that, so made out of my material, is yours or mine. Some think that the material and substance must be looked to, that is, that the thing should be held to belong to him out of whose materials it was made, and this was

§ 25. When a thing has been made by one person out of materials belonging to another, the question is often asked which of the two persons is, according to natural reason, the owner, he who made it, or he who was the owner of the materials. For instance, if a person has made wine, oil, or corn out of the grapes, olives, or ears of corn belonging to another, or has made some vessel out of gold, silver, or copper belonging to another, or has mixed a sweet drink with another's wine and honey, or has made a plaster or balsam out of another's drugs, or has made a garment out of another's wool, or has constructed a ship, a chest, or a bench with another's planks. After much diversity of opinion between the Sabi-

the better opinion, according to Sabinus and Cassius. Others think that the thing should be his who made it, and this is the opinion generally approved by the leaders of the opposite school. But he who owned the material and substance has an action for theft against him who took them, and a personal action is also available, in spite of the fact that, owing to the thing being destroyed, a suit for its recovery will not lie, for a personal action may be brought against thieves and certain other possessors.

nians and Proculians, an intermediate view has been followed in this way, that, if the thing made can be reduced to its former material, then the owner of the material is to be deemed the owner, but if the thing cannot be so reduced, then he is rather to be deemed the owner who made the thing. For example, a vessel which has been cast can be reduced to the raw mass of copper, silver, or gold, but wine, oil, or corn cannot be restored to the condition of grapes, olives, or ears of corn, nor can the sweet drink be resolved into the wine and honey. But if a man has made anything in part with his own materials, and in part with the materials of another, as, for example, if he has made the sweet drink with his own wine and another's honey, or a plaster or balsam out of his own and another's drugs, or a garment out of his own and another's wool, then in such cases no doubt is to be entertained that he is the owner who made the thing, for he not only gave his labour, but provided also part of the material.

§ 26. But if a person has woven another's purple in with his own garment, the purple, although the more valuable, falls as an accessory to the garment, and he who was owner of the purple has an action for theft, and a personal action against him who took it, whether it was he or someone else who made the garment. For, although things which have been destroyed cannot be claimed in a suit for their recovery, still against thieves and certain other possessors a personal remedy is available. § 27. If the materials belonging to two persons are mingled with their consent, the total result of the mixture is common to both, as, for example, in the case of their having mixed together their wines, or melted together masses of gold or silver. And although the materials be different, so that a new thing is the result, as when a sweet drink is made with wine and honey, or an artificial metal out of gold and silver, the rule is the same; for, in such a case, there need be no doubt entertained that the thing made is common. And if it is by chance, and not through the will of the owners that the mingling has taken place, still, whether the materials are of the same or of different kinds, it is laid down that the rule is the same. § 28. If the corn of Titius has become mixed with yours, and this is with your consent, the result will be common; because each separate body, that is, each single grain, which before was your particular property has, by your consent, become common; but, if the mixture were the result of accident, or if Titius mixed it without your consent, the result is not held to be common property, because the grains of corn continue distinct in substance, and therefore in such cases the corn is no more common than would a flock be held to be common property, because sheep belonging to Titius had become mixed with yours; but, if the whole quantity of corn is retained by either of you, the other has an action for the specific recovery of his proportion of the corn, and it is within the province of the judge to estimate the quality of the corn which belonged to each.

§ 29. If a man builds upon his own ground with the materials of another, he is held to be the owner of the building, because everything built on the ground goes as an accessory to it. But the owner of the materials does not cease to be the owner of them, only in the meantime he cannot claim the materials, nor does a suit for their production lie, on account of the law of the Twelve Tables, by which it is provided that no one can be compelled to remove another's beam which has been worked in as part of his own building, but that he may be made, by means of the action in respect of building materials used, to pay double the value. (By the term 'beam', all materials for building are included). The object of this law is to prevent the necessity of buildings being pulled down. But if the building should be from any cause destroyed, then the owner of the materials, if he has not already obtained the double value, may claim them and sue for their production.

§ 73. Moreover, that which a person has built on our land, although he may have built it for himself, becomes ours by natural law, because the superstructure goes as an accessory to the land.

§ 30. On the other hand, if a person builds a house with his own materials on another's ground, the house becomes his to whom the ground belongs. But in this case the owner of the materials loses his property in them, because he is held to have voluntarily parted with them, that is, if he was not ignorant that he was building upon another's land; and, therefore, although the building should be destroyed, he will not be able to claim the materials. But it is clear that, if the person who built was in possession of the soil, and the owner of the soil claims the house, and will not pay the price of the materials and the wages of the workmen, the owner may be defeated by a plea of fraud, that is, assuming that the possessor who erected the building acted bona fide. For, if he knew that the ground belonged to another, he is open to the charge of being in fault for rashly building on ground which he knew to belong to another.

§ 74. And this rule of accession applies more forcibly still in the case of a plant which a person has placed in our ground, provided it has become bound up with the land by its roots.

§ 31. If Titius puts another man's plant in his own ground the plant will belong to Titius; on the other hand, if Titius puts his own plant in the ground of Mævius, the plant will belong to Mævius, that is, if, in either case, the plant has taken root; for before it has taken root it remains his whose it was. But, from the time it has taken root, the ownership of it is changed; so much so that, if a neighbour's tree is so close on to the ground of Titius as to take root in it, we lay down that the tree becomes the property of Titius. For reason does not suffer a tree to be deemed the property of any one else than of him in whose ground it has taken root; and, therefore, if a tree placed near a boundary has extended its roots into the neighbour's land it becomes common property.

§ 75. The same rule applies in the case of corn sown in our ground by another person. § 76. But if we, as owner of the ground, claim the produce, or the building, and are not willing to repay the expenses incurred in the building, planting, or sowing, he will be able to defeat our claim by the plea of fraud, assuming that he was a bona fide possessor.

§ 32. By the same reason that plants rooted in the earth are an accessory to the soil, so corn which has been sown is held to be an accessory to the soil. But just as he who has built on the ground of another, may, as we have said, set up a plea of fraud if the owner of the ground claims the building; so he who, at his own cost and in good faith, has sown another man's field, may protect himself with the aid of a like plea.

§ 77. By this rule it is held that that which a person has written on my paper or parchment, even with letters of gold, is mine, because the letters are an accessory to the paper or parchment. Hence also, if I claim these books or parchments, and will not pay the cost of the writing, I may be defeated by the plea of fraud.

§ 33. Written characters, although of gold, are an accessory to the paper or parchment, just as whatever is built on, or sown in, the ground, is an accessory to the ground. Hence, if Titius has written a poem, a history, or an oration on your paper or parchment, you, and not Titius, are to be held the owner of the substance. But if you claim your books or parchment from Titius,

§ 78. But if a person has painted on my tablet, for example, a portrait, the opposite rule holds, for it is rather to be laid down that the tablet is an accessory to the picture. For this difference scarcely a satisfactory reason can be given. Still, it will be in accordance with this rule, that, if you claim the portrait as yours whilst I possess it, and do not pay the price of the tablet, you can be met by the plea of fraud. But if you are the possessor, the consequence is that an equitable action must be granted to me against you; and in this case, unless I pay the cost of the picture, you can resist my claim by the plea of fraud, assuming that you are a bona fide possessor. It is clear that, whether you or another have stolen the tablet, an action for theft can be brought by me.

and are not ready to pay the cost of the writing, Titius can defend himself by a plea of fraud, assuming that he obtained possession of the paper or parchment in good faith. § 34. If a person has painted on the tablet of another, some think that the tablet goes as an accessory to the picture, others that the picture, whatever it be, is an accessory to the tablet. But it appears to us to be the better opinion, that the tablet should go as an accessory to the picture; for it is ridiculous that a painting by Apelles or Parrhasius should go as an accessory to the most worthless tablet. Hence, if the owner of the tablet is in possession of the picture, the painter, should he claim it from him, but does not pay the price of the tablet, may be met by the plea of fraud; but, if the painter is in possession of the picture, it follows that an equitable action should be given to the owner of the tablet against him; and in this case, if the owner of the tablet does not pay the value of the picture, he may also be met by a plea of fraud, assuming that the painter became possessed of the tablet in good faith; for it is clear that, if the tablet has been stolen, whether by the painter or anyone else, an action for theft is available to the owner of the tablet.

§ 35. If anyone has purchased in good faith land from a person not the owner, but whom he believed so to be, or has received it in good faith from such a person, by gift or other lawful title, it is in accordance with natural reason that the produce which he has gathered should be his in return for his care and culture; and, therefore, if the true owner subsequently appear and claim the land, he cannot sue in respect of the produce consumed; but this allowance is not granted to him who has been in possession of another's estate with knowledge of the fact; and therefore he is compelled to account, together with the land, for all the produce, although consumed. § 36. He to whom the use and enjoyment of land belongs, does not become owner of the produce until he has himself gathered it; and, therefore, if he should die before the produce, though ripe, has been gathered in, it does not belong to his heir, but is the property of the owner of the soil; and nearly the same reasoning will apply to the case of the farm tenant. § 37. The produce of animals includes their young as well as their milk, hair, and wool; and therefore lambs, kids, calves, colts, and sucking pigs, are immediately, by the law of nature, the property of him who has a right to the produce; but the offspring of a female slave is not reckoned as produce, and therefore belongs to the owner of the property. For it seemed absurd that a man should be reckoned amongst produce when it is for the benefit of man that, in the nature of things, all produce is provided. § 38. But if a person has the use and enjoyment of a flock, he is bound to replace, by young ones, any of the flock that die; and Julian was of this opinion. So, too, the usufructuary ought to replace dead vines or trees, for he ought to cultivate with fairness and like a good head of a family.

§ 39. The Emperor Hadrian, following the rules of natural equity, granted to the finder any treasure which he found in his own land, and settled the same rule in the case of treasure found by chance in a sacred or religious place. If, however, a person found it by chance in another's ground, without expressly working for it, half of it was granted to the owner of the ground. In accordance with this view, he decided that if anything is found in a place belonging to the emperor, half belongs to the finder and half to the emperor. Consistently with this is the rule that, if a person finds anything in a place belonging to the imperial treasury, or to the public, or to a city, half is to belong to the finder, and half to the imperial treasury or to the city.

§ 40. Delivery is also, according to natural law, a mode of acquiring things, for nothing is more consonant with natural equity than that the wishes of the owner of property, desirous of transferring it, should be deemed binding; and, therefore, a corporeal thing of whatever kind, may be delivered over, and when so delivered over by the owner, it is alienated. In this way are transferred senatorial, provincial, and imperial provincial lands, that is, lands in the provinces, between which and Italian lands there is now, by our constitution, no difference, so that when delivery is made of them on account of a gift, a marriage portion, or other reason, they are undoubtedly transferred. § 41. But things sold and delivered, are not acquired by the purchaser until he has paid the price to the vendor, or otherwise satisfied him, as by finding a surety, or giving a pledge. And, although this is a provision of the Twelve Tables, yet it may be rightly said to be deducible from the law of nations, that is, from the law of nature. But, if the vendor has trusted the purchaser, it is to be laid down that the thing immediately becomes the property of the purchaser. § 42. It is immaterial whether the owner deliver the thing himself, or some one else by his direction. § 43. For this reason, if anyone is entrusted by the owner with the uncontrolled management of all his affairs, and in transacting these affairs he sells and delivers a thing, he passes the property in it to the person who receives it. § 44. Sometimes, too, the mere intention of the owner, without delivery, is sufficient to transfer the property in a thing, as, for example, if a person has lent, or let to, or deposited anything with you, and then sells it, or gives it to you; for, although he has not delivered it to you, as the result of the sael or gift, yet in that he suffers it to become yours, you instantly acquire the ownership of it, just as if it had actually been delivered to you for that purpose. § 45. So, too, if a person sells goods deposited in a warehouse, as soon as he has handed over the keys of the warehouse to the purchaser, he transfers the ownership of the goods to the purchaser. § 46. Nay, more, sometimes the intention of the owner, although directed towards an uncertain person, transfers the ownership of a thing, as, for example, the prætors or consuls throwing largess to the crowd, cannot tell what part of it anyone in the crowd may succeed in getting; yet, as it is their intention that each should have what he gets, they make what each gets to immediately belong to him. § 47. For this reason it seems quite correct to hold that the first occupant of a thing, treated by its owner as abandoned, immediately becomes owner of it; and that is held to be abandoned which its owner has thrown away with the intention that it may no longer form part of his property, as he thereupon immediately ceases to be the owner of it. § 48. It is otherwise with respect to those things which are thrown overboard in a storm for the purpose of lightening the vessel; for they remain the property of their owners, because it is clear that they were not thrown overboard through a wish not to have them, but in order that the ship might escape the perils of the sea. Hence, anyone who, with a view to make a profit of them, carries them off when washed on shore, or even found at sea, is guilty of theft. There is little difference to be discerned between these things and those which, without their owner's knowledge, drop from a vehicle in motion.

Title ii. Of corporeal and incorporeal things.

§ 12. Again, some things are corporeal, others incorporeal. § 13. Corporeal things are those which are tangible, as land, a slave, a garment, gold, silver, and, indeed, other things innumerable. § 14. Incorporeal things are those which are not tangible, such are those consisting in a right, as an inheritance, a usufruct, and obligations in any way contracted. Nor does it affect the matter, that corporeal things are comprised in an inheritance, for produce gathered from the soil is corporeal; and that which is due to us by virtue of an obligation is usually corporeal, as land, a slave, or money; for it is the right of succession, or the right to the use and enjoyment, or the right arising out of the obligation, which is incorporeal. Amongst things incorporeal are to be included the rights over urban and rural estates, which are also called servitudes.

Some things are corporeal, others incorporeal. § 1. Corporeal things are those which are by their nature tangible, as land, a slave, a garment, gold, silver, and, indeed, other things innumerable. § 2. Incorporeal things are those which are not tangible, such are those consisting in a right, as an inheritance, a usufruct, use, or obligations in any way contracted. Nor does it affect the matter that corporeal things are comprised in an inheritance; for produce gathered from the soil is corporeal, and that which is due to us by virtue of an obligation is usually corporeal, as land, a slave, or money; for it is the right itself of inheritance, or the right to the use and enjoyment, or the right arising out of the obligation, which is incorporeal. § 3. Among things incorporeal are to be included the rights over urban and rural estates, which are also called servitudes.

Title iii. Of servitudes.

Rights appertaining to rural estates are: "iter", "actus", "via", "aquaeductus". "Iter" is the right enabling a man to go and pass along, but not to lead a beast of burden or a vehicle. "Actus" gives the right of leading a beast of burden or a vehicle. Hence, he who has the first right has not the second, but he who has the second, has the first also, and can make use of his right without having a beast of burden with him. "Via" gives the right of passing, whether driving or walking; for both "iter" and "actus" are included in this right of way. "Aquaeductus" is the right of leading water across another's estate.

§ 14A. The rights appertaining to urban estates are, the right of

§ 1. The servitudes of urban estates are those attaching to

raising buildings so as to obstruct the lights of the neighbouring building, or of preventing the raising of buildings that would obstruct the access of light. § 14B. And so as to the rights of receiving rain water in drops, or flowing in the gutter . . . . . (three lines illegible).

buildings, and they are said to be servitudes of urban estates, because we call all edifices urban estates, although built in the country. Now, servitudes of urban estates are such as these: that a neighbour must support the weight of his neighbour's house; that he must let his neighbour insert a beam into his wall; that he must receive, or need not receive, the water that drops from the roof, or that flows from the gutter of another's house, on to his house, or into his courtyard or drain; that he must not raise his house higher nor block out his neighbour's lights. § 2. Some consider that it is proper to reckon amongst servitudes of rural estates the right of drawing water, of driving cattle to water, of pasturage, of burning lime, of digging sand.

§ 3. These servitudes are called servitudes of estates, because they cannot exist without estates. For no one can acquire or be liable in respect of a servitude over a rural or urban estate, unless he has an estate belonging to him. § 4. If a person wishes to create such a right in favour of his neighbour, he must effect the purpose by agreements and stipulations. A person may, also, by testament, forbid his heir to raise his house higher, to obstruct his neighbour's lights, or make him suffer the insertion by a neighbour of a beam into his wall, or to receive the water from his roof, or allow a neighbour to pass or drive beasts of burden or vehicles, or conduct water across his land.

Title iv. Of usufruct.

Usufruct is the right of using and taking the produce of another's property, without altering the substance, for it is a right over the substance, and, if this perish, the usufruct itself necessarily disappears also. § 1. The usufruct is capable of being detached from the ownership, and this takes place in many ways, for example, if a person leaves the usufruct to another by way of legacy, for the heir has then the bare ownership, and the legatee has the usufruct; conversely, if he leaves the estate as a legacy, minus the usufruct, the legatee has the bare ownership, and the heir has the usufruct. Again, he may leave the usufruct, by way of legacy, to one, and the estate, minus the usufruct, to another. But, if a person wishes to establish a usufruct otherwise than by testament, he should do it by agreements and stipulations. But, lest ownerships should be rendered valueless by reason of the usufruct being for ever detached, it has been thought right that there should be certain ways in which the usufruct should become extinguished, and revert to the ownership. § 2. A usufruct may be established, not only in respect of land and buildings, but also over slaves and beasts of burden, and other things, except those which are consumed by the use of them, for, neither by natural or civil law are these susceptible of usufruct. Amongst these are wine, oil, corn, garments, and akin to these is coined money; for it, in the very use, by perpetual interchange, is consumed. However, on the score of utility, the senate resolved that usufruct might be established even over these things, provided that sufficient security were given on account of them to the heir; and, therefore, if the usufruct of money is left by legacy, the money is so given to the legatee as to become his own, and he has to give security to the heir for the repayment of an equal sum in the event of his death, or undergoing a change of status. The other things mentioned above are delivered to the legatee in such a way as to become his property; but their value is estimated, and security given for the payment of the amount at which they are valued, in the event of his dying, or undergoing a change of status. Hence, the senate has not, indeed, established the usufruct of these things, for that could not be done, but, by means of the security, has established a right in the nature of usufruct. § 3. The usufruct terminates by the death of the usufructuary, and by the two kinds of change of status, namely, the greatest and the intermediate, and by not using it in the manner, and at the time fixed; all which points have been settled by our constitution. The usufruct is also terminated if the usufructuary surrenders it to the owner of the property (for a surrender to a stranger would effect nothing); or, conversely, by the usufructuary acquiring the ownership of the thing, which is called consolidation. And further than this it is settled that if a building is destroyed by fire, or by an earthquake, or fall by reason of the usufructuary's neglect, the usufruct is extinguished, and the ground on which the building stood is not deemed liable. § 4. When the usufruct is entirely extinguished, it reverts to the ownership; and, the person who had the bare ownership, begins from that moment to have complete power over the thing.

Title v. Of use and habitation.

The bare use is established and extinguished by the very same means as the usufruct. § 1. But the use is a less extensive right than usufruct; for he who has the bare use of an estate is held to have no further right than that of taking herbs, fruit, flowers, hay, straw, and wood, sufficient for his daily use, and he may stay on the estate so long as he neither annoys the owner of it, nor hinders those who are engaged in its cultivation. He cannot let or sell, or assign gratuitously his right to another, whereas a usufructuary can do all these. § 2. So he who has the use of a house is only held to have a right to the extent of living in it himself, and he cannot transfer this right to another; indeed, it seems to have been hardly conceded that he had a right to receive a guest, or to have his wife and children, and freed-men, and other free persons in his service like slaves; or in the case of a wife having the use, of having her husband to live with her. § 3. In the same way, he to whom the use of a slave belongs, has only the right of himself using the labour and services of the slave; for in no way is he permitted to transfer his right to another: the same rule of course holds good in respect of a beast of burden. § 4. But if the use of a flock or of a herd be given as a legacy, the person who has the use cannot take the milk, the lambs, or the wool, because these are included in the produce; but he may certainly make use of the flock to manure his land.

§ 5. But if the right of habitation be left to anyone by way of legacy, or granted in any other way, this does not seem to be either a right of user or usufruct, but a peculiar right in itself; and on the ground of utility, following the opinion of Marcellus, we have delivered a decision permitting those who have this right of habitation, not only to live in the place themselves, but also to let it out to others.

§ 6. This much must here suffice for the subject of servitudes, as well as of usufruct, use, and habitation. We shall treat of inheritances and obligations in their turn. We have already set out briefly the modes by which things are acquired by the law of nations. Let us now pass to the modes in which they are acquired by processes of the civil law.

§ 15. All things are either things requiring for transfer the formal conveyance by copper and scale, or are things not requiring that form of transfer. Things requiring transfer by a formal conveyance are estates on Italian soil, whether rural, as a farm, or urban, as a house; also slaves and those quadrupeds which have been habituated to the saddle and the collar, as oxen, mules, horses and asses; and the leaders of our school consider that these animals are things requiring transfer by formal conveyance immediately they are born, whilst Nerva, Proculus, and other leaders of the opposite school, do not hold them to be so until they are broken in: and if, on account of their great ferocity, they cannot be broken in, then they are held to begin to be things requiring transfer by a formal conveyance when they have reached that age at which such animals are usually broken in. § 16. But wild beasts, such as bears and lions, are things not requiring transfer by a formal conveyance; as also those animals which are commonly reckoned amongst wild beasts, such as elephants and camels; and the point is not material that these animals are accustomed to the collar and the saddle, because, at the time the division into things requiring transfer by a formal conveyance, and things not so requiring, was made, there was no mention of these animals. § 17. Nearly all incorporeal things are things not requiring transfer by a formal conveyance, with the exception of servitudes of rural estates, for it is held that these are things requiring transfer by a formal conveyance, although they are amongst the number of incorporeal things.

§ 18. A great difference exists between things requiring transfer by a formal conveyance and things not so requiring. § 19. For things not requiring transfer by a formal conveyance may lawfully become the property of another by mere delivery, if only they are corporeal, and on that account susceptible of delivery. § 20. Therefore, if I have delivered to you a garment, or gold or silver, whether as the result of a sale, or as a gift, or on any other ground, that thing immediately becomes yours if I was the civil law owner of it. § 21. It is the same with provincial estates, of which we call some stipendiary, others tributary; stipendiary are those situated in those provinces which are regarded as the peculiar property of the Roman people; tributary are those situated in those provinces which are considered as peculiar to the emperor. § 22. "Res mancipi" are those things which are transferred to another by "mancipatio", whence also they are so called. But what stands good when done privately by this method of formal conveyance, also stands good when done by way of surrender in court. § 23. In what manner the formal conveyance by copper and scale is effected we have already explained in the previous commentary.* § 24. The process of surrender in court is done in the following way: Being in the presence of a magistrate of the Roman people, as, for example, a prætor or a governor of a province, he to whom the thing is surrendered in court, and whilst holding it, speaks thus:—"I assert that this slave is mine by the law of the quirites." After he has thus claimed the thing, the prætor asks him who is surrendering it, whether he counterclaims it, and, upon his denial or silence, the prætor declares the thing to be his who has claimed it. This is called an action of the law, and can be carried out, even in the provinces, in the presence of the governors. § 25. Commonly, however, indeed almost always, we proceed to effect the transfer by formal conveyance, because we can do this ourselves in the presence of friends, as it is not proper or necessary to make any application (involving considerable difficulty) to perform it in the presence of a prætor or a governor of a province. § 26. But if a thing requiring transfer by a formal conveyance has been neither so conveyed nor surrendered in court . . . . (thirty-one lines illegible). . . . § 27. Finally, it is necessary to observe that the conveyance by means of the copper and the scale is a process peculiar to Italian soil, and there can be no such process employed in respect of provincial soil, for this process refers only to a thing which requires transfer by a formal conveyance, but provincial soil is a thing not requiring such a mode of transfer. . . . . (one line illegible).

* *ante* i, § 119.

§ 28. It is clear that incorporeal things are not subject matter for delivery. § 29. But rights appertaining to urban estates can be surrendered in court, whilst those appertaining to rural estates can also be transferred by means of a formal conveyance. § 30. Usufruct is only susceptible of transfer by surrender in court; for the owner of the property can surrender in court the usufruct to another, so that the latter has the usufruct, and he himself retains the mere naked ownership. When the usufructuary himself surrenders in court the usufruct to the owner of the property, the effect is that the usufruct departs from him and merges in the ownership; but if he surrenders it in court to another person than the owner, he retains his rights, for it is held that such a surrender in court effects nothing. § 31. But these remarks of course apply only to estates in Italy, because these are capable of being the subject of transfer by formal conveyance and of surrender in court, whereas in the provinces, whether a person wishes to establish a usufruct, or a right of passing, or of driving cattle, or of leading water, or of raising or not raising buildings higher so as to block out his neighbour's lights, and other similar rights, he must do it by agreements or stipulations, because the estates themselves are incapable of transfer, either by the formal conveyance or by surrender in court. § 32. But since usufruct can be established in respect of slaves and the other animals mentioned above, we must understand that the usufruct of these can be established, even in the provinces, by a surrender in court. § 33. Now what we have said as to the usufruct being established only by a surrender in court, has not been rashly asserted, as though it may be established by a formal conveyance, in that it can be detached from the ownership in the process of formal conveyance, yet here it is not the usufruct that is formally conveyed; but by being withdrawn from the property to be formally conveyed, the result is that the usufruct will be in one person, and the ownership in another. § 34. An inheritance also is only susceptible of surrender in court. § 35. For if he, to whom an inheritance has fallen by legal succession, on an intestacy, surrenders it in court to another before he has entered upon it, that is to say, before an heir exists, the result is that he, to whom the surrender in court was made, becomes heir just as if he himself had been called to the inheritance by law; but if it is surrendered after he has incurred liability respecting it, he will remain heir, and will therefore be liable to the creditors, but the debts are lost, and in this way debtors to the inheritance are benefited. The corporeal things belonging to the inheritance are, however, transferred to him to whom the inheritance was surrendered, as if each single object had been surrendered in court to him. § 36. But if the heir, named in a testament, before he has entered upon the inheritance, surrenders it in court to another, he effects nothing; but, if he surrenders it after entering upon it, the same results follow, as we have just stated, in respect of him, to whom the inheritance belongs by law on an intestacy, if he surrenders it in court after incurring liability. § 37. The leaders of the opposite school hold that the same applies to the case of necessary heirs, because it seems to be immaterial whether a person becomes heir on entering upon the inheritance, or immediately and against his will; but how this is will appear in its proper place.* Our teachers, however, are of opinion that the necessary heir effects nothing when he surrenders the inheritance in court.† § 38. Obligations in whatever way contracted are not susceptible of these modes of transfer. For if I wish that that which is owed by some one to me, should be owed to you, I cannot effect my purpose by any of those modes by which corporeal things are transferred to another; but it will be necessary for you, by my order, to stipulate for the thing from him,‡ the result of which will be that he is released from me, and begins to be bound to you, and this is called a novation of the obligation. § 39. And without this novation you cannot sue in your own name, but would have to bring your action in my name, as my cognitor or procurator.**

* *post*, § 152.

† *post*, iii, § 87.

‡ *post*, iii, § 176.

** *post*, iv, § 82, etc.

§ 40. The next point to mention is that among foreigners there is only one kind of ownership; for a person is either held to be, or not to be, owner, and this rule was formerly in use amongst the Roman people, for a person was either owner, by the law of the quirites, or was not looked upon as owner at all. But afterwards ownership became susceptible of division, in such a way that one person could be the owner by the law of the quirites, while another could hold it as part of his goods. § 41. For, if I have neither conveyed to you by the process of the copper and the scale a thing requiring to be so conveyed, nor surrendered it in court, but have only delivered it, the thing has thereby, indeed, become part of your goods, but it will remain mine, by the law of the quirites, until you have acquired it by use through the required period of possession; for when the period of acquisition by use is once completed, the thing will become completely yours in law, that is, it will be yours both as part of your goods, and by the law of the quirites, just as if it had been formally conveyed or surrendered in court.

§ 42. The acquisition by use of movables is completed in one year, that of lands and of buildings in two years, and this is so provided by the Twelve Tables.

§ 43. But the acquisition by use

Title vi. Of acquisition by use, and of possession of long standing.

By the civil law it was provided that he who bona fide bought a thing, or received it by way of gift, or any other lawful means, from a person who was not the owner, but whom he thought to be so,

of those things even which have been delivered to us by another person than the owner, whether they are things requiring transfer by a formal conveyance or not, is available in our favour, if only we have received them bona fide, believing that he who delivered them was owner. § 44. This rule appears to have been adopted to prevent the ownership of things remaining for a longer time in uncertainty than the period of one or two years, which is required to entitle a possessor to acquire by use, this period affording a sufficient interval within which an owner can make inquiries after his property.

should acquire the thing through having had the use of it for one year, if it were a movable, wherever it might be, or for two years in the case of an immovable, but this only if it were on Italian soil, the object of the rule being to prevent the ownership of things remaining in uncertainty; but though this was so settled by the ancients, on the ground that the above-mentioned time was sufficient for owners to inquire after their property, we have come to a better decision, in order to prevent owners being defrauded of their property too quickly, and to prevent the benefit of the rule being restricted to any fixed locality; and, therefore, we have made a constitution, providing that movables may be acquired by a use during three years, but immovables by the possession through a long period (that is, ten years between persons present, and twenty between persons absent): and that by these means not only in Italy, but in every land ruled by us, the ownership of things may be acquired, provided a lawful ground for possession precedes.

§ 45. But sometimes, although a person possesses the property of another in perfect good faith, yet no acquisition by use flows from that possession: as, for example, if a person possesses a thing stolen, or taken by force; for the Twelve Tables forbids the acquisition by use of a thing stolen, and the Julian and Plautian law, that of a thing taken by force. § 46. So provincial land is not susceptible of acquisition by use. § 47. So, also, before the Claudian law, such things belonging to a woman under agnate guardianship, as required transfer by the formal conveyance of copper and scale, could not be acquired by use, except when they had been delivered by herself with the authority of her tutor, and this was so provided by the Twelve Tables. § 48. So it is clear that free men, as well as sacred and religious things, cannot be acquired by use.

§ 1. But, sometimes, although a person possesses the property of another in perfect good faith, no acquisition by use flows from the possession, however long it may be: as, for example, when anyone possesses a free person, a sacred or religious thing, or a fugitive slave. § 2. Things stolen, or taken by force, cannot be acquired by use, although they have been bona fide possessed during the above-mentioned period; for such acquisition by use is prohibited, as to things stolen, by the Twelve Tables, and the Atinian law, as to things taken by force, by the Julian and Plautian law.

§ 49. When it is commonly said that the acquisition by use of things stolen or taken by force, is forbidden by the Twelve Tables, this does not mean that the thief, or he who gets possession of the thing by force, is unable to acquire by use (for another reason prevents the acquisition by use, viz., that, of course, his possession is mala fide), but that no other person, even though he may have purchased from him in good faith, has the right of acquiring by use. § 50. Whence, in respect of movables, it does not easily happen that a bona fide possessor can avail himself of acquisition by use. Because he who has sold and delivered another's property commits theft, and the same holds good if he have delivered the thing on any other ground. But yet this may sometimes be otherwise; for, if a thing lent or hired out to the deceased, or deposited with him, has been sold or given away by the heir, supposing it to be part of the inheritance, he does not commit theft; so, if he who has the usufruct of a female slave has sold or given away her offspring, believing it to belong to him, he does not commit theft; for theft is not committed without the intention of stealing. It may also happen in other ways, that a person may transfer to another property not his own, without its being infected with the vice of theft, so that the possessor may acquire it by use. § 51. For a person may become possessed, without violence, of land belonging to another; when, for example, it is vacant through the negligence of the owner, or because the owner has died without a successor, or has been absent from it for a long time; in which

§ 3. When it is said that the acquisition by use of things stolen or taken by force is forbidden by these laws, this does not mean that the thief himself, or he who possesses himself of the thing by force, is unable to acquire the property (for another reason prevents the acquisition byuse, viz., that, of course, their possession is mala fide), but no one else, although he has in good faith purchased or received it on any other ground, has the right of acquiring by use. Whence, in respect of movables, it does not easily happen that a bona fide possessor can avail himself of acquisition by use. For whenever a person sells, or delivers for any other reason, a thing belonging to another, it is theft. § 4. But this may sometimes be otherwise; for, if an heir, supposing a thing lent or hired out to the deceased, or deposited with him, to be part of the inheritance, sells or gives it as a gift or dowry to a person who receives it bona fide, there is no doubt that the person receiving it may acquire the property in it by use, and the thing will not be infected by the vice of theft, for in that the heir has bona fide alienated it as his own, he has not committed theft. § 5. So, if he to whom the usufruct of a female slave belongs, sells or gives away her offspring, believing it to belong to him, he does not commit theft; for theft is not committed without the intention of stealing. § 6. It may also happen in other ways that a person may transfer to another property not his own, without its being infected with the vice of theft, so that the possessor may acquire it by use. § 7. But, in respect of things of the class of immovables, the case may more easily arise, as, if a person, without violence, has taken

cases, if it has been conveyed to another person who receives it bona fide, the possessor will be able to acquire by use; and, although he who had taken the vacant possession, knew that the land belonged to another, this does not interfere to prevent the bona fide possessor acquiring by use, for the opinion is disapproved of those who have thought that land can be the subject of theft.

possession of a place vacant through the absence or negligence of the owner, or because he has died without a successor; and although he possesses mala fide (since he knows that he has occupied land belonging to another), yet, if he delivers it to a third person who receives it bona fide, this person may acquire the property in it by long possession, as the thing he receives has neither been stolen nor taken by force. The opinion of certain of the ancients, who thought that there could be theft of land or of a place, has been abandoned; and there are imperial constitutions which provide that no possessor of things of the class of immovables shall be deprived of the benefit of a long and undoubted possession. § 8. Sometimes even a thing stolen or taken by force may be acquired by use, as where it has returned into the power of the owner; for, then, the vice being purged, the acquisition by use may take place. § 9. Things belonging to our imperial treasury cannot be acquired by use; but Papinian has laid down that, if before property comprising an escheated succession has been reported to the imperial treasury, a bona fide purchaser has received delivery of any part of it, he can acquire the property by use; and the late Emperor Antoninus Pius, and the late Emperors Severus and Antoninus, have issued rescripts in accordance with this view. § 10. Lastly, it is to be observed that a thing must be in such a condition as not to be infected with any vice, in order that a bona fide purchaser or person who possesses it on any other lawful ground, may acquire it by use.

§ 11. But a mistake as to the ground of possession is not available for acquisition by use; as, for example, if a person possesses in the belief that he has bought the thing when he has not bought it, or that he possesses on the ground of a gift, when no gift has been made to him.

§ 52. Again, on the other hand, it may happen, that he who knows that he possesses the property of another, may yet acquire by use, as, for example, if anyone should possess himself of property belonging to an inheritance, of which the heir has not yet obtained possession, for in such a case the right of acquiring by use is conceded, provided the property in question is susceptible of acquisition by use.

This kind of possession and acquisition by use is known as that "in the place of the heir". § 53. And this acquisition by use has been conceded to such an extent that even things belonging to the class of immovables may be acquired by use in one year. § 54. But the reason why, in this case, acquisition by use of things belonging to the class of immovables has been allowed to take place in one year, is because it was formerly thought that the things belonging to the inheritance could, like the inheritance itself, be acquired by use in the course of one year; for by the Twelve Tables it is ordered that things appertaining to the soil may be acquired by use in two years, but other things in one year. Therefore, an inheritance seemed to be included among the other things, because it does not appertain to the soil, nor is it a corporeal thing; and, although it has been subsequently admitted that inheritances themselves cannot be acquired by use, still, in respect of all things included in inheritances, even those appertaining to the soil, the acquisition by use in one year remained. § 55. But the reason why such an unjust possession and acquisition by use have been admitted at all is, because our ancestors wished inheritances to be entered upon with all speed, so that there might be persons to perform the sacred rites, the observance of which was of very great importance at that time, and also that the creditors might have some one to proceed against for their claims. § 56. But this kind of possession and acquisition by use is also known as that by way of gain: for anyone, knowingly possessing the property of another, thereby makes gain. § 57. But, now, it is no longer by way of gain; for, by the authority of . . . Hadrian, a decree of the senate decided that such kinds of acquisition by use should be revoked; and, therefore, the heir, by claiming the inheritance from him who has acquired the thing by use, obtains it just as if acquisition by use had not taken place. § 58. And, moreover, if there is a necessary heir in existence, then the acquisition by use, known as that "in the place of the heir",* cannot, by mere operation of law, be made available.

* *ante*, § 52.

§ 59. There are, however, still, other grounds by which a person can, knowingly, acquire by use the property of another. For he who has given a thing to another, by the process of the copper and scale, or surrendered it in court, subject to a fiduciary agreement, and becomes possessed of it again, can acquire it by use in the course of one year, even if it be land.

This kind of acquisition by use is called retaking by use, because we re-acquire, by means of the use, that which we formerly possessed. § 60. But, when a fiduciary contract is made, it is either with a creditor in a contract of pledge, or with a friend, in order that our property may be in greater safety with him. If the fiduciary contract is made with a friend, then, indeed, retaking by use is allowable in any case; but, if it be with a creditor, it is always allowable when the debt has been paid; but, if the money has not been paid, it only applies if the debtor has neither hired his property from the creditor, nor begged the creditor to allow him to hold it at will. § 61. So, if the state has sold a thing pledged to it, and if the owner become possessed of it, retaking by use is allowed, but in this case, if the thing pledged be land, possession for two years is required. And this is what is commonly called the recovery of possession in respect of forfeited property, for the person who thus buys from the state is called a purchaser of forfeited pledges.

§ 12. Long possession, which has been running in favour of the deceased, is continued in favour of the heir, or the possessor of the goods, although he may know that the estate belongs to another; but, if the deceased commenced an unlawful possession, the possession does not avail the heir or the possessor of the goods, although ignorant of this. And, our constitution has settled the same rule as to acquisitions by use, that is, that the time may continue to run on. § 13. The late Emperors Severus and Antoninus have decided by rescript that the times of possession of vendor and purchaser shall be reckoned together.

§ 14. An edict of the late Emperor Marcus Aurelius provides, that a person who has purchased from the imperial treasury a thing belonging to another person, may defeat the owner of the thing, if five years have elapsed since the sale, by setting up a plea of that fact. But a constitution of Zeno, of sacred memory, has wisely provided that those who receive anything from the imperial treasury by sale, gift, or other title, shall be immediately secure, and be victorious, whether they sue, or are themselves sued. Whilst those who think that they have a right of action in respect of the ownership or mortgage of the things alienated, may proceed against the sacred treasury within four years. An imperial constitution, which we ourselves have recently issued, extends to those who have received anything from our palace, or from that of the august empress, the above-mentioned provisions of the constitution of Zeno, relative to alienations by the treasury.

Title vii. Of gifts.

There is, again, another mode of acquisition, that by gift, of which there are two kinds, that "mortis causa", and that "non mortis causa". § 1. A gift "mortis causa" is that which is made in view of death, as when anything is given upon condition that if any mischance befalls the donor, the person to whom it is given shall keep it, but that if the donor should survive, he should have it back again, whether because he repents of having made the gift, or because the person to whom it has been given dies first. These gifts, "mortis causa", have been placed exactly on the footing of legacies; for, since it was much debated by the jurists whether they ought to be considered as a gift, or as a legacy, partaking as they did in some respects of the character of both, so that some included them in one class, and some in the other, we have decided, by a constitution, that they shall in almost every respect be reckoned amongst legacies, and shall be made in accordance with the forms our constitution has settled, and, in short, it is a gift, "mortis causa", when a person wishes that the thing given should belong to himself rather than to the donee, and to the donee rather than to his own heir. It is in this manner that, according to Homer, Telemachus made a gift to Piræus:—

> "Piræus, as we cannot tell how this matter will end,
> If the proud suitors should secretly slay me,
> And divide my ancestral goods amongst themselves,
> I would rather that you possessed this than one of them;
> But if I hurl death and destruction amongst them,
> Then, full of joy like myself, bring it to me again in my palace." (*Odyssey*, xvii, 78-83.)

§ 2. But other gifts are made without any consideration of death, and are called "inter vivos". These cannot, in any way, be compared to legacies, and, if they have been completed, they cannot be revoked without a motive. They are completed when the donor has manifested his intention with or without writing. Our constitution has declared that, as in the case of sales, they shall also involve the necessity of delivery, so that, even although they have not been delivered, they have their full and complete effect, and place the donor under the necessity of delivering them. The enactments of former emperors required their registration amongst public documents, if exceeding two hundred solidi, but our constitution has raised the amount to five hundred solidi, so that up to that sum registration is not necessary. Our constitution also refers to certain classes of gifts which need no registration at all, but are completely valid of themselves. Besides this, we have introduced many other provisions for more fully protecting the effect of gifts, which may be collected from our constitutions, which we have prepared in this matter; but it must be noted that however complete the gifts may be, yet if men upon whom the benefit has been cast prove ungrateful, the donor is permitted by our constitution, on certain specified grounds, to revoke the gift, lest those who have bestowed their property on others should suffer through them injury, or loss of the kinds enumerated in our constitution.

§ 3. There is another kind of gift, "inter vivos", entirely unknown to the ancient jurists, but subsequently introduced by later emperors, and termed a gift before marriage, and made under a tacit condition that it should only be realised by the marriage. Hence, it was called a gift before marriage, because such a gift was effected before the marriage, and never after its celebration. But as it had been allowable to increase the dowry, even after marriage, the late Emperor Justin, our father, was the first to permit by a constitution, that where the dowry was increased, the gift before marriage might, even during the marriage, be increased also; but the gift still retained what was now an inconsistent name, as it was still called a gift before marriage, although such an increase had been made to it after marriage. We, therefore, being desirous of completing the rules on this subject, and of making names accord with things, have enacted that such gifts may not only be increased, but may also have their origin during marriage, and that they shall be called not gifts before marriage, but gifts on account of marriage; and, that they shall be assimilated to dowries, in the sense that, just as dowries may not only be increased, but created, during marriage; so gifts, on account of marriage, may not only precede the marriage, but also, after the contract of marriage has been entered into, may be increased or created.

§ 4. There was formerly another civil law mode of acquisition, viz., that by right of accrual, which occurs in this way: if a person owned a slave in common with Titius, and he alone gave him his liberty, whether by the process of fictitious vindication, or by testament, his share was lost, and accrued to the co-owner. But, as it was an example of the worst kind, that both the slave should be defrauded of his liberty, and that more humane masters should suffer loss, whilst harder masters profited, we have thought it necessary to apply, by our constitution, a beneficent remedy to what seemed so odious, and have devised a way by which the manumittor and the co-owner, and he who receives his liberty, may all benefit; whilst the freedom (in favour of which it is abundantly obvious that ancient legislators have often violated the ordinary rules of law) shall be really effectual, and he who has given this freedom shall have the gratification of seeing it maintained; and his co-owner shall be indemnified by receiving a price for the slave, in proportion to his share in him, according to the rates fixed by us.

§ 62. It sometimes happens that he who is owner of a thing cannot alienate it, and that he who is not owner can alienate it. § 63. Thus, the husband is, by the Julian law, forbidden to alienate dowry immovables without the wife's consent, although they belong to him, whether as the result of a formal conveyance by copper and scale, grounded on the dowry, or surrendered in court, or acquired by use through the statutory period of possession. But whether this law applies only to immovables in Italy, or extends also to those in the provinces, is matter of doubt.

Title viii. Of those who can, and of those who cannot alienate.

It sometimes happens that he who is owner of a thing cannot alienate it; whilst, on the contrary, he who is not owner, has the power of alienating it. Thus, the husband is, by the Julian law, forbidden to alienate dowry immovables without the wife's consent, although they belong to him, having been given him by way of dowry. We, however, amending the Julian law, have introduced a great improvement. This law only applied to immovables in Italy, and forbade alienations made against the wishes of the wife, and mortgages made even with her consent, but we have effected a remedy for both these points in that it is now forbidden to alienate or mortgage even immovables in the provinces, and that no alienation or mortgage shall be effectual, even with the consent of the wife, lest the weakness of the female sex should be turned to the detriment of her fortune.

§ 64. On the other hand, an agnate curator of a lunatic can alienate the property of the lunatic by virtue of the Twelve Tables; the same is the case with a procurator, that is, one

§ 1. On the other hand, a creditor can, by virtue of the contract, alienate a pledge, although the thing pledged is not his property. But, perhaps, this

to whom free management has been accorded. So, a creditor can alienate a pledge by virtue of the contract, although the thing pledged is not his property. But, perhaps, this may be held to result from the consent of the debtor who had originally agreed that, if the money should not be paid, the creditor should be at liberty to sell the thing pledged.

may be held to result from the consent of the debtor, who agreed at the outset that, if the money should not be paid, the creditor should be at liberty to sell the thing pledged. But, lest creditors should be impeded in the pursuit of their rights, and debtors seem too easily deprived of their property, it has been provided by our constitution that a fixed mode of procedure for the sales of pledges be followed, by which the interests of both parties, that is, of creditors and debtors, have been sufficiently secured.

Of pupils, whether they can alienate anything.

§ 80. It is now necessary to observe that neither a woman nor a pupil can alienate a thing requiring transfer by a formal conveyance without the authority of a tutor, but a woman can alienate a thing not requiring such a mode of transfer, though a pupil cannot. § 81. And, therefore, as often as a woman lends money to a person without the authority of her tutor, she contracts an obligation, because she transfers the property in the money to him who receives it, since a fixed sum of money is a thing not requiring transfer by formal conveyance. § 82. But if a pupil does the same, he does not contract any obligation, because he cannot, without the authority of his tutor, make the money the property of him who receives it. Hence the pupil can claim the coin itself as long as it is in existence, that is to say, he can sue for it as being his by the law of the quirites; and, if it has been expended mala fide, he can reclaim it, just as if it still remained in possession. On this account, and in respect of a pupil, the question arises whether money lent can be

§ 2. It is now necessary to observe that neither a male or female pupil can alienate anything without the authority of a tutor; and, therefore, if a pupil, without the tutor's authority, lend money to anyone, he does not contract an obligation, for he does not make the money the property of the receiver, and he may bring a suit claiming the coin itself, if it still exist; and if the money which the minor has lent has been consumed by the receiver, bona fide, a personal action lies, and, if mala fide, an action for the production of the money. On the contrary, the pupil of either sex may acquire anything whatsoever without the authority of the tutor; and, therefore, if a debtor pays a pupil, the authority of the tutor will be required, or the debtor will not be released. And we have, for a very obvious reason, declared, by a constitution which we published to the advocates of Cæsarea, on the suggestion of the very eminent Tribonian, quæstor of our sacred palace, that the debtor of a pupil may pay the tutor or curator, on first obtaining permission by the

reclaimed from him who has received it in good faith after it has been disposed of, since he would seem to have made the money the property of the recipient. § 83. But, on the other hand, women and pupils can receive in payment without the authority of their tutor, both things which require transfer by a formal conveyance and those which do not, because it is agreed that they may improve their condition without the authority of their tutor. § 84. Therefore, if a debtor pays money to a pupil, he makes the money the property of the pupil, but he himself is not released, because a pupil cannot dissolve an obligation without the authority of his tutor (since no power of alienation, without his tutor's authority, has been conceded to him). But still, if he has become richer by means of this money, and he, nevertheless, claims it, he can be defeated by a plea of fraud. § 85. But a payment may be validly made to a woman without the authority of her tutor, for he who pays is released from his obligation, because the woman, as we have just said, can alienate a thing, not requiring transfer by a formal conveyance, without the authority of her tutor, although this is only so if she actually receives the money; but if she does not receive it, but declares that she has had it, and wishes to free the debtor, without the authority of the tutor, by a formal release,* she cannot do this.

* *post*, iii, § 169.

order of a judge, pronounced without any expense; and, if these forms are observed, a payment made in accordance with the order of the judge will give the debtor the most complete security. As to a payment made otherwise than in accordance with the mode we have directed, if the pupil has the money still in his possession, or if he has been made richer by it, and if he again demand the same sum, he may be defeated by a plea of fraud. But, if he has spent the money uselessly, or lost it through theft, the plea of fraud will not avail the debtor, and he will be condemned in spite of it, because he acted incautiously in paying the money without the authority of the tutor, and without conforming to our rules. On the other hand, neither a male nor female pupil can pay without the authority of the tutor, because that which they pay does not thereby become the property of the person who receives it, as no power of alienation is conceded to them without the authority of their tutor.

§ 86. Property is acquired for us, not only by ourselves, but also by those whom we have in our power, whether as being descendants or slaves, or as being in our marital power, or being freemen in a state of bondage; also by those slaves of whom we have the usufruct,

Title ix. Of the persons through whom we can acquire.

Property is acquired for us, not only by ourselves, but also by those whom we have in our power; also by those slaves of whom we have the usufruct; and by those freemen and slaves of others

as well as by those freemen and slaves of others whom we bona fide possess. Let us inquire carefully into these different cases.

whom we bona fide possess. Let us examine carefully into these different cases.

§ 1. Formerly, whatever our children, of both sexes and under power acquired, excepting, of course, property gained in war, was, without any distinction, acquired for the benefit of their parents; and to such an extent was this the case, that that which the ascendant had thus acquired through one of his children, he could give, or sell, or apply in any way he pleased for the benefit of another child, or a stranger. As this appeared very harsh to us, we have, by a general constitution, relieved the children, and yet reserved for the ascendants their due; for it has been declared by us that all which comes to the child through the property of the father, shall, according to the old rule, be acquired entirely for the ascendant's benefit (for what objection can be made to that which comes from the father returning to him?). But whatever the son in power acquires in any other way, of this the father shall have the use and enjoyment, but the son shall retain the ownership, so that that which the son has gained by his labour or good fortune, may not be a source of grief to him by its passing over to another. § 2. We have also laid down rules in respect of that power which, by virtue of former constitutions, a father had, when emancipating his children, of retaining, if he so chose, a third part of the property over which he had no right of acquisition, as it were, by way of the price of the emancipation; and it seemed hard that the son should thus be deprived, by emancipation, of the ownership of a part of his property, and that the honour added to him as the result of becoming emancipated, should be decreased by a diminution of his property. We have, therefore, enacted, that the father, instead of retaining the third part of the property, which he could do as owner, he shall retain the use and enjoyment, not the ownership of half. Thus the whole property will remain intact with the son, while the father will enjoy the benefits of a larger portion, getting the half instead of the third.

§ 87. Therefore, that which comes to our children whom we have in our power; also that which our slaves receive by formal conveyance or by delivery; and that which they acquire by stipulation, or in any other way, is acquired for us; for he who is in our power can have

§ 3. So, too, all that your slave acquires by delivery, or by a stipulation, or in any other way, is acquired for you, and that even without your knowledge and against your wish. For a slave who is in the power

nothing of his own; and, therefore, if he be appointed heir, he cannot enter upon the inheritance, except by our order; and, if he shall have entered by our order, he acquires the inheritance for us, just as if we ourselves were the appointed heirs. And of course a legacy is also, in like manner, acquired through them for us. § 88. But we must understand that, if one person holds a slave as part of his goods, whilst another owns him by the law of the quirites, then, in all cases, only he who holds him as part of his goods will acquire through the slave. § 89. But not only is ownership acquired for us by those whom we have in our power, but also possession. For, of whatever thing they have become possessed, we are held to be possessed. Hence, also, acquisition by use through the statutory period of possession takes effect through them.

of another cannot have anything of his own. And, if he is appointed heir, he cannot enter on the inheritance except by your order. And, if he should enter by your order, the inheritance is acquired for you, just as if you had yourself been appointed heir; and of course a legacy is acquired in the same way for you by your slaves. Not only is ownership acquired for you by those whom you have in your power, but also possession, for everything of which they have obtained possession, you are held to possess; and hence you may acquire, through them, the ownership arising from possession through the statutory period or through that of long standing.

§ 90. But, though we acquire ownership, under all circumstances, through those who are in our marital power, or through those free persons in bondage to us, just as in the case of those who are in our paternal power, still, whether we can also acquire possession, is a matter of doubt, because we do not possess the persons themselves. § 91. In respect of those slaves of whom we have only the usufruct, it has been held that whatever they acquire from anything belonging to us, or by their own labour, is acquired for us; but what they may have acquired from other sources belongs to their owner; and, therefore, if such a slave be appointed heir, or if a legacy is left to him, it is acquired, not by me, but by the owner of the slave. § 92. The same rule holds in respect of him whom we bona fide possess, whether he be a free-man or the slave of another, because that which holds good with regard to the usufructuary, is equally approved of in the case of the bona fide possessor; and, therefore, whatever is acquired outside these two sources, belongs either to him

§ 4. In respect of those slaves of whom you have only the usufruct, it has been held that whatever they acquire by means of anything belonging to you, or by their own labour, belongs to you; but all that which they acquire from any other source belongs to their owner. So, if such a slave be appointed heir, or anything is left him by way of a legacy, or given him as a gift, it is acquired for the owner, not for the usufructuary. The same rule holds in respect of him whom we bona fide possess, whether he be a free-man or the slave of another, for that which holds good with regard to the usufructuary, holds good with regard to the bona fide possessor. Hence everything acquired out-

himself, if he be free, or to his owner, if he be a slave. § 93. But if a bona fide possessor has acquired the slave by use through the statutory period of possession, then, since he has in this way become the owner, he can acquire for himself, in all cases, through the slave; though the usufructuary cannot acquire by possession through the statutory period, first, because he does not possess, but has only the use and enjoyment; and, secondly, because he knows that the slave belongs to another. § 94. Here the question arises whether we can possess anything, and acquire by use through a slave of whom we have the usufruct, since we do not possess the slave himself. But, by means of the slave whom we bona fide possess, we can, without doubt, both become possessors, and acquire by use. But, in respect of both these classes of persons, we are speaking in accordance with the qualification previously laid down, that is, if they acquire anything by means of our property, or by their own labour, it is acquired for us. § 95. From this it appears that we cannot, on any ground, acquire through free persons whom we neither have in our power nor possess bona fide; and so, too, as to the slave of another of whom we have neither the usufruct nor lawful possession. And this is what is meant by the common saying, that we cannot acquire through a stranger; but, in respect of possession, it is a question whether an agent can acquire it for us.

side these two sources, either belongs to himself, if he be a free-man, or to his master if he be a slave. But, when the bona fide possessor has acquired the slave by possession through the statutory period, since he has in this way become the owner, he can acquire for himself in all cases through the slave, though the usufructuary cannot acquire by such possession, first, because he does not possess, but has only the use and enjoyment; and, secondly, because he knows that the slave belongs to another. It is not only ownership that is acquired through those slaves, of whom you have the usufruct, or whom you bona fide possess, or through a free person who is bona fide serving you, but also possession. But, in respect of both these classes of persons, we are speaking in accordance with the qualification previously laid down, that is, if they have acquired possession through property belonging to you or by their own labour.

§ 5. From this, it therefore appears that in no way can anything be acquired for you through free persons who are neither in your power nor bona fide possessed by you; and so as to the slaves of others of whom you have neither the usufruct nor lawful possession. And this is the meaning of the saying, that nothing can be acquired by means of a stranger, with this exception, however, that, according to a constitution of the late Emperor Severus, possession may be acquired for you by a free person, as, for example, by an agent, not only with, but even without your knowledge; and, by this possession, the ownership, if it was the owner who delivered the thing, or the statutory period of possession or prescription of long standing, will avail, if he was not owner.

§ 96. Finally, we must know that to those who are in paternal or marital power, or to those freemen who are in bondage to us, nothing can be surrendered in court. For, since such persons can have no property of their own, it of course follows that they cannot set up a claim in court for anything as their own.

§ 97. What we have now said as to the mode in which individual things are acquired for us, must suffice for the present, as we shall have a better opportunity hereafter* of dealing with the law of legacies, by which also we acquire individual things. Let us now inquire in what way things are acquired by us in the aggregate. § 98. If, then, we have been made heirs to any one, or have claimed the possession of any person's goods, or have bought the property of an insolvent person, or have adopted any one, or a wife has come under our marital power, the property of that person passes to us.

§ 6. What we have now said as to the mode in which individual things are acquired for us, must suffice for the present, as we shall have a better opportunity hereafter† of dealing with the law of legacies, by which, also, we acquire individual things, and also of bequests in trust, where individual things are left to us.‡ Let us now inquire in what way property is acquired in the aggregate. If, then, you are made heir to a person, or if you demand possession of the goods of any one, or if you arrogate any one, or if the goods of a person are adjudged to you in order to preserve the liberty of slaves, all the property of that person passes to you.

§ 99. And first let us deal with inheritances, of which the nature is two-fold; for they belong to us, either by virtue of a testament, or as the result of an intestacy.

And first let us deal with inheritances, of which the nature is twofold; for they belong to you either by virtue of a testament, or as the result of an intestacy.

§ 100. And it will be better, first, to inquire as to those things which fall to us by virtue of a testament.

And it will be better, first, to inquire as to those things which fall to us by virtue of a testament, for which purpose it is necessary, at the outset, to explain the formalities relating to testaments.

§ 101. There were originally two kinds of testaments, for they were made in the general assemblies when called together for private business, which was done for the purpose of making testaments twice in the year; or they were made when in battle array, that is, when arms had been taken up on account of a war, for "procinctus"

Title x. Of the formalities of testaments.

A testament is so called because it testifies to the intention. § 1. That nothing of antiquity may be altogether ignored, it must be known, that formerly two kinds of testament were in use, of which one was employed in time of peace and tranquillity, and was known as that made in the general assembly when called together for pri-

* *post*, § 191, etc.

† *post*, tit. xx.

‡ *post*, tit. xxiv.

means an army equipped and ready for battle. Consequently, the one kind was made at a time of peace and tranquillity, the other at a time when about to engage in battle. § 102. Subsequently, a third kind of testament was added, which is made by means of the copper and the scale. For he who had neither made a testament in the assembly called together for private business, nor in the presence of the army, if he was suddenly in apprehension of immediate death, could give his whole property, that is, his patrimony, by the process of formal conveyance by copper and scale, to a friend who asked him as to his wishes in respect of the disposition of his property after his death. This testament is, of course, called that of the copper and the scale, because it is carried out by means of that mode of conveyance. § 103. But the first two kinds of testament have fallen into disuse, and only that by copper and scale has been retained, though, in fact, the testament is now made in a different way to that which was formerly customary, for in earlier times the purchaser of the patrimony, that is to say, he to whom the patrimony was conveyed by the testator by the process of the copper and the scale, occupied the place of heir, and in this character the testator charged him as to his wishes in respect of the disposition of his property after his death; but now another heir is appointed in the testament, who is charged with the legacies, while for form's sake, and in imitation of the old law, another is joined to him as the purchaser of the patrimony.

§ 104. The proceeding is conducted as follows: He who makes the testament, being in the presence (as in the case of other conveyances by copper and scale) of five witnesses, Roman citizens over the age of puberty, and a scale-bearer, after he has written the tablets of his testament, conveys to another, for form's sake, by the process of the copper and the scale, his patrimony, in doing which the purchaser of the patrimony makes use of these words: "I declare that your household and money are in my charge, guardianship, and custody, and since, according to the public law, you can rightly make a will, let these things be now bought by me with this copper," and, as some would add,

vate business; the other when about to engage in battle, and was known as that made when in battle array. A third kind was afterwards added, called that of the copper and the scale, of course because it was carried out by means of the process of conveyance by copper and scale, that is, an imaginary sale in the presence of five witnesses and the scale-bearer, all Roman citizens above the age of puberty, together with him who was called the purchaser of the patrimony. But the two first kinds of testament fell into disuse in ancient times, and though that made with the copper and the scale remained longer in vogue, still it also has, to some extent, ceased to be in use.

"and with this copper scale". He then strikes the scale with the copper, and gives that piece of copper to the testator, as if it were the price of the sale. After this the testator, holding the tablets of the testament, says as follows: "The dispositions, as they are here written in these tablets and in this wax, so I give them, so I bequeath them, so I dispose of them, and you, O Quirites, bear witness to me." And this is called the formal declaration, for "nuncupare" means to declare openly; and, in fact, by the general statement, the testator is held to declare and confirm that which he has specially written on the tablets of the testament.

§ 2. The above-mentioned forms of testament belonged to the civil law, but afterwards another form for the making of testaments was introduced by the edict of the prætor. For, by prætorian law, no sale was required, but the seals of seven witnesses sufficed, although, by the civil law, the seals of witnesses were not necessary. § 3. But when, by degrees, as much by custom as by the corrections introduced by imperial constitutions, the civil and prætorian law began to be fused into one consistent whole, it was established that the testament should be made all at one time (a matter to some extent required by the civil law), in the presence of seven witnesses, and with the subscription of the witnesses (a formality introduced by the constitutions), and with their seals impressed (according to the edict of the prætor); so that the law seems to be threefold, in that the witnesses, and their presence at one continuous time, for the purpose of going through the formalities of the testament, are derived from the civil law; the subscriptions of the testator and of the witnesses are necessary in order to conform to the sacred constitutions; whilst the seals and the number of the witnesses come from the edict of the prætor. § 4. And to all these formalities has been added by our constitution, (to secure the genuineness of testaments, and prevent the interference of fraud), the additional precaution that the name of the heir shall be in the handwriting either of the testator or of one of the witnesses; and that everything shall be done according to the tenor of that constitution.

§ 5. All the witnesses may seal the testament with the same seal; for, (as Papinian suggests), what if all the seven rings were engraved in the same way? and a witness may seal the testament with a ring belonging to another person.

§ 6. Those persons can be present as witnesses with whom the right of going through the formalities of a testament exists. But neither women nor persons under the age of puberty, nor slaves, nor dumb persons, nor deaf persons, nor lunatics, nor interdicted prodigals, nor persons declared by law to be infamous and incapable of giving testimony, can be included amongst the number of witnesses. § 7. If, however, one of the witnesses was believed, at the time of making the testament, to be free, but it appeared afterwards that he was in truth a slave, the late Emperor Hadrian, in his rescript to Catonius Verus (and afterwards the late Emperors Severus and Antonius, equally by rescript) declared, "that he would come in aid of such a testament, so that it should be treated as if it had been made as it ought to have been; since, at the time when the testament was sealed, this witness was, by the common accord of all, deemed a freeman, and there was no one present who raised a question as to his status". § 8. A father, and a son under his power, or two brothers under the power of the same father, may both be witnesses to the same testament, for there is no impediment to several witnesses from the same family being concerned in the business of a stranger.

§ 105. He, however, must not be among the witnesses who is under the power either of the purchaser of the patrimony or of the testator himself; because, in imitation of the old law, the whole of this matter, which is gone through for the purpose of making a testament, is viewed as taking place between the purchaser of the patrimony and the testator, since formerly, as we have just said, he who received by way of formal conveyance the patrimony of the testator, stood in the position of heir, and for that reason the testimony of members of the same family was considered improper in such a transaction. § 106. Hence, also, if he who is under the power of his father, is present as purchaser of the patrimony, his father cannot be a witness, nor can he be a witness who is

§ 9. He, however, must not be among the witnesses who is under the power of the testator; and if a son in power, after his discharge from the army, make a testament disposing of his property acquired in war, neither his father, nor anyone under the power of his father, can properly be a witness; for, in a matter of this kind, it is not considered right to admit the testimony of members of the same family. § 10. And neither the appointed heir, nor anyone under his power, nor his father in whose power he is, nor his brothers under the power of the same father, are admissible as witnesses, for this whole matter, which is gone through for the purpose of making a testament, is in the present day looked upon as a transaction between the heir and the testator. In fact, although, by reason of the complete confusion which had arisen in this part of the law, the ancients, rejecting the testimony of the purchaser of the patrimony and of the members of his family, had admitted that of the

under the same paternal power, as, for example, his brother; but if a son under paternal power, after his discharge from the army, makes a testament disposing of his property acquired in war, neither can his father be a witness, nor anyone else in the power of his father. § 107. That which we have said in regard to witnesses, is to be understood as applying to the scale-bearer, for he also is included in the number of the witnesses. § 108. But he who is under the power of the heir, or of the legatee, or he in whose power the heir himself or the legatee is, and anyone who is under the same power as the heir or the legatee, can be present as a witness and as a scale-bearer, just as the heir himself or the legatee can legally be. But still, so far as this extends to the heir, and to anyone under his power, or to the person in whose power he may be, this right should be sparingly used.

heir and of those who were connected with him by the ties of paternal power, and contenting themselves with exhorting them not to abuse their privilege; we have corrected these rules, turning into a legal necessity that which only existed as an exhortation. For, in imitation of the old law respecting the purchaser of the patrimony, we have refused to allow the heir, who stands in the place of the ancient purchaser of the patrimony, or any of those connected with him in the manner above mentioned, to be, as it were, witnesses in their own behalf; and, therefore, we have not permitted the ancient constitutions on the subject to be inserted in our code. § 11. But we do not deny to legatees, or to persons benefiting by bequests in trust, or to those connected with them, the right to give testimony, because they are not successors to the rights of the deceased. On the contrary, in a certain constitution of ours, we have specially granted them this privilege; and we give it still more readily to those who are in their power, or to those in whose power they are.

§ 12. It is immaterial whether a testament be written on tablets, or on paper, or parchment, or any other material. § 13. And a person may execute as many original copies of one and the same testament as he please, provided each be made with the prescribed formalities. This may be sometimes necessary; as, for instance, when a person who is going a voyage is desirous to carry with him, and also to leave at home, a proof of his last wishes, or for any other of the numberless grounds which arise from the imminent necessities of mankind. § 14. This all relates to testaments committed to writing. But if any one wishes to make an unwritten civil law testament, it may be done in the presence of seven witnesses, before whom he verbally declares his wishes, and this will be a testament absolutely valid according to the civil law, and confirmed by constitutions.

Of soldiers' testaments.

§ 109. This scrupulous attention has been relaxed by imperial constitutions in the case of the framing of soldiers' testaments, on account of their want of experience. For though the legal number of witnesses may not have been present, and though they may not have sold their patrimony, nor proclaimed their wishes by a formal declaration, still they are held to have made a valid testament. § 110. Besides, they are permitted to appoint as heirs both aliens and Latins, or to leave them legacies, although formerly aliens were prohibited by the civil law from taking the inheritance and legacies, and Latins by the Junian law. § 111. Unmarried persons, also, who are forbidden by the Julian law from taking inheritances or legacies, and married persons who have no children, whom the Papian law prohibits taking more than half an inheritance or legacy . . . . (one sheet missing and twenty-three lines illegible) . . . .

Title xi. Of a soldier's testament.

Scrupulous attention to the abovementioned formalities has been relaxed by imperial constitutions in the framing of soldiers' testaments, on account of their want of experience; for, although they do not have present the legal number of witnesses, nor observe the other requisite formalities of testaments, still they are held to have made a valid testament, that is to say, if made while they are on actual service, a proviso introduced by our constitution with good reason. Thus, in whatever mode his last wishes are given, whether ascertained from a writing or without writing, the testament is good, as an expression of his intentions; but during the time when he is at home or elsewhere, and not on actual service, a soldier is not permitted to claim this privilege; but, though he have the right as a soldier, in spite of being a son in power, to make a testament, still, in this case, the same formalities are required to be observed as we have already detailed as necessary in respect of the testaments of civilians.

§ 1. The Emperor Trajan wrote thus in a rescript to Statilius Severus, with special reference to military testaments: "The privilege given to soldiers, that their testaments, in whatever manner made, shall be held binding, is to be understood in the sense that it must first be clear that a testament has been made, for a testament may be made without writing, even by persons not on military service. If, therefore, the soldier, in respect of whose property the question now arises, so spoke in the presence of persons, called expressly for this purpose, as to declare who he wished should be his heir, and to whom he wished to give freedom, he may be held to have made in this way a testament without writing, and his wishes shall be deemed binding. But if (as often happens in the course of conversation) he said to some one, 'I appoint you my heir', or, 'I leave you my property', this is not to be treated as the making of a testament. No one is more interested than those to whom this privilege is accorded, that such a precedent should not be admitted; otherwise it would not be difficult to procure witnesses who, after the death of a soldier, would affirm that they had heard him say he left his property to whomsoever they pleased; and thus the real intentions might be defeated." § 2. A soldier, though dumb or deaf, may make a testament. § 3. This privilege is only granted by the imperial constitutions so long as they are on military service and are in camp. Therefore, veterans, after their discharge, or soldiers not in camp, if they make testaments, must make them according to the forms common to all Roman citizens. And if a testament be made in camp, not according to the regular forms, but in any way the soldier may have wished, it will be valid only for one year after his discharge. What, then, will be the consequence if the soldier should die within the year, but a condition attaching to the heir should not be accomplished until after the year? would his testament be valid as if it were that of a soldier? and it is held that it would be valid on that ground. § 4. And if a person, before entering on military service, had made a testament irregularly, and having become a soldier, and whilst on service broke the seal, and added or struck out something, or in any other way it was manifest that he intended it to be treated as the last wishes of a soldier, it must be deemed to be such, as being, as it were, a new testament made by a soldier. § 5. Finally, if a soldier should be given in arrogation, or, being a son in power, he is emancipated, his testament is valid, as being a new expression of wishes as a soldier; nor is it deemed to have become ineffectual by reason of the change of status he has undergone.

§ 6. But it is to be noted that the rules as to property acquired in war have established a precedent, which has been followed in both the ancient laws and imperial constitutions by allowing certain persons to hold private property by analogy to that acquired in war; and to some of these persons, also, permission has been given to dispose of this private property by testament, although they were under paternal power; and this our constitution has extended to all those who have this kind of private property, but their testaments must be made with the customary formalities. By reading this constitution, there will be no cause for ignorance of the subject matter connected with the above-mentioned rule.

Title xii. Of persons who are not permitted to make a testament.

Permission is not given to everyone to make a testament, for, in the first place, persons subject to the power of others have not the right of making a testament, so much so that although their ascendants should give them permission, still they cannot make a valid testament, except those whom we have already enumerated, and particularly those soldiers who are in the power of their ascendants, for the imperial constitutions have given them the power of making a testament in respect of that property which they have acquired whilst in camp, which right was at first granted by the late Emperors Augustus and Nerva, and the most excellent Emperor Trajan, to those on military service only; but, afterwards, it was conceded, by the late Emperor Hadrian, to soldiers who had received their discharge, that is, to veterans; hence, if such persons make a testament in respect of their property acquired in war, this will belong to him whom in such testament they make their heir; but, if they should die intestate, without children or brothers them surviving, the property will belong, according to the ordinary rule, to their ascendants. From this we can understand that whatever a soldier, who is in the power of his father, has acquired while on service, cannot be taken from him by his father, nor can the creditors of the father sell it, or otherwise interfere with it, nor on the death of his father is it to be shared with his brothers, but that which he has so acquired on service remains his sole property, although, according to the civil law, the private property of all those who are in the power of ascendants are included in the property of their ascendants, just as the private gains of slaves are reckoned as part of the property of their masters, except, of course, that property which, by sacred constitutions, and especially by our own, is, for different reasons, not so acquired. With the exception, therefore, of those who have property acquired in war, or property deemed analogous to it, if any other son in power make a testament, it is useless, although, at the time of his death, he had ceased to be under power.

§ 112. But the senate has, by the authority of Hadrian, and, as we have already stated above, permitted women, over the

§ 1. Again, persons under the age of puberty cannot make a testament, because they have not the requisite mental capacity, nor can lunatics, because they are deprived of their senses; nor does it make any difference

age of puberty, to make a testament without going through the forms of a fictitious sale, that is, if they are not less than twelve years of age, and act under the tutor's authority; so that those women who are not released from tutelage ought to make their testaments in this way. § 113. Females, therefore, appear to be in a better position than males; for, a male of less than fourteen years cannot make a will, although he is willing to make it with the authority of his tutor; but a woman, on attaining twelve years, gains the right of making a will.

that the persons under the age of puberty arrive at puberty, or that the lunatics regain their senses before they die. But, if a lunatic makes a testament during a lucid interval, it would seem that his testament is valid; and clearly a testament which he made before becoming a lunatic is valid; for subsequent lunacy cannot render invalid a testament validly made, or any other act validly performed. § 2. So, a prodigal who has been prohibited by injunction from managing his property cannot make a testament; but one which he had made before the injunction issued will be upheld. § 3. So, a deaf or a dumb person is not always capable of making a testament; but we are speaking of a deaf person, who cannot hear at all, not of one who hears with difficulty; and, by a dumb person, is to be understood one who cannot articulate anything, not one who speaks with difficulty. For, often, even men of letters and learning lose by various accidents the faculty both of hearing and of speaking. Hence, our constitution comes also to the aid of these, so that in certain cases and ways, according to a form given in that constitution, they can make a testament, and do other acts which are permitted them. But, if a person, after having made a testament, through illness, or other cause becomes deaf or dumb, his testament, nevertheless, remains valid. § 4. A blind man can only make a testament by observing the forms introduced by the law of our late father Justin. § 5. The testament made by a prisoner, whilst with the enemy, is not valid, although he should return from captivity. But one made whilst he was still in his own country is, if he should return, valid by the law restoring rights on return, or if he die in captivity, it is valid by the Cornelian law.

§ 114. Therefore, when the question arises whether a testament is valid, we ought, in the first place, to inquire whether the testator had the legal right to execute such an instrument. If he had, then, in the second place, whether he has made the testament according to the rules of the civil law, except in the case of soldiers to whom, as we have said, on account of their want of experience in such matters, permission is given to make a testament in any way they wish, or in any way they may be able.

Title xiii. Of disinheriting children.

Attention to the rules above explained, is not, however, sufficient in all cases to make a testament valid.

§ 115. Attention to the rules, above explained, concerning the sale of the patrimony, and as to the witnesses and the formal declaration, is not, however, sufficient in all cases to make a testament valid. § 116. Before all things it is essential to inquire whether the appointment of the heir has been done in solemn form; for, if it has been done otherwise, then it will not avail that the patrimony was sold by the testator, that the witnesses were present, and that the formal declaration as to the testament was made in the way mentioned above. § 117. The solemn form of appointment is this: "Let Titius be my heir", though this also seems now to be equally approved—"I order Titius to be my heir"; but this form of expression is not approved—"I wish Titius to be my heir." These following are also disapproved by the majority: "I appoint Titius heir", or "I make him heir".

§ 118. Further, it is to be observed that if a woman who is in tutelage make a testament she must do it with the authority of her tutor; otherwise it will be inoperative according to the civil law. § 119. But if the testament is sealed with the seals of seven witnesses, the prætor promises the possession of the property to the named heirs in accordance with the terms of the testament, and if there be no one to whom the inheritance would on intestacy legally belong, as, for example, a brother by the same father, or a paternal uncle, or a son of a brother, the named heirs could in this way retain the inheritance, for the same rule applies here as is the case if the testament is not valid on any other ground, as, for example, because the testator has not sold the patrimony, or because the testator has not pronounced the words of the formal declaration. § 120. But, let us see whether, although a brother or a paternal uncle exist, they would be preferred to the appointed heirs, for it is laid down, in a rescript of the Emperor Antonine, that those who have demanded possession of the property, in accordance with the provisions of a testament, not made according to law, can defend themselves by a plea of fraud against those who claim the inheritance as on an intestacy. § 121. It is clear that this decision applies to the testaments of males, as well as to the case of females who have made an ineffectual testament, either because, for example, they have not sold the patrimony, or not used the words of the formal declaration. But whether this constitution relates to those testaments of females which have been made without the authority of their tutor is a matter for consideration. § 122. We are speaking, however, of course, of women who are not under the legal guardianship of their ascendants or patrons, but of those who have tutors of another kind, and who can be compelled against their will to give their authorisation ; otherwise it is clear that an ascendant and a patron cannot be set aside by a testament made without their authority.

§ 123. Again, he who has a son in power must take care either to appoint him heir, or to exclude him by name, otherwise if he should pass him over in silence, the testament will be of no effect; and this is so true that, as the leaders of our school think, even if the son should have died in the lifetime of the father, no one can be heir under that testament, principally because, of course, the appointment was invalid from the beginning. But the leaders of the opposite school think that, if the son should be living at the time of the death of the father, he is in the way of the appointed heirs, and they say that he becomes heir, as on an intestacy; but that, if he die before his father, the inheritance can be entered upon by virtue of the testament, there being no son in the way, because they consider that the omission of the son did not render the testament invalid from the beginning. § 124. But, if the testator should have only passed over in silence other descendants, the testament is valid, but a share accrues to these persons passed over along with the appointed heirs; and if these appointed heirs were heirs who would take at law as co-owners of the patrimony, the children passed over will take an equal share; if the appointed heirs were strangers, then one half; that is to say, if a person has appointed, for example, his three sons, and omitted his daughter, the daughter comes in as an heiress for a fourth share, and hence it follows that her rights are considered as if her father had died intestate; but if the testator had appointed strangers heirs, and passed over his daughter, the daughter comes in as an heiress, entitled to half the inheritance. What we have said of the daughter is to be understood as equally applying to a grandson, and to all other

He who has a son in power must take care either to appoint him heir, or to exclude him from the heirship by name. Otherwise, if he should pass him over in silence, the testament will be of no effect; so much so, that even if the son should have died in the lifetime of the father, yet no one can be heir under that testament, because, of course, it was invalid from the beginning. But this was not so formerly in respect of daughters or other descendants of either sex through the male line; for if they were neither appointed heirs nor excluded, the testament was not invalidated, but they had a right of coming in to obtain a fixed share, and ascendants were not obliged to exclude them by name, but were at liberty to do this under the term "the others".

children, whether male or female. § 125. How does the matter stand, then? Although these women, as we have said, withdraw only one half of the inheritance from the appointed heirs, still the prætor promises them the possession of the property in spite of the testament, for which reason stranger heirs are deprived of the entire inheritance, and so become heirs without the beneficial interest, and this is the law as it stood, so that no distinction was drawn between males and females. 126. But the Emperor Antonine has recently decided by a rescript that females are not to acquire more by means of the possession of the goods than they would get by the right of having an additional share, and this applies to the similar case of emancipated women, that is, that what they would have had by right of having an additional share, if they had been in power, they will now have by the possession of the goods. § 127. But, if a son is disinherited by his father, he must be disinherited by name, otherwise the exclusion is of no avail. It is held that he is disinherited by name, whether he is thus disinherited—"Let my son Titius be disinherited", or thus—"Let my son be disinherited", without the addition of the proper name. § 128. Other children, whether of the male or female sex, are sufficiently disinherited by being included amongst the rest, that is, in these words—"Let all the rest be disinherited", which words are always added after the appointment of the heirs, but this rule is based on the civil law only. § 129. For the prætor orders all persons of the male sex, that is, grandsons and great-grandsons, to be excluded by name, but females in a general clause; and, if they are not thus disinherited, he promises them possession of the property in spite of the testament.

A person is held to be excluded by name, whether he is excluded in this way—"Let my son Titius be disinherited", or thus—"Let my son be disinherited", without the addition of a proper name in case no other son exist.

§ 130. Posthumous children ought to be either appointed heirs or excluded. § 131. And the condition of all such children is equal in this, that if a posthumous son, or any posthumous male or female descendant, is passed over, the testament is indeed valid; but it is subsequently revoked by the agnation of a male or female posthumous child, and for that reason it becomes invalid. And, therefore, if a woman, from whom a male or female posthumous child is ex-

§ 1. Posthumous children, also, must either be appointed heirs or excluded; and the condition of all such children is equal in this, that if a posthumous son, or any posthumous male or female descendant, is passed over, the testament is indeed valid, but it is subsequently revoked by the agnation of a male or female posthumous child, and for that reason it becomes invalid. And, therefore, if a woman, from whom a male or female posthumous child is expected, should miscarry, there is nothing to hinder the appointed heirs from entering upon the inheritance. § 132. But as to persons of the female sex, it was customary either to exclude them expressly, or under the general term "the others", though, if they were disinherited under the term "the others", something was left them as a legacy to prevent its being held that they had been passed over through forgetfulness. But posthumous male children, that is, sons and other descendants, could not be properly disinherited otherwise than by name, that is to say, in this way: "Whatsoever son may be born to me, let him be disinherited. § 133. Those, also, are to be included amongst posthumous children, who, by succeeding to the place of an heir, who would take at law as a co-owner of the patrimony, become, by quasi-agnation, heirs of that class to their ascendants, as, for example, if I have a son, and, through him, a grandson or granddaughter in my power, then, since the son is nearer in degree, he alone has the rights of an heir of that class, although the grandson, and granddaughter by that son, are under the same power. But if my son die in my lifetime, or for any reason should cease to be under my power, the grandson or granddaughter would thereupon succeed in his place; and thus, by quasi-agnation, obtain the rights of heirs of that class. § 134. Lest, therefore, by this means my testament should be revoked, just as I must, in order to make an effectual testament, appoint my son as heir, or exclude him by name, it is equally necessary for me to appoint as heir, or to exclude, a grandson or grand-

pected, should miscarry, there is nothing to hinder the appointed heirs from entering upon the inheritance. But as to persons of the female sex, it was customary either to exclude them expressly or under the general term, "the others"; though, if they were disinherited under the general term, "the others", something was left them as a legacy to prevent its being held that they had been passed over through forgetfulness. But posthumous male children, that is, sons and other descendants, could not be properly disinherited otherwise than by name, that is to say, in this way: "Whatsoever son may be born to me, let him be disinherited." § 2. Moreover, those are to be included amongst posthumous children, who, by succeeding to the place of an heir, who would take at law as a co-owner of the patrimony, become, by quasi-agnation, heirs of that class to their ascendants, as, for example, if a person has a son in power, and through him a grandson or granddaughter in power, then, since the son is nearer in degree, he alone has the rights of an heir of that class, although the grandson and granddaughter by that son are under the same power. But, if the son should die in the lifetime of the father, or for any other reason should cease to be under the power of the father, the grandson or granddaughter would thereupon succeed in his place, and would thus, by quasi-agnation, obtain the rights of heirs of that class. Lest, therefore, by this means, his testament should be revoked, the testator, just as he must, in order to make an effectual testament, appoint his son as heir, or exclude him by name, so is it

daughter, lest, by the death of my son during my lifetime, and my grandson or granddaughter succeeding in his place, my testament should be revoked through this quasi-agnation. Provision has been made for this by the Junian Velleian law, in which the mode of disinheriting by analogy to the case of posthumous children is pointed out, so that male children should be excluded by name, but females, either by name or "among the rest", with, nevertheless, something left to those who are excluded "among the rest".

equally necessary for him to appoint as heir, or to exclude, the grandson or granddaughter by that son, lest, by the son dying in the lifetime of the father, the grandson or granddaughter should succeed in his place, and, by this quasi-agnation, the testament should be revoked. Provision has been made for this by the Junian Velleian law, in which the mode of disinheriting by analogy to the case of posthumous children is pointed out.

§ 135. By the civil law it is unnecessary either to appoint as heirs or to exclude emancipated children, because they are not heirs who would take at law as being co-owners of the patrimony; but the prætor orders all children, whether male or female, if they are not appointed heirs, to be excluded, those of the male sex by name, females, either by name or under the general term "the others"; and, if they have neither been appointed heirs nor excluded in the way we have mentioned, the prætor promises them the possession of the property in spite of the testament.

§ 3. By the civil law it is unnecessary either to appoint as heirs or to exclude emancipated children, because they are not heirs who would take at law as being co-owners of the patrimony; but the prætor orders all children, whether male or female, if they are not appointed heirs, to be excluded, those of the male sex by name, but females under the general term "the others"; and if they have neither been appointed heirs nor excluded in the way we have mentioned, the prætor promises them possession of the property in spite of the testament.

§ 135A. They are not in the power of the father, who received the Roman citizenship with the father, if, on receiving the Roman citizenship, the father did not immediately claim the right from the Emperor to have them in his power, or if he did claim it but the right was not granted, for those who are brought under the power of the father by the Emperor differ in no way from heirs who take at law as being co-owners of the patrimony.

§ 136. Adopted sons, so long as they remain in adoption, are like children in blood; but after they have been emancipated by their adopting father, they are

§ 4. Adopted children, whilst under the power of their adopting father, have the same rights as children sprung from a lawful marriage; and, therefore, they must be appointed heirs, or excluded according to the rules we have explained

neither numbered amongst his children by the civil law, nor by the rules established by the prætor. § 137. For this reason it is that, conversely, and in respect of their actual father, so long as they are in the adopting family, they are considered strangers. But, if they are emancipated by their adopting father, they then begin to be in the same position in which they would have been if they had been emancipated by their actual father.

respecting children in blood. But children emancipated by the father who had adopted them are, neither by the civil law nor by the rules established by the prætor, reckoned among his children. For this reason it is that, conversely, and in respect of their actual father, so long as they are in the adopting family they are considered strangers, so that they need not be appointed heirs or excluded. But if they are emancipated by their adopting father, then they begin to be in the same position in which they would have been if they had been emancipated by their actual father.

§ 5. Such was the state of the ancient law; but we, thinking that there is no difference in this matter between the sexes, since both the male and the female equally contribute, according to their nature, to the procreation of the human species, and, besides, by the ancient law of the Twelve Tables, all were equally called to the intestate succession, which rule the prætors seem afterwards to have followed, we have, by our constitution, made the law the same, both as to sons and daughters, and also as to all other descendants in the male line, whether already born or posthumous; so that all, whether they are heirs who take at law as being co-owners of the patrimony, or emancipated, must either be appointed heirs or be excluded by name; and their omission produces the same result in destroying the effect of the testaments of their ascendants and taking away the inheritance from the appointed heirs, as would be caused by the omission of children who were heirs taking at law as being co-owners of the patrimony or emancipated, whether they have been already born, or, having been already conceived, are born afterwards. In respect of adopted children, we have introduced a distinction, which is explained in our constitution relating to adoption. § 6. If, however, a soldier, whilst on service, make a testament, and does not disinherit by name his children already born, or his posthumous child, but passes them over in silence, although he is not ignorant that he has children, it is provided by the imperial constitutions that his silence shall be held to be as if he had excluded them by name. § 7. Neither a mother nor a maternal grandfather need either appoint their children heirs or exclude them, but may omit them; for the silence of a mother or of a maternal grandfather, or other maternal ascendant, has the same effect as a father actually excluding them. For neither is a mother, in respect of her son or daughter, if she does not appoint him or her as heir, nor a maternal grandfather in respect of his grandson or granddaughter by a daughter, obliged to exclude them if they have not been appointed heirs; whether we consider the case according to the civil law or the edict of the prætor, under which possession of the property, in spite of the will, is promised to those children who have been passed over. But another remedy has been provided for them which we shall shortly* explain.

* *post*, tit. 18.

§ 185. Just as in the case of free persons, so can slaves, as well our own as those belonging to others, be appointed heirs. § 186. But our own slave ought to be declared at the same time both free and heir, that is, in this way—"Let my slave, Stichus, be free and heir", or, "Let him be heir and free". § 187. For, if he should be appointed heir without freedom, he cannot be heir even if he should have been subsequently manumitted by his master, because the appointment does not exist in his person; and, therefore, although he may have been alienated, he cannot declare his intention of entering upon the inheritance by order of his new master.

Title xiv. Of the appointment of heirs.

A man may appoint as his heirs either free-men or slaves, and either his own slaves or those of another. Formerly, according to the opinion of the majority, he could not properly appoint his own slaves, unless he also freed them. Now, however, by our constitution, he can appoint them heirs without giving them their liberty. And we have been led to do this, not as an innovation, but because it was the more equitable; and Paul, in his works, both on Masurius Sabinus and on Plautius, states that this was the opinion of Atilicinus. He is looked upon as being the testator's own slave, of whom he has only the bare ownership, another having the usufruct. But there is a case in which a slave is not validly appointed by his mistress, although his liberty is expressly given to him, as is laid down in a constitution of the late Emperors Severus and Antoninus, in these words: "Reason demands that a slave accused of adultery shall not be allowed, before his sentence is pronounced, to be made free by the woman who is accused as an accomplice in the same crime. Hence it follows that the appointment of such a slave by his mistress as her heir is void." He is held to be the slave of another, of whom the testator has the usufruct.

§ 188. But when he is appointed heir with freedom, if he has continued in the same state, he becomes free by virtue of the testament and then necessary heir. But if he has been manumitted by the testator himself, it is at his own choice that he enters upon the inheritance; and, if he has been alienated, he should enter upon the inheritance by the order of his new master, and by that means the master becomes heir through him; for he himself, when alienated, can be neither heir nor free. § 189. So, too, when the slave of another is appointed heir, and he remains in the same condition, he should enter upon the inheritance by order of his master. But if he should have been alienated by his master, whether in the lifetime of the testator or after his death, and before declaring that he would enter upon the inheritance, he ought, by the command of his new master, to declare his acceptance. If he has been manumitted, he can exercise his own discretion as to entering upon the inheritance. § 190. But if a slave belonging to another has been appointed heir, with the usual term for deliberation,* then the days for deliberation are held to run from the time when the slave himself first knew that he had been appointed, and no hindrance existed to his informing his master, in order that he might, by that master's order, declare his acceptance.

* *post*, § 173.

§ 1. A slave appointed heir by his master, if he has remained in the same condition, becomes, in virtue of the testament, free and necessary heir. But if he has been manumitted in the lifetime of the testator, he can please himself as to entering upon the inheritance, for he does not become a necessary heir, since he does not obtain both his liberty and the inheritance in virtue of the testament of his master. But, if he has been alienated, he should enter on the inheritance by order of his new master, who thus, through him, becomes heir; for, as he has been alienated, he can neither be free nor be heir, although he was appointed heir together with his freedom; and the master, in that he has alienated him, is held to have shown that he has renounced the intention of giving him his liberty. So, too, when the slave of another is appointed heir, and he remains in the same condition, he should enter upon the inheritance by order of his master; but if he should have been alienated by his master, whether in the lifetime of the testator, or after his death, but, before he has entered upon the inheritance, he should enter upon it by order of his new master. But, if he be manumitted in the lifetime of the testator, or after his death, and before he has entered upon the inheritance, he may please himself as to entering upon the inheritance.

§ 2. The slave of another may be properly appointed heir, even after the death of his master, because the legal capacity of receiving by testament can exist in slaves belonging to an inheritance; for an inheritance not yet entered upon, represents the deceased, not the future heir, and similarly the slave of an unborn child may be appointed heir. § 3. If a slave belonging to several masters, in all of whom the legal capacity of receiving by testament exists, is appointed heir by a stranger, he acquires a share of the inheritance for each one of his masters, by whose orders he enters upon it, proportionate to their ownership of him.

§ 4. A testator may appoint one man heir, or as many as he please. § 5. An inheritance is usually divided into twelve ounces, which are included under the total denomination of one pound, and these parts, from the ounce to the pound, have their peculiar names, as the ounce, the sixth, the fourth, the third, five ounces, the half, seven ounces, two-thirds, three-fourths, ten ounces, eleven ounces, the pound. But it is not always essential that there should be twelve ounces, for the pound may be made up of as many ounces as the testator please, and, if a man has appointed but one heir, and made him, for example, heir for six ounces, then the whole pound will consist of six parts; for no one can die partly testate and partly intestate, unless he be a soldier, whose intention is the only matter regarded in respect of his testament. On the other hand, a person may divide his inheritance into as many more ounces as he thinks proper. § 6. If several heirs be appointed, it is only necessary to point out their shares, if the testator does not wish them to be heirs in equal portions. For, if no shares are mentioned, it is sufficiently clear that they are heirs for equal portions. But if the shares of some should be stated, and another be named heir, without having any ascertained portion, he will become heir of that part which is wanting to make up the pound. And if several be appointed heirs, without having any ascertained portion, they will all divide that part between them. But if the whole pound has been distributed, then those whose shares are specified will be called to take one half, and he or they whose shares are not named, the other half. It is immaterial whether the heir, whose share is not specified be appointed first, intermediate, or last, for the vacant share is considered to have been given to him. § 7. Let us now see what is to be done when a part remains undisposed of, and yet there is no heir without a part? as, for example, if three heirs have been appointed with a fourth to each. It is clear, in this case, that the undisposed part would be deemed tacitly to accrue to each in proportion to his share in the inheritance, and the result would be the same as if each had been appointed heir for a third part. And, on the other hand, if the parts disposed of are too many, for example, if four are appointed, and a third be given to each, this would be dealt with as if each of the heirs had been appointed for a fourth only. § 8. If more than twelve ounces are distributed, then he who is appointed without any share will have what is wanting to complete the double pound; and so if the double pound has been distributed, he will have the amount necessary to make up the third pound. But all these parts are afterwards reduced to one pound, although there may have been more than the number of ounces.

§ 9. An heir may be appointed absolutely or conditionally, but not from or to any certain period, as, for example, "after five years from my death", or "from such calends", or "until such calends let him be heir". The term thus added is held to be mere surplusage, and the case is dealt with as if the heir had been appointed absolutely. § 10. An impossible condition in respect of appointments of heirs, and in the case of legacies, as well as in bequests in trust, and gifts of freedom, is looked upon as if it were not inserted. § 11. If several conditions are attached to an appointment, if they are conjunctive, as, for example, "if that and that shall have been done", all must be complied with. But if disjunctive, as "if that or that shall have been done", it is sufficient if either one has been complied with.

§ 12. Persons whom the testator has never seen may be appointed heirs, as, for example, if he should have appointed as heirs his brother's sons, born abroad and unknown to him; for this ignorance of the testator will not render the appointment useless.

Of substitution.

§ 174. Sometimes we make two or more degrees of heirs, in this way, "Lucius Titius, be heir and decide within the next hundred days after you know of your appointment, and are able to act, whether you will accept, and if you do not so accept, be disinherited, in which case Mævius be heir, and decide within a hundred days whether you will accept", and so on; and in this way we are able to make as many substitutions as we please, and, as a last resource, substitute a necessary heir.

Title xv. Of common substitution.

Any one may appoint several degrees of heirs in his testament, as, for instance, "if such a person will not be heir, let such a person be heir". And so on through as many substitutions as the testator pleases, and finally, as a last resource, he may appoint a slave his necessary heir. § 1. And several may be substituted in the place of one, or one in the place of several, or

§ 175. And we may substitute one or more in the place of one heir; and, on the other hand, one or more in the place of several. § 176. Therefore, the heir designated in the first degree, on declaring his acceptance of the inheritance, becomes heir, and the substitute is excluded. But, by not declaring his acceptance, he is set aside, even though he act as heir, and the substitute succeeds in his place. And so on, if there are several degrees; the same rule applying in each case. § 177. But if the right of declaring acceptance has been given without disinheritance, that is to say, in these words: "If you do not make the declaration of acceptance, then Publius Mævius be heir", a different rule applies; for, if the first person appointed, having omitted to declare acceptance, acts as heir, the substituted person comes in for a share, and they both become heirs in equal shares; but if the one first appointed, neither declares his acceptance nor acts as heir, then he is clearly set aside in respect of the whole, and the substituted heir succeeds to the entire inheritance. § 178. But, according to Sabinus, so long as the person first appointed can declare his acceptance, and in that way become heir, even though he may have acted as heir, the substituted heir cannot be admitted. But when the time for acceptance has expired, then by having acted as heir, the substituted person is admitted. Others, however, were of opinion that, even during the period fixed for declaring acceptance, if the appointed heir acted as heir, the substituted heir would be admitted for his share, and the first heir could not afterwards fall back upon his right to declare his acceptance.

one in the place of each one, or the appointed heirs themselves reciprocally to one another.

§ 2. And, if he has substituted reciprocally to one another, heirs appointed with unequal shares, and has made no mention of the shares they are to have in the substitution, he is held to have given the same shares in the substitution, which he mentioned in the appointment, and the Emperor Antoninus has so decided by rescript. § 3. If a co-heir be substituted to any appointed heir, and a third person to that co-heir, the late Emperors Severus and Antoninus have by rescript decided that the substitute is to be admitted to the share of both without distinction. § 4. If a person, thinking the slave of another to be free from power, appoint him heir, and if he does not become heir, Mævius is named as a substitute; then, if that slave should enter upon the inheritance by order of his master, Mævius would be admitted to a share. For those words, "if he do not become heir", in the case of a person whom the testator knew to be subject to the power of another, are taken to mean, "if he neither become heir himself, nor cause another to be heir"; but in the case of a person whom the testator supposed to be free from power, the words mean, "if he neither acquire the inheritance for himself, nor for him under whose power he may subsequently fall". This was so settled by Tiberius Cæsar, in the case of his own slave Parthenius.

§ 179. Not only can we substitute an heir in the way we have above pointed out for our children, under the age of puberty, and in our power, that is, so that if they do not become heirs, somebody else may be our heir; but, further, if they do become our heirs, and yet die under the age of puberty, somebody else may be heir in their place, as, for example, "Titius, my son, be my heir; if my son should not be my heir, or if he become heir, and die before he is free from tutelage, Seius be heir." § 180. In which case, if the son should not become heir, the substitute becomes the heir of the father; but if the son become heir, and die before attaining the age of puberty, the substitute becomes heir to the son himself.

Title xvi. Of pupillary substitution.

Not only can a person substitute an heir in the way we have above pointed out for his children, under the age of puberty, and in his power, that is, so that if they do not become his heirs, somebody else may be; but, further, if they do become his heirs, and yet die under the age of puberty, somebody else may be heir in their place; as, for example, if a testator declares his will to be thus: "Titius, my son, be my heir; if my son should not become my heir, or, becoming my heir, should die before he is free from tutelage" (that is, before he has come to the age of puberty) "then Seius be heir". In which case if the son do not become heir, the substitute becomes heir to the father; but if the son become heir, and die under the age of puberty, the substitute becomes heir to the son himself. For custom has established, that ascendants may make testaments for those of their children who are not of an age to make testaments for themselves. § 1. Impelled by a similar principle, we have had a constitution placed in our code, by which it is provided that, if a person have children, grandchildren, or great-grandchildren deprived of their intellect, of either sex, or any degree, he may, although they have attained the age of puberty, substitute certain persons as heirs in their place on the analogy of pupillary substitution. But, if they recover their reason, the substitution is to be void, on the analogy of pupillary substitution, which becomes void after the pupil attains to puberty.

Hence, there are, as it were, two testaments, one of the father, the other of the son, just as if the son had appointed an heir for himself; or, at any rate, there is one testament respecting two inheritances.

§ 181. But lest the pupil should seem exposed to the risk, after the death of the ascendant, of trickery, it has been usual to make the common form of substitution openly, that is to say, in the place in which we have appointed the pupil; for common substitution only calls the substitute to the inheritance if the pupil cannot possibly become heir, which happens when he dies during the lifetime of the ascendant, in which case no trickery can be suspected on the part of the substitute, because, during the lifetime of the testator, the contents of the testament are unknown.. But that kind of substitution by which we call in a substitute, if, although the pupil have become heir he should have died under the age of puberty; we write separately on the concluding tablets, and we seal up these tablets with a separate thread and separate seal, and we insert a clause in the earlier tablets that the latter ones are not to be opened during the lifetime of the son, and whilst he is under the age of puberty. But it is by far the safer plan, for both kinds of substitution to be separately sealed up in the concluding tablet, because, if the substitutions have been sealed or separated in the manner we have stated, it can be guessed from the first tablet that the same person has been substituted in the second.

§ 182. Moreover, we can not only substitute to our children under the age of puberty, whom we have appointed heirs, so that if they die before the age of puberty, he whom we have selected may be heir, but we may also provide a substitute for our disinherited

§ 2. Therefore, in a pupillary substitution, made in the above-mentioned way, there are, as it were, two testaments, one of the father, the other of the son, just as if the son had appointed an heir for himself; or, at any rate, there is one testament relating to two matters, that is, to two inheritances.

§ 3. If a person be so apprehensive as to fear that his son, being yet a pupil, should be exposed after his death to the risk of trickery, from another person being openly substituted to him, he should openly make a common substitution, and insert it in the first part of his testament; but should write the substitution, by which a substitute is called to the inheritance, if his son should become an heir, and then die under the age of puberty, separately in the lower part, and that part should be sealed and tied up with its own thread and seal, and he should insert a clause in the first part of his testament, forbidding the lower part to be opened while his son is alive and under the age of puberty though it is clear that a substitution to a son under the age of puberty, is not the less valid, because written on the same tablet in which the testator has appointed him his heir, although this may involve danger to the pupil.

§ 4. Ascendants may not only substitute to their children under the age of puberty, so that if such children become their heirs, and die under the age of puberty, anyone whom the testator please shall be made their heir, but they may also substitute to their disinherited children; so that in such a case, if anything has come to the pupil by way of inheritance or legacies, or gifts from relations, it will all belong to the substitute. § 183. Whatever we have said respecting substitution to children under the age of puberty, whether appointed heirs or disinherited, we intend to be understood as equally applying to the case of posthumous children.

children; so that, in such a case, if anything has come to the pupil by way of inheritance, by legacies, or by gifts from relations and friends, it will all belong to the substitute. Whatever we have said respecting substitution to children under the age of puberty, whether appointed heirs, or disinherited, we intend to be understood as equally applying to the case of posthumous children.

§ 5. But no one can make a testament for his children, unless he also make one for himself; for the pupillary testament is part of, and an accessory of the paternal testament, so much so, that if the testament of the father be invalid, so is that of the son. § 6. The substitution may be to each of the children, or to that one who shall die last under the age of puberty; to each, if he does not wish any of them to die intestate; to the last, if he wish that the order of succession established by law should be maintained among them. § 7. A substitution may either be made to a child under the age of puberty, by name, as, "Titius be heir", or generally, as, "whosoever shall be my heir". By which words those are called to the inheritance by substitution, on the death of the son, under the age of puberty, who have been appointed, and have become heirs to the father, and each for the share which they had assigned to them as heirs. § 8. Therefore, substitution may be made to a male, up to the age of fourteen years; and, to a female, up to twelve years; but, if this age be passed, the substitution vanishes.

§ 184. We cannot, however, make a substitution in such a way to a stranger, or a son above the age of puberty, appointed heir, so that if he should become heir, and die within a certain time, another shall be heir in his place, but this only is allowed us that we may bind him by a bequest in trust to restore our inheritance, either wholly or in part. What the law is on this point, we will explain in its proper place.*

§ 9. No one can make a substitution in such a way to a stranger, or son above the age of puberty, that if he should become heir, and die within a certain time, another shall be heir in his place; but this only is allowed, that the testator may bind him by a bequest in trust to restore the inheritance to another, either wholly or in part. What the law is on this point, we will explain in its proper place.†

* *post*, § 246.

† *post*, tit. xxiii.

§ 138. If anyone, after having made a testament, has adopted as his son, either by authority of the people, one who is free from power, or by the authority of the prætor, one who is under the power of an ascendant, in either case the testament is revoked by this quasi-agnation of an heir who would take at law as a co-owner of the patrimony. § 139. The same rule applies, if a man, after he has made a testament, acquires marital power over his wife, or marries a woman who was under marital power, for in this way she begins to occupy the place of a daughter, and is, as it were, an heir taking at law as a co-owner of the patrimony. § 140. Nor does it matter if she or he who has been adopted be appointed heir in that testament, for it seems superfluous to enter upon the question as to disinheriting, since, at the time of making the testament, he, or she, was not in the number of the class of heirs taking as co-owners of the patrimony. § 141. So the son, who is manumitted after the first or second sale, causes a revocation of the testament previously made, since he falls again under paternal power, and it is immaterial whether he has been appointed heir or disinherited in that testament. § 142. Formerly, the law was the same as to him in respect of whom a cause of mistake was proved, grounded on the decree of the senate,* because it may be he had been born of an alien or a Latin woman, whom his father had married under the mistake that she was a Roman citizen. For whether he had been appointed heir by his ascendant, or disinherited, or cause had been shown during the lifetime of the father, or after his death, in any case the testament was revoked by the quasi-agnation. § 143. But now, by virtue of the new decree of the senate, made under the authority of the late Emperor Hadrian, if cause is shown during the life of the father, the testament is altogether invalid, as formerly; but, if the error is proved after the death of the father, the testament is invalid in the case of the child being

* *ante*, I, § 67.

Title xvii. Of the modes in which testaments become invalid.

A testament duly executed continues valid until it is revoked or becomes ineffectual. § I. A testament is revoked when the testator still remaining in the same status, the effect of the testament is destroyed; for, if a person, after making his testament, adopts as a son, by the authority of the emperor, one who is free from power, or by the authority of the prætor, and in accordance with our constitution,* one who is in the power of an ascendant, then the testament would be revoked by this quasi-agnation of an heir who would take at law as a co-owner of the patrimony.

* *ante*, I, tit. 11, § 2.

passed over; but, if he be appointed heir or disinherited, the testament is not revoked, lest testaments carefully made should be rendered invalid at a time when they cannot be re-executed.

§ 144. An earlier testament is revoked, also, by a later one duly executed; and it is immaterial whether, under the later testament, anyone become heir or not; for the only question is, whether there could have been an heir under it. Therefore, if he who is appointed heir by the later testament duly executed, is unwilling to be heir, or dies before the testator, or after his decease, but before he has entered upon the inheritance; or if he be excluded by not having made the declaration,* or if the condition under which he was appointed heir, has failed, or if, on account of the rules as to celibacy under the Julian law, he has been set aside from the inheritance—in any of these cases the testator dies intestate; for the first testament is invalid, being revoked by the second, and the second is equally of no force, since no one becomes heir under it.

* *post*, § 168.

§ 2. An earlier testament is revoked, also, by a later one duly executed; and it is immaterial whether, under the later testament, anyone become heir or not; for the only question is, whether there could have been an heir under it. Therefore, if a person is unwilling to be heir, or dies, either during the life of the testator, or after his death, but before he enters upon the inheritance; or if the condition under which he was appointed heir, has failed—in any of these cases the testator dies intestate; for the first testament is invalid, being revoked by the second, and the second is equally of no force, as no one becomes heir under it. § 3. But if anyone, after having made a valid testament, makes another equally valid, although the heir is appointed therein for certain particular things only, yet, as the late Emperors Severus and Antoninus have settled by a rescript, the first testament is thereby destroyed. We have ordered the words of this constitution to be here inserted, as something further is also therein contained. "The Emperors Severus and Antoninus to Cocceius Campanus: The second testament, although the heir named in it be appointed only in respect of particular things, is as valid in law as if no mention had been made of the things, though there is no doubt but that the heir appointed in the second testament must be content with the things so given him, or with the fourth part, made up to him in accordance with the Falcidian law, and must restore the inheritance to those who were appointed in the first testament, on account of the words inserted in the second, declaring that effect is to be given to the first testament." Hence, therefore, in this way the testament is revoked.

§ 145. Testaments duly executed are also invalidated in another way, as if he who made the testament undergo a change of legal position. It has been shown in the first Commentary under what circumstances this may happen. § 146. In such a case as this, we say the testaments become ineffectual, although those revoked, and those which, from the beginning, were not validly executed, may be equally well termed ineffectual, and so those, which, although at first validly executed, subsequently, through a change of legal position, became ineffectual, may be said to be revoked. But, as it is more convenient to distinguish by different terms each cause, some are said not to be validly executed; others, which have been validly executed, are said to be revoked or rendered ineffectual.

§ 147. But those testaments, which, either at the outset were not validly executed, or, though validly executed, afterwards became ineffectual or were revoked, are not in all respects useless. For, if they have been attested by the seals of seven witnesses, the appointed heir can demand possession of the property, according to the terms of the testament, provided only the deceased testator was both a Roman citizen and free from power at the time of his death; for, if a testament becomes ineffectual, because, for example, the testator has lost citizenship or liberty, or because he had given himself in adoption, and was at the time of his death under the power of his adopting father, then the appointed heir cannot demand the possession of the property according to the terms of the testament.

§ 4. Testaments duly executed are also invalidated in another way, as if he who made the testament undergo a change of status. We have shown, in the First Book, under what circumstances this may happen. § 5. In such a case, testaments are said to become ineffectual, although those revoked and those which, from the beginning, were not validly executed, may be equally well termed ineffectual, and we may also say that those have been revoked which, though validly executed afterwards, by a change of status, become ineffectual. But, as it is more convenient to distinguish by different terms each cause, some are said not to be validly executed; others, validly executed, to be revoked or rendered ineffectual.

§ 6. But those testaments, which, though at the outset validly executed, afterwards become ineffectual by reason of a change of status, are not in all respects useless; for, if they have been attested by the seals of seven witnesses, the appointed heir can obtain possession of the goods according to the terms of the testament, provided only the testator was both a Roman citizen and free from power at the time of his death. For, if a testament becomes ineffectual because the testator has lost citizenship or liberty, or because he has given himself in adoption, and was at the time of his death under the power of his adopting father, then the appointed heir cannot demand possession of the goods according to the terms of the testament.

§ 148. But if those who are granted possession of the property, in accordance with the terms of a testament, which, from the very outset, was either not validly executed, or, though validly executed, was subsequently revoked or rendered ineffectual, if only they can obtain the inheritance, they will have the grant of the possession of the property, together with the beneficial interest; but, if the inheritance can be reclaimed, they will have the grant of the possession of the property without the beneficial interest.* § 149. For if a person has been appointed heir according to the civil law, either in the first or a subsequent testament, or if he be heir at law on an intestacy, he can withdraw the inheritance from them. But, if no one is heir according to the civil law, they themselves can retain the inheritance, and those who are deprived of their strict rights at law have no remedy against them, as we have elsewhere† pointed out. Nevertheless, sometimes, although an heir is appointed by a testament, made in accordance with the civil law, or there is an heir at law, those appointed (in a later testament) have the preference, as, for example, if the invalidity in the execution of this testament is due to such a cause as that, either the patrimony has not been sold, or the testator has not pronounced the formal words of the declaration. § 150. The position is different of those who have become possessed of the property when there is no heir, and yet have not received the grant of possession of the property from the prætor, for even such possessors used formerly to obtain the property before the Julian law, by which law the property now lapses, and is directed to be handed over to the state, if no successor to the deceased have appeared. § 151. Testaments, validly executed, may be invalidated by a contrary intention, but it seems that a testament cannot be rendered invalid on the mere ground only that the testator subsequently did not wish it to be valid; and this is so true that, even though he should cut the thread, nevertheless it would remain valid by the civil law, wherefore, also, if he should efface or smear over the tablets of the testament, the writing which previously stood there would not immediately cease to be valid, although there would be no direct proof of the contents. How, therefore, would it be? If a person demanded possession of the goods as on an intestacy, and he who was heir under the testament demanded the inheritance, the latter must of necessity succeed, but the Imperial treasury would deprive him of the inheritance on the ground of unworthiness, so that it could not in any way come to the heir whom the testator was unwilling to have, and this is so settled by a rescript of the Emperor Antonine.

* see *post*, iii, § 36.

† cf. *ante* § 120.

§ 7. A testament cannot be invalidated merely on the ground that, subsequently to its execution, the testator is unwilling that it should remain valid, and this is so true that, although a person who had made one testament, began to make a second, and then, being prevented by death, or because, having changed his mind, he did not complete it, it was provided, in an address by the late Emperor Pertinax, that the first testament shall not be invalidated, unless the subsequent one was regularly made according to law and complete, for an imperfect testament is undoubtedly null. § 8. It is laid down in the same address that he would not accept the inheritance of one who, on account of a law-suit, made the Emperor his heir; nor would he admit as valid a testament not executed according to law, and in which, in order to get over the defect, he himself was appointed heir; nor would he accept the title of heir given him by word of mouth only; nor would he take anything by virtue of any writing defective in point of law. The late Emperors Severus and Antoninus have also often issued rescripts based on the same principles; "for although", say they, "we are released from obedience to the laws, yet we live in accordance with them".

Title xviii. Of inofficious testaments.

In consequence of ascendants often disinheriting or omitting their children from their testaments, without any cause, children who complain that they have been improperly disinherited, or improperly passed over, have been permitted to bring the action on an inofficious will, based on the supposition that their ascendants were not sane when they executed their testament. This does not imply that the maker of the testament was really insane, but that, though he had regularly made the testament, he had not done so in a manner consistent with the duties of affection. For, if he had been really insane, the testament would be void. § 1. But not only children are allowed to attack the testaments of their ascendants as inofficious, but ascendants also those of their children. A sister, or a brother also, by the imperial constitutions, are preferred to infamous persons appointed heirs, and, therefore, they cannot so proceed against all heirs. Blood relations, beyond brothers and sisters, cannot either sue or succeed in this way at all. § 2. But actual children, as well as those adopted, and of the class referred to in our constitu-

* see *ante* I, xi, § 2.

tion,* can only bring the action on an inofficious will, if they are unable in any other way to get hold of the property of the deceased; for those who can come at the inheritance, whether in whole or in part, by any other process, cannot bring this action. So posthumous children, who are unable to attain their end by any other process, can make use of this action. § 3. But these rules only hold good if nothing whatever has been left them by the testators in their testament: a provision introduced by our constitution out of respect for the rights of nature. For if any portion whatever of the inheritance, or anything, has been left to them, they cannot bring the action on an inofficious will; but that which is wanting to make up the fourth part of what they would be entitled to at law on an intestacy, must be made up to them, although there is no direction in the testament that this is to be made up by the estimate of an honest arbitrator. § 4. If a tutor should receive in the name of a pupil, whose tutorship he has undertaken, a legacy derived from the testament of the tutor's father, when nothing has been left to the tutor himself by his father, nevertheless he may, in his own name, proceed by the action on an inofficious will. § 5. On the other hand, if a tutor, in the name of his pupil, to whom nothing has been left, sues by the action on an inofficious will, and is defeated, the tutor himself does not lose anything that may have been left him by way of legacy in the same testament. § 6. Therefore, in order that a person, who is entitled to a fourth, may be debarred from bringing the action on an inofficious will, he must have this fourth either by way of inheritance, or legacy, or bequest in trust, or gift "mortis causa", or gift "inter vivos", but in those cases only, of which our constitution makes mention, or in the other ways referred to in the constitutions. § 7. What we have said of the fourth is to be understood in the sense that, whether there be one or several persons, able to sue by the action on an inofficious will, only one fourth is to be given them, that is, distributed among all proportionally, so that each has his fourth share.

§ 152. Heirs are said to be "necessary", or "necessary and taking at law as co-owners of the patrimony", or "strangers".

Title xix. Of the descriptions of, and differences between, heirs.

Heirs are said to be "necessary", or "necessary and taking at law as co-owners of the patrimony", or "strangers".

§ 153. A "necessary" heir is a slave appointed heir and granted his freedom; and he is so called because, whether willing or unwilling, he is immediately, and in any case, after the death of the testator, free and heir. § 154. Hence, he who has suspicions of his own solvency, commonly makes such an one free and heir, in the first or second, or even in a lower place, so that, if there should not be sufficient for his creditors, the property may be sold rather as that of the heir, than of the testator himself; that is to say, so that the disgrace resulting from the sale may fall on this heir, rather than upon the testator; although Sabinus, according to Fufidius, held that the slave should be exempted from this disgrace, because he suffers the sale of the property by the requirement of the law, and not from his own fault; but we follow a different rule. § 155. But, to compensate for this inconvenience, a slave enjoys this benefit, that that property which he has acquired for himself after the death of his patron, whether before or after the sale of the property, is reserved for himself; and, although the property sold only pays part of the debts, there can be no second sale of property, on account of the inheritance, unless he has acquired anything in consequence of the inheritance, as, for example, if he has acquired the property of a Latin, and thereby become richer; whilst, as to all other persons, the sale of whose property has only paid a portion of the debts, if they acquire anything afterwards, their property is liable to be sold over and over again.

§ 1. A "necessary" heir is a slave appointed heir; and he is so called because, whether willing or unwilling, he is immediately, and in any case, after the death of the testator, free and necessary heir. Hence, he who is suspicious of his own solvency, commonly appoints a slave heir in the first or second, or even in a lower place, so that, if there should not be sufficient for his creditors, it may be rather the goods of this heir, and not those of the testator himself, which are seized, or sold by, or divided amongst the creditors. But, to compensate for this inconvenience, a slave enjoys this benefit, that property which he has acquired for himself after the death of his patron, is reserved for himself, and, although the goods of the deceased should be insufficient for the payment of the creditors, yet property acquired by the slave from other sources than the inheritance is not liable to be sold.

§ 156. Now heirs, succeeding as being "co-owners of the patrimony", and as being "necessary", are, for instance a son, or a daughter, a grandson or a granddaughter by a son, and their descendants who were in the power of the deceased at the time of his death. But in order that a grandson or granddaughter may be such an heir, it is not sufficient for him or her to have been under the power

§ 2. Now heirs, succeeding as being "co-owners of the patrimony", and as being "necessary", are, for instance, a son, or a daughter, a grandson or a granddaughter by a son, and their children who were in the power of the deceased at the time of his death. But in order that a grandson, or granddaughter may be such an heir, it is not sufficient for him or her to have been in the power of his or of his or her ancestor at the moment of his death; but it is necessary that his or her father should have ceased to be such an heir in the lifetime of his father, either through having been cut off by death, or through some other cause freed from the power, for then the grandson or granddaughter succeeds to the place of the father. § 157. But they are called heirs, succeeding as being "co-owners of the patrimony", because they are heirs of the family; and even during the lifetime of the ascendant, they are deemed, as it were, owners; and, hence, if a person die intestate, they occupy the first place in the succession of descendants. They are also called "necessary", because, in any case, whether they are willing or not, they become heirs, equally on an intestacy, as by virtue of a testament. § 158. But the prætor permits them to abstain from the inheritance, in order that the property may be sold rather as that of the ascendant than theirs. § 159. The same rule applies to the case of a wife in marital power, because she fills the place of a daughter; and so as to a daughter-in-law, who is in the marital power of a son, because she fills the place of a granddaughter. § 160. Similarly, the prætor gives the right of abstaining to the freeman who is in a condition of bondage, that is, to a person who has been sold by the process of the copper and the scale, when he is appointed heir, and declared free, since he, like a slave, is a necessary heir, though not also an heir taking at law as co-owner.

her ancestor at the time of his death; but it is necessary that his or her father should have ceased to be such an heir in the lifetime of his father, having been either cut off by death, or otherwise freed from power; for, then, the grandson, or granddaughter succeeds to the place of the father. But they are called heirs, succeeding as being "co-owners of the patrimony", because they are heirs of the family; and even during the lifetime of the father, are deemed, as it were, owners; and, hence, if a person die intestate, they occupy the first place in the succession of descendants. They are called "necessary", because, in any case, whether they are willing or not, they become heirs, equally on an intestacy, as by virtue of a testament. But the prætor permits them to abstain from the inheritance, if they so desire, in order that the property may be seized by creditors, rather as that of their ascendant than theirs.

§ 161. Those who are not subject to the power of the testator are called "stranger" heirs. Therefore, also, our children who are not in our power when they are appointed heirs by us are regarded as strangers. For which reason those also who are appointed heirs by their mother are reckoned in the same class, be-

§ 3. Those who are not subject to the power of the testator are called "stranger" heirs. Therefore, children who are not in our power when they are appointed heirs by us are regarded as stranger heirs. For which reason those who are appointed heirs by their mother are reckoned in the same class, because women do not have their children

cause women do not have their children in their power. Slaves also who have been appointed heirs with their freedom, and afterwards manumitted by their master, are reckoned amongst the same class.

in their power. A slave, also, appointed heir by his master, and, after the testament had been made, manumitted by him, is reckoned amongst the same class. § 4. In respect of stranger heirs, it is to be noted that they must have the capacity of taking under the testator's will, whether they themselves are appointed heirs, or those in their power. And this matter is to be considered at two periods: at the making of the testament, that the appointment may be valid, and at the testator's death, that it may take effect. Further, at the time the inheritance is entered upon by the heir, he must be capable of taking under the testator's will, whether he is appointed simply or conditionally; for the right of the heir is to be particularly looked to at that time. But, in the interval between the making of the testament and the death of the testator, or whilst the condition attaching to the appointment is in suspense, a change in the capacity of the heir has no prejudicial effect, because, as we have said, we look to these three periods. But not only is he held to have testamentary capacity who is able to make a will, but also he, who, under the testament of another, can take for himself, or acquire for another, although he may not be able himself to make a testament; and, therefore, the insane, the dumb, a posthumous child, an infant, a son in power, and the slave of another, are said to have testamentary capacity, for although they cannot make a testament, yet they can acquire by testament either for themselves or for others.

§ 162. A power of deliberation is given to stranger heirs, whether they will or will not enter upon the inheritance. § 163. But whether he who has the power of abstaining from the inheritance has intermeddled with the hereditary property, or whether he, who is permitted to deliberate as to the acceptance of the inheritance, has entered upon it, the power of renouncing the inheritance is gone, unless he is under twenty-five years of age. For to men of this age, as in all other cases where they have been deceived, so here, the prætor comes to their aid, if

§ 5. A power of deliberation is given to stranger heirs, whether they will or will not enter upon the inheritance. But whether he who has the power of abstaining from the inheritance, has intermeddled with the hereditary property, or whether a stranger heir, who is permitted to deliberate as to the acceptance of the inheritance, has entered upon it, the power of renouncing the inheritance is gone, unless he is under twenty-five years of age; for to men of this age, as in all other cases, where they have been deceived, so here, the prætor comes

they have rashly taken upon themselves a burdened inheritance; indeed, I am aware that the late Emperor Hadrian granted the indulgence to one more than twenty-five years of age, when, after having entered upon the inheritance, a heavy debt came to light, which was unknown at the time of entering upon the inheritance.

to their aid if they have rashly taken upon themselves a burdened inheritance. § 6. It must be known, however, that the late Emperor Hadrian granted this indulgence to one more than twenty-five years of age, when a heavy debt came to light, unknown at the time that he had entered on the inheritance. But this was granted as a special favour. The late Emperor Gordian afterwards extended this as a privilege to soldiers only. But we, in our goodness, have extended this benefit to all our subjects in common, and have drawn up a constitution as equitable as it is excellent, by which, if men attend to its provisions, they may enter upon an inheritance, and only be liable to the extent of the value of the estate; so that there will be no necessity for their calling in aid their right of deliberation, unless, neglecting to take advantage of our constitution, they think proper to deliberate, and prefer to risk the liabilities attending the old mode of entering upon the inheritance.

§ 164. Time for declaring their acceptance is usually given to stranger heirs, that is to say, a limited period for deliberation, so that within a certain time they may either enter upon the inheritance, or if they do not enter, they are, at the expiration of the time, set aside. This is called "cretio", from "cernere", which denotes, as it were, to deliberate and decide. § 165. When, therefore, it is thus written—"Titius be heir", we ought to add—"and decide as to accepting the inheritance within the next hundred days, after you know of the appointment, and are able to act upon it, but if you do not so decide, be disinherited." § 166. And he who is thus appointed heir, if he wishes to be heir, ought to make a declaration within the period allowed for deliberation, that is, he must pronounce the following words—"Since Publius Mævius has appointed me, Titius, his heir by testament, I enter upon and declare my acceptance of that inheritance." But if he has not thus decided, when the period for declaring his acceptance elapsed, he is excluded, and it avails nothing for him to have acted as heir, that is, if he has used the property of the inheritance as if he were heir. § 167. But he who is appointed heir without a period for deliberation, or who is called by law to the inheritance on an intes-

§ 7. So, a stranger heir appointed by testament, or called by law on an intestacy to the succession, may become heir, either by

tacy, can become heir, either by declaration of his acceptance, or by acting as heir, or even by the mere wish of taking over the inheritance; and he is at liberty to enter upon the inheritance whenever he please. But the prætor usually, on the demand of the creditors of the estate, fixes a period within which he may enter upon the inheritance if he please; and, if he does not, it is lawful for the creditors to sell the property of the deceased. § 168. But just as he who is appointed heir with a period for deliberation, does not become heir, unless he has declared his acceptance of the inheritance; so also he is not otherwise excluded than if he does not declare his acceptance within the period to which the declaration is limited. Therefore, though before the limit has expired for the declaration of acceptance, he may have resolved not to enter upon the inheritance, yet upon repenting this decision, he may become heir by declaring his acceptance during the time for the making of the declaration still unexpired. § 169. But since he who is appointed heir without a period for deliberation, and he who is called by law on an intestacy, become heir by the mere intention to act, so a contrary intention has the effect of immediately barring the inheritance. § 170. But every period for deliberation is limited to a fixed time; and in this matter the period of a hundred days seemed reasonable; nevertheless, according to the civil law, a longer or shorter period may be given, though the prætor sometimes abridges a longer period. § 171. And although every period for deliberation is limited to a certain number of days, still a distinction exists between that called the "common" period for deliberation, and that limited to a fixed number of days. The "common" period for deliberation, which we explained above,* is that in which

* *ante*, § 165.

acting as heir, or even by the mere wish to take over the inheritance. A person is deemed to act as heir if he use the hereditary property as if he were heir, by selling any part of it, or by cultivating the land, or letting it, or in any other way declare, either by act or word, his intention of entering upon the inheritance, provided only he know that he, in respect of whose estate he is acting as heir, has died, testate or intestate, and that he is heir to him. To act as heir is to act as owner, for the ancients used the term heirs to denote the owners.

Since a stranger heir becomes heir by the mere intention to act, so a contrary intention has the effect of immediately barring the inheritance. Nothing prevents a person who was born deaf or dumb, or who subsequently became so, from acting as heir, and acquiring the inheritance for himself, if only he understands what he is about.

these words are added, "within which he knows of the appointment, and is able to act upon it"; but that for a "fixed number of days" is that in which these words are omitted. § 172. There is an important difference between these two kinds of periods for deliberation. For in the "common" period for deliberation no days are counted, except those during which he who is appointed knows that he is heir, and is in a position to declare his acceptance. But in the case of the period for deliberation for a "fixed number of days" the days are counted continuously, even though he who is appointed does not know that he is heir. So, also, the time runs against him who is on any ground prevented from declaring his acceptance, and more especially against him who has been appointed heir, subject to a condition. § 173. Hence, this kind of period for deliberation is called "continuous". But since it presses hard, the other is the more usual, and hence, also, it is called "common".

Title xx. Of legacies.

§ 191. From these matters, let us now turn to legacies. This part of the law would seem, indeed, to be outside our present subject,* for we are engaged in discussing the means created by law for acquiring property in the aggregate; but as we have dealt generally with testaments and with the heirs who take under them, it will not be unreasonable to deal next with this branch of law.

From these matters, let us now turn to legacies. This part of the law would seem to be outside our present subject,† for we are engaged in discussing the means created by law for acquiring property in the aggregate; but as we have dealt generally with testaments, and with the heirs who take under them, it will not be unreasonable to deal next with this branch of the law.

§ 1. A legacy, then, is a certain kind of gift left by a deceased person.

Of legacies.

§ 192. Now, there are four kinds of legacies, for we may leave a legacy by way of "giving the legatee the right to claim it", or by way of "ordering the heir to give it to the legatee", or by way of "directing the heir to suffer the legatee to take it", or by way of "giving the legatee the right to take it before the division of the inheritance".

§ 193. We leave a legacy by way of giving the legatee the right to claim it thus: "To Lucius Titius", for example, "I give and bequeath the slave Stichus"; and although only one or other of the

* *ante*, § 97.

† *ante*, tit. ix, § 6.

words be used, as, for example: "I give", or "I bequeath"; still the legacy is equally by way of giving the legatee the right to claim it. So, it would seem to be held that if the legacy is given in this form: "Let him select", or thus: "Let him have for himself", or thus: "Let him acquire"; the legacy is equally by way of giving the legatee the right to claim it. § 194. Therefore, this legacy is called "that by way of giving the legatee the right to claim it", because, immediately after the inheritance is entered upon, the thing bequeathed becomes the property of the legatee by the law of the quirites; and if it should be necessary for the legatee to sue either the heir or any other person who has got the thing in his possession, he should proceed by the action laying claim to a thing, that is, ground his action on the fact that the thing is his by the law of the quirites. § 195. On one point the jurisconsults are not agreed; for Sabinus and Cassius, and the other leaders of our school, think that what has been so bequeathed vests in the legatee immediately after the inheritance is entered upon, although he may be ignorant that a legacy has been left to him; and not until he knows of it, and repudiates the legacy, is the case as if nothing had been bequeathed to him; but Nerva and Proculus, and the other leaders of that school, think that the thing does not otherwise become the property of the legatee than if he wishes that it should belong to him. But, at the present day, by virtue of a constitution of the late Emperor Antoninus Pius, we would seem rather to follow the rule laid down by Proculus; for, when a Latin had been bequeathed to a colony by way of giving it the right to claim him, "Let the members of the local senate deliberate", says this emperor, "whether they wish to become owners of this legacy, just as if the Latin had been bequeathed to a single individual." § 196. Only those things, however, can be properly bequeathed by way of giving the legatee the right to claim it, which belong to the testator by the law of the quirites; but, as to those things which consist in their weight, number, and measure, it is held sufficient if they were the property of the testator, by the law of the quirites, at the time of his decease, as in the case of wine, oil, corn, money in coin; but, as to other things, it is held that they ought to be the property of the testator by the law of the quirites, at both periods, that is, both when he made the testament and when he died, otherwise the legacy is invalid. § 197. And this is certainly so by the civil law; but afterwards, by direction of the Emperor Nero, a decree of the senate was made, by which it was enacted that, if anyone had left by legacy property which had never been his, the legacy should be as valid as if the thing had been bequeathed in the manner most advantageous to the legatee. The most advantageous manner in which a legacy is left to a legatee, is that by way of ordering the heir to give it, by which mode even the property of another can be bequeathed, as will appear below. § 198. But if a person has left a thing by legacy, and, after having made his testament, he alienate it, the majority are of opinion that the legacy is not only invalid, according to the civil law, but cannot be confirmed by virtue of the decree of the senate. This view is adopted, because, in the opinion of the majority, even though a person should have bequeathed his own property by way of ordering the heir to give it, yet, if he have subsequently alienated it, then, although the legacy may be due at law, the legatee, on suing for it, can be defeated by a plea of fraud, as claiming it against the wish of the deceased. § 199. One thing is clear, that if the same thing be bequeathed to two or more persons, by way of giving the legatee the right to claim it, whether conjointly or in the disjunctive, and, if all are in a position to take the legacy, equal portions belong to each, and the portion of anyone who fails to take accrues to the co-legatee. A legacy is left conjointly thus: "I give and bequeath to Titius and to Seius the slave Stichus." It is left in the disjunctive thus: "I give and bequeath the slave Stichus to Lucius Titius. I give and bequeath the same slave to Seius." § 200. The question arises, If a thing is bequeathed by way of giving the legatee the right to claim it, subject to a condition, whilst the condition is in suspense, whose property is it? The leaders of our school are of opinion that it is in the heir, by analogy to the case of a conditionally free person, that is, of a slave, who, by testament, is ordered to be free, subject to some condition, and who, it is agreed, is, during the interval, the slave of the heir. But the leaders of the opposite school think that the thing during the interval is the property of no one, and this, they say, is still more true of that which is bequeathed simply without any condition, before the legatee assents to the legacy.

§ 201. We leave a legacy, by way of ordering the heir to give it, in this way: "My heir be bound to give my slave Stichus"; but, if the words used are "let him give", the legacy is still by way of ordering the heir to give it. § 202. By this kind of legacy even things which belong to another can be bequeathed, so that the heir must procure it, and deliver it, or hand over the value of it. § 203. So a thing which is not yet in existence, provided it will come into existence, can be bequeathed by way of ordering the heir to give it, as, for example, "the produce which shall come from that estate", or "the offspring of that female slave". § 204. But that which is bequeathed in this way, after the inheritance is entered upon, and although the legacy is left absolutely, does not, as in the case of a legacy, by way of giving the legatee the right to claim it, vest immediately in the legatee, but remains in the heir, and therefore the legatee must sue by a personal action, that is, ground his claim on the fact that the heir ought to give it to him, and then the heir, if the thing be a thing requiring transfer by the formal conveyance of copper and scale, should give it by that process, or go through the forms of a surrender in court, and deliver possession; if it be a thing not requiring the above form of conveyance, it will be sufficient if he deliver it; for if he has only delivered a thing requiring the formal mode of conveyance;* and not gone through that process, then only when the period of acquisition by use is complete, does it absolutely become the property of the legatee at law. Now the acquisition by use is completed, as we have elsewhere said,† for movable things in one year, but, for those which belong to the soil, in two years. § 205. There is also another difference in this kind of legacy, for, if the same thing is left by legacy to two or more, by way of ordering the heir to give it, and it is bequeathed conjointly, no doubt equal shares are due to each, as in a legacy by way of giving the legatee the right to claim it. But, if it is left in the disjunctive, the whole thing is due to each, so that the heir should give the thing to one and the value of it to the other; and, if left conjointly, the portion of one, who does not come in for his share, does not accrue to his co-legatee, but remains in the inheritance.

* *ante*, § 41.

† *ante*, § 42.

§ 206. When, however, we said that in the case of a legacy by way of ordering the heir to give it, the share of a legatee, who fails to take, is retained in the inheritance, whilst, in the case of a legacy by way of giving the legatee the right to claim it, it accrues to the co-legatee, we must note that this was so by the civil law before the Papian law, but, after that law, the share of him who fails to take lapses, and falls to those taking under that testament who have children. § 207. And, although the right of suing for lapsed legacies belongs, in the first place, to those of the heirs who have children, and, secondly, if the heirs have no children, to the legatees who have children, yet it is provided, by this same law, that a conjoint legatee, if he have children, has a better right than the heirs, even though they have children. § 208. But it is the opinion of the majority that, so far as regards the rule established by this law as to conjoint legatees, it is immaterial whether the legacy is left by way of giving the legatee the right to claim it, or by way of ordering the heir to give it.

§ 209. We leave a legacy by way of directing the heir to suffer the legatee to take it, thus: "My heir be bound to suffer Lucius Titius to take and have for himself the slave Stichus." § 210. This kind of legacy involves more than the legacy by way of giving the legatee the right to claim it, but less than that by way of ordering the heir to give it, for in this way the testator can validly leave as a legacy not only his own property, but also that of his heir, whereas he can only leave as a legacy by way of giving the legatee the right to claim it, that which belongs to himself, though he can leave by way of ordering the heir to give it, the property of any outsider. § 211. But if, at the time of the testator's death, the thing was the property of the testator or of his heir, the legacy is clearly valid, even though, at the time of making the testament, it was not the property of either. § 212. But, suppose the thing became the property of the heir after the death of the testator, the question arises whether the legacy is valid? the majority hold that it is invalid. Now, how does the matter stand? And it seems that, although a person should leave by legacy a thing which was never his, and which never afterwards became the property of the heir, still, by virtue of Nero's decree of the senate, it is to be treated as having been left by way of ordering the heir to give it. § 213. But, just as a thing bequeathed by way of ordering the heir to give it, does not vest in the legatee immediately after the inheritance is entered upon, but remains the property of the heir, until the heir, by delivering it, or by going through the process of conveying it by copper and scale, or by surrender in court, has made it the property of the legatee, so does the same rule hold in the case of a legacy by way of directing the heir to suffer a legatee to take it; and, therefore, when suing for this kind of legacy, the action will be personal, viz., for "whatever the heir, by reason of the testament, ought to give or to do". § 214. There are, however, those who think that the heir would not seem to be bound by a legacy of this description to go through the process of conveying it by copper and scale, or to surrender it in court, or to deliver the thing; but that it will be sufficient if he suffer the legatee to take the thing, since the testator has ordered him to do nothing further than to permit, that is, to suffer the legatee to have the thing for himself. § 215. A greater diversity of opinion, in respect to this legacy, arises where you have bequeathed the same thing to two or more in the disjunctive, for some think that the whole is due to each, as in the case of a legacy by way of ordering the heir to give it, others deem the position of the first occupant to be the better, since, in this kind of legacy, the heir is bound to suffer the legatee to take the thing, and therefore it follows that, if he has made no opposition to the first of the two legatees, and this legatee has taken it, the heir will be safe against him who subsequently demands the legacy, for he neither has the thing, so as to allow it to be taken, nor has he been guilty of fraud in getting the thing out of his possession.

§ 216. We leave a legacy by way of giving the legatee the right to take it before the division of the inheritance, thus: "Lucius Titius is to take my slave Stichus beforehand." § 217. But the leaders of our school are of opinion that a legacy cannot be left in this way to any other than one who is appointed heir of some portion of the inheritance; for to take beforehand means to select specially, and this can only apply in respect of a person who is appointed heir of some portion of the inheritance, and who is to have a special legacy over and above his share of the inheritance. § 218. And hence, if such a legacy should be left to an outsider, it would be invalid, and so much so that, as Sabinus thought, it could not even become valid by virtue of Nero's decree of the senate, for he says by that decree only those legacies are rendered valid which were invalid, according to the civil law, through some defect in the wording, not those which lapse on account of something to do with the legatee himself. But, in the opinion of Julianus and of Sextus, even in this case the legacy is rendered valid by the decree of the senate, for here, also, it results from the words used, that the bequest is, by the civil law, invalid; whence it is obvious that a legacy left to such a person by other words would be valid. But then it also follows that, if there is a defect in the legatee, the legacy will not be valid, as when it has been made to one who can, under no circumstances, receive a legacy, as, for example to an alien in whom the legal capacity of taking under a will does not exist, in which case it is clear there is no ground for the application of the decree of the senate. § 219. Further than this, the leaders of our school hold that a legacy of this description can be sued for in no other manner by him to whom it has been left, than by means of the action for the partition of an inheritance, for it is involved in the duties of the judge to award that which has been bequeathed by way of giving the legatee the right to take it before the division of the inheritance. § 220. From this we must understand that, according to the opinion of the leaders of our school, nothing else can be bequeathed by way of giving the legatee the right to take it before the division of the inheritance, but what belongs to the testator; for no other than the hereditary property can be taken into account in this action; and, therefore, if the testator has bequeathed in this way property not his own, the legacy will, indeed, be invalid, according to the civil law, but it will be rendered valid by the decree of the senate. Still, however, in one class of cases our leaders admit that the property of another person can be left by legacy, by way of giving the legatee the right to take it before the division of the inheritance, as, for example, if a person has left as a legacy a thing which he had conveyed by the process of copper and scale to a creditor, with a clause for re-conveyance, in which case they think that the the co-heirs could be compelled, through the order of the judge, and after payment of the debt, to redeem the thing, in order that he to whom it has been left as a legacy may be able to take it beforehand. § 221. But the leaders of the opposite school think that a legacy may be left by way of giving the legatee the right to take it before the division of the inheritance, even to an outsider, just as if the bequest were in these words: "Titius, take the slave Stichus", the addition of the word, "beforehand", being superfluous; and hence the legacy seems to be made by way of giving the legatee the right to claim it: an opinion which is said to be confirmed by a constitution of the late emperor Hadrian. § 222. Therefore, according to this opinion, if the thing devised belonged to the deceased by the law of the quirites, it seems that the legatee could sue for it by the action laying claim to a thing, whether he were one of the heirs or an outsider; but, if the thing were only in the equitable ownership of the testator, the legacy would be valid, in the case of the outsider, by reason of the decree of the senate, whilst, in the case of an heir, it would be obtained through the aid of the judge, in an action for the partition of the inheritance. But, if it were not the property of the testator in either way, then the legacy would be rendered valid by the decree of the senate, as well for the heir as for the outsider. § 223. And, whether the same thing has been left by legacy to two or more, conjointly or in the disjunctive, and whether to heirs according to the opinion of our school, or to outsiders according to the leaders of the other school, each ought to have his share of the thing.

§ 2. Formerly there were four kinds of legacies, viz., that by way of giving the legatee the right to claim it, that by way of ordering the heir to give it to the legatee, that by way of directing the heir to suffer the legatee to take it, and that by way of giving the legatee the right to take it before the division of the inheritance; and certain set forms of words were proper to each, by which each of these kinds of legacies was distinguished. But the force of the form of words used has been entirely taken away by constitutions of the late emperors. A constitution of ours also, (which we have prepared with much labour, and with the desire of favouring the intention, and giving more weight to the wishes of the deceased than to the words employed), has provided that the nature of all legacies shall be the same; and that, whatever may be the words with which anything is left to them, legatees may sue, not only by personal actions, but also by real actions, and by those actions available for the assertion of mortgage rights. The perusal of this constitution will reveal the wisdom of these measures. § 3. But we have not considered it sufficient to rest on this constitution; for, finding that, anciently, legacies were confined within narrow limits, whilst bequests in trust, as deriving their origin rather from the wishes of the deceased, obtained greater indulgence and more latitude, we have been brought to think it necessary to make all legacies equal to bequests in trust, so that there should be no difference between them, and what is wanting to legacies may be borrowed from bequests in trust; and, if there is anything in favour of legacies, this is to be communicated to bequests in trust. But, lest we should put difficulties in the way of the young student, just commencing his studies in law, by treating these subjects together, we have been induced to take the trouble to deal first with the case of legacies separately, and afterwards with bequests in trust, so that, when acquainted with the law relating to both, the student, thus prepared, may easily grasp the fusion of the two.

§ 4. Not only can a testator bequeath as a legacy his own property, or that of his heir, but also the property of others, so that the heir must then either purchase and deliver it, or, if he cannot purchase it, give the value of it. But, if it be not a thing in commerce, or purchasable, the heir is not liable for its value, as, if a testator should bequeath the Campus Martius, the courts of justice, the temples, or any of the things appropriated to public purposes, for such a legacy is void. But, when we said that the property of another person may be left as a legacy, this is to be understood to mean if the deceased knew that the thing belonged to another, not if he were ignorant of that fact; for it may be that, had he known it belonged to another, he would not have bequeathed it, and hence a rescript of the late Emperor Antoninus lays down that it is the more correct view to consider that it lies on the plaintiff, that is, the legatee, to prove that the deceased knew that he had bequeathed the property of another, not upon the heir to prove that the deceased did not know that it was another's property, for the burden of proof always lies upon the person who is suing. § 5. If a testator should leave as a legacy a thing pledged to a creditor, the heir is under the necessity of redeeming it; and in this case, also, the same rule holds as in that of the property of another, viz., that the heir is only under the necessity of redeeming it if the deceased knew that the thing was pledged, and the late Emperors Severus and Antoninus have so decided by rescript. If, however, the deceased wished that the legatee should redeem, and has expressed this wish, then the heir need not redeem it. § 6. If a thing belonging to another has been given as a legacy, and the legatee has become the owner of it in the lifetime of the testator, then, if he had acquired it by purchase, the price may be recovered in an action grounded on the testament; but, if it was acquired by way of clear gain, as, for example, by gift, or by other similar method, he cannot bring such an action, for it is an admitted rule, "that two modes of acquiring, by way of clear gain, cannot unite in the same person and in respect of the same thing." According to this rule, therefore, if the same thing is due to the same person, by two testaments, it makes a difference, whether the legatee has obtained the thing or its value from one testament; for, if he has obtained the thing, he cannot bring an action, for he has received it by way of clear gain; but, if he has only got the value, he may bring an action. § 7. A thing also not in existence, if only it may hereafter be, may properly be bequeathed as a legacy, as, for instance, the produce which shall grow on such an estate, or the offspring to be born of such a slave. § 8. If the same thing is given as a legacy to two persons, either conjointly or in the disjunctive, and both are in a position to claim the legacy, it is divided between them. But, if one of the legatees should fail to be in a position to take it, either because he has refused it, or because he has died in the lifetime of the testator, or if it should fail to come to him for any other reason, the whole belongs to the co-legatee. A legacy is given conjointly, if, for example, a testator say: "I give and bequeath the slave, Stichus, to Titius and Seius"; but in the disjunctive, thus: "I give and bequeath the slave, Stichus, to Titius; I give and bequeath Stichus to Seius." And although he should have expressed himself thus: "The same slave Stichus"; yet the legacy is still held to be given in the disjunctive. § 9. If an estate belonging to another should have been left as a legacy to a person, and the latter should have purchased the ownership, minus the usufruct, and the usufruct should come to him, then, if he subsequently bring an action grounded on the testament, Julian is of opinion that such action may be properly brought and the estate claimed, because in the action the usufruct will be regarded as a servitude only; and it will be part of the duty of the judge to order the value to be handed over, deducting the usufruct. § 10. But if a person bequeath as a legacy a thing already belonging to the legatee, the legacy is void; for what is already the legatee's own property cannot be made more so. And although the legatee has alienated the thing, still neither the thing itself nor its value is due to him. § 11. If a person should have bequeathed his own property as if it belonged to another the legacy is valid; for the fact is rather to be regarded than an opinion about it, and if he thought it belonged to the legatee, still if such is not the case, the legacy holds good, because the wish of the deceased can be accomplished. § 12. If a testator should have bequeathed his own property as a legacy, and afterwards have alienated it,

Celsus is of opinion that the legacy is nevertheless due if it was not sold with the intention of revoking the legacy, and the late Emperors Severus and Antoninus have so decided by rescript. And the same emperors have also settled by rescript that he who, after making a testament, mortgages the estates which he had bequeathed by legacy is not to be held to have revoked the legacy; and, therefore, the legatee may bring an action against the heir to compel him to redeem the property out of the hands of the creditor. But if a part of the thing given as a legacy should have been alienated, the part not alienated is of course due, but the part alienated is only due if it was not alienated with the intention of revoking the legacy. § 13. If a testator gives his debtor, by way of legacy, a release of his debt, the legacy is valid, and the heir cannot recover the debt from the debtor himself or his heir, or anyone who stands in the place of his heir; but it is open to the debtor to compel the heir by action to release him from the debt, and a person may forbid his heir to sue for payment of a debt during a certain time. § 14. On the other hand, if a debtor bequeath as a legacy to his creditor that which he owes him, the legacy is void if nothing more is included in the legacy than in the debt, for the creditor gets nothing by the legacy. But if the debt was not due for a time, or was subject to a condition, and is left by way of legacy absolutely, the legacy is good, because it is due immediately; and Papinian lays down that if the term should have expired, or the condition become fulfilled, in the lifetime of the testator, the legacy is nevertheless valid, because it was once so. And this is the correct view, as the opinion may be rejected of those who think that the legacy is extinguished, because it has come under conditions which would have affected its validity at the outset. § 15. If a husband should leave his wife's dowry to her by way of legacy, the legacy is valid, because it is more beneficial than the action available for the recovery of the dowry. But if he should have bequeathed a dowry which he had not received, the late Emperors Severus and Antoninus have decided by a rescript, that if the legacy be simply of the dowry, the legacy is void; but if a fixed sum of money, or a certain thing is pointed out, or reference made to the deed constituting the dowry, and it be stated that this is to be taken by way of legacy, the legacy is valid. § 16. If the thing left by legacy should perish without the act of the heir, the loss falls upon the legatee; and if the slave of another, given as a legacy, should have been manumitted without the act of the heir, the heir is not liable. But if the slave of his heir should have been given as a legacy, and the heir manumits that slave, Julian lays down that he is answerable, whether he knew or was ignorant that the slave was left as a legacy away from him. And if the heir should have given the slave to another who had manumitted him, the heir would be liable, although he was ignorant that the slave had been left away from him. § 17. If a person bequeath his female slaves, together with their offspring, then, although the mothers should have died, the issue goes to the legatee. The same rule holds as to head slaves bequeathed together with their assistants, for although the head slaves die, yet the assistant slaves go to the legatee. But if a slave is bequeathed together with his private savings, then, on the death of the slave, or his manumission, or alienation, the legacy of the private savings fails to take effect. The same rule holds if an estate should be bequeathed with its appurtenances, or with its instruments of culture; for on the alienation of the land, the legacy of the accessories fails. § 18. If a flock should be left as a legacy, and it is afterwards reduced to one sheep, what remains can be claimed; and when a flock is given as a legacy, those sheep added to the flock after the testament was made, will, according to Julianus, go to the legatee. For a flock is one body, consisting of distinct heads, just as a house is one body, made up of stones united together. § 19. So, if a building is left as a legacy, any columns or marbles, added after the testament was made, pass with the legacy. § 20. If the private savings of a slave are left by way of legacy, there is no doubt but that accruals or diminutions in the lifetime of the testator are the gain or loss of the legatee. But, according to Julianus, if the slave should have acquired anything after the death of the testator, and before the inheritance is entered upon, and the private savings are given to the slave himself on his manumission, then, all that has been acquired before the inheritance was entered upon goes to the legatee, for the time when such a legacy can be claimed runs from the entering upon the inheritance. But if the private savings have been given to a stranger, then, anything acquired within this period will not go with the legacy, unless the increase has been acquired by means of that which already formed part of the private savings. Moreover, the private savings are not due to the slave on his manumission, unless given him as a legacy, although, if his master in his lifetime had manumitted him, it is enough if he had not taken them away; and the late Emperors Severus and Antoninus have so decided by rescript. The same emperors have also laid down by rescript that when the private savings are given as a legacy, this is not to be held to imply the right to sue for such sums as the slave may have expended in settling the accounts of his master. The same emperors have held in a rescript that the private savings will be deemed to be left as a legacy when he is ordered to be free, on making up his accounts and paying over any deficiency out of his private savings. § 21. Both corporeal and incorporeal things may be given by way of legacy. Hence, that which is due to the deceased may be left as a legacy to a person, and the heir must, then, give the legatee the benefit of his rights of action, unless the testator in his lifetime collected the money, for in this case the legacy becomes void; but such a legacy as this is good: "My heir be bound to repair the house of so and so, or to release him from his debts". § 22. If a slave or other thing be left as a legacy, generally, the election is in the legatee, unless the testator has declared otherwise. § 23. A legacy of election, that is, where a testator directed his legatee to choose one from among his slaves, or other things, had this condition implied, that unless the legatee had made the choice in his lifetime, the legacy did not pass to his heir. But, by our constitution, this matter also has been put on a better footing, and power is given to the heir of the legatee to elect, although the legatee in his lifetime had not done so. And dealing with the subject still more closely, we have in our constitution further added, that whether there be several legatees to whom the election is left, and they disagree as to the thing they would select, or whether there be several heirs of one legatee, and they disagree as to the choice, then, to prevent the legacy failing (which the majority of the juris-consults, contrary to the equity of the case, have held, would be the result), fortune must be the judge as to the choice, and the opinion of him is to prevail who is selected by lot.

§ 24. A legacy can only be given to those who possess the legal capacity of receiving a testamentary bequest from the testator.

§ 238. A legacy made to an uncertain person is invalid. Now, a person is considered to be uncertain in respect of

§ 25. Formerly the giving of legacies or bequests in trust to uncertain persons was not allowed; for not even a soldier could leave anything

whom the testator has no precise idea in his mind, as, for example, if the legacy is left thus: "Let my heir give ten thousand sesterces to the person who first comes to my funeral." The same rule holds if he has made a bequest to all generally, "whoever comes to my funeral". So, in the case of such a bequest as this: "My heir is to give ten thousand sesterces to him who marries his daughter to my son." The same applies to a legacy in these terms: "To those who shall be nominated consuls after the making of my testament", in all of which cases the legacy is equally held to be left to uncertain persons. There are many other examples of this nature. But a legacy may be left to an uncertain person under a certain description, as in this case: "My heir is to give ten thousand sesterces to that one out of my relations now living, who comes first to my funeral." § 239. So it is held that freedom cannot be given to an uncertain person, because the Fusian Caninian law orders slaves to be freed by name.

§ 241. A legacy to a posthumous stranger is also invalid. A posthumous stranger is one who, if born, would not be included among the heirs of the testator taking at law as being co-owners of the patrimony. Therefore, a grandson, conceived from an emancipated son, is a posthumous stranger. So the unborn child of her who is not held to be a wife, according to the civil law, is a posthumous stranger to the father.

to an uncertain person, as the late Emperor Hadrian decided by rescript. An uncertain person was held to be one of whom the testator had no precise idea in his mind, as if a person were to say: "Whoever marries his daughter to my son, to him let my heir give such an estate." So of that which was left in these terms: "Those who shall be nominated consuls after the making of the testament;" this also would have been held to be a gift to an uncertain person, and there are many other similar examples. Freedom, also, could not be given to an uncertain person, for it was held that all slaves must be freed by name. It was held, also, that the appointment of tutor must be of a definite person; but a legacy given with a certain description, that is, to an uncertain person amongst a number of certain persons, was valid, as, for example, "amongst my relations now living—if anyone shall marry my daughter let my heir give him such a thing". But, if legacies or bequests in trust to uncertain persons have been paid by mistake, they cannot be recovered back, for it has been so decided by the imperial constitutions.*

§ 26. Formerly, also, a legacy to a posthumous stranger was void. A posthumous stranger is one who, if born, would not be included among the heirs of the testator taking at law as being co-owners of the patrimony. And so a posthumous grandson, conceived from an emancipated son, was a posthumous stranger to his grandfather. § 27. But these matters have not been left without proper correction, for a constitution has been placed in our code by which we

* cf. III, xxvii, § 7.

§ 240. The person appointed as tutor ought also to be definite.

§ 242. A posthumous stranger cannot be appointed heir, for he is an uncertain person. § 243. But the other matters, to which we referred above,* apply properly to legacies, although some, not without reason, hold that an heir cannot be appointed under a penalty, for it is immaterial whether an heir is ordered to give a legacy if he do or do not do something, or a co-heir be joined with him, because he is as much compelled to do, or not to do, something against his will by the addition of a co-heir as by the giving of a legacy.

* § 229, 232, 233.

have amended this portion of the law, not only in respect of inheritances, but also as to legacies and bequests in trust; and this will clearly appear from the constitution itself. But not even by our constitution can an uncertain tutor be appointed, for a person is bound to take care to provide, in clear directions, for the guardianship of his posterity. § 28. But a posthumous stranger could formerly, and can now, be appointed heir, unless the child has been conceived by a woman whom, by our law, we cannot marry. § 29. Although a testator may have made a mistake as to the family name, surname, or christian name of the legatee, yet, if it is clear who the person is, the legacy is valid. The same holds good as to heirs, and properly so, for, since names were invented for the purpose of indicating persons, if they can be ascertained in some other way, it is of no consequence. § 30. Allied to this is that rule of law, that a legacy is not avoided by a false description, as, for instance, if a person left a legacy in this way: "I give and bequeath Stichus, born my slave", for, although Stichus was not born in his master's house, but had been bought, yet, if it is clear which slave it is, the legacy is valid. And, similarly, if he be pointed out thus: "The slave Stichus, whom I bought of Seius", and he was bought of somebody else, yet the legacy is good, if it is clear which slave is meant. § 31. Much less does a false reason invalidate a legacy, as, for example, when a person says this: "I give and bequeath Stichus to Titius, because he attended to my affairs during my absence," or thus: "I give and bequeath Stichus to Titius, because, by his defence of me, I was acquitted of a capital charge." For, although Titius never carried on the affairs of the testator, and though the testator was never acquitted through the advocacy of Titius, still the legacy is valid. But the rule is different if the reason is stated in the form of a condition, as, for example, thus: "I give and bequeath to Titius such an estate if he shall have attended to my affairs."

§ 244. The question has been raised whether we can properly leave a legacy to him who is in the power of him whom we have appointed heir. Servius thinks that a legacy can be legally so left, but that the legacy vanishes if the legatee, at the time when the right to the legacy begins to run, is still in power, and, therefore, whether the legacy be absolute, and the legatee cease to be in the power of the heir in the lifetime of the testator, or whether the legacy be subject to a condition, and before the accomplishment of the condition, that event has happened, the legacy is due. Sabinus and Cassius think that the legacy, subject to a condition, is valid, but not that given absolutely; for, although the legatee may cease to be in the power of the heir in the lifetime of the testator, yet that the legacy ought to be held invalid, because it would be absurd that what would have had no force if the testator had died immediately after making his testament, should become valid because his life has been lengthened out. The leaders of the opposite school think that even the legacy, subject to a condition, is invalid, because we cannot be any more indebted to those whom we have in our power conditionally than absolutely. § 245. On the other hand, it is clear that a legacy can be properly left to you through him who is in your power, if he be appointed heir; but, if you become heir through him, the legacy vanishes, because you cannot owe a legacy to yourself; but if the son should be emancipated, or the slave manumitted, or transferred to another, and he become heir, or has made another person heir, the legacy is due.

§ 32. The question has been raised whether a legacy can be properly left to the slave of the heir; and it is clear that such a legacy given absolutely is void, nor does it help matters if the slave should be freed from the power of the heir in the lifetime of the testator; for a legacy which would have been void if the testator had died immediately after the making of the testament, ought not to become valid because the testator happened to live longer. But he may properly leave a legacy subject to a condition, and then we must see whether, at the time when the right to the legacy began to run, the slave has ceased to be in the power of the heir. § 33. On the other hand, it is not doubted, but that, if a slave be appointed heir, a legacy may be properly left to his master, even unconditionally. For, though the testator should have died immediately after the making of the testament, still the right to the legacy does not immediately begin to run in favour of him who is heir; for the inheritance is separated from the legacy, and another person may become heir by means of that slave, if, before he has entered upon the inheritance by order of the master, he should be transferred to the power of another; or the slave himself, if manumitted, may become heir, in which cases the legacy is valid. But, if the slave should remain in the same condition, and should enter upon the inheritance by order of the legatee, the legacy vanishes.

Of legacies ineffectually bequeathed.

§ 229. A legacy placed before the appointment of the heir is void, because testaments derive their force from the appointment of the heir, and, on that account, the appointment of the heir is looked upon as being, as it were, the head and foundation of the whole testament. § 230. For a like reason, freedom cannot be given before the appointment of the heir. § 231. The leaders of our school hold that a tutor cannot be appointed in that part of the will; but Labeo and Proculus think that a tutor can be so given, as, by the appointment of a tutor, nothing is taken from the inheritance.

§ 232. A legacy is also void to take effect after the death of the heir, that is, made in this manner: "When my heir is dead, I give, I bequeath," or, "Let it be given". But a legacy is valid made in this way: "When the heir dies", because it is not left after the death of the heir, but at the last moment of his life. Again, a legacy cannot be made thus: "The day before my heir dies", but the adoption of this rule seems devoid of any reasonable ground. § 233. We wish to be understood as making the same remarks in respect of freedoms. § 234. But, to those inquiring whether a tutor can be given "after the death of the heir", perhaps the question will prove to be a matter for discussion, like that raised in the case of appointing tutors before the appointment of heirs.*

§ 34. Formerly, a legacy placed before the appointment of the heir was void, because testaments derive their force from the appointment of the heirs, and, on that account, the appointment of the heir is looked upon as being, as it were, the head and foundation of the whole testament. For a like reason, freedom could not be given before the appointment of the heir. But, since we have thought it unreasonable to follow the mere order of the writing (which the ancients themselves seem to have condemned), in defiance of the wishes of the testator, we have, by our constitution, also amended this defect, so that it is now lawful to give a legacy, and much more liberty, which is always favourably interpreted, not only before the appointment of the heir, but in between the appointments of heirs.

§ 35. A legacy, to take effect after the death of the heir or legatee, was also void; as if, for example, a person said this: "When my heir is dead, I give and bequeath", or thus: "The day before the death of the heir or legatee". But we have, in a similar way, corrected this matter, also, by giving all such legacies the same validity as bequests in trust, lest legacies should be found in this respect to be in a worse position than bequests in trust.

* *ante*, § 231.

Of legacies bequeathed by way of penalty.

§ 235. A legacy bequeathed by way of penalty is also void. A legacy is looked upon as left by way of a penalty which is bequeathed for the purpose of coercing the heir to do, or not to do, something; as, for example, a legacy bequeathed in this way: "If my heir gives his daughter in marriage to Titius, he shall give ten thousand sesterces to Seius"; or, thus: "If he does not give his daughter in marriage to Titius, he shall give ten thousand sesterces." So, also, if he orders a sum to be paid to Titius, if the heir has not, for example, raised, within two years, a monument to him, such a legacy is deemed to be by way of penalty; and, indeed, from the very definition of this sort of legacy, we can imagine many similar cases of the class. § 236. Nor can freedom be given by way of penalty, although this point has been doubted. § 237. But there can be no question as to the case of a tutor, because the heir cannot be forced, by the appointment of a tutor, to do, or not to do, anything; and, therefore, whenever a tutor is appointed by way of penalty, the appointment is looked upon as made rather subject to a condition than by way of penalty.

§ 36. So, formerly a legacy was void if given, revoked, or transferred by way of penalty. A legacy is looked upon as left by way of a penalty which is bequeathed for the purpose of coercing the heir to do, or not to do, something; as, for example, if a person write thus: "If my heir give his daughter in marriage to Titius" (or, on the contrary, "If he do not give her in marriage"), "let him give ten gold pieces to Seius"; or, if he had written thus: "If my heir alienates the slave Stichus"; (or, on the contrary, "If my heir does not alienate"), "let him pay ten gold pieces to Titius". And to such an extent was this rule observed, that it was laid down in many constitutions, that even the emperor would not receive a legacy which was given him by way of a penalty; nor was such a legacy valid, even in the testament of a soldier, although other wishes of soldiers expressed in their testaments were scrupulously followed. Hence, also, it was held that even freedom could not be given by way of a penalty; still less, in the opinion of Sabinus, could another heir be added by way of a penalty, as if, for example, a person said this: "Let Titius be heir, but if he give his daughter in marriage to Seius, let Seius also be heir"; for it was immaterial in what way Titius was coerced, whether by the giving of a legacy, or the addition of a co-heir. But scruples of this kind have not seemed to us desirable; and we have, therefore, settled generally as to things which are left, although so left, revoked, or transferred, by way of penalty, shall differ in no way from other legacies, whether given, revoked, or transferred, excepting of course legacies which are impossible, forbidden by law, or otherwise improper, for the manners of the age do not permit dispositions to be made by testators of such a character.

Title xxi. Of the revocation and transference of legacies.

The revocation of legacies made in the same testament, or in a codicil, is valid, whether the revocation is made by contrary words, as, for example, if that which a person had given thus: "I give and bequeath"; he revokes thus: "I do not give and do not bequeath"; or in terms not contradictory, that is, in any other form of words. § 1. A legacy may also be transferred from one person to another, as, for example, if a person said thus: "I give and bequeath to Seius the slave Stichus, whom I have given as a legacy to Titius", and this can be done in the same testament or in codicils; in which case the legacy is held to be at the same time taken from Titius and given to Seius.

Of the Falcidian law.

§ 224. Formerly, indeed, it was lawful to give away the whole patrimony in legacies and freedoms, leaving nothing to the heirs but the empty title of heir; and it was held that the law of the Twelve Tables* permitted this result, in that it provided, that what a person declared by testament concerning his property should be valid in these words: "The dispositions made by a deceased person as to his property are to be binding." Wherefore, those who were appointed heirs, abstained from the inheritance, and on that account many persons died intestate. § 225. In consequence of this the Furian law was passed, by which no one (with certain exceptions) could take more than the value of one thousand pound pieces of copper by way of legacy, or gift "mortis causa". But even this law failed in the object aimed at, for he who had, for example, the value of five thousand pound pieces of copper as his patrimony could, by leaving each of five persons the value of a thousand pound pieces of copper by way of legacy, take the whole from the heir. § 226. Hence, the Voconian law was subsequently passed, providing that no one should be able to take by way of legacy, or gift "mortis causa", more than the heirs. By this law

* see table v, law 3.

Title xxii. Of the Falcidian law.

It remains to discuss the provisions of the Falcidian law by which legacies received their latest limitations. For, as formerly, by the law of the Twelve Tables, the power of bequeathing by legacy was so unfettered that a person could even give away the whole patrimony in legacies (since by that law it was enacted that: "The dispositions made by a deceased person as to his property are to be binding"); it seemed necessary to restrain this power of bequeathing by legacy; and this was done for the sake of testators themselves, because on this account they frequently died intestate, the appointed heirs refusing to enter upon inheritances out of which they could derive little or no benefit. With this view the Furian

the heirs must clearly get something in every case; but a like defect lurked in it, for by distributing his patrimony amongst a number of legatees, a testator could leave so little to the heir, as to make it not worth while for the heir to gain so little to undertake the burdens of the entire inheritance. § 227. Therefore, the Falcidian law was passed, by which it is provided that it shall not be lawful to give away in legacies more than three-fourths; and hence it follows that the heir can get a fourth part of the inheritance; and this is the law now in force. § 228. As to the excessive licence in giving freedoms, it will be remembered, as we mentioned in the first commentary,* that this was restrained by the Fusian Caninian law.

* see 1, § 42.

law and the Voconian law were passed; but as neither of these appeared sufficient to attain the desired end, finally, the Falcidian law was passed, by which it is provided that it shall not be lawful to give more in legacies than three-fourths of the whole property; so that whether there be one or more heirs appointed, there must remain to him or them a fourth part.

§ 1. And since the question has been raised, whether, when two heirs are appointed, as, for example, Titius and Seius; and the share of Titius in the inheritance is either entirely exhausted or heavily burdened with legacies expressly charged upon him, while Seius is either wholly free, or his share diminished only up to half, then, since Seius gets a fourth part or more of the whole inheritance, will it not be lawful for Titius to retain anything out of the legacies charged upon his share? It has been decided that he is entitled to have a fourth of his share intact; for the rule laid down by the Falcidian law is to be applied to the case of each heir separately. § 2. For the application of the rule laid down by the Falcidian law the value of the estate at the time of the testator's death is looked to, so that, for example, if he who has a patrimony of one hundred gold pieces as his property, should have left the hundred gold pieces in legacies, it will not benefit the legatees, though before the inheritance is entered upon there should be by the acquisitions of slaves, the offspring of female slaves, or the young of cattle, such an increase in the value of the inheritance that after the hundred gold pieces have been taken away from the heir under the name of legacies, the heir would still have a fourth part of the inheritance, but a fourth part of the legacies is, nevertheless, to be deducted. On the other hand, if seventy-five have been given in legacies, and before the inheritance is entered upon, the estate should be diminished to such an extent by, perchance, fire, shipwreck, or the death of slaves, that not more, or even less than seventy-five gold pieces in value remain, still the whole legacies are due;

and this state of things is not prejudicial to the heir, since he need not enter upon the inheritance; the result being that the legatees have to come to terms with the heir as to the share of the inheritance he is to retain, otherwise by the abandonment of the inheritance they would get nothing. § 3. In order that the rule laid down by the Falcidian law may be applied, debts, funeral expenses, and the value of freed slaves, are first deducted, then, the rule is applied to the residue in such a way that a fourth part of that residue remains for the heir, and the other three parts are distributed amongst the legatees in proportion, of course, to the amount of their legacies. Hence, suppose that four hundred gold pieces have been given in legacies, and that the value of the patrimony out of which the legacies are to be paid is four hundred, then a fourth part must be deducted from the share of each legatee; but if we suppose that the legacies amount to three hundred and fifty, then an eighth is to be deducted. And if five hundred have been given in legacies, first, a fifth, and then a fourth must be deducted, for a deduction must first be made of the amount exceeding the value of the property, and then that which must remain with the heir.

Title xxiii. Of inheritances bequeathed in trust.

§ 246. Now let us pass to bequests in trust. § 247. And, first, as to inheritances.

Let us now pass to bequests in trust; and, first, let us deal with inheritances bequeathed in trust.

§ 1. Now, it must be understood that, originally, all bequests in trust were ineffectual, for no one could be compelled, against his will, to do that which he was only requested to attend to. When testators wished to leave an inheritance or legacies to persons to whom they could not do so, if they did leave them, they entrusted them to the good faith of those who could take under the testament; and, therefore, they were called bequests in trust, because they rested on no legal obligation, but only on the honour of those who were asked to carry them out. Subsequently, the late Emperor Augustus, being moved over and over again by consideration for the parties involved, or because he who was asked had promised, by the oath of the emperor's welfare, or on account of some striking cases of perfidy, ordered the consuls to intervene with their authority. As this seemed just and popular, the authority of the consuls gradually assumed the character of a regular jurisdiction, and bequests in trust grew into such favour that, after a time, a special prætor was appointed to adjudicate in these matters, and he was called the prætor for bequests in trust.

§ 248. In the first place, then, it is necessary to know that some one must be duly and legally appointed heir, and it must be entrusted to his good faith to hand over the inheritance to another, for otherwise a testament is ineffectual in which no one is duly and legally appointed heir. § 250. When, therefore, we have written "Lucius Titius be heir", we may add, "I ask you, Lucius Titius, and I beg you, as soon as you can enter on my inheritance, to hand it over and restore it to Gaius Seius". We can also ask that a portion be handed over, and there is full liberty to make bequests in trust, conditionally or absolutely, or from a certain time. § 251. Still, after the inheritance has been handed over, he who has handed it over nevertheless remains heir; but he who receives the inheritance is sometimes in the place of an heir, sometimes in that of a legatee.

§ 2. In the first place, it is necessary to know that some one must be duly and legally appointed heir in the testament; and it must be entrusted to his good faith to hand over the inheritance to another; for otherwise a testament is ineffectual in which no one is appointed heir. When, therefore, a person had written, "Lucius Titius, be heir," he could add, "I ask you, Lucius Titius, as soon as you can enter upon my inheritance, to hand it over and restore it to Gaius Seius". A person can also ask the heir to hand over a portion, and there is full liberty to make a bequest in trust absolutely or conditionally, or from a certain time. § 3. After the inheritance is handed over, he who has handed it over, nevertheless, remains heir. But he who receives the inheritance was sometimes looked upon as an heir, and sometimes he occupied the place of a legatee.

§ 252. But formerly he was neither in the place of an heir nor in that of a legatee, but rather in that of a purchaser; for it was then the custom for him (to whom the inheritance was restored) to, for form's sake, purchase it with a single piece of money; and those stipulations were entered into between the heir and him to whom the inheritance was restored, which were customary between the vendor and the purchaser of an inheritance; that is, in this way: the heir stipulated, from him to whom he restored the inheritance, that he should be personally indemnified as to all that he might have to give as heir, whether he was compelled to do so, or had done it bona fide, and that in any event he should be properly protected if anyone sued him in respect of the inheritance; and he who received the inheritance in his turn stipulated that, if anything belonging to the inheritance should come to the hands of the heir, it should be given up to himself, and that he should be suffered to conduct actions relating to the inheritance as the procurator or cognitor of the heir.

§ 253. But subsequently, in the time of Nero, and in the consulship of Trebellius Maximus and Annæus Seneca, a decree of the senate was passed, by which it is provided that, if an inheritance should have been handed over by reason of a bequest in trust, the actions which, by the civil law, are available to, and lie against, the heir, should be given to, and lie against, him to whom the inheritance had been handed over by reason of a bequest in trust. After this decree of the senate, these securities, by way of stipulations, ceased to be in use; for the prætor began to give equitable actions to and against him who received the inheritance, just as to and against an heir, and forms adapted to the case are set out in the edict. § 254. But again, since the appointed heirs, when requested to hand over the whole, or usually nearly the whole, inheritance, refused to enter upon it on account of the little or no benefit to be derived from it, and thus the bequests in trust failed, therefore, subsequently, in the time of the Emperor Vespasian, in the consulship of Pegasus and Pusio, the senate decreed that it should be lawful for him, who was asked to hand over an inheritance, to retain a fourth part, just as he is entitled to do by the Falcidian law, in respect of legacies, and the same right of retention is granted the heir in respect of separate things bequeathed in trust. By this decree of the senate, the heir himself sustains the burdens of the inheritance; but he who receives the residue of the inheritance by reason of the bequest in trust, is in the position of a legatee of part, that is to say, of a legatee to whom a portion of the whole property is bequeathed.

§ 4. In the time of the Emperor Nero, and in the consulship of Trebellius Maximus and Annæus Seneca, a decree of the senate was passed, by which it is provided that, if an inheritance should have been handed over by reason of a bequest in trust, all actions which, by the civil law, are available to, or lie against, the heir, should be given to, and against him, to whom the inheritance was handed over by reason of the bequest in trust. After this decree of the senate, the prætor began to give equitable actions to and against him who received the inheritance, as if to and against the heir. § 5. But, since the appointed heirs, when they were asked to hand over the whole, or, usually, nearly the whole inheritance, refused to enter upon it on account of the little or no benefit to be derived from it, and thus the bequests in trust failed. Subsequently, in the time of the Emperor Vespasian, in the consulship of Pegasus and Pusio, the senate decreed that it should be lawful for him, who was asked to hand over an inheritance, to retain a fourth part, just as he is entitled to do by the Falcidian law in respect of legacies, and the same right of retention is granted the heir in respect of separate things bequeathed in trust. After this decree of the senate, the heir himself sustained the burdens of the inheritance; and he who received a part of the inheritance, by reason of the bequest in trust, was in the position of a legatee of part, that is, a legatee to whom a portion of the whole property was bequeathed. This kind of legacy is called a share legacy, because the legatee shared the inheritance with the heir. Hence those stipulations, which were customary be-

This kind of legacy is called a share legacy, because the legatee shares the inheritance with the heir; and the result was that those stipulations, which were customary between an heir and a legatee of part, were interposed between him who receives the inheritance by reason of a bequest in trust, and the heir, that is, that both the profit and loss resulting from the inheritance should be borne by them in proportion to their respective shares. § 255. Therefore, if the appointed heir is not asked to hand over more than three-fourths of the inheritance, then he hands it over by virtue of the Trebellian decree of the senate, and actions relating to the inheritance are given against both in proportion to their respective shares, those against the heir according to the civil law, but those against him who receives the inheritance according to the Trebellian decree of the senate; although the heir, even for that part which he has handed over, remains heir, and actions as to the whole inheritance lie for and against him; but he is not burdened, nor are actions given to him, beyond the value of the portion of the inheritance which remains to him. § 256. But, if a person is asked to hand over more than three-fourths, or even the whole inheritance, the Pegasian decree of the senate comes into play. § 257. But he who has once entered upon the inheritance, if only he has done so voluntarily, whether he has, or has not, retained a fourth part, takes upon himself the whole burden of the inheritance; but, after having retained a fourth part, stipulations analogous to those termed "for his and for your part", should be interposed, as if between a legatee of a share legacy and the heir; but, if he has handed over the whole inheritance, stipulations analogous to those on the sale and purchase of an in-

tween the heir and the legatee of a share-legacy, were interposed between him who received the inheritance, by reason of a bequest in trust, and the heir, that is, that the profit and loss arising out of the inheritance should be shared between them in proportion to their respective interests. § 6. Therefore, if the appointed heir was not asked to hand over more than three-fourths of the inheritance, then the inheritance was handed over by virtue of the Trebellian decree of the senate, and actions relating to the inheritance were given against both, according to their respective shares—against the heir, however, by the civil law, but against him who received the inheritance by the Trebellian decree of the senate, as if against an heir. But, if he was asked to hand over more than three-fourths, or even the whole inheritance, then the Pegasian decree of the senate applied; and the heir who had once entered on the inheritance, provided he had done so voluntarily, whether he had or had not retained the fourth part, was obliged to sustain the whole burdens of the inheritance. But, when the heir did retain a fourth, then stipulations, analogous to those termed "for his and for your part", were entered into, as if between a legatee of a share legacy and the heir; but, if the heir handed over the whole inheritance, then stipulations analogous to those on the sale and purchase of an inheritance were entered into. But if the appointed heir refuse to enter upon the inheritance, on the ground that he is suspi-

heritance are to be entered into. § 258. But, if the appointed heir refuse to enter upon the inheritance, on the ground that he is suspicious that it would prove a loss to him, it is provided by the Pegasian decree of the senate, that, on the demand of him to whom he had been asked to hand over the inheritance, he should, by order of the prætor, enter upon the inheritance and hand it over, after which actions may be given to and against him who receives the inheritance, as if it were a case falling under the Trebellian decree of the senate, and, in this case, no stipulations are needed, for security is afforded at the same time both to him who hands it over, and the actions relating to the inheritance are transferred to, and against, him who has received the inheritance.

cious that it would prove a loss to him, the Pegasian decree of the senate provided that, on the demand of him to whom he had been asked to hand over the inheritance, he should enter, by order of the prætor, upon the inheritance, and hand it over, after which all actions would be given to and against him who received the inheritance, as if it were a case falling under the Trebellian decree of the senate, and, in this case, no stipulations are needed, for security is afforded at the same sime both to him who hands over the inheritance, and the actions relating to the inheritance are transferred to, and against, him who receives the inheritance, both decrees of the senate here applying concurrently.

§ 7. But, since the stipulations arising out of the Pegasian decree of the senate, were not satisfactory even to the ancients themselves, and in some cases are, by that man of great intellect, Papinian, considered to be dangerous; and, as we prefer simplicity rather than difficulty in law, therefore it has pleased us, after having had our attention drawn to all the points of agreement and difference in the two decrees of the senate, to reject the Pegasian decree of the senate, which was subsequent in time, and to give full force to the Trebellian decree of the senate, so that all inheritances bequeathed in trust shall now be handed over by virtue of the latter decree, whether the heir takes, by the wishes of the testator, a fourth, or more or less, or even nothing. So that, however, when either nothing, or less than a fourth, is left to him, he may, by our authority, retain either a fourth, or as much as will make up the deficiency, or demand repayment of it if he has paid it over, and actions are to lie both against the heir and the recipient of the trust inheritance, according to their respective shares, as if under the Trebellian decree of the senate. But, should the heir voluntarily hand over the whole inheritance, all actions relating to the inheritance are available to, or lie against, the recipient of the trust inheritance. And, as to the main point in the Pegasian decree of the senate, viz., that when the appointed heir refused to enter upon the inheritance which had been given him, he was under the necessity of handing over the whole inheritance at the request of the person beneficially entitled, and that all actions were transferred to and against him; this provision we have introduced into the Trebellian decree of the senate, so that, by it alone, the obligation is imposed upon the heir, if, when he is unwilling to enter upon the inheritance, the person beneficially entitled desires that the inheritance should be handed over to him, the heir in this case incurring neither gain nor loss.

§ 259. But it makes no difference whether a person, who is appointed heir for the whole, is asked to hand over the whole or a part of the inheritance, or whether an heir, appointed for a part, is asked to hand over the whole of that part, or a part of it, for in such a case, also, it is customary to apply the rule laid down by the Pegasian decree of the senate as to the retention of the fourth part of that part.

§ 8. But it makes no difference whether a person, who is appointed heir for the whole, is asked to hand over the whole or a part of the inheritance, or whether an heir, appointed for a part, is asked to hand over the whole of that part, or a part of it, as we desire the same rules to be followed which we have laid down in the case of the handing over of the whole inheritance.

§ 9. If a person is asked to hand over an inheritance after first taking or deducting some particular thing, equivalent to a fourth, as, for example, an estate or other thing, he will hand it over under the Trebellian decree of the senate, just as if he had been asked to hand over the remainder of an inheritance, after retaining one fourth. But there is this difference, that in the one case, that is, when the inheritance is handed over after deducting, or first taking, a particular thing, then, according to that decree of the senate, all actions are transferred, and the thing which remains with the heir is free from all charge in respect of the inheritance, just as if he had acquired it by way of legacy. But, in the other case, that is, when the heir is asked to hand over the inheritance, retaining his fourth part, and he does hand it over, the actions divide, and, in respect of three-fourths, pass to the recipient of the trust inheritance, whilst those affecting the one-fourth remain with the heir; and hence, although a person is asked to hand over an inheritance, first taking or deducting some particular thing, which comprises the largest part of the inheritance, still all actions are transferred to the recipient of the trust inheritance, and he to whom the inheritance is to be handed over should, therefore, deliberate whether it is advisable to have it handed over to him. The same remarks, of course, apply if the heir is asked to hand over the inheritance, after first taking or deducting two or more particular things, and the same rule holds in the case of the heir being asked to hand over the inheritance, after first taking or deducting a certain sum of money, which may be a fourth or even the greatest part of the inheritance. What we have said of him who is appointed heir for the whole inheritance, is to be held to apply also to him who is appointed heir for a part.

§ 10. Moreover, a person who is about to die intestate, may ask him on whom he sees his property will devolve, either by the civil or prætorian law, to hand over to another his whole inheritance, or a part of it, or any particular thing, as, for example, an estate, a slave, a sum of money: whereas legacies are only valid when given by testament. § 11. So he may ask him, to whom anything is handed over again, to hand over the whole or part of it to another, or even to hand over something else. § 12. As bequests in trust at the outset depended on the good faith of heirs, and so derived their name and essence, the late Emperor Augustus rendered them binding in law, and we, striving to surpass that prince, have recently—on account of a case brought to our notice by Tribonian, that eminent man and quæstor of our sacred palace—caused a constitution to be drawn up, by which we have enacted that, if a testator has entrusted to the good faith of his heir the handing over of the inheritance, or any particular bequest in trust, and evidence of the trust is not forthcoming, either by a writing or by five witnesses, which is the legal number required in matters of bequest in trust, but either fewer than, or no witnesses at all, were present, then, whether it is the father of the heir, or anyone else who has trusted to the good faith of the heir, and desired him to hand over anything, if the heir, incited by dishonesty, refuse to fulfil the trust, denying that anything of the kind occurred, the person beneficially entitled, having previously himself sworn to his own good faith, may put him on his oath, and so compel him either to take an oath that he never received any such directions from the testator, or, on his refusing to take the oath, he may be compelled to hand over to the person beneficially entitled the whole inheritance, or any particular thing, so that the last wishes of a testator, entrusted to the good faith of the heir, may not be frustrated. We have decreed that the same rules are to be observed in the case of something being left in the same way to a legatee or to a recipient of a bequest in trust; and, if anyone to whom such a trust has been committed, admits that something was so left, but relies upon defeating it by the subtleties of the law, he is to be compelled, in any event, to hand over the property.

Title xxiv. Of specific things bequeathed by way of trust.

§ 260. A person may also bequeath specific things by way of trust, as, for example, an estate, a slave, a garment, silver, or money; and ask either the heir himself, or the legatee, to hand it over to another; though a legatee cannot be charged with a legacy. § 261. And not only the testator's own property may be so bequeathed by way of trust, but also that of the heir, or of the legatee, or of any other person. Hence, a legatee may not only be asked to hand over to another that which has been left to him, as a legacy, but any other thing, whether it is the property of the legatee or of another. But it must be noted that no one can be asked to hand over to others more than he himself has taken under the testament, for the bequest as to the excess is void. § 262. And when the property of another is left by way of bequest in trust, the person who is asked to hand it over must either purchase the thing itself from the owner and hand it over, or pay its value, just as is the rule of law when a legacy of another person's property has been made by way of ordering the heir to give it to the legatee,* though some are of opinion, that if the owner of the thing bequeathed by way of trust will not sell it, the bequest in trust fails, which is not the case with a legacy by way of ordering the heir to give it to the legatee.

* *ante*, § 202.

A person may also bequeath specific things by way of trust, as, for example, an estate, a slave, a garment, silver, or pieces of money; and ask either the heir himself, or the legatee, to hand it over to another; though a legatee cannot be charged with a legacy. § 1. A testator may not only leave, by way of bequest in trust, his own property, but also that of the heir, of the legatee, of the recipient of a bequest in trust, or of any other person. Hence, a legatee, or recipient of a bequest in trust may not only be asked to hand over what has been left to him, but other property, whether his own or belonging to somebody else. But it must be noted that no one can be asked to hand over to another more than he has himself taken under the testament, for the bequest as to the excess is void. And when the property of another is left by way of bequest in trust, the person who is asked to hand it over must either purchase the thing itself from the owner and hand it over, or pay its value.

§ 263. Freedom may also be given to a slave by way of bequest in trust; as either the heir or a legatee may be asked to manumit him. § 264. And it is immaterial whether the testator ask this in respect of his own slave, or of the slave of his heir, or of a legatee, or of a stranger. § 265. Therefore, a slave belonging to another must be bought and manumitted. But if the owner refuse to sell him, the liberty given by way of bequest in trust fails, because in such a case there is no means of computing the value. § 266. But he who is manumitted by reason of a bequest in trust does not, however, become the freedman of the testator, even although he was the testator's own slave; but he becomes the freedman of the manumittor. § 267. But he who is ordered to be free directly from the testament, for example, thus: "Stichus, my slave, be free"; or, "I order my slave, Stichus, to be free", becomes the freedman of the testator; and no other slave can have his liberty directly by testament than he who was the property of the testator by the law of the quirites, both at the time when the testator made his testament, and at the time of his death.

§ 249. The proper words for bequests in trust, and those usually employed are: "I beg"; "I ask"; "I wish"; "I commit to your good faith"; and each word is as binding separately as if all were used together.

§ 2. Freedom may also be given to a slave by way of bequest in trust as the heir, or a legatee, or the recipient of a bequest in trust may be asked to manumit him. And it is immaterial whether the testator ask this in respect of his own slave, or of the slave of his heir, or of a legatee, or of a stranger; and, therefore, the slave of another must be bought and manumitted. But if the owner refuse to sell him, which he can only do if he has taken no benefit under the will of him who gave the freedom, then the freedom so given by way of trust is not defeated, but only deferred, as an opportunity may arise in the course of time of purchasing and freeing the slave. He who is manumitted by reason of a bequest in trust does not, however, become the freedman of the testator, even though he was the testator's own slave; but he becomes the freedman of the manumittor. But he who is ordered to be free directly from the testament, becomes the freedman of that testator, and is called "liberated by testament"; and no other slave can have his liberty directly by testament, than he who was the property of the testator, both at the time when the testator made his testament, and at the time of his death. Liberty is held to be given directly, when a testator does not ask that the slave may be manumitted by another, but wishes the freedom to result as it were from his testament.

§ 3. The words usually employed for bequests in trust are these: "I beg"; "I ask"; "I wish"; "I entrust"; "I commit to your good faith"; and each word is as binding separately as if all were used together.

§ 268. The things which may be bequeathed in trust differ much from those which are left in the ordinary legal form. § 269. For it is possible for an inheritance to be bequeathed in trust, even by a nod;

whereas, a legacy is void unless given by testament. § 270. Again, he who is about to die intestate, can charge him upon whom his property devolves with a bequest in trust for a third person, whereas he could not so charge him with a legacy. § 270A. Again, a legacy left by a codicil is not valid unless it has been confirmed by the testator, that is, unless the testator has declared in his testament that whatever he shall have written in his codicils is to be ratified, but a bequest in trust may be left by a codicil, although not confirmed. § 271. Again, a legacy cannot be charged upon a legatee, but a bequest in trust may be so left.* Hence, we can even again charge him to whom we have made a bequest in trust with a bequest in trust in favour of another. § 272. Again, freedom cannot be given directly to the slave of another, but it can be done by way of bequest in trust.† § 273. Again, no one can be appointed heir, nor disinherited by a codicil, even though confirmed by a testament; but he who is appointed heir by the testament may be asked in a codicil to hand over either the whole or a part of the inheritance to another, although the codicils have not been confirmed by testament. § 274. Again, a woman who, according to the Voconian law, cannot be appointed heir by anyone who is inscribed in the census as possessing property to the value of one hundred thousand pounds of copper pieces, may yet take by way of bequest in trust the inheritance left to her. § 275. Latins also, who, by the Junian law, cannot by the direct process of law take either inheritances or legacies,‡ can take by way of bequest in trust. § 276. Again, although a decree of the senate forbids the freeing of one's own slave, who is under thirty years of age by testament, and the appointment of him as heir;** yet it is the opinion of the majority that we can order him to be free when he is thirty years of age, and ask that, then, the inheritance may be handed over to him. § 277. Again, although we cannot appoint another as heir after the death of him who has actually been our heir;†† still we can ask him when he dies to hand over to another either the whole or part of the inheritance; and, since a bequest in trust can also be given after the death of the heir, so we can even effectually engraft a trust if we write this: "When my heir, Titius, is dead, I wish my inheritance to belong to Publius Mævius." In both ways, as well by the latter as the former, he leaves his heir Titius bound to carry out the bequest in trust. § 278. Further, we sue for legacies by formula;

* *ante*, § 260, 261.

† *ante*, § 264, 267.

‡ *ante*, i, § 23, 24.

** *ante*, i, § 18, 21.

†† *ante*, § 184.

but we claim bequests in trust at Rome before the consul, or before that prætor who has special jurisdiction in respect of bequests in trust; and in the provinces before the president of the province. § 279. Again, the law affecting bequests in trust may be declared at Rome at any time, but in respect of legacies only during the authorised sittings of the courts. § 280. In the case of bequests in trust he who delays handing over the property bequeathed in trust is liable for interest and produce; but interest is not due on legacies, and this is so laid down in a rescript of the late Emperor Hadrian. I am, however, aware that, according to Julianus, in respect of a legacy left by way of directing the heir to suffer the legatee to take it, the same rule of law applied as in the case of bequests in trust; and I see that even now-a-days this is considered the better opinion. § 281. Again, legacies written in Greek are invalid; but bequests in trust so expressed are valid. § 282. Again, if the heir deny that a legacy has been left by way of ordering him to give it to the legatee, the action brought against him is for double the amount, but the prosecution of bequests in trust is always restricted to the simple amount. § 283. Again, that which a person has by mistake paid over and above what was due, under a bequest in trust, can be recovered back again; but the excess erroneously paid on a legacy left by way of ordering the heir to give it to the legatee cannot be reclaimed. The same rule, of course, applies to a legacy not due, but which, by a mistake, arising from some cause or other, has been paid over.

§ 284. There were also other differences which do not now exist. § 285. As, for example, aliens could take bequests in trust, and probably this was the origin of bequests in trust, but subsequently this was put a stop to; and now, in consequence of the decree of the senate, passed at the instance of the late Emperor Hadrian, such bequests in trust are claimed by the imperial treasury. § 286. Unmarried persons also, who are forbidden by the Julian law to take the inheritances and legacies of others,* appear formerly to have been able to take bequests in trust. So, also, childless persons who by the Papian law, on account of not having children, lose half of inheritances and legacies, were able, it seems, formerly to take the whole by way of bequest in trust; but subsequently, by the Pegasian decree of the senate, they also were not allowed to take bequests in trust any more than legacies and inheritances, and these

* *ante*, § 111.

bequests in trust were transferred to those persons named in the testament who had children,* or if none of them had children, then to the state; just as is the law in respect of those legacies and inheritances which, on these or similar grounds, lapse. § 287. Again, bequests in trust could formerly be left in favour of an uncertain person, or a posthumous stranger, although he could not be appointed heir, or take a legacy.† But, by a decree of the senate, passed by the authority of the late Emperor Hadrian, the same rule was established for bequests in trust as for legacies and inheritances. § 288. Again, there is no doubt that now a bequest in trust cannot be left by way of a penalty.‡ § 289. But although in many branches of the law the latitude allowed to bequests in trust, is far greater than that permitted in the case of direct bequests, and in others stands on the same footing; yet a tutor cannot be appointed otherwise than directly by testament, as, for example, thus: "Titius be tutor to my children"; or, thus: "I give Titius as tutor to my children."** But he could not be appointed by way of bequest in trust.

* *ante*, § 206, 207.

† *ante*, § 238, 241.

‡ *ante*, § 235.

** *ante*, i, § 149.

Title xxv. Of codicils.

It is clear that the law relating to codicils was not established before the time of Augustus, as the introduction of them is due to Lucius Lentulus (to whom the origin of bequests in trust is also to be attributed), for when on the point of death in Africa, he wrote certain codicils, confirmed by his testament, by which he begged Augustus by way of bequest in trust to do something for him, and as the emperor carried out his wishes, other persons subsequently followed his example, and gave effect to bequests in trust; and the daughter of Lentulus paid over legacies which, legally speaking, she was not liable for. It is said, moreover, that Augustus called the jurisconsults together, and among them Trebatius, who had the greatest reputation at that time, and asked whether this innovation could be admitted, and whether the use of codicils was inconsistent with the principles of law; and it is said that Trebatius persuaded Augustus to admit them, asserting that they were most useful, and necessary to citizens on account of the lengthy journeys which they had at that time to take, during which, if a person could not make a testament, yet he might be able to make codicils. In later times when Labeo himself made codicils, no further doubt was felt, but that codicils should acquire complete validity.

§ 1. Not only can a person who has already made his testament make codicils, but a person also dying intestate may make bequests in trust by means of codicils. But when the codicils had been made before the testament, Papinian gave it as his opinion that they should not be valid unless subsequently specially confirmed. The late Emperors Severus and Antoninus, however, decided by rescript, that a bequest in trust made in a codicil, which preceded the testament, might be demanded, if it should appear that he who afterwards made the testament had not abandoned the intention expressed in the codicils. § 2. But an inheritance can neither be given nor taken away by codicils, otherwise the rules relating to testaments and codicils would be confounded, and, therefore, no heir can be disinherited by codicils. It is, however, only directly that an inheritance cannot either be given or taken away by codicils, for the inheritance may be lawfully left in codicils by way of bequest in trust. Nor can a condition be added by codicil to the appointment of the heir, nor a direct substitution made. § 3. But a person may even make several codicils, and they are not subject to any formalities as to the mode of making them.

INSTITUTES

OF

GAIUS, COMMENTARY III. JUSTINIAN, BOOK III.

Title i. Of intestate succession.

He dies intestate who has not made any testament, or not one according to law; or when the testament he has made has been revoked or become useless, or no one has become heir under it.

§ 1. According to the law of the Twelve Tables, the inheritances of intestates belong, in the first place, to the heirs succeeding as being co-owners of the patrimony. § 2. Now, those children are regarded as such heirs, as we have stated above,* who were in the power of the deceased at the time of his death, as, for example, a son or daughter, a grandson or granddaughter by a son, a great grandson or great granddaughter a descendant of a grandson born of a son, and it is immateral whether they are actual or adopted children.

§ 1. According to the law of the Twelve Tables, the inheritances of intestates belong, in the first place, to the heirs succeeding as being co-owners of the patrimony. § 2. Now, those are regarded as such heirs, as we have stated above,† who were in the power of the deceased at the time of his death, as, for example, a son or daughter, a grandson or granddaughter by a son, a great grandson or great granddaughter a descendant of a grandson born of a son; and it is immaterial whether they are actual or adopted children. We must also reckon among such heirs those who are not the offspring of a lawful marriage, but who have acquired the rights of such heirs by reason of their having been given to the senate of their cities; according to the tenor of those imperial constitutions enacted on this subject, and also those who are included in the constitutions of our own, by which we have ordained that, if a person has cohabited with a woman, not at the outset with any desire of marrying her, but with whom he could intermarry, and has had children by her, and subsequently impelled by affection has gone through the forms of marriage with her, and has had sons or daughters, not only are those born after the settlement of the dowry to be legitimate, and in the power of their father, but also those born previously who were the cause of the legitimacy of the children born subse-

* *ante*, II, § 156.

† *ante*, II, tit. 19, § 2.

quently. And this rule is to hold good, although no children are born subsequent to the execution of the dowry deed, or those born have all departed this life.

But a grandson or granddaughter, a great grandson or great granddaughter, are only reckoned amongst this class of heirs if the person who precedes them has ceased to be in the power of the ascendant, whether this arises from his death or from some other ground, as, for example, by emancipation; for if, when a person dies, his son is in his power, his grandson, by that son, cannot be such an heir; and this rule applies to the case of other descendants, ad infinitum. § 3. A wife, also, who is in the marital power of her husband, is one of this class of heirs, because she occupies the place of a daughter; so, also, a daughter-in-law, who is in the marital power of a son, for she occupies the place of a granddaughter;* but she will only be such an heiress if the son, in whose marital power she is when the father dies, is not in his power. The same rule holds as to her who is, by marriage, in the marital power of a grandson, because she occupies the place of a great granddaughter.

* *ante*, ii, § 159.

But a grandson or granddaughter, a great grandson or great granddaughter, are only reckoned amongst the class of heirs succeeding as being co-owners of the patrimony if the person who precedes them has ceased to be in the power of the ascendant, whether this arises from his death or from some other ground, as, for example, by emancipation; for if, when a person dies, his son is in his power, his grandson, by that son, cannot be such an heir; and this rule applies to the case of other descendants, ad infinitum.

§ 4. Posthumous children, also, who, if they had been born in the lifetime of their ascendant, would have been in his power, are heirs of this class. § 5. The same rule holds as to those in whose name, after the death of the father, cause has been shown, in accordance with the Ælian Sentian law, or the decree of the senate; for, if cause had been shown in the lifetime of the father, they would have been in his power.* § 6. We take it that this rule applies also to a son, who, after the death of his father, is manumitted after a first or a second formal sale.

* *ante*, i, § 67, etc.

Posthumous children, also, who, if they had been born in the lifetime of their ascendants, would have been in his power, are heirs of this class. § 3. Heirs of this class become so even without their knowledge, and may be such although they are insane; for, in those cases in which we can acquire without our knowledge, in all such cases lunatics can acquire, and, immediately on the death of the ascendant, the ownership is, as it were, continued, and, therefore, there is no necessity for the pupil to have the authority of a tutor, as the inheritance is acquired by heirs of this class, even without their knowledge; nor does a lunatic acquire it by the consent of his curator, but by operation of law. § 4. Sometimes, however, although an heir of this class is not in power at the time of the death, yet he becomes such an heir of his ascendant, as, for example, if a person returns from captivity after the death of his father, for this is the result of the law restoring rights on return. § 5. On the other hand, it may happen that, although a person was in the family of the deceased at the time of his death, he does not become such an heir, as, for example, if the father, after his decease, is condemned as guilty of treason, and his memory is thus rendered infamous, for he then cannot have such an heir, as the imperial treasury is his successor; but it may be said that there was such an heir by operation of law, but that he ceases to be such.

§ 7. When, therefore, there is a son or daughter, and, at the same time, grandsons or granddaughters by another son, they are all equally called to the inheritance; nor does the nearer in degree exclude the more remote, for it seemed equitable that grandsons or granddaughters should succeed to the place and share of their father. For the same reason, if there is a grandson or granddaughter by a son, or a great grandson or great granddaughter by a grandson, all are called together to the inheritance. § 8. And, since it was held that grandsons or granddaughters, and also great grandsons and great granddaughters, should succeed in the place of their ascendant, it seemed equitable that the inheritance should be divided, not according to individuals, but according to representation; so that the son takes one-half of the inheritance and the two or more grandsons by the other son the other half. So, if there are grandsons by two sons, one, or perhaps two, by one son, three or four by the other son, one-half belongs to the one or the two, and the other half to the three or the four.

§ 6. When there is a son or daughter, and, at the same time, a grandson or granddaughter by another son, they are all equally called to the inheritance of their ancestor; nor does the nearer in degree exclude the more remote; for it seems equitable that grandsons or granddaughters should succeed in the place of their father. For the same reason, if there is a grandson or granddaughter by a son, and a great grandson or great granddaughter by a grandson, they are all called together. And, since it is held that grandsons and granddaughters, as well as great grandsons and great granddaughters, are to succeed in the place of their ascendants, it seemed to follow that inheritances should be divided, not according to individuals, but according to representation; so that the son takes one-half of the inheritance and the two or more grandchildren by the other son the other half. So, if there are grandchildren by two sons, one or two, perhaps, by the one, and three or four by the other, half will belong to the one or the two, and the other half to the three or the four.

§ 7. The time to inquire whether anyone is an heir succeeding as being a co-owner of the patrimony, is when it is certain that the deceased died without a testament, which will include the case of the testament being abandoned. Hence, if a son should be disinherited, and a stranger appointed heir, and after the death of the son it becomes certain that the heir appointed by the testament will not be heir, either because he is unwilling to be heir, or because he is unable to be such, then the grandson becomes heir to his grandfather, as being co-owner of the patrimony, because, at the time when it is certain that the head of the family has died intestate, there is only the grandson existing, and of this rule there can be no question. § 8. And, although he be born after the death of the grandfather, yet, if he were conceived in the lifetime of the grandfather, he becomes such an heir if his father is dead, and the testament of the grandfather abandoned. But clearly, if he was both conceived and born after the death of the grandfather, he could not be such an heir to his grandfather, although his father died and the testament of the grandfather was subsequently abandoned, because he is not connected with his father's father by any tie of relationship. Similarly, he is not included amongst the descendants of the grandfather, whom an emancipated son has adopted. And, as these classes of persons are not descendants as regards the inheritance, so they cannot demand possession of the property on the ground of being, as it were, the nearest relations.* Thus much concerning heirs who succeed as being co-owners of the patrimony.

* *post*, tit. ix, § 3, 4.

§ 9. Emancipated children have no claim by the civil law, and are not heirs succeeding as being co-owners of the patrimony, because they have ceased to be in the power of their ascendant, nor are they called on any other ground, according to the law of the Twelve Tables. But the prætor, prompted by natural equity, gives them the possession of the property, on the ground of being descendants, just as if they had been in the power of their ascendant at the time of his death, and this, whether they are alone or competing with heirs who are taking as being co-owners of the patrimony. Therefore, if there are two children, the surviving one of whom was emancipated, and the other in power at the death of the ascendant, then, indeed, he who was in power is the only heir by the civil law; that is, he alone is an heir succeeding as being a co-owner of the patrimony; but, as the emancipated son, by the instrumentality of the prætor, is admitted to a share, the first-named heir becomes heir only of a share. § 10. But those who, after emancipation, have given themselves in adoption, are not allowed, as descendants, to take the property of their actual father, that is, if, at the time of his death, they are in the adopting family. For, if in his lifetime they have been emancipated by the adopting father, then they are allowed to take the property of their actual father, just as if they had been emancipated by him and had never been in the adopting family. Consequently, so far as regards their adopting father, they begin to occupy the position of strangers to him. But, if they are emancipated by the adopting father after the death of their actual father, then, so far as regards the former, they are equally in the position of strangers, and, in respect of the property of their actual father, they do not acquire the rank of descendants; and this has been so settled, because it was unjust that it should be in the power of an adopting father to determine to whom the property of the actual father should belong, whether to his children or to his agnates. § 11. Therefore, adopted children have less rights than actual children, for actual children, though emancipated, retain the rank of descendants, through the instrumentality of the prætor, although they lose it according to the civil law; but adopted children, on being emancipated, lose the rank of descendants by the civil law, and are not assisted by the prætor, and this is quite right, for a rule of the civil law cannot destroy natural ties,* and because they cease to be heirs succeeding as being co-owners of the patrimony they cannot cease to be sons or daughters, grandsons or granddaughters. But adopted children, on being emancipated, begin to occupy the position of strangers; for the right and title of son or daughter, which resulted from adoption, vanish by reason of the rules of the civil law relating to emancipation. § 12. The same rules are observed in respect of that possession of the property which the prætor promises, in spite of the testament of an ascendant, to those children who have been passed over, that is, who have neither been appointed heirs nor disinherited in the proper way. For the prætor calls to this possession of the property those children who were in the power of the ascendant at the time of his death, and those who were emancipated; but he excludes those who were in an adopting family at the time of the death of their actual father. Again, adopted children, emancipated by their adopting father, as they are not admitted to succeed to their adopting father on an intestacy, much less are they

* *ante*, I, tit. xv, § 3.

admitted to take the property of their adopting father, in spite of his testament, because they cease to be in the number of his descendants. § 13. We must, however, note that those who are in the adopting family, or who have been emancipated by the adopting father, after the death of their actual father who dies intestate, although not admitted by that part of the edict by which descendants are called to the possession of the property, yet are admitted by another part, that is, by that part of the edict by which the cognates of the deceased are called. But they are only admitted by this part of the edict when there are no descendants who succeed as being co-owners of the patrimony, and no emancipated descendants and no agnate is interposed. For the prætor first calls the descendants, both those succeeding as co-owners of the patrimony and those emancipated, then the heirs by statute,* and then the nearest cognates. § 14. Now, all these rules were held binding formerly; but they have received sundry amendments by our constitution, which we have passed affecting those persons who are given by their actual fathers in adoption to others. For, cases have come to our notice in which sons who have lost their succession to their actual ascendants on account of adoption, and through the tie of adoption being easily dissolved by emancipation, they have not been called to succeed either father. Correcting, therefore, as usual, such points, we have drawn up a constitution declaring, that when an actual ascendant has given his son to be adopted by another, all his rights are to remain intact, just as if he had remained in the power of his actual father, and no adoption had taken place, except, only in this, that on an intestacy, he may succeed to his adopting father. But, if he has made a testament, the adopted son cannot, either by the civil or prætorian law, obtain any part of the inheritance, neither by claiming admission to the possession of the property in spite of the testament, or by taking proceedings grounded on the testament being inofficious; as there is no obligation imposed on the adopting father, either to appoint him his heir, or to disinherit him, there being no natural bond connecting them; not even if he had been adopted out of three males, by virtue of the Sabinian decree of the senate, for, even in this case, a fourth share is not retained for him, nor is there any action available to him for its recovery. But a person, whom an actual ascendant has taken in adoption, is excepted from our constitution; for, as both natural and legal rights

* *post*, tit. ix, § 3.

concur in him, we have preserved the old rule in respect of such an adoption, as we have also done in the case of a head of a family, giving himself in arrogation. The details of these special rules may be gathered from a perusal of the above-mentioned constitution.

§ 15. Again, our forefathers in their favour for the descendants of males only, called to the succession, as being co-owners of the patrimony, grandsons or granddaughters descended from the male sex, preferring their claims to those of the agnates; but grandsons of daughters, and great grandsons of granddaughters, were reckoned among cognates, and were called after the agnates as well in the succession to their maternal grandfather or great grandfather, as to their grandmother or great grandmother, paternal or maternal. But the late emperors would not leave such an unnatural injustice without proper correction; and as the name of grandson and great grandson is common to both descendants of males and females, therefore, they put them in the same degree and order in the succession. But that something more might come to those whose rights rest not only on nature, but on the ancient law, they decided that the share of grandsons and granddaughters, and of the others, of whom we have spoken above, should be a little diminished, so that they should receive one-third less than their mother or grandmother would have received; or, when it is in respect of the succession to the inheritance of a woman, than their father, or paternal or maternal grandfather would have received; and though these persons only entered upon the inheritance, the agnates were not called to the succession. And, as upon the death of a son, the law of the Twelve Tables calls the grandsons or granddaughters, the great grandsons or great granddaughters to the succession of their grandfather in place of their father; so the rule introduced by the emperors calls them to the succession in the place of their mother or grandmother, subject to the deduction of the third part already referred to. § 16. But, as a point of dispute still remained between the agnates and the grandchildren referred to, the agnates claiming by virtue of a certain constitution a fourth part of the property of the deceased, we have removed this constitution from our code, and have not allowed it to be inserted into our code from that of Theodosius. By the constitution which we have issued we have altered all these provisions, and have enacted that the agnates shall not be able to claim any portion of the succession of the deceased, when there are grandchildren of a daughter or great grandchildren of a granddaughter, or their descendants surviving, in order that those coming in a collateral line may not be preferred to direct descendants. And we now declare that this our constitution is to take effect from the date when it comes into force, but in such a way, that just as the old law ordered, that between sons and grandsons by a son, the inheritance should be divided according to representation, and not according to individuals; so, also, we declare that the distribution shall in like manner take place between sons and grandsons by a daughter, and between all grandsons and granddaughters, and other descendants in a direct line; so that the children of either branch may obtain the share of their mother or father, or of their grandmother or grandfather, without any deduction; and so that if there are perhaps one or two surviving on the one side, and three or four on the other; then the one or two will take one half, and the other three or four the other half of the inheritance.

Title ii. Of the succession by law of agnates.

§ 9. If there be no one belonging to the class of heirs succeeding as being co-owners of the patrimony, then the inheritance belongs, by the same law of the Twelve Tables, to the agnates. § 10. Now, those are called agnates who are relations by law; and relationship by law is that which arises through the male sex. Thus, brothers sprung from the same father are agnates to each other, and are also called consanguineous, whether they have the same mother or not being immaterial. Again, a father's brother is an agnate of his brother's son, and conversely he is an agnate of his uncle. So as to brother's children, commonly called cousins. By following this rule, we may go through many degrees of

If there be no heir succeeding as being a co-owner of the patrimony, nor any of those whom the prætor or the constitutions include amongst that class, and who take the succession in any way, then the inheritance belongs, by the law of the Twelve Tables, to the nearest agnate. § 1. Now. agnates are, as we pointed out in the first book,* cognates related through males, that is, relations through the father. Therefore, brothers sprung from the same father are agnates, and are also called consanguineous, it being immaterial whether they have the same mother. Again, an uncle is the agnate of his brother's son, and inversely he is an agnate of his uncle. So in the same class are brother's children, who are also called cousins.† By following this rule we may go through many degrees of agnation. Those, too,

* 1, 15, § 1. † *post*, vi, § 4.

agnation. § 11. The law of the Twelve Tables does not, however, give the inheritance to all the agnates together, but to those who are next in degree at the time when it is certain that a person has died intestate. § 12. There is no succession in this class of heirs, so that if the nearest agnate should not take the inheritance or should have died before he entered upon it, no right arises by law in favour of his successor. § 13. Hence, also, we do not inquire who is the nearest in degree at the time of death, but at the time when it is certain that the person died intestate, because if a person should have died after having made a testament, it seemed the better plan to seek for his nearest agnate, only when it is certain that there would be no heir under the testament.

§ 14. But, in respect of women, it is held, according to this law, that there is one rule as to taking their inheritances, and another as to their taking the property of others, for the inheritances of females come to us, indeed, by the rule of agnation, just as those of males; but our inheritances do not belong to women who are beyond the degrees of consanguinity. Hence, a sister is by law heir to a brother or sister; though a paternal aunt, and a brother's daughter cannot be our heir at law. But a mother or step-mother, who, by a contract bringing her under the marital power of our father, has acquired the rights of a daughter, is in the position of a sister to us.

who are born after the death of their father acquire the rights of consanguinity. The law of the Twelve Tables does not, however, give the inheritance to all the agnates together, but to those who are next in degree at the time when it is certain that a person has died intestate. § 2. The right of agnation is acquired also through adoption, as, for example, it exists between the actual children and those whom their father has adopted, though there is no doubt but that such persons are improperly called consanguineous. Again, if one of your agnates, as, for example, a brother or a paternal uncle, or any other more remote agnate, should adopt a person, he will be amongst your agnates.

§ 3. The right of agnation gives males, however distant in degree, reciprocal claims to the succession of inheritances. But it has been laid down in respect of females that they should only take inheritances by right of consanguinity, if they were sisters, though not beyond; although males, even in the remotest degree, are admitted to their inheritances. For this reason the inheritance of the daughter of your brother or of your paternal uncle or aunt, will belong to you, but your inheritance did not belong to her. This was so settled because it seemed expedient that the law should be so arranged as that inheritances should tend for the most part to get into the hands of males. But as it was unjust to wholly exclude females as if they were strangers, the prætor admits them to the possession of the property by that part of his edict in which he promises the possession of the property on the ground of proximity; but in this part of the edict they are only, of course, admitted if there is no agnate, nor any nearer cognate. But the law of the Twelve Tables introduced none of these distinctions; but framed with the simplicity proper to laws, called all agnates, whether male or female, and of whatever degree, in their turn to the succession, in the same manner as heirs who succeed as being co-owners of the patrimony. It was an intermediate jurisprudence subsequent to the law of the Twelve Tables, but prior to the imperial rules, that, induced by a spirit of subtlety, worked out the above-mentioned difference, and entirely excluded females from agnate succession, no other method of succession being then known, until the prætors, correcting by little and little the asperity of the civil law, or filling in what was wanting, added by their edicts, with humane intent, another class; and the line of cognates being introduced on the score of proximity, females were aided by having the possession of the property given to them with those who were called to the succession as being cognates. But we, following the law of the Twelve Tables, and adhering to its dispositions on this point, whilst praising the humanity of the prætors, yet do not think that they have provided a complete remedy for the evil; for why, when they are in the same degree of relationship, and when the title of agnation is equally balanced between the males and females, should males be permitted to come into the succession of all agnates, whilst amongst agnate females there are none, except sisters, who are allowed to come into the succession of agnates? We, therefore, doing away with the whole of these rules, and making our arrangement correspond with that of the Twelve Tables, have, by our constitution, ordained that all persons entitled by law, that is, descendants from males, whether themselves male or female, shall be equally called to the rights of succession arising at law on an intestacy, according to the priority of their degree; and, therefore, females are not to be excluded because they have not, like sisters, the rights of consanguinity.

§ 15. If the deceased have a brother, and the son of another brother, it will be gathered from what we have said above,* that the brother has the prior claim, because he is of a nearer degree. But the law has been differently interpreted in respect of heirs succeeding as being co-owners of

* *ante*, § 11.

§ 4. We have also thought it desirable to add to our constitution that one degree should be transferred from the rights of cognates to those of the succession at law, so that not only the son and daughter of a brother, as we have already explained, may be called to the succession of the

the patrimony.* § 16. But if no brother of the deceased survives him, and there are children of brothers, the inheritance belongs to them all; but, the question is, suppose the children are unequal in number, as, for example, if there are one or two of one brother, and three or four of the other brother, is the inheritance to be divided according to representation, as is the rule amongst heirs succeeding as being co-owners of the patrimony,† or rather according to individuals? But it has now for some time been held that the inheritance must be divided according to individuals, so that whatever the number of persons on both sides may be, the inheritance must be divided into so many portions that each individual may get his share.

* *ante*, § 7.

† *ante*, § 8.

paternal uncle, but the son or daughter (but not their issue) of not only a consanguineous, but also of a uterine sister may also be admitted with them to the succession of their maternal uncle; and on the death of him who is a paternal uncle to the children of his brother, but maternal uncle to the children of his sister, then the children of both sides succeed just as if they were all entitled at law as being descendants of males; but this is, of course, assuming that there is no brother or sister surviving, for, if there are, such persons having prior rights, are admitted to the inheritance, and these other degrees are entirely excluded, as the inheritance would have to be divided according to individuals, and not according to representation. § 5. If there are many degrees of agnates, the law of the Twelve Tables expressly calls the nearest; and therefore if, for example, there is a brother of the deceased, and a son of another brother, or a paternal uncle, the brother is preferred. And, although the law of the Twelve Tables calls the nearest agnate using the singular number, yet there is no doubt but that if there are several of the same degree they are all admitted; for, although, properly speaking, the "nearest" means the nearest of several degrees; still there is no doubt that though there is only one degree of agnates the inheritance belongs to those in that degree. § 6. When anyone dies, without having made a testament, the "nearest" agnate must be looked for at the time of the death of him whose inheritance is in question. But, if he should have died after having made a testament, the inquiry must be gone into at such time as it becomes certain that there will be no heir under the testament, for it is only then that the person can, properly speaking, be said to have died intestate; and this sometimes is a matter for question during a long period, and in the interval it often happens that the nearest agnate dying, some one becomes the nearest who was not so at the time of the death of the testator. § 7. But it was held that in this order of succession there was no devolution, that is to say that, although the nearest agnate who was called to the inheritance in the way we have mentioned, either refused it, or died before he entered upon it, his successors were not admitted at law. Here, again, the prætors, only partially correcting the rule, did not leave them altogether without benefit, but called them in the rank of cognates, as they were shut out from any right of agnation. But we, desirous that nothing should be wanting to the completeness of the law, have directed by our constitution, which we have brought forward in a spirit of humanity, concerning the law of patronage, that devolution in the succession to inheritances of agnates is not to be denied them, since it was, indeed, absurd that that which, by the aid of the prætor, is open to cognates, should be denied to agnates, especially as the burden of tutelages devolved on the next degree if there was a failure of the first; so that a rule which obtained in respect of burdens was not allowed to govern the case of a benefit.

§ 8. Similarly, the ascendant who emancipates his son or daughter, grandson or granddaughter, or other descendant, with a redemption clause, is called to succeed at law. This is somewhat affected by our constitution, in that emancipations of children are always to be deemed made with a redemption clause, though formerly this was only so if the ascendant had manumitted under a special agreement as to redemption.

§ 17. If there is no agnate, the same law of the Twelve Tables calls all the descendants of the common ancestor collectively to the inheritance. Now, as to who these are, we refer to the first commentary —(N.B. the passage is missing from the MS.),—and as we there observed that the whole law relating to the subject has fallen into disuse, it is unnecessary here to deal with the matter further.

Title iii. Of the Tertullian decree of the senate.

The law of the Twelve Tables laid down so strict a rule, and so preferred the descendants of males, and so debarred those connected through females, that there was no right of reciprocal succession, even between a mother and her son or daughter, except so far as the prætors called these persons under their relationship as cognates to that possession of the property which they accorded in turn to cognates. § 1. But these restrictions, created by the law, were subsequently altered; for, first, the late Emperor Claudius made a mother, by way of solace for the loss of her children, successor by statute to them. § 2. Subsequently, by the Tertullian decree of the senate, which was passed in the reign of the late Emperor Hadrian, provision was made for a mother, but not a grandmother, having the sad privilege of succeeding to her children, so that in case of a freeborn mother with three children, or a freedwoman with four, she was admitted, although she might be in the power of an ascendant, to take the property of her deceased intestate children, but subject of course to this, that if she was in the power of another she must have the authority of him in whose power she was. § 3. But those descendants of the deceased who are heirs succeeding as co-owners of the patrimony, or who rank as such, whether in the first or in a lower degree, are preferred to the mother. And a son or daughter of her deceased daughter, is preferred by the constitutions to the mother of the deceased, i. e., to their grandmother. In both cases the father, but not the grandfather or great-grandfather, is preferred to the mother, assuming, of course, that it is between these only that the question as to the inheritance arises. The consanguineous brother of a son or daughter, also excluded the mother; but the consanguineous sister came in on equal footing with the mother. But if there were a consanguineous brother and sister, the brother excluded the mother, although she had the qualifying number of children, and the inheritance was shared in equal parts between the brother and sister. § 4. But we, by a constitution, inserted in the code which is adorned with our name, have deemed it right to come to the aid of the mother, from a consideration of the bond of nature and of childbirth, and its perils, and of the death which sometimes overtakes mothers at such times. We, therefore, have deemed it unjust that a fortuitous circumstance should be allowed to do them harm; for, if a free-born woman has not given birth to three children, or a freed-woman to four, she is unjustly debarred from the succession to her children. But how has she sinned in not having many, but a few, children? We have given to mothers full right to the succession by statute of their children, whether they are free-born or freed, and although they may not have had three or four, but only him or her who has been cut off by death. § 5. But as previous constitutions dealing with the right of succession by statute, in part came to the aid of the mother, in part denied her claim, and did not give her the whole inheritance, but in some cases depriving her of a third, gave it to certain agnates, and in other cases did just the opposite; it seemed to us that the straightforward and easy path should be followed of placing the mother before all heirs by statute, and that they should succeed to their children without any deduction, except as against a brother or sister, whether consanguineous or having only the rights of cognation; and, as we have placed the mother before all other heirs by statute, so we call all brothers and sisters, whether agnates or not, to the inheritance together with her, subject to the following rule, that if there are only agnate or cognate sisters surviving, together with the mother of the deceased, the mother takes half, and all the sisters the other half; but, if on the death of the intestate son or daughter, the mother is surviving together with a brother or brothers, whether alone or with agnate or cognate sisters, then the inheritance is to be divided according to individuals.

§ 6. But, as we have thus consulted the interests of mothers, so it behoves them to consult the interests of their offspring. Let it be known to them, therefore, that if they do not demand tutors for their children, or, for the space of a year, neglect to apply for a tutor in place of those removed or excused, they will be deservedly debarred from the succession of those of their children who die before the age of puberty.

§ 7. Moreover, although a son or daughter is born of an uncertain father, still the mother may take his or her property by virtue of the Tertullian decree of the senate.

Title iv. Of the Orphitian decree of the senate.

Reciprocally, the admission of children to the property of their intestate mothers has been brought about by the Orphitian decree of the senate, passed during the consulship of Orphitius and Rufus, in the reign of the late Emperor Marcus Aurelius, by which the succession at law goes to the son or daughter, although they may be in the power of another, and they are preferred both to consanguineous relations and to the agnates of the deceased mother. § 1. But, since grand-children were not, by this decree of the senate, called to succeed at law to their grandmother, this was subsequently corrected by imperial constitutions, and, in analogy to sons and daughters, grandsons and granddaughters were called. § 2. It is to be further noted that successions of the nature of those derived from the Tertullian and Orphitian decrees of the senate are not lost by a change of status, owing to the rule that newly-created successions at law are not affected by a change of status, as it only applies to those successions resulting from the law of the Twelve Tables. § 3. Lastly, it is to be noted that even those children who are born of an uncertain father are admitted to the inheritance of the mother by the Orphitian decree of the senate.

§ 4. If some out of a number of heirs by statute do not take the inheritance, or are prevented from entering upon it by death, or other cause, then their share accrues to those who have entered upon the inheritance; and, although these should be already dead, the accrual will, nevertheless, take place in favour of their heirs.

Title v. Of the succession of cognates.

§ 18. So far, succession on intestacy is regulated by the law of the Twelve Tables, and how strict this law was is easily perceived. § 19. For, immediately on being emancipated, children have, by that law, no right in the inheritance of their ascendant, since they have ceased to be heirs succeeding as co-owners of the patrimony. § 20. The same law applies if children are not in the power of their father, because they have had the gift of Roman citizenship with him, but have not been reduced into his power* by the emperor. § 21. Again, agnates, who have undergone a change of legal position, cannot be admitted under this law to the inheritance, because title by agnation is lost† through the change of legal position. § 22. Again, if the nearest agnate does not enter upon the inheritance, the next in degree has no title‡ at law. § 23. So, women who are agnates, but outside the degree of consanguinity, have no title to succeed** by this law. § 24 Similarly, cognates, whose tie of relationship is through the female sex, are not admissible, and this is carried to such an extent that, even between the mother and the son or daughter, there is no reciprocal right to succeed, unless the rights of consanguinity have been established between them by means of a contract bringing the female under marital power.

§ 25. But this unfairness in the rules of the Twelve Tables was corrected by the edict of

* *ante*, i, § 94.

† *ante*, i, § 158.

‡ *ante*, § 12.

** *ante*, § 14.

the prætor. § 26. For he calls to the inheritance all those who are deprived at law,* just as if they had been in the power of their ascendant at the time of his death; and this, whether they stand alone or compete even with heirs succeeding as being co-owners of the patrimony, that is, with those who were in the power of their father. § 27. But he does not call in the second degree, after the heirs who succeed as being co-owners of the patrimony, those agnates who have undergone a change of legal position, that is, he does not call them in that degree in which they would be called at law if there had been no change of legal position, but in the third degree, grounded on their nearness of relationship; for, although, by the change of legal position, they have lost their rights at law, yet they clearly retain the rights of cognation.† Hence, if another person possesses the rights of agnation intact, he will have the better right, even though he should belong to a degree more remote. § 28. Again, the rule is the same, according to some, in the case of that agnate, who, though the nearest agnate does not take the inheritance, is still not admissible at law. Some, however, are of opinion that such an agnate is called by the prætor in the same degree as that in which the inheritance is given at law‡ to the agnates. § 29. Female agnates, who are outside the degree of consanguinity, are undoubtedly called in the third degree,** that is, if there is no heir succeeding as being co-owner of the patrimony, and no agnate. § 30. In the same degree are also called those women who are related through females. § 31. Children, also, who are in an

After heirs, succeeding as being co-owners of the patrimony, and those whom the prætor, and the constitutions, call with them, and after the heirs by statute, in which number are agnates, and those whom the above-mentioned decrees of the senate and our constitution have placed amongst them, the prætor calls the nearest cognates. § 1. In this part of the edict it is natural relationship which is looked to; for agnates, who have undergone a change of status, and their descendants, are not reckoned amongst heirs at law by the Twelve Tables, but they are called by the prætor in the third order; but we must except the brother and sister, who have been emancipated, though not their children, as the Anastasian law calls them, with brothers whose rights remain intact to the succession at law of their brother or sister, though not with equal shares, but with a certain deduction, the details of which may be easily gathered by reference to the constitution itself; and it prefers them to all agnates of a lower degree, even though these latter have not undergone any change of status, and, of course, prefers them to cognates. § 2. Collateral relations, through females, are also called to the succession in the third degree by the prætor, on the ground of their proximity. § 3. Children, also, who are in

* See *Just. Inst.*, III, i, § 9.

† *ante*, i, § 158.

‡ *Just. Inst.*, III, ii, § 7.

** *Ibid.*, § 3.

adopting family, are called to the inheritance of their actual ascendants in this same degree.

an adopting family, are called to the inheritance of their actual ascendants in this same degree. § 4. It is obvious that children born of an uncertain father have no agnates, since agnation comes from the father's side, cognation from the mother's, and such children are looked upon as having no father.* For the same reason as between themselves, they cannot be said to be consanguineous, because the rule as to consanguinity is a species of the law of agnation. They can, therefore, only be cognates, as between themselves, by being related on their mother's side. Hence, under that part of the edict by which cognates are called on the ground of proximity, the possession of the property can be claimed by such children as these. § 5. At this point it is necessary to note, also, that, by right of agnation, a person can succeed to an inheritance, although he may be in the tenth degree, whether we are considering the law of the Twelve Tables or the edict by which the prætor promises that the possession of the property shall be given to heirs at law. But, on the ground of proximity, the prætor promises the possession of the property only up to the sixth degree of cognation, and, to the seventh degree in favour of children of a second cousin.

* *ante*, I, x, § 12.

§ 35. But it often happens that the grant of the possession of the property is made in such a way that he, to whom it is given, does not thereby get the inheritance, and this kind of possession of property is called possession without the beneficial interest. § 36. For if, by way of example, an heir appointed by a testament, made according to law, has duly declared* his intention of entering upon the inheritance, but is unwilling to claim possession of the property with the will annexed, being content to be heir by the civil law, nevertheless, those who are called to take on an intestacy, where no testament has been made, can claim possession of the property; but it then belongs to them without the beneficial interest, since an heir, appointed by the testament, can recover the inheritance. § 37. The same rule holds if, after the death of anyone intestate, the heir who succeeds as being co-owner of the patrimony, content to be heir at law, is unwilling to claim possession of the property, for here also the possession of the property belongs to the agnate, but without the beneficial interest, since the inherit-

* *ante*, ii, § 164.

ance can be undoubtedly recovered by the heir who takes as being co-owner of the patrimony. Similarly, the principle comes into play if the inheritance belongs, by the civil law, to an agnate, and he has entered upon it, but is unwilling to claim possession of the property; then, although a cognate from the nearest degree should claim it, still he will get possession of the property in the same way, without the beneficial interest. § 38. There are, also, other like cases, some of which we have dealt with in our preceding commentary.*

* see ii, § 119, 148, 149.

Title vi. Of the degrees of relationship.

It is necessary to show how the degrees of cognation are reckoned. In this matter we must note, in the first place, that one line of relationship is counted upward, another downward, and a third transversely, or, as it is also called, collaterally. The line reckoned upwards is that of ascendants; that downwards, of descendants; that transversely, of brothers and sisters and their descendants, and, agreeably with this plan, also that of paternal and maternal uncles and aunts. In the ascending and descending branch, counting begins from the first, but in the transverse, from the second degree. § 1. In the first degree in the ascending line is the father, the mother; in the descending line, the son, the daughter. § 2. In the second degree, ascending, the grandfather and grandmother; descending, the grandson or granddaughter; in the collateral line, the brother or sister. § 3. In the third degree ascending, the great-grandfather or great-grandmother; descending, the great-grandson or great-granddaughter; in the collateral line, the son or daughter of a brother or sister; and, agreeably to this plan, the paternal and maternal uncle and aunt. "Patruus" is the brother of a father, in Greek called πάτρως; "avunculus" is the brother of a mother, in Greek, μήτρως; and θεῖος being used equally for both; "amita" is the sister of a father, "matertera" the sister of a mother, both being called θεία, or, by some, τηθίς. § 4. In the fourth degree, in the ascending line is the great-great-grandfather and great-great-grandmother; in the descending line, the great-great-grandson and great-great-granddaughter; in the collateral line, the grandson and granddaughter of a brother or a sister; and, agreeably to the same plan, also the paternal great-uncle and great-aunt, that is, the brother or sister of a grandfather; also, the maternal great-uncle and great aunt, that is, the brother or sister of a grandmother; and, also, the male or female cousin, that is, those who are born of brothers or sisters. But some say that, properly speaking, "consobrini" are the children of two sisters, as if "consorini"; whilst the sons of two brothers are properly called "fratres patrueles"; the daughters, "sorores patrueles"; whilst the children of a brother and sister are, properly, "amitini"; the children of your paternal aunt call you "consobrinus", you call them "amitini". § 5. In the fifth degree, in the ascending line, the great-great-grandfather's father and mother; in the descending line the great-great-great-grandson and daughter; in the collateral line, a great-grandson or daughter of a brother or sister, and, agreeably to this plan, also, a paternal great-great-uncle and aunt, that is, the brother and sister of a great-grandfather, also, the maternal great-great-uncle and aunt, that is, the brother and sister of a great-grandmother; also, first cousins once removed, as being the son or daughter of cousins, whether descended from a son or daughter of a father's or mother's brother or sister; also, first cousins once removed, as being a son or daughter of a paternal or maternal great-uncle or aunt. § 6. In the sixth degree in the ascending line, the great-great-great-grandfather's father or mother; in the descending line, the great-great-great-great-grandson or daughter; in the collateral line, the great-great-grandson or daughter of a brother or sister; and, agreeably to this plan, the great-great-great-paternal or maternal uncle or aunt, that is, the brother or sister of a paternal or maternal great-great-grandfather or mother, also, second cousins, that is, those in the relationship of children, sons and daughters of cousins to one another, whether those cousins are the children of two brothers or two sisters, or of a brother and sister. § 7. It may suffice to have explained up to this point in what ways the degrees of cognation are reckoned. For, from this, it may be easily understood how we ought to count the more remote degrees, since a generation always adds one degree; so that it is far easier to say in what degree a person is than to denote him by the proper term of cognation.

§ 8. The degrees of agnation are reckoned in the same manner. § 9. But, as truth is much more readily grasped by the minds of men through the eyes than the ears, we have deemed it necessary, after this description of the degrees of relationship, to have a table of them inserted in this book—(see table of consanguinity annexed),—to the end that young students may be able, by means of both their ears and eyes, to acquire a perfect knowledge of the degrees.

§ 10. It is clear that that part of the edict, in which the possession of the property is promised on the ground of proximity, does not apply to the relationship of slaves, for neither does any other ancient law take such relationship into account; but by our constitution, which we have drawn up as to the law of patronage (a law sufficiently obscure even up to the present time, and full of cloud, and in every way confused), we have, under the promptings of humanity, conceded that, if a slave shall have a child or children, either by a free woman or a slave, or, on the other hand, if a female slave shall have children of either sex, by a freeman or a slave, then, on the parents attaining their freedom, and the children, whose mother was a slave, becoming also free, or if free mothers have children by slaves, who afterwards attain to freedom, in all these cases the children succeed to their father or mother, the right of patronage, under these circumstances, slumbering; for we have called these children to succeed, not only to their ascendants, but, also, mutually to each other, calling them, by the special provisions of this law, whether the case is that of those alone who have been born in servitude and afterwards freed, or it is the case of one succeeding with others, who were conceived after the enfranchisement of their parents; or, whether they all spring from the same father or mother, or from different unions, just as in the case of those born in lawful wedlock.

§ 11. Now, on summing up what we have said, it appears that those who stand in the same degree of cognation are not always called on an equal footing; and, further, that the cognate nearest in degree has not always the better right. For, as heirs succeeding as being co-owners of the patrimony, and those whom we have enumerated as classed with them, have the first claim, it appears that the great-grandson, or great-great-grandson of the deceased has a better right than the brother or the father and mother of the deceased, although the father and mother, as we have pointed out above, are in the first degree of relationship, the brother in the second, the great-grandson in the third, and the great-great-grandson in the fourth; nor is it material whether he was in the power of the deceased, at the time of his death,

					VI. G.G. G.G. grandfather.	VI. G.G. G.G. grandmother.					
				VI. Paternal G.G.G. uncle, and G.G.G. aunt.	V. G.G.G. grandfather.	V. G.G.G. grandmother.	VI. Maternal G.G.G. uncle, and G.G.G. aunt.				
			VI. Paternal G.G.-uncle and aunt's son and daughter (*i.e.*, first cousins twice removed).	V. Paternal G.G.-uncle and G.G.-aunt.	IV. G.G. grandfather.	IV. G.G. grandmother.	V. Maternal G.G.-uncle and G.G.-aunt.	VI. Maternal G.G.-uncle and aunt's son and daughter (*i.e.*, first cousins twice removed).			
		VI. Paternal G.-uncle and aunt's grandchildren (*i.e.*, second cousins).	V. Paternal G.-uncle and aunt's son & daughter (*i.e.* first cousins once removed).	IV. Paternal G.-uncle and G.-aunt.	III. G. grandfather.	III. G. grandmother.	IV. Maternal G.-uncle and G.-aunt.	V. Maternal G.-uncle and aunt's son & daughter (*i.e.*, first cousins once removed).	VI. Maternal G.-uncle and aunt's grandchildren (*i.e.*, second cousins).		
	VI. Paternal uncle and aunt's G. grandchildren (*i.e.*, first cousins twice removed).	V. Paternal uncle and aunt's grandchildren *i.e.*, first cousins once removed).	IV. Paternal uncle and aunt's children (*i.e.*, first cousins, cousins german).	III. Paternal uncle and aunt.	II. Grandfather.	II. Grand mother.	III. Maternal uncle and aunt.	IV. Maternal uncle and aunt's children (*i.e.*, first cousins, cousin german).	V. Maternal uncle and aunt's grandchildren (*i.e.*, first cousins once removed).	VI. Maternal uncle and aunt's G. grandchildren (*i.e.*, first cousins twice removed).	
VI. Brother's G.G.-grand son and G. G.-grand daughter (*i.e.*, G.G.G. nephew, G. G.G.-niece.	V. Brother's G.-grandson and G. granddaughter (*i.e.*, G.G. nephew, G.G.-niece).	IV. Brother's grandson and granddaughter (*i.e.*, G. nephew, G.-niece).	III. Brother's son and daughter (*i.e.*, nephew and niece).	II. Brother.	I. Father.	I. Mother.	II. Sister.	III. Sister's son and daughter (*i.e.*, nephew and niece).	IV. Sister's grandson and granddaughter (*i.e.*, G. nephew G.-niece).	V. Sister's G.-grandson and G. granddaughter (*i.e.*, G.G. nephew, G.G. niece).	VI. Sister's G.G.-grandson and G.G.-granddaughter (*i.e.*, G.G.G. nephew, G. G.G.-niece).
					I. Son.	I. Daughter.					
					II. Grandson.	II. Granddaughter.					
					III. G.-grandson.	III. G.-granddaughter.					
					IV. G.G.-grandson.	IV. G.G.-granddaughter.					
					V. G.G.G.-grandson.	V. G.G.G.-granddaughter.					
					VI. G.G.G.G.-grandson.	VI. G.G.G.G.-granddaughte r.					

or not, because he had been, or was, the issue of an emancipated descendant, or related through the female line. § 12. But, assuming that there are no heirs succeeding as being co-owners of the patrimony, nor any of those whom we have referred to as called with them, then an agnate, who possesses his rights as such intact, although he stand in the most distant degree, has generally a much better title than a cognate standing in a nearer degree; for the grandson or great-grandson of a paternal uncle is preferred to a maternal uncle or aunt. So that, as often as we say either that he who is nearer in degree of cognation has the better title, or that cognates in the same degree are all called equally, so often is it to be understood that there are no heirs succeeding as being co-owners of the patrimony, or those who are reckoned amongst them, or anyone whose claim is to be preferred, on the ground of agnation, according to the rules we have discussed; with the excepted case of the emancipated brother and sister, who, although they have undergone a change of status, are called to the succession of their brothers and sisters, being preferred to other agnates of a more remote degree.

§ 39. Let us now turn to the consideration of the property of freed-men. § 40. Formerly, a freed-man could, with impunity, take no notice of his patron in his testament, for the law of the Twelve Tables did not call the patron to the inheritance unless the freed-man had died intestate, leaving no heir taking at law as being a co-owner of the patrimony. Hence, though a freed-man had died intestate, if he should have left such an heir, none of his property came to his patron. Now, if he left as his heir one of his actual children, there would seem no cause for complaint; but, if an adopted son or daughter, or a wife under marital power, became his heir, it was clearly unjust that no right should be outstanding in the patron. § 41. For this

Title vii. Of the succession to freed-men.

Let us now turn to the consideration of the property of freed-men. Formerly, a freed-man could, with impunity, take no notice of his patron in his testament; for the law of the Twelve Tables did not call the patron to the inheritance unless the freed-man had died intestate, leaving no heir taking at law as being a co-owner of the patrimony. Hence, though the freed-man had died intestate, yet, if he should have left such an heir, none of his property came to his patron. Now, if he left as his heir one of his actual children, there would seem no cause for complaint; but, if it was an adopted son, it was clearly unjust that no right should be outstanding in the patron. § 1. For this reason, this unfair rule was subsequently amended by the edict

reason, this unfair rule was subsequently amended by the edict of the prætor, for he ordered that a freed-man should so make his testament as to leave half his property to his patron; and, if he left him nothing, or less than the half, possession of the property, to the extent of one-half share, was given to the patron, in spite of the will. And if he died intestate, leaving, as his heir taking at law as co-owner of the patrimony, an adopted son, or a wife under marital power, or a daughter-in-law under the marital power of his son, the possession of the property, to the extent of one-half share, was in like manner given to the patron as against these heirs. But his actual children can be used by the freed-man to exclude the patron; not only those in his power at the time of his death, but also those who have been emancipated and given in adoption, provided only they have been appointed heirs in respect of some portion of the estate, or if, being passed over, they have, under the edict, claimed possession of the property, in spite of the testament; for those who have been disinherited in no way exclude the patron. § 42. Subsequently, by the Papian law, the rights of patrons were increased so far as regarded the more wealthy freed-men, for it was provided by that law that the patron should take an equal share of the property of a freed-man who left a patrimony of one hundred thousand sesterces, or more, and had fewer than three children, whether he had made a testament or had died intestate. Hence, when the freed-man has left one son or one daughter as his heir, a half share goes to the patron, just as if he had died without any son or daughter; but, when he has left two sons or two

of the prætor, for he ordered that a freed-man should so make his testament as to leave half his property to his patron; and, if he left him nothing, or less than the half, possession of the property, to the extent of one-half share, was given to the patron, in spite of the will. And if he died intestate, leaving, as his heir taking at law as co-owner of the patrimony, an adopted son, the possession of half the property was, in like manner, given to the patron as against this heir. But children were available to the freed-man for the purpose of excluding his patron, not only those in his power at the time of his death, but also those who had been emancipated and given in adoption, provided only they had been appointed heirs in respect of some portion of the estate, or, if they had been omitted, had claimed, under the edict, possession of the property, in spite of the testament; for those who had been disinherited did not in any way exclude the patron. § 2. Subsequently, by the Papian law, the rights of patrons were increased, so far as regarded their more wealthy freed-men, for it was provided that the patron should take an equal share of the property of a freed-man, who has left a patrimony of one hundred thousand sesterces, and had fewer than three children, whether he had made a testament or had died intestate. Hence, when the freed-man left one son or a daughter as his heir, a half share would go to the patron, just as if he had died without any son or daughter; but, when he left two sons or two daughters, a

daughters, a third part goes to the patron; but, if he leaves three, the patron is excluded.

third part went to the patron, but, if he left three, the patron would be excluded.

§ 43. Patrons suffered no injustice, under the ancient law, in respect of the property of freed-women, for when they were in the legal guardianship of their patrons, of course they could not make a testament without the authority of the patron.* Hence, if he had authorised the making of the testament, he would either only have himself to blame, if nothing had been left to him, or he would take the inheritance as having been made heir, but, if he had not authorised the making of the will, or if the freed-woman had died intestate, the inheritance belonged to the patron, as women have no heirs succeeding as co-owners of the patrimony, and no other heir could complain, as the patron could not be excluded from the property of the freed-woman against his will. § 44. But subsequently, when the Papian law—releasing freed-women with four children from the tutelage of their patrons,† and thereby conceding to them the power of making testaments without the authority of their tutor—provided that the patron should take an equal share, according to the number of the surviving children of the freed-woman; and . . . . (two lines illegible) . . . .

§ 45. What we have stated in respect of the patron is to be understood as applying also to the case of the son of a patron, also to the grandson by a son, and to the great-grandson by a grandson born to a son. § 46. The daughter of a patron, also his granddaughter by a son, and his great-granddaughter by a grandson born to a son, formerly had the same rights which, by the law of the Twelve Tables, were given to the patron; but the prætor only calls to the possession of the property the male children of patrons. But, though such a daughter, on claiming the possession of the property—either in spite of the testament of a freed-man, or on an intestacy against the adopted son or the wife, or the daughter-in-law under marital power—will succeed by virtue of the right accorded to the mother of three children by the Papian law, yet, if she cannot rest her claim on this ground, she will fail. § 47. But according to some, this right to an equal share, resulting from the birth of three children, does not avail if the freed-woman who has made the testament has herself had four children. But if the freed-woman has died intestate, the express words of the Papian law apply to

* ii, § 118, 122.

† i, § 194.

give her an equal share, though, if the freed-woman dies after having made a testament, a similar right is given to her as is given to the children of patrons, in spite of the testament of a freed-man, that is, such as the male children of patrons have, in spite of the testament of a freed-man, although this part of the statute has been carelessly drawn. § 48. Hence, it appears that the stranger heirs* of a patron are far removed from any right available to the patron himself, whether in respect of the property of intestates or in spite of the testament.

* ii, § 161.

§ 49. Formerly, before the passing of the Papian law, patronesses only had that right, as to the property of freedmen, which is granted to patrons by the law of the Twelve Tables, for the prætor did not come to their aid, as he had done in the case of the patron and his children, as to claiming possession of the property to the extent of one-half share, in spite of the testament of an ungrateful freed-man, or on an intestacy against the adopted son, or the wife, or daughter-in-law. § 50. But the Papian law gave free-born patronesses with two children, and freed patronesses with three children, nearly the same rights as patrons have under the edict, and gave free-born patronesses, with three children, the rights which were given by the same law to a patron; but the same rights were not extended to the case of a freed-patroness. § 51. But, in respect of the property of freed-women, who have died intestate, the Papian law makes no innovation in favour of a patroness with children. Hence, if neither the patroness herself nor the freed-woman have undergone a change of legal position, the inheritance belongs to the former by the law of the Twelve Tables, and the children of the freed-woman are shut out; and this rule applies even if the patroness have no children. For, as we have stated above,† women never can have an heir succeeding as being co-owner of the patrimony; but, if either one or the other has undergone a change of legal position, then the children of the freed-woman exclude the patroness, since the right at law having been destroyed by the change of legal position, it follows that the children of the freed-woman have the better claim by reason of their relationship. § 52. But when a freed-woman dies, after having made a testament, the patroness, not favoured by reason of having children, has no claim available against the testament of the freed-woman; but she who is favoured on the ground of having children, has the same right afforded to her by the Papian law

† ? *ante*, § 43, or ii, § 161.

which the patron has, under the edict, in spite of the testament of his freed-man.

§ 53. The same law gave nearly all the rights of a patroness to the son of a patroness if he had children; but, in his case, the law was satisfied if he had one son or daughter.

§ 54 It must suffice, thus to have indicated, as it were, all these rights as to freed-persons: their interpretation is more fully gone into in a special work.

§ 55. We must now proceed to deal with the case of the property of Latin freed-men. § 56. In order that this part of the law may be clearer, we must bear in mind what we have said in another place,* viz., that those, who are now called Latin Junians, were formerly slaves by the law of the quirites; but, by the aid of the prætor, they were accustomed to enjoy a kind of liberty, on which account their property used to belong to their patrons by the right of being owners of their private savings, and subsequently, by the Junian law, all those whose liberty the prætor protected began to be free men, and were called Latin Junians, Latins, because the law wished them to be as free as if they had been free-born Roman citizens, who, having passed out of the city of Rome to Latin settlements, began, thereupon, to be Latin colonists, and Junians, because they were made free by the Junian law, although they were not Roman citizens. Hence, when the proposer of the Junian law perceived that the result of this fiction would be that the property of deceased Latins would no longer go to their patrons, because, of course, they had neither died as slaves, so that their property might belong to their patrons by right of owning their private savings, nor, as free Latins, could their property belong to their patrons by right of the manumission of a slave, he deemed it necessary to prevent the benefit given to these men being turned to the injury of their patrons, and he therefore provided that their property should belong to those who manumitted them, just as if the law had not been passed; and, therefore, the property of these Latins belongs, by virtue of this law, to those who manumitted them, as it were, by right of owning their private savings. § 57. Hence it happens that those rights, which by the Junian law arise in respect of the property of Latins, differ widely from those which govern the case of the inheritances of freed Roman citizens. § 58. For the inheritance of a freed Roman citizen in no

* *ante*, i, § 22.

case belongs to the stranger heirs of the patron; but, in any case, it belongs to the son of the patron, to his grandsons of a son, and to the great-grandsons of a grandson born to a son, even though they have been disinherited by their ascendant; but the property of Latins, like the private savings of a slave, belongs to stranger heirs, and does not belong to the disinherited children of the manumittor. § 59. Again, the inheritance of a freed Roman citizen belongs equally to two or more patrons, although they owned him as a slave in unequal shares; but the property of Latins is shared in proportion to the share in which each master owned them. § 60. Again, in respect of the inheritance of a freed Roman citizen, one patron excludes the son of another patron, and the son of one patron shuts out the grandson of another; but the property of Latins belongs to the one patron and to the heir of the other patron, in the proportion in which it would have belonged to the manumittor himself. § 61. Again, if there are, say, three sons of one patron, and one son of another, the inheritance of a freed Roman citizen is divided according to individuals, that is, the three brothers take three parts and the one the fourth part; but the property of Latins belongs to the successors of a patron, in the same proportion as it would belong to the manumittor himself. § 62. Again, if one of these patrons should reject his share in the inheritance of a freed Roman citizen, or, it he dies before declaring his intention of entering upon it, the whole inheritance goes to the other; but that part of the property of a Latin, which a patron fails to take, lapses, and belongs to the state.

§ 63. Subsequently, in the consulship of Lupus and Largus, the senate decreed that the property of Latins should, in the first instance, belong to him who had freed them; secondly, to such of his descendants as had not been expressly disinherited and stood nearest to him; and, finally, according to the old rule, to the heirs of those who had freed them. § 64. Some think that the result of this decree of the senate is that we should apply the same rule to the property of Latins which we apply in the case of the inheritance of freed Roman citizens; and this view was greatly in favour with Pegasus; but such an opinion is clearly erroneous, for the inheritance of a freed Roman citizen never belongs to the stranger heirs of the patron; but the property of Latins, even by this very decree of the senate, may pass to the stranger heirs if there are no children of the manumittor in the way. Again, in respect of the inheritance of a freed Roman citizen, disinheriting them does not affect the rights of the children of the manumittor; but, as to the property of Latins, it is laid down, in the decree of the senate itself, that an express disinherison bars the right. The better opinion is, therefore, that the only result of this decree of the senate is that the children of the manumittor, who are not disinherited by name, are to be preferred to the stranger heirs. § 65. Therefore, the emancipated son of a patron, who has been passed over in the testament, although he may not have claimed possession of the property of his ascendant, in spite of the will, has, nevertheless, a better right to the property of Latins than the stranger heirs. § 66. So a daughter and other heirs, taking at law as being co-owners of the patrimony, although they may have been excluded under the general clause and debarred from the whole inheritance of their father; yet, in respect of the property of Latins, unless they have been expressly disinherited by their ascendant, they will have a better right than the stranger heirs. § 67. Again, the property of Latins, resulting from the inheritance, belongs to the children who have abstained from the inheritance of their ascendant; for in no way can they be said to be disinherited any more than those who have been passed over in silence by the testament. § 68. From all this, it sufficiently appears that, if he who has made a Latin . . . . (twenty-five lines illegible) . . . § 69. Again, it also seems clear that, if a patron has left only his children as heirs in unequal shares, the opinion of those is the better who think that the property of the Latin will belong to them, according to the shares in the inheritance, because, as no stranger heir intervenes, the decree of the senate does not apply. § 70. But, if a patron should leave a stranger heir, together with his children, Cælius Sabinus lays down that all the property passes in equal shares to the children of the deceased, because, when a stranger heir intervenes, the Junian law does not apply, but the decree of the senate does. On the other hand, Javolenus says that the children of the patron would only get, by virtue of the decree of the senate, equal shares of that part which the stranger heirs would have taken under the Junian law before the passing of the decree of the senate, but that the remaining shares belong to them according to the shares in the inheritance. § 71. Again, the question arises whether this decree of the senate affects those descendants of the patron who are the issue of a daughter or granddaughter, that is, whether my grandson by a daughter has a better right to the property of my Latin than the stranger heir; and a further question is, whether this decree of the senate affects Latins belonging to the mother's side, that is, whether the son of a patroness has a better right to the property of a Latin belonging to his mother than the stranger-heir of the mother. Cassius considered the decree of the senate to apply to both cases; but the majority disapprove of this opinion, because the senate was not concerned with these children of patronesses, who belong to another family, and this also appears from the fact that the decree of the senate bars those expressly disinherited; for it seems to have in view those usually disinherited by an ascendant, when not appointed heirs; whereas, it is not necessary for the mother to disinherit the son or daughter, nor for the maternal grandfather to disinherit the grandson or granddaughter if neither is appointed heir, whether the question arises in respect of the civil law, or under the prætorian edict, by which the possession of the property, in spite of the testament, is promised to the children who are passed over.

§ 72. Sometimes, however, a freed Roman citizen dies as if he were a Latin, as, for example, if a Latin has obtained from the emperor the rights of the quiritarian law, but with a reservation of the rights of his patron, for the late Emperor Trajan decided that this should be so when a Latin obtained from the emperor the rights of quiritarian law against the will or without the knowledge of his patron. In which cases, whilst this freedman lives, he is like other freed Roman citizens, and begets legitimate children; but he dies subject to a Latin's rights, and his children cannot be his heirs; and he has testamentary power to the extent only of appointing his patron as his heir, and of substituting some one else if the patron is unwilling to act. § 73. And as it seemed to be the result of this constitution, that such men could never die with the rights of Roman citizens, although after being freed they had fulfilled the conditions by which, in virtue of the Ælian Sentian law or the decree of the senate, they could become Roman citizens, the late Emperor Hadrian, moved by the injustice of this matter, caused a decree of the senate to be passed, by which those who had obtained the rights of quiritarian law from the emperor, without the knowledge or against the consent of the patron, should be deemed to have obtained the Roman citizenship, as it were, by virtue of the Ælian Sentian law, or the decree of the senate, if, after being freed, they had fulfilled the conditions by which, under the Ælian Sentian law or the decree of the senate, supposing they had remained Latins, they would have obtained the Roman citizenship.*

§ 74. The property of those whom the Ælian Sentian law classes as surrendered persons,† belongs to their patrons; sometimes as if it were that of freed Roman citizens, at other times as if it were that of Latins. § 75. For, by the same law, the property of those who, if some defect had not existed would, on manumission, have become Roman citizens, goes to their patrons, as if that of Roman citizens; but this does not give them the power of making a testament,‡ at least it is so generally considered, and not without reason, as it seemed incredible that the person who proposed this law should have intended to give the right of making a testament to persons of the lowest class. § 76. But the property of those who, if some defect had not existed would, on manumission, have been Latins, goes to their patrons just as if they had died Latins. But it has not escaped me that in this matter the person who proposed the law has not expressed his intention in so many words.

* *ante*, i, § 29, 66, etc.

† *ante*, i, § 13.

‡ *ante*, i, § 25.

§ 3. But our constitution, which we have drawn up in the Greek tongue, and to which we have coupled, for the information of everyone, a short explanation, lays the following rules down for cases of this kind, viz., that if freed-men or freed-women are less than "centenarii", that is, possess less than one hundred gold pieces (for we have so reckoned the sum fixed by the Papian law, counting one gold piece as equal to one thousand sesterces), then, if they have made a testament, the patron is to have no claim upon the succession. But if they have died intestate, and have not left any children, then, the right of patronage, according to the law of the Twelve Tables, is preserved intact. But, when they possess more than one hundred gold pieces, and leave one or more descendants of either sex and any degree, as heirs or possessors of the property, then, these are to succeed to the inheritance of their ascendants, excluding in every way the patron and his descendants. But, if they should have died intestate without children, in that case we have called the patrons or patronesses to the whole inheritance. If, however, they have made a testament, and have passed over their patron

or patroness, though they have no descendants, or have disinherited them, or in the case of a mother or maternal grandfather, they have been omitted; but so that in all the above cases their testaments cannot be treated as inofficious; then, by our constitution, these patrons or patronesses take by way of possession of the property, in spite of the will, not the half as formerly, but the third part of the property of the freed-man, or by virtue of our constitution the deficiency is to be made up to them when the freed-man or freed-woman has left them less than a third of their property, and this third is to be without encumbrance, so that it is not to be liable even for legacies or bequests in trust in favour of the descendants of the freed-man or freed-women, but such charges are to be thrown upon the co-heirs. And we have provided for a number of other cases which are collected in the above-mentioned constitution, and in respect of which the law required adjustment, so that not only patrons and patronesses and their descendants, but also collaterals to the fifth degree, are called to the succession of freed-persons (as may be gathered from the constitution itself), and so that if there are descendants of one patron or patroness, or of two or more, the nearest in degree is called to the succession of the freed-man or freed-woman; and the property is divided according to individuals and not according to representation, and the same rule applies to collaterals; for we have made the laws affecting
* cf. *post*, tit. ix, § 5. the succession of free-born and freed-persons almost* the same. § 4. But these rules are to be considered as applying to those freed-persons who now-a-days obtain the Roman citizenship, since there are no other classes of freed-persons; the class assimilated to surrendered persons, and that of Latins, having been done away with, and since there never was really any succession at law to Latins; for, although during their lifetime they existed as free, yet at their last gasp they lost both life and liberty, and those who had freed them, kept, by virtue of the Junian law, their property as it were by right of taking their private savings as if that of slaves. Subsequently it was provided by the Largian decree of the senate that the descendants of a manumittor, not expressly disinherited by him, should be preferred to their stranger-heirs in the succession to the property of Latins. This was followed by the edict of the late Emperor Trajan, by which, if a slave, against the will or without the knowledge of his patron, contrived to procure a hasty grant of citizenship from

the emperor, though he became during his life a Roman citizen, yet died a Latin. But on account of these changes of condition and other difficulties, we have decided to abolish for ever the Junian law, the Largian decree of the senate, and the edict of the late Emperor Trajan, together with the class of Latins themselves, so that all freed-men may enjoy the Roman citizenship; and we have so admirably altered matters that, with certain further provisions we have made the very path which formerly led to the condition of a Latin, now to be the means of attaining Roman citizenship.

Title viii. Of the assignment of freed-men.

Finally, in respect of the property of freed-persons, we must notice that the senate has decreed that, although the property of freed-persons belongs equally to all the descendants of the patron who are of the same degree, yet that it shall be lawful for an ascendant to assign a freed-man to one of his descendants, so that after the assignor's death, the assignee is alone the patron, and the other descendants, who would have had equal rights to the property if no assignment had taken place, have no claim on the property, and they only recover their original right in the event of the assignee dying leaving no issue. § 1. The assignment may be not only of a freed-man, but also of a freed-woman, and the assignee may be not only a son or grandson, but even a daughter or granddaughter. § 2. And this power of assignment is given to him who has two or more descendants in his power in order that it may be lawful for him to assign the freed-man or freed-woman to one of those whom he has in his power. Hence, the question arose, if the assignee was subsequently emancipated, was the assignment thereby rendered void? and it has been held that it was void in accordance with the view entertained by Julianus and the majority. § 3. It is immaterial whether a person makes the assignment by testament or without a testament; and, by virtue of the decree of the senate, passed in the time of Claudius, during the consulship of Suillus Rufus and Osterius Scapula, patrons might do it in any form of words.

Title ix. Of the prætorian possessions of property.

The right of claiming possession of the property was introduced by the prætor for the purpose of amending the ancient law; and not only did the prætor amend the ancient law as to intestate inheritances, as we have already pointed out,* but also as to the inheritances of those who died after making a testament. For, if a posthumous stranger had been appointed heir, although he could not enter upon the inheritance by the civil law, as the appointment was invalid; yet by prætorian law he could be made possessor of the property, that is to say he could be assisted by the prætor. Such a person may now by our constitution† be properly appointed heir, for he is now recognised by the civil law.

* *ante*, titles 1, 2, 5.

† see *ante*, II, xx, § 27.

§ 34. Sometimes, however, the prætor promises the possession of property rather for the purpose of confirming the old law than to correct or do away with it, for he gives possession of the property, according to the terms of the testament, to those, also, who have been appointed heirs in a testament regularly made; again, he calls to the possession of the property, on an intestacy, the heirs who take at law as being co-owners of the patrimony and the agnates. In these cases, the grant would seem to have no other advantage than that he who claims, in this way, possession of the property, can use the interdict which begins, "Of which property", and the use of this interdict we shall point out in its proper place;* but, apart from this giving of the possession of the property, the inheritance belongs to them by the civil law.

§ 1. Sometimes, however, the prætor promises the possession of property rather for the purpose of confirming the old law than to correct or do away with it, for he gives possession of the property, according to the terms of the testament, to those, also, who are appointed heirs in a testament regularly made; again, he calls to the possession of the property, on an intestacy, the heirs who take at law as being co-owners of the patrimony, and the agnates, though apart from this giving of the possession of the property, the inheritance belongs to them by the civil law.

§ 32. But those whom the prætor calls to the inheritance do not become heirs at law; for the prætor cannot make heirs, heirs being only created by statute, or by appointment in law equal to it, as by virtue of a decree of the senate or imperial constitution. But, when the prætor gives them possession of the property, they occupy the position of heirs.

§ 33. For this purpose the prætor has also created many other degrees in respect of the grant of possessions of property, with a

* iv, § 144.

§ 2. But those whom the prætor alone calls to an inheritance do not become heirs at law; for the prætor cannot make an heir, heirs being only created by statute, or by an appointment in law equal to it, as by virtue of a decree of the senate or imperial constitutions; but, when the prætor gives them possession of the property, they occupy the position of heirs, and are called possessors of the property. For this purpose the prætor has created many other degrees in respect of the grant of possessions of pro-

view to prevent persons dying without successors; but we do not propose to deal further in these commentaries with this subject, because we have explained the whole of this branch of the law in a special commentary. It is sufficient here simply to note . . . . (thirty-six lines illegible). . . .

perty, with a view to prevent persons dying without successors; for the prætor has extended, according to the principle of what is good and equitable, those very narrow limits, within which the right of succession was restricted by the law of the Twelve Tables.

§ 3. Now, the possessions of property, which arise out of testamentary dispositions, are these. First, that which is given to descendants who have been passed over, and which is called "possession in spite of the testament". Second, that which the prætor promises to all those legally appointed heirs, and therefore called "possession in accordance with the terms of the testament"; and, having first dealt with the matter of testaments, he then passes to the case of intestacy, and he gives, in the first place, to the heirs who take at law as being co-owners of the patrimony, and to those whom the prætorian edict numbers with them, the possession of the property, which is called "that on the ground of being descendants"; secondly, that to the heirs by statute; thirdly, that to the ten persons whom he preferred to the stranger manumittor. These ten persons are the father, mother, grandfather and grandmother, whether paternal or maternal; also, the son, daughter, grandson, and granddaughter, whether by a son or a daughter, the brother and sister, whether consanguineous or uterine; fourthly, that to the nearest cognates; fifthly, that to the nearest member of the patron's family; sixthly, that to the patron or patroness, and to their children and ascendants; seventhly, that to the husband and wife; eighthly, that to the cognates of the manumittor. § 4. The above resulted from prætorian jurisdiction; but we, allowing nothing to escape our observation, and correcting everything by our constitutions, have allowed the possession of property given in spite of the testament, and that given in accordance with the terms of the testament, to stand, on the ground of their necessity, as, also, those possessions of property given on intestacy, on the ground of being descendants, and that on the ground of being heirs by statute. That, however, placed fifth in the edict of the prætor, viz., that given on the ground of being the ten blood relations, we have shown, in a kindly intended and brief discourse, to be superfluous, for the aforesaid possession of the property placed ten persons before the stranger manumittor; but, as the constitution which we have drawn up respecting the emancipation of children, imports an implied contract of redemption into all manumissions made by these ascendants, so that the manumission carries the right in itself, and makes the above-mentioned possession of the property superfluous; therefore, we have suppressed this fifth possession of the property, and inserted in its place what was formerly the sixth possession of the property, that is, making fifth that which the prætor promises to the nearest cognates. § 5. And the possession of the property, which formerly stood in the seventh place, viz., that on the ground of being the nearest member of the patron's family; and, in the eighth, viz., that on the ground of being descendants or ascendants of a patron or patroness, we have entirely suppressed by our constitution made on the subject of the right of patronage. For, as we have made the successions of freed-persons similar to those of the free-born, except that we have limited them to the fifth degree, so that there may be some difference between the free-born and the freed, it suffices to leave them the following possessions of property, by which they may assert their rights, viz., that given in spite of the testament, that given on the ground of being heirs by statute, and that given on the ground of being cognates, all the subtlety and inextricable confusion of two of the above-mentioned possessions of property being swept away. § 6. But the other possession of property, given on the ground of being husband and wife, which was placed ninth among the ancient possessions of property, we have maintained in full force, and have raised it to a higher place, that is, the sixth. The tenth possession of property, under the old rules, given on the ground of being cognates of the manumittor, has been very properly done away with, for reasons already set out; and there now only remain six of the ordinary possessions of property still in force. § 7. The seventh, which followed these, was introduced by the prætor for an excellent reason. For, at the end of the edict, possession of the property is promised to all those to whom it may be given by any law, decree of the senate, or constitution. This possession of the property has not been definitively classed by the prætor, either with the possessions of the property resulting from an intestacy, nor with those which are testamentary; but he has adapted it to serve as a last and extraordinary resource, according to the nature of the case, whether for those who apply under a testament, or on an intestacy, by virtue of any laws, decrees of the senate, or the later imperial constitutions. § 8. As, therefore, the prætor had introduced several kinds of successions, and arranged them in order; and, as in each kind of succession many persons of different degrees of relationship existed, he deemed it necessary to fix the time within which the possession of the property must be claimed, so that creditors might not be delayed in bringing their actions, and might have responsible persons to sue, as well as to prevent creditors easily getting possession of the property, and in that way consulting their own interests only. Therefore, he allowed a period of one year, within which ascendants and descendants, whether actual or adopted, could claim possession of the property. To all others one hundred days. § 9. And, if a person did not claim the possession of the property within this period, his right accrues to those persons who are in the same degree; and, if there be no such persons, the prætor, by the edict, on succession, promises the possession of the property to the next following, just as if he who preceded had been omitted altogether. If a person should refuse the possession of the property so offered to him, it is not necessary to wait until the time limited for applying for the possession of the property has expired, but the next in succession are immediately admitted under the same edict. § 10. In computing the time, however, available for claiming possession of the property, only the days on which the claim could be legally made are counted; and previous emperors have wisely provided in this matter, that no person need be at the trouble of expressly claiming the possession of the property, but that he is to have the full benefit of his rights on manifesting, in any way, within the specified period, his intention of accepting.

§ 77. Let us now deal with that succession which arises on the purchase of the patrimony. § 78. The property which is sold may belong either to the living or to the dead. To the living, as in the case of those who are hiding on account of some fraud, and, being absent, are undefended. So of those who have surrendered their property under the Julian law. So of judgment debtors against whom the time has run which was given them, partly by the Twelve Tables, and partly by the edict of the prætor, for satisfying the judgment. The property of deceased persons is sold, in the case of, for example, those to whom it has become clear that there is no heir or any possessor of the property, or any other lawful successor. § 79. If the property of a living person should have to be sold, the prætor orders it to be retained for thirty successive days, and public notice given. But, if the property is that of a deceased person, the creditors are ordered to assemble on the expiration of fifteen days, in order that, out of their number, a trustee may be appointed, that is, a person by whom the property may be sold. Then, if the property of a living person is to be sold, the prætor orders it to be done in (ten ?) days, if of the dead, in (five ?) days, and the order of the adjudication of the property to the creditor, in the case of a living person (is on the twentieth day), in the case of a deceased person (on the tenth ?) day. The reason of the longer interval to elapse in the case of the property of living persons, is to prevent the sale of the property of living persons being too easily effected.

§ 80. Things acquired by possessors of the property, or by purchasers of the property, do not become theirs at law, for such property is only held by an equitable title, and is only acquired at law when the period required for its acquisition by use has expired. Sometimes, however, this acquisition by use will not run in favour of purchasers of the property, as, where, for example, the purchaser only holds on behalf of those. . . . . (two lines illegible). . . : . § 81. Again, debts due to him whose property it was, and the debts he owes, are not due to or from the possessor or purchaser, by mere operation of law, but in all such matters the claims on either side are asserted by means of equitable actions, which we shall explain in the next commentary.*

* see iv, § 34, 35.

§ 82. There are other kinds of successions which have not resulted from the law of the Twelve Tables nor from the edict of the prætor, but from that law which is based on common consent. § 83. For, in the case of the head of a family giving himself in adoption, or a woman making a contract bringing her under marital power,† all their property, corporeal and incorporeal, and all that was owed them, are acquired by the adopting father, or by the

† II, § 86.

Title x. Of acquisition by arrogation.

There is another kind of universal succession which did not result from the law of the Twelve Tables, or from the edict of the prætor, but from that law which is based on common consent. § 1. For, in the case of the head of a family giving himself in arrogation, his whole property, corporeal and incorporeal, together with all that was owed to him, were formally acquired in full ownership by the arrogator, with the exception of those things which become extin-

fictitious purchaser, with the exception of those things which are extinguished by the loss of legal position; such as usufruct, the obligation in respect of the services of freedmen, which have been contracted by oath, and such things as are involved in an action at law.

guished by the loss of status; such as obligations in respect of services and rights of agnation; but, though formerly use and usufruct were numbered among these, a constitution of ours has prevented the extinction of these by the lowest form of loss of status.

§ 2. We have, however, restrained this mode of acquisition by arrogation, in analogy to that of actual ascendants; for nothing beyond the usufruct is now acquired by actual or adopting fathers through their children, of those things which come to the children from the extraneous source, the ownership remaining intact in the children; but, on the death of an arrogated son in the adopting family, the ownership also passes to the arrogator, unless there exist any of those persons who, by our constitution, are preferred to the father in respect of those things which cannot be acquired by him.

§ 84. On the other hand, that which is owed by him who gives himself in adoption, or by her who makes the contract bringing herself under marital power, does not become transferred to the fictitious purchaser, or to the adopting father, unless it was a debt belonging to the inheritance; for then, indeed, since the adopting father or the fictitious purchaser becomes heir, he is directly liable at law, but he who has given himself in adoption, or she who has made the contract bringing herself under marital power, cease to be heirs. But, in respect of debts owing to those on their own account, although neither the adopting father nor the fictitious purchaser can be liable, and though neither he who has given himself in adoption, nor she who has made the contract bringing herself under marital power, remains bound, because, of course, they are free, as the result of the loss of legal position, still an equitable action may be brought against him or her, as if the loss of legal position had not occurred, and if they are not defended (by the adopting father or the fictitious purchaser), when the action is brought against them, the prætor allows the creditors to sell all the property which would have remained theirs, if they had not subjected themselves to the power of another.

§ 3. On the other hand, the arrogator himself is not liable at law for the debts of him who has given himself in adoption, but he may be sued in his son's name, and, if he is unwilling to defend the action, the creditors may obtain an order from the proper magistrates to seize and dispose of, in the manner prescribed by law, that property which, together with the usufruct, would have belonged to the son if he had not subjected himself to the power of another.

[N.B.—The authenticity of §§ 85, 86, 87, is disputed.]

§ 85. If anyone is called to an inheritance at law, and before he declares his intention of entering upon it, or before he acts as heir, he goes through the form of surrendering it in court; he to whom the inheritance is surrendered becomes heir with full legal rights just as if he himself had been called to the inheritance by law. But if the heir, after he has become such, surrender the inheritance, he still remains heir, and is therefore himself liable to creditors; but the corporeal property becomes transferred, just as if he had surrendered each individual thing, though the debts vanish, and therefore those who were indebted to the inheritance are gainers. § 86. The same rule applies to the case of an heir appointed by testament, and, after he has become heir, going through the form of surrendering the inheritance in court, though if he surrenders before entering upon the inheritance his act amounts to nothing. § 87. Whether an heir who succeeds as being a co-owner of the patrimony, or as being a necessary heir, effects anything by going through the form of a surrender in court, is an open question. The leaders of our school think that nothing thereby results. The leaders of the opposite school are of opinion that the result is the same as in the case of those who surrender after having entered upon the inheritance; for that it is immaterial whether a person becomes heir by a declaration of his intention of accepting, or by acting as heir, or because he is compelled to be heir by operation of law.

Title xi. Of him to whom property is assigned in order to preserve gifts of freedom.

A new description of succession has resulted from a constitution of the late Emperor Marcus Aurelius. For, if those who have received liberty from their master, in a testament under which no one enters upon the inheritance, wish that the property should be assigned to them for the purpose of preserving the gifts of freedom, their claim is heard. § 1. And this results from a rescript of the late Emperor Marcus to Pompilius Rufus, couched in the following terms: "If the estate of Virginius Valens (who, by his testament, has granted freedom to certain slaves), has (through there being no one to succeed him as on an intestacy) fallen into that position that it must be sold, then the magistrate who is attending to the matter shall comply with your application, and assign the property to you in order that the liberty, as well of those to whom it was given directly, as of those to whom it was given by way of bequest in trust, may be preserved, on condition that you give satisfactory security to the creditors that each one's claim shall be paid in full. And those to whom freedom was given directly, shall become free just as if the inheritance had been entered upon; but those whom the heir was asked to manumit shall obtain their freedom through you; but if you do not wish to take an assignment of the property, unless those slaves also who received their liberty directly become your freed-men, and if those whose status this concerns consent to this, we are willing to sanction this alteration. And, lest the operation of this rescript should be defeated on another ground, viz., by the imperial treasury putting in a claim for the property, those who look after our interests are to understand that the cause of liberty is to be preferred to our pecuniary advantage; and the property is only to be seized in such a way as to preserve intact the liberty of those who would have acquired it if the inheritance had been entered upon under the testament." § 2. By the aid afforded by this rescript favour is shown both to freedoms and to deceased persons, as the creditors are prevented seizing and selling the property; for, clearly, if the property is on this ground assigned, the sale of the property is at an end, as a representative of the deceased exists, and that, too, a satisfactory one, who gives security to the creditors for the full amount. § 3. The ground for the application of this rescript is, in the first place, that freedoms have been conferred by testament. What, then, is to be done if a person dying intestate has given freedom by codicils, and the intestate inheritance is not entered upon? The benefit of the constitution ought to cover the case; clearly, if the deceased die testate, there is no doubt but that freedom given by codicils is effectual. § 4. Then the words of the constitution show that it applies when there is no successor on intestacy; therefore, as long as it is uncertain whether there is a successor or not, the application of the constitution is suspended; but when it is certain that no successor exists, then the constitution becomes available. § 5. If a person who is entitled to an entire restitution of his rights, should abstain from taking the inheritance, then, although he can claim restitution, still the constitution is applicable, and an assignment of the property may be made. What, then, will be the result, if, after the assignment has been made for the purpose of preserving the freedoms, he should be restored to his former rights. It must be held in such a case that the freedoms are not revoked which have once been obtained. § 6. This constitution was drawn up for the purpose of affording protection to gifts of liberty, and, therefore, when no freedoms are given, the constitution is not applicable. What, then, is to be done if a person has given freedoms "inter vivos", or "mortis causa", and to prevent the question being raised whether the creditors have been thereby defrauded or not, the slaves apply for an assignment of the property to them? Is their prayer to be granted? and we incline to the view that their prayer is to be heard, although the words of the constitution do not cover the point. § 7. But, as we perceived that much was wanting in this constitution, a very complete constitution has been drawn up by us, in which a number of cases are covered, so that full effect can be given to the law relating to this kind of succession, as may be easily ascertained by reading the constitution itself.

Title xii. Of abolished successions resulting from sale of the property, and from the Claudian decree of the senate.

There were formerly other universal successions existing, prior to the succession above-mentioned. Such was the sale of the property, which was introduced for selling with embarrassing formalities the property of debtors, and continued as long as the system of magistrate and judge lasted; but when subsequent generations used the extra-ordinary mode of trial, these sales of the property disappeared together with the ordinary mode of trial; and creditors can only now seize the property under an order, and dispose of it as they think expedient, all which will appear more clearly on reference to the fuller pages of the Digest. § 1. There was also, under the Claudian decree of the senate, a miserable mode of universal acquisition; when a free-woman, indulging in a union with a slave, lost her freedom by virtue of the decree of the senate, and with her freedom her property. As this seemed unworthy of our age, we have abolished it in our dominions, and forbidden it to be inserted in our Digest.

Title xiii. Of obligations.

§ 88. Let us now pass to obligations, of which the chief division is into two species; for every obligation arises either from contract or from tort.

§ 89. And, first, let us look into those which arise from contract. Of these, there are four kinds; for an obligation is contracted either by the thing, or by words, or by writing, or by consent.

Let us now pass to obligations. An obligation is a tie of law binding us to the fulfilment of something in accordance with the laws of this empire. § 1. The principal division of all obligations is into two kinds, for they are either civil or prætorian. Civil obligations are those directly established by statute, or at least approved by the civil law. Prætorian obligations are those which the prætor has created by his own authority; they are also called honorary. § 2. A further division separates them into four kinds, for they arise either from contract, or what is analogous to a contract, or from tort, or what is analogous to a tort. It will be necessary, first, to treat of those which arise from contract, of which again there are four kinds; for they are formed by the thing, or by words, or by writing, or by consent. We must consider each of these separately.

Title xiv. Of the modes in which an obligation is contracted by means of the thing itself.

§ 90. An obligation is contracted by means of the thing itself, as in the case of a loan in kind. The contract of loan in kind properly applies to those things which are estimated by weight, number, or measure, such as coined money, wine, oil, corn, copper, silver, gold, which things we give either by counting, or measuring, or weighing them, in order that they may become the property of those receiving them, and the identical things are not returned to us, but others of the same nature; and, hence, this is called a "mutuum", because that which has been so given by me to you from being mine becomes yours. § 91. He, also, who receives a thing which is not owed to him from a person who pays it by mistake, is bound by the thing, for he

An obligation is contracted by means of the thing itself, as in the case of a loan in kind. This contract of loan in kind applies to things which are estimated by weight, number, or measure, as, for example, wine, oil, corn, coined money, copper, silver, gold, which things we give either by counting, or measuring, or weighing them, in order that they may become the property of those receiving them, and the identical things lent are not returned to us, but others of the same nature and quality; and, hence, this is called a "mutuum", because the thing is so given by me to you that from being mine it becomes yours. From this contract arises the action termed a "condictio". § 1. He, also, who receives a thing which is not owed to him from a person who pays it by mistake, is bound by the thing, and the "condictitia" action

can be sued by the personal action, "if it appear that he ought to give", just as if he had received a loan in kind. Hence, some think that a pupil, or a woman to whom, without the authorisation of the tutor, something has been paid by mistake which was not due, is not liable to a personal action, any more than by the giving of a loan in kind. But this kind of obligation does not seem to arise out of contract, since he who gives with the intention of paying, is rather desirous of dissolving than of forming an obligation.

is available to the plaintiff against him for the recovery of the thing, for he can be sued by the personal action, "if it appear that he ought to give", just as if he had received a loan in kind. Hence, a pupil to whom, without the authorisation of his tutor, something has been paid by mistake which was not due, is not liable to a personal action, for that which is not due, any more than he would be by the giving of a loan in kind. But this kind of obligation does not seem to arise out of contract, since he who gives with the intention of paying, is rather desirous of dissolving than of forming an obligation.

§ 2. Again, he to whom something is given in order to be used, that is, lent, is bound by means of the thing itself, and is subject to the action for a specific loan. But his position is widely different from him who receives a loan in kind; for the thing is not given him in order that it may become his property, and therefore he is bound to restore the identical thing itself. And he who receives a loan in kind, if by any mischance, as, for example, by fire, by the fall of a building, by shipwreck, by the attack of thieves or enemies, he should lose what he receives, nevertheless remains bound. But he who receives a thing for use, is indeed required to employ the utmost diligence in the preservation of it, and it will not be sufficient for him to have given the same amount of care which he has been accustomed to give in respect of his own property, if a more careful person might have preserved it in safety; but he is not liable for loss occasioned by superior force, or unavoidable accident, provided only that this mischance was not due to his own fault; otherwise, if you choose to take with you on a journey the thing simply lent you to use, and you lose it by the attack of enemies or robbers, or by shipwreck, there is no doubt but that you are liable for its restitution. A thing is properly said to be lent in specie when the thing is given you to be used, no recompense being received or agreed upon; otherwise, if there is any recompense, the use of the thing is held to be hired out to you, for a loan in specie must be gratuitous.

§ 3. Further, he with whom something is deposited is bound by means of the thing itself, and liable to the action of deposit, for he also is liable for the restitution of the identical thing which he received. He is, however, only liable on the ground of having committed fraud, and is not liable under the head of failure of duty, that is, for carelessness or negligence. He is therefore safe, from whom a thing deposited with him, which he has not kept sufficiently carefully, has been stolen, for he who delivers a thing into the custody of a careless friend, should impute its loss to his own imprudence.

§ 4. The creditor, also, who receives a pledge is bound by means of the thing itself, and is liable by the action of pledge for the restoration of the identical thing which he receives. But since a pledge is given in the interest of both parties, of the debtor that he may the more readily borrow money, and of the creditor that the debt due to him may be better secured, it has been held to be sufficient if he employ the utmost diligence about the custody of the thing, and if he has done this, and he lose the thing by some accident, he is safe, and is not prevented claiming the sum advanced.

§ 92. A verbal obligation results from a question and answer, as, for example, Do you bind yourself to give? I do bind myself. Will you give? I will give. Do you promise? I promise. Do you become an additional debtor? I do so become. Do you become a surety? I do so become. Will you do? I will do. § 93. But that form of verbal obligation:—Do you bind yourself to give? I do bind myself—is peculiar to Roman citizens, the other forms belong to the law of all nations, and, therefore, are valid amongst all men, whether Roman citizens or aliens. And, although they may be expressed in the Greek language, as, for example thus:—Will you give? I will give. Do you agree? I do agree. Do you pledge your good faith? I do pledge my good faith. Will you do? I will do; still these forms are binding amongst Roman citizens, provided

Title xv. Of verbal obligations.

A verbal obligation is contracted by means of a question and answer, when we stipulate for anything to be given to or done for us. From this contract two actions arise, viz., a "condictio", when the stipulation is certain, and an action grounded on the stipulation when it is uncertain. The name stipulation comes from "stipulum", which signified, with the ancients, "firm", and, perhaps, comes from "stipes", the trunk of a tree.

§ 1. To form this contract, such words as the following were formerly used: Do you bind yourself? I do bind myself. Do you promise? I do promise. Do you become an additional debtor? I do so become. Do you become a surety? I do so become. Will you give? I will give. Will you do? I

they understand the Greek language. And, on the other hand, although they are expressed in Latin, they are binding amongst aliens, provided they understand the Latin language. But that form of verbal obligation, Do you bind yourself to give? I do bind myself to give, is so peculiar to Roman citizens that it cannot be translated into the Greek tongue, although the word "spondeo" is said to come from a Greek word. § 94. When, however, it is said that there is one case in which an alien can become bound by the use of this word, viz., if our emperor should thus interrogate the sovereign of a foreign nation concerning peace: Do you bind yourself to make peace? or, if the emperor himself were interrogated in this way, this is drawing the line too fine, for, if the agreement should not be carried out, the matter is not adjusted by means of an action founded on the stipulation, but by the laws of war. § 95. . . . . (twenty-four lines illegible). . . . (This paragraph probably dealt with the case of verbal contracts, made by a promise without a previous interrogation, as in the stipulation in respect of a wife's dowry, and then as to the stipulation being valid, although the promise and answer were in different languages.) § 96. . . . at least, when the question arises as to the Roman law; for, if we inquire what is the law amongst foreigners, we may find rules differing in each state.*

will do. But whether the stipulation is expressed in Latin, Greek, or any other tongue is immaterial, provided that both the parties to the stipulation understand it; and it is not necessary for both parties to use the same language, but it suffices if the answer agree with the question, and hence two Greeks may contract an obligation by means of the Latin tongue.

Formerly, these solemn words were in actual use, but, subsequently, the constitution of the Emperor Leo abolished the solemnity attaching to the words themselves, and required only concordant apprehension and mutual consent, in whatever words expressed.

§ 2. Every stipulation is either absolute, or has a limiting period attached, or is conditional. An example of an absolute stipulation is: "Do you bind yourself to give five gold pieces?" in which case the sum named may be immediately demanded. It has a limiting period attached when a day is mentioned on which the money is to be paid, as, "Do you bind yourself to give ten gold pieces on the next calends of March?" In such a case the money is owed at once, but cannot be sued for until the time has expired, and it cannot even be claimed on the day mentioned in the stipulation, for the whole of

* cf. *post*, § 120.

that day must be allowed the debtor for payment, as it can never be certain that payment has not been made on the day promised until that day is past. § 3. But if you stipulate thus: "Do you bind yourself to give ten gold pieces a year as long as I live?" the obligation is held to be absolute and perpetual, for a debt cannot be due for a time; but, if the heir should sue, he would be defeated by a plea founded on the agreement. § 4. A stipulation is conditional when the fulfilment of the obligation is subject to some uncertain event, so that the stipulation takes effect if something happens, or does not happen, as, for example, "Do you bind yourself to give five gold pieces if Titius should become consul?" A stipulation in this form, "Do you bind yourself to give such a sum if I do not go up to the capitol?" is just the same as if it had been stipulated that it should be given to him when he should die. A conditional stipulation gives rise merely to a hope that it will turn into a debt; and we transmit this hope to our heirs, if, before the condition is fulfilled, death has overtaken us. § 5. Particular places are often inserted in a stipulation, as, for example, "Do you bind yourself to give at Carthage?" This stipulation, although it would seem to be absolute, yet, from its nature, involves the period of time required for the promissor to pay the money at Carthage. And, therefore, if anyone being in Rome should stipulate thus: "Do you bind yourself to give at Carthage to-day?" the stipulation is void, as the promise given in reply would be impossible of fulfilment. § 6. Conditions which relate to the time, past or present, either at once make the obligation void or do not hinder its effect at all, as for instance, "If Titius has been consul", or, "If Mævius is living, do you bind yourself to give?" for, if these things are not so, the stipulation is void, and, if they are so, the stipulation is at once binding, for those things which are in their nature certain, do not suspend the obligation, although our knowledge of them may be uncertain.

§ 7. Not only may things be the subject of a stipulation, but acts also, as when we stipulate for something to be or not to be done. And, in stipulations of this nature, it is best to add a penal clause, so as to prevent the amount included in the stipulation being uncertain, and the plaintiff compelled to prove the value of performance to him. If anyone stipulate that something may be done, a penalty should be added in this manner: "If it is not so done, do you bind yourself to give ten gold pieces by way of penalty?" But, if a stipulation involve in one single interrogation the doing of some things and the not doing of others, a clause of this sort should be added: "If anything should be done contrary to this agreement, or, if that which is agreed on is not done, then do you bind yourself to give ten gold pieces by way of penalty?"

Title xvi. Of joint promisees and joint promisors.

Two or more persons may be jointly parties to a stipulation or promise. Such a case would arise in a stipulation, if, after the question has been asked by all, the promisor should answer, "I bind myself", as, for example, when two stipulators have each asked the question, the promisor answers, "I bind myself to give to each of you". For, if he first promise Titius, and then, on the other asking him the question, he again promise him, these will be distinct obligations, and they are not looked upon as standing in the position of joint stipulators. Two or more become joint promisors, thus: "Mævius, do you bind yourself to give five gold pieces?" "Seius, do you similarly bind yourself to give five gold pieces?" And then each separately answers, "I do bind myself." § 1. By such obligations as these, the whole subject matter of the stipulation is due to each stipulator and from each promisor. But, in both cases, only one thing is due, and, on any one of them receiving or paying what is due, the obligation is destroyed, and all are free. § 2. Where there are two joint promisors, one may be bound absolutely, the other for a term or subject to a condition, and neither the term nor the condition will be any impediment to a claim being made upon him who is bound absolutely.

Title xvii. Of stipulations by slaves.

A slave's power of stipulating is derived from the person of his master; but, as in many respects, the inheritance represents the person of the deceased, and therefore what a slave belonging to the inheritance stipulates for, before the inheritance is entered on, he acquires for the inheritance, and in this way it is acquired also for him who subsequently becomes heir. § 1. But whether a slave stipulate for his master, or for himself, or for his fellow-slave, or without stating for whose benefit he is stipulating, he acquires for his master. The same rule applies to children, in the power of their father,* in respect of

* *post* iv, tit. vii.

those matters in which they can acquire. § 2. But when the stipulation is in respect of an act, the stipulation is always confined to the person of the stipulator, as, for example, if a slave should stipulate that he is to have the right of passing and leading along, he only cannot be prevented, not his master. § 3. If a slave owned in common, stipulate, he acquires for each of his masters, proportionally to each one's share in him, unless he has stipulated by the order of one, or in the name of one of his masters; for, then, the subject-matter of the stipulation is acquired for him alone. The whole of that which a slave owned in common stipulates for, is acquired for one of his masters, if it cannot be acquired for the other, as, for example, if the thing which he has stipulated for is the property of one of his masters.

Title xviii. Of the classification of stipulations.

Some stipulations are judicial, others prætorian, others conventional, others common, that is, both prætorian and judicial. § 1. Simple judicial stipulations are those based entirely on the jurisdiction of the judge, as the stipulation by way of security against fraud, or as to pursuing a fugitive slave, or restoring his price. § 2. Prætorian stipulations are those which are based on the jurisdiction of the prætor, as, for example, the giving security against apprehended damage, or for the payment of legacies. The term prætorian is here to be understood as including stipulations required by the ædiles, for these also are based on the right of declaring the law. § 3. Conventional stipulations are those which derive their force from the agreement of both parties; that is, not resting on the order of a judge, or on that of the prætor, but on the consent of the contracting parties. And of these stipulations there are as many kinds, I might almost say, as there are things to be the subjects of contract. § 4. Common stipulations are such, for example, as that providing for the security of the property of a pupil, for sometimes the prætor, and sometimes the judge, if the matter cannot be otherwise managed, orders the security to be given by way of stipulation; another example is the stipulation as to ratification.

Title xix. Of useless stipulations.

Everything of which we can be owner, whether movable or immovable, may be the subject matter of a stipulation. § 1. But if anyone should have stipulated for a thing,

§ 97. If that which we stipulate to be given

us is of such a nature that it cannot be given, the stipulation is useless, as, for example, if a person should stipulate for a free man, whom he thought to be a slave; or for a dead slave, whom he thought to be alive, or for a plot of sacred or religious ground, which he thought to be the subject of commerce. § 97A. Again, if a person stipulate for a thing which does not, or cannot exist, as, for example, a hippocentaur, the stipulation is equally useless.

which does not, or cannot, exist, as, for example, for Stichus who is dead, but whom he thought living, or in respect of hippocentaurs, which are non-existent things, the stipulation is useless. § 2. The same rule holds good in the case of a person stipulating for a sacred or religious thing, which he thought to be the subject of commerce, or for public property appropriated to the perpetual use of the people, as a forum, or theatre, or for a free man, whom he thought to be a slave, or for a thing of which he has not the power of disposal, or for a thing belonging to himself, nor will the stipulation remain in suspense on the ground that public property may get into private hands, or the freeman may become a slave, or the stipulator may acquire the power of disposing of the thing, or the thing which now belongs to him may cease to be his; but it is then and there void. So, conversely, although a thing may have been validly made the subject-matter of a stipulation at the outset, yet, if it subsequently fall within any of the descriptions, to which we have above referred, without the act of the promissor, the stipulation is extinguished, and such a stipulation as the following, and others of a similar class, are not even valid at the outset: "Do you bind yourself to give Lucius Titius when he shall become a slave?" for things which, by their nature, are independent of our ownership, cannot in any way be made the subject-matter of an obligation.

§ 3. If a person has promised that another shall give or do something, he is not bound, as, for example, if he promise that Titius shall give five gold pieces. But if he has promised that he will bring it about that Titius shall give five gold pieces, he is bound.

§ 103. Moreover, a stipulation is useless if we stipulate on behalf of one, to whose power we are not subjected; hence, the question has arisen, to what extent is the stipulation valid, if a person stipulate for a sum to be given to himself, and to some one to whose power he is not subjected. The leaders of our school think that it is valid for the

§ 4. If a person stipulate on behalf of some other person than him in whose power he is, the stipulation amounts to nothing. But, clearly, it may be arranged that payment is to be made to a third person (as, if a person stipulate thus: "Do you bind yourself to pay me or Seius?") in which case the benefit of the obligation is acquired by the stipulator; but payment may be made to Seius, even against the will of the stipulator, and the obligor is released by operation of law, and the stipulator will have an action,

whole amount; and, further, that the whole is due to the stipulator alone, just as if he had not added the name of a third person. But the leaders of the opposite school are of opinion that half is due to him, for that the stipulation, so far as the other half is concerned, is useless . . . (three lines illegible.) . . .

grounded on gratuitous agency, against Seius. If a person stipulate that ten gold pieces shall be paid to him, and to a third person to whose power he is not subjected, the stipulation is valid; but it has been a matter of doubt whether the whole sum, which formed the subject-matter of the stipulation, is due, or only half; and we think that only half can be claimed. If you have stipulated on behalf of another person who is your power, you acquire for yourself; because your words are, as it were, the words of your son, just as your son's words are deemed to be yours, in respect of those things which can be acquired for you.

§ 102. So a stipulation is useless if a person's answer is not in accord with the question; as, for example, if I stipulate for ten thousand sesterces to be given by you, and you promise five thousand sesterces; or if I stipulate absolutely, and you promise subject to a condition.

§ 5. Moreover, a stipulation, again, is useless, if the answer should not agree with the question put; as, for example, if a person stipulate for ten gold pieces to be given by you, and you promise five, or vice versa, or if he stipulate absolutely, and you promise conditionally, or vice versa; provided, of course, that you express this disagreement, that is, if, when a person stipulates conditionally, or for a limited period, you answer: "I bind myself for to-day"; but if you answer only: "I promise", you will seem briefly to have promised, in respect of the time or the condition mentioned; for it is unnecessary that everything should be repeated in the answer, which the stipulator may have expressed.

§ 104. Again, the stipulation is useless if I stipulate with one who is in my power, or if he stipulate with me. And a slave, a free man in bondage, a daughter in our power, and a woman under marital power, are not only unable to become liable to those in whose power they are, but they cannot be liable to anyone else.

§ 6. Again, the stipulation is useless if you stipulate with a person who is in your power, or if he stipulate with you, and a slave not only cannot become liable to his master, but he cannot become liable to anyone else, though a son in power can be under an obligation to others.

§ 105. It is evident that the dumb can neither stipulate nor promise, and the same restriction applies to the deaf; because, he who stipulates ought to be able to hear the words of the promisor, and he who promises the words of the stipulator. § 106. A lunatic cannot transact any business, because he

§ 7. It is evident that the dumb can neither stipulate nor promise, and the same restriction applies to the deaf; because, he who stipulates ought to be able to hear the words of the promisor, and he who promises, the words of the stipulator. Hence it follows that we are not speaking of a person who hears with difficulty, but of one who does not hear at all. § 8. A lunatic cannot transact any business, because he does

does not understand what he is doing. § 107. A pupil can transact any business, provided that where the authority of the tutor is necessary, the tutor is a party to the transaction; for example, if the pupil binds himself, for he may bind others towards himself without the authority of his tutor. § 108. The same rule applies to women who are under tutelage. § 109. But what we have said of the pupil is to be understood as applying to him who has attained to some intelligence; for an infant, and one only a little above that age, do not differ much from a lunatic; for a pupil of the former age has no intelligence; but with respect to the latter class of pupils, a more favourable interpretation of the law has been adopted.

§ 98. Again, if a person stipulate subject to a condition which cannot be fulfilled, as, for example, if he shall touch the sky with his finger, the stipulation is useless. But the leaders of our school are of opinion that a legacy left subject to an impossible condition is just as good as if no condition had been inserted. The leaders of the opposite school, however, think that the legacy is no less useless than the stipulation, and it certainly seems difficult to give a satisfactory reason for the difference. § 99. Moreover, a stipulation is useless if a person stipulate for a thing to be given to him, not knowing that it is his, for that which is already a person's property cannot be given to him.

not understand what he is doing. § 9. A pupil can transact any business, provided that where the authority of the tutor is necessary, the tutor is a party to the transaction, as, for example, when the pupil binds himself, for he may bind others towards himself without the authority of his tutor. § 10. But what we have said of pupils is to be understood as applying to those who have attained to some intelligence; for an infant, and one only a little above that age, do not differ much from a lunatic, because pupils of that age have no intelligence. But for the benefit of those a little above the age of infancy, a more favourable interpretation of the law has been adopted, so as to give them the same rights as those have who are little removed from puberty. But a person below the age of puberty, and in the power of his ascendant cannot bind himself, even with his father's authority.

§ 11. If an impossible condition is added to the obligations entered into, the stipulation is void. Now, a condition is deemed impossible to the fulfilment of which an impediment exists from the nature of things; as, for example, if a person should say this, "Do you bind yourself to give if I touch the heavens with my finger?" But if a stipulation is made thus, "Do you bind yourself to give if I do not touch the sky with my finger?" the obligation is considered as absolute and performance may be at once claimed.

§ 12. Again, a verbal obligation entered into between absent persons is useless. But as this rule gave ground for law-suits with contentious men, who, perhaps, after some time had elapsed, set this up in bar, alleging that either they or their opponents were not present, therefore our constitution,—which is intended to secure the speedy termination of disputes, and which we addressed to the advocates of Cæsarea,—has provided that documents showing that the parties were present are to be in all cases believed, unless he who uses such unworthy testimony shall have made it evident by the clearest proofs, whether by writing or by credible witnesses, that either he or his opponent was in some other place during the whole of that day on which the document was prepared.

§ 100. Lastly, the stipulation is useless if a person stipulate that a thing be given in such a way as this, "Do you bind yourself that it shall be given after my death?" or thus, "Do you bind yourself that it shall be given after your death?" but it is valid if a person stipulate for it to be given thus, "Do you bind yourself that it shall be given when I die?" or thus, "Do you bind yourself that it shall be given when you die?" that is, that the obligation is to be fulfilled at the last moment of the life of the stipulator or promisor. For it seemed anomalous that the obligation should begin to take effect by means of the person of the heir. Again, we cannot stipulate in this way: "Do you bind yourself that it shall be given on the day before I die?" or, "the day before you die", because, which is the day before the death of anyone cannot be ascertained until after death has happened; again, when death has happened, the stipulation relates to the past, and is something like this: "Do you bind yourself that it shall be given to my heir?" which is clearly useless. § 101. What we have said in respect of death is to be understood as applicable also to the case of a change of legal position.

§ 13. No one could stipulate that a thing should be given him after his own death, any more than after the death of him of whom he stipulated. So, neither could he who was in the power of another stipulate that anything should be given him after the death of him in whose power he was, because he is held to speak with the voice of his father or master. But if any one stipulated thus, "Do you bind yourself that it shall be given the day before I die?" or "the day before you die?" the stipulation was useless, but since stipulations (as has already been stated) are binding by reason of the consent of the contracting parties, we have thought it right to introduce a necessary amendment to this rule of law, so that the stipulation is to hold good, whether referring to after the death or the day before the death of the stipulator or promisor.

§ 14. Again, if anyone had stipulated thus: "If the ship hereafter arrives from Asia, do you bind yourself to give to-day?" the stipulation was useless, as being preposterously drawn up. But, since the Emperor Leo of glorious memory held that a stipulation of this sort, which is called preposterous, was not to be rejected when relating to marriage portions, we have thought it right to give it full force, so that every stipulation of this sort may be binding, not only when relating to marriage portions, but to anything else. § 15. A stipulation so drawn up, as where, for example, Titius says, "Do you bind yourself to give when I die?" or, "when you die?" was considered valid by the ancients, and is so now. § 16. So we may validly stipulate for a thing after the death of a third person. § 17. If the document state that a person has promised, this is to be taken as if an answer had been given to a precedent question. § 18. Whenever several things are included in one stipulation the promisor is bound in respect of all if he simply answer: "I bind myself to give." But if he answer as to giving only one, or some of them, the obligation only extends to those in respect of which he has promised. For, of the several included stipulations, one or some are deemed to have been concluded, for each of the things should be stipulated for and answered singly. § 19. No one (as has been already stated*) can stipulate on behalf of another, for this class of obligations has been invented to enable each person to acquire for himself what will benefit himself, but if it is to be given to another, it is of no benefit to the stipulator. If, however, anyone wish to do this, he should stipulate for a penalty, so that if the thing is not done as is intended the stipulation will involve a penalty to him who has no other interest in it, for when a penalty is stipulated for, the interest of the stipulator is not the point considered, but what is the amount payable under the condition. Therefore, if a person stipulate that a thing shall be given to Titius he effects nothing, but if he should add as a penalty: "Do you bind yourself to give so many gold pieces if you do not give?" then the stipulation is binding. § 20. But if a person stipulate for another, having himself an interest in the matter, it has been decided that the stipulation is valid. For if he who had begun to act as tutor afterwards surrendered the administration to his co-tutor, and had stipulated for the security of the estate of his pupil, since it is to the interest of the stipulator that what he has stipulated shall be performed, as he would be responsible to the pupil if his affairs were badly conducted, the obligation is binding. So, if a person has stipulated that a thing shall be given to his procurator, the stipulation is valid. So, too, if a person has stipulated that a thing shall be given to his creditor, and the stipulator is interested in the performance of the promise; in that otherwise he may become liable to a penalty, or the estates which he had mortgaged should be sold, the

* *ante*, § 4.

stipulation is valid. § 21. On the other hand, he who has promised that another shall do, is held not to be liable unless he himself promise to be liable under a penalty. § 22. Again, no one can validly stipulate that a thing which will hereafter be his shall be given him when it becomes his. § 23. If the stipulator has one thing in his mind and the promisor another, an obligation is no more contracted than if there had been no answer to the question; as, for example, if a person has stipulated that you should give the slave Stichus, but you are thinking of Pamphilus, whom you thought was called Stichus. § 24. A promise grounded on a base purpose, as, for example, if a person promise to commit homicide or sacrilege, is not binding.

§ 25 If a person has stipulated subject to some condition, then, although he should die before the fulfilment of the condition, if the condition is subsequently fulfilled, his heir can sue upon the promise. The same holds good on the side of the promisor. § 26. A person who has stipulated that a thing shall be given to him in such a year or in such a month cannot validly sue until the whole of the year or month has elapsed. § 27. If you stipulate for an estate, or a slave, you cannot immediately sue unless such a period has elapsed within which delivery could have been made.

§ 110. We can, however, join another to stipulate for that for which we stipulate. This person is commonly called an adstipulator. § 111. But an action is then equally open to him, and payment may be just as properly made to him as to us. But whatever he obtains thereby he may be compelled to hand over to us by means of the action based on gratuitous agency.* § 112. This additional creditor may, however, use other words than those which we have used. Therefore, if for example, I have stipulated (with the principal debtor) thus: "Do you bind yourself to give?" he may stipulate in addition (with a guarantor) thus: "Do you become an additional debtor in respect of the same thing?" or (with a surety), thus: "Do you become surety in respect of the same?" or vice versa. § 113. Again, he can adstipulate for less, but not for more. Therefore, if I have stipulated for ten thousand sesterces, he can stipulate for five thousand; but, on the other hand, he cannot stipulate for more. So, if I have stipulated absolutely, he can stipulate conditionally, but not the other way. But more and less are to be understood as referring, not

* *post*, § 117.

only to quantity, but also to time, for to give something immediately is to give more; to give it after a time is to give less. § 114. To this branch of the law some special rules apply. For the heir of the adstipulator has no right of action.* Again, a slave acting as adstipulator effects nothing, though in all other cases he acquires by the stipulation for his master. The same rule, according to the better opinion, holds in respect of a free person who is in bondage, for he is in the position of a slave. He, however, who is in the power of his father does an act valid in itself, but he does not acquire for his ascendant, although in all other cases when stipulating he acquires for him, and he does not even get a right of action himself unless he has passed out of the power of his ascendant without loss of legal position, as, for example, by the death of the ascendant, or because he has himself been solemnly invested as a priest of Jupiter. The same rules are to be understood as applying to a daughter in power, or to a woman under marital power.

* iv, § 113

Title xx. Of sureties.

It is usual for other persons to become liable for him who promises. These persons are called sureties, and they are commonly required by creditors in order that their security may be more ample.

§ 115. It is also usual for other persons to become liable for him who promises, of whom some are called sponsors, others fidepromissors, others fidejussores. § 116. A sponsor is interrogated thus: "Do you bind yourself that the same thing shall be given?" A fidepromissor: "Do you become an additional debtor for the same?" A fidejussor thus: "Do you become surety for the same?" We shall have to consider as to the class into which those fall who are interrogated thus: "Will you give the same?" "Do you promise the same?" "Will you do the same?" § 117. We are in the habit of taking sponsors, or fidepromissors, or fidejussors, when we are anxious to have better security. But we commonly only employ an adstipulator, when we are stipulating in such a way as that something is to be given after our death; for since by so stipulating we ourselves effect nothing,* an adstipulator is added in order that he may be able to sue after our death, and if thereby he should have acquired anything, he is liable under the action of gratuitous agency to hand it over to my heir.

* *ante*, § 100.

§ 118. The position of a sponsor and of a fidepromissor are of a similar character, but that of a fidejussor is widely different. § 119. For the two former cannot intervene in any obligations except those created by the verbal contract, and yet sometimes he, who has so promised as principal debtor, has not become liable; as, if a woman or a pupil has promised without the tutor's authority, or if anyone has promised that something shall be given after his death; but the point is doubtful whether, if a slave or an alien has promised, the sponsor or fidepromissor is bound for him.

But a fidejussor may be joined in any obligation, that is, whether the obligation has been contracted by means of the thing itself, or by words, or by writing, or by consent; and it is immaterial whether the obligation to which he is added is civil or natural, so much so that he may even bind himself for a slave, whether he is a stranger, who takes the surety from the slave, or the master himself, as to a thing which may be due to him. § 120. Further, the heir of the sponsor or fidepromissor is not bound unless we are considering the case of an alien fidepromissor, whose country follows a different rule.* But the heir of a fidejussor is liable. § 121. Again, the sponsor and the fidepromissor are, by the Furian law, released at the end of two years; and the obligation is divided into as many shares as there are sureties liable at the time when the debt can be claimed,† and each is liable for an equal share. But the liability of fidejussors is not limited as to time, and, whatever their number may be, each is bound for the whole amount. Hence the creditor is at liberty to select anyone he pleases to sue for the whole amount. But now, by a rescript of the late Emperor Hadrian, the creditor is compelled to sue each of those who are solvent at the time, for their shares. This rescript, therefore, differs from the Furian law, in that, if any of the sponsors or fidepromissors are insolvent, their liability in respect of their shares falls on the others. But, since the Furian law applies only to Italy, it follows that, in

§ 1. They may be joined in any obligation, that is, whether the obligation is contracted by means of the thing itself, or by words, or by writing, or by consent; and it is immaterial whether the obligation to which the surety is added, is civil or natural; so much so, that he may even bind himself for a slave, whether he is a stranger, who takes the surety from the slave, or the master himself, as to a thing which is due to him under a natural obligation. § 2. The surety himself is not only bound, but he leaves his heir bound also. § 3. A surety may be added either before an obligation is entered into or afterwards. § 4. If there are several sureties, whatever their number may be, each is liable for the whole amount, and, therefore, the creditor is at liberty to select anyone he please to sue for the whole amount. But, by a rescript of the late Emperor Hadrian, the creditor is compelled to divide his demand between all those who are solvent at the time of the joinder of issue.

* cf. *ante*, § 96; and iv, § 113. † iv, § 22.

the provinces, sponsors and fidepromissors are, like fidejussors, bound without any limitation as to time, and each for the whole amount, unless they are aided by the rescript of the late Emperor Hadrian as to their liability for a share only. § 122. Besides this, the Apuleian law has introduced a sort of partnership between sponsors and fidepromissors, for, if any one of these has paid more than his share, this law gives him an action against the rest for the excess, and this law was passed before the Furian law, at a time when each was bound for the whole: hence the question arises whether, after the Furian law, the benefit of the Apuleian law continues. It does continue outside Italy, for the Furian law is confined to Italy, whilst the Apuleian law applies to other provinces, but, whether it still survives in Italy, is an open question. However, to fidejussors, the Apuleian law does not apply. Hence, if a creditor has obtained the whole from one, the loss will fall upon that one alone, that is, of course, if the principal debtor is insolvent. But, as appears from what has been said above, he from whom the creditor claims the whole, could require, under the rescript of the late Emperor Hadrian, that the action against him should be restricted to his share. § 123. Moreover, it was provided, by the Cicereian law, that he who required sponsors or fidepromissors should declare openly, beforehand, both as to the amount of the security, and how many sponsors or fidepromissors he was about to require in respect of that contract; and, unless he did make this declaration beforehand, the sponsors and fidepromissors are allowed, within thirty days, to demand a preliminary investigation, with a view to ascertain whether the declaration required by that law has been made; and, if judgment is given that no such declaration has been made, they are released. No mention is made of fidejussors in this law, but it is customary, on accepting fidejussors, also to make a similar declaration.

So that, if any one of the sureties should not be solvent at that time, the rest are proportionally burdened. But, if the creditor had obtained the whole from one of the sureties, the loss falls upon that one alone, if the principal debtor is not solvent. And for this he has only himself to blame, as he might have claimed the benefit of the rescript of the late Emperor Hadrian, and required that the action against him should be restricted to his share.

§ 124. But the benefits of the Cornelian law are common to all. This law forbids the same person to become liable on behalf of one and the same borrower of money to the same creditor, in the same year, for a larger sum than twenty thousand sesterces;

and, although a sponsor or fidepromissor has bound himself in respect of a larger sum, as, for example, for one hundred thousand sesterces, he will not be liable. We include, in the expression "borrowed money", not only that money which we give for the purpose of creating a loan, but all that which, at the time the obligation is contracted, it is certain will become a debt, that is, that which is made the subject matter of an obligation without any condition. Hence that money also is included which we stipulate to be given on a certain day, because it is certain that it will become due, although it can only be sued for after the expiration of the time. Under the expression "money", as used in this law, everything is included. Therefore, if we stipulate for wine, or corn, or for an estate, or a slave, this law applies. § 125. But, in certain cases, the law allows security to be taken to an unlimited amount, as, for example, in the matter of a dowry, or in respect of that which is due to you under a testament, or where security is ordered to be given by a judge. And, further, it is provided by the (Julian) law, relating to the tax of one-twentieth on inheritances, that the Cornelian law is not to apply to the classes of security required under that law.

§ 126. The position of all sureties, whether sponsors, fidepromissors, or fidejussors, is, on one point of law, identical, viz., that they cannot be so made liable as to owe themselves more than he, for whom they are bound, owes. But, on the other hand, they may bind themselves so as to be liable for less, as we have already stated to be the case with an adstipulator.* For, like the adstipulator, their obligation is an accessory to the principal obligation, and there cannot be more in the accessory than in the principal thing. § 127. They are, also, all alike on another point, viz., that if anyone of them has paid for the principal debtor, he has against him the action of gratuitous agency for the purpose of recovering the

§ 5. Sureties cannot be so bound as to be liable for more than he for whom they are surety is liable, since their obligation is an accessory to the principal obligation; and there cannot be more in the accessory than in the principal thing. But, on the other hand, they may be bound so as to be liable for less. Hence, if the principal debtor has promised ten gold pieces, the surety may be lawfully liable for five, but he cannot be liable in the opposite way. Again, if the principal debtor has promised absolutely, the surety may promise conditionally, but not vice versa, for more or less are to be understood as referring not only to quantity, but also to time, as to give something immediately is to give more, to give it after a time is to give less.

§ 6. If a surety has paid anything on behalf of the principal debtor, he has against him the action of gra-

* *ante*, § 113.

amount, and sponsors have in addition, under the Publilian law, a special action for double the amount, called the "actio depensi".*

tuitous agency for the purpose of recovering the amount.

§ 7. A surety becomes such if he promise, in the Greek language, thus: "I order", or "I affirm", or "I wish", or "I desire it upon my credit", and, if he uses the words "I say", it will be held equivalent to "I affirm". § 8. It is to be noted that it is a general rule, in all stipulations of sureties, that, whatever is stated in writing to have been done, is deemed to have been done; hence, if a person has stated in writing that he has become liable as a surety, it will be presumed that all the required formalities have been complied with.

* see *post*, iv, § 9, 22, 25.

Title xxi. Of obligations contracted by entries in writing.

§ 128. An obligation arises by writing, as, for example, in the case of accounts transferred to the ledger. This transfer of the entries of accounts may occur in two ways, either from thing to person, or from one person to another. § 129. A transfer of the entry of an account from thing to person occurs in the case of, for example, the entry of a sum by me as due from you, which you owe me as the result of a sale, a letting, or a partnership. § 130. A transfer of the entry from person to person occurs, for example, if I enter to your debit a sum which Titius owes me, that is, if Titius substitute you for himself. § 131. The entries which are called "arcaria" stand on quite a different footing, for in these the obligation arises out of the thing itself, and not by the writing, because they are not binding unless the money has been paid; for the paying over the money makes an obligation arising out of the delivery of the thing, not a contract by writing, and hence we shall be correct in saying that entries, in respect of such payments, give rise to no obligation, but afford evidence of one having been made. § 132. Hence, also, it may be properly said that aliens may bind themselves by means of such entries of payment, because they are not bound by the entry itself, but by the paying over of the money, which kind of obligation falls under the law of nations. § 133. But, whether aliens can be bound by transferred entries is, very properly, open to question, for such an obligation, contracted in this way, belongs to the civil law; and this is the opinion of Nerva; but, according to Sabinus and Cassius, if the transferred entry were from thing to person, then even aliens were bound, but not if it were from person to person. § 134. Further, it is held that an obligation by writing may be formed by means of a document given by the debtor only, or one exchanged by debtor and creditor, that is (where no stipulation on the subject has been entered into), a writing stating that a person owes something, or that he will give something, and this form of contract is peculiar to aliens.

Formerly a kind of contract was created by writing, which was said to be made by entries, but these entries are not now in use. Clearly, if a person has stated in writing that he owes a sum which has not been paid over to him, it has been repeatedly decided that he cannot, after a long period has elapsed, set up a plea of not having received the money; and it thus happens that, even at the present day, as he has no redress, he is bound by the writing, and, upon this, a personal action is grounded, that is, of course, in the absence of any obligation contracted by words. The period of time within which this plea was allowed was formerly fixed, under the imperial constitution, as not less than five years. But, in order that creditors may not run the risk of, perhaps, being defrauded of their money after a longer period, we have, by our constitution, abridged the time, so that this plea is not available after the lapse of two years.

§ 135. Obligations are created by consent in buying and selling, letting and hiring, partnerships and gratuitous agencies. § 136. We, therefore, say that obligations are contracted in these ways by consent, because there is no form of words or of writing required, but it is sufficient that those who are transacting the business have come to an agreement. Hence, also, such obligations may be contracted between absent parties, as, for example, by letter or by messenger, though a verbal obligation cannot be formed between absent parties. § 137. Again, in contracts of this nature, both parties are under a mutual obligation to do all that is fair and

Title xxii. Of obligations by consent.

Obligations are created by consent in buying and selling, letting and hiring, partnerships and gratuitous agencies. An obligation is, in these ways, said to be contracted by consent, because there is no need either for a writing or for the presence of the parties, nor is it necessary that anything should be given to make the obligation acquire binding force; but it is sufficient if those who are transacting the business agree. Hence, also, such obligations may be contracted between absent persons, as, for example, by letter or messenger. Again, in contracts of this nature, both parties are under a mutual obligation to do all that is fair and equitable in respect of the subject matter of the contract, whereas, in verbal obligations, one party stipulates and the other promises, and, in contracts made by entries, one binds the other by making an entry to his debit, whereby the other is bound. § 138. But a contract may be made by an entry debiting an absent person, although a verbal obligation cannot be contracted with an absent person.

equitable in respect of the subject matter of the contract, whereas, in verbal obligations, one party stipulates and the other promises.

Title xxiii. Of the contract of sale.

§ 139. The contract of sale is complete when the price is agreed upon, although the money may not yet have been paid, nor even any earnest given, for what is given by way of earnest, is only evidence that a contract of sale has been formed.

The contract of sale is complete as soon as the price is agreed upon, although the money has not yet been paid, nor even any earnest given, for what is given by way of earnest is only evidence that a contract of sale has been formed. But this is the case with sales made without writing; for no alteration has been made by us in such sales. But, in respect of those which are committed to writing, we have enacted that a sale is not to be complete unless an instrument of sale has been drawn up, being either written by the contracting parties, or at least signed by them, if written by another hand; or, if drawn up by a notary, it must be accepted by the parties as completely setting out the contract in all its parts; for, as long as any of these points are wanting, there is opportunity to retract, and either vendor or purchaser may withdraw from the contract without incurring any penalty. We, however, have only allowed the contracting parties thus to withdraw without loss, if nothing has already passed by way of earnest; for, if earnest has been given, whether the contract of sale has been created with or without writing, he who declines to complete the contract, if he is the purchaser, is to forfeit the earnest; but, if he is the vendor, he must hand over double the amount, although nothing has been agreed upon about the earnest.

§ 140. The price, however, should be certain, for, otherwise, if the parties have agreed that the price shall be what Titius shall value the thing at, Labeo denies that such a

§ 1. A price should have been agreed upon, for there can be no sale without a price. And the price should be certain; otherwise, if the parties have agreed that the price shall be what Titius shall value the thing at, then it was a point much debated amongst the ancients, whether this was or was not a sale.

transaction can have any effect, and this opinion is approved by Cassius, though Ofilius thinks that a contract of sale exists, and this view is followed by Proculus.

But our decision settles the matter in this way, viz., that, whenever a sale is made, the price being "so much as he shall determine", the contract shall stand on this condition, that, if he who has been so named fix the price, then the price is to be paid according to the amount fixed by him, and the thing delivered, so that the sale may be completed, the purchaser having an action grounded on the purchase, and the vendor an action grounded on the sale. But, if he who has been named is either unwilling or unable to fix the price, then the sale is void, on account of no price having been agreed upon. This rule, as we have adopted it in respect of sales, may, without absurdity, be applied to contracts of letting and hiring.

§ 141. Again, the price should consist of a sum of money, for it is a point rightly open to question, whether the price can consist of anything else, as, for example, whether a slave, a garment, or a piece of land can be the price of another thing. The leaders of our school think that the price may consist of some other thing; whence arises the common opinion, that a contract of sale is formed by the exchange of things, and that this is the oldest form of the contract of sale, and they support this view by quoting the Greek poet Homer, who somewhere says as follows:

§ 2. Again, the price should consist of a sum of money, for it was a point much disputed whether the price can consist of anything else, as, for example, whether a slave, or a piece of land, or a garment can be the price of another thing. Sabinus and Cassius thought that the price could consist of another thing, whence arises the common opinion that a sale is formed by the exchange of things, and that this is the oldest form of the contract of sale, and the Greek poet Homer was quoted, who somewhere says that the army of the Greeks procured themselves wine in exchange for certain things. These are his words:

"Then straightway the long-haired Greeks bought wine,
Some with copper, others with flashing steel,
Others with ox-skins, and others with the oxen themselves,
Others with prisoners of war."—*Iliad*, vii, 472-5.

and so on. The leaders of the opposite school take a different view, and think that an exchange of things is one thing and the contract of sale quite another, otherwise there would be no means of ascertaining, on an exchange of things, which was to be taken to be the thing sold and which given by way of price; and, again, it would seem absurd that both things should be regarded as sold and

The leaders of the opposite school viewed the matter otherwise, and thought the exchange of things was one thing and the contract of sale quite another, otherwise there would be no means of ascertaining, on an exchange, which was to be taken to be the thing sold and which given by way of price, for it seemed unreasonable to hold that both were sold and given by way of price; but the opinion of Pro-

both given by way of price. But Cælius Sabinus lays down that if I should propose to buy a thing which you have for sale, as, for example, an estate, and I should give, say, a slave for it, the estate will then be held to have been sold, and the slave to have been given by way of price.

culus, who maintained that exchange was a peculiar kind of contract apart from sale, has very properly prevailed, for it is supported by other verses of Homer, and confirmed by adducing more weighty grounds; and this has been admitted by the late emperors, who have preceded us, and is more fully discussed in our Digests. § 3. As soon, then, as the contract of sale has been made (which will be, as we have said, when the parties are agreed about the price, assuming the transaction is carried out without writing), the risk as to the thing sold immediately falls upon the purchaser, although the thing has not yet been delivered to him. Hence, if the slave die or receive an injury in some part of his body, or the whole or some portion of the house is burnt, or the whole or some portion of the land is swept away by the force of the waters, or is much diminished or deteriorated in value by an inundation, or by the trees being thrown down by tempest, the loss is on the purchaser, and, although he does not get the thing, he must pay over the price, for the vendor is not responsible for that which happens without fraud or negligence on his part. But if, after the sale, the land is increased by alluvion, the purchaser profits by it, for he who incurs the risk should take the gain. If, however, a slave, who had been sold, runs away or is stolen, without any fraud or negligence on the part of the vendor, it will be necessary to inquire whether the vendor undertook the safe custody of him until delivery, for, if he undertake this, the risk will clearly be on him; but, if he has not undertaken this, he is safe. The same rules are to be understood as applying to other animals or things; but, in any case, the vendor is bound to assign to the purchaser his right to a real or personal action; for, of course, he who has not yet delivered a thing to the purchaser, is still the owner of it, and the same remarks apply to the action of theft and the action for unlawful injury. § 4. A contract of sale may be made conditionally or absolutely; conditionally, as, for example, "If you approve of Stichus, before such a day, he is to be bought by you for so many gold pieces". § 5. The purchase, with knowledge of the fact, of a sacred or religious place, or a public place (as, for example, a forum or basilica), is void; but if, deceived by the vendor, he has bought it supposing it to be private property or unconsecrated, he will have an action on the purchase, not for the purpose of getting the property, but for damages for the loss he has sustained by being deceived. The same rule applies to the case of a free man bought as a slave.

Title xxiv. Of the contract of letting and hiring.

§ 142. The contract of letting and hiring is subject to similar rules; for, unless a fixed sum for the hire has been agreed upon, it is held that there is no contract of letting and hiring. § 143. Hence the question arises whether a contract of letting and hiring is made if the amount to be paid for the hire is left to the decision of a third party, as, for example, at the sum which Titius shall fix. For this reason, also, the question arises whether a contract of letting and hiring has been made when I have given clothes to a fuller for the purpose of cleaning and pressing, or to a tailor to mend, without, at the same time, having agreed upon the sum to be paid, but only that so much shall be given as we subsequently agree upon. § 144. Or if I have given you a thing for use, and in return have received another thing for my use, the question arises whether this is a contract of letting and hiring.

The contract of letting and hiring closely resembles that of buying and selling, and is regulated by the same rules of law. For, as the contract of sale is formed when the price is agreed upon, so is the contract of hiring held to be complete when the sum to be paid for the hire is settled; and the person letting has an action on the letting, and the hirer an action on the hire. § 1. And what we have stated above,* as to the case of the price being left to the decision of a third party, is to be understood as applying also to the contract of letting and hiring, if the sum to be paid by way of hire has been left to the decision of a third party. For this reason, if a person should give clothes to a fuller to be cleaned and pressed, or to a tailor to be mended, without, at the same time, having agreed upon the sum to be paid, but only that so much shall be given as we subsequently agree upon, a contract of letting and hiring cannot properly be held to have been made, but an action on the case, based upon the agreement of the parties, will be available. § 2. Moreover; just as it was commonly doubted whether a contract of sale resulted from an exchange,† or a similar doubt was raised in the case of the contract of letting and hiring, if, say, a person gave you something to use or take the produce of, and, in return, received from you another thing for his use, or of which he was to have the produce. And it has been decided that this is not a letting and hiring, but a peculiar kind of contract. So, for example, if a person has an ox, and a neighbour of his also has one, and it is agreed between them that the oxen are to be lent to

* *ante*, tit. xxiii, § 1. † *ante*, tit. xxiii, § 2.

each other to work for ten days at a time, and the ox of one dies whilst in the possession of the other, no action of letting or of hiring, or of loan, lies, since the loan was not gratuitous, but an action on the case must be brought.

§ 145. Hence, also, the contracts of buying and selling, and of letting and hiring, seem to have some resemblance to each other, as, in certain cases, it is commonly a matter of doubt whether a contract of buying and selling, or of letting and hiring, has been made. As, for example, if something has been let out in perpetuity, as is the case with the estates of municipalities, which are let out under the condition that, so long as the rent is paid, the land shall not be taken away from the hirer himself, nor from his heir. But the better opinion is that this is a contract of letting and hiring.

§ 3. Hence, also, the contracts of buying and selling, and of letting and hiring, seem to have some resemblance to each other, so that, in certain cases, it is a matter of doubt whether a contract of buying and selling, or of letting and hiring, has been made, as, for example, in the case of those lands which are delivered to persons to be enjoyed in perpetuity, that is, that, as long as the rent or price of hire is paid for these lands to the owner, he cannot take away the lands from the hirer or his heir, or anyone to whom the hirer or his heir has sold or delivered over the lands by way of gift or dowry, or otherwise alienated them. But, as this contract was a matter of dispute amongst the ancients, some holding it to be a letting, and others a sale, a law was passed, by the Emperor Zeno, which declared the contract of emphyteusis to be of a special nature, neither inclining to the contract of hire or to that of sale, but to rest on its own agreements; and that, if any special pact was made on the subject, it was to be as binding as if it were the nature of the contract to contain such pact; but if no agreement was made respecting the risk, then, if the thing was totally destroyed, the loss should be thrown back on the owner, but a partial loss should fall upon the lessee, and this rule is now in force.

§ 146. Again, it becomes a question whether a contract of buying and selling, or of letting and hiring, is formed, when I have delivered gladiators to you on condition that I am to receive, by way of hire for their labour, twenty silver pieces in respect of each one who comes out unhurt, but one thousand silver pieces for each one killed or maimed; and the better opinion is, that, as to those who come out unhurt, there is a contract of letting and hiring, but that, as to those who are killed or maimed, the contract is one of buying and selling, and this results from the event, just as if there had been a condition attached to the sale or hire of each one, for it is now no longer doubted but that a thing may be sold or hired under a condition.

§ 147. Again, the question arises whether a contract of buying and selling, or of letting and hiring, is formed if I come to an agreement with a goldsmith that he is to make some rings for me of a certain weight and of a certain form out of his gold, and that he is to receive, say, two hundred silver pieces. Cassius lays down that there is a sale of the material and a hiring of the work. But the majority are of opinion that a contract of sale has been formed, though, if I had given him my gold, and agreed with him as to the price for his workmanship, then a contract of letting and hiring would have been concluded.

§ 4. Again, the question arises whether a contract of buying and selling, or of letting and hiring, is formed when Titius has come to an agreement with a goldsmith that the latter, out of his gold, is to make him rings of a certain weight and of a certain form, and to receive, say, ten gold pieces. Cassius lays down that there is a sale of the material and a hiring of the work; but it has been decided that only a contract of buying and selling has been formed, though, if Titius gave the gold and came to an agreement as to the price to be paid for the work, there is no doubt but that the contract is one of letting and hiring.

§ 5. The hirer ought to do everything according to the terms of the contract of hiring, and, if any condition has been omitted, he ought to supply it, according to what is fair and equitable. He who has given or promised a sum for the hire of clothes or silver, or a beast of burden, must bestow as much care for the preservation of the thing he hires, as the most careful head of a family bestows on the care of his own property; and if he does do so, and yet the thing is lost through some accident, he is not liable for its restoration.

§ 6. On the death of the hirer during the period of the hire, his heir acquires the contract in the original terms.

Title xxv. Of partnership.

§ 148. We are in the habit of entering into the contract of partnership, either in respect of our whole property, or in respect of some one particular business, as, for example, the purchase or sale of slaves.

We are in the habit of entering into the contract of partnership, either in respect of our whole property, to which the Greeks give the special name of *κοινοπραξία*, or in respect of some one particular business, as, for example, the sale or purchase of slaves, or of wine, oil, or corn. § 1. And if there has been no express agreement as to the shares of profit and loss, the shares both of profit and loss are deemed equal; but if the shares have been the subject of express agreement this is binding, and it has never been doubted that the agreement is valid if two persons have agreed that, say, two-thirds of the profit and loss shall belong to one, and one-third to the other.

§ 149. But the question has been much debated whether a partnership can be so constituted that one of the partners shall take the greater part of the profit, but bear only a smaller proportion of the loss. This Quintus Mucius deemed contrary to the nature of the contract of partnership; but Servius Sulpicius, whose opinion has prevailed, thought that a partnership could be so created; for he has said that a partnership could be entered into in this way, viz., that one should not be liable for any loss at all, but should take part of the profit, provided his services were deemed so valuable that it would be just for him to be admitted into the partnership under such an agreement. For it is clear that a partnership may be constituted so that one partner contributes the money, the other none, and yet the profit may be common to both, for the services of one are often an equivalent for money.

§ 2. But doubts have been raised whether an agreement like the following should be considered binding, viz., if Titius and Seius have agreed that two-thirds of the profit and one-third of the loss shall go to Titius, and two-thirds of the loss and one-third of the profit to Seius. Quintus Mucius deemed such an agreement contrary to the nature of the contract of partnership, and therefore not to be treated as binding. Servius Sulpicius, whose opinion has prevailed, was of the contrary opinion, because the services of some partners are so valuable that it is just that they should be admitted into the partnership on better terms; for there can be no doubt that a partnership may be constituted so that one partner contributes money, the other none, and yet the profit may be common to both, because the services of one are often an equivalent for money. Hence, an opinion, contrary to that of Quintus Mucius, has prevailed, that a partnership may be so created that one partner may share the profit and not be liable for the loss, and this view Servius consistently held; but this, however, is to be understood in this sense, that if profit result from one transaction and loss from another, the one must be set off against the other, and only the excess reckoned as profit.

§ 150. And this is certain, that if nothing has been agreed upon between them as to the respective shares of profit and loss, still the profit and loss will be shared equally between them; and if the shares have been expressed on one side of the account, say, that of profit, but omitted on the other, then on that side also of the account which has been omitted the shares will be the same.

§ 3. It is settled that if the share is stated in respect of one side of the account only, as, for example, in respect of the profit only, or the loss only, but no mention of the other side of the account, the same share is also to be held on the side omitted.

§ 151. The partnership continues as long as the partners

§ 4. The partnership continues as long as the partners continue to wish

continue to wish it to do so, but, when one of them has renounced, the partnership is dissolved. But, clearly, if one of the partners has withdrawn from the partnership in order that he may alone get some coming profit, as, for example, if my partner, in a business in which our whole property is embarked, upon being left heir by some one, withdraw from the partnership in order that he alone may profit by the inheritance, he may be compelled to bring in this profit to the joint account; but if he make a profit by something which he had not been seeking, the benefit belongs to him only; and whatever is acquired after his withdrawal from the partnership is acquired by me alone. § 152. A partnership is also dissolved by the death of a partner; for he who enters into the contract of partnership selects that particular person as his partner. § 153. It is also said that a partnership is dissolved by change of legal position because it is said that in view of the civil law a change of legal position is equivalent to death; still, if the partners consent to go on, a new partnership would seem to begin. § 154. Again, the partnership is dissolved, if the property of one of the partners is sold* publicly or privately. But this partnership of which we are speaking may be contracted again by mere consent, for, as it belongs to the law of nations, it may exist between any persons according to the principle upon which that law is based.

* *ante*, § 78, 79.

it to do so, but, when one of them has renounced, the partnership is dissolved. But, clearly, if one of the partners has craftily withdrawn from the partnership in order that he may alone get some coming profit, as, for example, if a partner in a business in which all the property of the partners is embarked, when he has been left heir by some one, on this account withdraw from the partnership so that he alone may profit by the inheritance, he may be compelled to bring in this profit to the joint account; but if he make a profit by something which he had not been seeking, the benefit belongs to him only, but the partner from whom he has withdrawn takes everything that is acquired after his partner has renounced the partnership. § 5. A partnership is also dissolved by the death of a partner, for he who enters into the contract of partnership selects that particular person as his partner. And, even if the partnership has been formed by the consent of several persons, the death of one dissolves the partnership, although several still survive, unless when the partnership was formed it was otherwise agreed. § 6. Again, if the partnership has been formed in respect of one transaction, and this matter is completed, the partnership is ended. § 7. It is clear, also, that the partnership is dissolved by confiscation, that is. of course, the confiscation of the whole of the property of a partner, for as another person succeeds to the place of the partner, the latter is considered dead. § 8. Again, if one of the partners, borne down by the weight of his debts, surrender his property to his creditors, and his property is therefore sold to satisfy his debts, public or private, the partnership is dissolved. But, in this case, if the partners agree to go on, a new partnership would seem to begin.

§ 9. It has been a question whether a partner can only be sued by his co-partner by the action based on the partnership, when he has been guilty of fraud, as is the case with him who has become a depositary, or whether a partner is liable also for failure of duty, that is, for carelessness and negligence, and the better opinion is that he is also answerable for failure of duty, but not such as is measured by the most absolute carefulness, for it is sufficient if a partner use such care in partnership matters as he is accustomed to use in his own affairs. For he who takes to himself a careless partner, has only himself to blame.

Title xxvi. Of the contract of gratuitous agency.

§ 155. A contract of gratuitous agency arises whether we commission a person to do something for us or for another. Hence, whether I commission you to carry on my affairs, or those of another person, this contract is formed, and we are reciprocally bound to each other to do all that which I ought equitably to do for you in the matter, or you for me. § 156. Though, if I commission you to do anything for your own sake, the commission is useless; for what you may do for your own sake, you will be deemed to do in accordance with your own judgment, and not because of my commission:

This contract may be formed in five ways, whether by a person commissioning you to act for his benefit, or for his and yours, or for another person's only, or for his and another person's, or for yours and another person's, but a commisson given you for your benefit only is useless, and therefore no obligation arises out of it, nor does any right of action on the commission exist between you. § 1. A contract of gratuitous agency arises for the benefit of the mandator only; if, for example, a person commission you to conduct his business, or to buy an estate for him, or to become surety for him. § 2. It arises for your benefit, and that of the mandator; if, for example, he commission you to lend money at interest to a person who borrows it for the affairs of the mandator; or, if, when you, as a creditor, are about to sue him on his suretyship, he commission you to sue the principal debtor at his risk, or to stipulate at his risk, from a person whom he appoints as his substitute for a sum which he owes to you. § 3. The contract is created for the benefit of a third person; if, for example, you are commissioned to manage the affairs of Titius, or to buy an estate for him, or to become surety for him. § 4. It arises for the benefit of the mandator and a third party, if, for example, the mandator commission you to see to some business transactions in which he and Titius are jointly interested, or to buy an estate for him and Titius, or to become surety for him and Titius. § 5. It arises for your and a third party's benefit, if, for example, you are commissioned to lend money at interest to Titius, but if you are to lend the money without interest, only the benefit of the third person would be involved. § 6. It arises for your benefit only, if, for example, you are commissioned to place your money out in the purchase of land rather than at interest, or, on the other hand, that you should put it out at interest rather than invest it in land. But this form of gratuitous agency is rather advice than a commission, and on that account is not obligatory, because no one is liable, on the ground of having given advice, even though it may not have been beneficial to him to whom it was given, since every one is free to consider for himself whether the advice is good.

therefore, if I advised you to put out at interest the money you have lying idle at home, then, although you may have entered into a loan of it in kind with some one from whom you cannot recover it, still you will have no action, grounded on the commission, against me. Again, if I advised you to buy something, then, although it may not have been advantageous to you to have bought it, still I shall not be liable to you on the mandate, and this rule is carried to such an extent that it may be doubted whether he is liable on the mandate who has commissioned you to lend money at interest to Titius. Servius lays down that he is not liable, but we incline to the opinion of Sabinus, who says he is liable, because you would not have lent the money if you had not been commissioned to do so.

Hence, if a person should advise you to purchase something with, or lend, the money which you have lying idle at home, although it may not have been advantageous to you to have bought that thing, or to have lent the money, still he is not liable to you on the mandate, and this is so much so that it has been doubted whether he would be liable to an action on the mandate, if he commissioned you to lend money at interest to Titius; but the opinion of Sabinus has prevailed that a mandate in such a case would be obligatory, because you would not have lent your money to Titius, unless you have been commissioned to do so.

§ 157. It is clear that if a person give a mandate in respect of a matter which is contrary to good morals, no obligation is contracted; as, for example, if I commission you to steal from Titius, or to do him an injury.

§ 7. So a mandate is not obligatory which is contrary to good morals; as, for example, if Titius commission you to steal, or do damage, or commit an unlawful act; for although you incurred the penalty arising from the act you have no action against Titius.

§ 161. When he whom I have duly commissioned has exceeded the terms of the mandate, I have an action on the mandate against him to the extent to which it was to my interest that he should have fulfilled the mandate, provided it was in his power to fulfil it; but he cannot sue me. Hence, if I have commissioned you to buy me an estate for, say one hundred thousand sesterces, and you have bought it for one hundred and fifty thousand, you will have no action on the mandate against me, even though you should be willing to let me have the estate for the sum which I had commissioned you to give. And this opinion was especially approved by both Sabinus and Cassius. But if you have bought it for less you will of course have an action against me, because he who commissions a person to buy for one hundred thousand sesterces will be deemed at the same time to have given a commission to buy it for less if possible.

§ 8. He who executes a mandate should not exceed its limits, as, for example, if a person has commissioned you to go as far as one hundred gold pieces in buying an estate, or in becoming surety for Titius, you must not exceed this sum in the purchase or the suretyship, otherwise you will have no action on the mandate against your principal; and this is carried so far that, according to Sabinus and Cassius, even though you proposed to limit your claim to the hundred gold pieces, the action would fail; but the leaders of the opposite school think that you may properly bring an action up to the one hundred gold pieces, and this opinion is doubtless the more consonant to the justice of the case. If you lay out less on the purchase you will, of course, have an action against him, for he who commissions a person to buy an estate for him for one hundred gold pieces, will be deemed at the same time to have commissioned him to buy it for less if possible.

§ 158. Again, if a person commission me as to the doing of something after my death, the mandate is useless, because the rule holds generally that an obligation cannot begin to arise in the person of the heir.*

* *ante.* § 100.

§ 159. But, though a mandate has been properly constituted, it is extinguished if, before anything has been done under it, it is revoked. § 160. Again, the mandate is dissolved, if, before it is executed, either of the parties should die, that is, either the principal or the agent. But, on the ground of utility, the rule has been adopted, that if, in ignorance of the death of my principal, I have executed the mandate after his death, I can still bring an action on the mandate, otherwise a want of knowledge, which was excusable and

§ 9. A mandate properly constituted is, nevertheless, extinguished, if, before anything has been done under it, it is revoked. § 10. Again, a mandate is extinguished, if, before it is executed, either of the parties should die, that is, either the principal or the agent. But, on the ground of utility, the rule has been adopted, that if, in ignorance of the death of your principal, you have executed the mandate after his death, you can still bring an action on the mandate, otherwise a want of knowledge, which was excusable reasonable, would involve me in loss. Similar to this, is the rule adopted by the majority that my debtor is discharged, who has paid my steward in ignorance of the fact that the latter has been manumitted by me, although in strict law, he would not be discharged, for he has paid another person, and not him whom he ought to have paid.

and reasonable, would involve you in loss. Similar to this, is a rule which has been adopted, viz., that debtors are discharged if they have paid, in ignorance of the manumission, the steward of Titius after he has been freed, although in strict law they cannot be discharged, as they paid another than him whom they ought to have paid.

§ 11. Every one is free to refuse to undertake a mandate, but, once undertaken, it must be carried out, or renounced in time to enable the principal to execute it himself, or through the agency of another. For, otherwise, if the renunciation has not been so made as to leave the principal full opportunity of carrying out the thing, an action on the mandate will lie, unless a lawful ground of excuse has arisen, either for having renounced, or for having done so at an inconvenient time.

§ 12. A mandate may be given not to be carried out for a time, or subject to a condition.

§ 162. Finally, it must be noted that an action on the mandate will lie whenever I give something to be done gratuitously, which, if I had at the time settled the cost, would have fallen within the contract of letting and hiring, as, for example, if I have given clothes to a fuller to be cleaned and pressed, or to a tailor to be mended.

§ 13. Finally, it must be noted that, unless a mandate is gratuitous, it falls under the head of some other contract, for, if the remuneration is agreed upon, it is a contract of letting and hiring. And we lay down, generally, that, in those cases in which the duty is undertaken without any remuneration being agreed upon, and, therefore, a contract of mandate or deposit is formed, in such cases, if remuneration comes in question, the contract is one of letting and hiring; and hence an action on the mandate lies, if a person gives clothes to a fuller to be cleaned and pressed, or to a tailor to be mended, without any remuneration being agreed upon or promised.

Title xxvii. Of obligations arising from quasi-contracts.

After having thus discussed the various kinds of contracts, let us now consider those obligations which are not held, properly speaking, to spring from contract; but yet, as they do not derive their origin from tort, seem to arise, as it were, from contract. § 1. Thus, when a person has carried on the affairs of another during his absence, actions result reciprocally between them, which are called "negotiorum gestorum", the action available to him whose affairs have been carried on being the "direct", and that available to him who has carried them on being the "contrary" action. It is clear that these actions cannot properly be said to result from contract, for they arise out of the fact that one person has, without being commissioned so to do, undertaken the management of another person's affairs, and consequently, those whose affairs have been so carried on are bound even without their knowing it. This rule has been adopted, on the ground of utility, in order to prevent the affairs of those being entirely neglected who have been compelled suddenly to go abroad, without having had an opportunity of entrusting the management of them to anyone; and, obviously, no one would concern himself about them if he had no action for the recovery of any expenses incurred. But, just as he who has carried on the affairs of another to good purpose, has rendered the latter liable to him, so, on the other hand, he himself is bound to render an account of his management. In such a case, the account rendered must show the most scrupulous care, and it is not enough to have bestowed as much care as he is in the habit of bestowing on his own affairs, if another person, with more care, might have managed the matter better. § 2. Tutors, also, who are liable to the action in respect of their guardianship, are not, properly speaking, bound by contract (for no contract arises between the tutor and the pupil); but, as they are clearly not tortiously liable, they seem to be bound as if by contract; and in this case, too, there are reciprocal actions, for not only has the pupil an action grounded on the tutorship against the tutor, but, on the other hand, if the tutor has incurred expenses on behalf of the pupil, or become bound for him, or pledged his own property with the pupil's creditors, he has a "contrary" action arising out of the tutorship. § 3. Again, if a thing is common to several persons, without any partnership existing between them, as, for example, by its having been given, or left to them, by way of legacy, jointly, and one of them has become liable to the other in an action for the division of the common property,—either because he alone has drawn the produce of the thing, or because the other has incurred necessary expenses in respect of the thing—he cannot be held, properly speaking, to be bound by contract (for no contract has been entered into between them); but, as he is not liable tortiously, he seems to be bound as if by contract. § 4. The same rule applies to him who, for similar reasons, is liable to his co-heir in an action for the division of the inheritance. § 5. So, an heir cannot be said, properly speaking, to be liable, as by contract, in respect of legacies due, for the legatee cannot be said, properly speaking, to have transacted any business either with the heir or with the deceased; and yet, as the heir is not tortiously liable, he is held to be liable as if by contract. § 6. Again, he to whom a person has, by mistake, paid that which is not due, seems to be liable by quasi-contract, for he cannot properly be deemed bound by contract, inasmuch as, if we follow out the reasoning, he is rather bound (as we have remarked above)* in respect of an act for dissolving than forming a contract, for he who hands over money, with the intention of making a payment, seems rather to do this with the view of dissolving than forming a contract; but still, he who receives it is bound, just as if a loan in kind had been made to him, and he is, therefore, liable to a personal action. § 7. In some cases, however, that which was not due, but paid by mistake, cannot be recovered back, for the ancients have settled this to be so in those cases where the liability increases if it is denied, as, for example, in the case of the Aquilian law, and again in the case of a legacy.† This rule, however, the ancients only applied in respect of those legacies, which were for a fixed sum, which the heir was ordered to give the legatee.‡ But, by our constitution, which has assimilated all legacies and bequests in trust, we have extended the doctrine to all legacies and bequests in trust; though it does not avail all legatees, but only applies to prevent the recovery, as not due, of those legacies and bequests in trust paid over by mistake to churches or other places dedicated to religion or charity.

* *ante*, tit. xiv, § 1.

† cf. Gai. IV, § 9.

‡ cf. Gai. II, § 282.

Title xxviii. Of the persons through whom we can acquire obligations.

§ 163. Having treated of the kinds of obligations which arise out of contract, we must observe that obligations may not only be acquired by ourselves, but also by those who are in our power,** whe-

** III, § 104.

Having treated of the kinds of obligations which arise out of contract and quasi-contract, we must observe that obligations may not only be acquired by ourselves, but also by those who are in our power,

ther as being descendants or slaves, or as being in our marital power, or as being freemen in a state of bondage.*

as, for example our slaves and children; but the whole of whatever is acquired for us by our slaves becomes ours, but that which has been acquired as the result of an obligation by our children, who are in our power, is divided, according to the rule enunciated in our constitution,†† as to the ownership and use and enjoyment of things. So that, as to what resulted from an action, the father has the use and enjoyment, but the ownership is reserved for the son, that is, of course, when the action is brought by the father according to the provision in our constitution.

§ 164. We acquire, also, by those freemen, and slaves belonging to others, whom we bona fide possess, but only in two cases,† that is, if they acquire anything by their labour or by means of our property. § 165. Similarly, we acquire in the same two cases by means of a slave, of whom we have the usufruct.‡ § 166. But he who has the bare legal right in a slave, although he is the owner, is, nevertheless, held to have less right in this respect than the usufructuary or the bona fide possessor,** for it is settled that on no ground can anything be acquired for him, and this rule is carried to such an extent that, according to some, he will not acquire anything, though the slave should have expressly stipulated for it, or taken a formal conveyance of it in his name.

§ 1. We acquire, also, by those freemen, and slaves belonging to others, whom we bona fide possess, but only in two cases, that is, if they acquire anything by their labour or by means of our property. § 2. Similarly, we acquire, in the same two cases, by means of a slave of whom we have the usufruct or use.

§ 167. It is clear that a slave, owned in common, acquires for his masters in proportion to their several interests in him, except that when stipulating, or going through the formal sale with the copper and the scale, for one owner expressly named, he acquires for this one alone, as, for example, when he stipulates thus: "Do you bind yourself to give to my master Titius?" or when he goes through the formal mode of conveyance, thus: "I declare this thing to belong to my master, Lucius Titius, by the law of the quirites, and be it now bought for him by means of this copper and this copper-scale." § 167A. It

§ 3. It is clear that a slave, owned in common, acquires for his masters in proportion to their several interests in him, except that, when stipulating or receiving by delivery for one owner expressly named, he acquires for this one alone, as, for example, when he stipulates thus: "Do you bind yourself to give to my master Titius?" But, if the slave has stipulated by order of one master, then, although the point was formerly disputed, it is now settled by our deci-

* *ante*, II, § 86.
† *ante*, II, § 92.
‡ *ante*, II, § 91.
** *ante*, II, § 88.

†† *ante*, II, ix, § 1.

is a disputed point whether, although the name of one of the masters being added makes that one only acquire, the same rule applies to the case of the slave acting on the order of one of his masters only. The leaders of our school think that it is acquired for him alone who gave the order, just as if the slave had expressly stipulated for him, or had gone through the formal mode of conveyance on his behalf. But the leaders of the opposite school are of opinion that it is just as much acquired for both masters as if neither of them had given any order.

sion, and, (as we have stated above,*) he acquires for him alone who gave him the order.

* *ante*, tit. xvii, § 3.

Title xxix. Of the modes in which obligations are dissolved.

§ 168. An obligation is dissolved, primarily, by the payment of that which is due. Hence the question arises whether, if with the consent of his creditor, one thing be paid for another, the debtor will be discharged at law, as our leaders affirm, or whether he continues bound in law, but should be allowed to defeat the suit of the claimant by means of a plea of fraud, as is the opinion of the founders of the opposite school.

§ 169. Again, an obligation is dissolved by crediting it as fulfilled; for "acceptilatio" is, as it were, an imaginary payment. For, if you are willing to release me from that which I owe you by virtue of a verbal contract, it may be done by your allowing me to say these words: "Have you received that which I promised you?" and you reply, "I have". § 170. By this process, as we have just stated, properly speaking, only those obligations can be dissolved which arise out of the verbal contract, and no others, for it seemed consistent that an obligation, consti-

Any obligation is dissolved by the payment of that—or, with the consent of the creditor, of something else as an equivalent for that—which is due. And it is immaterial who pays, that is, whether the debtor himself pays, or some one else for him; for the debtor is discharged by the payment made by a third person, whether that payment was made with, or without, the knowledge, or against the will of the debtor. Again, if the debtor should pay, then those who have become surety for him are also discharged, just as happens when, on the other hand, the surety pays, for he thereby is not only himself discharged, but the principal also.

§ 1. Again, an obligation is dissolved by crediting it as fulfilled; for "acceptilatio" is an imaginary payment. For, if Titius is willing to release his debtor from that which the latter owes him by virtue of a verbal contract, it may be done by his allowing the debtor to say these words: "Have you received that which I promised you?" and Titius answers, "I have"; and this mode of release may be effected in the Greek language, if only similar words are employed to those in use in Latin, as, "Do you acknowledge to have received so many silver pieces?"

tuted verbally, should be capable of dissolution by other words; but, further, that which may be owed in other ways, may be thrown into the form of a stipulation, and then be dissolved by crediting it as paid. § 171. But a woman cannot, without the authority of her tutor, give a release by this mode of imaginary payment, although payments may be made to her without the authority of her tutor.* § 172. So the part payment of a debt is valid, but whether there can be an imaginary payment of a part is doubtful.

* *ante*, ii, § 85.

"I do." By this process (as we have said), only those obligations can be dissolved which arise out of the verbal contract, but no others; for it seemed consistent that an obligation, constituted verbally, should be capable of dissolution by other words; but, further, that which may be owed in other ways, may be thrown into the form of a stipulation, and then be dissolved by an imaginary payment. And, just as a part of a debt may be paid, so a release by way of imaginary payment may be made of a part only. § 2. A stipulation has been introduced which is commonly called the Aquilian, by which an obligation, arising in any way, may be thrown into the form of a stipulation, and then dissolved by way of imaginary payment. For this Aquilian stipulation effects a novation of all obligations, and was drawn up by Gallus Aquilius, in the following terms: "Whatever you ought, now or hereafter, on any ground to give or to do for me, and in respect of whatever things I have now, or shall have, against you, the right to a personal or real action, or to the extra-ordinary aid of the magistrate, and whatever you have, hold, or possess of mine, or which you have fraudulently ceased to possess: now, whatever is the value of these things, so much money Aulus Agerius has stipulated to be given him, and Numerius Negidius has bound himself to do so;" and then, on the other side, Numerius Negidius interrogated Aulus Agerius thus: "Have you received all that I, this day, by the Aquilian stipulation, promised you?" And Aulus Agerius answered: "I have, and I have credited it as received."

§ 173. There is, also, another kind of imaginary payment, viz., that by means of the copper and the scale. This kind of release has been adopted in certain cases, as, for example, when anything is due by reason of a contract formed with the copper and the scale, or due by virtue of a testament or a judicial sentence. § 174. And this proceeding is carried out, in the presence of not less than five witnesses and the scale-bearer,† in this way. He, who is being released, should speak thus: "Since I have been condemned in so many thousands, from that sum I pay and I discharge myself with this copper and this copper scale, and I balance this scale for you from first to

† *ante*, i, § 119.

last, in accordance with the public law." He then strikes the balance with a copper coin, which he gives to the person from whom he desires to be released, as if by way of payment. § 175. In a similar way, the legatee releases the heir from a legacy, which the latter has been ordered, by his testator, to give him,* but, of course, just as the debtor implies that he has been condemned by the judgment to pay, so must the heir admit that he has been ordered to give by virtue of the testament. But the heir can only be released in this way in respect of things which are estimated by weight or number, if certain in quantity, though some think that things which are estimated by measure are included in the rule.

* *ante*, ii, § 201.

§ 176. Moreover, an obligation is dissolved by novation; as, for example, if I have stipulated that what you owe me shall be paid by Titius. For a new obligation arises from the intervention of a new person, and the first is dissolved by its transference into the second, so that sometimes, although the subsequent stipulation is void, nevertheless the first is dissolved by the effect of the novation, as, for example, if I have stipulated from Titius, to receive after his death† what you owe me, or from a woman or a pupil without the authorisation of the tutor. In these cases I lose the thing owing to me, for the first debtor is released, and the subsequent obligation is void. The rule is not the same if I have stipulated from a slave, for, in this case, the original debtor continues liable, just as if I had not made any subsequent stipulation. § 177. But, if the person with whom I make the subsequent stipulation is the same, then novation only arises if there is something new in the subsequent stipulation, as, say, a condition, or a term, or a surety is added or withdrawn. § 178. But what I have said regarding the surety is disputed, for the leaders of the opposite school hold that the addition or withdrawal of a surety has no effect in the matter of novation. § 179. And what we have said as to novation being effected where a

† *ante*, § 100.

§ 3. Moreover, an obligation is dissolved by novation; as, for example, if Seius stipulate from Titius that which you owe to Seius. For a new obligation arises from the intervention of a new person, and the first is dissolved by its transference into the second; so that sometimes, although the subsequent stipulation is void, nevertheless the first is dissolved by the effect of the novation, as, for example, if Titius stipulate from a pupil, without the authorisation of his tutor, for that which you owe Titius. In this case the thing is lost, for the first debtor is released and the subsequent obligation is void. The rule is not the same if a person has stipulated from a slave, for then the original debtor continues liable, just as if there had been no subsequent stipulation. But, if the person with whom I make the subsequent stipulation is the same, then novation only arises if there is something new in the subsequent stipulation, as, say, a condition, or a term, or a surety added or withdrawn. And what we have said as to novation

condition is added, must be understood in the sense that we mean to say that a novation is effected if the condition is fulfilled; otherwise, if it should fail, the former obligation remains. But let us see whether he, who on that account brings an action, can be defeated by a plea of fraud, or one based on the agreement, for it would seem to have been agreed that the thing shall only be demanded if the condition of the subsequent stipulation is fulfilled. Servius Sulpicius, however, was of opinion that novation was immediately, and during the pendency of the condition, effected; and, if the condition failed, no action could be brought upon either ground, and, in that way, the thing was lost; and hence he also averred that, if a person stipulated from a slave that which Lucius Titius owed the former, a novation was effected and the thing lost, because an action could not be brought against the slave. But, in both these cases, we adopt a different rule, for a novation no more arises in these cases than if I had used the words, "Do you bind yourself?" in stipulating in respect of what you owe me, with an alien incapable of joining with me in that form of verbal contract.*

being effected where a condition is added, must be understood in the sense that we mean to say a novation is effected if the condition is fulfilled, otherwise, if it fail, the former obligation remains. But, as the ancients were agreed in this, that novation was effected when the second obligation had been entered into, with the intention of effecting a novation, but the matter was doubtful as to when this intention of effecting a novation should be held to have been manifested, and different presumptions were drawn by different persons to meet various cases, therefore a constitution of ours has been issued, which has clearly laid down, that novation shall only be effected when the contracting parties have expressly stated that their object in making the new contract is to dissolve the old one; otherwise, the first obligation will continue in force, and the second be added to it, so that an obligation will exist, resting on both grounds, according to the provisions of our constitution, which will appear more clearly by a perusal of the constitution itself.

§ 4. Further, those obligations, which are formed by consent, are dissolved by a contrary intention; for, if Titius and Seius have agreed together that Seius shall become the purchaser of the Tusculum estate for one hundred gold pieces, and then, whilst the contract is still executory, that is, before the price has been paid or the estate delivered over, it is agreed between them that the contract of sale shall be annulled, they are both released. The same rule applies to the contract of letting and hiring, and to all other contracts resulting, as we have just stated, from consent.

* *ante*, § 93.

§ 180. Further, an obligation is dissolved by joinder of issue, provided the action is one resulting from the civil law.† For then the original obligation

† *post*, iv, § 104.

is dissolved, and the debtor begins to incur a liability by reason of the issue joined, and, if he is condemned, the issue joined is gone, and a liability then arises, grounded on the judgment. And this is what is meant when the ancient writers say that, "before joinder of issue, the debtor ought to pay, after the joinder of issue, he ought to be condemned; after condemnation he ought to satisfy the judgment". § 181. Hence it is that, if I have sued for a debt by an action based on the civil law, I cannot again sue in respect of the same right, for I uselessly state my claim to be "that it ought to be given me",* since, by the joinder of issue, the original claim has ceased to be due; but it is otherwise if I have sued by an action based on the authority of the magistrate, for, in such a case, the obligation nevertheless remains, and therefore I can subsequently sue in respect of the same right, but I ought to be defeated by a plea of judgment awarded or of pending suit.† In the next commentary‡ we shall deal with the nature of actions resulting from the civil law and those based on the authority of the magistrate.

* *post*, iv, § 107.

† *post*, iv, § 106, 123.

‡ iv, § 103-109.

INSTITUTES OF JUSTINIAN, BOOK IV.

Title i. Of obligations arising from wrongs.

§ 182. Let us now pass to obligations arising from wrongs, as, for example, if a person has been guilty of theft, or taken property by violence, or inflicted damage, or committed an outrage; all which misdeeds give rise to one kind of obligation only, whilst obligations arising from contract (as we have above explained),* are reducible to four kinds.

* *ante*, § 89.

As in the preceding book we have discussed the subject of obligations arising from contract and quasi-contract, it follows that we should now deal with obligations arising from wrongs. The former class, as we pointed out at the time, are divided into four kinds, but of these latter there is only one kind, for they all arise from the act itself, that is, from the wrong, as, for example, from theft, from robbery, or damage, or outrage. § 1. Theft is a fraudulent dealing with the use, or possession of a thing, and this is forbidden by natural law. § 2. The word "furtum" is said to come from "furvum", that is, "black", because it is done secretly and darkly, and generally by night; or from "fraus", or from "ferre", that is, "auferre" (to carry away), or it is derived through the Greeks, who call a thief, φὼρ, which, too, comes from φέρειν, to carry off.

§ 183. According to Servius Sulpicius and Masurius Sabinus, there are four kinds of thefts, viz., that which is manifest, and that which is not manifest, that which arises from the discovery of the thing after solemn search, and that which arises from the stolen thing being deposited elsewhere. According to Labeo, two kinds, viz., manifest and non-manifest; the two other kinds being rather forms of actions relating to theft than kinds of thefts, and this seems the better opinion, as will appear below.* § 184. Some lay down that it is a manifest theft when the thief is taken in the act, but others extend it to cover the case of the thief being taken in the place where the act was committed, as, for example, if olives have been stolen in an olive-grove, or grapes in a vineyard, as long as the thief is in the olive-grove, or in the vineyard; or if the theft has been committed in a house, so long as the thief is in that house it is manifest theft. Others go further, and say that it is manifest theft until the thief has carried the stolen property to the place to which he intended carrying it. Others, again, go further, and say that it is manifest theft whenever the thief has been seen holding the thing in his hand, but this opinion has not gained ground; and the opinion of those who have thought that the theft is manifest if the thief is caught before he has carried the stolen property to the place he intended seems also unsatisfactory, because it raises grave doubts whether it would extend over the space of one or even of several days, which is material in this way, that a thief often intends to convey property stolen in one city to another city, or another province. Of the two first-mentioned opinions, both have met with approval, but the majority incline to the second. § 185. As to what is non-manifest theft may be gathered from what we have said, for that which is not manifest is non-manifest. § 186. Theft is said to be "conceptum" when the

* § 186, 187.

§ 3. There are two kinds of thefts, viz., that which is manifest; and that which is not manifest; for that which arises from the discovery of the thing af er solemn search, and that which arises from the stolen thing being deposited elsewhere, are rather forms of actions relating to theft than kinds of thefts, as will appear below. A manifest thief is he who the Greeks call "caught in the act" (ἐπ' αὐτοφώρῳ), being not only he who is taken in the act of thieving, but also he who is taken in the place where it is committed, as, for example, he who has committed theft in a house, and has been caught before he has got out of the door, or has stolen olives in an olive-yard, or grapes in a vineyard, and has been caught whilst in the olive-yard, or in the vineyard. Manifest theft must be further extended to include the case of the thief having been seen or caught, in a public or private place, by the owner or anyone else, whilst still holding the thing, and before he has reached the place to which he intended to carry it. But if he has carried the thing to the place he intended, although he may be caught with the stolen thing, he is not a manifest thief. As to what is non-manifest theft may be gathered from what we have said, for that which is not manifest is, of course, non-manifest. § 4. Theft is said to be "conceptum" when the stolen thing has been searched for, and found in the presence of witnesses in a person's possession; for a special action, known as the action based on the discovery of the stolen thing after formal search, lies against him, even though he may not be the thief. § 187. Theft is said to be "oblatum" when the stolen thing has been brought to you by someone, and has been found in your possession, that is, if it has been given you with the view of its being found in your possession rather than in his who gave it. For you, in whose possession the thing has been found, are entitled to a special action, known as the action based on the deposit of the stolen thing elsewhere, against him who placed the thing in your possession, although he may not be the thief. § 188. There is also an action for opposing a search against him who has prevented a person from searching for stolen goods.

stolen thing has been searched for, and found in the presence of witnesses in a person's possession; for a special action, known as the action based on the discovery of the stolen thing after formal search, lies against him, even though he may not be the thief. Theft is said to be "oblatum" when the stolen thing has been brought to you by some one, and has been found in your possession, that is, if it has been given you with the view of its being found in your possession rather than in his. For you, in whose possession the thing has been found are entitled to a special action, known as the action based on the deposit of the stolen thing elsewhere, against him who placed the thing in your possession, although he may not be the thief. There is also an action for opposing a search against him who has prevented a person from searching, in the presence of witnesses, for stolen goods. Moreover, under the edict of the prætor, he who does not produce stolen property searched for, and found in his possession, incurs a penalty by means of the action for not producing stolen goods. But these actions, based on the discovery of the stolen thing after search, on the deposit of the stolen thing elsewhere, on the opposition offered to a search, and on the non-production of stolen goods, have fallen into disuse; for, as searching for stolen property is not now conducted according to the ancient practice, therefore these actions have very properly ceased to be in common use, and it is abundantly clear that all who have knowingly received and concealed stolen property are liable to the action for non-manifest theft.

§ 189. The punishment for manifest theft, by the law of the Twelve Tables, was of a nature to cause the loss of the legal position of a citizen. For a free man, after being scourged, was adjudged to him whose property he had stolen; but whether, in consequence of this adjudication, he became a slave, or was only in the position of an ad-

§ 5. The penalty for manifest theft is quadruple the value, whether the thief be a slave or a free man; that for non-manifest theft is double.

judged debtor, was a disputed point. A slave after being equally scourged, was hurled from the Tarpeian rock. But, subsequently, the severity of the punishment met with disapproval, and, under the edict of the prætor, an action for the quadruple* was established as well for slaves as for free persons. § 190. The penalty inflicted for non-manifest theft, by the law of the Twelve Tables, was double the value, and this the prætor has retained. § 191. The penalty for theft discovered after formal search, and that arising out of the stolen property being deposited elsewhere, was, by the law of the Twelve Tables, threefold, and this the prætor has also retained. § 192. The action for preventing a search for stolen property was for the quadruple, and was introduced by the edict of the prætor. The law of the Twelve Tables had established no penalty under this head; it only enjoined that he who wishes to search shall do so naked, girt with a "linteum", and holding a plate; and if he found anything, the law directs the theft to be deemed manifest. § 193. As to what the "linteum" was is open to question, but it is highly probable that it was a sort of girdle to cover the private parts. Hence, the whole law is absurd. For he who hinders the search of a man clothed, will also hinder the search being made by a naked one, especially as he would be liable to a heavier penalty if the thing sought for in this way were found. Then, as to the plate, was he directed to carry this in order that, as his hands were occupied, nothing could be brought with him, or that he might put in it whatever might be found? but neither of these explanations would avail, if what is sought were of such a size or nature, that it could not be so brought in, nor placed thereon. There is no doubt, however, on one point, that of whatever material the dish may be made the law will be satisfied. § 194. Since, however, the law directs that, on this ground, the theft shall be deemed manifest, there are some writers who lay down that theft is manifest, either by law or by nature; by law, in the case of which we are speaking; by nature, in the case we have detailed above. But the better opinion is that theft is only to be deemed to be manifest by nature; for the law can no more make a non-manifest thief a manifest thief, than it can make him a thief, who is not a thief at all; or a man an adulterer or murderer, who is not an adulterer or a murderer; but the law can, of course, cause a man to be liable to a penalty as if he had committed theft, or adultery, or murder, although he has not done any of these things.

* iv, § 111.

§ 195. Theft is committed, not only when a person takes away the property of another in order to appropriate it, but generally when a person deals with the property of another against that other's will. § 196. Hence, if a person uses a thing which has been deposited with him, he commits theft, and, if he who has the use of a thing uses it for another purpose than that intended, he is liable to an action of theft; as, for example, if a person has borrowed silver plate, as if about to invite friends to supper, and carries it abroad with him; or, if anyone, having borrowed a horse for a ride, takes it away with him a longer distance than agreed upon, as in the case of him whom the ancient authors quote as having taken the horse into battle. § 197. It is, however, settled that those who use things, otherwise than was agreed upon when they were lent, only commit theft if they know that they are doing so against the will of the owner, and that he, if he knew of it, would not allow it; but, if they believe that they would be allowed, they are clear of the crime of stealing; and this is a most salutary distinction, for theft cannot be committed without a fraudulent intent. § 198. But, although a person thinks that he is dealing with the borrowed thing in a way contrary to the will of the owner, yet, if the owner is a consenting party, it is laid down that no theft has been committed. Whence arises this question: If Titius has persuaded my slave to steal some things from me, and to bring them to him, and the slave has disclosed the proposal to me, and I, in order to detect Titius in the wrongful act, have allowed my slave to take those things to him,

§ 6. Theft is committed, not only when a person takes away the property of another in order to appropriate it, but generally when a person deals with the property of another against that other's will. Hence, if a creditor uses the pledge, or a depositary the thing deposited, or if he, who has the use of a thing, uses it for another purpose than that for which it has been given, he commits theft; as, for example, if a person has borrowed silver plate, as if about to invite friends to supper, and carries it abroad with him, or if anyone, having borrowed a horse for a ride, takes it away with him a long distance, as in the case of him whom the ancient authors quote as having taken the horse into battle. § 7. It is, however, settled that those who use things otherwise than was agreed upon when they were lent, only commit theft if they know that they are doing so against the will of the owner, and that he, if he knew of it, would not allow it, but, if they believe that they would be allowed, they are clear of guilt; and this is a most salutary distinction, for theft cannot be committed without the intention of stealing. § 8. But, although a person thinks that he is dealing with the borrowed thing in a way contrary to the will of the owner, yet, if the owner is a consenting party, it is laid down that no theft has been committed. Whence arises this question: When Titius had persuaded the slave of Mævius to steal some things from his master, and to bring them to him, the slave disclosed this to Mævius. and Mævius, wishing to detect Titius in the wrongful act, allowed his slave to take those things to Titius, is Titius liable, either in an action for theft, or in an action for the

is Titius liable to me, either in an action for theft, or in an action for the corruption of my slave, or in neither? It has been held that neither action lies, for there can be no action for theft against him, since he has not dealt with the thing against my will, nor is he liable in an action for the corruption of my slave, because my slave has not been depreciated in value by corruption.

corruption of the slave, or in neither? The doubt here arising having been submitted to us, we have considered the conflicting opinions of the ancient jurists on the subject, some of whom held that neither the action of theft, nor that for corrupting a slave, were available, while others thought only the action of theft lay; and we, to cut short crafty distinctions of this short, have decided that both the action of theft and that for the corruption of a slave may be brought against him; for, although the slave has not been depreciated in value by the corruption of the tempter, and, therefore, the rules upon which the action for the corruption of a slave are based do not apply, yet the intention of the corrupter to destroy the honesty of the slave is involved, and he may, therefore, be rendered liable to the penal action, as if the slave had been corrupted by this very act, lest the impunity, in a case of this sort, should incite others to the perpetration of a similar misdeed towards a slave who could be easily corrupted.

§ 199. Sometimes theft may be committed of free persons, as, for example, if a person has carried off one of our children in our power, or our wife under marital power, or my adjudicated debtor,* or my hired gladiator. § 200. A person may even steal his own property, as, for example, if a debtor deprives his creditor of a thing pledged to him,† or if I have secretly withdrawn property belonging to me from a bona fide possessor. Hence it has been held that he who concealed his slave, who had returned to him whilst bona fide possessed by another, commits theft. § 201. Again, on the other hand, sometimes, the property of another may be occupied and acquired by use, without it being deemed a theft, as, for example, in the case of property belonging to an inheritance, of which the heir has not yet acquired possession, provided he is not a necessary heir; for, if the necessary heir is in existence, it is held that nothing can be acquired by way of use which is grounded on being in the place of the heir.‡ Again, a debtor may sometimes (as we have pointed out in the previous commentary)**

§ 9. Sometimes theft may be committed of free persons, as, for example, if a person has carried off one of our children in our power. § 10. A person may even steal his own property, as, for example, if a debtor deprives his creditor of a thing pledged to him.

‡ see II, § 9, 52, ** II, § 59, 60.

* *post*, IV, § 21. † *post*, § 204.

possess and acquire by use, without committing a theft, the property which he had sold by the process of the copper and the scale, or surrendered in court to a creditor, subject to a redemption clause.

§ 202. Sometimes a person is liable to an action for theft, though he himself has not committed the theft, as in the case of him by whose intentional co-operation theft has been committed. In this class may be included him who has knocked money out of your hand to enable another to run off with it, or got in your way to enable another to steal, or has scattered your sheep or oxen to enable another to catch them; and the ancient writers include, in the same class, him who, with a piece of red cloth, has frightened a herd of cattle. But, although this was done from wantonness, and not with that intention necessary to constitute theft, still we shall have to consider whether, even then, an equitable action will not lie in respect of such an act, as, by the Aquilian law, if damage has been sustained, even an unintentional wrongful act* may be punished.

* *post*, § 211.

§ 11. Sometimes a person is liable to an action for theft, though he himself has not committed the theft, as in the case of him by whose intentional co-operation theft has been committed. In this class may be included him who has knocked money out of your hand to enable another to run off with it, or got in your way to enable another to steal, or has scattered your sheep or oxen to enable another to catch them, and the ancient writers include in the same class him who, with a piece of red cloth, has frightened a herd of cattle. If, however, this was done from wantonness, and not with that intention necessary to constitute theft, the action should be one based on the circumstances of the case. But where Titius has committed a theft with the assistance of Mævius, both are liable in an action for theft. So he is held liable, as for theft, on the ground of his intentional co-operation, who enables another to commit theft by placing ladders to windows, or breaking open windows or a door, or who, knowing the purpose for which they have been borrowed, has lent tools for housebreaking, or ladders for placing against windows. But a person who does not assist in the commission of a theft, but only advises and urges its commission, is not liable in an action for theft. § 12. If those who are in the power of ascendants or masters steal a thing from them, they are guilty of stealing from them, and the thing falls under the head of stolen property (so that no one can acquire it by use until it has again returned into the power of its owner), but an action for theft does not lie, because no action on any ground can arise between them. But, if such a theft has been committed with the intentional assistance of another, then, as a theft has been committed, this person may properly be held liable to an action for theft, because, in fact, it was by his intentional cooperation that the theft was committed.

§ 203. An action for theft is available to him whose interest it is that the property should be safe, although he may not be the owner; and, therefore, it is only available to the owner when it is to his interest that the property should not perish. § 204. Hence it is clear that a creditor may bring an action for theft in respect of a stolen pledge; and this is carried so far that, although it is the owner himself, that is, the debtor, who has stolen the thing, nevertheless an action for theft lies in favour of the creditor. § 205. Again, if a fuller has received clothes to be cleaned and pressed, or a tailor has received them to mend for a fixed remuneration, and the clothes are stolen, it is he, and not the owner, who has the action for theft, because the owner is not interested in their preservation, since he can, in an action based on the letting, sue the fuller or the tailor for his property, provided the fuller or the tailor is good for the amount; but, if he is insolvent, then, as the owner cannot get redress from him, he is entitled to the action for theft, because, in such a case, it is to his interest that the thing should be safe. § 206. What we have said in respect of the fuller or the tailor may be repeated as to him to whom a thing has been lent; for, as he who receives remuneration is answerable for the safe custody of the thing, so also in this case, in consequence of

§ 13 An action for theft is available to him whose interest it is that the property should be safe, although he may not be the owner; and, therefore, it is only available to the owner if it is to his interest that the thing should not perish. § 14. Hence it is clear that a creditor may bring an action for theft in respect of a stolen pledge, even though his debtor is solvent, because it is to his advantage, rather, to rely upon the security than to bring a personal action; and this is carried so far that, although the debtor himself has stolen the thing, nevertheless an action for theft lies in favour of the creditor. § 15. Again, if a fuller received clothes to be cleaned and pressed, or a tailor has received them to mend for a fixed remuneration, and the clothes are stolen, it is he, and not the owner, who has the action for theft, because the owner is not interested in their preservation, since he can, in an action based on the letting, sue the fuller or tailor for his property. But, if a thing be stolen from a bona fide purchaser, he is entitled, as in the case of a creditor, to the action for theft, although he may not yet be owner. But the action for theft does not lie in favour of the fuller or the tailor, unless they are solvent, that is, unless they are in a position to pay the owner the value of the thing; for, if they are insolvent, then, as the owner cannot get redress from them, he is entitled to the action for theft, because, in such a case, it is to his interest that the thing should be safe; and the same rule holds although the fuller or the tailor may be partially solvent. § 16. What we have said in respect of the fuller and of the tailor was deemed, by the ancients, to be capable of application, also, to the case of the borrower. For, as the fuller, by accepting remuneration, becomes answerable for the safe custody of the

the benefit received by the use of the thing, a liability for its safe custody is entailed.

thing; so, also, he who derives benefit by the use of the thing incurs a liability for its safe custody. But our forethought has here, also, introduced an improvement by our decisions, for the owner is to have the right to decide whether he will bring an action based on the loan against him who borrowed the thing, or an action for theft against him who stole it; but, having made his election to sue either of them, he cannot afterwards fall back on an action against the other, and, if he elect to sue the thief, the borrower is released altogether from liability; but, if he elect to sue the borrower, he cannot bring an action for theft against the thief, but the borrower can sue the thief by the action for theft; though this is to be so only if the owner, knowing the thing to have been stolen, has proceeded against the borrower, for, if he is ignorant of this, or being uncertain whether the property is in the hands of the borrower or not, has commenced an action based on the loan, and then afterwards, on ascertaining the facts, wishes to withdraw from the action based on the loan, and commence one for the theft, liberty will be given to do so without any difficulty being thrown in his way, as it was in ignorance of the facts that he sued the borrower, unless reparation has been made to the owner by the borrower, for then the thief is released from any liability to an action for theft on the part of the owner, but the person who has made reparation to the owner, in respect of the thing lent to him, has the right of action transferred to him. In the case, however, of the owner having at the outset, in ignorance that the thing had been stolen, commenced an action against the borrower, based on the loan, but, on discovering the truth, has gone against the thief, then it is most clear that the borrower is to be altogether released from liability, whatever may be the result of the action against the thief, just as, in the opposite case, the thief would be released from liability, whether the borrower was in a state of absolute or partial solvency.

§ 207. But he with whom a thing is deposited is not answerable for its safe custody, and the only liability he incurs, in respect of it, is that arising out of any fraudulent act of his own; for which reason, if the thing is stolen from him, as he is not liable to restore it by an action based on

§ 17. But he with whom a thing is deposited is not answerable for its safe custody, and the only liability he incurs, in respect of it, is that arising out of any fraudulent act of his own; for which reason, if the thing is stolen from him, as he is not liable to restore it by an action based on the deposit, and, for the same reason, has no interest in the preservation of the thing, therefore, he cannot sue by an action for theft, but that action is available to the owner.

§ 208. Finally, it must be noted that the question has been raised whether a person under the age of puberty, by carrying off another person's property, commits theft. In the opinion of the majority, since theft turns on the intention, a person under the age of puberty can only be liable if he is approaching the age of puberty, and, consequently, understands that he is doing wrong.

the deposit, and, for the same reason, has no interest in the preservation of the thing, therefore, he cannot sue by an action for theft, but that action is available to the owner.

§ 18. Finally, it must be noted that the question has been raised whether a person under the age of puberty, by carrying off another person's property, commits theft. And it is settled that, since theft turns on the intention, a person under the age of puberty can only be liable if he is approaching the age of puberty, and, consequently, understands that he is doing wrong.

§ 19. The action for theft, whether for double or quadruple, is only for the purpose of recovering the penalty. For the owner can separately sue for the recovery of the thing itself, either by a real or a personal action.* The real action lies against the possessor, whether it is the thief himself who possesses or anyone else; the personal action lies against the thief himself or his heir, although not in possession of the thing.

* *post*, tit. vi, § 14, 18.

Title ii. Of the action for robbery with violence.

§ 209. He who takes, by violence, another's property, is, indeed, also liable to an action for theft; for who takes another's property more against the owner's will than he who takes it by force? and, therefore, he is rightly said to be a violent thief; but the prætor has introduced a special action for this kind of wrong, which is called the action for robbery with violence, and, if brought within the year, it is for the fourfold, but, after the year, for the simple value. The action is available though only one single thing has been taken by force, and that of the least possible value.

He who takes, by violence, another's property, is, indeed, also liable to an action for theft; for who takes another's property more against the owner's will than he who takes it by force? and, therefore, he is rightly said to be a violent thief; but the prætor has introduced a special action for this kind of wrong, which is called the action for robbery with violence, and, if brought within the year, it is for the fourfold, but, after the year, for the simple value. The action is available although only one single thing has been taken by force, and that of the least possible value. The whole of the quadruple is not, however, a penalty, and, besides the penalty, an action for the recovery of the thing, as we stated to be the case in respect of the action for manifest theft, but the recovery of the thing is included in the quadruple, so that the penalty is threefold,* whether the robber was caught in the act or not. For it would be ridiculous that a person, who takes a thing by force, should be in a better condition than he who secretly removes it. § 1. This action, however, only lies when a person has committed the forcible robbery with fraudulent intent, so that he ought to be held free from liability who, under a mistake, thinking it to be his own property, and, unmindful of law, takes a thing by force, with the idea that the owner may take his own property by force away from persons in whose possession it is; and it is, of course, consistent to hold that a person who, with this view, took a thing by force, would not be liable to an action for theft. But lest, in working out such distinctions as these, a loophole should be discovered, by which robbers may practice, with impunity, their nefarious schemes, it has been wisely provided, by the imperial constitutions dealing with this subject, that it shall be unlawful for anyone to carry off by force a thing that is movable, or moves itself, although he may believe that thing to be his own; and, if anyone should do so in spite of these constitutions, he is to lose the ownership of the thing if it belong to him, and, if it belong to some one else, he must, after making restitution of the thing, also pay the estimated value of it. These constitutions are held to apply, not only to movables capable of being carried off by force, but also to the case of forcible entry upon land, in order that every kind of robbery by force may, on this ground, be prevented. § 2. For this action to lie it is not essential that the thing should have formed part of the plaintiff's property, for, whether it was part of his property or not, yet, if it has been taken from amongst his property, the action is available. Hence, if anything has been let, lent, or pledged to Titius, or even deposited with him in such a way that it was to his interest not to have had the thing carried off, as, for example, if he had undertaken to be responsible for negligence in the case of the thing deposited, or if he possess it bona fide, or if a person has the use and enjoyment of the thing, or any other right in it that makes it to his interest not to have it taken by force, it is to be laid down that this action lies, not in order that he may get the ownership, but to enable him to get again that which

* see *post*, tit. 6, § 19.

he has lost by violence from amongst his goods, that is, that which has been carried away out of his property; and, generally, it may be taken that the acts which, if committed secretly, are grounds for an action for theft, will be grounds for this action.

Title iii. Of the Aquilian law.

§ 210. The action for damage wrongfully inflicted is established by the Aquilian law; the first head of which provides that, if a person has wrongfully killed a slave, or a quadruped (of the class denominated cattle), the property of another person, he is to be condemned to pay to the owner the highest market value of the slave or animal during the previous year.

The action for damage wrongfully inflicted is established by the Aquilian law; the first head of which provides that, if a person has wrongfully killed a slave, or a quadruped (of the class denominated cattle), the property of another person, he is to be condemned to pay to the owner the highest market value of the slave or animal during the previous year. § 1. As the provision of the law is not in respect of quadrupeds generally, but relates only to those which are included under the head of cattle, we must observe that it does not cover the case of wild animals or dogs, but applies only to animals which can properly be said to feed in flocks, such as horses, mules, asses, sheep, oxen, goats. Swine are also held to be included, since they come under the term cattle, for they feed in flocks, as Ælius Marcianus notes in his Institutes that Homer, in the "Odyssey", says:

> "You will find him sitting by his swine, which are feeding
> By the rock of Corax, near the spring of Arethusa"
> (*Od.*, xiii, 407-8)

§ 211. He is deemed to kill wrongfully, by whose malicious act, or culpable negligence, death has ensued, for damage not caused unlawfully is neither censured by this nor any other law, so that he goes unpunished, who, by accident, without malicious intent, or culpable negligence, commits damage.

§ 2. He is deemed to kill wrongfully who does so unlawfully. Hence, he who kills a robber is not liable, that is, if he could not otherwise escape the danger. § 3. Nor is he liable under this law who kills by accident, provided there was no culpable negligence, for every one is liable under this law, not only for his malicious acts, but also for culpable negligence. § 4. Hence, if a person, whilst practising with javelins, or being exercised therein, has transfixed your passing slave, a distinction is made; for, if it was done by a soldier in camp, and in the place where it is usual to exercise, he will be deemed free from culpable negligence, but if it was done by another person he would be guilty. The same rule would hold in the case of the soldier, if it had been done in some other place than that set apart for military exercises. § 5. Again, if a person, whilst pruning a tree, let a bough fall and killed your passing slave, and this was done near a public way or a local passage, and he had not called out, so that the accident might have been avoided, he is guilty of culpable negligence; but, if he called out, and the passer-by did not take care to avoid the danger, he is not liable. He would also be deemed equally free from blame if he was lopping the bough away from the road, or in the middle of a field, although he had not called out, for in such a place no stranger had a right to be walking. § 6. Further, if a physician, who had performed an operation on your slave, should have neglected to attend to his cure, so that the slave's death was thereby occasioned, he is liable for culpable negligence. § 7. Want of skill is included under the head of culpable negligence, as, in the case of a physician causing the death of your slave, either because he performed an operation badly, or administered improper medicine to him. § 8. So, also, if your slave is trampled upon by mules, which a mule-driver from want of skill could not manage, the latter is guilty of culpable negligence; and if a stronger person could have held them in, but he, through weakness, could not, he is equally liable. The same rules have been held to apply to him who, whilst riding a horse, is unable, either from weakness or want of skill, to manage the horse. § 9. These words in the law, "the highest market value of the thing during the previous year", are intended to mean, that if a person has killed your slave, who was, at the time of his death, lame, maimed, or blind of an eye, but quite sound, or of considerable value during that year, the liability is not limited to what he is now worth, but is reckoned at his highest market value within the year. Hence, the action resulting from this law is looked upon as penal, because a person is not only liable for the actual damage he has done, but sometimes for a great deal more, and therefore it is clear that the action does not lie against the heir as it would do if the liability never exceeded the actual loss. § 10. It has been decided, not by the very words of the law, but by

§ 214. The effect of the words which are added to this law, viz., "the highest market value of the thing during the previous year", is, that if the slave, when killed, was, say, lame, or had lost an eye, but had been sound at some time during the year, the value would be so estimated; and thus a person may sometimes obtain compensation beyond the damage he has sustained.

§ 212. Nor is it the mere value of the deceased slave himself that is estimated in this action, for if the owner of the deceased slave sustains greater damage than the value of the slave, this also is estimated; as, for example, if my slave has been killed before he has declared his acceptance, by my order, of an inheritance, of which he had been appointed heir, then not only the value of the slave is estimated, but also that of the lost inheritance. Again, if one out of a pair, whether of actors, or of musicians, has been killed, not only is the value of the one killed estimated, but the estimated depreciation in the value of the remainder is also calculated, The same rule holds if one of a pair of mules, or even one out of a set of four chariot horses has been killed. § 213. He whose slave is killed is free to choose whether he will prosecute the slayer for the capital offence, or sue him under this law for damages.

their interpretation, that not only is the value of the object destroyed to be estimated, in accordance with what we have said, but also the loss which we may have incurred by the destruction of the object; as, for example, if a person has killed your slave before he could, by your order, enter upon an inheritance, of which he had been appointed heir; for it is clear that a calculation must be made of the lost inheritance also. Again, if one of a pair of mules, or one of a set of four chariot horses, or one slave out of a company of actors is killed, not only is the value of the object killed to be calculated, but also the depreciation in the value of the remainder is to be reckoned. § 11. He, however, whose slave has been killed may sue by the civil action, given under the Aquilian law, for the damages sustained, and also prosecute the offender for the capital offence.

§ 215. By the second head an action is established to recover the amount against the adstipulator,* who, in fraud of the stipulator, has released a debt by the process of imaginary payment.† § 216. It is clear that this action has been introduced in this part of the law as falling under the head of damage. But it would not have been necessary to have provided for it here, since an action on the mandate would have sufficed for the purpose;‡ had it not been that, by suing under this law, the action will be for double the amount, if the liability for the extinction of the debt is denied.

§ 12. The second head of the Aquilian law is not now in use.

* *ante*, § 110.

† *ante*, § 169.

‡ *ante*, § 111.

§ 217. By the third head provision is made for every other kind of damage. Therefore, if a person has wounded a slave or a quadruped, included under the class of cattle, or has wounded or killed a quadruped, not included under that class, as a dog, or a wild beast, as a bear, or a lion, an action lies under this head. In respect of all other animals, also, as well as in

§ 13. By the third head provision is made for every other kind of damage. Therefore, if a person has wounded a slave or a quadruped, included under the class of cattle, or has wounded or killed a quadruped not included under that class, as a dog, or a wild beast, an action lies under this head. In respect of all other animals, also, as well as in re-

respect of those things which are devoid of life, any loss wrongfully sustained may be claimed under this part of the law. For, if anything has been burnt, broken, or fractured, an action lies under this head; although the single expression "broken" would suffice to cover all these grounds; as the term "broken" means that which has been in any way damaged. Hence, this word comprises, not only that which is burnt or fractured, but also that which is torn and crushed, and spilt, and in any way spoiled, destroyed, and deteriorated.

spect of those things which are devoid of life, any loss wrongfully sustained may be claimed under this part of the law. For, if anything has been burnt, broken, or fractured, although the single expression "broken" would suffice to cover all these grounds; as the term "broken" means that which has been in any way damaged. Hence, this word comprises, not only that which is burnt or fractured, but also that which is torn and crushed, and spilt, and in any way destroyed, and deteriorated. Finally, it has been decided that he who has mixed anything with the oil or wine of another, so as to destroy the natural goodness of the wine or oil, is liable under this head of the law. § 14. It is clear that, just as a person is liable under the first head, if, through his malicious intent or culpable negligence, a slave or quadruped has been killed; so, under this head, a person is to be liable for all other kinds of damage, if resulting from malicious intent or culpable negligence.

§ 218. Under this head, however, he who has caused the damage is not liable for the value during the previous year, but for the value during the preceding thirty days; and the word "highest" is not even added, and, hence, some have thought that the judge was at liberty to fix the value, either at a time, within the thirty days, when it was highest, or when it was lower. But Sabinus held that the case was to be dealt with as if the word "highest" had been inserted in this part also of the law, on the ground that the proposer of the law was satisfied with the use of the word in the first part. § 219. But it was held that the action resulting from the law only lay if a person caused the damage by his own bodily act; and if the damage was caused in any other way, equitable actions are given; as, for example, if a person has shut up another's slave or cattle, so that they

Under this head, he who has caused the damage is not liable for the value within the year, but within the thirty preceding days. § 15. Even the word "highest" is not added. But Sabinus rightly held that the value was to be estimated as if this word had been inserted in this part also of the law, on the ground that the plebeians who carried this law, on the proposition of the tribune Aquilius, were satisfied with the use of the word in the first part. § 16. But, it was held that the action under this law only lay if a person has, by his own bodily act, done damage; and therefore it has been usual to give equitable actions against him who does damage in any other way; as, for example, if

perished by starvation, or has driven a beast of burden so violently as to have caused its death; so, if a person has persuaded another's slave to climb a tree, or descend into a well, and in ascending or descending the slave has fallen, and been either killed, or injured in some part of his body. If, however, a person has hurled another's slave from a bridge or bank into a river, and the slave has been drowned, it is not difficult to understand that, in this case, the damage has resulted from the bodily act, in that he threw him over.

a person has shut up another's slave or cattle, so that they perished by starvation, or has driven a beast of burden so violently as to have caused its death, or frightened cattle to such a degree as to cause them to precipitate themselves headlong, or if a person persuaded another's slave to climb a tree or descend into a well, and in climbing or descending the slave is killed, or injured in some part of his body, then an equitable action is given against him. But, if a person has hurled another's slave from a bridge or bank into a river and the slave is drowned, then, in that he has thrown him over, there can be no difficulty in holding that he has caused the damage with his own body, and therefore he is liable under the Aquilian law itself. But, if no damage has been done by the body, nor to the body, but the damage has happened in some other way, then, as neither the direct nor the equitable Aquilian action apply, it is held that the offender is liable to an action on the case, as, for example, if a person has been impelled by compassion to loose the fetters of another's slave, so as to enable him to escape.

Title iv. Of outrages.

The word "injuria", in its general acceptation, means anything done contrary to law; in a special sense it means sometimes outrage ("contumelia", which comes from "contemnere", the Greek ὕβρις); sometimes culpable negligence ("culpa", which the Greeks call ἀδίκημα), as in the Aquilian law, where damage is spoken of as done wrongfully ("injuria"); sometimes, again, it is used in the sense of iniquity and injustice, which the Greeks call ἀδικία; and the person, against whom the prætor or a judge pronounces an unjust sentence, is said to have had a wrong ("injuria") done to him.

§ 220. Now, an outrage is not only committed when a person is struck with, say, the fist, or a stick, or even scourged; but, also, if a crowd has been caused to assemble round him, or if a person has

§ 1. Now, an outrage is not only committed when a person is struck with the fist or with clubs, or even scourged, but if a crowd has been caused to assemble round him, or if his goods have been seized, as if he were the debtor of one who knows that nothing is due to

advertised for sale, by auction, the property of another, as if he were his debtor, when he knows that the latter does not owe him anything; or if a person has written a libel or verses in defamation of another's character; or if a person has persistently followed a respectable woman or a boy, and, in short, in many other ways. § 221. But we are held to suffer outrage, not only in our own person, but also in the persons of our children whom we have in our power, and in the persons of our wives, when they are in our marital power. Therefore, if, for example, you have committed an outrage on my daughter, who is married to Titius, not only can an action be brought against you in the name of my daughter, but I, also, and Titius can sue.

§ 222. No outrage can be deemed to be committed on a slave himself, as it is held to be done to the master through him; but we are not held to suffer an outrage through them, by the same means as would amount to such in the persons of our children or our wives, but only when such a gross outrage has been committed as makes it a manifest insult to the master, and in which case the formula would run, as, for example, "if a person has scourged another's slave". But, if a person has caused a crowd to assemble round a slave, or struck him with the fist, no formula is provided, and one would not easily be obtained by a claimant.

him; or if a person has written, composed, and published a libel or verses defamatory of his character, or has maliciously brought it about that another person did any of these things; or if a person has persistently followed a respectable woman, or a boy or girl, or is alleged to have attempted the chastity of a person, and, in short, it is clear that an outrage may be committed in many other ways. § 2. A man may suffer an outrage, not only in his own person, but also in the persons of his children in power, and even in the person of his wife, according to the opinion that has prevailed. Therefore, if you commit an outrage on a person's daughter who is married to Titius, not only can an action for the outrage be brought against you in the name of the daughter, but the father and the husband may also sue in their own right. On the other hand, if an outrage has been committed on the husband, the wife cannot bring an action, based on the outrage, for it is just that wives should be protected by their husbands, but not husbands by their wives; a father-in-law can however sue for an outrage in the name of the daughter-in-law whose husband is in his power. § 3. No outrage can be deemed to be committed on slaves themselves, as it is held to be done to the master through them, not however in the same ways as would be considered outrages in the case of our children and wives, but only when a gross outrage has been committed, and one which clearly amounts to an insult to the master, as, for example, if a person has scourged another's slave, in which case an action lies; but a master cannot bring an action against a person who has caused a crowd to collect round his slave, or struck him with his fist. § 4. If an outrage has been committed on a slave, held in common, it is just that the outrage should be estimated, not according to the share each owner has in him, but according to their rank, for the outrage is done to them. § 5. But, if Titius has the usufruct of the slave, and Mævius is the owner, the outrage is considered to be done rather to Mævius. § 6. But, if the outrage has been done to a free man who is bona fide serving you, no action is given to you, but he can sue in his own name, unless he has been beaten in order to insult you; for, then, an action, based on the outrage, is available to you. The same rule holds in the case of the slave of another who is bona fide serving you, for you may bring an action, based on the outrage, whenever the outrage has been committed for the purpose of insulting you.

§ 223. The penalty for outrages, according to the law of the Twelve Tables, was retaliation for a bodily member destroyed; but, for a bone broken or crushed, the penalty was three hundred copper pound pieces, that is, if a free man's bone was broken, but one hundred and fifty such pieces if it were that of a slave, and for other outrages the penalty was fixed at twenty-five such pieces, and, considering the great poverty of all classes in those times, these sums seem to have been sufficient by way of compensation. § 224. But we now follow a different rule, for we are now allowed, by the prætor, to estimate the outrage for ourselves, and the judge, in his discretion, and by his sentence, either awards the sum we have estimated or a smaller amount; but, when the prætor deems an outrage of a grave character, if he has at the same time settled the amount of the security for reappearance,* we insert this sum in the formula as the measure of our damages, and the judge, although he may, in his sentence, award a smaller sum, yet, generally, on account of the authority of the prætor, he does not venture to diminish the amount of the condemnation.

* *post*, IV, § 184.

§ 7. The penalty for outrages, according to the law of the Twelve Tables, was retaliation for bodily members destroyed; but, for a broken bone, a scale of pecuniary compensation was fixed in accordance with the great poverty of the ancients. But, subsequently, the prætors allowed those who had suffered outrages to estimate the damages themselves, so that the judge would, in his discretion, either award, by his sentence, the damages estimated or a smaller amount. The penalty for outrage, introduced by the Twelve Tables, has fallen into disuse, but that which the prætors have introduced, and which is called "honorary", is in use in the courts of justice. For the damages for the outrage increase or diminish according to the rank and character of the individual, and the same rule is very properly followed even in the case of a slave, so that a different amount of compensation is awarded in the case of a slave who is a steward to that awarded for a slave filling an intermediate position, or for one of the lowest rank, or wearing fetters. § 8. The Cornelian law, also, deals with the subject of outrages, and introduced an action for outrages, which is available on the ground that a person alleges that he has been beaten, or scourged, or that his house has been entered by force; and the word "house" includes the case of a person living in his own house, or in a hired one, or occupying one gratis or as a guest.

§ 225. An outrage is deemed grave, either from the nature of the act; as, for example, if a person has been wounded, or scourged, or beaten with rods by another; or from the place, as, for example, if the outrage has been committed in the theatre or in the forum; or from the rank of the person, as, if it is a magistrate who has suffered the outrage, or an outrage has been done to a senator by a person of low repute.

§ 9. An outrage is deemed grave either from the nature of the act, as, for example, if a person is wounded or beaten with rods by another, or from the place, as, for example, if the outrage has been committed in the theatre or in the forum, or in the presence of the prætor, or from the rank of the person, as, if it is a magistrate who has suffered the outrage, or an outrage has been done to a senator by a person of low repute, or to an ascendant or patron, by descendants or freed-men (for an outrage committed on a senator, an ascendant, or a patron, is estimated differently from that committed on a person of low repute, or a stranger); sometimes it is the part of the body injured that makes the outrage grave, as, if anyone has been struck in the eye. It matters little whether such an outrage has been done to the head of a family or to one in power, as it is, in either case, considered grave.

§ 10. Finally, it is to be noted that in all cases of outrage the sufferer may proceed criminally or civilly. If the injured party elect to pursue his remedy by civil action, the penalty is imposed according to the measure of damages ascertained in the way we have pointed out. If, however, he proceeds criminally, an extraordinary penalty is inflicted on the guilty party, by virtue of the powers vested in the judge, observing, however, the rule introduced, by a constitution of Zeno, permitting those of illustrious rank, and those above that rank, to bring or defend a criminal prosecution for outrage by a procurator, in accordance with the terms of that enactment, which will be better understood by reference to it.

§ 11. Not only, however, is he liable to an action for the outrage who has committed the outrage, that is, he who struck the blow, but he, also, may be sued who has maliciously acted or contrived to bring it about, that another should get (for example) his ears boxed. § 12. The action is extinguished by concealing the fact of the outrage having occurred; and hence, if a person has neglected to take notice of the outrage, that is, if he has not immediately, on suffering the outrage, shown an intention of resenting it, he cannot subsequently change his mind, and revive the outrage he has condoned.

Title v. Of obligations arising from quasi-delicts.

If a judge has drawn upon himself the responsibility of a suit, he cannot be said, properly speaking, to be liable for what is technically known as a wrong. But, as he is neither bound by such a wrong, nor by contract, and yet is deemed to have erred, even though inadvertently, therefore, he is held liable for a quasi-delict, and will incur such a penalty as will, in the opinion of the judge settling the case, justly cover the loss sustained. § 1. Again, he is held liable for a quasi-delict, out of whose upper room something has been thrown, or poured down, so as to injure another person; and this is so whether the room is his own, or hired, or occupied gratuitously, for he cannot be deemed, properly speaking, liable for a wrong, because, in the majority of such cases, he becomes liable for the culpable negligence of some other person, as a slave or a child. The same remark applies to the case of him who has, in a place in which the public are accustomed to pass, placed or suspended that which, if it should fall, would injure a person, the penalty, in this case, being fixed at ten gold pieces. But, in the case of things being thrown or poured down, the measure of damages, awarded by the action, will be double the amount of the loss sustained; and, if a freeman was killed, the penalty was fifty gold pieces, though, if he should survive, and it is shown that he has sustained injury, such an amount will be recovered by action as the judge deems equitable, under the circumstances, taking into account the medical charges incurred, as well as the other expenses which his illness has involved, and the value of the employment which he has lost, or may lose, through being incapacitated. § 2. If a son in power live apart from his father, and from his upper room anything is thrown, or poured down, or if he keeps a thing so placed, or suspended, that its fall would be attended with danger, Julianus laid down that no action would lie against the father, but that the son himself must be sued. The same remark applies to the case of a son in power, who, as a judge, has drawn upon himself the responsibility of a suit. § 3. The owner of a ship, or the keeper of an inn, or of a stable, is liable for a quasi-delict in respect of any loss or theft committed in the ship, or in the inn, or stable, that is, if there is no wrongful act on his own part, but on the part of one of those whom he employed to work in the ship, or in the inn or stable. For, as the action which lies against him is not grounded in contract, and yet he is liable for culpable negligence in making use of the labour of worthless servants, therefore he seems to be liable for a quasi-delict. In these cases an action, based on the circumstances of the case, lies, and it may be brought by the heir of the injured party, though it does not lie against the heir of the party who was liable for the injury.

INSTITUTES OF GAIUS, COMMENTARY IV.

§ 1. It now remains for us to treat of actions.

And, if we inquire how many kinds of actions there are, it would seem the better opinion to say that there are two, viz., real and personal; for those who have laid down that there are four kinds, arising out of the different classes of preliminary stipulations, have not considered that some of these classes of actions resolve themselves into the kinds we have mentioned. § 2. The action is personal whenever we sue another who is liable to us, either in contract or in tort, that is, when the basis of our claim is that he ought to give, do, or perform. § 3. The action is real when we claim a corporeal thing as ours, or claim some right as ours; as, for example, a right of using, or of using and taking the produce, or a right of way, or of leading cattle or water along, or of raising our buildings

Title vi. Of actions.

It now remains for us to treat of actions. An action is nothing else than the right of suing in a court of law for that which is due to us.

§ 1. The principal division of all actions, brought before judges or arbitrators for the settlement of any issue between the parties, is into two kinds, viz., real or personal. For everyone sues either a person who is liable to him in contract or in tort, in which the actions available are personal, in that the basis of the claim is that the adversary is to give, do, or otherwise act in other cases. Or he sues a person who is bound to him by no legal obligation, but with whom he raises a contention about some certain thing, in which case the actions available for the purpose are real, as, for example, if a person is in possession of a corporeal thing, which Titius contends is his property, whilst the possessor asserts that it is his, the action commenced by Titius is real. § 2. So, again, if the ground

higher, or a right of view. So, again, the contrary action available to our adversary is also a real action, although negative in form.

of his suit is that he asserts that he has a right to the use and enjoyment of an estate, or of a house, or that he has a right of passing along, or leading his cattle across his neighbour's land, or of leading water from his neighbour's land, the action is real. The action is the same which relates to urban servitudes, as, for example, if he claim the right of raising his house, or a right of view, or a right of projecting his house over his neighbour's land, or of inserting a beam into his neighbour's wall. On the other hand, there are actions relating to such use and enjoyment and to rural and urban servitudes, which are available in the contrary sense, as when the basis of a person's claim is that his adversary has no right to such use and enjoyment, or to go along, or lead cattle or water along, or raise his house, or have a view, or project his house, or put a beam into his neighbour's wall, and these actions are also real though negative. This kind of action is not available in disputes about corporeal things, for in these the person out of possession is plaintiff, and no action lies in favour of the possessor to deny that the thing is the claimant's. There is only this one case in which he who possesses acts the part of plaintiff, as will more clearly appear in the larger books of the Digest.

§ 3. The actions mentioned above, and others of a similar character, derive their origin from others, both real and personal, which the prætor has established by virtue of his jurisdiction, the nature of which it is necessary to show by some examples: thus, the prætor often allows a real action to be so brought as that the plaintiff may assert that he has, as it were, acquired by use something which he has not so acquired, or, on the contrary, that the possessor may deny that his adversary has acquired by use something which he has so acquired. § 4. For, if he to whom a thing has been delivered over on some lawful ground, as, for example, by reason of a sale, gift, dowry, or legacy, to a person who has not yet become owner of the thing, and he, by accident, loses the possession, he has no direct action for the recovery of the thing, for actions are only available by the civil law to enable a person to claim the ownership. But, as it was clearly hard that an action should be wanting in such a case, an action was established by the prætor in which he who has lost the possession asserts that he has acquired by use the thing, and, on that account, claims it as his own. This action is called "Publician", because it was first introduced into the edict by the prætor Publicius. § 5. So, on the other hand, if a person whilst absent abroad on service of the state, or a prisoner with the enemy, has acquired by use a thing which is the property of another who has remained at home, then the owner is allowed within a year after the return of the possessor to claim the thing, and treat the acquisition by use as rescinded, that is, he may claim it in such a way as to assert that the possessor has not acquired the thing by use, and that, therefore, the thing is his. Prompted by similar equitable motives the prætor adapts this kind of action in certain other cases, as may be gathered from the larger work of the Digest or Pandects. § 6. Again, if a person has, in fraud of his creditors, delivered over some property to another, and, by order of the president of the province, the debtor's goods have been seized by his creditors, the latter are allowed to rescind the delivery, and bring an action to recover back the portion of the property delivered over, that is, to allege that that portion of the property has not been delivered over, and therefore has remained a part of the debtor's goods. § 7. Again, the Servian and the quasi-Servian action (the latter also called hypothecarian), derive their origin from the jurisdiction of the prætor. By the Servian action a person sues for the effects of a tenant which are liable to seizure by way of pledge for the rent due in respect of the estate. By the quasi-Servian action creditors follow things pledged or mortgaged to them. As far as this hypothecarian action is concerned, there is no difference between a pledge and a mortgage, for the title of this action equally covers any case, where it has been agreed between debtor and creditor that a certain thing shall be security for the debt; but, in other respects, there is a difference, for, under the term pledge, is properly included that which, at the time, is delivered over to the creditor, especially if a movable; but, properly speaking, we denote by mortgage that which becomes security by the mere agreement of the parties without delivery. § 8. The prætor has, also, by virtue of his jurisdiction, introduced some personal actions, as, for example, the action in respect of an agreement to pay a pre-existing debt on an appointed day, to which the action based on a day having been named for payment, bore much resemblance; but the latter has been, by our constitution, struck out of the list of valid actions, as, after any additional advantages it possessed had been transferred to the former, it became superfluous. So, again, the prætor has provided an action in respect of the private savings of slaves, and of sons in power, and one in which the issue involved is whether the plaintiff has taken an oath, besides very many others. § 9. The action in respect of an agreement to pay a pre-existing debt on an appointed day lies against whoever has engaged to pay money, either for himself or another, where no stipulation has been interposed; for, otherwise, if he has promised a stipulator, he is bound by the civil law. § 10. The prætor has provided the actions in respect of private savings, against a father or master, because, although they are not liable by the mere operation of law on the contracts of their children or slaves, yet it is only equitable that they should be liable to the extent of the private savings, which is, as it were, the patrimony of sons and daughters, as well as of slaves. § 11 So, again, if a person, when called upon by his adversary, has taken an oath that the money he claims is due and unpaid, an action is most properly given to the creditor, in which the issue involved is, not whether the money is due to him, but whether the oath has been taken. § 12. A number of penal actions have also originated from his jurisdiction, as, for example, against him who has obliterated anything posted on the official notice-board, so against him who has summoned his patron or ascendant before a court of justice without obtaining a previous order for the purpose; so, again, against him who has, by force or fraud, got out of the way a person summoned to appear in a court of justice. § 13. Prejudicial actions are deemed real actions; such are those in which the issue involved is whether such an one is a free or a freed-person, or as to his paternity. Of these only the one in which the issue involved is whether a person is free belongs to the civil law. The others derive their efficacy from the prætor's jurisdiction.

§ 4. It is clear from this division of actions that we cannot claim our own property from another person, in this way: "If it appear that he ought to give", for that which is ours already cannot be given to us, since that only is held as given to us, which is given in order that

§ 14. It is clear from this division of actions that a plaintiff cannot claim his own property from another, thus, "If it appear that he ought to give", for it does not lie on the defendant to give the plaintiff what is already his, since that only is held as given to a

it may become ours, and a thing which is ours already cannot become more so. It was manifestly from a sense of detestation of thieves, and in order that they might be exposed to a greater number of actions, that they are liable, over and above the penalty of double or quadruple the amount taken, to an action for the recovery of the property, in the form, "If it appear that they ought to give", although the action also lies against them in which we claim "the thing as ours". § 5. Real actions are called "vindicationes", but personal actions, in which the basis of our claim is that a person ought to give or to do, are called "condictiones".

person which is given in order that it may become his, and a thing which is already the property of the plaintiff cannot become more so. It was manifestly from a detestation of thieves, and in order that they might be exposed to a greater number of actions, that they are rendered liable, over and above the penalty of double or quadruple the amount taken, to an action for the recovery of the property in the form, "If it appear that they ought to give", although the action also lies against them in which a person claims the thing as his. § 15. Real actions are called "vindicationes", but personal actions, in which the basis of the claim is, that a person ought to give or to do, are called "condictiones"; for "condicere", in the old tongue, is equivalent to "denuntiare", and we now, improperly, use the word "condictio" to indicate the personal action by which the plaintiff asserts that something ought to be given to him, for, now-a-days, there is, in such a case, no formal summons of the defendant by the plaintiff.*

* cf. Gai. IV, § 18.

§ 6. We sometimes sue for the purpose of recovering only the thing, sometimes only to get a penalty, at other times both for the thing and a penalty. § 7. We sue for the thing only, for example, by those actions by which we enforce a liability arising out of contract.

§ 16. The next division is that based upon the distinction between those actions provided for the purpose of recovering the thing, those for recovering a penalty, and those of a mixed character. § 17. All real actions are provided for the purpose of recovering the thing; and, of personal actions, nearly all those arising out of contract would seem intended for the recovery of the thing, as, for example, the action by which a plaintiff claims a sum of money lent or stipulated for; so, also, in the case of the action based on a specific loan, or on a deposit, or on gratuitous agency, or partnership, or sale, or hire. But, clearly, if the action on a deposit is brought in respect of a thing deposited at a time of tumult, or fire, or on account of the fall of a building, or shipwreck, the prætor allows the action to go for double the value, provided the action is brought against him with whom the deposit was made, or against his heir, grounded on the latter's personal fraud, in which case the action is mixed. § 18. Of actions arising out of

§ 8. We sue for a penalty only, as, for example, by the action for theft and for outrage, and, according to the opinion of some, by the action for robbery with violence; as for the recovery of the thing itself, both a real and a personal action are available. § 9. But we sue for the recovery of the thing and for a penalty, for example, in those cases in which we sue for the double value against a person denying his liability, as occurs in the actions for the recovery of a judgment debt,* of a sum paid by a surety,† of wrongful damage, under the Aquilian law,‡ or in order to obtain those legacies which the heir has been ordered to give.**

* *post*, § 21, 25.

† *ante*, iii, § 127.

‡ *ante*, iii, § 216.

** *ante*, ii, § 201.

wrongs, some are provided only for the sake of recovering a penalty, some for both the thing and the penalty, and, therefore, they are mixed. A person only sues for a penalty in an action of theft; for whether he sues for the quadruple, as in manifest theft, or for the double, where the theft is not manifest, he sues only for a penalty, for a person follows the property itself by a separate action, that is, by claiming it as his, whether the thief himself is in possession of it, or anyone else. Further than this, there also lies against the thief a personal action for the thing. § 19. The action for robbery with violence is mixed, because the pursuit of the thing taken is included in the quadruple, and so the penalty is for triple the amount only;†† and the action under the Aquilian law, for wrongful damage, is also mixed, not only when the action is for double against a person denying the fact, but sometimes when a person is suing for the simple value only, as, for example, if a person has killed a lame, or one-eyed slave, who within the year previous had been sound and of great value, for the condemnation is, then, for the highest value of the slave during that previous year, according to the rule we have already discussed.‡‡ So, again, the action is mixed which is brought against those who have delayed handing over a legacy, or bequest in trust, made in favour of the holy churches, or other sacred places, until it became necessary to summon them before a court of justice, for, then, they are compelled to hand over both the thing itself, or the money bequeathed, and an equivalent amount, by way of penalty, so that the condemnation in such a case is for double the amount.

§ 20. Some actions appear to have a mixed character as being both real and personal. Such is the action for the partition of an inheritance which is available to co-heirs, in order to obtain the division of the property descended; so the action for the division of property held in common, which lies for the division of such property between those who so hold it in common; so the action for the settlement of boundaries, which lies between those who have adjoining lands. In these three actions the judge is allowed to assign, to each of the litigant parties, a portion of the property, according to what is just and right, and if it appear to him that the portion of one is in excess of his share, to condemn him to pay to one of the others a certain sum of money.

†† *ante*, tit. ii. ‡‡ *ante*, tit. iii, § 9.

§ 21. All actions are for the purpose of recovering the single, double, triple, or quadruple value; beyond this no action extends. § 22 The action is for the single value, for example, in the case of actions arising out of a stipulation, a loan in kind, a sale, a hiring, a gratuitous agency, and in numberless other cases. § 23. We sue for the double value, for example, in the action for non-manifest theft, for wrongful injury, under the Aquilian law, and on a deposit in certain cases. So, in the case of the action for the corruption of a slave, which lies against him by whose instigation or advice another person's slave has fled, or become insolent to his master, or has begun to live licentiously, or, in a word, has been made in anywise less valuable; and in this action the value also is to be calculated of any property, which, when he fled, he stole from his master. So, also, in the case of the action for a legacy bequeathed to a sacred place, as we have already stated.* § 24. Triple the amount is sued for when a person inserts in his statement of claim a greater sum than the true amount, by which means the bailiffs, that is, the officers of the court, are enabled to demand a larger sum by way of fees; for then the defendant may sue the plaintiff for triple the amount of damage he has sustained through their demand, but in this triple is included the simple loss actually sustained. This has been introduced by a constitution of ours which shines in our code, and under which, there is no doubt, a personal action, based on the law, can be founded. § 25. Quadruple the amount is sued for, in, for example, an action for manifest theft, or in an action for being coerced through fear into doing an act, and an action in respect of money given to induce a person to set on foot, or to desist from a vexatious suit. So, again, a personal action, based on the law, arises out of our constitution, by which officers of the court who demand anything from the defendants, contrary to the provisions of the constitution, will be condemned in quadruple the amount. § 26. But the action for non-manifest theft, and that for corrupting a slave, differ from the others which we enumerated at the same time, in that the former are always brought for double the value; but the latter, that is, the action under the Aquilian law for wrongful damage, and sometimes the action for a deposit, entail the double value if the liability is denied, but, if admitted, they only lie for the simple value, whilst in the action which lies in respect of property bequeathed to sacred places, double is recovered, not

* *ante*, § 19.

only if liability is denied, but also if payment of that which is due is delayed until summoned to pay by a magistrate's order; though the simple value only will suffice if the liability be admitted, and the amount handed over before the magistrate summons the party to pay. § 27. So, again, the action for being coerced through fear into doing an act, differs from the other actions mentioned at the same time, in that it is tacitly implied by the nature of this action that he who, in accordance with the judge's order, restores the thing to the plaintiff, ought to be absolved from liability; but this is not so in the other actions, as the condemnation is always for the quadruple, as in the case of the action for manifest theft.

§ 10. Moreover, there are some actions which are related to an action of the law, whilst others stand on their own strength.* In order to make this clear, it will be necessary for us, in the first place, to describe the actions of the law.

* *post*, § 33.

§ 11. The actions which were formerly in use were called "actions of the law", either because they were created by statutes, for at that time the edicts of the prætor, by means of which very many actions have been introduced, were not yet published, or because they followed the very terms of the statutes, and therefore were regarded as unchangeable as if they were laws themselves. Hence, we shall find that he lost his suit who, on bringing an action for cutting his vines, used the word "vines", whereas he ought to have called them "trees", because in that part of the law of the Twelve Tables, on which an action for cutting vines is based, the general expression "trees" is used.

§ 12. There were five forms for suing by statute, viz., by way of "sacramentum", "judicis postulatio", "condictio", "manus injectio", "pignoris capio".

§ 13. The sacramental action was the general form; for the procedure by way of wager was applicable in all cases where the law had not otherwise provided. This action was just as perilous to those who proved to be in the wrong as now-a-days is the action for money lent, on account of the preliminary stipulation, by which the defendant becomes liable to pay a penalty if he rashly deny the claim, and the reciprocal stipulation by which the plaintiff becomes similarly liable if he claims that which is not due;† for he who lost the suit was liable for the amount of the sacramentum, by way of penalty; and this was guaranteed to the prætor by sureties, and went to the treasury, not as now, when the penalty involved in

† *post*, § 171, 180.

the preliminary reciprocal stipulations goes to the profit of either the creditor or debtor, according to which is victorious. § 14. The penalty in the sacramental action was either five hundred or fifty pounds of copper, for it was provided by the law of the Twelve Tables, that for suits involving property of the value of one thousand pounds of copper or more, the wager should be five hundred pounds of copper; but for property under that amount fifty pounds of copper. If, however, the dispute was about the freedom of a slave, then, however valuable the slave might be, still the suit was carried on under a penal sum for costs of only fifty pounds of copper, and this was a special provision of the law in favour of liberty, to prevent claimants of liberty being too heavily weighted by the security required of the guarantors for costs. § 15. . . . (twenty-four lines illegible, probably giving the forms used before the prætor for settling the amount of the wager, that is, the penal sum deposited as security for costs in the case of a personal action, at the close of which proceedings the parties asked for the appointment of a judge) . . . they came in order to receive a judge. On their subsequent return the judge was assigned to them. The rule that the judge should be assigned to them on the thirtieth day was introduced by the Pinarian law, for, previous to that law, the judge was assigned immediately. From the foregoing we see that, if the suit was in respect of a matter of less value than one thousand pounds of copper, the penal sum for costs was usually fifty pounds of copper, and not five hundred. After a judge had been assigned, the parties summoned each other to appear before him on the third day. When they did come before him, it was customary, before proceeding regularly with the trial, to give him briefly an outline of the case, which was called a summary of the case, it being, as it were, a brief statement of the points in dispute on each side. § 16. If it was a real action in respect of movables or moving things, which could be brought or led into court, they were claimed before the prætor, thus: The claimant, holding a staff, took hold of the thing, for example, a slave, and spoke as follows: "I say this slave is mine, according to the law of the quirites, by the title which I have shown. Thus, upon him I place my lance", at the same time placing the staff on the slave. His adversary then said and did the same, and when both had thus laid claim to the slave, the prætor said: "Both claimants quit hold of the slave." Upon this, they both let go. The first claimant then said: "I demand of you the ground of your claim?" The other replied: "I declared my right when I placed my lance upon him." Then, the first claimant said: "Since you claim him in defiance of right, I challenge you to stake five hundred pounds of copper upon the issue of a trial." His adversary replied by a similar challenge; but if the subject-matter of the suit was of less value than one thousand pounds of copper, then they named fifty pounds of copper as the sum reciprocally staked. Then, the same proceedings were gone through as in a personal action,* after which the prætor temporarily assigned to one of the parties the subject-matter of the suit, that is, appointed one of them to be interim possessor, and ordered him to give security to his opponent for the subject-matter of the suit, and the interim possession, that is, for the thing in dispute and the produce, whilst the prætor himself took security from both parties in respect of the penal sum for costs, as that would be forfeited to the public treasury. A staff was used, as it were, in the place of the spear, which was the symbol of lawful ownership; since that was especially looked upon as a man's own property which had been taken from the enemy, and for this reason a spear is placed before the centumviral tribunal. § 17. If the thing was of such a nature that it could not be conveniently brought or led into court, as, for example, if it were a column, or a ship, or a herd of cattle of any sort, some part of it only was taken, aud the claim was made in respect of that part as if the whole were before the court. Hence, one sheep or goat out of the flock was led into court, or even a tuft of wool was taken from the flock and brought into court, but from a ship or a column some portion was broken off. Similarly, when the dispute was about a piece of land, or a building, or an inheritance, some part was taken and brought into court, and the claim was made in respect of this portion as if in the presence of the whole, as, for example, a clod was taken from the piece of land, or a tile from the house, and if the dispute were about an inheritance . . . . (a leaf missing, in which Gaius probably completed the description of the sacramental action, and then treated of the action, "per judicis postulationem", after which he commenced describing the "condictio".†)

§ 18. . . . . for they ought to be ready to receive a judge in thirty days, for "condicere", in the old tongue, is equivalent to "denuntiare". Hence, this

* *ante*, § 15.

† cf. Just. IV, vi, § 15.

action was properly named "condictio", for the plaintiff warned his adversary to appear in thirty days for the appointment of a judge. Now-a-days we improperly use the word "condictio" to indicate the personal action, by which we assert that a thing ought to be given to us, for there is not now, in such cases, any formal summons of the defendant by the plaintiff. § 19. This form of action of the law was established by the Silian and Calpurnian laws; by the Silian law in respect of the recovery of a certain sum of money, and by the Calpurnian law in respect of any certain thing. § 20 But the question has often, very properly, been asked what necessity there was for this action, since, in regard to that which was due to us, we could sue by the sacramental action, or by that for the demand of a judge.

§ 21. Similarly, by the action of "manus injectio", those things could be sued for in respect of which this remedy was provided by any law, as, for example, the action upon a judgment resulting from the law of the Twelve Tables.* This action proceeded in the following way. He who sued said thus: "Since you have been adjudicated—or condemned—towards me in the sum of ten thousand sesterces, which you have fraudulently withheld, therefore I now lay hands upon you for this judgment debt of ten thousand sesterces"; and at the same time he took hold of some part of his body. He, against whom the judgment had been given, was not allowed to remove the hand, and defend himself in the suit, but gave a surety, who undertook his defence for him; but he who did not find a surety was led away by the plaintiff to his house, and put in chains. § 22. Subsequently, certain laws gave this form of action upon a judgment; in other cases against other persons, as, for example, by the Publilian law it is given against the original debtor for whom a surety had paid, if he had not paid the money to the surety within six months of its being paid on his behalf.† So, again, the Furian law of suretyship gave it against him who had demanded from a surety more than his proportion;‡ and many other laws have made this action available in many cases. § 23. But other laws have, in certain cases, established actions of this kind; but, simply, that is, not as upon a judgment; as, for example, the Furian law concerning testaments gave it against him who had received by way of legacy, or gift, "mortis causa", more than one thousand pounds of copper, when he was not within the exceptions of the law, so as to be able to take more.** So, again, the Marcian

* tab. iii, 2, 3.

† *ante*, iii, § 127.

‡ *ante*, iii, § 121, 122.

** *ante*, ii, § 225.

law gave it against money-lenders, so that this kind of action could be used against them, to compel the restitution of usurious interest obtained by them. § 24. In the action based on these and any similar laws, it was lawful for the defendant to remove the hand of the plaintiff, and conduct his own defence; for in such a case the plaintiff did not add the words, "on account of the judgment"; but, after stating the cause of action, said thus: "On that account I lay hands upon you;" whilst those for whom an action on account of a judgment was available, stated the ground upon which they were suing, thus: "Therefore, I now lay hands upon you for this judgment." It has not escaped my notice that in the formula, under the Furian law concerning testaments, the words, "pro judicato", are inserted, though they are not found in the law itself; and, therefore, the insertion seems to be devoid of reason. § 25. But, subsequently, by the Vallian (?) law, except in the cases of an action upon a judgment, and of an action for money paid by a surety, in all other cases in which an action of this sort was used, the defendant could remove the hand, and conduct his own defence. Hence, the judgment-debtor, and he for whom a surety had paid, were required, even after this law, to find a surety, and unless they found one they were carried off to the plaintiff's house; and so long as the actions of the law were in use this was also so; hence it is that, at the present day, he who is sued on a judgment, or for money paid by a surety, is compelled to find security for the payment of that which shall be adjudged.

§ 26. The action "pignoris capio" originated from custom in respect of certain claims, and from statute in respect of others. § 27. It was introduced by custom in respect of a soldier's pay. For a soldier could take a pledge, in respect of his pay, from him whose duty it was to distribute it, unless it was paid. This money, which was given under the name of pay, was called "æs militare". So, again, it was lawful for a soldier to take a pledge as security for the money required for the purchase of a horse, which money was called "æs equestre". So, again, he could take a pledge for the money to be provided for fodder for the horse, and which money was called "æs hordiarium". § 28. The action was introduced by statute, as, for example, by the law of the Twelve Tables, which gives it against him who had bought a victim for sacrifice and did not pay the price of it; also, against him who did not pay for the hire of a beast of burden, which a person had let out to him, in order that the money when received might be spent on a feast, that is, for a sacrifice. So, again, by a law called "censoria", this action was given to farmers of the public revenues of the Roman people against those who, in virtue of any law, were liable for taxes. § 29. In all these cases the pledge was taken possession of with a certain form of words, and, therefore, the majority have held that this was an action of the law; but this view was scarcely satisfactory to some, because, in the first place, the seizure of the pledge took place out of court, that is, not before the prætor, and even, generally, in the absence of the opposite party, whereas the other actions of the law could not be proceeded with otherwise than before the prætor and in the presence of the opposite party; and, further, because the pledge could be seized on a "nefastus" day, that is, on a day when it was not lawful to proceed with an action of the law.

§ 30. But all these actions of the law gradually fell into discredit; for, by reason of the excessive subtlety of the ancients who built up the system, the result was brought about that he who made the smallest mistake lost the suit.* On this account these actions of the law were done away with by the Œbutian law and the two Julian laws; and hence it is that we now conduct our actions in set forms of words, that is to say, by formulæ. § 31. The form of procedure, by action of the law, was only allowed in two cases, viz., for apprehended damage, and if the case had to be brought before the centumviral tribunal. For, as often as the case is to be carried to the centumvirs, the sacramental action is proceeded with before the urban prætor or the prætor for aliens;† but, in the case of apprehended damage, no one desires to proceed by an action of the law, but rather by that stipulation which is set forth in the edict, and which binds his adversary, and gives a more convenient and complete right . . . . (twenty-four lines illegible). . . . § 32. On the other hand, in that formula which is available to a farmer of the revenue, there is a fiction to this effect, that the defendant is to be condemned in such a sum as he would formerly have had to give to redeem a pledge, if a seizure by way of pledge had been made. § 33. But no fiction is introduced into the formula based on the "condictio", for, whether we claim a certain sum of money, or other certain thing, due to us, we allege that that thing "ought to be given to us", and we do not add any fiction of a demand. Hence we

* cf. *ante*, § 11.

† cf. *post*, § 95.

perceive, at once, that those formulæ by which we allege that money or something "ought to be given", stand on their own strength. Of this class are the actions of loan, of redemption, of conducting another's affairs, and innumerable others.

§ 34. Further, we have fictions of another kind in certain formulæ; as, for example, he who founds his claim on the edict for possession of the property, sues as feigning himself heir. For, since he succeeds in the place of the deceased according to prætorian law, and not according to the civil law,* he has no direct actions, and he cannot allege that to be his by the law of the quirites, which was the property of the deceased, nor can he allege that what was owing to the deceased ought to be paid to him; hence, on the fiction that he is the heir, he draws up the claim, for example, in this way: "— be judge. If Aulus Agerius" (that is, the plaintiff himself) "were the heir of Lucius Titius, then, if it appear that the estate, which is the subject matter of the action, ought to be his by the law of the quirites", or, if he is suing by a personal action, a similar fiction is prefixed, and the claim then goes on to say: "If it appear that Numerius Negidius ought to give ten thousand sesterces to Aulus Agerius." § 35. In the same way, the purchaser of an insolvent's goods† sues on the fictitious assumption that he is heir; but sometimes he may sue in another way, for, making out the claim in the name of him whose goods he has bought, he turns the wording of the condemnation so as to apply in his own favour, that is, so that the defendant is to be condemned to give him what was the property of, or what ought to have been given to, the insolvent; and this form of action is called Rutilian, because it was drawn up by the prætor, Publius Rutilius, who is also said to have introduced the mode of selling an insolvent's goods.‡ But the form of action first mentioned, in which the purchaser of an insolvent's goods feigns himself heir, is called Servian. § 36. To the same class belongs the action called Publician. This action lies in favour of him who claims a thing which he had not yet acquired by use, and of which he has lost the possession, after it had been delivered to him by some title recognised in law. For, as he cannot allege that the thing is his by the law of the quirites,** he fictitiously assumes that he has acquired it by use; and so, as if he had become owner by the law of the quirites, he asserts his claim, for example, thus: "— be judge. If Aulus Agerius has bought that slave, and if he has been

* *ante*, iii, § 32.

† *ante*, iii, § 80, 81.

‡ *ante*, iii, § 77.

** *ante*, ii, § 41.

delivered to him, and assuming the slave to have been possessed by him for a year, then, if that slave, about whom the suit is brought, ought to be his by the law of the quirites", and so on. § 37. So the Roman citizenship may be fictitiously assumed by an alien when he sues, or is sued, as such in a case where the action is established by our laws, provided the action can be legally extended to the case of an alien; as, for example, if an alien has committed theft, and he is sued, the formula is drawn up thus: "— be judge. If it appear that a theft was committed on Lucius Titius, by Dinon, son of Hermæus", or, "If it appear that, by the advice and assistance of Dinon, son of Hermæus, a theft was committed on Titius of a golden bowl, for which, if he were a Roman citizen, he would have to make amends for the loss as a thief," and so on. Again, if an alien sues for theft, the Roman citizenship is fictitiously ascribed to him. So, again, if an alien sue, or is sued, for wrongful damage, on the ground of the Aquilian law, a suit is instituted under the fiction that he has the Roman citizenship. § 38. Moreover, sometimes we fictitiously assume that our opponent has not undergone a change of legal position. For, if a man or a woman, who is liable to us under an obligation, has undergone a change of legal position, as, for example, happens to a woman by going through the forms of a fictitious purchase, or to a man by adrogation, he or she ceases to be liable to us by the civil law;* and it cannot be directly alleged that he or she ought to give, but, to prevent it being in their power to destroy our right, there was introduced, against him or her, an equitable action with the change of legal position disregarded, that is, in which it is fictitiously assumed that he or she has not undergone a change of legal position.

* *ante*, iii, § 84.

§ 39. The principal parts of a formula are these: the "demonstratio", "intentio", "adjudicatio", "condemnatio". § 40. The "demonstratio" is that part of the formula which is inserted for the purpose of indicating the subject matter of the suit; as, for example, this part of the formula: "Whereas, Aulus Agerius sold a slave to Numerius Negidius," or thus: "Because Aulus Agerius deposited a slave with Numerius Negidius." § 41. The "intentio" is that part of the formula in which the claim of the plaintiff is comprised, as, for example, this part of the formula: "If it appear that Numerius Negidius ought to give to Aulus Agerius ten thousand sesterces;" or this: "Whatever it appear that Numerius Negidius ought to give or do for Aulus Agerius;" or, again, this: "If it appear that the slave belongs to Aulus Agerius by the law of the quirites." § 42. The "adjudicatio" is that part of the formula by which the judge is authorised to adjudge a thing to one of the litigants, as, for example, in the case of a suit between co-heirs for the partition of an inheritance, or between partners for a division of common property, or between neighbours for the settlement of boundaries; for here it runs thus: Let the judge assign to Titius as much as ought to be adjudged. § 43. The "condemnatio" is that part of the formula by which power is given to the judge to condemn or to absolve;* as, for example, this part of the formula: "Judge, condemn Numerius Negidius in — sesterces to Aulus Agerius; if it do not appear, absolve him." Or, again, the following: "Judge, condemn Numerius Negidius to Aulus Agerius in a sum not exceeding ten thousand sesterces; if it do not appear, absolve him." So, again, this: "Judge, condemn Numerius Negidius to Aulus Agerius in ten thousand," and so on, without adding "not exceeding". § 44. But all these parts are not found together in all formulæ, but some are inserted, some are not. It is evident that the "intentio" is sometimes found alone, as in the prejudicial formulæ, as where the question, whether a person is a freed-man, or how much the dowry amounts to, and many others; but the "demonstratio", the "adjudicatio", and the "condemnatio", are never found alone; for the "demonstratio" cannot possibly have any effect without the "intentio" or the condemnatio"; so the "condemnatio" without the "demonstratio" or the "intentio"; or the "adjudicatio" without the "demonstratio" and the "intentio", and the "condemnatio" have no force; and, on that account, these are never found alone.

* cf. *post*, § 48.

§ 45. But those formulæ, in which a civil law issue is raised, we call "in jus conceptæ". Of such are those by which we allege a certain thing to be ours by the law of the quirites, or that it ought to be given us; or that satisfaction ought to be given us for loss occasioned by theft; in all which the claim involves a question of civil law. § 46. But other formulæ we call "in factum conceptæ", that is, in which no such claim is embodied; but, in the beginning of the formula, after having set out what has been done, those words are added by which the power is given to the judge of condemning or absolving. Such is the formula used by the patron against his freed-man, who, in contravention of the edict of the prætor, has summoned his patron to appear in court, for, in such an action, the wording of the formula is as follows: "— be recuperators. If it appear that this patron has been summoned by his freed-man to appear in court, in contravention of the edict of the prætor, recuperators condemn this freedman in ten (? a clerical error for five) thousand sesterces to this patron, if it do not so appear, absolve him."* The other formulæ which are treated of under the title in the edict, "De in jus vocando", are also drawn up "in factum"; as, for example, that against him who, on being summoned to appear in court, has neither come or found a surety to defend him, so, again, that against him who has, by force, kept out of court anyone so summoned. And, finally, numberless other formulæ, of the same kind, are set out in the album. § 47. But, in some classes of suits, the prætor has framed formulæ, both involving a civil law issue and resting on the facts of the case; as, for example, that in respect of a deposit† and that for a loan. For a formula framed thus: "— be judge. Whereas, Aulus Agerius has deposited with Numerius Negidius a silver dish, which is the subject-matter of this action, whatever on that account it behoves Numerius Negidius, in good faith, to do, or to give to Aulus Agerius, in that same, unless he make restitution, judge, condemn Numerius Negidius to Aulus Agerius. If it do not so appear, absolve him"—is drawn up on a civil law basis. But the formula, which is framed thus: "— be judge. If it appear that Aulus Agerius has deposited a silver dish with Numerius Negidius, and that Numerius Negidius has, in fraud of Aulus Agerius, not returned it, judge, condemn Numerius Negidius to pay to Aulus Agerius its ascertained value. If it do not so appear, absolve him"—is drawn up on the facts of the case. The formulæ in the case of a loan are similar.

* cf. Just. IV, xvi, § 3.

† cf. *post*, § 60.

§ 48. The "condemnatio" of all formulæ which contain a condemnation is now framed on a pecuniary valuation. Hence, although we are suing for some specific thing, as a piece of land, a slave, a garment, gold, or silver, the judge does not condemn the defendant in respect of that very thing which is the subject-matter of the suit, as was formerly done, but condemns him in the estimated money value of the thing. § 49. But the condemnation, inserted in the formula, may be either for a certain or for an uncertain sum. § 50. It is for a certain sum in such a formula, for example, as that in which we claim a certain sum of money; for, in that case, the concluding part of the formula runs thus: "Judge, condemn Numerius Negidius to Aulus Agerius in ten thousand sesterces. If it do not so appear, absolve him." § 51. A condemnation for an uncertain sum has a twofold meaning. For, in one sense, the expression is employed to cover the case of some maximum being fixed, when the condemnation is commonly called "cum taxatione"; for example, if we are claiming something uncertain, for then the concluding part of the formula runs thus: "Judge, condemn Numerius Negidius to Aulus Agerius in a sum not exceeding ten thousand sesterces. If it do not so appear, absolve him." But an unlimited condemnation is also uncertain, as, for example, if we claim something as ours from the person in possession of it, that is, if we are suing by a real action or for the production of a thing; for, in such a case, the condemnation would be worded thus: "Whatever the value of the thing may prove to be, judge, condemn Numerius Negidius to Aulus Agerius in that amount of money. If it do not so appear, absolve him." § 52. Wherefore, it results that, if the judge condemn, he must condemn in a fixed sum, although no fixed sum has been inserted in the condemnation. But the judge must be careful that, when a fixed sum has been inserted in the condemnation, he condemn for neither more nor less than the sum so inserted, otherwise he draws the suit upon himself. So, again, if words limiting the amount are inserted, he must not condemn for more than the limited sum, otherwise he will, in the same way, draw the suit upon himself; but he may condemn in a less sum. . . . (seven lines illegible) . . .

§ 61. In actions belonging to the class of those of good faith, full power is deemed vested in the judge to estimate how much in fairness and equity the plaintiff is entitled to. In this power is included that of taking into account what the plaintiff ought in his turn to hand over to the defendant in respect of the same matter, and the judge ought to condemn the defendant for the balance only. § 62. The following are actions of good faith, viz., those based on buying and selling, letting and hiring, carrying on another's affairs, gratuitous agency, deposit, redemption,

§ 28. Again, some actions fall under the class of those of good faith; some are of strict right. The following are actions of good faith, viz., those actions based on buying and selling, letting and hiring, carrying on another's affairs, gratuitous agency, deposit, partnership, guardianship, loan, pledge, partition of an inheritance, division of common property, and the action based on the circumstances of the case arising out of a commission for sale at a fixed price, or on an exchange, and the claim of an inheritance. For, although it was up till now uncertain whether the claim of an inheritance should be included or not amongst actions of

partnership, guardianship, loan. § 63. The power given to the judge does not arise out of the doctrine of set-off, for no words are prefixed to the formula for that purpose, but it seems to rest on its being in accordance with an action of good faith, and therefore it is deemed involved in his duty. § 64. It is otherwise as to the action by which a banker sues, for he is compelled to frame his action so as to allow for set-off, and that set-off is expressed in the words of the formula, so that immediately from the commencement, the set-off having been allowed, he draws his statement of claim for the reduced amount due to him; for suppose he owes Titius ten thousand sesterces, and twenty thousand are owed to him, he frames his claim thus: "If it appear that Titius ought to give him ten thousand more than he himself owes Titius."

good faith, our constitution has positively settled that it is to be included amongst them. § 29. Formerly, the action to compel the restitution of the wife's property was included amongst actions of good faith; but, finding the action based on a stipulation more effectual, we have transferred all rights formerly included under the action for the recovery of the wife's property, with all its varieties, to the action based on a stipulation, and which is brought for the recovery of the dowry; and the action for the recovery of the wife's property being thus abolished, the action based on a stipulation, introduced in its place, has naturally acquired the good faith character when specially applied to the recovery of a dowry; and we have also given the wife an implied mortgage, but we only give her the preference over other mortgagees when she herself is suing in respect of her dowry, as we have been induced to do this for her protection alone. § 30. Now, in actions of good faith, full power is deemed vested in the judge to estimate how much in fairness and equity the plaintiff is entitled to. In this power is included that of taking into account what the plaintiff ought, in his turn, to hand over to the defendant, which being set off, the judge ought to condemn the defendant for the balance. But, even in actions of strict right, set off was introduced through the plea of fraud, allowed to be opposed to the claim, by a rescript of the Emperor Marcus Aurelius, and our constitution has given still greater latitude in the admission of claims of set off which are founded on a clear right, so that actions, whether real, personal, or of any other kind, are reduced by mere operation of law, with the single exception of the action of deposit, in respect of which we have deemed it highly improper for anything in the shape of set off to be opposed, lest, under pretext of a set off, a person should be defrauded of his right of recovering the thing deposited.

§ 65. So, again, when the purchaser of a fraudulent debtor's* property sues on the latter's behalf, he is

* *ante*, iii, § 78.

required to allow a set off, so that the adversary is only condemned in the balance which remains after the deduction of that which the purchaser of the property owes him on account of the fraudulent debtor. § 66. But between the set off which is allowed by the banker, and the deduction which has to be set off by the purchaser of the property, there is this difference; that in the former only matters of the same kind, and of the same nature, are taken into account, as, for example, money is set off against money, wheat with wheat, wine with wine; but, in the opinion of some, not any kind of wine can be set off against wine, or wheat with wheat, but only if they are of the same sort and quality. In deduction, however, may be included that which is not of the same kind; hence, if the purchaser of the property claim money from Titius, whilst he owes Titius on a cross account for corn or wine, the purchaser of the property, after deducting the value of this, sues for the balance. § 67. So, again, that which is not yet due is taken into account in striking the balance in the case of deduction, but in the case of set off, only that which is now due. § 68. Moreover, the allowance, by way of set off, is made in the claim itself; whence, it follows that, if the banker, after having allowed the set off, claims one single sesterce too much, the action falls to the ground, and therefore his claim is gone; but the deduction is placed in the condemnation, where claiming too much does not involve any danger,* at least in the case of an action by a purchaser of the property, who, although he is suing for a certain sum, yet draws up the condemnation in the uncertain form.

* *post*, § 57.

§ 31. Moreover, we call some actions arbitrary, that is, depending upon the discretion of the judge. In these, unless the defendant make satisfaction to the plaintiff, in accordance with the award of the judge, as, for example, to restore produce, or pay, or give up a slave who has been guilty of an injury, he ought to be condemned. Actions of this kind are to be found, both real and personal; real, as, for example, the Publician action, the Servian, in respect of the goods of a tenant-farmer, and the quasi-Servian, which is also called hypothecarian; personal, as, for example, those by which a person sues on account of something done through fear or occasioned by fraud; so, also, the action which claims that which was promised at a particular place; the action for production also depends on the discretion of the judge. In these actions, and others of a like character, the judge is allowed to estimate in fairness and equity, and according to the nature of the subject-matter of the suit, what ought to be given by way of satisfaction to the plaintiff.

§ 32. A judge ought to take care, in all cases, as far as he possibly can, to make his sentence an award of a certain sum or thing, although the issue before him involves an uncertain quantity.

§ 53. If a person has demanded too much in his claim, the suit is at an end, that is, he loses the thing claimed, nor is he restored to his rights by the prætor, except in certain cases . . . . (two lines illegible) . . . . More than a person is entitled to may be claimed in four ways, viz., in respect of the thing, the time, the place, the conditions attached. In respect of the thing, as, for example, if a person, instead of the ten thousand sesterces owed him, should claim twenty thousand, or, if he who owns a definite share in a thing should claim the whole or the greater part of it. In respect of time, as, for example, if a person should make the demand before the day for payment had arrived, or the condition had been fulfilled. In respect of place, as, for example, when a person sues in another place for that which has been promised in a certain place, without taking any notice of the place which had been named, as, suppose the stipulation was to this effect: "Do you bind yourself to give at Ephesus?" the plaintiff would be deemed to demand too much if he framed his claim at Rome, simply to the effect that, "if it appear that he ought to give me"; or even if at Rome he claimed, "if it appear that he ought to give me at Ephesus", because, either way, he deprives the debtor of any advantage as to the place of payment; still, he who has stipulated in this way: "Do

§ 33. If a plaintiff had included in his claim in the formula more than he was entitled to demand, his action fell to the ground, that is, he lost the thing, nor was he easily restored to his rights by the prætor, unless he was under the age of twenty-five years, for, just as he was assisted, on application to the court, in other cases, if he had sustained loss by reason of his youth, so, also, in such a case as this, it was usual to come to his aid. If, however, the case involved such a considerable ground of justifiable mistake, that even the most cautious might have fallen into it, then relief was afforded, even to persons above twenty-five years of age; as, for example, if a legatee had claimed the whole legacy, and afterwards codicils were produced, by which either a part of the legacy was taken away, or legacies were given to some other persons, the effect of which was that the claimant would appear to have demanded more than three-fourths, as, by the Falcidian law, legacies were diminished to that extent.

More than a person is entitled to may be claimed in four ways, viz., in respect of the thing, the time, the place, and the conditions attached. In respect of the thing, as, for example, if a person, instead of the ten gold pieces owed him, has claimed twenty; or if he, who owns a definite share of a thing, claim the whole or the greater part of it. In respect of time, as, for example, if a person should make the demand

you bind yourself to give at Ephesus", can properly sue at Ephesus simply, that is, without naming the place.

§ 53A. More is claimed in respect of the conditions attached, as, for example, if a person, by his claim, deprives the debtor of his election, which he enjoys by the terms of the obligation; as, if a person has stipulated, thus: "Do you bind yourself to give ten thousand sesterces, or the slave Stichus?" and then, one or other merely of these is claimed; for although he may claim that which is less in value, still he is deemed to claim more, because it may be sometimes easier for an adversary to give that which is not claimed. Similarly, if a person had stipulated for a certain class of thing, and then claims a specific kind; as, for example, if any one have stipulated generally for purple, and afterward specifically claim Tyrian purple, and even, though he claim the cheapest kind, the same rule applies on account of the reason just stated. The same rule holds if a person have stipulated generally for a slave, and afterwards claims one by name, as, for example, Stichus, although he may be of the least value. Therefore, the claim in the formula should be drawn up in the same way that the stipulation itself was framed.

before the day for payment had arrived, or the condition had been fulfilled; for, just as he who is behindhand in paying is deemed to pay less than he ought, so he who makes his demand before the time demands more than his due. A demand of more than is due is made in respect of place when, for example, a person claims at another place that which he has stipulated for delivery at a certain place, without taking any notice of the place which had been named, as, for example, if he who had stipulated thus: "Do you bind yourself to give at Ephesus?" claim at Rome, simply, that the defendant ought to give. In this case, he is held to demand more than his due, because, by drawing the claim in this simple form, he deprives the promisor of the advantage he might derive from paying at Ephesus; and, on this account, an arbitrary action lies for the plaintiff in the other place, in which the allowance to be made for the advantage which the promisor might have derived, if he could have paid in the place agreed upon, is taken into consideration. This advantage is chiefly found in relation to merchandise, as, for example, in wine, oil, corn, which have different prices in different places; and even money is not lent everywhere at the same rate of interest. But if a person sue at Ephesus, that is, brings his action at the place where it has been stipulated that the thing should be given him, it will be quite correct if he sue simply for the amount, as the prætor himself points out, for, in this case, the debtor preserves all his advantages. The case of him who claims more than is due in respect of the conditions attached, closely approaches the case of him who is held to be claiming more in respect of place; for, if a person has stipulated with you, thus: "Do you bind yourself to give the slave Stichus, or ten gold pieces?" and then sues for one or the other, as, for example, for the slave only, or the ten gold pieces only, he would, in this case, be deemed to have claimed more than his due, because, in a stipulation of this kind, the right of election is in the promisor, whether he would rather give the slave or the money; and he, therefore, who claims that either the money only, or the slave only, ought to be given him, deprives his adversary of his right of election, and so makes his own condition better, and that of his adversary worse. For this reason an action is provided to meet a case of the sort, by which a person can claim either the slave Stichus, or the ten gold pieces; that is, the action conforms to the stipulation made. Further, if a person has stipulated generally for a slave, and sues specifically for Stichus, or has stipulated generally for wine, and sues specifically for Campanian, or has stipulated generally for purple, and afterwards sues specifically for Tyrian, in all such cases he is held to sue for too much, because he deprives his adversary of the right of election, as, by the terms of the stipulation, he was at liberty to pay over something else than that which he is sued for. So much is this so, that though that which is sued for be of the lowest value, still he is held to have claimed too much, because it is often easier for the debtor to pay that which is of higher value. Now, this was the law formerly in use. But subsequently, a constitution of the Emperor Zeno, and one of our own, has altered this; and if it is in respect of time that more is claimed than due, the constitution of Zeno, of divine memory, applies; but, if more is claimed, in respect of quantity, or in any other way, then, as in the case of the fees of the officers of the court,* all loss, falling on him against whom too much has in this way been claimed, is to be punished by a condemnation of triple the amount.

* *ante*, § 24.

§ 54. From this it sufficiently appears that too much cannot be claimed in formulæ which are of the "uncertain" class, because, where there is no demand of a certain quantity, but the claim is for that which the adversary ought to give, or do, no one can demand too much. The same rule applies to the case of a real action given in respect of an uncertain part, as, for example, such as this: "Such part as appears to be due to the plaintiff of that piece of land which is the subject of this action," which kind of action is very rarely allowed.

§ 55. Again, it is clear that if a person claim one thing instead of another, he runs no risk, and can commence an action over again, because he is not

§ 34. If the plaintiff has included less in his

deemed to have sued; as if he, who should have claimed the slave Stichus, has claimed Eros; or if a person has framed his claim on his right to have something, by virtue of a testament, when the obligation arose out of a stipulation, or if a cognitor or procurator* has claimed something as due "to himself". § 56. But though, as we have stated above,† it is dangerous to demand more, it is allowable to frame the claim for less; but the residue of the claim cannot be sued for during that prætorship, for he who so sues is defeated by the plea which is called that "litis dividuæ".‡ § 57. But, if more than was right has been inserted in the condemnation, there is no risk to the plaintiff; but the defendant, on the ground that an unjust formula has been received, is restored to his original rights, so that the condemnation may be diminished. But, if less than was right has been inserted, the plaintiff only gets that which was inserted; for, though the whole matter is brought before the judge, a limit is fixed by the condemnation beyond which the judge cannot go.** Nor does the prætor accord a restitution of rights on account of a matter growing out of this part of the formula; for the prætor more readily gives his aid to defendants than to plaintiffs. We are speaking now without reference to minors under twenty-five years of age, for, in all cases of loss, the prætor gives relief to persons under that age.†† § 58. If either more or less is inserted in the preliminary description, there is nothing to come before the judge, and therefore the matter remains intact; and this is what is meant by saying that a matter is not concluded by a false description. § 59. But there are some who think that less may be included, so that, for example, he who has, say, bought both Stichus and Eros, may be deemed to have drawn the preliminary statement properly thus: "Whereas, I have bought the slave Eros of you;" and, if he choose, he can sue for Stichus by another similar formula, for it is true that he, who has bought two, has also bought each one; but if he who has bought one, should sue for two, his preliminary statement would be false. The same remarks apply in the case of other actions; as, for example, in that of loan, and of deposit, and this was the opinion adopted by Labeo. § 60. But we have found it laid down by some that, in the action of deposit, and, indeed, in all those other actions in which, if condemned, ignominy follows,‡‡ he, who has claimed, by his preliminary state-

* *post*, § 83, 84.
† *ante*, § 53.
‡ *post*, § 122.
** *ante*, § 52.
†† *ante*, ii, § 163.
‡‡ *post*, § 182.

claim than he is entitled to demand, as, for example, if, when ten gold pieces are owed to him, he has claimed five, or, when he was entitled to the whole estate, he has claimed only the half as his, he incurs no risk, for the judge can, nevertheless, in the same action, condemn the adversary in the balance due to the plaintiff, in accordance with the constitution of Zeno of divine memory. § 35. If a person claim one thing instead of another, it is settled that he runs no risk; but, on the fact being ascertained, we allow him to correct the error in the same suit; as, for example, if he who should claim the slave Stichus, has sued for Eros, or if a person has claimed to have something by virtue of a testament when the obligation arose out of a stipulation.

ment, more than he ought, loses the case, as, for example, if a person, who has deposited a single article, set out in the preliminary statement that he has deposited two or more, or if he who has been struck with the fist on the cheek, frames his preliminary statement, in an action for outrage, so as to show that some other part of the body was struck. But, whether we should accept this as true, requires a more careful investigation. Clearly, as there are two formulæ for an action of deposit, the one involving a civil law issue, the other based on the facts, as we have already observed;* and in that formula, which involves a civil law issue, there is, at the outset, an indication of the subject matter of the suit in the form of a preliminary statement, and then follows the claim containing the legal right asserted in these words: "Whatever, on account of that matter, it behoves him to give or do for me," whilst in the formula framed on the facts of the case, the thing, which is the subject matter of the suit, is indicated in another way, immediately at the commencement of the claim, in these words: "If it appear that he has deposited that thing with him," we cannot doubt but that, if in a formula drawn up on the facts a person has included more things than he has deposited, he loses the cause, because he would be deemed to have inserted too much in the claim . . . (forty-eight lines illegible) . . .

* *ante*, § 47.

§ 36. There are, besides, certain actions by which we do not get all that is due to us, but sometimes all, sometimes less; as, for example, when we are sued in respect of the private savings of a son or a slave, for, if the private savings do not amount to less than what we claim, the father or master is condemned for the whole amount; but, if it turn out that it amounts to less, the judge only condemns to the extent of the private savings. As to how the private savings are to be dealt with, we shall explain in its proper place.*

* *post*, tit. vii.

§ 37. So again, if a woman bring an action for her dowry, it is held that the husband should be condemned to pay as far as he is able, that is, as far as his means allow. Hence, if his means are equal to the amount of the dowry, he is condemned in the whole amount, if less, then only to the extent he is able. The recovery of the dowry is also liable to be diminished by the right of retention possessed by the husband in respect of expenses incurred in connection with the dowry property, for the dowry is liable, by operation of law, to be diminished by necessary expenses, as may be seen by reference to the larger work of the Digest. § 38. So, if a person sue his ascendant or patron, or if one partner sue another in an action of partnership, the plaintiff cannot recover more than his adversary can pay. The same rule applies to the case of a donor sued on the ground of a gift he has made. § 39. The effect of a set-off, also, when opposed to a plaintiff's demand, is generally to cause less to be recovered than was due to him; for a calculation being made of what, in fairness and equity, the plaintiff, on his side, is liable for in respect of the same matter, the judge condemns the defendant in the balance, as has already been stated.* § 40. He, also, who has surrendered his property to his creditors, if he subsequently should acquire anything which yields a sufficient profit, his creditors can commence fresh proceedings against him to compel him to pay to the extent he is able, for it would be inhuman that he, who has already been deprived of all his property, should be condemned in the whole amount of the debt.

* *ante*, § 30.

Title vii. Of actions granted in respect of transactions with a person in the power of another.

§ 69. As we have referred above† to the action used to enforce claims against the private savings of sons in power, and of slaves, it is necessary that we should now carefully consider this and the other actions which are usually granted against ascendants or masters in respect of their descendants or slaves.

As we have referred above‡ to the action used to enforce claims against the private savings of sons in power or of slaves, it is necessary that we should now carefully consider this and the other actions which are usually granted against ascendants or masters in respect of their descendants or slaves. But, as the law governing the case of transactions with slaves, or with those who are in the power of an ascendant, being nearly the same, we shall, to avoid prolixity, direct our attention to the case of the slave and the master, leaving what we say of them to be understood as applicable, also, to children and to those ascendants in whose power they are. For, if anything is peculiar to their case, we will point it out separately.

§ 70. In the first place, then, if any business has been transacted by the order of the father, or of the master, the prætor has established an action against the as-

§ 1. If, therefore, any business has been transacted with a slave, who was acting under the orders of his master, the prætor has promised an action against the

† ? in the illegible part of § 60.

‡ *ante*, tit. vi, § 36.

cendant or the master for the whole amount; and justly so, because he who has so contracted rather relies upon the credit of the ascendant or of the master, than upon that of the son or the slave. § 71. For the same reason the prætor has established two other actions, viz., the exercitorian and the institorian. The exercitorian action is available when the father or the master has made the son or slave master of a vessel, and some transaction has been entered into relating to the matters over which the master of the vessel has charge. For, since this transaction seems to be entered into by the intention of the father or master, it appeared most just that an action should be granted for the whole amount; and, further, although a person has appointed some stranger, whether slave or free, as master of the vessel, still this prætorian action is given against him. And this action is styled exercitorian, because he is called "exercitor" to whom the daily earnings of a ship belong. The institorian formula is, however, available when a person has appointed his son, or his slave, or any stranger he pleased, whether slave or free, to manage a shop or any particular business, and any transaction has been entered into with him in respect of the business he has been appointed to manage. This action is styled institorian, because he who is placed at the head of a shop is called "institor". This formula, also, is used to recover the whole amount.

§ 72. Further, a tributorian action has been established against the father or master when a son or slave, with the knowledge of the father or master, trades with the money or goods contained in his private savings. For, if any con-

master for the whole amount, for he who thus contracts is deemed to rely upon the credit of the master. § 2. For the same reason the prætor has promised two other actions for the whole amount, one of which is called exercitorian, the other institorian. The exercitorian action is available when a person has made his slave master of a vessel, and some transaction has been entered into with him relating to the matters over which the master of the vessel has charge; and this action is styled exercitorian because he is called "exercitor" to whom the daily earnings of a ship belong. The institorian action is available when a person has appointed his slave to manage a shop or any particular business, and any transaction has been entered into with him in respect of the business he has been appointed to manage. This action is styled institorian, because persons appointed to manage a business are called "institores", and the prætor grants these two actions, whether the person appointed to the management of the ship, or of the shop, or of any other business, be a free person or the slave of another, because the same rule of equity would be involved in any such case.

§ 3. The prætor has also established another action called tributorian, for if a slave, with the knowledge of his master, trades with the goods contained in his private savings, and any contracts are made with him

tracts are made with the son or slave in relation to this trading, the prætor declares that, whatever shall result from these transactions, and tending to the profit of the private savings, shall be divided between the father or the master, if anything be due to him, and the rest of the creditors in proportion to their claims. And, as the prætor allows the father or master himself to make the distribution, if any one of the creditors complain that a smaller share has been distributed to him than he is entitled to, the prætor provides this action for him, which is called tributorian.

§ 73. Moreover, the action in respect of private savings, and that in respect of what has turned to the profit of the father or master, have been introduced; so that, although the business has been transacted without the consent of the father or master, yet they must, if the result of the transaction has turned to their profit, be treated as liable for the whole amount; but, if no profit has resulted to them, then they must be deemed liable to the extent of the private savings. Now, whatever the son or slave has necessarily expended on behalf of his father's or master's property, is deemed to have turned to their profit, as, for example, if their creditors have been paid, or dilapidated buildings repaired, or corn bought for the household, or an estate or any other necessary thing has been bought with borrowed money. Hence, if out of, say, ten thousand sesterces which your slave has borrowed from Titius, he has paid five thousand to your creditor, and spent the other five thousand in any other way, you would be condemned to pay the whole of the five thousand, and as much of the

in relation to this trading, the prætor declares that, whatever shall result from these transactions, and tending to the profit of the private savings, shall be distributed between the master, if anything be due to him, and the rest of the creditors, in proportion to their claims. And, as the prætor allows the master himself to make the distribution, if any one of the creditors complain that a smaller share has been distributed to him than he is entitled to, the prætor provides this action for him, which is called tributorian.

§ 4. Moreover, the action in respect of private savings, and that in respect of what has turned to the profit of the master, have been introduced; so that, although the business has been transacted without the consent of the master, yet the master must, if the result of the transaction has turned to his profit, be treated as liable for the whole amount; but, if no profit has resulted to him, then he must be deemed liable to the extent of the slave's private savings. Now, whatever the slave has necessarily expended on behalf of his master's property is deemed to have turned to the master's profit, as, for example, if the slave has paid his master's creditors, or repaired dilapidated buildings, or bought corn for the household, or has bought an estate, or any other necessary thing, with borrowed money. Hence, if out of, say, ten gold pieces which your slave has borrowed from Titius, he has paid five to your creditor, and spent the other five in any other way, you would be condemned to pay the whole of the five and as much of the other five as the private savings would cover; whence it appears

other five thousand as the private savings would cover; whence it appears that, if the whole ten thousand sesterces had turned to your profit, Titius could recover the whole ten thousand, for, although the action is one and the same by which the plaintiff seeks to obtain the private savings, and the amount by which the father or master has profited, yet the action has two condemnations. Hence the judge, before whom the action is brought, usually commences with the inquiry whether the father or master has received any profit, and does not proceed to the valuation of the private savings otherwise than if either nothing or not the whole can be deemed to have turned to the profit of the father or master. But, in estimating the value of the private savings, a deduction is first made of any sum owed by the son or the slave to the father or master, or anyone in his power; and the residue only is deemed to be the private savings. Sometimes, however, that which a son or a slave owes to him who is in the power of the father or master is not deducted from the private savings, as when, for example, he to whom he owes it forms a part of his own private savings.

§ 74. However, there is no doubt but that he who contracts with a son or slave acting under the order of his father or master, and who can make use of the exercitorian or institorian formula, can also sue by the action in respect of private savings, or that in respect of profit to the father or master. But no person who, by one of these actions, could, without doubt, recover the whole, will be so foolish as to involve himself in the difficulty of proving that he, with whom he has contracted, has pri-

that, if the whole ten gold pieces had turned to your profit, Titius could recover the whole ten, for, although the action is one and the same by which the plaintiff seeks to obtain the private savings, and the amount by which the master has profited, yet the action has two condemnations. Hence the judge, before whom the action is brought, usually commences with the inquiry whether the master has received any profit, and does not proceed to the valuation of the private savings otherwise than if either nothing or not the whole can be deemed to have turned to the profit of the master. But, in estimating the value of the private savings, a deduction is first made of any sum the slave owes to his master, or to anyone in the power of the master, and the residue only is deemed to be the private savings. Sometimes, however, that which a slave owes to him who is in the power of his master, is not deducted, as, for example, if that person forms part of his own private savings, because it belongs to him; so that if a slave owes anything to his own under slave, it cannot be deducted from his private savings.

§ 5. However, there is no doubt that a person who has contracted with a slave acting under the order of his master, and who can make use of the exercitorian or institorian action, can also sue by the action in respect of private savings, or that in respect of profit to the father or master; but it would be very foolish for anyone not to avail himself of an action by which he might easily recover the whole amount due under the contract, without involving himself in the difficulty of proving that the trans-

vate savings, and that there is sufficient to be obtained from that source to satisfy him, or that that which has been gained has gone to the profit of the father or master. He, also, to whom the tributorian action is open, can also use the action in respect of private savings, or that in respect of profit to the father or master, but, in most cases, it will obviously be better for him to make use of the last-mentioned action than the tributorian action, for, in the latter action, account is only taken of that portion of the private savings with which the business was carried on by the son or slave; and of what thence resulted, whilst in the action in respect of private savings, the whole of the private savings comes in question—and it may be that the slave has carried on the business with a third or a fourth, or, possibly, even a smaller portion of his private savings, whilst the greater portion was employed in other things—much more then should this action be used if it can be proved that the transaction has turned to the profit of the father or master, for, as we have stated above*, the same formula embraces both the action in respect of private savings and that in respect of profit turned to the father or master.

* *ante*, § 73.

action has turned to the profit of the master, or that the slave had private savings, and that they were sufficient to cover the whole claim. He, also, to whom the tributorian action is open, can also use the action in respect of private savings, or that in respect of profit to the master; and it may be expedient for him, in some cases, to use the tributorian, in other cases the action in respect of private savings, and that in respect of profit to the master. The tributorian action may be advantageous, because in this no preferential position is accorded to the master, that is, no deduction is made of what is owing to the master, but he and the rest of the creditors stand on an equal footing; but, in the action in respect of private savings, a deduction is first made of that which is due to the master, and then the master is condemned in respect of the balance to the creditor. On the other hand, it is so far advantageous to sue by the action in respect of private savings, in that the whole of the private savings comes in question in that action, whereas, in the tributorian action, only that portion of it which was involved in the conduct of the business, and it may be that a slave has traded only with, perhaps, a third or fourth, or even a smaller part of his private savings, whilst the rest was invested in lands and slaves, or lent at interest. Hence, therefore, a person should select this or that action as may be most advantageous in the given case; and clearly, he who can prove that the transaction has turned to the profit of the master, should bring the action available in respect of such profit.

§ 6. What we have said in respect of the slave and his master, the same is to be understood as applying to the case of a son and daughter, or a grandson and granddaughter, and to their father or grandfather in whose power they are. § 7. To them specially, however, apply the provisions of the Macedonian decree of the senate, which prohibits the lending of money to those who are in the power of an ascendant, and refuses an action to him who has lent the money, as well against the son or daughter, grandson or granddaughter (whether still in power or become free from power by the death of the parent, or by emancipation), as against the father or grandfather, whether he still has them in his power, or has emancipated them. This was so decreed by the senate, because those who had become loaded with debt in the shape of money borrowed and squandered in luxury, often laid plots against the lives of their ascendants. § 8. Finally, we must note that, in respect of that which has been the result of a contract made by order of a father or master, and in respect of that which has turned to his profit, a direct personal action may be brought against the father or master, just as if the transaction had originally been made with him as principal. So, when anyone is liable to the exercitorian or institorian action, it is held that he may be sued by a direct personal action, because the contract is deemed made in this case, also, by his order.

Title viii. Of noxal actions.

§ 75. The wrongful acts of sons in power, or of slaves, as, for example, if they are guilty of theft, or commit an outrage, give rise to noxal actions, in which it is lawful for the father or master either to pay the estimated damages or to abandon him by way of reparation; for it was unjust that their wrongful acts should involve their ascendants or masters in greater loss than the value of their persons.

The wrongful acts of slaves, as, for example, if they are guilty of theft or violent robbery, or cause damage or commit an outrage, give rise to noxal actions, in which the condemned master is allowed either to pay the estimated damages or to abandon his slave by way of reparation. § 1. Now, the word "noxa" means the thing which does the damage, that is, the slave, and "noxia" means the wrongful act itself, as, for example, the theft, the damage, the robbery with violence, or the outrage. § 2. It is in the highest degree reasonable that liability should be got rid of by the surrender of the offending person, for it was unjust that their wrongful acts should involve their masters in greater loss than the value of their persons. § 3. A master who is sued in a noxal action on account of his slave, is released from liability on surrendering the slave to the plaintiff by way of reparation, and the ownership of that slave is transferred for ever from the master; so that if the slave can get money, and compensate him to whom he has been surrendered for the damage done, he may be manumitted, by the aid of the prætor, against the will of his master.

§ 76. Noxal actions owe their origin either to the laws, or to the edict of the prætor; to the laws, for example, in the case of theft, by the Twelve Tables, and of wrongful damage, by the Aquilian law, to the edict of the prætor, for example, in the case of outrages and robbery with violence. § 77. All noxal actions follow the delinquent; for, if your son or your slave has been guilty of a wrongful act, so long as he is in your power, an action lies against you; if he has fallen under the power of another, the action lies against that other; if the delinquent has become free from power, a direct action lies against him, and any ground for his surrender is removed. On the other hand, the direct action may become noxal; for, if the head of a family has been guilty of a wrongful act, and then arrogate himself to you, or become your slave (which may happen in such cases as we have pointed out in the first commentary),* the action, which was previously direct, becomes a noxal action against you. § 78. But, if a son has been guilty of a wrongful act against his father, or a slave against his master, no action lies; for no obligation can in any way arise between me and the person who is in my power, and therefore, although he should have passed into the power of another, or has become free from power, no action can be brought either against the man himself, or against him in whose power he may now be. Whence arises the question whether, if another's slave, or son, has been guilty of a wrongful act against

* *ante*, i, § 160.

§ 4. Noxal actions owe their origin either to the laws, or to the edict of the prætor; to the laws, for example, in the case of theft, by the Twelve Tables, and of wrongful damage, by the Aquilian law, to the edict of the prætor, for example, in the case of outrages and robbery with violence. § 5. Every noxal action follows the delinquent; for, if your slave has been guilty of a wrongful act, so long as he is in your power, an action lies against you; if he has fallen under the power of another, the action lies against that other; but if he has been manumitted, he is himself directly liable, and any ground for his surrender is removed. On the other hand, a direct action may become noxal; for, if a freeman has been guilty of a wrongful act, and then become your slave (which may happen in such cases as we have pointed out in the first book),† then the action, which was previously direct, becomes a noxal action against you. § 6. If a slave has been guilty of a wrongful act against his master, no action lies; for no obligation can arise between the master and him who is in his power; and, therefore, although he should have passed into the power of another, or has been manumitted, no action can be brought either against the man himself, or against him in whose power he may now be. Hence, if another's slave should have been guilty of a wrongful act against you, and afterwards pass into your power, the right of action is lost, because matters have fallen into that position in which

† *ante*, I, tit. xvi, § 1.

me, and he afterwards fall into my power, the right of action is lost, or is only in abeyance. The leaders of our school think that the right of action is lost, because matters have fallen into that position in which no action could in any way arise; and, therefore, though he should pass out of my power I cannot sue. The leaders of the opposite school think, that so long as he is in my power, the action is in abeyance, since I cannot sue myself; but that it revives when he ceases to be in my power. § 79. But when a son in power is surrendered by the process of formal sale, on the ground of having committed a wrongful act, the leaders of the opposite school think that the forms of formal sale should be gone through three times,* because, by the Twelve Tables, it is provided that a son shall not otherwise pass out of the power of the father than by three formal sales; Sabinus and Cassius, and the other leaders of our school, believe that one formal sale is sufficient, as they think that those three formal sales referred to in the Twelve Tables, relate to cases of voluntary formal sales.

* *ante*, i, § 132, 140.

§ 80. Thus much as to those persons who are in the power of another, whether the action is brought in respect of their contracts or delicts. But as to those persons who are in marital power, or those free persons who are in a state of bondage, the law may be stated in this way: that in the case of a suit at law arising out of a contract of theirs, unless the action be defended for the whole liability by him to whose power they are subject, the property which would have belonged to them, if they had not been subjected to his power, is sold, the change of legal position being treated as not having taken place; but when the action is based on the authority of the magistrate .... (twenty-four lines illegible) .... § 81. ... how does the matter then stand? for although, as we have said, the surrender of dead slaves in a noxal action would not have been allowed, yet if a person give up one who has died from natural causes, he is equally discharged from liability.

no action can arise; and, therefore, although he should subsequently pass out of your power, you cannot sue, just as if a master have injured his slave in any way, and the slave has been manumitted or alienated, no action can be brought against the master.

§ 7. The ancients allowed these rules to apply to children of both sexes in the power of ascendants, but the feeling of later times has rightly deemed that harshness of this sort should be discarded, and these rules have, therefore, passed wholly into disuse. For who could bear to surrender, by way of reparation for a wrong, his son, or still more his daughter, for in the person of his son the father would be a heavier sufferer than the son, whilst in respect of daughters, regard for modesty alone excludes such rules. Hence noxal actions are held to be only capable of being used in the case of slaves, and we find it often laid down by the ancient commentators on the law that sons in power may be themselves sued for their own wrongful acts.

Title ix. Of damage caused by animals.

* viii, § 6.

The Twelve Tables* provided a noxal action to meet the case of animals devoid of reason causing damage through sportiveness, bad temper, or ferocity; and, according to the Twelve Tables, if such animals were surrendered by way of reparation for the damage, the defendant was released from liability; as, for example, if a kicking horse should have kicked some one, or an ox, prone to use his horns, has tossed some one. But this action only lies in respect of those animals which act at the time in a way not in accordance with their ordinary nature, as no action can be brought where the animal is untamable. Hence, if a bear escape from his owner, and damage has resulted, the owner cannot be sued; for he ceased to be owner when the wild beast escaped. The word "pauperies" means damage done without legal wrong on the part of the doer; for an animal cannot be said to have done a legal wrong, since it is devoid of reason. Thus much appertains to the subject of noxal actions.

§ 1. But it must be observed that by the Ædilitian edict we are prohibited from keeping a dog, a boar pig, a wild boar, a bear, or a lion, in a place where the public are in the habit of passing, and if this rule be disobeyed, and a freeman is injured, the owner is to be condemned in such a sum as the judge thinks just and fair, and in respect of other things damaged, the condemnation is to be double the loss sustained. Besides the Ædilitian actions, the action in respect of damage caused by an animal also lies, for actions, especially penal actions, capable of being used concurrently in respect of the same matter, never extinguish one another.

Title x. Of those by whom we may sue.

§ 82. We must now note that we can sue either in our own name or in that of another. In the name of another, as, for example, when

We must now note that a person may sue either in his own name or in that of another. In the name of another, as, for example, suing by a cognitor, a procurator, a tutor, or a curator; although formerly, in strictness, it was not lawful to sue in the name of another, except in certain cases. § 83. Now, a cognitor is substituted for oneself in the suit by certain set words in the presence of the adversary. For the plaintiff appoints a cognitor thus: "As I am claiming from you," for example, such and such an estate: "I appoint in this matter Lucius Titius as cognitor against you." The adversary appoints him thus: "Since you claim the estate from me, I appoint in this matter Publius Mævius as cognitor against you." The plaintiff may also say as follows: "As I am desirous of suing you, I appoint a cognitor in the matter;" and the defendant may say: "Since you wish to sue me, I appoint a cognitor in the matter." And it is immaterial whether the cognitor so appointed be present or absent; but if he was absent at the time of his appointment he will only become cognitor when it has come to his knowledge, and he has undertaken the duty.

when suing as procurator, tutor, or curator; although, formerly, a person could not sue in the place of another, except on behalf of the people, or freedom, or a pupil. The Hostilian law afterwards allowed an action for theft to be brought in the names of those who were prisoners with the enemy, or who were absent on the service of the state, or who were in the tutelage of such persons. But, as the impossibility of suing or pleading to an action in the name of another was productive of no small inconvenience, the custom grew up of suing by procurators; for illness, age, an unavoidable journey, and many other causes often prevent persons being able themselves to attend to their own affairs.

§ 84. But a procurator is substituted in the suit without any special form of words, and by a simple mandate, and he may be appointed in the absence, and without the knowledge of the adversary. Indeed, some are of opinion that he is to be deemed a procurator who has not received a mandate, if only he has entered upon the matter bona fide, and has found security that his acts shall be ratified by his principal. Although, even he who holds a mandate ought usually to give security; because often, at the commencement of a suit, the mandate is not produced, and is subsequently brought forward before the judge.

§ 1. A procurator is not appointed with any particular form of words, or in the presence of the adversary; indeed, the appointment is generally made without his knowledge; for any person is held to be your procurator who is employed to sue, or defend an action in respect of your affairs.

§ 85. In what way tutors and curators are appointed we have explained in the first commentary.*

§ 2. In what way tutors and curators are appointed has been explained in the first book.†

* 1, § 144–200.

† 1, tit. xiii–xxiii.

§ 86. Now he who sues in the name of another lays the claim in the person of his principal, but turns the condemnation to his own person; for if, by way of example, Lucius Titius is suing on behalf of Publius Mævius, the formula is drawn up thus: "If it appear that Numerius Negidius ought to give ten thousand sesterces to Publius Mævius, judge, condemn Numerius Negidius in the sum of ten thousand sesterces to Lucius Titius. If it do not appear, absolve him." If he is suing in a real action, he lays the claim thus: "The thing is the property of Publius Mævius by the law of the quirites," and turns the condemnation to his own person. § 87. So, if a person appear on behalf of the defendant, he who has brought the action alleges, by his claim, "That the principal ought to give", but the condemnation is turned against the person who has undertaken the defence. But, when the action is real, nothing appears in the claim as to the person against whom the action is brought, whether such person is defending in his own name or in that of another; for the allegation in the claim is only, "that the thing is the property of the plaintiff".

§ 88. Let us now see in what cases he who is sued, or he who sues, may be called upon to give security. § 89. Thus if, for example, I am suing you by a real action, you ought to give me security, for it has seemed just that you should give me security in respect of that thing which you are permitted in the interval to possess, but about your ownership of which a doubt has been raised, so that if you lose the suit, and do not hand over the thing itself, or pay the estimated damages, I may have it in my power to proceed either against you or against your sureties. § 90. And much more ought you to give me security if you defend the action in the name of another. § 91. Real actions are however of two sorts, for the suit may be either by the formula framed to claim the thing itself, or by the wager method. If the first mentioned formula is used, then the stipulation called "judicatum solvi" is introduced, if the second

Title xi. Of security.

Formerly, in respect of taking security, one system was in force; in modern times, another system has developed itself through custom.

For formerly, if the action was real, the possessor was obliged to give security, so that if he lost the suit, and did not either hand over the thing itself, or pay the estimated damages, the plaintiff might have the power of either suing him or his sureties. This security is called "judicatum solvi", and it is not difficult to understand why it is so styled, for a person stipulates that his adversary shall satisfy the judgment. With still greater reason was he who was sued in a real action compelled to give security if he was acting on behalf of another.

method is employed, then that called "pro praede litis et vindiciarum". § 92. The petitorian formula* is that by which the plaintiff alleges in his claim that the thing is his. § 93. But we sue by the wager method in the following way. We challenge our adversary by a wager of this sort: "Do you bind yourself to give me twenty-five sesterces if the slave, the subject matter of this suit, is mine by the law of the quirites?" Then we draw up a formula in which we allege, in the claim, that the amount of the wager ought to be given us, and by such a formula we are only victorious if we prove that the thing is ours. § 94. Yet the amount of the wager is not exacted; for it is not a penal sum, but pre-judicial, and only introduced to obtain by means of it a decision in respect of the thing, and hence no counter stipulation is required from the defendant, and the stipulation is called "pro praede litis vindiciarum", because it takes the place of guarantors; for formerly, when the process was by an action of the law*, guarantors were given by the possessor to the claimant, "pro lite et vindiciis", that is, for the subject matter of the suit and its produce. § 95. But, if the action is brought before the centumvirs, we do not claim the amount of the wager by formula, but by the procedure of an action of the law, and the sacramental challenge is in a larger sum, for this wager is usually fixed at a hundred and twenty-five sesterces, by virtue of the Creperian (?) law. § 96. But he who sues by a real action, if he sue in his own name, gives no security. § 97. And if the action is conducted by a cognitor, no security is required either from him or from his principal; for, since a cognitor is substituted for his principal by a special, and, as it were, a solemn form of words, he is rightly regarded as taking the place of his principal. § 98. If, however, the suit is carried on by a procurator, he is ordered to find security "that his principal will ratify his acts", for there is a risk that the principal may again sue in respect of the same thing; but this danger does not arise when the action is brought by a cognitor, because he who has sued by a cognitor has no further action in respect of that thing than if he himself had sued. § 99. Tutors and curators are required, by

* *ante*, § 41.

* *ante*, § 16.

He, however, who sued by a real action, if he was plaintiff on his own behalf, was not obliged to give security.

But a procurator, suing in a real action, was called upon to give security that his acts would be ratified by his principal; for there was a risk that the principal might put the very same matter in issue again.

Tutors and curators were

the terms of the edict, to give security in the same way as procurators, but sometimes security is dispensed with in their case. § 100. These were the rules in real actions; but, if the inquiry is made as to when the plaintiff, in a personal action, should give security, we shall find that the same rules apply as stated by us in respect of a real action. § 101. But in respect of him who is sued, if he has intervened in the name of another, he ought always to give security, because, unless security is given, no one is deemed a competent defendant in another's cause; and if the defence is conducted by a cognitor, the principal is required to give the security, but, if a procurator has appeared, then the procurator himself must give it. The same rule applies to the case of both the tutor and the curator. § 102. But if anyone defend a personal action in his own name, it is usual for security to be given in certain cases, which the prætor himself has pointed out. The grounds for the giving of this security are twofold, for, by the prætor's edict, it is provided that security should be given either on account of the nature of the action or on account of the character of the defendant, because he is suspected. On account of the nature of the action; as, for example, in the action upon a judgment, or an action for money paid by a surety*, or when grounded on immorality on the part of a wife. On account of the person; as, for example, if the action be against a person who has been made bankrupt, or whose property has been seized by creditors, and publicly offered for sale, or if the action be against an heir whom the prætor has deemed suspected.

* *ante*, § 25.

required, by the terms of the edict, to give security in the same way as procurators, but sometimes the security was dispensed with when they were plaintiffs. These were the rules in the case of a real action. § 1. But, as to personal actions, and in respect of the plaintiff, similar rules applied, as those stated by us in the case of real actions. But, in respect of him who is sued, if he appeared on behalf of another, he was always obliged to give security; for, unless security is given, no one is deemed a competent defendant in another's cause. But, if a person defended a personal action in his own name, he was not obliged to give security that the judgment would be satisfied.

§ 2. But these matters are now-a-days otherwise dealt with. For whether a person is sued in a real or personal action in his own name, he is not obliged to give any security for the value of the subject-matter of the action, but only on his own behalf, that he will remain in attendance to the end of the suit, for which purpose he is either bound by his promise, with an oath attached (which security is called that by oath), or by his simple promise, or by security given according to his rank. § 3. But where an action is commenced or defended by a procurator, if acting on behalf of a plaintiff, and his authority has not been registered, or if his principal has not appeared in person before the judge to confirm the appointment, then the procurator must himself give security that his principal will ratify his acts; and the same rules apply to the case of a tutor, a curator, or other persons of that class who have undertaken the management of the affairs of others, and who bring an action through another person. § 4. But if a person is sued, then, if he is present and ready to appoint a procurator, he may either himself come into court and support the appearance of the procurator in his behalf by entering into solemn stipulations by way of security that the judgment will be satisfied, or he may find security out of court by which he becomes a surety for his own procurator in respect of all the conditions involved in the security that the judgment will be satisfied. For this purpose, whether he give the undertaking in court, or enter into the security out of court, he is obliged to subject his property to a mortgage, so that both he and his heirs become liable. He has also to give another undertaking, or find security on his own behalf, that he will be in attendance in court when judgment is pronounced, or, if he is not in attendance, that his surety will do all that is required by the judgment, unless appealed against. § 5. But, if from any cause, a defendant is not ready, and another person desire to undertake his defence, he can do so without any distinction being drawn between real and personal actions, provided he find security to the amount of the subject-matter of the action that the judgment will be satisfied. For, according to the old rule already mentioned,* no one is deemed a competent defendant in another's cause unless security is forthcoming. § 6. All these points will be more clearly and perfectly known from observing the daily practice of the courts in respect of these very matters. § 7. We direct that these rules shall obtain, not only in this royal city, but also in all our provinces; although from ignorance the practice may now perhaps be different; for it is necessary that all the provinces should follow the practice of this royal city, the head of all our dominions.

* *ante*, § 1.

§ 103. All actions either result from the civil law, or are based on the authority of the magistrate.† § 104. Actions resulting from the civil law are those which take place in the city of Rome, or within the first milestone thereof, between Roman citizens and before a single judge, and these, by the Julian law

† *ante*, iii, § 180, 181.

regulating procedure in civil suits, expire if not decided within one and a half years, and hence the meaning of the common saying that by the Julian law a suit dies in a year and a half. § 105. But actions heard by recuperators are based on the authority of the magistrate, as well as those which take place before a single judge where either the judge or one of the litigants is an alien. In the same class fall all those actions which take place beyond the first milestone of the city of Rome, whether between Roman citizens or aliens. These actions are said to be based on the authority of the magistrate, because they are effectual so long as he who authorised them retains his authority. § 106. Now, if an action based on the authority of the magistrate has been concluded, whether it was real or personal, and whether the formula was one drawn up on the facts, or contained a civil law claim,* another action can nevertheless be subsequently brought as a matter of right about the very same thing; and, therefore, a plea of judgment awarded, or of pending suit, becomes necessary. § 107. But where the action was personal and resulting from the civil law, with a formula setting up a civil law claim, an action in respect of the very same matter cannot be subsequently brought as a matter of right, and therefore such a plea is superfluous; but if the action was either real or based on the facts, the plaintiff can nevertheless as a matter of right subsequently bring another action, and on that account a plea of judgment awarded, or of pending suit, is necessary. § 108. The case was different formerly with actions of the law, for when a matter had once been the subject of litigation, no action could again be brought as a matter of right in respect of that thing, and the use of exceptions was not in vogue then as now.† § 109. But an action may result from some law, and yet not be of the civil law, and, conversely, an action may not result from a law, and yet be of the civil law; for if, for example, an action be commenced in the provinces based on the Aquilian or Ollinian (?) or Furian law, the action will rest on the authority of the magistrate; and the same rule applies if we sue at Rome before recuperators, or before a single judge, when he or one of the parties is an alien. On the other hand, if, on some ground forming the basis of an action given by the edict of the prætor, the action takes place at Rome before a single judge, and to which all the parties are Roman citizens, it is an action resulting from the civil law.

* *ante* § 45.

† *post*, § 116.

§ 110. We must here note that the prætor usually allows actions resulting from a law, or from decrees of the senate, to be brought at any time, but he generally limits within the year those actions which spring from his own jurisdiction. § 111. Sometimes, however, the prætor makes these latter perpetual, as, for example, those actions in which a civil law right is taken as a precedent, as in the case of those which the prætor renders available to the possessors of property,* and to others who stand in the place of the heir. So also the action for manifest theft, although it now depends on the jurisdiction of the prætor himself, may be granted at any time; and rightly, since a pecuniary is imposed instead of the capital penalty.

§ 112. Not all actions which lie against anyone, as a matter of right, or by the grant of the praetor, equally lie, or are usually given, against his heir. For it is a clear rule of law that penal actions arising out of torts do not lie, and are not given by the prætor, against the heir; as, for example, the actions for theft, for violent robbery, for outrages, and for wrongful damage. But actions of this kind are available for heirs, and are not refused by the prætor, except the action for outrages and any other that may seem to resemble it. § 113. Sometimes, however, even an action arising from contract does not lie either for or

* *ante*, iii, § 32; iv, § 34.

Title xii. Of perpetual and temporary actions, and of those available for and against heirs.

We must here note that those actions which resulted from a law, or a decree of the senate, or from the imperial constitutions, were formerly available at any time, until imperial constitutions set limits to both real and personal actions; but those actions springing from the prætor's own jurisdiction for the most part only last during one year, for the authority of the prætor himself was only annual. Sometimes, however, they were made perpetual, that is, made to last to the limit introduced by the constitutions; such are those available to the possessor of goods and to others who stand in the place of the heir. The action for manifest theft, also, though arising from the jurisdiction of the prætor, is yet perpetual, for he deemed it absurd to limit its duration to a year.

§ 1. Not all actions which lie against anyone as a matter of right, or by the grant of the prætor, equally lie, or are usually given, against his heir. For it is a clear rule of law that actions arising out of torts do not lie against the heir; as, for example, the actions for theft, for violent robbery, for outrages, and for wrongful damage. But actions of this kind are available for heirs, except the action for outrages, and any other that may seem to resemble it. Sometimes, however, even an action arising from contract does not lie against an heir; as where the testator has fraudulently appropriated (? a thing de-

against the heir. For the heir of an adstipulator has no action,* and the heir of a sponsor, and of a fidepromissor, is not liable.†

* *ante*, iii, § 114. † *ante*, iii, § 120.

posited with him), and no benefit has accrued to the heir from the fraud. But if issue has been joined by the principals in the penal actions which we have mentioned above, then they are available both for and against the heirs.

§ 114. It remains for us to inquire what is the duty of the judge when the defendant, after having joined issue, and before judgment is pronounced, makes satisfaction to the plaintiff. Ought he to absolve, or rather condemn, because, when issue was joined, the defendant was in such a position that he ought to be condemned. The leaders of our school think he ought to absolve him, and that it is immaterial what kind of action it was: and this is what is meant by the common saying that Sabinus and Cassius held that all actions are capable of being absolved. But the leaders of the opposite school hold otherwise in respect of actions of strict law, though they are of the same opinion as to actions of good faith, because, in actions of that class, the judge is not restricted in his functions, and they think the same as to real actions, because . . . . (sixteen lines illegible) . . . .

§ 2. It remains for us to remark that, if before judgment is pronounced, the defendant make satisfaction to the plaintiff, the judge ought to absolve him, although from the time that issue was joined the defendant was in such a position that he ought to be condemned, and this is what was meant when, in former times, it was commonly said that all actions admit of the defendant being absolved.

Title xiii. Of exceptions.

§ 115. In pursuing our subject we must now treat of exceptions. § 116. Exceptions have been introduced as a means of defence for those against whom an action is brought; for it often happens that a person is liable according to the civil law, but it would be unjust to condemn him in the action; as, for example, if I have stipulated from you the payment of a sum of money, which I was

In pursuing our subject, we must now treat of exceptions. Exceptions have been introduced as a means of defence for those against whom an action is brought; for it often happens that, although the suit brought by the plaintiff is in itself just, yet it is unjust against him whom he is suing. § 1. For example, if compelled by fear, or induced by fraud, or through mistake, you have, on the stipulation of Titius, promised that which you should not have promised, it is clear that according to the civil law you are liable, and an action, claiming that you ought to give, is sustainable; but it is unjust that you should be condemned, and therefore, to defeat the action, a plea of fear or fraud, or one setting out the facts, is allowed you. § 2. The rule is the same if a person should have stipulated money from you, as if for money lent, but does not hand the

about to hand over to you by way of loan, but have not handed it over, in which case it is clear that the money can be claimed from you, for you are bound to give it, as you are liable on the stipulation; but, as it is unjust that you should be condemned on such a ground, it is held that you should be protected by a plea of fraud. So, again, if I have agreed with you that I will not demand what you owe me, still I can sue you, "that you ought to pay me", because the obligation is not destroyed by the agreement we have come to, but it is held that a plea of the agreement made should defeat my action. § 117. In those actions, also, which are not personal, exceptions may be used; as, for example, if you have compelled me by fear, or induced me by fraud, to transfer to you, by a formal conveyance, a thing requiring such a mode of transfer, then, if you claim that thing from me, a plea is allowed me by which, if I show that you have caused me to do this through fear or fraud, you will be defeated. So, again, if, knowing an estate to be the subject matter of a law

money over to you. For in such a case it is clear that he could claim the money from you, and you are bound to give it, for you are liable under the stipulation; but, as it would be unjust that you should be condemned on such a ground, it is held that you ought to be able to protect yourself by a plea of the money not having been handed over. The time within which this plea is available, has, as we have said in a former book,* been reduced by our constitution. § 3. Further, if a debtor has agreed with his creditor that no demand shall be made upon him, still the debtor remains liable, for obligations are not always dissolved by an agreement; and hence an action by which the plaintiff asserts "if it appear that he ought to give" is sustainable; but, as it would be unjust that the debtor should be condemned in contravention of the agreement, he may defend himself by a plea of the agreement made. § 4. So, too, if the debtor, on the creditor putting him to his oath, swear that he ought not to give, he still remains bound; but, as it would be unjust to inquire whether he has been guilty of perjury, he defends himself by a plea of having taken the oath. In real actions exceptions are equally necessary; as, for example, if the possessor, on being put to his oath by the claimant, swear that the thing is his, and yet the claimant goes on with his action claiming it; for, though what he asserts may be true, viz., that the thing is his, still it is unjust for the possessor to be condemned. § 5. So, again, if an action has been brought against you, whether real or personal, nevertheless the obligation subsists, and, therefore, according to strict law, an action may be subsequently brought against you in respect of the same matter, but you are to be protected by the plea of judgment awarded. § 6. These cases, brought forward by way of example, will suffice. Besides, in what numerous and varied cases exceptions are necessary, may be gathered from the larger work of the Digest or Pandects. § 7. Some of these exceptions result from laws, or from enactments having the force of law, or from the jurisdiction of the prætor.

* *ante*, III, tit. xxi.

suit, you buy it of one not in possession, and then bring an action for it against the possessor, an exception may be opposed to you by which you will be non-suited in any case. § 118. Some exceptions the prætor has published in his edict; others he inserts after inquiry into the matter; but all either result from laws or from those enactments which have the force of law, or have proceeded from the prætor's jurisdiction.

§ 119. Now all exceptions are drawn up in the negative to the affirmation of the opposite party. For if, for example, a defendant allege that the plaintiff is acting fraudulently, because, perhaps, he is claiming a sum of money which he never handed over,* the exception is drawn up in this form: "If nothing fraudulent has been or is now being done by Aulus Agerius." So, again, if he allege that the money is claimed in contravention of an agreement, the exception is drawn up thus: "If no agreement has been entered into between Aulus Agerius and Numerius Negidius that this money should not be sued for." And so, in other cases, it is customary to draw it up in a similar way, because, of course, every exception is put in by way of opposition by the defendant, and is so inserted in the formula as to make the condemnation conditional, that is, that the judge can only condemn the defendant if no fraud has been committed by the plaintiff in relation to the subject matter of the action; or, again, the judge can only condemn him if no agreement has been entered into that the money should not be sued for.

* *ante*, § 116.

§ 120. Exceptions are said to be either peremptory or dilatory. § 121. Peremptory exceptions are those which are good at any time, and which cannot be avoided; as, for example, that grounded on fear, or fraud, or that something has been done in contravention of a law, or decree of the senate, or that judgment has been awarded, or that there is a pending suit;† or, again, the exception of a concluded agreement where it has been agreed that the money should never be sued for. § 122. Dilatory exceptions are those which offer a bar for a time only; as, for example, that arising from an agreement made that no claim shall be

† *ante*, § 106.

§ 8. Some exceptions are called perpetual and peremptory, others temporary and dilatory. § 9. Perpetual and peremptory exceptions are those which always stand in the way of the party suing, and always put an end to the matter involved in the suit. Such is the exception of fraud, that it was done through fear, and that of a concluded agreement, when an agreement has been entered into that the money

made for, say, five years, for at the expiration of that time the exception is of no avail. Of a similar character to this is the exception that the cause of action has been divided, or that the actions have been separated, for if a person sue for a part of a thing, and within the term of office of the same prætor claim the remainder, he will be defeated by this exception, which is called that "litis dividuæ".* So, again, if he who has several actions in respect of the same matters against the same person goes on with some actions but postpones others, he will be defeated by the exception called that "rei residuæ", if, during the term of office of the same prætor, he goes on with the actions which he has so postponed. § 123. It must be noted that he, against whom a dilatory exception is opposed, should delay the action; otherwise, if, notwithstanding the exception opposed to him, he goes on with the action, he loses his cause, nor does the right of suing survive to him even after the time in which he could have avoided its effect, as having a clear right of action, for the matter having been brought into court, the right of action has been destroyed by the exception.

* *ante*, § 56.

shall never be sued for. § 10. Temporary and dilatory exceptions are those which offer a bar for a time only, and afford an extension of time. Such is that arising from an agreement made when it has been agreed that no action shall be brought within a certain time, as, for example, for five years; and when this period has expired, the plaintiff is not prevented from following up the matter. Therefore, those who, on attempting to sue within the fixed time, are met by an exception of agreement made, or any similar one, should put off the action, and sue after the time has elapsed; hence, these exceptions are termed dilatory. Otherwise, if they have sued within the time, and the exception has been opposed to them, nothing will result to them in that action on account of the exception, nor could they formerly have sued after the time had expired, because they had rashly brought the matter into court, and used up their right, and so lost all claim to the thing. At the present day however we do not desire to proceed so strictly, but he who has ventured to bring an action before the time fixed by the agreement, or obligation, is to be brought under the constitution of Zeno, which that most sacred legislator introduced respecting those who in point of time claim more than their due, so that if the delay is disregarded, which the plaintiff had voluntarily granted, or which is involved in the nature of the action, the delay is doubled for the benefit of those who have suffered such a wrong; and, after the expiration of the time, the suit can only be recommenced if the defendants have been previously reimbursed all the costs incurred by the former action, so that plaintiffs alarmed by such a penalty may be taught to observe the proper delays in commencing suits.

§ 124. But dilatory exceptions are held to relate not only to time but also to persons. Such are those concerning cognitors; as, for example, if he who cannot, according to the edict, appoint a cognitor,* bring an action by a cognitor, or if, having the right to appoint a cognitor, he appoints a person who cannot lawfully undertake the office, for if an exception grounded on the person of the cognitor be opposed, and he who brings the suit is a person who cannot lawfully appoint a cognitor, he can himself sue; but if the exception be that the cognitor whom he has appointed cannot lawfully act, he has full power to sue by another cognitor, or in his own person. In this or the other way he can avoid the effect of the exception; but if he take no notice of it, and sue by the cognitor, he loses his cause. § 125. Whenever the defendant has by mistake not made use of a peremptory exception, he will be restored to the entirety of his rights, in order that the exception may be inserted; but whether he can be restored to the entirety of his rights, if he has not availed himself of a dilatory plea, is a question.

* *ante*, § 83.

§ 11. There are also dilatory exceptions by reason of the person. Such are those relating to a procurator; as, for example, if a person wishes a soldier or a woman to sue on his behalf, for the right of acting as procurators on behalf of their father or mother, or wife, or even under an imperial rescript, is not conceded to soldiers, though they may attend to their own affairs if they can do so without any breach of discipline. But we have observed that those exceptions which were formerly opposed to procurators on account of the infamy, either of the person appointing the procurator, or of the procurator himself, are no longer used in practice, and we have sanctioned their abolition, lest whilst discussions arose in respect of them, the trial of the action itself should be prolonged.

§ 126. It sometimes happens that an exception, which prima facie seems just, may affect the plaintiff inequitably. When this happens, another addition becomes necessary for the purpose of aiding the plaintiff, and this addition is called a replication, because by its means the force of the exception is rebutted and resolved. For if, for example, I have agreed with you not to demand from you the money you owe me, and then subsequently we come to an opposite agreement, that is, that I may sue you; and if on my bringing an action against you, you oppose me with the exception that you

Tit. xiv. Of replications.

It sometimes happens that an exception, which prima facie seems just, may work injustice. When this happens, another addition becomes necessary for the purpose of aiding the plaintiff, and this is called a replication, because by its means the force of the exception is rebutted. For when a person has agreed with his debtor not to demand payment from him, and subsequently they have come to a contrary agreement; that is, that the creditor may sue, if the creditor does sue, and the debtor opposes the exception that he ought only ought only to be condemned towards me if no agreement has been come to "that I would not sue for the money", this exception of a concluded agreement will prejudice my suit, for this pact, nevertheless, remains true, although we have subsequently come to a contrary agreement; but as it is unjust that I should be defeated by this exception, a replication is given to me setting up the subsequent agreement in this way: "If it was not subsequently agreed that I might sue for the money." So, again, if a banker, suing for the price of a thing which he has sold by auction, is opposed by the exception that the purchaser should only be condemned "if the thing which he bought has been delivered to him", which is a proper exception; but if it was declared at the time of the sale that the thing would not be delivered to the purchaser until he paid the price, the banker is aided by a replication in this form: "Or if it has been declared that the thing would not be delivered to the purchaser unless the purchaser paid the purchase-money."

§ 127. But it sometimes happens that the replication itself, which, prima facie seemed just, unfairly prejudices the defendant. When this happens, it becomes necessary, for the purpose of aiding the defendant, to make another addition, which is called the "duplicatio". § 128. And if, again, this appear prima facie just, but for some reason unjustly prejudices the plaintiff, it again becomes necessary to make an addition in aid of the plaintiff, which is called the "triplicatio". § 129. The variety of transactions has brought about the use of all these additions, sometimes even beyond those we have referred to.

to be condemned "if it was not agreed that the creditor should not demand payment", this exception will prejudice his suit, for he has so agreed, and it remains true, although subsequently they came to a contrary agreement. But as it is unjust that the creditor should be defeated, a replication is given him setting up the subsequent agreement.

§ 1. Again, it sometimes happens that the replication, which prima facie seemed just, is unfairly prejudicial. When this happens, it becomes necessary, for the purpose of aiding the defendant, to make another allegation, which is called the "duplicatio". § 2. And if, again, this appear prima facie just, but for some reason unjustly prejudices the plaintiff, it again becomes necessary to make another allegation for the purpose of aiding the plaintiff, which is called the "triplicatio". § 3. The variety of transactions has brought about the use of all these exceptions, sometimes beyond those we have referred to. A knowledge of the subject may be easily obtained from the larger work of the Digest.

§ 4. The exceptions by which a debtor defends himself are, in the majority of cases, usually accorded to his sureties also, and rightly so, for that which is claimed from them is to be deemed as if claimed from the debtor himself, because, by the action based on gratuitous agency, he may be compelled to repay them that which they have paid for him.* For which reason, if a person has agreed with the defendant not to demand payment, it has been held that his sureties may avail themselves of the exception based on the agreement, just as if the agreement not to sue had been made with themselves. But there are, however, some exceptions which are not so allowed them. For if, for example, a debtor has surrendered his property, and a creditor sue him, he may defend himself by the exception "unless he has surrendered his property"; but this exception is not available to the sureties, for, of course, he who takes others as surety for the debtor, has mainly in view the power of suing those who become surety for the debtor, in the event of the latter's insolvency.

* *ante*, iii, tit. 20, § 6.

§ 130. Let us now turn to the subject of those prescriptions which are admissible on behalf of the plaintiff. § 131. For it often happens that, as the result of one and the same obligation, something ought now to be performed, and something hereafter; as, for example, when we have stipulated for a certain sum of money every year or every month; for then, at the end of any given number of years or months, the money due in respect of that period ought to be paid; but, although an obligation has indeed been contracted in respect of future years, still there is, as yet, no liability for performance. If, therefore, we wish to claim that which ought to be done, and to bring the matter into court, but to leave that which has to be done hereafter under the obligation in uncertainty, it is necessary to sue with this prescription: "That thing is sued for of which the time for performance has expired;" otherwise, if we have sued without this limiting clause, and with that formula by which we demand an uncertain thing, the claim of which is drawn up in these words: "That which it appears Numerius Negidius ought to give or to do to Aulus Agerius," we have made the whole obligation (that is, that also of which the performance is due hereafter) the subject matter of this action, and that portion of the obligation, of which the time for performance has not yet arrived, is destroyed on the joinder of issue, and cannot afterwards be again brought before the court. So, again, if, for example, we are suing by an action arising out of a purchase, that an estate should be transferred to us by a formal conveyance, we ought to insert a prescription in this way: "The matter sued for is in respect of the formal conveyance of the estate," so that, if we are subsequently desirous of having undisturbed possession delivered to us . . . . (one line illegible? to the effect that:—we may be able to sue for its delivery, either by action based on the stipulation, or on the purchase, for, if we have not inserted the limiting clause) the obligation in respect of the entire right involved in the uncertain action: "Whatever, on account of that thing Numerius Negidius ought to give, or to do to Aulus Agerius," is destroyed on the joinder of issue; so that, if we are afterwards desirous of suing for the delivery of the vacant possession, no action is available. § 132. That prescriptions are so called, because they are inserted at the commencement of the formula, is, of course, obvious.

§ 133. But now-a-days, as we have already pointed out,* all prescriptions are inserted by the plaintiff. Formerly, indeed, some were also inserted on behalf of the defendant; as in the case of such a prescription as this: "That thing may be the subject of the action, in so far as it does not prejudice the question of the inheritance," a form which has now been reduced to a kind of exception, and is employed when a claimant of the inheritance, by another kind of action, may get a preliminary decision as to the inheritance; as, for example, when he is making a claim in respect of particular things, as it is unjust that, in a suit about particular things in it, a decision should be obtained as to the whole inheritance . . . . (twenty-four lines illegible, probably to the effect that a prescription was allowed to be inserted in the place of the demonstration, where, for example, the master brought an action in respect of a stipulation of his slave, which related to present and future obligations, and he wished to limit it to that portion now due. In such cases it was necessary that the name of the slave should appear in the prescription) . . . . § 134. Then, by the claim in the formula, it is pointed out who it is that is entitled to receive, and, of course, it is to the master that that which the slave stipulates for has to be given; but, in the prescription, the question of the matter of (fact?) is raised, and this ought to be correctly stated, according to its natural import. § 135. And, whatever we have stated in respect of slaves, we are to understand as said of those other persons who are subjected to our power. § 136. So, again, we must note that, if we sue the person himself who has promised us an uncertain thing, the formula is so drawn up for us as to insert the prescription in the place of the demonstration of the

* *ante*, § 130.

formula in this way: "— be judge. Since Aulus Agerius has stipulated for an uncertain thing from Numerius Negidius, whatever on account of that thing, so far as now due, Numerius Negidius ought to give or to do to Aulus Agerius, etc." § 137. If the action is against a sponsor or fidejussor,* the prescription usually runs in the case of the sponsor, thus: "The subject matter of the action is that which is now due of what Aulus Agerius has stipulated in respect of an uncertain thing from Lucius Titius, on whose behalf Numerius Negidius is sponsor;" but, in the case of the fidejussor, thus: "The subject matter of the action is that which is now due of what Numerius Negidius has become surety for Titius in respect of an uncertain thing," then the rest of the formula follows.

* *ante*, iii, § 115.

Title xv. Of interdicts.

It follows that we should now treat of interdicts or of the actions which are used in their place. Interdicts were certain set forms of words, by which the prætor either ordered something to be done, or forbade the doing of something, and he chiefly made use of them when disputes had arisen between persons about possession or quasi-possession.

§ 138. It remains for us to treat of interdicts. § 139. Now, the prætor or pro-consul interposes his authority in certain cases, mainly with a view to putting an end to disputes; and this he chiefly does when there is a dispute between persons about possession or quasi-possession; and, finally, he orders something to be done, or forbids something being done, and the formulæ and forms of words used for this purpose are called interdicts or decrees. § 140. They are called decrees when he orders something to be done; as, for example, when he makes a preliminary order that something shall be produced or restored; but they are called interdicts when he forbids something being done; as, for example, when he makes a preliminary order that no violence is to be done to the other party bona fide possessing, or that something shall not be done on sacred ground. Hence, all interdicts are called restitutory, or exhibitory, or prohibitory. § 141. The matter, however, is not at an end so soon as he has ordered something to be done or forbidden the doing of something, for the matter goes before a judge or recuperators, and there the question is raised, on the formula prepared for the purpose, whether anything has been done contrary to the edict of the prætor, or whether that which he ordered to be done has not been done. And the action then sometimes involves a penalty, sometimes does not. It involves a penalty, for example, when the action is by way of wager; without a penalty, when an arbitrator is claimed. In the case of prohibitory interdicts it is usual always to sue by way of wager; but, in the case of restitutory or exhibitory interdicts, the action is sometimes by way of wager and sometimes by the formula which is called "arbitraria".*

§ 142. The principal division, therefore, consists in this, that interdicts are either prohibitory, restitutory, or exhibitory.

§ 143. The next division arises from this, that they are either prepared for the purpose of acquiring possession, or for retaining it, or for recovering it.

§ 144. In order to acquire possession, an interdict is given to the possessor of the property,† of which the commencement is "quorum bonorum", and of which the force and effect is, that whatever por-

* *post*, § 163.

† *ante*, iii, § 34.

§ 1. The main division of interdicts is that they are either prohibitory, or restitutory, or exhibitory. Prohibitory interdicts are those by which the prætor forbids something to be done; as, for example, to use violence towards a bona fide possessor, or towards one carrying a dead body to a place where he has a right to carry it, or as to building in a sacred place, or as to the doing of anything in a public river, or on its bank, tending to impede the navigation. Restitutory interdicts are those by which he orders something to be restored; as, for example, possession to the possessor of the goods of an inheritance, which possession a person has taken on the ground of occupying the place of heir or possessor, or when he orders the possession of land to be restored to him who has been forcibly dispossessed. Exhibitory interdicts are those by which the prætor orders to be produced, for example, him in respect of whose liberty a suit is raised, or the freed-man on whom a patron wishes to impose services, or the children to the ascendant in whose power they are. There are some, however, who think that those are interdicts, properly so called, which are prohibitory, because to interdict is to denounce and to forbid, whilst restitutory and exhibitory should, properly, be called decrees; but the term interdict is applied to all alike, because they are said to be between two parties. § 2. The next division of interdicts is based upon this, that some are prepared for the purpose of acquiring possession, some for retaining it, some for recovering it.

§ 3. In order to acquire possession, an interdict is provided for the possessor of the property which is termed "quorum bonorum", and of which the force and effect is that, whatever portion of the

tion of the property, of which possession has been given to another, is possessed by a person in the character of heir or possessor, that portion is to be handed over to him to whom the possession of the property is given. But both he who is heir, as well as he who thinks he is heir, appear to possess as heir. He possesses as possessor who possesses, without title, some portion of, or the whole of, the inheritance, knowing that it does not belong to him. Hence, the interdict is called that for acquiring possession, because it is only of service to him who now, for the first time, is endeavouring to acquire the possession, and, therefore, if a person who has gained possession has lost it, this interdict ceases to be of use to him. § 145. Similarly, an interdict is available to the purchaser of an insolvent's property,* which some call "possessory". § 146. So, again, an interdict of a similar character is available for him who has purchased confiscated property, and it is called "sectorium", because those persons who purchase confiscated property are termed "sectores". § 147. There is also an interdict, called "Salvianum", available for the purpose of acquiring possession. This the owner of land uses in respect of that property of a tenant, which the latter has pledged as security for the rent of the land.

* *ante*, iii, § 80.

§ 148. An interdict for the purpose of retaining possession is usually granted when, in a dispute between two parties as to the ownership of a certain thing, the preliminary question arises as to which of the litigants should be put in possession, and which should be claimant. For this purpose the interdicts "uti possidetis", and "utrubi", have been provided. § 149. The first of these two interdicts is available in the case of disputes about the possession of land

property, of which possession is given to another, is possessed by a person in the character of heir or possessor, that portion must be restored to him to whom the possession of the property is given. A person is held to possess as heir who thinks he is heir. He possesses as possessor who, without right, possesses a part or the whole of an inheritance, knowing that it does not belong to him. Hence, the interdict is called that for acquiring possession, because it is only of service to him who now, for the first time, is endeavouring to acquire possession of the thing, and, therefore, if a person who has gained possession has lost it, this interdict is useless to him.

There is also an interdict, called "Salvianum", available for the purpose of acquiring possession. This the owner of land uses in respect of the property of a tenant, which the latter has pledged as security for the rent of the land.

§ 4. The interdicts, "uti possidetis", and "utrubi", are available for the purpose of retaining possession when, in a dispute between two parties as to the ownership of a certain thing, the preliminary question arises as to which of the litigants should be put in possession, and which should be claimant. For, unless it is first ascertained who is to have possession, an action claiming it cannot be commenced, for both law and reason require that one should

or buildings, but the other interdict is for the possession of movable things. § 150. And if an interdict is applied for in respect of land or buildings, the prætor orders him to be deemed to have the better right who, when the interdict is granted, is in possession, as against his adversary, neither by force nor secretly, nor at will, but in respect of movable things, he orders him to be deemed to have the better right, who, during the greater part of that year should have possessed as against his adversary, neither by force, nor secretly, nor at will, and this is indicated clearly by the very words of the interdicts. § 151. But in the interdict "utrubi", not only is his own possession of advantage to him, but also that possession of another which rightfully falls to him, as, for example, of him to whom he has become heir, and of him from whom he has purchased, or from whom he has received it by way of gift or dower. Therefore, if the lawful possession of another joined to our possession exceeds the possession of our adversary, we come off victorious on the interdict. But no accession of time is given, or can be given, to him who has no possession of his own; for to that which amounts to nothing, nothing can be added; and so if he have a possession infected with a vice, that is, acquired from his adversary either by force, or secretly, or at will, it is not given, for an accession not his own avails him nothing. § 152. But the year is reckoned backwards. Therefore, if you, for example, have been in possession for eight months previously, and I for the seven subsequent months, I shall have the better right, because

possess, and the other claim it from the possessor. And as it is far more advantageous to possess than to claim the possession; there is generally, indeed, nearly always, a great effort made to obtain the possession. The advantage of possessing consists in this, that even though the thing be not his who possesses it, yet if the plaintiff cannot prove that it is his, the possession remains where it is, and, for this reason, when the rights of both parties are doubtful, it is usual to decide against the claimant. The interdict, "uti possidetis", is used in disputes about the possession of land or buildings, the interdict, "utrubi", in respect of movables; and with the ancients there were differences in the force and effect of these two, for, in the first-mentioned interdict, he came off victorious who was in possession at the time of the interdict, provided he had not acquired possession as against his adversary by force, or secretly, or at will, although he had expelled some other person by force, or had secretly deprived him of the possession, or had asked some one to allow him to possess at will; but in the case of the other interdict, he came off victorious, who, for the greater part of that year, had possession, as against his adversary, neither by force, nor secretly, nor at will. At the present day, however, a different rule is observed, for the effect of the two interdicts, so far as regards the possession, is put on an equality, so that he is victorious, both in respect of an immovable, as of a movable, who, at the time of the joinder of issue, holds the possession neither by force, nor secretly, nor at will, as against his adversary. § 5. A person is

possession for the three earlier months, avails you nothing in respect of this interdict as it is possession in another year. § 153. Moreover, we are deemed to possess, not only if we ourselves are in possession, but also if a person is in possession in our name, although he may not be subject to our power, such as a tenant of a farm, or of a house. We are also deemed to possess through those with whom we have deposited or lent anything, or to whom we have given the use of a house rent free; and this is what is meant by the common saying that possession may be retained through any one who is in possession in our name. And, some even think that possession may also be retained by the intention, although neither we ourselves are in possession, nor any other person in our name, if only we have departed, not with the intention of giving up possession, but of subsequently returning. We have pointed out in the second commentary* who those persons are by whom we may obtain possession; and there is no doubt but that we cannot acquire possession by intention only.

§ 154. An interdict for the purpose of recovering possession is usually given if any one has been deprived of the possession by force; for in such a case the interdict is granted which commences: "Whence you have forcibly ejected him," by which he who has forcibly ejected the other is compelled to restore the possession of the thing to him, provided that he who has been ejected does not possess, as against the other, either by force, or secretly, or at will; since he who has possession as against me, by force, or secretly,

* *ante*, ii, § 89, 94.

deemed to possess, not only if he himself is in possession, but also if a person is in possession in his name, although he may not be in his power, such as the tenant of a farm, or of a house. He is also deemed to possess through those with whom he has deposited or lent anything. This is what is meant, when it is said that a person may retain possession by any one who is in possession in his name. And it is even held that possession may be retained by the intention; that is, that although he himself is not in possession, nor any one else in his name, yet, if he has departed from the place, not with the intention of giving up possession, but of subsequently returning, he is deemed to retain the possession. We have pointed out in the second book† through whom a person can acquire possession, and there is no doubt that no one can acquire possession by the intention only.

§ 6. For the purpose of recovering possession an interdict is usually given if anyone has been forcibly deprived of the possession of land or of buildings. For the interdict, "unde vi", is then granted him, by which he who has ejected him is compelled to restore the possession to him, although he, who was forcibly ejected, possessed as against that other by force, or secretly, or at will. But, according to the imperial constitutions, as we have stated above,‡ if a person has taken possession of a thing by force, and it is his own

† II, tit. ix. ‡ IV, tit. ii, § 1.

or at will, may be ejected by me with impunity. § 155. Sometimes, however, although I have forcibly ejected him who possessed as against me by force, or secretly, or at will, I may be compelled to restore possession to him; as, for example, if I have ejected him by force of arms; for, on account of the atrocity of the wrongful act, I must submit to an action compelling me in any event to restore possession. By the term arms, we understand not only shields, swords, and helmets, but also sticks and stones.

§ 156. The third division of interdicts is based on the distinction that they are either simple or double. § 157. Simple are those in which one of the two parties is plaintiff, and the other defendant; such are all restitutory or exhibitory interdicts; for the plaintiff is he who asks either for the production or restitution; the defendant is he of whom the production or restitution is asked. § 158. But of prohibitory interdicts some are double, others are simple. § 159. Simple are, for example, those by which the prætor prohibits the defendant from doing anything in a sacred place, or in a public river, or on its bank; for the plaintiff is he who requires that nothing be done; the defendant is he who is endeavouring to do something. § 160. Double interdicts are, for example, such as "uti possidetis", and "utrubi". These are called "double", because in them the condition of each litigant is equal, for neither can be deemed to be rather defendant than plaintiff, but each sustains the part as much of defendant as of plaintiff, for the prætor addresses both in the same terms, the general form of these interdicts

property, he is deprived of the ownership of it, and if it belongs to another, he is obliged, after restoring it, to pay to him who was subjected to the violence the value of the thing. Moreover, he who has forcibly deprived another of his possession, is liable under the Julian law relating to private or public violence; and for private violence if the violence was done without arms, but for public violence if he expelled the other from the possession with arms. By the term arms, we understand not only shields, swords, and helmets, but sticks and stones.

§ 7. The third division of interdicts is based on this, that they are either simple or double. Simple are those in which one out of the two parties is plaintiff, and the other defendant; such are all restitutory or exhibitory interdicts; for the plaintiff is he who asks for the production or restitution, the defendant is he of whom the restitution or production is asked. But of prohibitory interdicts some are simple, others are double. Simple are, for example, those by which the prætor prohibits anything being done in a sacred place, or in a public river, or on its bank; for the plaintiff is he who requires that nothing be done, the defendant, he who is endeavouring to do something. Double interdicts are, for example, such as "uti possidetis", and "utrubi". These are called double, because in them the condition of each litigant is equal, for neither can be deemed to be rather defendant than plaintiff, but each sustains the part as much of defendant as of plaintiff.

running in the one case thus: "I forbid force to be used to prevent you possessing as you now possess"; and in the other case thus: "I forbid force to be used to prevent the slave, who is the subject-matter of this action, from being removed by that one of the two litigants, whichever he be, who has possessed him during the greater part of this year."

§ 161. Having enumerated the kinds of interdicts, it follows that we should now discuss the mode of using them and their result. Let us begin with simple interdicts. § 162. If, therefore, a restitutory or exhibitory interdict is granted, as, for, example, that possession should be restored to him who has been forcibly ejected, or that a freed-man should be produced, to whom the patron desires to appoint his services, sometimes the result is attained without the risk of a penalty, sometimes with that risk. § 163. For, if he who is sued has demanded an arbitrator, he receives a formula, which is called "arbitraria"; and by which, if under the award of the judge, anything is required to be restored or produced, it may be produced or restored without involving a penalty, and in this way he is discharged from liability; but, if he do not restore or produce, he is condemned to pay the value of the thing. But the plaintiff also proceeds without the risk of a penalty against him who, it appears, is not under any obligation to produce or restore anything, except in the case of an action for vexatious litigation,* being opposed to him for the tenth part, although, according to Proculus, an action for vexatious litigation was not available to a defendant who had demanded an arbitrator, inasmuch as he must thereby be held to have admitted that he was bound to restore or produce; but we follow a different rule, and rightly; for a person claims an arbitrator rather because he is desirous that the matter should be more dispassionately litigate than because he might lose his case. § 164. But he who desires to claim an arbitrator should be careful to make the demand before he leaves the prætor's court, for the petition will not be granted later in the case. § 165. Therefore, if he has not claimed an arbitrator, but leave the prætor's court in silence, the matter is brought to an end by the process involving a penalty. For the plaintiff challenges his adversary by the wager, if in spite of the edict of the prætor, he shall not have produced, or not have restored, and then the defendant puts a counter stipulation to the

§ 8. Of the mode in former times, of using, and the result of interdicts, it is now superfluous to speak; for, whenever the trial is conducted in the extra - ordinary manner (as now all trials are conducted), there is no necessity for the granting of an interdict; the trial going on without interdicts, just as if an equitable action had been allowed as a consequence of an interdict.

* *post*, § 175.

plaintiff against his own wager. Then the plaintift frames a formula against his adversary, grounded on the wager, and the latter in his turn on the counter stipulation. But the plaintiff joins to the matter of the wagers another action for the restitution or production of the thing, so that if he should win on the wager, and the thing is not produced or restored (? the defendant is condemned for the value of the thing) . . . . (forty-eight lines illegible.) . . . . § 166. (? After the interdict had been granted) interim possession was given to him who had made the highest bidding for the produce, provided he gave security to his opponent under the stipulation guaranteeing the restoration of the produce, the force and effect of which is, that if (? the decision finally) goes against him, he has to pay the guaranteed amount to his adversary. This struggle by way of bidding is called "the bidding for the produce", because (? the prætor sells the interim possession to the highest bidder), after which each challenges the other by a wager, "unless contrary to the edict of the prætor, violence has been done to the possessor", and both parties reciprocally restipulate against the wager . . . . (three lines illegible; ? or the two stipulations are united so as to make one wager and one counter stipulation, the result being) that the judge before whom the suit comes, investigates, of course, in the first place, the point covered by the prætor in the interdict, that is, which of them possessed that estate, or that house, during the time when the interdict was granted, neither by force, nor secretly, nor at will.* When the judge has ascertained this, and has, say, decided the point in my favour, he condemns my adversary in the amount both of the wager and of the counter stipulation, which I have entered into with him; and consistently with that view, he releases me from the wager and counter stipulation which had been entered into with me, and, in addition, in case my adversary has possession on account of his having been victorious at the bidding for the produce, and he does not hand over the possession to me, he may be condemned in the Cascellian or secutorian action. § 167. Hence, if he who was victorious at the bidding for the produce does not prove that he has a right to the possession, he is ordered to pay by way of penalty the amount of the wager, and of the counter stipulation, and of the bidding for the produce, and must moreover give up possession; and, in addition to this, he delivers over the produce, which he has

* *ante*, § 150.

gathered in the interval; as the sum bid for the produce does not represent the value of that produce, but is a payment made by way of penalty, because the interim possessor has endeavoured during this period to retain a possession that belonged to another, as well as to acquire the power of enjoying the produce. § 168. But if he who has failed at the bidding for the produce does not prove that he has a right to the possession he is only liable to pay by way of penalty the amount of the wager and counter stipulation. § 169. But we must note that if the stipulation guaranteeing the restitution of the produce has been omitted, he, who has failed at the bidding for the produce, is at liberty, in the same way as he can sue for the recovery of possession by means of the Cascellian or secutorian action, so also he may sue in respect of the bidding for the produce, for which purpose a special action is provided called "fructuarium", by means of which the plaintiff may obtain security that the judgment will be satisfied.* This action is also called "secutorian", because it follows on success as to the wager, but it is not, properly speaking, also called Cascellian. § 170. But inasmuch as some persons, on the interdict being granted, were unwilling to do the other things arising out of the interdict, and therefore the object sought could not be attained, the prætor provided for this and prepared interdicts which we call secondary, because they are granted in the second place, and of which the force and effect is this, that he who does not do the other things arising out of the interdict, as, for example, if he will not give security not to do violence, or does not bid for the produce, or does not give security in respect of the bid for the produce, or does not challenge by wager, or make the counter stipulations, or will not defend the actions arising out of the wagers, if he is in possession, he is ordered to deliver over the possession to his adversary; if he does not possess he is ordered to do no violence to the possessor. Therefore, although it was possible to come off victorious by means of the interdict "uti possidetis", if he were willing to do the other things consequent on the interdict, yet by the secondary interdict . . . . (thirty-three lines illegible) . . . .

* *ante*, § 91.

§ 171. . . . . An action for double is also provided by the prætor in cer-

Title xvi. Of the penalties on rash litigation.

We must now note that those who have upheld the laws have

tain cases against those who deny their liability; as, for example, if an action is brought on a judgment, or for money paid as a surety, or for wrongful damage, or for legacies which the heir has been ordered to give.* In certain cases the wager method is allowed; as, for example, in the case of an action for a fixed sum lent, and for that on an agreement to pay a pre-existing debt; but in the first case the wager is for the third part of the money, in the second case for half. § 172. But if the defendant is not involved in the risk of a wager, or of an action for double, and if the action itself be not from the outset for more than the simple value, the prætor allows an oath to be required, "that the defence is not set up vexatiously"; hence, although heirs and those who occupy the place of heirs are only liable for the simple amount,† and though, again, women and pupils are exempt from the risk of the wager, yet the prætor orders them to take the oath. § 173. But sometimes, from the outset, the action is for more than the simple value; as, for example, the action for manifest theft is for the quadruple, the action for non-manifest theft is for the double, the action based on the discovery of the stolen thing after solemn search, and that based on the stolen thing being deposited elsewhere, for treble value;‡ for in these and in some other cases, whether a person denies or admits the claim, the action is for more than the simple value.

bestowed much care in devising means for preventing men easily engaging themselves in lawsuits, and this is also our study. This is best effected both as to the rashness of plaintiffs and of defendants by restraining them, sometimes by a pecuniary penalty, sometimes by the solemnity of a judicial oath, sometimes by the fear of infamy. § 1. For instance, by our constitution, an oath is tendered to all defendants; and a defendant is not permitted to avail himself of his pleas, unless he first swear that he is induced to defend because he believes he has grounds for so doing. But against those denying liability, in certain cases the action is established for the double or treble value; as, for example, if the action is grounded on wrongful damage, or in respect of legacies left to sacred places. In some cases the action is from the outset for more than the simple value; as, for example, the action for manifest theft is for the quadruple, the action for non-manifest theft for the double; for in these cases and in some others,** whether a person denies or confesses the claim, the action is for more than the simple value.

** *ante*, tit. vi, § 19, 26.

§ 174. Vexatious litigation on the part of a plaintiff is sometimes restrained by the action for vexatious litigation, sometimes by a cross action, sometimes by a judicial oath, sometimes by a re-stipulation. § 175. Indeed, the action for vexatious litigation may be used against all actions, and is for the tenth part of the subject

Again, vexatious litigation on the part of the plaintiff is restrained; for the plaintiff is also obliged, by our constitution, to

* *ante*, § 9 † *ante*, § 112.
‡ *ante*, iii, § 186, 187, 191.

matter, but against a claimant of liberty it is for the third part. § 176. But he who is sued can either oppose the action for vexatious litigation, or require a judicial oath that "the action is not vexatiously brought". § 177. But the cross action is established for certain special cases; as, for example, where a person has been sued in an action for outrage, or in the case of a woman who has been sued on the alleged ground that she had fraudulently transferred to another the possession given her on behalf of her unborn child; and so in the case of a person suing on the ground that he alleged he had been prevented entering after the prætor had put him into possession. The condemnation in the cross action is for the tenth part, when brought against the action for outrage, but against the other two actions it is for the fifth part. § 178. But the restraint imposed by the cross action is more rigorous, as, in the action for vexatious litigation, no one is condemned in the tenth or the fifth part except he who is held not to have properly brought his action, but to have instituted it for the purpose of annoying his adversary, and in the hope of coming off victorious rather through the error or injustice of the judge than through the goodness of his cause. In the cross action, however, the plaintiff is always condemned if he has not been able to maintain his action, although, misled by an erroneous opinion, he thought he had a good cause of action. § 179. Although in those cases in which a person can bring a cross action, the action for vexatious litigation also lies, yet only one of the two is allowed to be brought. For this reason, if a judicial oath of not suing vexatiously has been exacted, then, inasmuch as the action for vexatious litigation is not allowed,* so the cross action ought not to be permitted to be brought. § 180. The penalty of re-stipulation is also usually involved in certain cases; and, just as in the cross action, the (former) plaintiff is always condemned if he has not been able to maintain his action, and the question is not gone into whether he knew that he had no good ground of action, so, also, the plaintiff is always condemned in the penalty of re-stipulation. § 181. Clearly, if the penalty of re-stipulation is claimed from the plaintiff, the action for vexatious litigation cannot be opposed to him, nor is he liable to have a judicial oath exacted from him, for it is obvious that a cross action does not lie in these cases.

swear that he is not proceeding litigiously. The advocates, also, on both sides, take the oath provided for in another constitution of ours. All these methods have been introduced in the place of the old action for vexatious litigation, which has fallen into disuse because it subjected the plaintiff to a penalty of the tenth part of the subject matter in dispute, which we do not find to have ever been enforced. In place of this the above-mentioned judicial oath has been introduced, as, also, that the dishonest litigant is compelled to bear the loss and expenses incurred by his adversary.

* *ante*, § 176.

§ 182. In certain actions those who are condemned become infamous, as, for example, in cases of theft, of robbery with violence, outrages, also in actions of partnership, mortgage, tutelage, gratuitous agency, deposit; but, in the case of theft, or violent robbery, or outrage, not only are those who are condemned branded as infamous, but even those who have come to terms about the action, as is declared in the edict of the prætor, and rightly, for there is an important difference whether a person lies under an obligation arising out of a delict or a contract. It is likewise expressly declared, in that part of the edict, that a person who has compromised the matter is to be deemed infamous, and forbidden to claim an action on behalf of another, or to ask for a procurator to be given, or to appoint a procurator or cognitor, or to intervene in a trial as a cognitor . . . . (half a line illegible) . . . .

§ 2. In certain actions those who are condemned become infamous, as, for example, in cases of theft, of robbery with violence, outrages, fraud; also in the case of the direct, but not the cross, actions of tutelage, gratuitous agency, and deposit, also in the case of the action of partnership, which is direct by whichever of the parties it is brought, and on that account any one of the partners condemned in that action is branded with infamy. But, in the case of the actions for theft, or robbery with violence, or outrage, or fraud, not only are the condemned branded with infamy, but also those who have compromised the action, and rightly, for there is an important difference whether a person lies under an obligation arising out of a delict or a contract.

§ 183. Finally, it must be understood that he . . . (half a line illegible, ? who wishes to sue a person must summon him into court) . . . and he who is summoned . . . (one line illegible, ? is bound to appear in court or find a surety) . . . . but certain persons cannot be summoned into court without the permission of the prætor; as, for example, ascendants, and patrons, and the children of patrons, and the ascendants of a patron or patroness, and a penalty falls upon those who act contrary to these rules.

§ 3. The process to be pursued in commencing all actions is set out in that part of the edict in which the prætor treats of the summons into court; for the first thing to be done is to summon the adversary into court, that is, to summon him before him who has jurisdiction in the matter. In this part of the edict the prætor accords this distinction to ascendants and to patrons, as well as to the descendants and ascendants of patrons and patronesses, that their children and freedmen cannot otherwise summon them into court than if they have first demanded and obtained permission to do so from the prætor; and, if a person summon them without this permission, the prætor inflicts upon them a penalty of fifty gold pieces.

§ 184. But, when an adversary has been summoned into court, and the matter cannot be concluded that day, security must be given by him that he undertakes to appear on a certain day. § 185. Now, the security is in some cases given simply, that is, without sureties; in other cases with sureties; in some cases a judicial oath is taken; in other cases recuperators are appointed, that is, so that, should a person not put in an appearance on the day fixed, he may be immediately condemned by the recuperators in the amount of the security given; and the rules relating to each of these cases are carefully laid down in the edict of the prætor. § 186. If the action is on a judgment or in respect of money paid by a guarantor,* the security will be for the amount involved in the suit; but, if it is in respect of other matters, security will be taken to the amount that the plaintiff swears, on oath that he is not proceeding vexatiously, ought to be given him, but not for more than half the sum sued for, or over one hundred thousand sesterces, and, therefore, if the matter in dispute amount to one hundred thousand, and the action is not one in respect of a judgment, or for money paid by a guarantor, the security to be given will not exceed fifty thousand sesterces. § 187. But, as to those persons whom we cannot with impunity summon before the court without the permission of the prætor,† we cannot, against their will, compel them to give security unless the prætor accedes to an application made to him for this purpose.

* *ante*, III, § 127.

† *ante*, § 183.

Title xvii. Of the duty of a judge.

It remains for us to treat of the duty of the judge. In the first place, the judge should take care not to give a decision otherwise than in accordance with the laws, the constitutions, and customs. § 1. Hence, if judgment has to be pronounced in a noxal action he should be careful, if he consider the master ought to be condemned, to make the condemnation run in this form: "I condemn Publius Mævius to pay ten gold pieces to Lucius Titius, or to surrender that which caused the damage." § 2. In the case of a real action, if he decide against the claimant, the defendant possessor should be absolved from liability; if against the possessor, he ought to order him to restore the property together with the produce. But if the possessor allege his inability to restore the property immediately, and his demand for time, within which to make the restitution, does not seem wrongful, his petition should be granted, provided he give security, with sureties, for the value of the property in litigation, if within the time accorded to him the property is not restored. If the claim is in respect of an inheritance, the same rules apply in respect of the produce, which we have referred to as involved in a claim for specific property. In the case of a mala fide possessor nearly the same rule is observed in either action as to that produce which, through his own fault, has not been gathered. A bona fide possessor, however, does not have to account for produce consumed or not gathered, but after the commencement of the action, an account is taken both of the produce which, through the fault of the possessor, has not been gathered, and of that which has been gathered and consumed. § 3. If the action was for the production of a thing, it is not sufficient for the defendant to produce the thing, but he must produce it with its accessories, that is, in such a way that the plaintiff may recover the thing in the state it would have been in, if, when the demand for production was first made, the thing had been produced. Hence, if, during the delay, acquisition by use of the thing is completed in favour of the possessor, he is nevertheless to be condemned. In addition, the judge ought also to have an account taken of the interim produce, that is, of that which has arisen between the granting of the action for production, and the delivery of judgment. If the defendant allege his inability to produce the thing at once, and his demand for time does not seem wrongful, time should be given him, provided he find security that he will deliver up the thing; but if he neither produce the thing at once, upon the order of the judge, nor find security for its subsequent production, he is to be condemned in an amount measured by the interest of the plaintiff that the thing should have been produced at the outset. § 4. In the case of an action for the partition of an inheritance, the judge should assign specific things to specific heirs, and if it seem that too much has been conveyed to one, he should condemn that one, as we have already stated,* by way of compensation, to pay a fixed sum to his co-heir. So, also, a person must be condemned towards his co-heir in respect of the value of the produce of the inheritance which he alone has enjoyed, or in respect of property belonging to the inheritance which he has deteriorated or con-

* *ante*, tit. vi. § 20.

sumed, and these rules are to be similarly applied also in the case of there being more than two co-heirs. § 5. The same rules are to be observed in the case of an action for the division of a number of things held in common. But if the division is required of one single thing, as, for example, of an estate, and the estate is capable of being conveniently divided, the judge ought to assign to each his specific share, and if it should appear that one has obtained more than his share, he should be condemned to pay the other a fixed sum of money by way of compensation; if, however, the subject-matter is not susceptible of convenient division, as, for example, if the action is in respect of, say, a slave, or a mule, then, the whole is to be assigned to one, and he should be condemned to pay the other a fixed sum by way of compensation. § 6. If the action is for the settlement of boundaries, the judge should examine whether an adjudication is necessary, which can only be in one case, viz., if it would be desirable that the fields should be marked out by more conspicuous boundaries than formerly separated them; for, then, it becomes necessary for a portion of the field of one of the neighbours to be assigned to the owner of the neighbouring field, in which case it is reasonable that the last-mentioned should be condemned towards the other in a fixed sum of money. In this action, also, condemnation should fall on him who has done any fraudulent act in respect of the boundaries, as, for example, if he has removed the boundary stones, or cut down the boundary trees. A person may also be condemned in this action for contempt of court, as, for example, if a person, in spite of an order of the judge, has not allowed his fields to be measured. § 7. That which in these actions is adjudged to a person immediately becomes the property of him to whom it is adjudged.

Title xviii. Of public prosecutions.

Public prosecutions are not conducted like actions, nor have they any similarity to the other modes of procedure of which we have spoken, and there is a great difference both in the way of commencing and of carrying them on. § 1. They are called public because the conduct of them is generally given to any citizen. § 2. Some public prosecutions are capital; others are not. We call 'capital' those which entail the extreme penalty of the law, or interdiction from fire and water, or deportation, or the mines. The rest, which involve infamy and a pecuniary penalty are, indeed, public, but they are not capital.

§ 3. Amongst public prosecutions are those resulting from the Julian law of high treason, the rigour of which is directed at those conspiring against the emperor or the state. The penalty of this law extends to the loss of life, and the memory of the guilty person is condemned even after death. § 4. So the Julian law for the repression of adultery, which punishes with death not only the violators of another's marriage bed, but also those who dare to indulge in infamous practices with males. By this same Julian law the crime of seduction is also punished, when a person, without violence, seduces a virgin or a widow of good morals. The law inflicts a penalty on guilty persons, if of honourable condition, of confiscation of half their property, whilst persons of low estate are subject to corporal punishment and banishment to a fixed place. § 5. So the Cornelian law on assassination, which overtakes with an avenging sword those guilty of homicide and those who go about armed with a dart for the purpose of killing a man. The word "telum", according to the explanation given by our Gaius, in his interpretation of the Twelve Tables, is commonly applied to that which is fired from a bow; but it also includes everything which is hurled by hand: hence it follows that under this term are included stones, and pieces of wood or iron, for it refers to that which is hurled to a distance, from the Greek word signifying "afar", and we find the same signification in the Greek term, for what we call "telum" they call βέλος, from a word signifying to throw. Zenophon makes this clear, for he writes* thus: "They carried projectiles (βέλη), spears, arrows, slings, and a great quantity of stones." Assassins are called "sicarii" from "sica", which means a knife made of iron. By the same law poisoners are condemned to death, who, by odious artifices, whether by poisons or magic charms, kill men, or who publicly sell injurious drugs. § 6. Another law, called the Pompeian law of parricide, punishes with a peculiar penalty a most frightful crime: as it provides that, if a person has hastened the death of an ascendant or child, or of any other relation whose murder is included under the term parricide, whether he has dared to do it openly or secretly, and whoever is an instigator, or an accomplice in the crime, al-

* Anab. v. 2, 14.

though a stranger, is subjected to the penalty of a parricide, and not punished by the sword, or by fire, or by any usual penalty, but is sewn up in a leathern sack with a dog, a cock, a viper, and an ape, and, shut up in this deadly prison-house, he is thrown, according to the nature of the locality, into the neighbouring sea, or river, so that during life he may begin to want the use of the elements, and that the air may be withdrawn from him whilst living and the earth when he is dead. If, however, a person should kill others allied to him by blood or marriage, he will be subjected to the penalty imposed by the Cornelian law respecting assassins. § 7. So the Cornelian law as to falsifications, also called the Cornelian law concerning testaments, inflicts a penalty on him who knowingly, and with wrongful intent, writes, seals, reads aloud, or substitutes, a forged testament or other document, or who makes, engraves, or impresses a forged seal. The punishment imposed by this law on slaves is the extreme penalty, just as is the case under the Cornelian law concerning assassination and poisoning, but deportation in the case of free persons. § 8. So the Julian law concerning public or private violence takes effect against those who have committed violence, whether armed or unarmed. If the violence has been conducted with armed force, the penalty of deportation is inflicted by the Julian law dealing with public violence; but, if without arms, a confiscation is made of the third part of the offender's property. But, in the case of the forcible abduction of a virgin, or widow, or nun, or other woman, the guilty person, and those who had aided him in the commission of the offence, are punished with death, in accordance with the terms of our constitution, from the perusal of which further information on this subject will be obtained. § 9. So the Julian law concerning peculation punishes those who have made away with money or property belonging to the state, or sacred or religious. If magistrates themselves, during their term of office, embezzle public money, they are punished by the penalty of death, as well as those through whose assistance the act was effected, or who knowingly received the money so embezzled; but others who fall under the penalties of this law are punished with deportation. § 10. Amongst public prosecutions, there are, also, those resulting from the Fabian law concerning kidnapping, which sometimes inflicts, according to the constitutions, the punishment of death, in other cases a lighter punishment. § 11. The following also relate to public prosecutions, viz.: the Julian law against bribery at elections, the Julian law against public functionaries taking bribes, the Julian law against coalitions affecting the price of corn, and the Julian law against the misapplication of public money, which all deal with distinct subjects, and do not inflict the punishment of death, but subject those offending against their provisions to various penalties.

§ 12. We have stated thus much concerning public prosecutions in order to indicate the subject to you, and to enable you to have touched it, as it were, with the tip of your finger, but, with God's help, you may look forward to arriving at a more complete knowledge by the study of the larger volumes of the Digest or Pandects.

FRAGMENTS

OF

THE TWELVE TABLES,

WITH

TRANSLATION.

DUODECIM TABULARUM FRAGMENTA.	FRAGMENTS OF THE TWELVE TABLES.
Tabula prima.	**Table i.**
[*De in jus vocando.*]	*Of summoning before the magistrate.*
1. Si in jus vocat, ni it, antestator; igitur em capito.	1. If a person be summoned to appear before a magistrate, and he do not go, call witnesses, and then let him be seized.
2. Si calvitur, pedemve struit; manum endojacito.	2. If he evade the notice to appear, or arrange for flight, let him be detained by force.
3. Si morbus aevitasve vitium escit, qui in jus vocabit jumentum dato; si nolet, arceram ne sternito.	3. If illness or age are obstacles, he who summons him must find a conveyance; but he is not bound to provide a covered carriage.
4. Assiduo vindex assiduus esto; proletario quoi quis volet vindex esto.	4. The surety for a tax-payer must also be a tax-payer; for the untaxed, anyone who chooses may be bail.
5. Rem ubi pagunt, orato.	5. Where the parties come to terms, let the matter be settled.
6. Ni pagunt, in comitio aut in foro ante meridiem causam conjicito, quom perorant ambo praesentes.	6. If the parties do not come to terms, let their case be stated before noon in the consilium, or in the forum, in the presence of both.
7. Post meridiem, praesenti stlitem addicito.	7. After midday, judgment by default in favour of the party present.
8. Sol occasus suprema tempestas esto.	8. Let the proceedings terminate at sunset.
9. Vades . . . subvades . . .	9. Sureties—Counter sureties (i.e., recognizances to be entered into by both parties for reappearance).

Tabula secunda.

[*De judiciis.*]

1. [De sacramento quingenario et quinquagenario.]

2. Morbus sonticus . . . status dies cum hoste . . . quid horum fuit unum judici, arbitrove, reove, dies diffisus esto.

3. Cui testimonium defuerit, is tertiis diebus ob portum obvagulatum ito.

4. [Si pro fure damnum decisum escit, furti ne adorato.]

Table ii.

Of judicial proceedings.

1. Of the sacramental action involving a wager of five hundred, or fifty, pound pieces of copper to be deposited in court as security for costs.

2. The case may be adjourned on account of the serious illness of the judge, or arbitrator, or one of the parties, and so if one of these is an alien.

3. Let him, who wants a person as a witness, go to his house and summon him in a loud voice to attend on the third market day.

4. If a theft has been compromised the action is extinguished.

Tabula tertia.

[*De aere confesso rebusque jure judicatis.*]

1. Aeris confessi rebusque jure judicatis triginta dies justi sunto.

2. Post deinde manus injectio esto, in jus ducito.

3. Ni judicatum facit, aut quips endo em jure vindicit, secum ducito; vincito, aut nervo, aut compedibus, quindecim pondo ne majore, aut si volet minore vincito.

4. Si volet, suo vivito; ni suo vivit, qui em vinctum habebit, libras farris endo dies dato; si volet plus dato.

Table iii.

Of execution after confession or condemnation.

1. Let thirty days be allowed for the payment of debts admitted or adjudged due.

2. After this period has elapsed, let the defaulter be seized by the creditor and led before the magistrate.

3. If the judgment be not satisfied, and no surety be forthcoming, let the creditor take his debtor and bind his hands or feet with fetters, not exceeding fifteen pounds in weight, or less if the creditor please.

4. Let the debtor find his own sustenance, if he will, otherwise the creditor must give him daily one pound of meal, or more if he please.

5. [. . . sexaginta dies endo vinculis retineto. . .]

5. (In default of payment or satisfactory security, the debtor) to be kept chained for sixty days, (proclamation of the sum due being made on three market days, in the presence of the prætor and the debtor).

6. . . . tertiis nundinis partis secanto; si plus minusve secuerint, ne fraude esto. . . .

6. After the third market day (the debtor may be put to death, or sold beyond the Tiber, or if more than one creditor), let the debtor's body (?) be cut up in pieces. If the parts are greater or less than they should be, no liability will be entailed.

Tabula quarta.

[*De jure patrio.*]

Table iv.

Of paternal power.

1. [Pater insignem ad deformitatem puerum . . . cito necato.]

1. Malformed infants may be immediately destroyed by the father (in the presence of five neighbours).

2. [Endo liberis justis jus vitae necis . . .]

2. Absolute power of the father over his legitimate children throughout their life (involving the right of imprisoning, flogging, chaining, selling, or killing them, however exalted their position may be.)

3. Si pater filium ter venumduit, filius a patre liber esto.

3. If a father sell his son three times, the son shall be free from the power of the father.

4. [Si qui ei in decem mensibus proximis posthumus natus escit, justus esto.]

4. A posthumous child born within ten months (after the dissolution of the marriage) to be deemed legitimate.

Tabula quinta.

[*De haereditatibus et tutelis.*]

Table v.

Of inheritance and tutelage.

1. [Virgines vestales a tutela liberas esse.]

1. (Regulations as to the perpetual tutelage of women.) Vestal virgins to be free from this tutelage, (and from paternal power).

2. [Res mancipi mulieris quae in tutela agnatorum sit ne usucapiantur.]	2. Such property of a woman, under the guardianship of her agnates, as requires a formal conveyance for its transfer, cannot be acquired by use (unless alienated by the ward with the authority of her tutor).
3. Uti legâssit super pecunia tutelave suae rei, ita jus esto.	3. Testamentary dispositions as to the property and guardianship of the substance shall be binding.
4. Si intestato moritur, cui suus haeres nec sit, adgnatus proximus familiam habeto.	4. On intestacy and in default of an heir succeeding as co owner of the patrimony, let the nearest agnate take the inheritance.
5. Si adgnatus nec escit, gentilis familiam nancitor.	5. In default of an agnate, the inheritance is to fall to the gens.
6. [. . . agnatus proximus tutelam nancitor.]	6. (In default of guardians appointed by testament,) the nearest agnate is to become the statutory tutor.
7. Si furiosus est, adgnatorum gentiliumque in eo pecuniaque ejus potestas esto, ast ei custos nec escit.	7. If a lunatic be not provided with a curator, let the care of his person and property fall to the agnates, or, in default, to the gens.
8. Ex ea familia . . . in eam familiam.	8. Out of that family . . . into that family. (In default of an heir succeeding as co-owner of the patrimony, the patron succeeds to the freed-man's property.)
9. [Nomina inter heredes pro portionibus hereditariis ercta cita sunto.]	9. Debts due to or from the inheritance divide by operation of law between the heirs in proportion to their respective shares.
10. [Hereditatem actione familiae erciscundae esse dividendam.]	10. A division of the inheritance can be attained by an action for its partition.
11. [Statu liber, emptori dando, liber esto.]	11. The slave freed by testament, on condition of giving a certain sum to the heir, is, if parted with by the heir, to acquire his freedom on paying this sum to the alienee.

Tabula sexta.	Table vi.
[*De dominio et possessione.*]	*Of ownership and possession.*
1. Quum nexum faciet mancipiumque, uti lingua nuncupassit, ita jus esto.	1. Let the legal effect of a contract or conveyance be determined by the declarations made at the time.
2. [Si inficias ierit, duplione damnator.]	2. The penalty for denying the declarations so made to be double the amount.
3. Usus auctoritas fundi biennium . . . caeterarum omnium . . . [annuus] . . .	3. The prescriptive guarantee against eviction (is to be acquired) after two years' possession in the case of land, and of one year in the case of other property.
4. [De trinoctio usurpandi causa.]	4. Of defeating the husband's acquisition of marital power through one year's possession, by the wife absenting herself for three consecutive nights in each year.
5. Adversus hostem aeterna auctoritas.	5. Title by possession to a Roman citizen's property can never be acquired by an alien.
6. Si qui in jure manum conserunt [secundum eum qui possidet, ast si qui quem liberali causa manu adserat secundum libertatem vindicias dato.]	6. After the preliminary inquiry as to the right to property, let interim possession be given to him who already possesses; but, if the suit is touching the liberty of a person, the interim possession must be given so as to favour that liberty.
7. Tignum junctum aedibus vineaeque et concapet ne solvito.	7. Timber built into a house, or forming supports for vines, shall not be removed.
8. [In eum qui junxit actionem dupli dari.]	8. But the owner can bring an action to recover double their value.
9. Quandoque sarpta, donec dempta erunt . . .	9. And, if they become separated, they may then be claimed by their owner.
10. [Res vendita transque data emptori non adquiritor, donicum satisfactum escit.]	10. The property in a thing sold and delivered not to pass until the vendee has paid or otherwise satisfied the vendor.

11. [In jure cessio et mancipatio.]	11. Regulations as to the process of surrender in court, and that of conveyance by copper and scale.

Tabula septima.	Table vii.
[*De jure aedium et agrorum.*]	*Of the law of real property.*
1. [Ambitus parietis sestertius pes esto.]	1. A space of two and a half feet must be left round each neighbouring building.
2. [De finium ratione ad exemplum legis Soloniae instituta.]	2. Of limitations imposed, in accordance with Solon's laws, in the case of neighbouring plantations, constructions, and excavations (i.e., a fence must be kept within the boundary line; a foot of space must be left outside a wall, two feet outside a house; a space must be left as broad as an excavation is deep, and, in the case of a well, six feet. Olives or vines must be kept within nine feet, other trees five feet of the boundary).
3. . . . Hortus . . . haeredium . . . tugurium . . .	3. . . . a villa . . . an estate . . . a hut . . .
4. [Intra v pedes aeterna auctoritas esto . . .]	4. A space of five feet, not susceptible of acquisition by use, must be left between neighbouring fields for the purposes of access and the use of the plough.
5. Si [vicini] jurgant . . .	5. If neighbours disagree (on the subject of boundaries, three arbitrators are to be appointed by the magistrate for the settlement of the question).
6. [Via in porrecto viii pedes; in anfracto xvi pedes lata esto.]	6. A road must be eight feet broad where straight, and sixteen feet in the bends.
7. [Si via . . . immunita escit, qua volet jumentum agito.]	7. If the road is impassable, the charioteer may diverge.

8. Si aqua pluvia nocet . . .	8. If rain water is causing damage (or the owner of the property is prejudiced by the construction of an aqueduct, he may demand security).
9. [De arboribus circumcidendis.]	9. Of the lopping of trees. (This must be done below fifteen feet in the case of a tree extending over adjoining property.)
10. [De glande legenda.]	10. Of collecting fruit. (This may be done by the owner when it has fallen from his tree on to a neighbour's ground.)

Tabula octava.	**Table viii.**
[*De delictis.*]	*Of wrongs.*
1. [Si quis occentaverit, sive carmen condiderit quod infamiam faciat flagitiumve alteri, eum fustibus feriri.]	1. If anyone shall have slandered or libelled another by imputing a wrongful or immoral act to him, he shall be scourged to death.
2. Si membrum rupit, ni cum eo pacit, talio esto.	2. If a man break another's limb, and do not compromise the matter with the injured party, let him be retaliated upon.
3. [Propter os fractum CCC assium poena.]	3. For a broken bone the penalty (if of a free man) to be three hundred, (or in the case of a slave one hundred and fifty), pound pieces of copper.
4. Si injuriam faxit alteri, viginti quinque aeris poenae sunto.	4. If a man injure another, let the penalty be twenty-five pound pieces of copper.
5. . . . Rupitias . . . sarcito.	5. (Unlawful damage accidentally occasioned to be repaired.)
6. [Si quadrupes pauperiem faxit. .]	6. If an animal has caused damage (the owner must repair the damage or forfeit the animal).
7. [Qui pecu endo alieno impescit . . .]	7. He who pastures flocks on another's crops (is to be scourged).

8. Qui fruges excantasset.... Neve alienam segetem pellexeris . . .	8. He who shall, by magic acts, destroy crops . . . or remove them from one field to another (penalty, death).
9. [De furto frugum noctu commisso.]	9. Of cutting or pasturing off crops at night (penalty, death; but, if the culprit be under the age of puberty, he may be scourged by order of the magistrate, and made liable for double the amount of damage).
10. [De eo qui aedes acervumve frumenti combusserit.]	10. Of him who sets on fire a house or corn-rick near it (if of sound mind, and the act intentional, he is to be punished by scourging and burning alive. If the act was the result of negligence, the damage must be repaired; but, if he be too poor, he is to be moderately chastised).
11. [Si injuri alienas arbores caesit, in singulas 25 aeris luito.]	11. The penalty for unlawfully felling another's tree to be twenty-five pound pieces of copper.
12. Si nox furtum factum sit, si im occisit, jure caesus esto.	12. If a theft be committed at night, and the thief be killed, let his death be deemed lawful.
13. [Si luci furtum faxit . . .]	13. If in the daytime (only if he defend himself with weapons).
14. [De poena furti manifesti.]	14. Of the penalty for theft detected at the time. (A freeman caught in the act of thieving in the daytime, and not having defended himself with arms, is to be scourged and delivered over to the party aggrieved; if under the age of puberty, he is, in the discretion of the magistrate, only to be scourged and compelled to repair the damage. A slave is to be scourged and then hurled from the Tarpeian rock.)

15. [Si furtum lance licioque conceptum escit . . .]	15. If the stolen property be discovered in the thief's possession after a solemn search, wearing a girdle only and holding a plate (the penalty to be the same as for manifest theft); but for theft discovered without these prescribed formalities ("conceptum"), or for the clandestine deposit of the stolen property on the premises of another ("oblatum"), the penalty to be three times the value of the property.)
16. Si adorat furto quod nec manifestum escit . . .	16. If the proceedings are in respect of a theft not falling under the former heads (the penalty is to be double the value).
17. [Furtivae rei aeterna auctoritas esto.]	17. Stolen property is not susceptible of acquisitive prescription.
18. [Si qui unciario foenere amplius foenerâsset quadruplione luito.]	18. Penalty of quadruple for exceeding the legal interest of one-twelfth of the principal.
19. [Si quid endo deposito dolo malo factum escit, duplione luito.]	19. Penalty of double for fraudulent conduct on the part of him with whom property has been deposited.
20. [De tutore suspecto, et de condemnatione in duplum].	20. Of a suspected tutor, and of condemnation in double. (Any citizen may bring an action for the removal of a suspected tutor, and the latter is to incur a penalty of double the value of any of the property of the pupil appropriated by him.)
21. Patronus si clienti fraudem fecerit, sacer esto.	21. Let the patron abusing his position towards his client be sacrificed to the gods.

22. Qui se sierit testarier libripensve fuerit, ni testimonium fariatur, improbus intestabilisque esto.	22. Let him who has acted as a witness or a scale-bearer, and who refuses to give evidence, be deemed infamous and incapable of being a witness or of calling upon others to be a witness for him.
23. [De poena falsi testimonii].	23. Of the penalty for false testimony. (False witnesses to be hurled from the Tarpeian rock.)
24. [De homicidio.]	24. Of homicide (Penalty, death).
25. Qui malum carmen incantasset. . . Malum venenum. . .	25. He who affects another by magic arts or with poisonous drugs (shall incur the penalty of death).
26. [Si qui in urbe coetus nocturnos agitassit, capital esto.]	26. Seditious meetings by night in the city forbidden under penalty of death.
27. [Sodales legem quam volent, dum ne quid ex publicâ corrumpant, sibi ferunto.]	27. Corporate bodies may make their own rules (provided they do not conflict with the law).

Tabula nona.	**Table ix.**
[*De jure publico.*]	*Of public law.*
1. [Privilegia ne irroganto.]	1. No laws shall be passed affecting an individual only.
2. [De capite civis, nisi per maximum comitium ne ferunto.]	2. Only the great comitium ("comitia centuriata") has the right of legislating so as to inflict a punishment on a citizen involving his life, his liberty, or his civic rights.
3. [Ne judex arbiterve ob rem judicandam pecuniam accipiat.]	3. No judge or arbitrator can be suffered to receive a bribe (if found guilty of so doing he is to be put to death).
4. [De quaestoribus parricidii et de provocatione.]	4. Of the commissioners for the punishment of homicide, and of the right of appeal (to the people).
5. [Si qui perduellem concitassit, civemve perduelli transduit; capital esto.]	5. If a person has incited an enemy to make war, or has given up a citizen to them, he is to be punished with death.

Tabula decima.	Table x.
[*De jure sacro.*]	*Of sacred law.*
1. Hominem mortuum in urbe ne sepelito, neve urito.	1. Let no dead bodies be interred or burned within the city.
2. Hoc plus ne facito. . . Rogum ascia ne polito.	2. Let no more be done than this. . . . Do not smooth with the axe the wood of the funeral pile.
3. [Sumptus et luctum a Deorum Manium jure removeto . . . Tribus riciniis et decem tibicinibus foris efferre jus esto.]	3. Regulations forbidding lavish expenditure in funerals, (and limiting the burial or burning of the dead) in more than three mourning robes (with purple bands) and not more than ten flute players are to be hired.
4. Mulieres genas ne radunto; neve lessum funeris ergo habento.	4. Let not the women disfigure their faces or indulge in ostentatious lamentation.
5. Homini mortuo ne ossa legito, quo post funus faciat.	5. The bones of a deceased person are not to be collected for the purpose of a subsequent funeral (except in the case of death on the field of battle or abroad).
6. [De unctura, circumpotatione, respersione, coronis.]	6. Of regulations forbidding slaves' bodies to be embalmed; also all funeral potations, costly besprinklings of the funeral pile, long rows of crowns, or incense vessels borne before the corpse.
7. Qui coronam parit ipse, pecuniave ejus, virtutis ergo duitor ei.	7. But the deceased is entitled to be crowned at the funeral with a wreath won by himself or his slaves or horses.
8. [Uni plura funera ne facito, neve plures lectos sternito.]	8. Prohibition as to several funerals or biers for one deceased person.
9. Neve aurum addito. Quoi auro dentes vincti escunt, ast im cum illo sepelire urereve se fraude esto.	9. Let no gold be thrown in with the body; but, if the teeth are fastened with gold, it will not be unlawful to let it be buried or burned with the body.

10. [Rogum bustumve novum propius lx pedes aedes alienas, si dominus nolet, ne adjicito.]

10. In the absence of consent, a funeral pile or sepulchre cannot be placed within sixty feet of another man's house.

11. [Fori bustive aeterna auctoritas esto.]

11. Neither a tomb nor its enclosure is susceptible of acquisition by use.

Tabula undecima.

[*Supplementum V priorum tabularum.*]

1. [Patribus cum plebe connubii jus nec esto.]

Table xi.

Supplement to the first five tables.

1. No right of intermarriage between patricians and plebeians.

Tabula duodecima.

[*Supplementum V posteriorum tabularum.*]

1. [De pignoris capione adversus eum qui hostiam emit.]

2. Si servus furtum faxit noxiamve nocuit. . .

3. Si vindiciam falsam tulit . . . rei si velit is . . . tor arbitros tres dato; eorum arbitrio . . . fructus duplione damnum decidito

4. [Si rem de quâ stlis siet, in sacrum dedicassit; duplione decidito.]

5. [Quod postremum populus jussit id jus ratum esto.]

Table xii.

Supplement to the five last tables.

1. A creditor may distrain for the unpaid price of a victim (or the hire of a beast of burden), when the amount was to be devoted to sacrificial purposes.

2. If a slave commit theft, or do any other damage (he may be surrendered by way of reparation to the party aggrieved).

3. Let him who has wrongfully acquired interim possession, be condemned in double the value of the produce, by the three arbitrators appointed to investigate the case.

4. Penalty of double for consecrating the subject of litigation.

5. Subsequent legislation repeals previous enactments inconsistent therewith.

GREEK TEXT

OF

THE CXVIIITH NOVEL,

AND PART OF THE CXXVIITH,

WITH

LATIN AND ENGLISH TRANSLATION.

ΔΙΑΤΑΞΙΣ ριη΄.

Διάταξις ἀναιροῦσα τὰ adgnatica δίκαια, καὶ τυποῦσα τὰς ἐξ ἀδιαθέτου κλήσεις.

Αὐτοκράτωρ Ἰουστινιανὸς Αὔγουστος Πέτρῳ τῷ ἐνδοξοτάτῳ ἐπάρχῳ τῶν ἱερῶν τῆς ἕω πραιτωρίων.

Προοίμιον. Πολλοὺς καὶ διαφόρους νόμους ἐν τοῖς παλαιοτέροις χρόνοις ἐκπεφωνημένους εὑρίσκοντες, δι' ὧν οὐ δικαίως διαφορὰ τῆς ἐξ ἀδιαθέτου διαδοχῆς μεταξὺ τῶν συγγενῶν ἐξ ἀῤῥένων τε καὶ θηλειῶν εἰσενήνεκται, ἀναγκαῖον εἶναι συνείδομεν πάσας ὁμοῦ τὰς ἐξ ἀδιαθέτου τῆς συγγενείας διαδοχὰς διὰ τοῦ παρόντος νόμου σαφεῖ καὶ συντόμῳ διαιρέσει διατυπῶσαι, ὥςτε τῶν προτέρων νόμων τῶν ὑπὲρ ταύτης τῆς αἰτίας τεθειμένων ἀργούντων, τοῦ λοιποῦ ταῦτα μόνα παραφυλάττεσθαι, ἅπερ νῦν διατυποῦμεν. Ἐπει-

Novella cxviii.

CONSTITUTIO QUAE JURA AGNATIONIS TOLLIT, ET SUCCESSIONES AB INTESTATO DEFINIT.

IMPERATOR JUSTINIANUS AUGUSTUS PETRO GLORIOSISSIMO PER ORIENTEM SACRO PRAETORIO PRAEFECTO.

PRAEFATIO. Quum multas et diversas leges antiquis temporibus promulgatas inveniamus, per quas non juste differentia successionis ab intestato inter cognatos ex masculis et feminis descendentes introducta est, necessarium duximus hac lege omnes simul successiones cognationis ab intestato clara et compendiosa distinctione definire, ut cessantibus prioribus legibus, quae hac de causa latae sunt, in posterum ea solum observentur, quae nunc definimus. Iam igitur quia omnis ab intestato familiae successio tribus

Novel cxviii.

CONSTITUTION WHICH TAKES AWAY THE RIGHTS OF AGNATION, AND PRESCRIBES THE ORDER OF SUCCESSION ON INTESTACY.

THE AUGUST EMPEROR JUSTINIAN TO PETER MOST GLORIOUS PRÆTORIAN PREFECT OF THE EAST.

PREFACE. As we find that many and different laws have been issued in ancient times, by which an unfair difference has been introduced in intestate succession between relations tracing their descent through males and those tracing their descent through females, we have felt it necessary, by means of this present law, and in respect of all successions arising out of relationship, to lay down a clear and short distinction, so that all previous laws which dealt with this subject now ceasing, for the future only that shall be observed which we now declare. As the whole of the intestate succession of a family is con-

δὴ τοίνυν πᾶσα ἡ τοῦ γένους ἐξ ἀδιαθέτου διαδοχὴ τρισὶ γνωρίζεται τάξεσι, τουτέστι τῇ τε τῶν ἀνιόντων, καὶ τῇ τῶν κατιόντων, καὶ τῇ τῶν ἐκ πλαγίου, ἥτις εἰς adgnatους καὶ cognatους διαιρεῖται, πρώτην εἶναι διατυποῦμεν τὴν τῶν κατιόντων διαδοχήν.

ordinibus cognoscitur, scilicet ascendentium, descendentium, et eorum, qui ex latere sunt, qui in agnatos et cognatos dividitur, ut descendentium successio prima sit, sancimus.

Κεφ. α'. Εἴ τις τοίνυν τῶν κατιόντων ὑπείη τῷ ἀδιαθέτῳ τελευτήσαντι οἱασδήποτε φύσεως ἢ βαθμοῦ, εἴτε ἐξ ἀῤῥενογονίας, εἴτε ἐκ θηλυγονίας καταγόμενος, καὶ εἴτε αὐτεξούσιος, εἴτε ὑπεξούσιος εἴη, πάντων τῶν ἀνιόντων καὶ τῶν ἐκ πλαγίου συγγενῶν προτιμάσθω. Κἂν γὰρ ὁ τελευτήσας ἑτέρου ὑπεξούσιος ἦν, ὅμως τοὺς αὐτοῦ παῖδας, οἱασδήποτε ἂν ὦσι φύσεως ἢ βαθμοῦ, καὶ αὐτῶν τῶν γονέων προτιμᾶσθαι κελεύομεν, ὧν ὑπεξούσιος ἦν ὁ τελευτήσας, ἐπ' ἐκείνοις δηλαδὴ τοῖς πράγμασιν, ἅτινα κατὰ τοὺς ἄλλους ἡμῶν νόμους τοῖς πατράσιν οὐ προσπορίζεται. Ἐπὶ γὰρ τῇ χρήσει τῶν πραγμάτων τούτων ὀφειλούσῃ προσπορίζεσθαι ἢ φυλάττεσθαι τοὺς περὶ τούτων ἡμῶν νόμους τοῖς γονεῦσι φυλάττομεν, οὕτω μέντοι γε, ὥστε εἴ τινα τούτων τῶν κατιόντων παῖδας καταλιπόντα τελευτῆσαι

CAP. I. Itaque si descendentem habeat is, qui intestatus moritur, cujuscunque sexus aut gradus, sive ex masculorum, sive ex feminarum progenie descendat, et sive sui juris, sive sub potestate sit, ille omnibus ascendentibus quique a latere sunt cognatis praeponatur. Licet enim defunctus sub alterius potestate fuerit, liberos tamen ejus, cujuscunque sint sexus aut gradus, ipsis etiam parentibus, sub quorum potestate defunctus erat, praeferri jubemus, in illis scilicet rebus, quae secundum alias nostras leges parentibus non acquiruntur. Quantum enim ad illarum rerum usumfructum, qui illis acquiri vel servari debet, leges de his latas parentibus servamus, ita tamen, ut, si quem ex his descendentibus liberis relictis mori contigerit, filii ejus aut filiae,

---

tained in three orders, that is, in that of ascendants, in that of descendants, and in that of collaterals, who are divided into agnates and cognates, so we sanction that the first succession shall be that of descendants.

CHAPTER I. If, therefore, he who dies intestate leaves a descendant, this descendant—without distinction of sex, and irrespective of degree, and whether tracing descent through males or females, and whether free from paternal power or not—is to be preferred to all ascendants and collaterals. For, although the deceased was subject to the paternal power of another, still we direct that his children, of whichever sex they may be, or in whatever degree they may stand, shall be preferred even to the ascendants in whose power the deceased was, that is, in respect of those things which are not acquired for their ascendants by other laws of ours. For in respect of the use and enjoyment of those things which should be acquired and preserved for them, we retain in force the laws passed on behalf of these ascendants; in such a way, however, that if one of such descendants should die, leaving children behind, his sons or

συμβαίη, τοὺς ἐκείνου υἱοὺς ἢ θυγατέρας ἢ τοὺς ἄλλους κατιόντας εἰς τὸν τοῦ ἰδίου γονέως τόπον ὑπεισιέναι, εἴτε ὑπεξούσιοι τῷ τελευτήσαντι, εἴτε αὐτεξούσιοι εὑρεθεῖεν, τοσοῦτον ἐκ τῆς κληρονομίας τοῦ τελευτήσαντος λαμβάνοντας μέρος, ὅσοι δήποτε ἂν ὦσιν, ὅσον ὁ αὐτῶν γονεύς, εἰ περιῆν, ἐκομίζετο, ἥντινα διαδοχὴν in stirpes ἡ ἀρχαιότης ἐκάλεσεν. Ἐπὶ ταύτης γὰρ τῆς τάξεως τὸν βαθμὸν ζητεῖσθαι οὐ βουλόμεθα, ἀλλὰ μετὰ τῶν υἱῶν καὶ τῶν θυγατέρων τοὺς ἐκ τοῦ προτελευτήσαντος υἱοῦ ἢ θυγατρὸς ἐγγόνους καλεῖσθαι θεσπίζομεν, οὐδεμιᾶς εἰσαγομένης διαφορᾶς, εἴτε ἄῤῥενες εἴτε θήλειαι ὦσι, καὶ εἴτε ἐξ ἀῤῥενογονίας εἴτε ἐκ θηλυγονίας κατάγωνται, εἴτε ὑπεξούσιοι εἴτε καὶ αὐτεξούσιοι εἴησαν. Καὶ ταῦτα μὲν περὶ τῆς τῶν κατιόντων διαδοχῆς ἐτυπώσαμεν. Ἀκόλουθον δὲ εἶναι συνείδομεν καὶ περὶ τῶν ἀνιόντων διατάξασθαι, ὅπως ἂν εἰς τὴν τῶν κατιόντων κληθεῖεν διαδοχήν.

Κεφ. β'. Εἰ τοίνυν ὁ τελευτήσας κατιόντας μὲν μὴ καταλίποι κληρονόμους, πατὴρ δὲ ἢ μήτηρ ἢ ἄλλοι γονεῖς αὐτῷ ἐπιζήσουσι, πάντων

aut reliqui descendentes, in parentis sui locum succedant, sive sub potestate defuncti, sive sui juris inveniantur, et tantam ex hereditate defuncti partem capiant, quotquot sint, quantam parens ipsorum, si superstes esset, accepisset, quam successionem in stirpes antiquitas vocavit. In hoc enim ordine gradum requiri nolumus, sed ut cum filiis et filiabus nepotes ex praemortuo filio vel filia vocentur, sancimus, nulla differentia facienda inter masculos et feminas, eosve, qui ex masculorum aut feminarum progenie descendant, sive sub potestate, sive sui juris sint. Et haec quidem de successione descendentium disposuimus. Consequens autem nobis videtur de ascendentibus etiam, quomodo ad successionem descendentium vocentur, constituere.

CAP. II. Quare si defunctus descendentes heredes non reliquit, pater vero et mater aliique parentes ei superstites sunt, sanci-

---

daughters, or other descendants, succeed in the place of their ascendant (father or mother), whether they were in the power of the deceased, or were free from power, and however many they may be, they take such portion of the inheritance of the deceased as their ascendant if he had lived would have taken, and this is the kind of succession, called by the ancients that by representation; for, in this order of succession, we are not willing to have any inquiry as to degree, but we direct that the grandchildren sprung from a deceased son or daughter are to be called along with sons and daughters, without making any difference between males and females, or whether they trace their descent through males or females, or whether they are under paternal power or not. These, then, are the rules we have established respecting the succession of descendants. It seems, however, expedient to settle, also, the order in which ascendants should be called to the succession of descendants.

CHAPTER II. Hence, then, if the deceased does not leave any descendant heirs, but his father or mother, or other ascendants survive

τῶν ἐκ πλαγίου συγγενῶν τούτους προτιμᾶσθαι θεσπίζομεν, ἐξῃρημένων μόνων ἀδελφῶν ἐξ ἑκατέρου γονέως συναπτομένων τῷ τελευτήσαντι, ὡς διὰ τῶν ἑξῆς δηλωθήσεται. Εἰ δὲ πολλοὶ τῶν ἀνιόντων περίεισι, τούτους προτιμᾶσθαι κελεύομεν, οἵτινες ἐγγύτεροι τῷ βαθμῷ εὑρεθεῖεν, ἄῤῥενάς τε καὶ θηλείας, εἴτε πρὸς μητρός, εἴτε πρὸς πατρὸς εἶεν. Εἰ δὲ τὸν αὐτὸν ἔχουσι βαθμόν, ἐξ ἴσης εἰς αὐτοὺς ἡ κληρονομία διαιρεθήσεται, ὥςτε τὸ μὲν ἥμισυ λαμβάνειν πάντας τοὺς πρὸς πατρὸς ἀνιόντας, ὅσοι δήποτε ἂν ὦσι, τὸ δὲ ὑπόλοιπον ἥμισυ τοὺς πρὸς μητρὸς ἀνιόντας, ὅσους δήποτε ἂν αὐτοὺς εὑρεθῆναι συμβαίη. Εἰ δὲ μετὰ τῶν ἀνιόντων εὑρεθῶσιν ἀδελφοὶ ἢ ἀδελφαὶ ἐξ ἑκατέρων γονέων συναπτόμενοι τῷ τελευτήσαντι, μετὰ τῶν ἐγγυτέρων τῷ βαθμῷ ἀνιόντων κληθήσονται, εἰ καὶ πατὴρ ἢ μήτηρ εἴησαν, διαιρουμένης εἰς αὐτοὺς δηλαδὴ τῆς κληρονομίας κατὰ τὸν τῶν προςώπων ἀριθμόν, ἵνα καὶ τῶν ἀνιόντων καὶ τῶν ἀδελφῶν ἕκαστος ἴσην ἔχοι μοῖραν· οὐδεμίαν χρῆσιν ἐκ τῆς τῶν υἱῶν ἢ θυγατέρων μοίρας ἐν τούτῳ τῷ θέματι δυναμένου τοῦ πατρὸς ἑαυτῷ παντελῶς ἐκδικεῖν,

mus, ut hi omnibus ex latere cognatis praeferantur, exceptis solis fratribus defuncto ex utroque parente conjunctis, sicut in sequentibus declarabitur. Si autem multi ascendentium supersunt, eos praeferri jubemus, qui gradu propinquiores inveniantur, masculos et feminas, sive materni, sive paterni sint. Si eundem gradum obtinent, aequaliter inter eos hereditas dividetur, ut dimidiam partem omnes paterni ascendentes, quotcunque sint, accipiant, reliquam vero dimidiam materni ascendentes, quotcunque inveniri contigerit. Si cum ascendentibus inveniantur fratres vel sorores defuncto per utrumque parentem coniuncti, cum ascendentibus gradu propinquioribus vocabuntur, licet pater aut mater sint, hereditate scilicet inter eos pro numero personarum dividenda, ut quilibet ascendentium et fratrum aequalem partem habeat. Neque in hoc casu pater in filiorum aut filiarum parte ullum usumfructum sibi omnino vindicare queat, quoniam pro illo usufructu partem hereditatis dominii jure ipsi per

---

him, we direct that these shall be preferred to all collateral relations, except brothers (or sisters) related to the deceased through both parents (i.e., of the whole blood), as will be subsequently more particularly stated. If, however, there are many ascendants living, we order that those shall be preferred who are nearest in degree, whether males or females, and whether they belong to the paternal or maternal side. When they are found in the same degree, the inheritance is to be divided equally between them in such a way that all the paternal ascendants, however numerous, may receive one half, and the maternal ascendants the other half, whatever their number may be found to be. If, along with the ascendants, brothers or sisters exist, related to the deceased through both parents, these are to be called with the nearest ascendants, although the latter may be a father or mother, and the inheritance must be divided between them according to the number of persons, so that each of the ascendants, and each of the brothers (or sisters) may have an equal share, and in such a case the father shall not lay claim to the use and enjoyment of the share of his sons or daughters,

ἐπειδὴ ἀντὶ ταύτης τῆς χρήσεως μέρος αὐτῷ τῆς κληρονομίας καὶ κατὰ δεσποτείας δίκαιον διὰ τοῦ παρόντος δεδώκαμεν νόμου· οὐδεμιᾶς φυλαττομένης διαφορᾶς μεταξὺ τῶν προςώπων τούτων, εἴτε θήλειαι, εἴτε ἄῤῥενες εἴησαν οἱ πρὸς τὴν κληρονομίαν καλούμενοι, καὶ εἴτε δι' ἄῤῥενος ἢ θήλεως προςώπου συνάπτονται, καὶ εἴτε αὐτεξούσιος, εἴτε ὑπεξούσιος ἦν, ὃν διαδέχονται. Ὑπόλοιπόν ἐστιν, ἵνα καὶ τὴν τρίτην ὁρίσωμεν τάξιν, ἥτις ἐκ πλαγίου καλεῖται, καὶ εἰς adgnatους καὶ cognatους διαιρεῖται, ἵνα καὶ τούτου τοῦ μέρους διατυπωθέντος πανταχόθεν ὁ νόμος τέλειος εὑρεθείη.

hanc legem dedimus. Neque ulla differentia inter illas personas observetur, sive feminae, sive masculi sint, qui ad hereditatem vocantur, et sive per masculum, sive per feminam conjungantur, et sive sui juris, sive sub potestate fuerit, cui succedunt. Reliquum est, ut tertium quoque ordinem definiamus, qui ex latere appellatur, et in agnatos et cognatos dividitur, ut hac quoque parte definita lex undique perfecta inveniatur.

Κεφ. γ'. Εἰ τοίνυν ὁ τελευτήσας μηδὲ κατιόντας μηδὲ ἀνιόντας καταλείψῃ, πρώτους πρὸς τὴν κληρονομίαν καλοῦμεν τοὺς ἀδελφοὺς καὶ τὰς ἀδελφάς, τοὺς ἐκ τοῦ αὐτοῦ πατρὸς καὶ τῆς αὐτῆς μητρὸς τεχθέντας, οὓς καὶ μετὰ τῶν πατέρων πρὸς τὴν κληρονομίαν ἐκαλέσαμεν. Τούτων δὲ μὴ ὑπόντων, ἐν δευτέρᾳ τάξει ἐκείνους τοὺς ἀδελφοὺς πρὸς τὴν κληρονομίαν καλοῦμεν, οἵτινες ἐξ ἑνὸς γονέως συνάπτονται τῷ τελευτήσαντι, εἴτε διὰ τοῦ πατρὸς

CAP. III. Quamobrem si defunctus neque descendentes neque ascendentes relinquat, primo ad hereditatem vocamus fratres et sorores ex eodem patre et eadem matre natos, quos etiam cum parentibus ad hereditatem vocavimus. His vero non exstantibus in secundo ordine illos fratres ad hereditatem vocamus, qui ex uno parente defuncto iunguntur, sive per patrem solum, sive per matrem. Quodsi defunctus fratres

---

because, by this law, we have given him, in lieu of this use and enjoyment, the absolute ownership of a portion of the inheritance, and no difference is to be observed between those persons who are called to an inheritance, whether they are males or females, or whether related through males or females, or whether he to whom they succeed was, or was not, under paternal power. It now remains for us to regulate the succession for the third degree, who are called collaterals, and divided into agnates and cognates; so that when we have defined the rules covering their case the law may be found complete in all respects.

CHAPTER III. Hence, therefore, if the deceased leave neither descendants nor ascendants, we call in the first place to the inheritance brothers and sisters born of the same father and mother, and whom we have also called to the inheritance with ascendants. But when there are none such existing, we call in the second rank to the inheritance, those who are related to the deceased through one parent, whether through the father only or the mother (i.e., brothers or sisters of the half-blood.) If, however, the deceased leave brothers (or sisters), and

μόνου, εἴτε διὰ τῆς μητρός. Εἰ δὲ τῷ τελευτήσαντι ἀδελφοὶ ὑπείησαν, καὶ ἑτέρου ἀδελφοῦ ἢ ἀδελφῆς προτελευτησάντων παῖδες, κληθήσονται πρὸς τὴν κληρονομίαν οὗτοι μετὰ τῶν πρὸς πατρὸς καὶ πρὸς μητρὸς θείων, ἀῤῥένων δὲ καὶ θηλειῶν, καὶ ὅσοι δή ποτε ἂν ὦσι, τοσοῦτον ἐκ τῆς κληρονομίας λήψονται μέρος, ὅσον ὁ αὐτῶν γονεὺς ἤμελλε λαμβάνειν, εἰ ἐπέζησεν. Ὅθεν ἀκόλουθόν ἐστιν, ἵνα εἰ τυχὸν ὁ προτελευτήσας ἀδελφός, οὗ οἱ παῖδες περίεισι, δι' ἑκατέρου γονέως τῷ νῦν τελευτήσαντι προςώπῳ συνήπτετο, οἱ δὲ περιόντες ἀδελφοὶ διὰ τοῦ πατρὸς μόνου τυχὸν ἢ τῆς μητρὸς αὐτῷ συνήπτοντο, προτιμηθῶσιν οἱ τούτου παῖδες τῶν ἰδίων θείων, εἰ καὶ τρίτου εἰσὶ βαθμοῦ, εἴτε πρὸς πατρός, εἴτε πρὸς μητρὸς εἴησαν οἱ θεῖοι, καὶ εἴτε ἄῤῥενες, εἴτε θήλειαι, ὥςπερ ὁ αὐτῶν γονεὺς προετιμᾶτο, εἰ περιῆν. Καὶ ἐκ τῶν ἐναντίων, εἰ ὁ μὲν περιὼν ἀδελφὸς ἐξ ἑκατέρου γονέως συνάπτεται τῷ τελευτήσαντι, ὁ δὲ προτελευτήσας δι' ἑνὸς γονέως συνήπτετο, τοὺς τούτου παῖδας ἐκ τῆς κληρονομίας ἀποκλείομεν, ὥςπερ καὶ αὐτός, εἰ περιῆν, ἐξεκλείετο. Τὸ δὲ τοιοῦτον

habeat, et alterius praedefuncti fratris aut sororis liberos, hi cum thiis paternis et maternis, masculis et feminis, ad hereditatem vocabuntur, et quotcunque tandem sint, tantam ex hereditate partem capient, quantam parens eorum fuisset habiturus, si vixisset. Unde consequens est, si forte praemortuus frater, cujus liberi supersunt, per utrumque parentem defunctae personae conjunctus fuerit, superstites vero fratres per patrem forte solum aut matrem illi conjungantur, ut liberi ejus patruis suis praeferantur, etsi tertio gradu sint, sive paterni sive materni sint thii, sive masculi sive feminae, sicut pater ipsorum praelatus fuisset, si vixisset. Contra si superstes frater per utrumque parentem defunctum cognatione attingat, qui vero praemortuus est per unum parentem conjungatur, liberos ejus ab hereditate excludimus, quemadmodum et ipse, si viveret, excluderetur. Hoc autem privilegium in hoc cognationis ordine solis concedimus fratrum masculorum vel feminarum filiis vel filiabus, ut in

---

also nephews by another previously deceased brother or sister, these nephews are to be called to the inheritance with the brothers or sisters of their father or mother; but however many these may be, they only take such a share of the inheritance as would have fallen to their parent if he had lived. From this it follows that if, say, a predeceased brother (or sister) whose children survive, was related to the deceased through both parents (i.e., of the whole blood), and there are brothers (or sisters) surviving, only related through the father or the mother (i.e., of the half-blood), then the children of that brother (or sister) are preferred to their father's or mother's brothers (or sisters), although they are in the third degree, just as their parent (father or mother) would have been preferred if he (or she) had lived. On the other hand, if a surviving brother is related to the deceased through both parents (i.e., is of the whole-blood), but a predeceased brother was only related through one parent (i.e., was of the half-blood), then the children of the latter are excluded from the inheritance, just as he himself would have been had he lived. We grant this privilege, however, in this

προνόμιον ἐν ταύτῃ τῇ τάξει τῆς συγγενείας μόνοις παρέχομεν τοῖς τῶν ἀδελφῶν ἀῤῥένων ἢ θηλειῶν υἱοῖς ἢ θυγατράσιν, ἵνα εἰς τὰ τῶν ἰδίων γονέων δίκαια ὑπεισέλθωσιν, οὐδενὶ δὲ ἄλλῳ παντελῶς προσώπῳ ἐκ ταύτης τῆς τάξεως ἐρχομένῳ τοῦτο τὸ δίκαιον συγχωροῦμεν. Ἀλλὰ καὶ αὐτοῖς τοῖς τῶν ἀδελφῶν παισὶ τότε ταύτην τὴν εὐεργεσίαν παρέχομεν, ὅτε μετὰ τῶν ἰδίων κρίνονται θείων ἀῤῥένων τε καὶ θηλειῶν, εἴτε πρὸς πατρός, εἴτε πρὸς μητρὸς εἶεν. Εἰ δὲ μετὰ τῶν ἀδελφῶν τοῦ τελευτήσαντος καὶ ἀνιόντες, ὡς ἤδη προείπομεν, πρὸς τὴν κληρονομίαν καλοῦνται, οὐδενὶ τρόπῳ πρὸς τὴν ἐξ ἀδιαθέτου διαδοχὴν τοὺς τοῦ ἀδελφοῦ ἢ τῆς ἀδελφῆς παῖδας καλεῖσθαι συγχωροῦμεν, οὐδὲ εἰ ἐξ ἑκατέρου γονέως ὁ αὐτῶν πατὴρ ἢ μήτηρ συνήπτετο τῷ τελευτήσαντι. Ὁπότε τοίνυν τοῖς τοῦ ἀδελφοῦ καὶ τῆς ἀδελφῆς παισὶ τοιοῦτο προνόμιον δεδώκαμεν, ἵνα τὸν τῶν γονέων ὑπεισιόντες τόπον μόνοι τρίτου ὄντες βαθμοῦ μετὰ τῶν ἐκ [πρώτου καὶ] δευτέρου βαθμοῦ πρὸς τὴν κληρονομίαν καλῶνται, ἐκεῖνο πρόδηλόν ἐστιν, ὅτι τῶν θείων τοῦ τελευτήσαντος ἀῤῥένων τε καὶ θηλειῶν, εἴτε πρὸς πατρός, εἴτε πρὸς μητρὸς εἴησαν, προτιμῶνται, εἰ καὶ ἐκεῖνοι τρίτον ὁμοίως συγγενείας βαθμὸν ἔχοιεν.

parentum suorum jura succedant, nulli vero alii omnino personae ex hoc ordine venienti hoc jus concedimus. Sed et ipsis fratrum liberis tum illud beneficium praebemus, quando certant cum thiis suis, masculis et feminis, sive paterni sive materni sint. Si vero cum fratribus defuncti ascendentes etiam, ut ante diximus, ad hereditatem vocantur, nullo modo ad successionem ab intestato fratris aut sororis liberos vocari permittimus, nec si ex utroque parente pater ipsorum vel mater defuncto conjunctus fuerit. Quandoquidem igitur fratris et sororis liberis ejusmodi privilegium dedimus, ut soli, quum tertio gradu sint, in parentum locum succedentes cum illis, qui primo et secundo gradu sunt, ad hereditatem vocentur, illud manifestum est, defuncti patruis, masculis et feminis, paternis et maternis, eos praeponi, licet illi quoque tertium similiter cognationis gradum obtineant.

---

order of relationship only to the sons and daughters of brothers and sisters, so that they may step into the rights of their parents; but we do not concede this right to any other person in this order of relationship, and we accord this benefit only in the case when these brother's or sister's children concur with their father's or mother's brothers or sisters, for, when together with the brothers or sisters of the deceased, ascendants are (as we stated above) called to the inheritance, we do not in any way permit the children of a brother or sister to be called to the intestate succession; not even though their father or mother was related to the deceased through both parents. Since then we have given to the children of a brother or sister this privilege that they alone, although in the third degree, shall be called to the inheritance in the place of their parents, along with those who are in the first and second degree, it is clear that they are preferred to the brothers or sisters of the father or mother of the deceased, although these latter similarly stand in the third degree of relationship.

§ α΄. Εἰ δὲ μήτε ἀδελφοὺς μήτε παῖδας ἀδελφῶν, ὡς εἰρήκαμεν, ὁ τελευτήσας καταλείψει, πάντας τοὺς ἐφεξῆς ἐκ πλαγίου συγγενεῖς πρὸς τὴν κληρονομίαν καλοῦμεν κατὰ τὴν ἑνὸς ἑκάστου βαθμοῦ προτίμησιν, ἵνα οἱ ἐγγύτεροι τῷ βαθμῷ αὐτοὶ τῶν λοιπῶν προτιμῶνται. Εἰ δὲ πολλοὶ τοῦ αὐτοῦ βαθμοῦ εὑρεθῶσι, κατὰ τὸν τῶν προσώπων ἀριθμὸν μεταξὺ αὐτῶν ἡ κληρονομία διαιρεθήσεται, ὅπερ in capita οἱ ἡμέτεροι λέγουσι νόμοι.

Κεφ. δ΄. Οὐδεμίαν δὲ εἶναι βουλόμεθα διαφορὰν ἐν οἱᾳδήποτε διαδοχῇ ἢ κληρονομίᾳ μεταξὺ τῶν πρὸς τὴν κληρονομίαν καλουμένων ἀῤῥένων ἢ θηλειῶν, οὓς πρὸς τὴν κληρονομίαν κοινῶς ὡρίσαμεν καλεῖσθαι, εἴτε δι' ἄῤῥενος, εἴτε διὰ θήλειος προσώπου συνήπτοντο τῷ τελευτήσαντι, ἀλλ' ἐπὶ πασῶν τῶν διαδοχῶν τὴν τῶν adgnatων τε καὶ cognatων διαφορὰν ἀργεῖν κελεύομεν, εἴτε διὰ θῆλυ πρόσωπον, εἴτε δι' ἐμαγκιπατίωνα ἢ ἕτερον οἱονδήποτε τρόπον τοῖς προτέροις ἐτρακτατίζετο νόμοις, καὶ πάντας δίχα τινὸς τοιαύτης διαφορᾶς κατὰ τὸν τῆς ἰδίας συγγενείας βαθμὸν εἰς τὴν ἐξ ἀδιαθέτου τῶν συγγενῶν διαδοχὴν ἐλθεῖν κελεύομεν.

§ 1. Si defunctus neque fratres neque fratrum liberos, ut diximus, reliquerit, omnes ex latere cognatos ordine ad hereditatem vocamus secundum uniuscujusque gradus praerogativam, ut propinquiores gradu reliquis praeponantur. Si multi ejusdem gradus inveniantur, pro numero personarum inter eos hereditas dividatur, id quod leges nostrae in capita appellant.

CAP. IV. Nullam vero differentiam esse volumus in qualibet successione aut hereditate inter masculos et feminas ad hereditatem vocatos, qui ut ex aequo ad hereditatem vocentur definivimus, sive per masculum, sive per feminam defuncto conjungantur, sed in omnibus successionibus agnatorum et cognatorum differentiam cessare volumus, sive propter femininam personam, sive propter emancipationem vel alium quemlibet modum in prioribus legibus tractata fuerit, omnesque sine ejusmodi differentia secundum cognationis suae gradum ad cognatorum ab intestato successionem venire jubemus.

---

§ 1. But if the deceased does not leave, (as we have stated), either brothers (or sisters) or brother's (or sister's) children, we then call all (the other) collaterals, according to the precedence accorded to their respective degrees, so that the nearer in degree are preferred to the more remote. If, however, several are found in the same degree, the inheritance is to be divided between them according to the number of persons, that is, according to the distribution which our laws call that by individuals.

CHAPTER IV. It is our wish, however, that in no order of succession, or inheritance, shall any distinction hereafter be drawn between males and females called to the inheritance, whom we have defined as to be called to the inheritance together, whether they are related to the deceased through males or females; and we wish that in all successions the distinction between agnates and cognates shall disappear, whether the matter has been dealt with in earlier laws on the ground of female sex, or on account of emancipation from paternal power, or for any other reason, and we order that all, without any distinction of this nature, shall come into the intestate succession of their relatives, according to the degree of their relationship.

Κεφ. ε΄. Ἐξ ὧν δὲ περὶ τῆς κληρονομίας εἰρήκαμέν τε καὶ διετυπώσαμεν, καὶ τὰ περὶ τῆς ἐπιτροπῆς δῆλα καθέστηκε. Θεσπίζομεν γάρ, ἕκαστον κατὰ τὸν βαθμὸν καὶ τὴν τάξιν, καθ' ἣν πρὸς τὴν κληρονομίαν καλεῖται ἢ μόνος ἢ μεθ' ἑτέρων, καὶ τὸ λειτούργημα τῆς ἐπιτροπῆς ὑπελθεῖν, οὐδεμιᾶς οὐδὲ ἐν τούτῳ τῷ μέρει διαφορᾶς εἰσαγομένης ἐκ τῶν adgnaticῶν ἢ cognaticῶν δικαίων, ἀλλὰ πάντων ὁμοίως εἰς τὴν ἐπιτροπὴν καλουμένων, τῶν τε δι' ἀῤῥενογονίας, τῶν τε διὰ θηλυγονίας τῷ ἀνήβῳ συναπτομένων. Ταῦτα δὲ λέγομεν, εἰ ἄῤῥενες καὶ τέλειοι τὴν ἡλικίαν εἴησαν, καὶ ὑπὸ μηδενὸς νόμου κωλύονται τὴν ἐπιτροπὴν ὑπελθεῖν, μηδὲ ἐξκουσατίωνι ἁρμοζούσῃ αὐτοῖς κέχρηνται. Ταῖς γὰρ γυναιξὶ καὶ ἡμεῖς ἀπαγορεύομεν τὰ τῆς ἐπιτροπῆς ὑπελθεῖν λειτουργήματα, εἰ μὴ μήτηρ ἢ μάμμη εἴη. Ταύταις γὰρ μόναις κατὰ τὴν τῆς κληρονομίας τάξιν καὶ τὴν ἐπιτροπὴν ὑπελθεῖν ἐφίεμεν, ἐὰν ἐν ὑπομνήμασι καὶ γάμοις ἑτέροις, καὶ τῇ βοηθείᾳ τοῦ Βελλιανείου δόγματος ἀπαγορεύσωσι. Ταῦτα γὰρ φυλάττουσαι πάντων τῶν ἐκ πλαγίου συγγενῶν εἰς τὴν

CAP. V. Ex his autem, quae de hereditate diximus et disposuimus, etiam ea, quae ad tutelam pertinent, clara sunt. Sancimus enim, ut unusquisque eo gradu et ordine, quo ad hereditatem vel solus, vel cum aliis vocatur, etiam munus tutelae suscipiat, neque ulla differentia neque hac in parte ex jure agnationis aut cognationis introducatur, sed omnibus similiter ad tutelam vocentur, cum ii, qui per masculos, tum ii, qui per feminas impuberibus junguntur. Haec autem dicimus, si masculi et perfectae aetatis sint, et nulla lege tutelam suscipere prohibeantur, neque excusatione sibi competente utantur. Mulieres enim etiam nos tutelae munus subire prohibemus, nisi mater vel avia sit. His enim solis secundum ordinem hereditatis etiam tutelam suscipere permittimus, si apud acta et secundis nuptiis, et beneficio senatus-consulti Velleiani renunciaverint. Haec enim si observent, omnibus cognatis ex latere ad tutelam praeferentur, testamentariis solum tutoribus eas praecedentibus. Nam defuncti volun-

---

CHAPTER V. Now, from these matters, which we have stated and laid down in respect of the inheritance, those also which relate to tutorship are clear. For we order that each one according to his degree of relationship and to the order in which he is called, either alone or with others to the inheritance, so also he shall take upon him the burden of the tutorship, and no difference in respect of this matter shall arise from the law of agnation or cognation, but all shall be equally called to the tutorship, as well those who are related through males as those who are related through females to the person under the age of puberty. This, however, is only to be the rule in respect of males who are of full age, who are not prohibited by any law from undertaking the tutorship, and who have not availed themselves of any excuse which they had a right to bring forward; for we forbid women to undertake the burden of the tutorship, except in the case of a mother, or grandmother, and we only allow these to enter upon the duties of the tutorship in the order of inheritance, after they have formally given an undertaking that they will not enter into a second marriage, and

ἐπιτροπὴν προτιμηθήσονται, τῶν testamentariων *μόνων ἐπιτρόπων προλαμβανόντων αὐτάς· τὴν γὰρ τοῦ τελευτήσαντος βούλησίν τε καὶ ἐπιλογὴν προτιμᾶσθαι βουλόμεθα. Εἰ δὲ πολλοὶ τὸν αὐτὸν τῆς συγγενείας ἔχοντες βαθμὸν καλοῦνται πρὸς τὴν ἐπιτροπήν, κελεύομεν αὐτοὺς κοινῇ συνελθόντας παρὰ τῷ ἄρχοντι, ᾧ τούτου μέλει τοῦ μέρους, ἕνα ἢ καὶ πλείονας, ὅσοι πρὸς τὴν διοίκησιν τῆς οὐσίας ἀρκοῦσιν, ἐξ αὐτῶν ἐπιλέξασθαι καὶ ὀνομάσαι καὶ τοῦτον ἢ τούτους τὰ τοῦ ἀνήβου πράγματα διοικεῖν, τοῦ τῆς ἐπιτροπῆς κινδύνου πᾶσιν ἐπικειμένου τοῖς πρὸς τὴν ἐπιτροπὴν καλουμένοις, καὶ τῶν οὐσιῶν αὐτῶν σιωπηρῶς ὑποκειμένων τῷ ἀνήβῳ ὑπὲρ ταύτης τῆς διοικήσεως.*

tatem electionemque praeferri volumus. Si vero multi qui eundem cognationis gradum obtinent, ad tutelam vocantur, jubemus, ut in unum conveniant, et apud magistratum, cui haec res curae est, unum vel etiam plures, quotquot ad bonorum administrationem sufficiunt, ex illis eligant et nominent, atque ille vel illi res impuberis administrent, periculo tutelae omnibus imminente, qui ad tutelam vocantur, eorumque bonis tacite pupillo pro hac administratione oppigneratis.

Κεφ. ϛʹ. *Ταῦτα δὲ πάντα, ὅσα περὶ διαδοχῶν τοῦ γένους ἐθεσπίσαμεν, ἐπ' ἐκείνοις βουλόμεθα κρατεῖν, ὅσοι τῆς καθολικῆς ὑπάρχουσι πίστεως. Ἐπὶ γὰρ τοῖς αἱρετικοῖς τοὺς ἤδη παρ' ἡμῶν τεθέντας νόμους βεβαίους εἶναι κελεύομεν, μηδένα καινισμὸν ἢ ἐλάττωσιν ἐκ τοῦ παρόντος ὑφισταμένους νόμου. Ἅπερ τοίνυν διὰ ταύτης τῆς δια-*

CAP. VI. Haec vero omnia, quae de successionibus familiae sancivimus, in illis obtinere volumus, qui catholicae sunt fidei. In haereticis enim leges a nobis jam latas firmas esse, nullamque eas innovationem vel deminutionem ex hac lege sustinere jubemus. Quae igitur hac constitutione in perpetuum observanda serenitas

---

that they renounce the benefit of the Velleian decree of the senate. On complying with these conditions they are to be preferred in respect of the tutorship to all collaterals, tutors appointed by testament alone taking precedence of them, for we desire that the will and choice of the deceased should be first taken into consideration. If, however, several, standing in the same degree of relationship, are called to the tutorship, we direct that all of them should appear before the magistrate, whose duty it is to see to this matter, in order that they may select and nominate out of their number, one or several, as will suffice for the administration of the property, and he, or they, shall administer the affairs of the person under the age of puberty, at the risk of all who are called to the tutorship, and their property shall be subject, in respect of this administration, to a tacit mortgage in favour of the pupil.

CHAPTER VI. It is our wish, however, that all these rules which we have laid down in respect of family succession shall apply only to those holding the catholic faith. In respect of heretics we direct that the laws already introduced by us shall still be in force, and shall undergo

τάξεως τῆς εἰς τὸ διηνεκὲς φυλαχθησομένης ἡ ἡμετέρα ἐθέσπισε γαληνότης, ἐπ' ἐκείνοις βουλόμεθα κρατεῖν τοῖς θέμασιν, ἅτινα ἐκ προοιμίων τοῦ Ἰουλίου μηνὸς τῆς παρούσης ἕκτης ἐπινεμήσεως συνέβη ἢ καὶ μετὰ ταῦτα συμβήσεται. Τὰ γὰρ προλαβόντα θέματα τὰ μέχρι τοῦ μνημονευθέντος χρόνου ἀποβάντα κατὰ τοὺς παλαιοὺς νόμους τέμνεσθαι παρακελευόμεθα.

nostra sancivit, in illis casibus obtinere volumus, qui ab initio mensis Julii sextae hujus indictionis contigerunt vel postea contingent. Casus enim praeteritos qui usque ad dictum mensem contigerunt, secundum veteres leges decidi volumus.

Ἐπίλογος. Ἡ ἐνδοξότης τοίνυν ἡ σὴ τὰ διὰ τοῦ παρόντος νόμου παρ' ἡμῶν διατυπωθέντα εἰς τὴν ἁπάντων γνῶσιν ἐλθεῖν προνοησάτω, ἐπὶ ταύτης μὲν τῆς βασιλίδος πόλεως ἐδίκτων κατὰ τὸ σύνηθες προτιθεμένων, ἐν δὲ ταῖς ἐπαρχίαις προστάξεων πεμπομένων πρὸς τοὺς λαμπροτάτους τούτων ἡγουμένους, ὥστε μηδενὶ τῶν τῇ ἡμετέρᾳ βασιλείᾳ ὑποκειμένων ἄγνωστον γενέσθαι τὴν τῆς ἡμετέρας ἡμερότητος περὶ τούτους πρόνοιαν, οὕτω μέντοι ὥστε δίχα πάσης ζημίας τῶν πολιτῶν καὶ ἐπαρχεωτῶν ἐν παντὶ τόπῳ τὴν τοῦ παρόντος νόμου ἐμφάνειαν γενέσθαι. DAT. VII. KAL. AUG. IMP. DN. JUSTINIANI PP. AUG. ANNO XVII. POST CONS. BASILII V. C. ANNO II.

EPILOGUS. Tua igitur gloria quae hac lege a nobis disposita sunt ad omnium notitiam venire curet, in hac quidem regia urbe edictis more solito propositis, in provinciis vero mandatis ad clarissimos earum rectores missis, ut nemini, qui imperio nostro subjectus est, mansuetudinis nostrae providentia circa eos ignota sit, ita tamen, ut absque ullo civium et provincialium damno in omni loco hujus legis insinuatio fiat.

Dat. vii. Cal. Aug. Imperii DN. Justiniani PP. Aug. Anno xvii, post consulatum Basilii V.C. Anno ii.

---

no change or diminution by reason of the present law. It is our imperial pleasure that the rules which we now, by this constitution, sanction for all time, are to hold good for all cases arising on and after the beginning of the month of July of this sixth year of the tax period, and we direct that all cases which arose before the aforesaid date shall be decided according to the old laws.

CONCLUSION. Let it be now your care that that which we have ordained by this present law come to the knowledge of all. As regards this royal city, let it be done in the accustomed way by publicly posting up edicts; but, in the provinces, by orders transmitted to their honoured governors; so that no one of those who are subject to our imperial sway may be ignorant of our gracious solicitude on their behalf, and yet in such a way that the publication of this our law in all places may not involve any inhabitant of the city or the provinces in any loss.

Given the 26th July, in the seventeenth year of the reign of the Emperor Justinian, in the second year after the consulship of the most noble Basilius (A.D. 543).

ΔΙΑΤΑΞΙΣ ρκζʹ.

Περὶ ἀδελφοπαίδων κληρονομούντων ὕμα τοῖς ἀνιοῦσι.

Ὁ αὐτὸς Βασιλεὺς Βάσσῳ τῷ ἐνδοξοτάτῳ ἐπάρχῳ πραιτωρίων.

Προοίμιον. Τοὺς ἡμετέρους νόμους ἐπανορθοῦν ἡμεῖς οὐκ ὀκνοῦμεν, πανταχοῦ τὸ συμφέρον τοῖς ὑπηκόοις εὑρίσκειν βουλόμενοι. Μεμνήμεθα τοίνυν γράψαντες νόμον, δι' οὗ παρεκελευσάμεθα, ἵνα, εἴ τις τελευτήσοι καταλιπὼν ἀδελφοὺς καὶ παῖδας ἑτέρου προτελευτήσαντος ἀδελφοῦ, παῖδες πρὸς τὴν κληρονομίαν καλῶνται, τὴν πατρῴαν ὑπεισιόντες τάξιν καὶ τὴν ἐκείνου κομιζόμενοι μοῖραν. Εἰ δὲ ὁ τελευτήσας καταλίποι τῶν ἀνιόντων τινά, καὶ ἀδελφοὺς ἐξ ἑκατέρων γονέων συναπτομένους αὐτῷ, καὶ παιδας ἐκ προτελευτήσαντος

Novella cxxvii.

DE FRATRUM FILIIS UNA CUM ASCENDENTIBUS SUCCEDENTIBUS.

IDEM IMPERATOR BASSO GLORIOSISSIMO PRAEFECTO PRAETORIO.

PRAEFATIO. Non piget nos leges nostras emendare, quum ubivis id, quod subditis nostris conducit, invenire velimus. Jam igitur meminimus, nos legem scripsisse, qua jussimus, ut, si quis moriatur relictis fratribus et liberis alterius praedefuncti fratris liberi ad hereditatem vocentur ita, ut paternum subirent locum, ejusque portionem acciperent. Si vero defunctus quendam ex ascendentibus, et fraires ex utroque parente illi junctos, liberosque ex praedefuncto fratre reliquerit, fraties quidem cum parentibus vocari ea-

---

Novel cxxvii.

OF THE SUCCESSION OF THE CHILDREN OF BROTHERS (AND SISTERS) ALONG WITH ASCENDANTS.

THE SAME EMPEROR TO BASSUS MOST GLORIOUS PRÆTORIAN PREFECT.

PREFACE. To amend our laws is no source of displeasure to us, as we desire to find out everywhere that which will be beneficial to our subjects. Now we call to mind that we have issued a law (Nov. 118) by which we have ordered that if a person die leaving brothers (or sisters), and children of another previously deceased brother (or sister), these children are to be called to the inheritance in such a way as to take the place of their father (or mother), and receive his (or her) share. If, however, the deceased leave some ascendants along with brothers (or sisters) related through both parents (i.e., of the whole blood), and children of a predeceased brother (or sister), then by that same law (C. III), we have directed that the brothers (or sisters) are to be called

ἀδελφοῦ, τοὺς μὲν ἀδελφοὺς ἐκελεύσαμεν διὰ τοῦ αὐτοῦ νόμου μετὰ τῶν γονέων καλεῖσθαι, τοὺς δὲ ἀδελφόπαιδας ἀπεκλείσαμεν.

Κεφ. α′. Ταῦτα τοίνυν δικαίως ἐπανορθοῦντες θεσπίζομεν, ἵνα, εἴ τις τελευτήσας καταλείψει τῶν ἀνιόντων τινά, καὶ ἀδελφοὺς δυναμένους μετὰ τῶν γονέων καλεῖσθαι, καὶ ἑτέρου ἀδελφοῦ προτελευτήσαντος παῖδας, μετὰ τῶν ἀνιόντων καὶ τῶν ἀδελφῶν καλῶνται καὶ οἱ τοῦ προτελευτήσαντος ἀδελφοῦ παῖδες, καὶ τοσαύτην λαμβάνωσι μοῖραν, ὅσην ἔμελλεν ὁ αὐτῶν πατὴρ κομίζεσθαι, εἰ περιῆν. Ταῦτα δὲ θεσπίζομεν περὶ ἐκείνων τῶν ἀδελφοπαίδων, ὧν ὁ πατὴρ ἐξ ἑκατέρου γονέως συνήπτετο τῷ τελευτήσαντι, καὶ ἁπλῶς εἰπεῖν, οἵαν αὐτοῖς δεδώκαμεν τάξιν, ὅτε μετὰ μόνων καλοῦνται τῶν ἀδελφῶν, ταύτην αὐτοὺς ἔχειν κελεύομεν, καὶ ὅτε μετὰ τῶν ἀδελφῶν καλοῦνται τῶν ἀνιόντων τινὲς πρὸς τὸν κλῆρον.

. . . .

Dat. kal. septembr. Constantinop. DN. Justiniani PP. Aug. anno XXI. post Basilii. V. C. cons. anno VI.

dem lege jussimus, fratrum autem liberos exclusimus.

Cap. I. Haec igitur juste emendantes sancimus, si quis moriens reliquerit quendam ex ascendentibus, et fratres, qui cum parentibus vocari possint, alteriusque fratris praemortui liberos, ut cum ascendentibus et fratribus praedefuncti etiam fratris liberi vocentur, et tantam partem accipiant, quantam pater ipsorum accepturus fuisset, si viveret. Haec autem de illis fratrum liberis sancimus, quorum pater ex utroque parente defuncto junctus erat; et, ut brevi dicamus, quem locum illis dedimus, quando cum solis fratribus vocantur, eum quoque illos habere volumus, quando cum fratribus quidam ex ascendentibus ad hereditatem vocantur.

. . . . . .

Dat. Cal. Septemb., Constantinop., Imp. DN. Justiniani, PP. Aug. Anno xxi, post consulatum Basilii V.C. Anno vi.

---

along with the parents (i.e., ascendants), but we have shut out the children of the brother (or sister).

Chapter I. As an amendment of these rules is therefore desirable, we order that, if a person die leaving some ascendants and brothers (or sisters) who can be called to the inheritance along with the parents (i.e., ascendants), and children of another predeceased brother (or sister), these children of the predeceased brother (or sister) shall be called along with the ascendants and the brothers (or sisters), and shall receive such a share as their father (or mother) would have received had he (or she) lived. These rules, however, are to apply to brothers' (or sisters') children, whose father (or mother) was related to the deceased through both parents (i.e., of the whole blood), and, shortly stated, we wish that they shall occupy the same position when called to the inheritance along with brothers and some ascendants, as we have given them when called with brothers (or sisters) only.

. . . .

Given at Constantinople, on the 1st September, in the twenty-first year of the reign of the Emperor Justinian, in the sixth year after the consulship of the most noble Basilius (A.D. 547).

INDEX.

INDEX.

N.B.—pp. i to lx, include the *Introduction*.
pp. 1 to 250 the text } of the *Institutes* of *Gaius* and *Justinian*.
pp. 252 to 576 the translation }
pp. 579 to 590 the *Twelve Tables*.
pp. 593 to 605 the CXVIIIth and CXXVIIth *Novels*.

T. RICHARDS, PRINTER, 37, GREAT QUEEN STREET.

www.ingramcontent.com/pod-product-compliance
Lightning Source LLC
LaVergne TN
LVHW102102300926
849161LV00001B/3
* 9 7 8 1 5 8 4 7 7 4 4 0 2 *